ENCYCLOPEDIA OF AFRICAN PEOPLES

The Diagram Group

Facts On File, Inc.

Encyclopedia of African Peoples

Copyright © 2000 by The Diagram Group

Diagram Visual Information Ltd
195 Kentish Town Road, London, NW5 2JU
e-mail: diagramvis@aol.com

Editorial director:	Bridget Giles
Contributors:	Trevor Day, Theodore Rowland Entwistle, David Lambert, Keith Lye, Oliver Marshall, Christopher Priest
Editors:	Nancy Bailey, Paul Copperwaite, Margaret Doyle, Moira Johnston, Ian Wood
Design:	Bounford.com, Philip Patenall
Artists:	Chris Allcott, Darren Bennett, Bob Garwood, Elsa Godfrey, Brian Hewson, Pavel Kostal, Kyri Kyriacou, Janos Marffy, Kathy McDougall, Patrick Mulrey, Rob Shone, Graham Rosewarne, Peter Ross
Production:	Trevor Bounford, Denise Goodey, Richard Hummerstone, Lee Lawrence, Oscar Lobban
Researchers:	Carole Dease, Peter Dease, Pamela Kea, Chris Owens, Catherine Michard, Neil McKenna, Matt Smout

With the assistance of:
Dr. Elizabeth Dunstan, International African Institute, School of Oriental and African Studies, University of London
David Hall, African studies bibliographer at the School of Oriental and African Studies, University of London
Horniman Museum, London
Museum of Mankind library, British Museum
Survival International
WWF-UK

Facts On File Inc.
11 Penn Plaza
New York NY 10001

Library of Congress Cataloging-in-Publication Data
Encyclopedia of African peoples/by the Diagram Group.
    p.cm.
  Includes index.
  ISBN 0-8160-4099-0
    1. Africans—Encyclopedias. 2. Ethnology—Africa—Encyclopedias. I. Diagram Group.

  DT15 .E53 2000
  305.896′003—dc21   99–055125

Facts On File books are available at special discounts when purchased in bulk quantities for businesses, associations, institutions, or sales promotions. Please call our Special Sales Department in New York at 212/967-8800 or 800/322-8755.

Cover design by Cathy Rincon

Printed in the United States of America

RRD DIAG 10 9 8 7 6 5 4 3 2 1

This book is printed on acid-free paper

Foreword

Africa is a vast continent, home to many millions of people. Its history stretches back millennia and encompasses some of the most ancient civilizations in the world. Modern Africa boasts a rich cultural heritage, the legacy of many diverse influences from all around the world, reflecting the central role Africa plays in world history. You will read about Africa's cultures, history, geography, economics, and politics in this book, which provides an invaluable overview of the whole continent, region by region, ethnic group by ethnic group, nation by nation, and celebrity by celebrity. The sections discussed below can be read together to reveal a portrait of Africa as a whole, or accessed separately for vital and interesting facts.

Africa Today The contemporary political and economic status of the five main regions of Africa – North, East, West, Central, and Southern Africa – are introduced in this section. Maps describe the regions' main features, national boundaries, and major cities, roads, and railroads.

The Peoples of Africa This section covers the most identifiable of the continent's several thousand ethnic groups. The entries are arranged alphabetically. Ethnic groups are dynamic and difficult-to-define populations that change, break up, disappear, or emerge, sometimes surprisingly quickly. For the purposes of this book, "ethnic group" is used to refer to people who are linked by a common language, history, religion, and cultural and artistic legacy. The members of an ethnic group can number in the millions or just a few hundred; several groups have histories that stretch back thousands of years.

The larger ethnic groups are dealt with in fascinating detail, with descriptions of their history, language, culture, religion, and society. Specially drawn artworks illustrate the text, and timelines place the group's unique history in the context of the region's history. Thousands of other entries give succinct and insightful descriptions of a great variety of ethnic groups, ranging from Black African cultures to Asian and European communities. Cross-references help you to find groups known by different names. Population figures have been included wherever possible, but they are only estimates since few official figures are available. Maps show the general area a group is concentrated in. Personalities appearing in this section who warrant an entry in "Biographies" are marked '(q.v.)'. In addition, (q.v.) refers to other "Peoples" entries within this section.

Culture and History Taking a completely different approach to the previous section, this section looks at interesting cultural and historical topics that cut across ethnic and national boundaries. Cash crops, Christianity in Ethiopia, tourism, and the lost colony of Carthage are all topics covered here. Historical features on, for example, Ancient Egypt and the four great medieval West African empires of Mali, Songhay, Kanem-Borno, and Ghana describe the rise and fall of some of the world's most powerful and important civilizations. Readers will learn how history can forge new ethnic groups and destroy old ones. Other features detail the horror of more recent events, such as South Africa's apartheid era, which still has a huge influence today on all Southern Africans. The less recent but equally significant slave trade is also covered in this section. Cultural topics are explored in features that cover music, from drumming through South African jazz to global pop stars; hairstyles, both real and imagined; buildings; and food and drink. Both the prehistoric rock art of the Sahara and contemporary African art and its influence on the West are discussed in separate features. Environmental threats such as deforestation and desertification as well as the refugee problem are also covered in detail. Personalities appearing in this section who warrant an entry in "Biographies" are marked '(q.v.)'.

The Nations Each of Africa's fifty-three nations are covered separately in this section, which is arranged alphabetically. This includes the island nations of Madagascar, São Tomé and Príncipe, and the Seychelles. The disputed territory of the Western Sahara also has its own entry. A wealth of facts and figures are given for each country, ranging from a color-coded illustration of the national flag and the title of the national anthem to the figures for life expectancy, employment, and level of urbanization. The geography sections describe the country's landscape, features, and climate. Timelines capture the main events in each nation's recent history.

Biographies Since the earliest civilizations, important Africans have shaped history and culture both inside and outside of Africa. The biographies of more than three hundred of these famous Africans appear in this section. Entries describe the life and legacy of each personality, illustrating that while ethnicity is important in Africa it is not the only trait that defines a person. A wide range of people are covered, from marathon runners and novelists to ancient royals and twentieth-century dictators and heroes. Within "Biographies," individuals who have their own entry appear in upper case where they occur in other entries.

Glossary and Index An extensive glossary defines unfamiliar words used throughout the book. The comprehensive index can be used to research related topics throughout the book and to find ethnic groups.

Contents

Africa today: North

North Africa is one of the continent's more prosperous regions. This is largely because of the huge reserves of oil and natural gas beneath the deserts, especially in Algeria and Libya. Another reason is that most North African countries have more stable economies than other African countries. With few exceptions, the sub-Saharan countries are economically dependent on agriculture and the export of raw materials – agricultural and mineral – the prices of which fluctuate on the world market. North Africa faces its own problems, however. The economy of Sudan, the region's poorest country, has been drained by a long civil war between the Muslim north and the mainly non-Muslim south. In Algeria and Egypt, many people resent Western influences and support radical Islamic

fundamentalist movements, which they see as the best means of preserving their culture. A hangover from colonial days is the unresolved issue of Western Sahara. This phosphate-rich desert territory has been occupied by Morocco – for a while jointly with Mauritania – since Spain withdrew in 1975. Support for Saharan nationalists from other African countries has isolated Morocco, which left the Organization of African Unity (OAU) in protest.

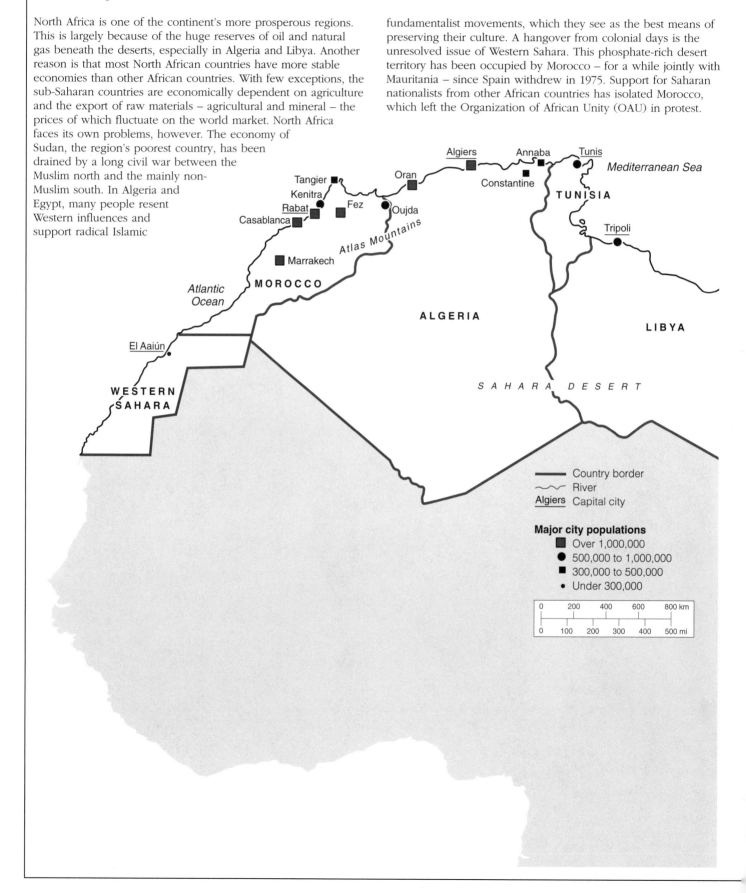

Country border
River
Algiers Capital city

Major city populations
■ Over 1,000,000
● 500,000 to 1,000,000
▪ 300,000 to 500,000
• Under 300,000

| 0 | 200 | 400 | 600 | 800 km |
| 0 | 100 | 200 | 300 | 400 | 500 mi |

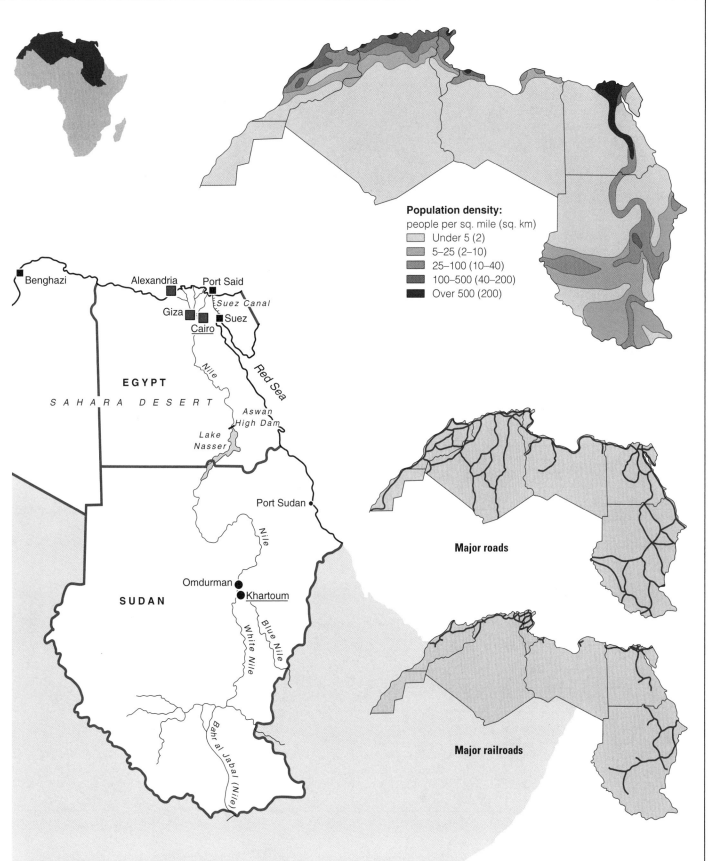

Population density:
people per sq. mile (sq. km)
- Under 5 (2)
- 5–25 (2–10)
- 25–100 (10–40)
- 100–500 (40–200)
- Over 500 (200)

Benghazi

Alexandria

Port Said

Suez Canal

Giza

Suez

Cairo

EGYPT

SAHARA DESERT

Nile

Red Sea

Aswan High Dam

Lake Nasser

Port Sudan

Nile

Omdurman

Khartoum

SUDAN

White Nile

Blue Nile

Bahr al Jabal (Nile)

Major roads

Major railroads

Africa today: East

East Africa, the cradle of human evolution, is one of Africa's most majestic regions. It contains snowcapped mountains, huge lakes, and abundant, though threatened, wildlife, which is partly preserved in vast national parks. Economically, however, East Africa is the continent's poorest region. It lacks the mineral and fossil fuel reserves of other areas and its economic development has been hampered by many problems. About eighty-five percent of the people make their living by farming. The quality of life of most farmers is low because they live at subsistence level (producing only enough to provide for the basic needs of their families). This precarious way of life collapses when natural disasters – especially prolonged droughts – ruin harvests, causing famine and suffering on a vast scale. Judged by their per capita (for each person) gross national products (GNPs), Rwanda, Eritrea, and Ethiopia, are the poorest countries, followed closely by Tanzania, Malawi, and Somalia. The economic growth of several countries has been put into reverse by civil war. Eritrea, which was united with Ethiopia in 1952, broke away in the early 1990s after a long and bitter war. Burundi and Rwanda have been rocked by appalling conflict between the Tutsi and the Hutu. Rival clans in Somalia have torn the country apart, effectively dividing it into three separate regions, while Uganda, following much bloody civil conflict, is still struggling to maintain national unity. Kenya is the most stable East African country. It has developed a strong tourist industry alongside its cash crop farming and a small but important manufacturing sector. Kenya has been held together by autocratic one-party rule and many of its leaders fear that a multiparty system could result in division and strife.

Major roads

Major railroads

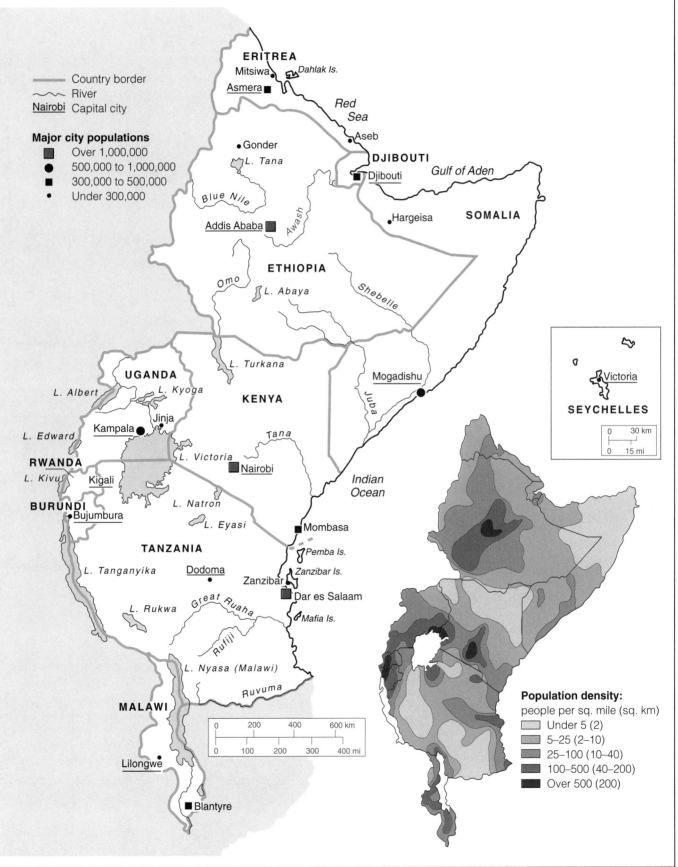

Country border
River
Nairobi Capital city

Major city populations
- Over 1,000,000
- 500,000 to 1,000,000
- 300,000 to 500,000
- Under 300,000

ERITREA
Mitsiwa
Dahlak Is.
Asmera

Red Sea

Gonder
L. Tana
Aseb
DJIBOUTI
Djibouti
Gulf of Aden

Blue Nile
Awash
Hargeisa
SOMALIA

Addis Ababa

ETHIOPIA

Omo
L. Abaya
Shebelle

L. Turkana

UGANDA
L. Albert
L. Kyoga
KENYA
Mogadishu

Kampala
Jinja
L. Edward
Tana
Juba
RWANDA
L. Victoria
Nairobi
L. Kivu
Kigali
Indian Ocean

BURUNDI
Bujumbura
L. Natron
L. Eyasi
Mombasa

TANZANIA
Pemba Is.
L. Tanganyika
Dodoma
Zanzibar Is.
Zanzibar
L. Rukwa
Great Ruaha
Dar es Salaam
Mafia Is.
Rufiji
L. Nyasa (Malawi)
Ruvuma

MALAWI

Victoria
SEYCHELLES

| 0 | 30 km |
| 0 | 15 mi |

| 0 | 200 | 400 | 600 km |
| 0 | 100 | 200 | 300 | 400 mi |

Lilongwe

Blantyre

Population density:
people per sq. mile (sq. km)
- Under 5 (2)
- 5–25 (2–10)
- 25–100 (10–40)
- 100–500 (40–200)
- Over 500 (200)

Africa today: West

In under forty years, West Africa has emerged from colonialism into nationhood. The path has not been smooth. Ethnic and religious differences combined with economic problems – including falls in commodity prices for such key exports as cocoa – have caused instability. Most countries have resorted to one-party or military rule to maintain order. By the mid-1990s, however, many West African nations had either returned to democratic rule or were in transition to democracy. Sierra Leone, Gambia, Liberia, and Nigeria are exceptions. While Gambia enjoyed nearly thirty years of democracy until a coup in 1994, Nigeria has had civilian rule for only nine years since 1960. This oil-rich nation is West Africa's giant, containing almost half the region's population. Yet its gross national product (GNP) per capita (for each person) is below the regional average. West African countries with lower per capita GNPs than Nigeria include Sierra Leone and Liberia, which have both suffered civil wars. By contrast, Cameroon and Senegal have enjoyed relative stability; their governments have led the way in successfully exploiting limited resources.

Population density: people per sq. mile (sq. km)
- Under 5 (2)
- 5–25 (2–10)
- 25–100 (10–40)
- 100–500 (40–200)
- Over 500 (200)

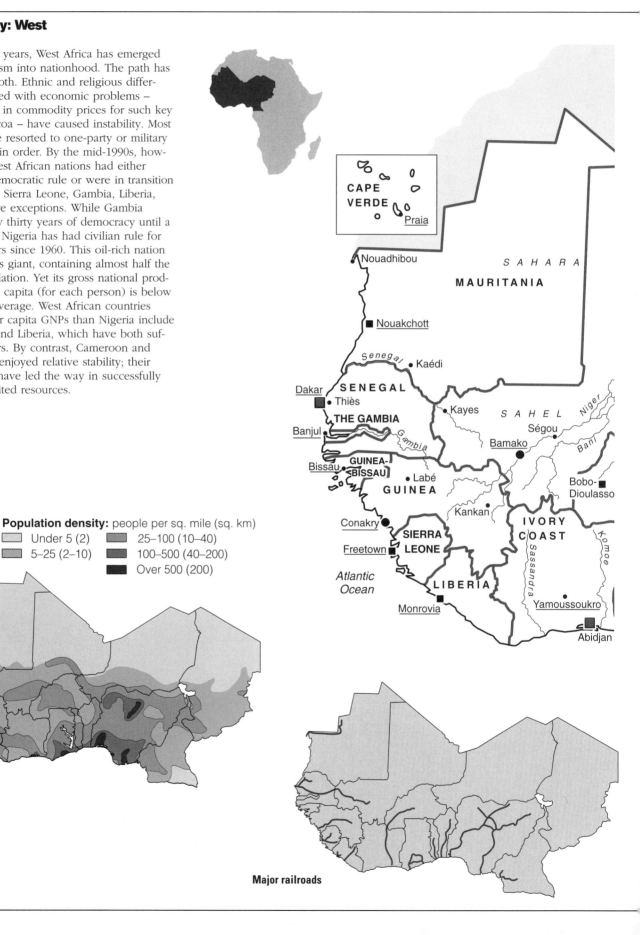

Major railroads

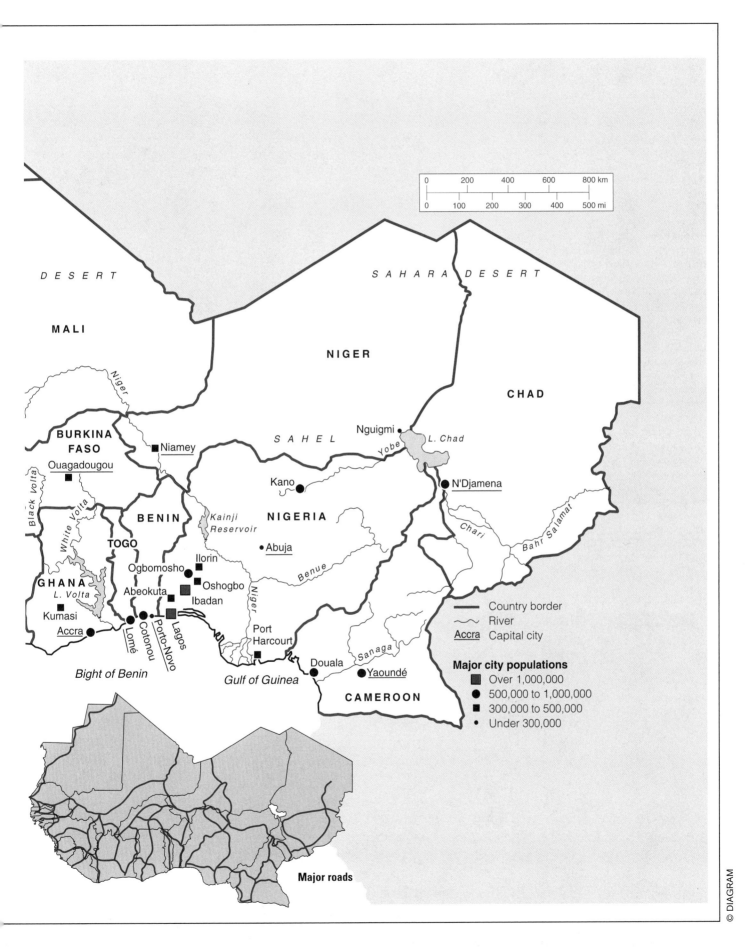

Africa today: Central

In recent years, the progress of many Central African countries has been hampered by instability. The Democratic Republic of Congo, the region's largest country, exploded into civil war when, as Zaire, it became independent in 1960. Despite autocratic rule by President Mobutu Sese Seko from 1965 to 1997, secessionist groups – especially in the mineral-rich southern region of Shaba (formerly Katanga) – periodically made the country ungovernable. Angola has been disrupted by a twenty-year civil war, which has only recently ended. The people of two other countries, the Central African Republic (CAR) and Equatorial Guinea, lived through years of rule by brutal despots. In 1966, the tyrannical Jean-Bédel Bokassa seized power in CAR and went so far as to declare himself "emperor," changing the name of his country to the "Central African Empire" between 1976 and 1979. Francisco Macías Nguema, dictator of Equatorial Guinea, executed and imprisoned thousands of people without trial between 1970 and 1979. The economic success of Central Africa is Gabon, whose exploitation of oil, gas, uranium, and various metal deposits has made it one of Africa's most successful countries in terms of its per capita (for each person) gross national product (GNP). Most of its citizens, however, practice subsistence agriculture, obtaining little benefit from the exploitation of their country's resources. Gabon's stability was bolstered by a long period of one-party rule. Although banning opposition parties may create stability, it also fosters inefficiency and corruption. Most countries in Central Africa are now restoring democratic institutions, despite ethnic tensions and recurring civil war.

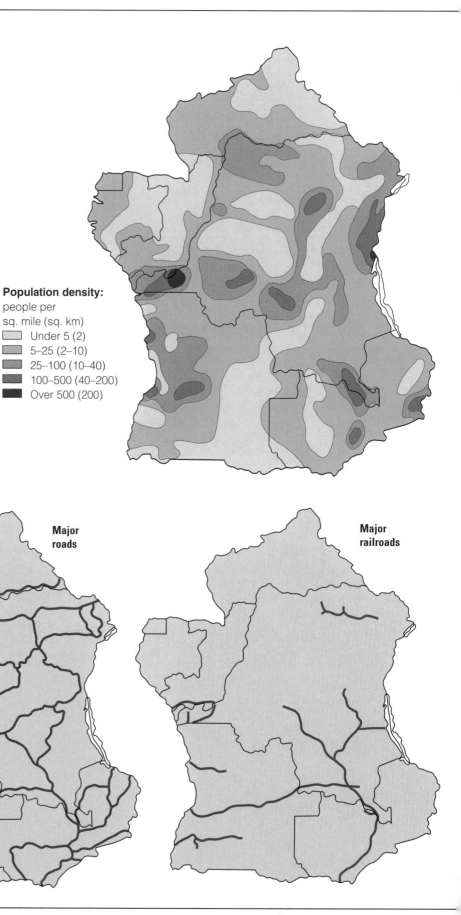

Population density:
people per
sq. mile (sq. km)

- Under 5 (2)
- 5–25 (2–10)
- 25–100 (10–40)
- 100–500 (40–200)
- Over 500 (200)

Major roads

Major railroads

Country border
River
Lusaka Capital city

Major city populations
- ■ Over 1,000,000
- ● 500,000 to 1,000,000
- ■ 300,000 to 500,000
- • Under 300,000

CENTRAL
AFRICAN
REPUBLIC

Oubangui

Bangui ●

Uele

EQUATORIAL
GUINEA

Malabo

Bioko Is.

Congo

Aruwimi

Lake
Albert

Bata

Sanga

Oubangui

C O N G O
B A S I N

Kisangani
≠*Boyoma Falls*

Lake
Edward

São Tomé

Libreville

Ogooué

Tshuapa

Lomami

Lake Kivu

SÃO TOMÉ
AND
PRÍNCIPE

GABON

CONGO
(REP.)

Congo

*Lake
Mai-Ndombe*

Lokolo

Lomela

Lukenie

Elila

Brazzaville

Kasai

Sankuru

CONGO
DEM. REP.

Lualaba (Congo/Zaire)

Lake
Tanganyika

Pointe-Noire

Kwilu

Kananga

Mbuji-Mayi

Luvua

CABINDA
(ANGOLA)

Cabinda

Cuango

Wamba

Loange

Chicapa

Kasai

Lulua

Lubilash

Lake
Mweru

*Atlantic
Ocean*

Luanda

Cuanza

L. Bangweulu

Luapula

ANGOLA

Cassai

Lubumbashi

Ndola

Lobito

Huambo

ZAMBIA

Luangwa

Kunene

Cuito

Cuando

Kafue

Lusaka

Zambezi

Kariba Dam

Cubango

Cunene

Okavango

Lake Kariba

Victoria Falls

0	200	400	600 km

0	100	200	300	400 mi

Africa today: Southern

South Africa, Africa's most powerful and wealthiest nation, has dominated Southern Africa for many years. It occupied Namibia from 1915 – illegally from 1969 – until 1990 and supported rebel forces in Mozambique and Angola. South Africa also aided the white-minority regime in Rhodesia until that country became independent as Zimbabwe in 1980. South Africa's intervention in the affairs of its neighbors was part of a destabilizing strategy aimed at preserving its system of racial segregation known as apartheid. Since 1994, however, the government of Nelson Mandela has sought to replace racial hatred with reconciliation, while in other parts of Africa the country has begun to act as a mediator in disputes. The Republic of South Africa faces great problems arising from the inequalities of apartheid. In 1993, the white population controlled about eighty-eight percent of the country's wealth, while almost half of the people of South Africa lived below subsistence level with a family income of less than US $200 per month. Other countries in Southern Africa with relatively high per capita (for each person) gross national products (GNPs) are mineral-rich Botswana, one of Africa's most stable democracies, and Namibia. The poorest countries are Mozambique and Madagascar, whose economies are based on subsistence agriculture. Mozambique's economy has been shattered by both civil war and drought.

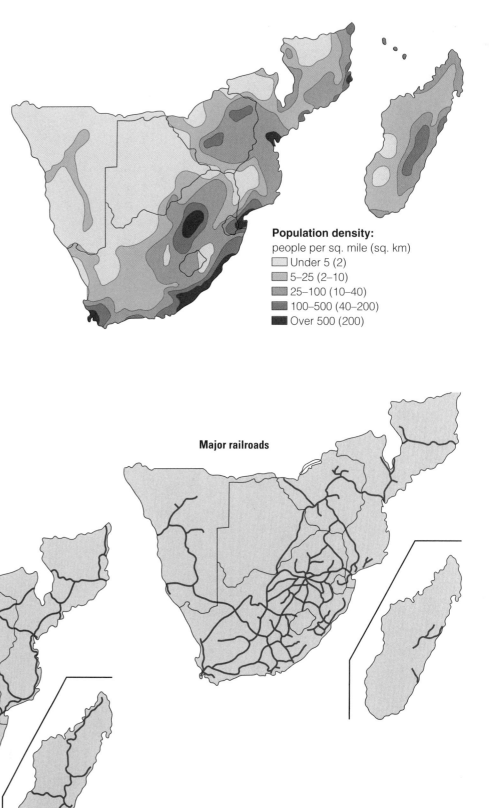

Population density:

people per sq. mile (sq. km)

- Under 5 (2)
- 5–25 (2–10)
- 25–100 (10–40)
- 100–500 (40–200)
- Over 500 (200)

Major railroads

Major roads

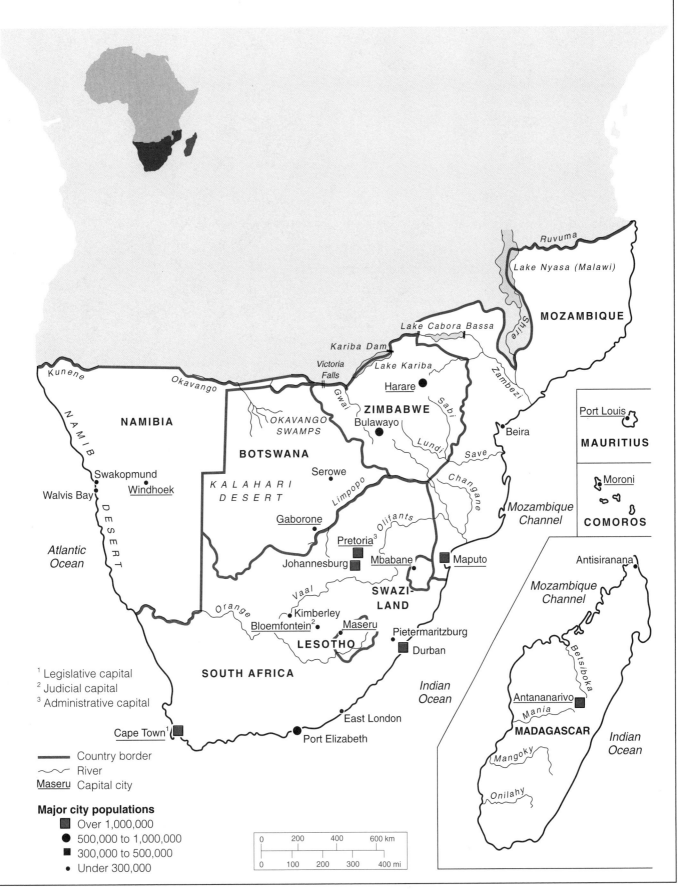

¹ Legislative capital
² Judicial capital
³ Administrative capital

Country border
River
<u>Maseru</u> Capital city

Major city populations
■ Over 1,000,000
● 500,000 to 1,000,000
■ 300,000 to 500,000
• Under 300,000

© DIAGRAM

Regions of Africa

This map gives the regions of Africa used within this book.

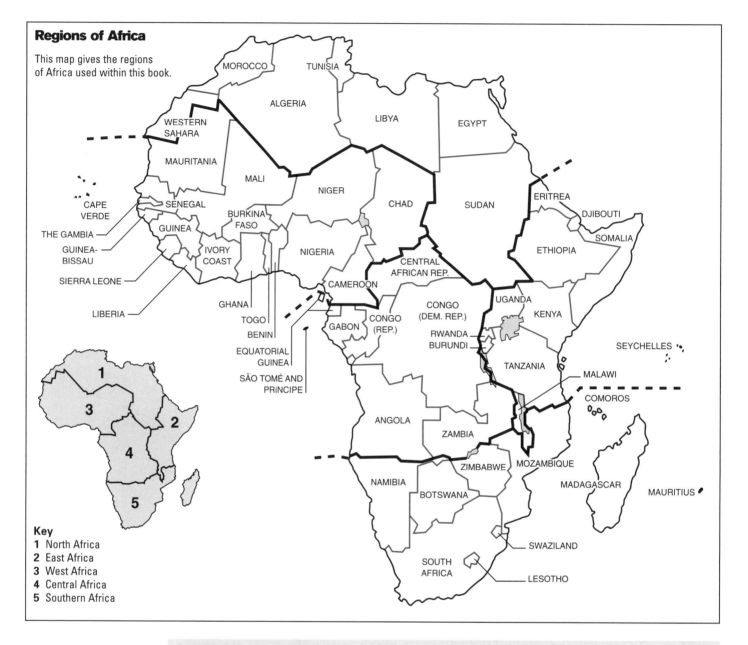

Key
1 North Africa
2 East Africa
3 West Africa
4 Central Africa
5 Southern Africa

A word about ethnic groups

The *Encyclopedia of African Peoples* focuses on ethnic groups or peoples, useful but difficult-to-define terms. In the past, the word "tribe" was used to describe ethnic groupings, but this is today considered an offensive and arbitrary label. It is incorrect to refer to a group of people who may number in the hundreds of thousands and who have a long history of nation building as a tribe. "Tribe" is now generally used only to describe a basic political unit that exists within some larger ethnic groups, not to describe the group itself. So what is an ethnic group? An ethnic group is distinct from race or nationality; the former is rarely used today because it requires broad and inaccurate generalizations; and the latter describes only the national boundaries within which a person is born or lives. Both categories are fraught with difficulty. For the purposes of this book, the term "ethnic group" is used to describe people who have a common language, history, religion, and cultural and artistic heritage; they may also have a common way of life and often live within the same geographical area.

There are probably more than a thousand ethnic groups in all of Africa. Many are related to one another, often in complex ways. Groups have subgroups and even sub-subgroups. Intermarriage, colonialism, conquest, and migration through the ages have led to many combinations and to an intermixing of influences. In this book we have chosen to focus on only a fraction of Africa's many ethnic groups. A number of factors – including population figures, available information, and recognition outside Africa – were used in making the selection. To a certain extent, however, it was an arbitrary choice, but one that we hope offers a vibrant picture of the people of this continent.

SECTION

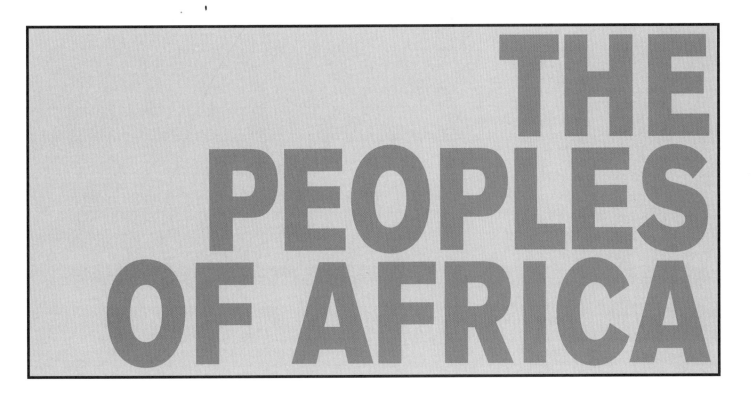

Ababa *see* **Ababda**

Ababda

The Ababda (or Ababa) are a subgroup of the Beja (q.v.) people of Sudan. The majority of the Ababda live along Sudan's Red Sea coast. There are more than 200,000 Ababda Beja people.

Abadja

The Abadja are are one of the many subgroups that make up Nigeria's Igbo (q.v.) population. The Igbo live in southeastern Nigeria.

Abaluyia *see* **Luyia**

Abam

The Abam are are one of the many subgroups that make up Nigeria's Igbo (q.v.) population. The Igbo live in southeastern Nigeria.

Abarue

The Abarue are a subgroup of the Shona (q.v.) people of Zimbabwe and Mozambique.

Abbe

The Abbe (Abbey or Abé) are a people living mostly along the southeastern coast of the Ivory Coast who number more than 20,000. The Abé are part of the so-called Lagoon cluster (q.v.) of peoples, and they are an Akan (q.v.) people.

Abbey *see* **Abbe**

Abé *see* **Abbe**

Abgal

The Abgal are the largest clan-based subgroup of the Issa (q.v.) people. The Issa are a Somali (q.v.) people who can be found throughout the Horn of Africa in Ethiopia, Djibouti, Eritrea, and Somalia. There are around 400,000 Abgal people.

Abidji

The Abidji (or Ari) are a small ethnic group living along the southeastern coastal region of the Ivory Coast. There are probably around 50,000 Abidji, the majority of whom are farmers. They are part of the so-called Lagoon cluster (q.v.) of peoples.

Abora

The Abora (or Abura) are a subgroup of the Fante (q.v.), an Akan (q.v.) people largely found in the southern half of Ghana. The Abora live mostly in central Ghana and number only a few thousand.

Abron *see* **Brong**

Abu Charib *see* **Abu Sharib**

Abu Sharib

The Abu Sharibs (or Abu Charibs) are one of the many Tama-speaking ethnic groups of Chad. Tama (q.v.) is a Nilo-Saharan language. There are more than 50,000 Abu Sharib.

Abura *see* **Abora**

Acholi

The Acholi live in a region that includes the borders of southern Sudan, Uganda, and northwestern Kenya. They are descended from Lwo (q.v.)-speaking ancestors who migrated into Eastern Africa from their homeland in southern Sudan several centuries ago. The Acholi began to emerge as a distinct ethnic group in the seventeenth century from the melding of three main ethnic groups: the Patiko (the Lwo ancestors who first migrated into what is now Acholiland), the local Ateker-speaking people, who had migrated there earlier), and Sudanic-speaking peoples coming in from the west. In the nineteenth century, slave raiders reached Acholi land from the east coast, and the Acholi suffered greatly from the slave trade.

Like other Nilotes (q.v.), the Acholi have a long history of pastoralism (herding livestock). They were once a largely cattle-keeping society, but many now farm or work in urban areas.

Acholi sleeping hut
The small doorway and the stilts provide protection from the rain.

Adare *see* **Harari**

Adhola *see* **Padhola**

Adjukru

The Adjukru (or Boubouri or Odjukru) are an ethnic group of the Ivory Coast who have both Kru (q.v.) and Akan (q.v.) ancestors. There are around 100,000 Adjukru people. They are part of the so-called Lagoon cluster (q.v.) of peoples.

Afar

The Afar (or Danakil) live in the Danakil Desert in Eritrea and Ethiopia, and in neighboring Djibouti. There are approximately 700,000 Afar.

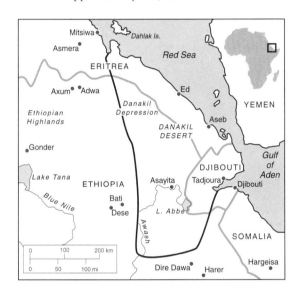

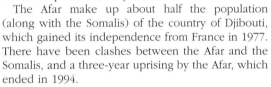

History

The ancestors of the Afar were settled livestock raisers in Ethiopia, but before 1000 they gradually shifted to a nomadic (unsettled) lifestyle and moved from the highlands to the area they occupy today. Their history has often been a violent one marked by fighting with invading armies and, later, imperial and national governments. Disputes with neighboring peoples have also continued until well into the twentieth century.

RECENT EVENTS In 1975, an Afar nationalist insurrection movement began in Ethiopia. The Afar Liberation Front (ALF) was established after an unsuccessful rebellion led by a former Afar sultan. Although the military government established the Autonomous Region of Assab (modern Aseb), the Afar were not satisfied with the degree of autonomy they were given and the insurrection continued until Eritrea became independent from Ethiopia in the early 1990s.

The Afar make up about half the population (along with the Somalis) of the country of Djibouti, which gained its independence from France in 1977. There have been clashes between the Afar and the Somalis, and a three-year uprising by the Afar, which ended in 1994.

Language

The Afar language (or Danakil) is a Cushitic language.

Ways of life

NOMADIC PASTORALISM Although today some Afar have migrated to cities like Addis Ababa and the port of Djibouti, the majority have long been nomadic pastoralists, tending herds of goats, sheep, and cattle in the harsh desert. They move from one waterhole to the next, eking a subsistence living from the barren soil. As the dry season advances, most Afar head for the banks

Camels with burdens
The camel is the essential beast of burden for nomadic peoples of the desert, like the Afar. The search for water dominates the lives of these people, and as they move the camels carry everything, including, as shown here, the light poles and mats that are used to build the Afar houses.

© DIAGRAM

Afar man
Rural Afar men often wear the traditional sanafil, which is wrapped around the waist and tied on the right hip. Some also wear a top called a harayto. In the past, men would wear a jile, a 15-in.- (38-cm-) long dagger, the blades of which were curved and extremely sharp.

of the River Awash, where they make camps. Because this is the only important river in the region, they compete for the best places and carefully guard the positions they take along the banks. The Awash River rises in the mountains and carries a great deal of water, but the heat is so great that it never meets the sea, ending instead in Lake Abbe.

The end of the dry season is hard on both the people and the animals. Food and grazing are scarce. Some Afar head for Asayita, regarded as the capital of the Afar, hoping to find land they can cultivate.

When the short rainy season arrives in November, most of the Afar move to higher ground. Mosquitoes and floods are the hazards of the plains in winter.

Like other nomadic peoples, the Afar carry their houses and beds with them. The Afar house is called an ari and is made with a number of flexible sticks, covered with mats. If the camp – known as the burra, and usually consisting of one or two ari – is to be occupied for some time, the Afar assemble beds for use inside the ari. These too are made with mats resting on pliable wooden sticks, and are cool and comfortable for sleeping.

The women are responsible for looking after the camp. They build the houses and beds, but they are also responsible for keeping the camp clean, taking care of the children, and looking after the animals.

The milk and hides of the livestock are used for the Afar's own needs and are also traded for grain and vegetables. Salt is also sold; blocks of it are dug out of the desert. The two main markets for selling and trading are Senbete and Bati, both in inland Ethiopia.

Social structure

SOCIAL STRUCTURE The Afar are organized into clans, groups of extended families who trace their descent from a common ancestor or ancestors. They also divide themselves between two classes: the asaimara (the "reds") and the adoimara (the "whites") or the lower class. The asaimara tend to be politically dominant; the adoimara are generally the workers.

Descent is traced through the male line, and it is said that men inherit strength of character from their fathers. Physical characteristics such as height, and also spiritual aspects are said to come from the mother.

The Afar practice circumcision rites on both boys and, much more controversially, the more serious operation on girls. A man is frequently judged for the bravery with which he bore the pain of circumcision.

Kwosso game
Kwosso is a fast ball game played by the Afar. The ball is made of rolled goatskins, and the object is to keep it away from the opposing teams. In the past, teams were made up of as many as one hundred players.

On becoming an adult, such a man would be able to marry the young woman of his choice, as he would be admired by his people. People ideally marry a partner from their own ethnic group, preferably a cousin. The emphasis on families leads to powerful feelings of loyalty.

POLITICAL STRUCTURE In the past, Afar society was organized into various sultanates, each of which comprised several villages. Each sultanate was headed by an appointed figure known as a dardar. Today, the Afar live in a semiautonomous region of federal Ethiopia.

Culture and religion

RELIGION The Afar were converted to Islam by Arabs in the tenth century. Although Islam is now of great importance to the Afar and they observe Muslim rules in most aspects of life, they have modified Islamic practices according to their own culture and religion, which is based on a Sky-god.

CLOTHING The basis of traditional Afar dress is the sanafil, a cloth tied around the waist: for men it is undyed, but women's sanafils are dyed brown using a dye produced from the bark of mimosa trees. Today, many women replace this brown cloth with brightly-colored, imported fabrics. "Western" dress is preferred by many Afar, especially those who live and work in the cities.

Afar woman (above)
A married Afar woman customarily wears a black cloth, known as a shash or mushal, as a headdress.

Scouring for salt (right)
Some Afar search for salt, the only thing produced by the desert. Above, an Afar man chips away at a large block of salt.

Ari (left)
Light and portable, the ari, or Afar house, provides cool shelter from the blistering sun. The house can be built and dismantled quickly, a job usually reserved for women.

Afar timeline

by 1000s Afar settled in present lands	**1967** French Somaliland renamed French Territory of the Afars and the Issas	**1979** In Djibouti, Afar form illegal prodemocracy movement	arrested; Afar commence rebel activities
1200s–1600s Afar Muslim states at war with Christian Ethiopia		**1980s** Severe *droughts* cause famine in Ethiopia	**1992** Unsound multiparty elections end one-party state in Djibouti
1884 French Somaliland (Djibouti) formed	**1974** Military coup in Ethiopia overthrows Haile Selassie I	**1981** Djibouti made a one-party state	**1993** Eritrea officially independent from Ethiopia
1935–1941 Ethiopia invaded and occupied by Italy	**1975** Afar Liberation Front (ALF) formed. ALF active on Ethiopian-Djibouti border	**1987** In Ethiopia, autonomous Afar region created	**1994** Afar state created in Ethiopia. Peace talks end Afar insurrection in Djibouti
1961 Eritreans begin struggle for independence from Ethiopia	**1977** Djibouti wins independence. Maj. Mengistu Haile Mariam takes power in Ethiopia	**1991** Mengistu loses power; end of civil war; Eritrean liberation In Djibouti, 100 Afar dissidents	**1995** 300 former Afar rebels join Djibouti army

Afar hairdo
This distinctive hairstyle is worn by many men following initiation, usually at around age fifteen. It is seen as a demonstration of manhood.

Afrikaners

Over three million Afrikaners live in South Africa, representing about sixty percent of the country's so-called "white" population and less than ten percent of all South Africans. In addition, about 70,000 Afrikaners live in Namibia, comprising roughly five percent of the country's population. Elsewhere in Africa, many of the large-scale farmers in Kenya and Zimbabwe were Afrikaners, but recently their numbers and economic importance have declined. Today, because of drought (inadequate rainfall) and pressure on farming land, small but increasing numbers of Afrikaner farmers are emigrating and taking their skills and capital to other parts of Africa as part of government relocation schemes, especially to Congo (Rep.), Zambia, Mozambique, and Tanzania.

History

In 1652, the Dutch East India Company founded a garrison and supply station on the Cape of Good Hope for ships sailing between Holland and Asia. In 1688, 156 French Protestant refugees (Huguenots) arrived in the Cape. The Company encouraged the establishment of farms around Cape Town to supply the garrison and passing ships. The African-born children of the settlers became known as "Afrikaners," the first recorded use of the term being in 1707. Until the early nineteenth century, "Afrikaner" carried few racial connotations, being applied to people of mixed European, African,

and Malay origin as well as those of solely European ancestry. Later, being an Afrikaner came to imply being "white," with people of mixed descent classified as "colored." Many Afrikaners are descendants of interracial unions, though few admit so.

Over the years, tension developed between the Dutch authorities and the Boers (the Dutch for "farmer" and the historical name of the Afrikaners), many of whom moved inland to escape what they felt was oppressive rule. In the interior, away from Company influence, the Afrikaner as a distinct group emerged. In 1806, the British took permanent control of Cape Town. Unwilling to live under British rule, many more Afrikaners journeyed north and east into the African interior in the Great Trek of the 1830s, which became a legendary event in Afrikaner history. These migrants, the Voortrekkers, met fierce resistance from Bantu-speaking inhabitants such as the Zulu and Xhosa. Their victories in battle are still celebrated as proof of divine intervention and of the righteousness of their mission. The 1838 victory at Blood River, when 500 Boers defeated 10,000 Zulu, is especially remembered and is claimed to be the result of a pact with God – though this pact was never mentioned until after the event. The Voortrekkers established independent republics that became Transvaal, Orange Free State, and Natalia. The British annexed these republics but later returned them to independence (except Natalia, which became Natal).

Trekboers
A group of Afrikaner farmers (Boers) accompanied by their Khoikhoi herdsmen and herds of sheep and cattle. During the 1700s, such trekboers (migrant farmers) led the colonization of areas inland as they moved farther away from the Cape in search of new pastures.

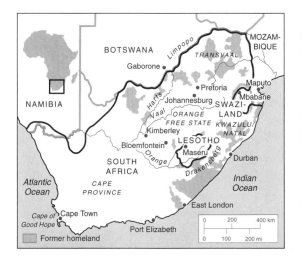

***Piet Retief** (above)*
An Afrikaner of French Huguenot descent and the commander of a militia, Piet Retief (q.v.) published a manifesto in 1837 setting out the reasons behind the Great Trek (1836–48). His complaints included:

We despair of saving the colony from the turbulent and dishonest conduct of vagrants...the severe losses which we have been forced to sustain by the emancipation of our slaves...the continual plunder which we have endured from the Caffres [the Xhosa] and other colored classes....

***The Great Trek and the first Boer republics (1836–54)** (right)*
Large-scale treks begun in 1836 came to be called the Great Trek and its participants Voortrekkers. Afrikaner farmers wishing to be independent, especially from British rules and regulations, organized large family groups to travel inland away from the Cape. For the years that they were on the move, the trekkers led a nomadic existence, stopping for a few days wherever grass and water were found. Progress was slow and only a few miles were covered each day. Some groups ventured east over the Drakensberg Mountains where they encountered the Zulu. Despite their victory over the Zulu at Blood River in 1838 and the establishment of the Natalia republic in 1839, the Afrikaners trekked back over the mountains after Natalia was annexed by the British in 1843. West of the Drakensberg, on the Highveld north of the Orange River, several independent Boer republics had been established. Annexed by the British in 1848, they were recognized as independent from 1852 and came to form the Orange Free State and the South African Republic (which became Transvaal).

In 1886, gold was discovered in Transvaal, leading to the arrival of thousands of fortune seekers. When the British sent troops into Transvaal they met fierce resistance, resulting in the Anglo-Boer War (1899–1902). Even today, bitterness toward the British remains, with memories of the loss of some 7,000 men in battle and of the 18,000 to 28,000 women and children who died in British concentration camps.

APARTHEID In 1948, the National Party came to power in South Africa – mainly thanks to the support of poor and rural Afrikaners. Apartheid (the racist doctrine of "separate development") was the government's main political platform, with many of its ideals inspired by Nazi Germany. Most Afrikaners supported apartheid, but some were fierce critics and joined nonracial churches, the illegal Communist Party, or the African National Congress. Branded as traitors, some were forced into exile, imprisoned, or put under house arrest.

RECENT EVENTS In 1991, a reformist National Party government ended all apartheid laws, and in 1994, South Africa's first nonracial elections were held, bringing to an end Afrikaner-dominated rule. Unlike many South Africans of British origin, Afrikaners have not been leaving the country in significant numbers. Afrikaners consider themselves to be Africans and, in the immediate future, they are likely to remain an economically-privileged minority within South Africa.

Language

Afrikaners speak Afrikaans, a language closely related to Dutch. The early European settlers' need to communicate with their slaves encouraged the grammatical restructuring of Dutch and the incorporation of words from Malay and African languages. The Afrikaans vocabulary further developed with the necessity of finding new words to express observations and sentiments relating to Africa, as well as incorporating French, German, and English influences. Afrikaans played an important role in the growth of Afrikaner nationalism, especially in terms of resistance to British

Boer guerrillas
Facing a much better equipped enemy during the Anglo-Boer War (1899–1902), the Boers adopted guerrilla tactics. At first, they were successful in resisting the British. After the establishment of concentration camps by the British and the destruction of their farms, however, the guerrillas found it hard to continue their successes.

rule and English influence, and the language remains central to Afrikaner identity. For 250 years, Dutch was the official language of the Afrikaners' church and schools. Official recognition of Afrikaans was hampered as it had no tradition as a written language, but in 1925 Afrikaans replaced Dutch as South Africa's official language alongside English. Today, most Afrikaners speak English as well as Afrikaans, with many rural Afrikaners also speaking other African languages. In 1995, the status of Afrikaans was reduced to one of eleven official South African languages, to the dismay of many Afrikaners.

Ways of life

In 1946, only about forty percent of Afrikaners lived in urban areas, but fifty years later the figure was over eighty percent. While fifty years ago poverty, especially

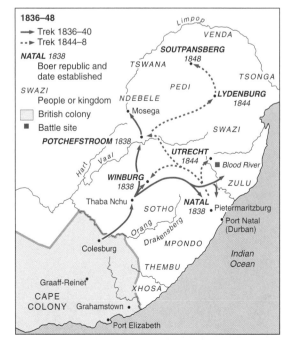

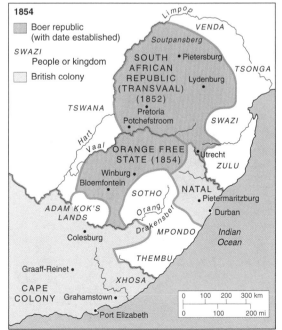

The Anglo-Boer War (1899–1902) *(left)*
These Afrikaner women are being taken to a British concentration camp. After the discovery of gold and diamonds in the region, the British set about conquering most of present-day South Africa including the Boer republics. In an attempt to wipe out Boer resistance, the British adopted a "scorched earth" policy – Afrikaner women and children were forcibly moved to concentration camps and their farms were destroyed in order to deny the Boer guerrillas access to food and supplies. Housed in wooden huts or tents with inadequate food and water supplies, many camp internees died from disease or starvation.

in rural areas, was still widespread, today the majority of Afrikaners have a lifestyle that is comparable to that of middle-class or wealthy North Americans.

Under apartheid, the Afrikaners' economically privileged position was protected by law, with most of South Africa's best land and jobs reserved for them and their white compatriots. Business was largely controlled by English-speaking South Africans. Following the National Party victory in 1948, however, Afrikaners became a significant business presence. When apartheid was no longer sustainable, it was working-class and junior-level white-collar Afrikaners who felt most threatened. The jobs of many such individuals were dependent on their race rather than on their skills and, as such, they were in the forefront of the stubborn resistance to political change.

Social structure

Afrikaner social structure differs little from that of North Americans or Europeans. Most Afrikaners can trace their ancestry to a relatively small number of Dutch or French Protestant settlers, but this ancestry is more important for social standing than for wealth.

Culture and religion

RELIGION Most Afrikaners are members of the Calvinist Dutch Reformed Church, which bases its teachings on the Old Testament. Early Afrikan-

ers saw themselves as Israelites – God's chosen people – with the British representing the Pharaoh, and the grasslands of the African interior the Promised Land. The Dutch Reformed Church sanctioned apartheid by arguing that it was God's will. Today, all but the most conservative churches have, at least officially, rejected apartheid.

LITERATURE Although prior to 1900 Afrikaans was not a written language (the Afrikaans translation of the Bible only appeared in 1933), Afrikaners have a rich literary heritage. Especially significant has been poetry, an ideal means to experiment with a rapidly developing language. Since the 1960s, poets and novelists such as Breyten Breytenbach and André Brink (q.v.) have shocked and angered the Afrikaner establishment because of the sexual content and antiapartheid themes of their work, much of which was banned from publication.

MUSIC Due to their religious backgrounds, most early Afrikaner households owned a harmonium, or pedal organ, which was used at evening prayer meetings. This instrument, along with the concertina and guitar, formed the basis of Boeremusiek – light, danceable country music, using arrangements popular with Afrikaners. As it is easier to transport, the accordion has replaced the harmonium to a great extent. Many of the melodies originated in Europe, but the lyrics have been adapted to suit local interests. Boeremusiek can be heard at large-scale music festivals or at private braaivleis parties (barbecues).

SPORT Competitive sport is extremely popular among Afrikaners, who are most associated with rugby. Banned from international competitions until recently, the South African rugby team (which is still dominated by white players) reentered world sport with a resounding victory in the 1995 rugby World Cup.

Voortrekker Monument
Opened in 1949 by Prime Minister Malan, the Voortrekker Monument near Pretoria commemorates the Great Trek of the mid-nineteenth century. It has become an important symbol for the Afrikaner people.

Paul Kruger *(right)*
President of the Transvaal Republic (1883–1902), Kruger had no formal education but established himself as a leader by fighting heroically in a commando unit against both other Africans and the British. He was a strong and forceful champion of Afrikaner interests and tried to free his republic from British domination.

Eugene Terre' Blanche *(right)*
As leader of the Afrikaner Resistance Movement, or Afrikaner Weerstandsbeweging (AWB), Terre' Blanche represents the fears of mostly poorer, rural Afrikaners who felt they would lose most from the end of apartheid. His extreme right-wing party formed in 1973 and adopted many Nazi symbols. The AWB is only one of many militant white right-wing groups.

Ajibba see **Murle**

Aka

The Aka are a subgroup of the Mbenga. The Mbenga are one of the major groupings of tropical forest-foragers – the so-called pygmies (q.v.) – of Central Africa. There are roughly 20,000 Aka living in northern Congo (Rep.) and southern Central African Republic. See **Mbuti, Twa and Mbenga**.

Fertility doll
This Fante doll closely resembles the Ashanti akua ba, except for its rectangular head. It was thought that both dolls were Ashanti fertitlity symbols, this one worn in hope of a boy and the other of a girl, but they are the work of different peoples.

Akan

The Akan make up a large family of related ethnic groups in southern and coastal Ghana and the southeast of the Ivory Coast. The Asante (q.v.) and the Fante (q.v.) of Ghana are Akan peoples, as are the Baulé (q.v.) and the Anyi (q.v.) of the Ivory Coast.

Between the 1200s and 1400s, a number of small groups of Akan-speaking peoples, such as the Asante and the Fante, settled in the forest regions of what is now modern-day Ghana. Several important Akan states developed in the area in response to the profitable gold trade. In fact, the region eventually came to be known as the Gold Coast. The Asante Empire was the greatest of these states, reaching the height of its power in the late nineteenth century. While Asante's wealth was based on trade with the Europeans, the gold mining industry in the Akan Forest region was well developed before contact with Europeans. Dyula (q.v.) traders to the north had long bought Akan gold to sell to Arab traders traveling across the Sahara Desert.

Akebou

The Akebou number only a few thousand. They live along and near the southern half of the border that separates Togo and Ghana. The Akebou live in both Ghana and Togo.

Akem see **Akyem**

Akie

The Akie are a subgroup of the Okiek. The Okiek are, in turn, part of the Kalenjin (q.v.). The Akie live in northeastern Tanzania.

Akié see **Attie**

Akoko

The Akoko live in southwestern Nigeria in Ondo State. They are a Yoruba (q.v.) people and are concentrated in the northeastern parts of Ondo.

Akpafu

The Akpafu are in a region of eastern Ghana that stretches from the Togo–Ghana border in the east to Lake Volta in the west. There are around 20,000 Akpafu people and they speak a Kwa language.

Akuapem see **Akwapim**

Akunakuna

Numbering more than 350,000, the Akunakuna are a large group of Bantu (q.v.) origin living in Nigeria's southeastern Cross River State.

Akwa

The Akwa are a significant Dyula (q.v.) subgroup, the majority of whom live in coastal regions of Cameroon. Originally a family-based grouping, the Akwa have been prominent politically and economically in Cameroon's history.

Akwamu

The 50,000 plus Akwamu live in southeastern Ghana around Lake Volta. The Akwamu Kingdom reached its height in the eighteenth century.

Akwapim

Numbering around 500,000, the Akwapim (or Akuapem) are a large subdivision of the Akan (q.v.) people. The majority live in southeastern Ghana.

Akyé *see* **Attie**

Akyem

The Akyem (or Akem) are a major subdivision of the Akan (q.v.) peoples. The majority of the more than 500,000 Akyem live in southeastern Ghana.

Alaba

The Alaba (or Halaba) are a subgroup of the Sadama (q.v.) people of southwestern Ethiopia. There are around 50,000 Alaba people.

Alagia *see* **Alladian**

Alago *see* **Alagoa**

Alagoa

The Alagoa (Alago or Arago) number more than 100,000 residents of Nigeria's central Plateau State. They are related to the Idoma and Ankwe (q.v.).

Aleta

The Aleta are one of the two main Sadama (q.v.) subgroups. The Sadama live in Ethiopia.

Ali

The Ali are one of the Central African Republic's (CAR's) smallest ethnic groups. They live in a region of southwestern CAR and across the border in Congo (Rep.). The Ali are descended from Baya (q.v.) and Bantu (q.v.) ancestors.

Alladian

The Alladian (or Alagia, Jack-Jacks, or Nladja-Wron) are an ethnic group living in the southeast of the Ivory Coast. Part of the so-called Lagoon cluster (q.v.) of the Ivory Coast, they are an Akan (q.v.) people who number around 20,000.

Alur

The Alur live in northwestern Uganda and neighboring parts of Congo (Dem. Rep.). The historical Alur homeland is around the northwestern shores of Lake Albert and the Albert Nile, though many Alur now live in Uganda's larger cities, including Kampala, the capital city. There are probably around 500,000 Alur, the majority of whom live in Uganda. The language the Alur speak is called DhaAlur, which is a Lwo (q.v) language.

The Alur are Nilotes (q.v.) originally from the cradleland of the so-called River-Lake Nilotes – southern Sudan. The ancestors of the Lwo-speaking River-Lake Nilotes migrated southward sometime after 1000 c.e., settling at Pubungu on the northernmost tip of Lake Albert. A group led by a man called Nyipir moved west across the Nile (from c. 1450), founding several chiefdoms. The followers of Nyipir and the people they colonized came to be called the Alur.

Amarar

The Amarar are one of the subdivisions of the Beja (q.v.) people. The majority of the 350,000 plus Amarar Beja live in northeastern Sudan along the coast with the Red Sea, and they are especially concentrated around Port Sudan.

Amba

The Amba (or Bulebule, Hamba, Kibera, or Kukamba) are related to the Azande (q.v.) and the Mangbetu (q.v.). They live south of Lake Albert, largely in Uganda but some also across the border in Congo (Dem. Rep.). There are very roughly 100,000 Amba people.

Americo-Liberians

Until recently, the Americo-Liberians formed the dominant political, economic, and social elite in Liberia – even though at few more than 100,000 they accounted for less than 3 percent of that country's population. A coup in 1980, which sparked a long-running civil war, ended more than a century's political domination by Americo-Liberians. In recent decades, intermingling between different ethnic groups in Liberia has led to the more widespread use of the term Kwi for people of part Americo-Liberian descent.

Monrovia, now the capital of Liberia, was founded in 1847 by a white philanthropic group called the American Colonization Society. The society settled more than 16,000 African Americans in Liberia, though settlers had already been arriving in the region since the 1820s. These freed slaves, or Congoes as they were then called, declared Liberia's independence in 1847, although this was not recognized by the US government until 1862. Many of the Congoes took African husbands or wives, leading to the emergence of the Americo-Liberian community.

The non-Americo-Liberian community was treated harshly by the settlers, however, who maintained they were "civilizing" the "barbarous shores of Africa." Until 1944 only Americo-Liberians were allowed to vote in Liberia's elections. Since the outbreak of civil war, however, many Americo-Liberians (along with other Liberians) have fled from Liberia. The pattern of Liberia's dominance by Americo-Liberians has been hard to break, however, since there are fewer members of the less-privileged other groups who are able to fill posts once held by Americo-Liberians due to a lack of education and skills.

Amhara

There are about fifteen million Amhara, who make up roughly thirty-five percent of Ethiopia's population and dominate the country's political and economic life. Most live in the rolling hills of the plateau to the north of Addis Ababa (Ethiopia's capital).

History

The Amhara are a Cushitic people whose ancestors lived in Ethiopia over two thousand years ago. The Cushites were the first food producers in Africa. The facts that for thousands of years the region has been the site of international trade routes, and that the Amhara have been influenced by the Semitic cultures of Arabia, suggest that Arabs and Greeks are probably among the Amhara's ancestors as well as Africans.

The earliest Ethiopian kingdom was centred on Axum (in what is now Tigre province). According to tradition, the Queen of Sheba (now part of Yemen) visited King Solomon in Jerusalem, and together they produced a son, Menelik. Solomon allowed Menelik to make a copy of the Ark of the Covenant, one of the most sacred Jewish objects. Menelik secretly exchanged the copy for the real Ark and took it to Axum, where he founded a kingdom, reigning between about 975 and 950 BCE. Historical records place the emergence of this kingdom in the 100s CE, however. The Axumite Kingdom grew to dominate much of what is now Ethiopia and southern Sudan and had great influence over southern Arabia. When the Axumite Kingdom's power declined from about 400, the Amhara from the south of the kingdom gradually gained political dominance over the Ethiopian

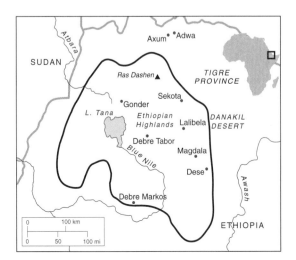

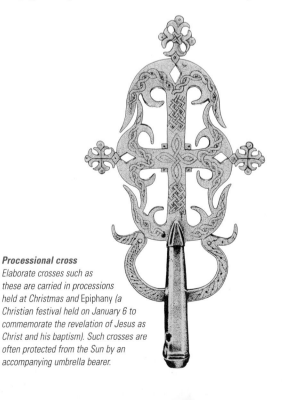

Processional cross
Elaborate crosses such as these are carried in processions held at Christmas and Epiphany (a Christian festival held on January 6 to commemorate the revelation of Jesus as Christ and his baptism). Such crosses are often protected from the Sun by an accompanying umbrella bearer.

George and the dragon (above)
Saint George (or Ghiorghis) is the patron saint of Ethiopia. This nineteenth-
century picture is from the seventeenth-century church of Debre Berhan
Selassie in the Gonder region of Ethiopia. Drawn on canvas fixed directly
on to the wall, it shows Saint George slaying the dragon.

Amharic script (above)
The Amharic script developed in
Ethiopia over two thousand years
ago and it is still used today. It is a
modified version of an ancient
Arabian script.

Highlands. After Syrians converted Ezana, king of Axum 320–55, to Christianity, the Amhara gradually adopted the religion too. The spread of Islam in surrounding areas from the seventh century resulted in the isolation of the Amhara until the arrival of the Portuguese in the 1500s.

For centuries, emperors ruled Ethiopia, many of whom claimed to be descended from King Solomon and the Queen of Sheba, the dynasty having been restored in 1270 by King Yekuno Amlak. This Solomonic dynasty survived both Muslim encroachment and European colonization (apart from Italian occupation from 1935 to 1941) until 1974 when the Emperor Haile Selassie I (q.v.) was overthrown by the military in an initially popular revolt.

RECENT EVENTS The military government claimed to follow a Marxist ideology, seeking popular support by pursuing land reform. Military rule was often ruthless, however, with attacks not only on the landowning class but on all opposition, especially peoples seeking independence or autonomy from what they regarded as centuries of Amhara domination. In 1991, the military was overthrown and Eritrea – after a thirty-year civil war – was liberated from Ethiopia.

Language

Since about the fourteenth century, the Amhara's language has been Amharic, now Ethiopia's former official language. Amharic is a Semitic language related to Geez, the ancient language of Ethiopia that is still used by the church today and which also forms the basis of the Amharic system of writing, but is rarely used in speech.

Ways of life

AGRICULTURE Nearly ninety percent of the Amhara are rural. The Ethiopian Highlands, where most Amhara live, is high, bleak, and hilly and many Amhara can grow just enough food for themselves and their families. Until the 1974 revolution, an unequal relationship was maintained between the (often absentee) landlords

and sharecropping farmers, many of whom were in a virtual state of slavery as a result of accumulated debts. The revolution did not improve the circumstances of the farmers, only changed them: rural officials maintained strict control, farmers were forced into villages and large-scale, state-controlled farms, or sent to face the alien conditions of the remote south of Ethiopia where many died.

Amhara farmers grow barley, corn, millet, wheat, and, teff (a small grain rich in protein and iron) as well as beans, peppers, and other vegetables. Lowland farmers are able to produce two crops a year, but in the colder and less fertile highlands only a single crop is achieved. Oxen are used for plowing, though the poorer farmers may have to borrow or hire oxen for this purpose. Poultry, sheep, and goats are commonly kept, as are donkeys and mules – for transportation. Wild coffee, which originates in Ethiopia, is gathered, though it is generally of poor quality. The basic diet consists of vegetable or meat stews, accompanied by injera (a pancakelike fermented bread made from teff), coffee, beer, mead, or milk.

The revolution, civil war, and droughts (periods of inadequate rainfall) have all had their effect on farming in Ethiopia. Throughout the 1980s drought, rebel and government troop activities, inadequate infrastructure, and bureaucratic indifference all conspired to trigger a major famine during which many Amhara and other Ethiopians lost their lives or became refugees or migrants. Aid programmes since the 1980s have been aimed at small-scale farmers in the hope that they can be prosperous enough to be vulnerable to famine no longer.

DIVISION OF LABOR Men's primary responsibility is tilling the soil and caring for the larger animals. From the age of seven, boys are expected to work, at first helping to look after smaller animals and later herding cattle. Amhara girls over the age of seven are expected to help with the housework. Amhara women have

Amharic homes
In general, Amhara houses are circular with walls made of wattle-and-daub, *sometimes of stone, and with a thatched roof – the frame of which is supported by a central post.*

Salt trading
Salt is one form of currency used by the Amhara. It is cut in blocks from the Danakil Desert in northeastern Ethiopia.

many responsibilities, including cooking, making beer, collecting fuel (dried animal dung and wood), taking water from the nearest well or stream, spinning cotton, weaving mats and baskets, and caring for the children.

Social structure

A typical Amhara household consists of a husband (generally regarded as head of the family) and wife, their children, and other unmarried or elderly relatives.

Social and community life is centered on the local church. Marriages are generally arranged by the families, with boys usually marrying between seventeen and twenty-two, and girls sometimes as young as fourteen. Civil marriages are most typical, but some Amhara marry in church, though after such marriages divorce is prohibited. Two wedding feasts follow, one held by each family. A week after the birth of a baby a priest visits to bless and, if the child is a boy, to circumcise it. The mother and baby remain in seclusion for forty days after the birth, finally emerging to go to church for the baptism. When a person dies, a priest officiates at the funeral. A forty-day period of intense mourning follows, after which the priest holds a memorial service.

Culture and religion

RELIGION Christianity has been the religion of the Amhara for many centuries and the church is widely regarded as the guardian of Amhara culture. Most Amhara are members of the Towahedo (Orthodox)

Christian Church which maintains close links with the Egyptian Coptic Church. There are numerous religious festivals – with Easter and Epiphany (the revelation and baptism of Christ) the most important – that are celebrated not only with religious services but with feasting and dancing.

ART Amhara art is closely linked with religion, and the Amhara decorate their churches with elaborate paintings, many of which were commissioned by wealthy landlords. Ethiopian church art is similar to that of other Orthodox churches and the influence of this style still persists.

Amhara timeline

100 Axumite Kingdom emerges	**1270** Amhara Solomonic dynasty established	**1930** Emperor Haile Selassie I begins reign	**1977** Somalia invades Ethiopia. Maj. Mengistu Haile Mariam takes power in Ethiopia.
300s Axumites issue gold currency	**1400s–1500s** Expansion of Ethiopian Empire through conquest	**1935–1941** Ethiopia invaded and occupied by Italy	**1980s** Drought and famine in Ethiopia
c. 320–355 Rule of Ezana, first Christian king of the Axumite Kingdom	**1700s** Ethiopia splits into several separate states	**1961** Eritrean rebels launch independence movement	**1991** Mengistu loses power; end of civil war for Eritrean liberation
640 on Rise of Islam; slow decline of Axumite Kingdom	**1855–1930** Series of Ethiopian rulers rise to reclaim Empire in an attempt to prevent colonialism	**1964** Ethiopia at war with Somalia	**1993** Eritrea officially independent from Ethiopia
1117 Zagwe dynasty founded in Ethiopia	**1896** Battle of Adowa (modern Adwa): Italians defeated by Ethiopians	**1970s** Drought and famine in Ethiopia	**1994** Ethiopia organized into nine states based on ethnicity; widespread Amhara lose out as the Tigre dominate the new government.
1268 Zagwe dynasty overthrown		**1974** Military coup overthrows Haile Selassie; socialist state declared	

Anaang see **Anang**

Anakaza

The Anakaza (or Annakaza) are a subgroup of the Daza (q.v.), who in turn are a subgroup of the Tebu (q.v.). They are a largely nomadic, semiautonomous people of northern Chad.

Anang

Numbering more than 800,000, the Anang (or Anaang or Annang) are a large ethnic group living in southeastern Nigeria's Cross River region. They are related to the Efik (q.v.) and speak an Ibibio (q.v.) language.

Ancheya see **Chewa**

Anglophones of Cameroon

The Anglophones, or Westerners, of Cameroon make up 20 percent of the population of that country and number well over two million. They inhabit the ex-British southwestern and northwestern provinces of western Cameroon. Although they are referred to as Anglophones, the Westerners actually speak various African languages, and a minority speak English and French.

What is now Cameroon was formed by the unification of British and French colonies in the 1960s. An independent republic of Cameroon was created in 1960 when the previously French-ruled Cameroun became independent. In 1961, the inhabitants of the then British-ruled territory of Western Cameroon voted on whether to join with Nigeria to the north or Cameroon to the south. Those living in the southern provinces of Western Cameroon voted to join the Republic of Cameroon, while those in the north voted to join Nigeria.

Many Anglophones of Cameroon feel that they are treated like second-class citizens. The Anglophones claim that they are under-represented in government, and the Anglophone regions have long been less advanced economically compared to Francophone regions. Some even want independence for the western region, but this would be strongly resisted by the government.

Ankwai see **Ankwe**

Ankwe

The Ankwe (or Ankwai, Gomei, or Groemai) are an ethnic group found in the region of the Jos Plateau, central Nigeria.

Anlo

The Anlo are a major subgroup of the Ewe (q.v.). The several thousand Anlo Ewe are concentrated in Ghana west of the River Volta.

Annakaza see **Anakaza**

Annang see **Anang**

Anniya

The Anniyia are a major subgroup of the Oromo (q.v.) of Ethiopia. They are concentrated in a region around Harer in the east of that country.

Antaifasy

The Antaifasy are a Madagascan people (q.v.) numbering more than 150,000. The majority live in a small region on the island's southeast coast around the city of Farafangana. Many Antaifasy have migrated to the other parts of Madagascar in recent decades, however, to look for work. Some people consider the Antaifasy to be a subgroup of the Antaisaka (q.v.).

Antaimoro

With more than 500,000 members, the Antaimoro are one of Madagascar's larger ethnic groups. The majority live in a region to the north of the Antaifasy (q.v.) on the island's southeast coast. Some people consider the Antaimoro to be a subgroup of the Antaisaka. See **Madagascan people**.

Antaisaka

The Antaisaka are a large grouping of Madagascan peoples (q.v.). They live in a region on the island's southeast coast to the south of the Antaimoro (q.v.), Antambhoaka (q.v.), and the Antaifasy (q.v.), who are sometimes considered to be Antaisaka subgroups. There are more than 600,000 Antaisaka people.

Antambahoaka

The Antambhoaka are probably Madagascar's smallest indigenous ethnic group. The Antambhoaka number only roughly 50,000 people, the majority of whom live in a region on the island's southeast coast just south of the city of Mananjary. They are sometimes considered to be a subgroup of the Antaisaka (q.v.). See **Madagascan people**.

Antandroy

The Antandroy are a large grouping of Madagascan peoples (q.v.). The majority of the 600,000 plus Antandroy live in the southernmost region of the island.

Antankarana

Although they have a population of more than 50,000, the Antankarana are one of Madagascar's smallest ethnic groups. The majority live in the northernmost tip of Madagascar. Although sometimes considered a subgroup of the Sakalava (q.v.) people, they are descended from Arabs (q.v.) and Betsimisiraka (q.v.) people as well. See **Madagascan people**.

Antanosy

Concentrated in the southeastern corner of Madagascar, the Antanosy number more than 360,000. They are descended from Antambahoaka (q.v.), Arab (q.v.), French, and Indian ancestors.

Anuak

The Anuak people occupy an area that straddles the border of southern Sudan and western Ethiopia. The civil war in Sudan lead to many Anuak migrating to Ethiopia. There are probably around 80,000 Anuak people. The Anuak language is also called Anuak; it is closely related to the Shilluk (q.v.) language.

The Alur are Nilotes (q.v.), originally from the cradleland of the so-called River-Lake Nilotes – southern Sudan. Sometime after 1000 c.e. the ancestors of the Anuak migrated south from their cradleland, reaching present-day Juba in southern Sudan. From Juba the Anuak returned north, settling in their present lands. Most Anuak today are farmers, but in the past cattle herding was their main occupation. Relics of this pastoral lifestyle can be found in their language, which includes many cattle-raising terms and names for bulls. The Anuak religion is similar to the Shilluk religion, involving a belief in the creator-god Juok.

Ancestral figure
This unusual Anyi carving has a shiny finish, white paint around the eyes and upper torso, and is sitting on a two-legged stool.

Anyi

The Anyi are an Akan (q.v.) people living in the Ivory Coast. Numbering more than 200,000 people in that country, the Anyi can be subdivided into such groups as the so-called Anyi proper, Nzimas, Aburés, and Brong. The Anyi are closely-related to the Baulé (q.v.) people of central southeastern Ivory Coast.

The Anyi proper are a Twi-speaking people who are concentrated in southeast Ivory Coast, in particular in the region that lies between the Komoé River and the border that separates Ghana and Ivory Coast. This subgroup alone accounts for at least 100,000 people, the vast majority of whom are Christian.

In the mid-eighteenth century, sections of the Asante (q.v.) Empire in what is now Ghana broke away in search of fresh lands to the west. Some groups, led by a woman called Awura Poku, settled on the lands to the east of the Bandama River. These and later migrations from the Akan homelands formed the present-day Baulé and Anyi populations.

Anyuak *see* Anuak

Apindji

The Apindji are a Gabonese ethnic group that has been decimated in size in the last century after a series of epidemics and a famine in 1922. Today, most live in the cities of west-central Gabon such as Lambarené and Fougamou. The Apindji religion, Bwiti, has gained many converts in the 20th century, including large numbers of Fang (q.v.) people.

Aquamboes *see* Akwamu

Arabs of North Africa

Arabs originate from Arabia (present day Saudi Arabia), where millions still live today. Now, however, there are more Arabs in North Africa than in Saudi Arabia. Their occupation of Africa came about as a result of the creation of a new religion, Islam.

Numbering over 100 million, Arabs are the most numerous ethnic group in North Africa. In many countries, Arabs have intermarried with the original people. Most Egyptians are a mixture of Arabs and the descendants of Ancient Egyptians. Nearly 90 percent of Libyans are descended from both Arabs and Berbers, and nearly half of the Sudanese population is Arab. The other North African countries (Morocco, Algeria, and Tunisia) form the Maghreb – an Arabic term meaning "the West." Tunisia's population is 98 percent Arab, Algeria's 83 percent, and Morocco's 70 percent.

Arab expansion

After the death of the Prophet Muhammad in 632, his Arab followers began the invasion and conquest of North Africa. These maps show the expansion of Arab peoples in the region. As they gained new territories, the Arabs brought Islam to the region.

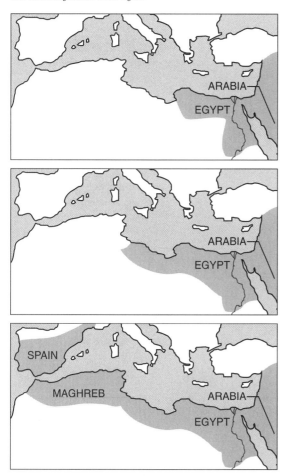

Gravestone

The gravestone of a king of the Marinid dynasty of Morocco, Sultan Abu Yaqub Yusuf, who reigned from 1286–1307. The Arabic inscriptions commemorate the dead king and quote from the Koran (Islamic holy book). The stone is made from marble and would have stood at the head of the grave or been embedded in a wall.

History

An Arab general, Amr ibn al As, led an army 4,000 strong into Egypt in 640, beginning the Arab invasion of North Africa. At that time, Egypt was part of the Byzantine, or East Roman, Empire. In 642, the Byzantines surrendered Egypt to the Arabs. The country came under the rule of governors appointed by the caliphs, the rulers of the Arab world. In 670, Uqba ibn Nafi, an Arab general, raided the Barbary Coast, the northwest African territory of the Berbers. By 711, Arabs controlled all of North Africa as well as southern Spain, where they were known as "Moors." The Arabs colonized Cyrenaica and Tripolitania, the coastal regions of what is now Libya, pushing out or absorbing the Berbers who lived there. Many Berbers soon converted to Islam.

Language

The Arabic language is a Semitic language. This is a language group that also includes Hebrew and the Ethiopian languages of Amharic and Tigrinya. There are many different forms of Arabic. Colloquial, or spoken, Arabic comprises all the dialects spoken in different Arabic countries. The Arabic spoken by a Tunisian, for example, is different from that spoken by an Egyptian. Written Arabic, however, descends directly from the classical language of the Koran (Islamic holy book) and is the standard written language of all Arab nations. A spoken form of it – Modern Standard Arabic – is used in broadcasting, films, and for communication between Arabs who would otherwise speak different dialects. Classical Arabic is now only used in the Koran.

Arabic is the official language of Algeria, Egypt, Libya, Morocco, Sudan, and Tunisia. The legacy of French colonialism remains, however, in that French is widely spoken throughout the Maghreb countries. Even since independence, the region's links with France have grown through tourism and migrant labor.

Ways of life

Arab ways of life vary as they are usually influenced by local cultures. About one-third of North African Arabs live and work in cities and towns. The rest are either farmers or herders – such as the widely-scattered Bedouin Arabs. Town life varies. Wealthy Arabs may live in modern houses and work in commerce or in industry. They may shop in modern, Western-style stores. Most urban Arabs, however, live in crowded, older parts of the towns, where the streets are often too narrow and winding for vehicles. Many streets are lined with stalls and open-fronted stores where people sell food and make and sell craft products.

Rural Arabs tend to live in small villages. In Egypt, for example, each village has a mosque (Islamic house of worship), perhaps a bathhouse, and a few stores. Some Arabs have their own plots of land, but many have to work for large, wealthy landowners growing cash crops such as grapes, dates, cotton, cereals, and citrus fruits.

ECONOMY In the twentieth century, the discovery of oil

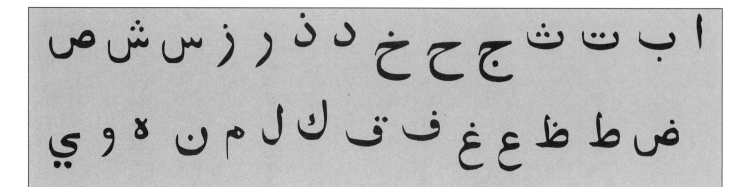

Arabic script *(above)*
Arabic is written from right to left. The Arabic alphabet has twenty-eight symbols, which are mostly consonants. Vowels are shown by diacritics – marks like accents – above or below the letters. These are normally omitted; they are generally only shown in the Classical Arabic of the Koran (Islamic holy book) and in elementary schoolbooks.

Kufic and Nashki *(above right)*
Arabic script has two main styles, angular Kufic and the more rounded Nashki. Kufic was more popular in the early years of Islam. From the eleventh century onward, Nashki became more frequently used. The example shown uses the Kufic style for a silk tapestry from tenth-century Egypt.

and mineral deposits in many North African countries has enriched Arab economies. For example, Libya, Egypt, and Algeria are now major oil exporters; Morocco and Tunisia have some of the world's largest supplies of phosphates, which are used in fertilizers. Manufacturing industries have also been developed: Algeria, Libya, and Tunisia are all major concrete manufacturers and Egypt exports cotton cloth. Inevitably, these industries have affected the lifestyles of many Arabs in North Africa – bringing new job opportunities and greater affluence to some.

BEDOUIN The Bedouin are an Arab subgroup who are chiefly nomadic pastoralists – they travel with their herds of sheep, goats, and camels in search of water and pasture. The Bedouin are mostly found in and around the Sahara Desert. Algeria, Libya, and Sudan have the greatest number of Bedouin. The Bedouin still use camels as their main form of desert transportation, but the great camel caravans (companies of travelers) of the past are being steadily replaced by trucks.

Social structure

The family is the most important part of Arab society. Arranged marriages are common, but gradually more young people are choosing their own partners. Men tend to be the heads of Arab households. They go out to work or work in the fields, while the women work in the home. Few women have jobs after they marry. In some parts, however, and especially in cities, women are able to work outside the home and hold responsible jobs. Men and women usually eat separately and sometimes pray separately as well – the women at home if they are not allowed into the local mosque. For social contact, women visit neighbors, friends, and relatives in their own homes. Egyptian women tend to have more freedom than in other parts of the Arab world, although the recent rise in radical Islamic fundamentalism threatens to reverse this.

Culture and religion

RELIGION The vast majority of Arabs are Muslims. Islam was founded in 622 by Muhammad – an Arab religious leader who lived in what is now Saudi Arabia. Muhammad is revered throughout the Islamic world as the Prophet of Allah. Islam united the Arab peoples, and it inspired them, after Muhammad's death in 632, to spread the new religion. Islam was the driving force behind the Arab invasion and conquest of North Africa.

Perfume sprinkler
Dating from the 1300s, this Egyptian brass qumqum was used to sprinkle perfume. It is inlaid with silver and gold inscriptions. The main inscription is a dedication to the Arab Sultan Al Malik al Nasir.

Wooden coffer
Perhaps used to store books in a mosque, this carved wooden coffer was made between 1300 and 1500. The style of the Arabic inscriptions suggests that it was made in Fez, Morocco.

Arab town *(above)*
The medina is the old section of an Arab town, and often has narrow winding streets. Part of it is always the souk, a marketplace.

Arabs of North Africa timeline		
632 Death of the Prophet Muhammad	**c. 1000** Fatimids begin to lose North African territories	**1798** Napoleon conquers Egypt
640 Arab invasion and conquest of North Africa begins	**1069** Berber Almoravid dynasty begins rule in Morocco	**1805** Egypt independent
642 Arabs conquer Egypt	**1169** Last remaining Fatmids in Egypt overthrown	**1914** North Africa under colonial rule
661 Omayyad rule over Arab empire in North Africa begins	**1200s** Much of North Africa is controlled by Berbers	**1945** League of Arab States founded
710 Omayyad conquest of western Maghreb and Spain begins	**1250** Mamluk rule in Egypt begins	**1950s** Many North African countries become independent
711 North Africa and southern Spain conquered by Arabs	**1510** Some cities under European rule	**1960s** Military coups in both Algeria and Libya
750 Abbasids overthrow Omayyads	**1517** Ottomans conquer Mamluks	**1973** Worldwide oil crisis begins after Arabs impose oil embargo
789 Independent Arab dynasties begin to emerge in North Africa	**1574** Ottomans control all of North African coast except Morocco	**1990s** Resurgence of Arab nationalism and Islamic militancy in many North African nations
909 Fatimids begin conquest of North Africa	**1610** Morocco divides into two warring kingdoms	
969 Fatimids control North Africa	**1670** Morocco reunited by Alawids	

Clothing
Arab men in cities generally wear Western-style clothes, but often cover a formal suit with a jalabiya (a loose, cotton robe).

Arago see Alagoa

Argobba

The Argobba (or Argobbinya) are a small ethnic group, numbering only a few thousand. They live in east-central Ethiopia.

Argobbinya see Argobba

Ari see Abidji

Arisi see Arusi

Arma

Numbering around 20,000, the Arma are a subgroup of the Songhay (q.v.) people of Mali. The majority of the Arma live in and around Tombouctou (formerly Timbuktu), where they once formed the ruling class. Arma ancestors include European soldiers captured by the Moroccan king in the sixteenth century. The Amar are descended from the offspring of these soldiers and their Songhay wives.

Aro

A politically and economically important Igbo (q.v.) subgroup, the Aro number more than 700,000. The Aro live in southeastern Nigeria and have long been well known as successful merchants and traders.

Arsi see Arusi

Arssi see Arusi

Arusha

The Arusha are a Maasai (q.v.) people living in northern Tanzania numbering more than 150,000. They have often been called the "agricultural Maasai" since they have largely abandoned nomadic pastoralism (livestock herdering) and become settled farmers.

Arusi

The Arusi (or Arsi, Arisi, or Arssi) are one of the larger Oromo (q.v.) subgroups. The Arusi are concentrated in central Ethiopia and the majority are Muslim.

© DIAGRAM

Asante

The Asante (or Ashanti) mostly live in the forest regions of south-central Ghana and are the largest ethnic group in that country. A number also live in the neighboring states of Togo and Ivory Coast. There are probably 1,500,000 Asante.

Gold pendant
The Asante are masters of gold working, not surprisingly since they have been mining and trading gold for centuries. This gold pendant is exquisitely decorated and comes from the royal regalia of the asantehene.

History

The Asante are descended from people who settled in West Africa thousands of years ago. A number of small groups of Akan-speaking peoples, including the Asante, settled in the forest regions of modern Ghana between the eleventh and thirteenth centuries.

ASANTE EMPIRE The separate Asante chiefdoms were united by Osei Tutu (q.v.) in the 1670s, when he took the title of asantehene (king) and founded the Asante Empire. Osei Tutu fell in battle in 1717 and was succeeded by Opoku Ware, who continued the Asante expansion. By the time of his death in 1750, the Asante Empire was the largest and most powerful state in the region. Much of the Asante success lay in the strength and flexibility of its fighting units and battle formations.

Its wealth and prosperity was based on mining and trading in gold and trading in slaves, with both the Europeans who visited the coast (which came to be known as the "Gold Coast") and with other African kingdoms to the north of the Asante Empire.

At its height under Osei Bonsu (q.v.), who ruled 1801–24, the Asante Empire covered all of modern-day Ghana as well as parts of Togo, Burkina Faso, and Ivory Coast. The Fante people on the Gold Coast were conquered by 1816. This brought the Asante increasingly into conflict with the British, who wanted to control the gold trade. The result was a series of Anglo-Asante wars. In the first, in 1824, the Asante defeated the British; in the second, in 1826, the Asante were defeated, but the British did not pursue their victory. In 1863, the Asante twice defeated joint Anglo-Fante troops. When Asante troops crossed the Pra River in 1874 – to reconquer the Fante – they were driven back by the British, who invaded the Asante capital, Kumasi, and blew up the royal palace, leaving the empire in disarray. Agyeman Prempe I became asantehene in 1888 and began reuniting the Asante; nervous of his success the British forced him into exile in 1896 and declared the Asante Kingdom (Prempe never recovered the full empire) a protectorate (colony). A further war followed in 1900, led by the ohemmaa (most senior woman). Despite great resistance, the Asante were defeated and the British annexed their lands in 1902.

Royal musicians
These musicians are blowing side-blown ivory horns at an Asante state ceremony. These horn blowers play an important part at any major event; every regional chief has his own blower who follows him, sounding his horn in the distinctive notes that identify each particular chief.

Asante architecture
Until relatively recently, Asante dwellings were usually constructed of four linked huts around a courtyard. The walls had a wooden framework and were built up with mud. The sides of the huts facing the courtyard were often left open or partly open. The outside walls were decorated with elaborate and beautiful relief patterns. Roofs were usually thatched. Many dwellings now have brick or concrete walls and roofs of sheet metal.

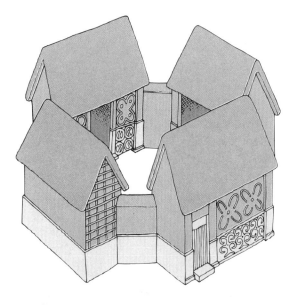

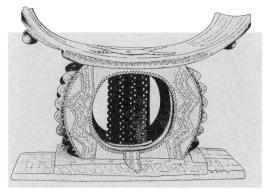

Silver Stool (above)
This wooden stool, which is decorated with silver sheeting, was made for the most senior Asante woman – the ohemmaa. When a new asantehene is selected, the ohemmaa inaugurates the selection in her capacity as owner of her own Silver Stool.

Language

The Asante language is also called Asante and is a dialect of Twi – one of the Akan group of languages.

Ways of life

Most Asante people make their living as farmers. Cash crops are grown as well as crops such as rice and yams for food. The most important cash crop is cocoa, Ghana's chief export. Other crops grown include coconuts, kola nuts, and palm kernels (seeds). Mining of diamonds, gold, bauxite, and manganese provides employment for some Asante; still others work in forestry. In urban areas, many Asante are employed in business or work for the government as civil servants. Producing wood carvings for the tourist trade is a source of funds for some Asante.

Social structure

POLITICAL STRUCTURE In the nineteenth century, the asantehene Osei Tutu introduced the Golden Stool, declared to embody the soul of the Asante nation. It symbolized the political unity of the Asante and was never sat on. The British attempted to confiscate the stool, so it was kept in hiding for many years. Its remains have been incorporated into a new stool, which is still a potent symbol of Asante unity today. The Asante Kingdom is now part of modern Ghana. Although the asantehene is still an important figure in Ghanaian society, his role is now largely ceremonial and symbolic.

Culture and religion

RELIGION Most Asante people are either Christian or Muslim. The Asante royalty, however, still follow the Asante religion as part of their role in maintaining Asante culture. It involves the worship of a supreme god called Nyame, who communicates through various lesser gods.

METAL CASTING The Asante are famous as the producers of probably the most beautiful goldwork in Africa. To this day, Asante state ceremonies and celebrations are occasions for a show of gold regalia worn and used by the Asantehene and his chiefs, all devised as symbols of their political and moral authority. Asante goldsmiths and other metal workers use a casting technique called the lost-wax method. The flourishing of representational forms of brass gold-weights – used to measure gold dust and nuggets – from the 1700s onward was, in part, allowed by the use of this effective method. Small, intricate pieces as well as larger, simpler pieces can be produced by lost-wax casting.

First, a wax model is made of the object to be cast. Modern metal casters usually use purified beeswax. The model is then covered with a clay mold in which a hole is pierced. When the mold is heated, the wax melts and is poured out of this hole. Molten metal is then poured into the cavity. After the metal has hardened and cooled, the mold is broken and the casting is removed for polishing and perhaps further decorative work. A possibly older method of metal casting is the lost-beetle method. The technique is the same as for lost-wax casting except a real object such as a beetle, seed, or flower is encased in the mold. When heated, the object in the mold turns to ash.

WEAVING The Asante are famous for weaving the colorful kente cloth, from which the national dress of Ghana is made. Kente cloth is distinctive for its complex patterns.

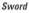

Sword
This Asante sword has a gold-plated wooden hilt, a rounded pommel and a decorated blade. Swords such as this are used for ceremonial purposes – they are carried in front of processions and state funerals.

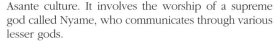

Asante battle formation
Asante battle formation was a precision instrument that few enemies resisted successfully. In outline, it bore a striking resemblance to a modern airplane. At the "nose" is a party of scouts; the "fuselage" is made up of a column of warriors, followed by the Commander-in-Chief and his military staff; the "tail" section comprises a rearguard; and the "wings" consist of five columns of men each. At the rear of each wing is a group of medical personnel – rather like wing flaps. This awesome arrangement of men was the secret of the Asante Empire's military success.

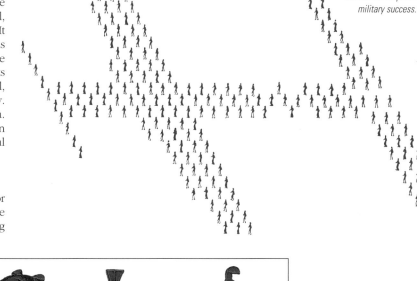

Gold-weights
Brass weights used to measure gold dust or nuggets have been made and used by the Asante for centuries. They are generally accurate to 0.2 oz (0.5 g). The weights were produced using the lost-wax or lost-beetle methods of casting.

Asante timeline			
1000s–1200s Early Akan-speaking peoples settle forests of modern Ghana	**1863** Third Anglo-Asante War	**1902** British annex Asante territories to Gold Coast colony	**1979** Military coup led by Jerry Rawlings forces elections
1640 Fante states emerge on coast.	**1874** Fourth Anglo-Asante war: Asante Empire in disarray	**1954** National Liberation Movement (NLM) formed in Asante region	**1981** Military coup led by Rawlings ends civilian rule in Ghana
1670s Asante united by Osei Tutu; Asante Empire founded	**1883–1888** Civil war as Asante Empire begins to disintegrate	**1957** Gold Coast gains independence as Ghana; nationalization begun	**1983** Process of denationalizing some state enterprises begins
1717–1750 Under Opoku Ware, empire becomes most powerful in region	**1888** Agyeman Prempe I attempts to revive Asante Empire	**1960s** Many large, mechanized, state-run farms created	**1992** Elections end military rule; Rawlings is elected president
1816 Asante defeat Fante states	**1896** Prempe exiled by British; colony established over Asante	**1966** Military coup in Ghana	**1999** Asante King Opoku Ware II died and Nana Kwaku Dua was crowned asantehene.
1824 First Anglo-Asante War	**1900** Asante rebel against British	**1969** Return to civilian rule in Ghana	
1826 Second Anglo-Asante War			

Ashanti *see* Asante

Asians of Africa

Asian people have contributed to the rich and varied history of Africa for centuries. Among the earliest Asian settlers were those who settled on the east coast of Africa and islands in the region, such as Madagascar, Zanzibar, and Mauritius. During the nineteenth century and early twentieth century, when India and a lot of Africa were British colonies, a great influx of Asians to Africa occurred. They settled in Kenya, Tanzania, Uganda, Zambia, Malawi, and South Africa. The majority of African Asians originate from the Indian subcontinent (South Asia), mostly from Gujarat and Punjab, though a small minority originally came from China.

Although many East African Asians (q.v.) and Central African Asians left Africa after independence from colonial rule – some forcibly, as in Idi Amin's (q.v.) Uganda – Indian South Africans (q.v.) have largely stayed in that country.

Assin

The Assin of central Ghana are a large grouping of Akan (q.v.) peoples. There are roughly 140,000 Assin.

Athi

Athi is a term originally used disparagingly by the Maasai (q.v.) to refer to non-Maasai people. The Okiek (q.v.) are sometimes called the Athi.

Atié *see* Attie

Attie

There are roughly 280,000 Attie (Akié, Atié, or Akyé) living north of Abidjan in Ivory Coast. The Attie are often considered to be part of the Lagoon cluster (q.v.) of peoples though are similar culturally to the Anyi (q.v.) and Baulé (q.v.).

Attuot

The Attuot (or Atuot or Atwat) number more than 50,000, the majority of whom live in the Upper Nile River region of southern Sudan. They are a Nilotes (q.v.) and are closely associated with the Nuer (q.v).

Atuot *see* Attout

Atwat *see* Attout

Avikam

The Avikam (or Brignan, Gbanda, Kwaka, or Lahou) are an Akan (q.v.) people of the Ivory Coast's so-called Lagoon cluster (q.v.) of peoples. There are around 10,000 Avikam people.

Awi

The Awi are an ethnic group of western Ethiopia. They speak an Agew language and are closely related to the Agaw. There are more than 90,000 Awi people.

Azande

The Azande, an ethnic group with several sub-groups, live in northeast Central African Republic and neighboring regions of Congo (Dem. Rep.), and Sudan. "Azande" is the plural of "Zande." The total number of Azande – who were formerly known as Niam-Niam – is estimated at between 750,000 and 2,000,000.

History

The Azande are of very mixed origins. More than 200 years ago, a people known as the Ambomou lived on the banks of the Mbomou River, which forms part of the present-day border between the Central African Republic and Congo (Dem. Rep.). The Ambomou were dominated by the royal Avongara clan, who led them in a campaign of conquest of neighboring subgroups. This campaign led them into Sudan. Some of the conquered subgroups retained their own languages, but most of them regard themselves as Azande, no matter how much they differ from one another.

Language

The Azande language, also called Azande (or Pazande), belongs to the Adamawa-Eastern language group. It is one of the African languages in which plurals and other word changes are made by altering the beginnings of words rather than their ends. There are several dialects, the most important being Dio, Nzakara, and Patri.

Ways of life

The Azande once lived by subsistence agriculture, growing corn, millet, sweet potatoes, and peanuts for their own use, raising chickens, and hunting for meat.

Since the 1920s, however, Azande life has been radically altered by government relocation schemes that encouraged them to move away from the banks of rivers and streams, sites where they historically settled, and attempted to impose territorial boundaries.

In part, these early schemes were to protect Azande homesteads from the tsetse fly, which thrives along riverbanks and is dangerous to cattle and people; the presence of the tsetse fly made keeping cattle impossible for the Azande. But these schemes were also a way to control the population, and they restricted the freedom of movement that Azande people previously enjoyed. Later schemes altered the way homesteads operated by introducing cotton as a crop grown for cash. This made homesteads more reliant on money and, eventually, less self-sufficient.

Social structure

The Azande recognize a king, who is a member of the royal clan. The nonroyal Azande are organized into more than 180 clans (several families descended from a common ancestor or ancestors) – organized along the male line – whose members come together for important occasions such as marriages and funerals. This unites what is otherwise a fairly scattered people, living in widely separated family groups. These family homesteads, surrounded by the families' fields, were until fairly recently the basic social unit in terms of the Azande's political and economic structure.

Culture and religion

RELIGION The Azande believe in an all-powerful god, Mboli, but many also hold parallel belief systems, including reverence for ancestors. Although they know that people die of disease or old age, and that crops fail because of drought, the Azande attribute natural events to the work of male witches. They believe that sons inherit witchcraft powers from their fathers, but every Zande is sure that he himself is not a witch, and that his male ancestors were not witches either.

When he believes he is being bewitched, a Zande decides on a few likely suspects, and consults oracles to find out if his suspicions are correct. The usual method is to put poison on the beak of a chicken, and then ask the chicken about a suspect. If the chicken dies, the Zande decides his suspicions are confirmed. If the chicken survives, the Zande asks other chickens about his other suspects. When a suspect is identified, the Zande asks him to stop his witchcraft. Apparently, a witch's power for evil can work without his knowing, so the accused man is grateful to hear what it has been doing, and takes steps to behave like a model citizen.

The Azande also use diviners for finding out about the future. Some Azande are specialists in this art, and people consult them to find out whether the time is right for certain actions, such as planting crops. In cases of dispute, they appeal to the king's diviner, who is regarded as supreme.

ARTS AND CRAFTS The Azande are famous for the shongo, a multibladed throwing knife. The shongo spins as it flies, so it does the maximum amount of harm to an enemy. The Azande smiths make the

Musician with harp *(above)*
In the past, Azande musicians wore elaborate costumes, like the one shown here. Most played a simple harplike instrument, which was often decorated with a sculpted human head.

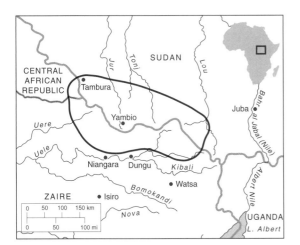

Yanda and the Mani initiation society
This figure of wood and beads is a yanda, a depiction of a protective spirit also called yanda. Yanda were introduced by the Mani initiation society around the beginning of the twentieth century. The expansion of Mani influence from the Congo River area throughout the whole of the Azande lands was fiercely opposed by the Azande royalty and the colonial powers. This was because the society allowed previously-excluded members of the Azande population – women, for example – to participate in meetings. This helped to foster feelings of revolt and triggered social change that could have upset the balance of power.

© DIAGRAM

Azande knives

The shongo *is a throwing knife used and made in the past by the Azande among others. It was a fearsome weapon for the Azande's enemies to face. Its multiple blades were so cunningly balanced that the knife spun in flight and thus caused maximum damage. It was generally aimed at the legs. A simpler form of Azande knife (top) was shaped like a sickle. Many of these knives were beautifully engraved.*

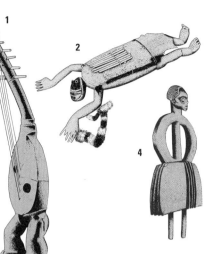

knives of copper or steel and decorate them with elaborate patterns. Another form of Azande knife is shaped like a sickle, and there is also a daggerlike pattern. These daggers are used not only as weapons but also as money, particularly for bridewealth gifts, which compensate a woman's family for the loss of her services when she marries.

Azande artwork includes carved wooden sculptures that were probably given as gifts by chiefs and were purely works of art. More common were functional items such as boxes made from wood and bark or pottery and used to store honey and other goods. Such box-statues, and other artworks, were often made in the shape of a human, or decorated with human features. Yanda figures, used for religious purposes, were made in more abstract human forms.

Musical instruments

The Azande produce a great variety of musical instruments. Human and animal forms are the basis of the design of many Azande musical instruments.

1 *This bow-harp is styled in the form of a human figure.*

2 *This* sanza *(a xylophonelike instrument) shows a dancing woman. Sanzas are made of wood or hollowed gourds, and have keys of flexible iron or bamboo.*

3 *This huge slit drum is carved in the shape of a cow or buffalo.*

4 *A carved wooden bell takes the form of a stylized human figure.*

Azande timeline			
1700s Ambomou people conquer neighboring peoples, forging Azande group in the process	**1905** Azande king, Gbudwe, defeated by British. Azande in Sudan come under control of Anglo-Egyptian forces	crop; Azande homesteads are reorganized around this	**1996** Widespread civil unrest in northeast Zaire follows spread of Rwanda/Burundi conflict
1885 Belgian king's colony of Congo Free State established (Zaire). French colony of Middle Congo established	**1908** Belgian government takes over Congo Free State after international outcry over human rights abuses and exploitation	**1960** Belgian and French Congo both independent as Republic of Congo; Central African Republic (CAR) independent (previously Oubangui-Chari colony)	**1997** Rebel forces led by Laurent Kabila overthrow the government and rename the country Democratic Republic of Congo
1894 French colony of Oubangui-Chari established	**1920s** Rehabilitation scheme resettles Sudanese Azande near roads	**1971** Former French Congo is renamed Zaire	**1998–9** Further fighting in northeastern Congo (Dem. Rep.)
c. 1900 Mani initiation society spreads revolt through Azande lands	**1943** "Zande scheme" in Sudan sees introduction of cotton as a cash	**1994** CFA franc is devalued by fifty percent; Congo and CAR suffer from economic hardship and widespread civil unrest	

Baboute see **Bafou**

Bache see **Rukuba**

Badiu

The Badiu inhabit the interior of the Cape Verdean island of São Tiago. They are descendants of runaway slaves who sought refuge on the isolated island. The Badiu speak a Creole language called Crioulo.

Bafia

The Bafia are a Bantu (q.v.) people living in central Cameroon. They migrated into that region under pressure from Fulani (q.v.) to the north. The Bafia language is called Rikpak.

Bafou

The Bafou (or Bafut, Baboute, Bute, Nbule, Voutere, Wute, or Vute) are a Bantu (q.v.) people who live in the forested regions of southern Cameroon. They number more than 35,000 people.

Bafut see **Bafou**

Baganda see **Ganda**

Baggara

The Baggara (or Baqqara) of southwestern Sudan are descended from Bedouin Arabs and Black Africans with whom the Bedouin intermarried. There are over one million Baggara divided into more than twenty subgroups; some of the major subgroups are the Messiriya, Habbania, and Reizegat of Darfur province and the Humr of the Bahr al Arab region.

History

Bedouin Arabs are thought to have entered North Africa from southwest Asia sometime after or during the eleventh century. By the eighteenth century, the descendants of these Bedouin who became the Baggara were settled in present-day southern Sudan.

MAHDISTS Some Muslims believe that a holy person, the Mahdi, will one day come to earth as a savior and liberator. In 1881, a religious leader called Muhammad Ahmad (q.v.) announced that he was the Mahdi and in 1882 led a revolt against the British and Egyptian conquerors of Sudan. His armies won several spectacular victories and drew much of their support and troops from the Baggara. After his death in 1885, the Mahdi was succeeded by a Baggara man called Abdullah ibn Muhammad, who was called the Khalifa (successor). Under the Khalifa, the Mahdist State expanded and the Sudanese were united. Although the Khalifa lead the Mahdist armies with great success, they were eventually defeated, and the Khalifa killed, by an Anglo-Egyptian force in 1898.

RECENT EVENTS In 1983, the Sudanese government adopted Sharia (Islamic holy) law against the wishes of the mainly non-Muslim south. Long-standing animosities between the north and south erupted in a civil war between government troops and southern-based rebels. Although living in the south, the Baggara have aligned themselves with their fellow Muslims in the

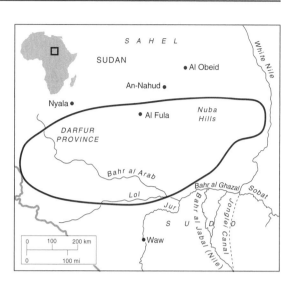

north. This has meant that they are at war with many of their neighbors – in particular, the Nuba.

The Baggara began organizing themselves for operations against the Nuba as early as 1984. In 1985, rebels attacked a Baggara village in the Nuba Hills. The government responded by beginning its policy of supplying arms and military training to the Baggara groups. One branch of these local militias was organized into the Popular Defense Force (PDF) by the government in 1988. Since then, the Baggara militias have fought many battles against the rebels, often alongside government troops. They have also been accused of burning and looting Nuba villages and killing Nuba civilians. During the 1990s, the PDF has been heavily involved in the government's policy of "ethnic cleansing" against the Nuba people. Despite many cease-fires, the civil war continues today and many ordinary Baggara are caught between government troops, rebels, and their own militias.

Baggara woman

This Baggara woman is wearing necklaces and other items of jewelry made from gold and silver. Some Baggara women wear a lot of jewelry. Baggara women generally manage their own finances and often this jewelry is literally a woman's savings.

Headgear
Many Baggara men shave their heads as a defense against insects and then wrap their heads in white cloth, as shown above.

Baggara man
Pictured in the early twentieth century, this spear-carrying Baggara man sitting astride his bull depicts a disappearing way of life. Although the Baggara rarely carry spears in modern Sudan, cattle are still of central importance. In fact, the name "Baggara" is derived from the Arabic word for cow – "bagar."

Traditional Baggara tent
The tents used by the Baggara have to be portable and easy to dismantle, so they are made from materials that are either readily available in the local area or are easy to carry. Sticks to make the basic framework can be cut at the campsite itself. Strips of bark and then mats, plastic sheeting, or cow hides are arranged to cover the sticks – these materials are usually carried from place to place. Traditional tents are beehive-shaped, cylindrical, or hemispherical, depending on which Baggara group they are made by. Some Baggara people give their tents conical thatched roofs.

Language
The Baggara speak a dialect of Arabic.

Ways of life
Most Baggara are cattle herders, and some men – only men own cattle – have herds several thousand strong. The land they live in is largely savanna (grasslands with a few trees and shrubs) and lies between the semidesert Sahel to the north and the seasonally swampy Sudd to the south. The Sahel does not always have enough rain to support cows, and the presence of disease-bearing tsetse flies and mosquitoes in the Sudd prevent cattle-rearing. So, during the summer rains, the Baggara and their herds move north to benefit from seasonal pastures. The Baggara temporarily settle and grow crops of sorghum and cotton, which is sold for cash. As the rainfall gets heavier, mosquitoes and tsetse flies flourish and the men move farther north with their herds, leaving the women to continue cultivating the crops. A few weeks later, the women and children join the men. When the northern grasslands become parched, the Baggara move back to harvest their crops. During the dry season, they move farther south – the mosquitoes and flies have now mostly died – to seek water and pastures.

Some men travel abroad for a year or two and work in various industries. The money earned is often used to pay their children's school fees or to buy more cattle.

Improvements in cattle-rearing and greater access to veterinary care have meant that the natural wastage of herds through disease has decreased. The Baggara have, therefore, been able to amass larger herds of cattle. Also, in order to control the Baggara better, the Sudanese government has adopted policies to encourage them to settle down – such as the boring of water holes and making school education compulsory for children. Larger herds, combined with more-settled lifestyles, have put a great strain on the fragile semidesert and savanna environments. Overgrazing of the land is fast becoming a severe problem. These changes have threatened the seminomadic lifestyle of the Baggara, which is ideally suited to an environment of scarce water resources and little vegetation.

Social structure
POLITICAL STRUCTURE Each group has a leader called a nazir – an Arabic word meaning "overseer." A large group may have two nazirs. The nazir acts as the official link with the Sudanese government. Every group also has several lesser officials called omda, who each look after a particular section. The omda are responsible for collecting taxes and settling disputes.

SOCIAL STRUCTURE The basic domestic unit is a woman and her young children, with an associate male such as the husband – who may have more than one wife, and therefore household of which he is a part. Married women control the domestic finances and earn significant amounts of money from the sale of milk to cheese factories and of butter and yogurt at markets.

MARRIAGE When a Baggara man marries, he gives his new wife's parents a gift of cattle, the bridewealth. By custom, his first wife is usually a cousin. A man can have several wives if he is rich enough to support them, but all wives should be treated equally.

Culture and religion
RELIGION The majority of Baggara are Muslims. Many Baggara men make the pilgrimage (Hajj) to Mecca, often staying for a few years to earn some money.

Ceremonial camel
Elaborate ceremonial decorations – such as the one shown, which is made of leather set with cowrie shells – are used by some well-off Baggara women to adorn their camels.

Baggara timeline		
c. 1000s Bedouin Arabs enter North Africa from Arabia	**1882** Anglo-Egyptian forces conquer Sudan	**1972** South granted regional autonomy; civil war ends
1500s Baggara migrate into present-day eastern Sudan	**1882–1883** Mahdist revolution overthrows Anglo-Egyptian rulers	**1983** Sudan adopts *Sharia* (Islamic holy) law against wishes of non-Muslim south; civil war erupts again
1700s Baggara settled in present-day southern Sudan	**1885** Mahdists take Khartoum. Abdullah ibn Muhammad succeeds Mahdi as Khalifa	**1985** Government begins training and arming Baggara militia
1821 Trade routes opened from north to south Sudan	**1898** Anglo-Egyptian force conquers Mahdist State; Khalifa killed	**1988** Formation of Baggara Popular Defense Front (PDF)
1840s Arab slave trade develops; Baggara active as traders	**1955** First civil war between south and north Sudan begins	**1990s** PDF accused of "ethnic cleansing" of Nuba people as civil war continues
1881 Muhammad Ahmad declares himself "Mahdi"	**1956** Sudanese independence	

Bagirmi

Originally comprising an historical state, today's Bagirmi are a multiethnic society made up of Arab (q.v.), Barma, and Fulani (q.v.) peoples and their descendants. Bagirmi people live in southern Chad along the Chari River from roughly N'Djamena, the capital city, to Bousso. The Bagirmi regional capital is Massénya, also on the Chari River. There are probably around 200,000 Bagirmi people. Arab Bagirmi speak Arabic, which is one of Chad's main languages, Fulani Bagirmi speak Fulfulde, and the Barma speak Tar Barma – a Central Sudanic language related to that spoken by the Sara (q.v.).

The first Bagirmi king, Dala Birni, founded the Bagirmi kingdom in the early sixteenth century. By the start of the seventeenth century Bagirmi had become an Islamic state and for much of the following two centuries jostled for power with the larger states of Borno (see Kanem-Borno) to the northwest and Wadai to the northeast. At times Bagirmi was part of the Borno empire, but in the late eighteenth century the Bagirmi rejected Borno's overlordship.

Bagyi see Gbagyi

Baham

The Baham belong to the Bamileke (q.v.) kingdom, or chiefdom, of the same name. The Bamileke are large ethnic group of West Africa.

Bahemba see Hemba

Bai see Beri

Baju see Kaje

Baka

The Baka are a subgroup of the Mbenga (q.v.). The Mbenga are one of the major groupings of tropical forest-foragers – the so-called pygmies (q.v.) – of Central Africa. There are roughly 20,000 Baka living in Cameroon, Congo (Rep.), and Gabon.

Bakahonde see Kaonde

Bakele

Perhaps the most scattered ethnic group in Gabon, there are around 20,000 Bakele people living throughout much of mainland Gabon. Those in eastern Gabon are being absorbed into the Bakota (q.v.) population.

Bakgalagadi see Kgalagadi

Bakhurutshe see Khurutshe

Bakongo see Kongo

Bakota

The Bakota (or Koto or Kota) are a Bantu (q.v.) people of Central Africa. The main areas that they inhabit are in the north and east of Gabon and across the border in neighboring parts of Congo (Rep.). They are one of the largest ethnic groups in Gabon, and the total Bakota population probably numbers well over 25,000 people.

The Bakota were probably driven into their current region from the north and west during the nineteenth century by the people pushed onto Bakota lands by Fang (q.v.) expansions.

Kota sculptures can be found in museums around the world. In particular, the Kota mbulu-ngulu sculptures are especially admired. These metal-covered wooden sculptures are reliquary figures – that is they were used to guard the relics (such as bones) of dead ancestors. The figures sat on top of baskets containing the bones and skulls, but many figures and their baskets have been separated so that the mbulu-ngulu can be put in a museum. Early Christian missionaries were responsible for breaking or removing many reliquary figures because they misunderstood the role they played and thought that they were fetishes or icons that the Bakota worshiped.

Bakota funerary figure
Known as the Mbulu Ngulu, *or 'image of the spirit of the dead', each of these figures is unique.*

Bakoukouya

The Bakoukouya are a part of the larger Teke (q.v.) cluster of people. They inhabit a region that stretches from eastern Gabon across the border into Congo (Rep.) and as far east as Kinshasa in the neighboring Congo (Dem. Rep.). There are well over 150,000 Bakoukouya.

Bakuba see Kuba

Balanta

The Balanta (or Balente) are the largest ethnic group in Guinea-Bissau, where they are concentrated in the central and northern areas and number more than 250,000.

Bale

The Bale are one of the three closely related groups that make up the Suri (q.v.). The Suri live in Ethiopia and Sudan.

Balente see Balanta

Baloumbou see Loumbou

Bamana see Bambara

Bambara and Malinke

The Bambara (or Bamana) and the Malinke are the two main subgroups of the Manding peoples (also called Mandinka or Mandingo). The Bambara people live chiefly in the grasslands around Bamako in the upper Niger River region of southern Mali. The Malinke have tended to settle more wooded areas, and now live largely in Mali, Guinea, and the Ivory Coast. Many also live in Gambia, Senegal, Guinea-Bissau, and Burkina Faso. There are approximately 2,500,000 Bambara and 1,500,000 Malinke people.

History

All Manding peoples originate from a mountainous region of the same name that sits astride the border of Guinea and Mali. This area was the base of the vast medieval Empire of Mali. In 1235, Sundiata (q.v.) – the Muslim ruler of the Malinke Kingdom of Kangaba – won a decisive battle against the leader of the Susu, Sumanguru, who ruled the region at that time. Malinke settlers and troops pushed west to the Atlantic, and the Empire of Mali came to control one of the largest-ever West African realm. Fertile soils, gold mining, iron-working, and trade led Mali to prosperity. Under Mansa Musa in the 1300s, Mali reached its height. After his

death in 1337, Mali began to disintegrate and by the 1400s, it was no longer important. In c. 1490, Mali's power was eclipsed by the dominant Songhay Empire and by c. 1550 it had ceased to exist.

The Bambara founded the upper Niger state of Segu (based around modern Ségou) in 1600, which reached its peak between 1740 and 1800. In 1754, the Bambara founded the state of Kaarta (based around modern Nioro du Sahel) to the west of Segu. These were the strongest states in the region by 1800. In the mid-nine-

Antelope dance
Two masked youths jumping like antelopes perform a Tyi-wara dance. Tyi-wara is a mythical half-man, half-antelope attributed to the introduction of cultivation to the Bambara. The straight-horned headress depicts a female; the maned, curved-horned headdress a male. Until recently, Tyi-wara dances were performed to make the crops grow, to celebrate a harvest, or to praise the best farmer. The dances are still performed, but with the onset of Islam and changing farming techniques they are becoming less common.

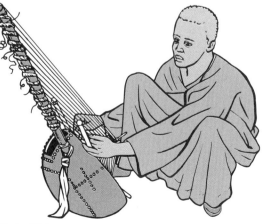

Musical history
A twenty-one-stringed harplike instrument called a kora *accompanies a Malinke* dyeli *(bard) as he sings and recites stories from Manding history.*

Mud cloth
Bambara mud cloths are traditionally woven by men but bear geometric designs applied by women. The designer starts by soaking the cloth in water colored with crushed leaves or bark. This dyes the cloth brown or black. Next, she paints a pattern onto the cloth with mud. When this is dry, the artist repaints the pattern in a soap made from ash and vegetable oil. Then she applies more mud to the pattern. When the cloth is dry, the mud is scraped off, the dye beneath comes off as well, and the pale pattern is exposed. The linear shapes at the top of this cloth represent crocodiles.

teenth century, a Dyula man (part Malinke, part Bambara in origin) called Samori Toure attempted to revive the medieval Empire of Mali. By 1881, Toure had established a huge empire in West Africa covering much of the present-day nations of Guinea and the Ivory Coast as well as southern Mali. It took the French seven years to defeat Samori Toure's empire; but, by 1898, the Second Mandinka Empire (as it was called) had fallen. By 1900, European colonial powers controlled the whole region.

RECENT EVENTS In the 1950s, one of West Africa's most important nationalist leaders was a descendant of Samori Toure – Sekou Touré (q.v.), who lead the bitter struggle for Guinean independence from the French. In 1958, Guinea became the first French West African nation to achieve independence, with Sekou Touré as prime minister.

Language
The Bambara and Malinke speak different dialects of Manding, which is a Mande language.

Ways of life
FARMING The Malinke and Bambara are mostly farming people, although many now live and work in towns. They grow corn, millet, and sorghum and also keep cattle, though milking cows was probably introduced from outside Manding culture.

TRADE Trade has always figured strongly in both people's economies. Products such as rice, corn, and cloth are sold, while butter, milk, livestock, and salt are bought. Islamic traders of mixed Malinke and Bambara ancestry have long dominated the southern end of trans-Saharan commerce. They are still active traders in much of West Africa today. Indeed, their dialect has become an international language of trade. These people and their language both go by the Mande name of "Dyula," which literally means "trader."

Social structure
From early times, Manding villages have been grouped into distinct units. A group of Bambara villages formed a district overseen by a fama (leader) who was drawn from a dominant family. A group of Malinke villages would make up a kafu with its own king or mansa. Bambara and Malinke families are also organized into dyamu. This is the Malinke word for groups of people who share the same name, male ancestors, and taboos – for instance, a ban on eating the animal that a dyamu has as its totem. Two famous, noble Malinke dyamu are the Keita and Traoré families. Both the founder of the Empire of Mali, Sundiata (q.v.), and the first president of the Republic of Mali, Modibo (q.v.), were Keitas, while the second president of Mali, Moussa, was a Traoré. There are also nyamakala, which are basically craft or profession groups. There are nyamakala for people such as dyeli (bards), farmers, leatherworkers, and blacksmiths.

A system of "secret" societies helps to regulate how people live their lives. For example, ntomos prepare young boys for circumcision and initiation into adult society. Joining such societies and obeying their rules and taboos helps to make people conform to what are considered acceptable kinds of behavior.

Figurine
Malinke female figurines like this one are more naturalistic and less geometric than their Bambara counterparts. The artists who carved them were usually blacksmiths.

Malinke town
Round houses with mud walls and thatched roofs form the Malinke town of Kirina, near Ségou in Mali. The barrel-like structures are grain stores. Hundreds of years old, Kirina is where the famous battle that lead to the foundation of the Empire of Mali was fought between Sundiata and Sumanguru in 1235.

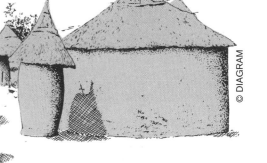

© DIAGRAM

Standing mask
Cowrie shells and stylized horns ornament this wooden "standing mask" of the Bambara. Such masks figure in the intiation ceremonies of ntomo societies, which prepare young boys for entry into the adult community.

Culture and religion

RELIGION Islam is now the main faith of both the Bambara and Malinke. It was introduced to the Malinke Kingdom of Kangaba in the 1100s by Berber traders from North Africa. Almost all the Malinke adopted Islam, but the Bambara gave up their old beliefs and rituals more slowly.

MUSIC Music has long played an important role in Manding culture. Dyeli sing of the deeds performed by the heroes of ancient Mali. Salif Keita (q.v.) is one internationally famous Manding singer who follows this tradition – updating it with topical references. Many dyeli accompany themselves on stringed instruments called koras or the three-stringed kontingo. Also used are gourd harps called bolombatos; ngonis – four-stringed lutes once played by Bambara musicians to inspire men to fight; and balafons, wooden percussion instruments similar to xylophones.

TEXTILES Bambara women are famous for their dresses of cloth decorated with abstract patterns depicting symbolically important animals such as lizards, tortoises, and crocodiles. In the past, most Bambara men would wear mud cloths, distinctive for their light patterns on dark backgrounds. Women design these cloths by an elaborate process using mud, ash, and soap.

Bambara and Malinke timeline

c. 750 Malinke Kingdom of Kangaba established	Empire **c. 1550** Mali ceases to exist	**1890s** Mandinka Empire relocates in east to resist French	military coup in Mali **1977** Keita's death in detention leads to widespread popular unrest
1100s Islam introduced to Kangaba	**c. 1740** Bambara found state of Segu	**1898** French conquer Mandinkas	**1979** Traoré elected president
1235 Sundiata founds Empire of Mali	**1754** Kaarta founded by Bambara	**1958** Guinea independent, with Sekou Touré as president	**1991** Traoré overthrown in coup
1240s Expansion of Empire of Mali	**c. 1800** Dyula kingdom of Kong south of Segu is a rich trading empire	**1960** Mali independent, with Modibo Keita as president	**1992** Alpha Konare elected president of Mali
1312–1337 Mali reaches height during reign of Mansa Musa	**1850s–1860s** Muslim Tukolor Empire conquers Kaarta and Segu	**1960s–1980s** Recurring *drought* causes famine in Sahelian countries	**1994** CFA franc devaluation causes widespread hardship
1324 Mansa Musa travels to Mecca	**1870s–1880s** Samori Toure founds the Second Mandinka empire	**1968** Moussa Traoré takes power in	
c. 1490 Mali Empire eclipsed by Songhay			

Bamileke

The Bamileke are made up of some 90 or more small kingdoms, or chiefdoms, in northwestern Cameroon. The largest kingdoms include Bafou, Bansoa, Foto, Banjoun, and Baham. There are probably between half and one million Bamileke. The Bamileke rarely refer to themselves as Bamileke (except when talking to a non-Bamileke person) but will use the name of the particular kingdom to which they belong. There are more than 10 Bamileke languages, which form a subgroup of the Bantu group of languages. Not all of the languages can be understood by other Bamileke. Unlike English, Bamileke languages are tonal, meaning that the pitch, or tone, of a spoken word affects its meaning.

The origins of the Bamileke are unclear – it is thought that they migrated into northwestern Cameroon after coming under pressure from the Fulani (q.v.) in the seventeenth century. The first Bamileke kingdoms emerged in the region in that century. More recently, the Bamileke region suffered a devastating civil war (sometimes called the Bamileke rebellion) from 1958 to 1972.

Bamileke mask
This heavily stylized representation of a buffalo is made from dark wood for ritual use and comes from the grasslands of Cameroon.

Bamom see Bamum

Bamum

The Bamum, Bamom, or Mom number somewhat less than 500,000 people living in the western region of Cameroon. The Bamum are a Bantu-speaking (q.v.) people whose language is also called Bamum.

The Bamum kingdom was established in the eighteenth century by Nchare, the first mfon (or king). The capital was established at present-day Foumban, which is now a major Cameroonian town on the eastern edge of the southern end of the Adamawa plateau. The most famous Bamum mfon was Njoya, the seventeenth king, who wrote a book on the history of the Bamum that was translated into French. At the end of the nineteenth century Njoya invented a written language that used 510 pictographic symbols. Pictographs are symbols that are used to represent words. Njoya's language was eventually condensed into an "alphabet" of 73 pictographs and 10 digits.

Today, the majority of the Bamum are Muslim. The Islamic religion was introduced to the Bamum by Njoya, who converted in 1918.

Banana see Massa

Banda

With a population in excess of one million, the Banda are one of the largest ethnic groups in the Central African Republic. They probably originate from western Sudan's Darfur Mountains, from where they migrated in the nineteenth century after refusing to except the rule of the sultans of Wadai and Darfur.

Bandi

More than 60,000 Bandi (or Ghandi) people live in Liberia, mostly in a region on the northwestern coast. They speak a Mande (q.v.) language.

Bandia

The Bandia (or Bandiya) are a subgroup of the Azande (q.v.) of Congo (Dem. Rep.). They are the westernmost Azande peoples and live near the northern border of Congo (Dem. Rep.) where the Uele and Ubangi rivers meet.

Bandiya see Bandia

Banjoun

The Banjoun belong to the Bamileke (q.v.) kingdom, or chiefdom, of the same name. The Bamileke are large ethnic group of West Africa.

Bansoa

The Bansoa belong to the Bamileke (q.v.) kingdom, or chiefdom, of the same name. The Bamileke are large ethnic group of West Africa.

Janus mask
This Bamileke court mask features anthropomorphic heads in the hair and beard, and a woman's head on the rear.

Bantu

There are three main divisions of Black African people: the Bantu, the Nilotes (q.v.), and the Cushites (q.v.). These groupings are based on cultural and linguistic similarities. A large number of the hundreds of Central, southern, and East African languages are Bantu.

The Bantu originated in eastern Nigeria several thousand years ago. At first, they spread over West Africa and through the equatorial rainforest belt and then, between 500 BCE and 300 CE, eastward and southward into East and Southern Africa. Later migrations – from the south to the east – further dispersed them through-out Africa. The Bantu settlers brought iron working and hoe cultivation with them.

In southern Africa there are two main divisions of Bantu peoples: the Nguni (q.v.) and Sotho–Tswana (q.v.) peoples. The Bantu-speaking peoples were established in southern Africa by the start of the Common Era, at least thirteen centuries before the arrival of Europeans in the 1600s. In East Africa, the larger Bantu groups include the Kikuyu, Ganda, Nyoro, and Nyamwezi.

Banyoro see Nyoro

Bapedi see Pedi

Bapounou

The Bapounou (or Pounou) are one of the largest ethnic groups in Gabon, where they are concentrated in the southwest. There are more than 20,000 Bapounou.

Baqqara see Baggara

Bara

Numbering around 400,000, the Bara are one of Madagascar's major ethnic groups. They live in an inland region in the southern half of the island. There is a great deal of mixing between the Bara and the Betsileo (q.v.) cultures. See also Madagascan peoples.

Barabaig

The Barabaig number more than 45,000, the majority of whom live south of Lake Eyasi in northern Tanzania. They are a Nilotic (q.v.) people considered to be part of the Nandi (q.v.) cluster of peoples.

Bararetta

The Bararetta are one of the nine main subgroups of the Oromo. They live in Ethiopia.

Bareshe see Reshawa

Bargu see Bariba

Bari see Beri

Bariba

Also known as the Bargu, Berba, Batonu or Borgawa, the Bariba are a widespread ethnic group found in the West African countries of Benin, Burkina Faso, Togo, and Nigeria. In total the Bariba number well over 650,000. Around 500,000 live in Benin, 100,000 in Nigeria, and probably at least 10,000 in Togo.

In Benin, the Mariba are concentrated in northern and central regions, in particular in the central city of Parakou. Neighboring regions of Nigeria are also home to the Mariba, especially in the far west of Nigeria's Kwara State, which borders north and central Benin. In recent decades, however, increasing numbers have moved to the major cities of Benin and Nigeria, such

as Cotonou, Benin's capital, which is on the southern coast. Nevertheless the vast majority of Mariba are still rural farmers, typically growing food crops such as yams, sorghum, millet, and vegetables as well as crops such as groundnuts, cotton, and rice, to sell. In the not-too-distant past Fulani (q.v.) herders would raise the Mariba's cattle for them.

The Mariba of Nigeria are known as the Busa, while the Mariba of Benin are the Nikki. Together the Nikki and Busa comprise the two main Mariba subgroups. Nearly 50 percent of the Busa are Muslim, but only around 30 percent of the Nikki.

Barma

The Barma are part the multiethnic Bagirmi (q.v.) society. They number between 50,000 and 90,000 people living in southern Chad.

Barotse see Lozi

Barutshe see Hurutshe

Basese

The Basese are a subgroup of the Ganda (q.v.). They inhabit the Ugandan islands of Lake Victoria.

Bashikongo see Shikongo

Bashilele see Lele

Basoga see Soga

Basolongo see Solongo

Basotho see Sotho

Bassa

The Bassa are a relatively large ethnic group in Liberia. There are more than 350,000 Bassa people, who live on the Atlantic coast of Liberia.

Bassi

The Bassi are one of the main subdivisions of the Gusii (q.v.). The Gusii are a large ethnic group of western Kenya.

Bateke see Teke

Batonu see Bariba

Batswana see Tswana

Baulé

The Baulé are an Akan (q.v.) people living in the Ivory Coast. They are one of that country's largest ethnic groups, numbering more than 1.5 million. They are closely-related to the Anyi (q.v.) people of the Ivory Coast and Ghana. The Baulé are concentrated in a central southeastern region of the Ivory Coast – between the Bandama River, which cuts through the middle of the Ivory Coast's southern half, and the Komoé River, which lies farther to the east near the border with Ghana.

In the mid-eighteenth century, sections of Asante (q.v.) Empire in what is now Ghana broke away in

search of fresh lands to the west. Some groups, led by a woman called Awura Poku, settled on the lands to the east of the Bandama River. These and later migrations from the Akan homelands formed the present-day Baulé and Anyi populations. Under Queen Akwa Boni, the Baulé took over the gold-bearing lands to the west of the Bandama region, but Baulé influence decreased after her death.

The Baulé are famous as sculptors and carvers of wood. Baulé works of art are known to have greatly influenced the US artist, Jacob Epstein.

Baulé pendant
This decorative jewelry features a pair of crossed crocodiles and is made of gold.

Baya

The Baya (or Gbaya) are the second largest ethnic group in the Central African Republic (CAR). There are roughly 700,000 Baya, the majority of whom live in western CAR.

History

The origins of the Baya are uncertain. By the tenth century, they were residents of the savanna (grasslands) of northwest Central Africa. They migrated southward at the beginning of the 1800s in response to incursions by the Fulani ruler Usman dan Fodio into northern Central Africa. As the Baya moved southward and westward, they assimilated or displaced the peoples they met. Once the Baya had consolidated themselves in their Central African territory, they were able to resist further incursions by slave-traders from the north and west.

This part of Central Africa became the French colony of Oubangui-Chari in 1894. It suffered greatly from the activities of companies that were granted exclusive rights to large areas. Labor was conscripted from local populations and those who refused or deserted were often killed or tortured. Armed resistance against the colonial regime occurred until the 1930s, with the Baya playing a major role. In 1960, independence as the Central African Republic was finally gained.

RECENT EVENTS Jean-Bédel Bokassa (q.v.) took power in a coup in 1965. In 1976, Bokassa declared himself emperor and was crowned (in 1977) in an extravagant ceremony, reputedly costing one quarter of the country's gross national product for that year. His regime was particularly brutal. Widespread corruption among the ruling elite led to revolts by students and schoolchildren in 1979, which helped topple Bokassa's

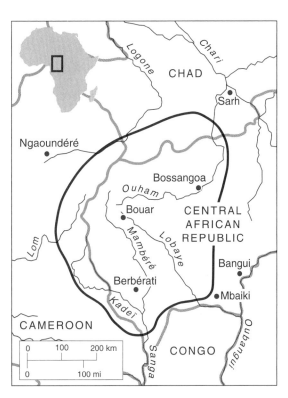

regime with a French-backed coup. In 1981, however, General André Kolingba (q.v.) instituted military rule and later established a one-party state. Strikes and demonstrations throughout 1991 and 1992 led to a return to multiparty politics in 1993.

Language

The Baya language is also called Baya. Most Baya speak Sango, however, which is CAR's common language, and some also use French, the former official language.

Ways of life

The Baya are largely a farming people, with cassava as the staple crop plus sweet potatoes, yams, groundnuts (peanuts), squashes, beans, leafy vegetables, and bananas. Some cotton and coffee are grown for export. Goats, chickens, and hunting dogs were historically the main domesticated animals, with cattle, horses, and donkeys being introduced before the beginning of the twentieth century. Many Baya work in diamond mines, and diamonds contribute over twenty-five percent of CAR's foreign earnings. Tourism exists, though on a fairly small scale. Some wildlife safaris are organized on the parks and game reserves in savanna lands.

Social structure

Precolonial Baya communities comprised extended family groupings living in hamlets, which were themselves grouped together to form "clan territories." Clans comprised several families descended from a common ancestor or ancestors. Within a hamlet, the head of each household was a male who controlled the labor of his family. Nuclear families usually worked alone to cultivate their fields and there was quite high economic equality between families within an area.

Baya sculpture
This Baya carving dates from the 1930s and is a female figure. Baya sculpture is rare. The few examples that exist are usually of male figures, which appear to represent boys undergoing initiation. Initiation for teenage boys was once widely practiced, involving as much as two or three years seclusion in camps away from the village. There, the boys studied and trained in the skills necessary for adult life. It is assumed that the sculptures may have been used as a part of this teaching process.

Baya crafts
This pot was probably produced for use on special or ritual occasions as it has been highly polished. Baya crafts include barkcloth making, basketry, mat weaving, and pottery. Foundry working and blacksmithing are also widely practiced.

By the late nineteenth century, these hamlet-based communities had begun to band together to form larger villages. These were stronger and more able to counter the threat of raiding parties from the west and the north, intent on capturing slaves for trade. River communities sometimes allied themselves with the slave traders, and strong animosity has existed between some savanna and river communities since that time.

Culture and religion

RELIGION Many Baya are Christians but elements of the Baya religion still thrive. Baya religious beliefs include the recognition of sorcerers – members of the community who have special magical gifts. The power of sorcery is inherited from the mother and conferred on her offspring. Sorcerers specialize either in using evil forces to harm others, or in refusing to use such forces and remaining a force for good. The latter are regarded as more powerful.

Baya timeline	
c. 900s Baya resident in northwest Central Africa	**1976** Bokassa makes himself emperor
c. 1820 Baya migrate to western Central Africa	**1979** Bokassa ousted with help of French and Moroccan troops
1894 French colony of Oubangui-Chari established; Baya active in armed resistance until 1930s	**1981** Military rule begins
	1991–1992 Strikes and demonstrations plague government
1958 Oubangui-Chari becomes the Central African Republic (CAR)	**1993** Multiparty politics introduced
1960 CAR independent and becomes a one-party state	**1994** CFA devalued by fifty percent; hardship and unrest follows
1965 Coup led by Jean-Bédel Bokassa	**1996** French troops helped to put down an army rebellion

Beafada *see* Biafada

Bedouin

The Bedouin are chiefly nomadic Arabs (q.v.) living throughout much of North Africa's desert and semidesert regions. The Bedouin can also be found in the Middle East, the original homeland of the Arabs. The Bedouin arrived in North Africa soon after the eighth-century Arab conquest of that region. Like other Arabs, the Bedouin speak dialects of Arabic. The vast majority of Bedouin are Muslim. The Baggara (q.v.) of southwestern Sudan are the descendants of Bedouin Arabs and Black Africans.

Nomads are pastoralists (livestock raisers) who travel from place to place in search of pasture and water for their herds. The Bedouin keep sheep, goats, camels, and, less frequently, cattle. They also plant crops along well-used migration routes that can be harvested on their return journey. Trade with settled populations provides the Bedouin with items they do not produce themselves. Many Bedouin today use trucks rather than camels as their beasts of burden.

Beja

The Beja live in northeastern Sudan and northern Eritrea, between the Red Sea and the Nile River. There are half a dozen main Beja groups. The Hadendowa live along the Gash watercourse (a seasonally dry river) and are the most numerous group. Other groups include the Ababda, who live near the coast; the Amarar, who live around Port Sudan; and the Beni Amer and the Tigre, who live mostly in the south of northeastern Sudan and the north of Eritrea. Today, there are probably over 800,000 Beja.

History

The Beja have lived in the region where they are today for at least 5,000 years and are mentioned in ancient Greek, Egyptian, and Roman writings.

Language

Different Beja groups speak different languages. The Beni Amer and the Tigre speak Tigrinya, a Semitic language derived from an ancient Ethiopian language. Most Ababda speak Arabic. The rest of the Beja speak a language that is also called Beja (or To Bedawi).

Ways of life

For many years, the Beja have lived by herding sheep and goats, with cattle in the south and camels in the north. One group, the Bisharin, are famous camel breeders. These animals provide them with milk, butter, and meat. The men tend the flocks and do the

milking, while the women grow crops, mostly sorghum and cotton. Most Beja are nomadic (they travel with their herds in search of pasture and water). Some keep on the move all year round, while others move seasonally.

RECENT CHANGES As with other nomadic groups, the Sudanese government has encouraged the Beja to settle down. In the more fertile areas of the south, this has been achieved with success by some groups.

Cotton and grain are the most common crops grown. The Hadendowa, in particular, have adopted sedentary cotton farming in large numbers. In fact, cotton cultivation along the Gash watercourse is largely controlled by Hadendowa farmers.

Other changes have been brought about by economic growth. The development of Port Sudan into a busy commercial centre has changed the lifestyles of many Beja. The Amarar, for example, previously lived in north Sudan but are now settled around Port Sudan and many work in its docks. Farther inland, other Amarar now graze cattle and sheep to sell in Port Sudan.

Social structure

Social organization differs from group to group. Some groups comprise one or more family units led by the most senior male. Others, such as the Tigre, have a distinct class system, with divisions between the nobility and ordinary citizens.

Culture and religion

RELIGION Under the influence of Christian Ethiopia, the Beja converted to Christianity about twelve centuries ago. However, after the seventh-century invasion of North Africa by the Arabs – who brought with them Islam – many converted to Islam. Since the fourteenth century, the majority of Beja have been Muslims.

Beja warrior
Pictured in the early twentieth century, the look of this Amarar man recalls the reputation the Beja had for being great warriors.

Beja sword
The design of this Beni Amer sword and scabbard is thought to have been influenced by swords that were used during the European crusades of the eleventh to thirteenth centuries.

Beja timeline

c. 3000–2000 BCE Ancient Egyptians mine gold in northern Beja territories	begins: Islam introduced **c. 1150–1300s** The vast majority of Beja convert to Islam	**1898** Britain and Egypt conquer Mahdist State	enlargement begins **1983** Sudan adopts Sharia (Islamic holy) law against wishes of the mainly non-Muslim south; civil war breaks out again
100s CE Axumite Kingdom emerges in Tigre lands: southern Beja adopt Tigrean class structure and language, Tigrinya	**1882** Mahdist revolution in Sudan begins; many Hadendowa become Mahdist warriors	**1955** First civil war between north and south Sudan begins	
600s Beja convert to Christianity. Decline of Axumite Kingdom	**1885** Battle at Tofrek between Anglo-Egyptian force and Mahdists. Anglo-Egyptian force supported by Bisharin and Amarar is defeated	**1956** Sudanese independence	**1990s** Despite many cease-fires, the Sudanese civil war continues
640 Arab conquest of North Africa		**1972** South granted regional autonomy; end of first Sudanese civil war	**1993** Eritrea officially independent from Ethiopia
		1978 Port Sudan: modernization and	

Bemba

Most Bemba live on the high, forested plateau of northern Zambia. The Bemba population of Zambia is about 1.7 million and there are 150,000 or so in neighboring countries such as Congo (Dem. Rep.).

History

The Bemba are descended from Luba-Lunda people who migrated from what is now the Shaba Province of Congo (Dem. Rep.) over three hundred years ago. Gradually, they conquered or absorbed the original inhabitants of the region. One of the most important of the migrant groups was the Bena Yanda (the Crocodile Clan), possibly descendants of Lunda chiefs, who settled on the banks of the Chambeshi River in the second half of the seventeenth century. They were led by a chief called Chiti. Bemba kings have adopted the name Chitimukulu, which means

"Chiti the Great," ever since. This small kingdom steadily expanded during the eighteenth and nineteenth centuries. It became one of Central Africa's most important kingdoms and the name "Bemba" was applied to all people who acknowledged the rule of the current Chitimukulu.

In 1889, the British government authorized Cecil Rhodes' British South Africa Company (BSA) – basically a mining company with its own army – to administer territories north of the Limpopo River and to control their mineral resources and trade. As a result, the Bemba kingdom became part of Northern Rhodesia. In 1924, control of Northern Rhodesia was transferred from BSA to the British government and the country became a British colony until its independence in 1964 as Zambia. The Bemba played a major role in the struggle for independence, which

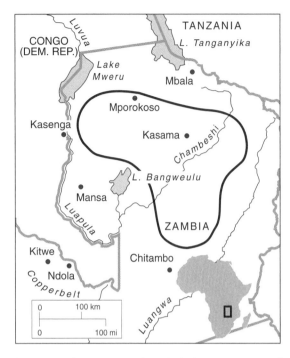

began in the 1950s and included a campaign of widespread civil disobedience.

RECENT EVENTS After independence, Zambia was ruled as a one-party state under President Kenneth Kaunda (q.v.). In 1991, Kaunda was defeated by Frederick Chiluba (q.v.) – a Bemba – in the country's first multiparty elections.

Language

The Bemba language is spoken not only by the Bemba but also by many other people in Zambia and Congo (Dem. Rep.). The total number of Bemba speakers is around 2.5 million.

Ways of life

Since the discovery of Zambia's vast reserves of copper in the 1920s, many Bemba have left their homes to work as migrant laborers in the mines of the Copperbelt, along the border with southern

Congo (Dem. Rep.). Most Bemba, however, remain on the high plateau where they live in villages of 100 to 300 people and grow crops such as millet, sorghum, corn, and cassava. The Bemba also keep some sheep and goats, but very few cattle because the tsetse fly is common in the area. The tsetse fly spreads diseases that affect both humans and cattle.

Social structure

Bemba society is organized into about thirty clans (several families descended from a common ancestor or ancestors), which are named after animals or other natural features. Previously these clans were governed by a hierarchy of village heads, priests, subchiefs, and chiefs, under the authority of the Chitimukulu. These positions of power were held by men but inheritance of them is matrilineal – through the female side of the family. They can pass from brother to brother, but when they pass to the next generation, it is to the sisters' sons, not those of the brothers. In present-day Zambia, the Bemba are incorporated into the modern political system.

Culture and religion

RELIGION The majority of the Bemba are Christians but the Bemba religion has left its mark on modern religious practice. The matrilineal aspects of Bemba society found expression in Bemba religious practices – the focus of the Bemba religion was a small shrine in each home, which was presided over by the married woman of the house. She conducted rituals at the shrine to keep in contact with the spirits of her ancestors, often through possession. The importance of house shrines was undermined in the 1700s by the growth of the worship of spirits of dead chiefs. It was further eroded during the 1900s by the widespread adoption of Christianity. Newer, Zambianized forms of Christianity incorporate many aspects of the Bemba religion, however, including spirit possession practiced by women (and now sometimes by men as well).

Musical pot (below)
This musical instrument consists of an upturned clay water pot and a three-legged stool. When the stool is turned, the legs rub against the pot and make a rasping sound. These instruments are played by women as an accompaniment to men's drumming.

Ancestor statue (left)
This wooden carving depicts a sitting ancestor and is a rare example of a larger Bemba carving; most Bemba carvings are smaller.

Bemba timeline	
c. 1600s Luba-Lunda people migrate into north of modern Zambia	**1953–1963** Northern Rhodesia part of white-minority ruled Central African Federation (CAF)
c. 1650 Bena Yanda *clan* led by Chiti found Bemba kingdom	**1964** Northern Rhodesia independent as Zambia
1700s–1800s Bemba kingdom expands its territory and power	**1981** Many Bemba arrested and accused of attempting to overthrow Zambia's president
1889 British South Africa Company (BSA) establishes control over Bemba, who become part of Northern Rhodesia	**1991** Kenneth Kaunda, president since 1964, is defeated in first multiparty elections by Frederick Chiluba – a Bemba
1920s Copper mining develops in	
1930s Copperbelt in north	**1994** Divisions in ruling party between Bemba and non-Bemba groups increase
1924 BSA hands over Northern Rhodesia to British government. White settlers are encouraged; Africans are restricted to "native reserves"	

Bemdzabuko

Together with the Emafikamuva (q.v.) and Emakhandzambili (q.v.), the Bemdzabuko are one of the three major subgroups of the Swazi (q.v.) of Swaziland and neighboring parts of South Africa. They consider themselves to be the "true Swazi," the founders of the Swazi kingdom, who moved into the present homeland from wider southern Africa.

Ben *see* Beng

Beng

The Beng (or Ben, Ngan, or Nguin) number approximately 20,000 and are located in the north of Ivory Coast and across the border in southern Burkina Faso. The Beng speak a Manding (q.v.) language and are sometimes considered to be a Lobi (q.v.) subgroup.

Beni Amer

One of the larger subdivisions of the Beja (q.v.) people, the Beni Amer population exceeds 300,000. They are concentrated in the eastern Sudan and northwestern Ethiopia.

Berba *see* Bariba

Berber

There are about fifteen million Berbers spread out over North Africa from Egypt to Morocco and south to the Sahel – the semidesert strip south of the Sahara Desert. The majority – about seven million – live in the Atlas Mountains of Morocco and Algeria. Others live in the oases (fertile pockets) that dot the Sahara. There are many different Berber groups: the Irifiyen of northeast Morocco; the Imazighen of central and southeast Morocco; and the Iqbailiyen of Algeria are just a few. The name "Berber" was given to them by the ancient Greeks. "Imazighen" is sometimes used to refer to all Berbers, as well as the Imazighen proper.

History

The Berbers are the earliest known inhabitants of North Africa and they were settled along the Mediterranean coast by 3000 BCE. By about 250 BCE, they had set up three kingdoms in what is now northern Morocco, Algeria, and Tunisia. At times, the Berbers were in conflict with their neighbors, the city-state of Carthage – near present-day Tunis – or the Romans who colonized parts of the coast. The Romans made an alliance with the Berber king, Masinissa, who ruled over a large area of North Africa called Numidia. He forced many Berbers to settle on the land as farmers and built up a strong kingdom, which broke up after his death. Another Numidian ruler, Juba I (q.v.), created a Berber kingdom but was deposed by the Roman general Julius Caesar in 46 BCE.

ALMORAVIDS AND ALMOHADS The modern history of the Berbers, and the history traced by the Berbers themselves, begins with their conversion to Islam by the Arabs, who began to move into North Africa in 640 CE. Over the years, Arab invasions forced many Berbers out of the coastal regions and into the mountains and desert. Others were absorbed into the Arab population.

In 1054, a confederation of Muslim Berber groups formed a new and powerful dynasty in the west, in what is now southern Morocco and Western Sahara. They were known as the Almoravids. The whole of Morocco was under Almoravid rule by 1069. In 1086, they invaded Spain and had conquered much of its south by 1106. In 1147, another Berber confederation formed – the Almohads – and by 1150 the Almohads

Mud castles
Mud-and-straw castlelike homes, such as the one shown here, can be found in Berber communities in the Atlas Mountains. They are not typical dwellings but would be lived in by the wealthy, by holy men, or by landowners.

Facial tattoo

This Berber woman has tattoos on her face. Tattoos are traditionally used to identify which Berber group the wearer belongs to. The designs are often based on an ancient Libyan script. The jewelry that she is wearing is also very traditional and distinctively Berber. It incorporates coins, amber, silver, glass, and cloth.

North African country. This reflects the fact that Berbers are often treated as second-class citizens by the dominant Arabs. In Algeria in 1990, for example, Arabic was made the sole official language and Berber was outlawed. Thousands demonstrated to demand that Berber be taught in schools. Both Morocco and Algeria finally gave Berber official recognition as a second language in 1994.

Ways of life

Although lifestyle varies from one Berber group to another and some Berbers live in cities, the vast majority are farmers. Vineyards and olive trees clothe the mountain slopes where many Berbers live. Staple crops include wheat, barley, and vegetables – turnips are commonly grown in the higher mountains. Apples and potatoes have become major cash crops since the 1980s. The Berbers raise a variety of animals such as cattle, sheep, goats, horses, and camels. Many Berbers rely on their animals for their livelihood and move with their herds according to the season to find the best pastures. Although nomadic in this sense, they still maintain permanent settlements where crops are grown. In farming communities, women tend to carry out domestic work while men farm and build houses. Exceptions to this include harvesting, collecting newly-cut grain, and whitewashing houses – tasks often done by women.

Since independence, many Moroccans and Algerians – including Berbers – have migrated to Europe, in particular France, where they work in various industries.

Social structure

POLITICAL STRUCTURE Berbers in the coastal regions are largely absorbed into the predominantly Arab culture and politics of the countries in which they live. In the more remote mountain and desert regions, however, traditional systems persist to a certain extent. Villages still have regular meetings of adult men, which in the past would decide questions of law and government. Nowadays, they usually deliberate on local issues.

SOCIAL STRUCTURE Southern Berber groups still maintain their precolonial social divisions. The top level comprises people who claim descent from the Prophet Muhammad. A middle level comprises the so-called "white Berbers" and the lower level of settled oasis cultivators are commonly known as haratin. In the past, the haratin – who are usually Black Africans – existed in a client relationship with a specific Berber group and would provide them with provisions when needed.

had taken over the whole Almoravid Empire, including their conquests in Spain. The Almohad Empire later collapsed, and they lost their last possessions in 1269. In Spain, the Almoravids and Almohads were known as "Moors" (not to be confused with the present-day Moors of Mauritania).

COLONIALISM All of North Africa was under at least nominal colonial rule by 1914. Resistance to European rule was strongest in Berber-speaking areas. The Berber leader Abd al Krim (q.v.) led a war against the French in 1921 and against the Spanish and French from 1925 to 1926. North Africa was free from colonial rule by the 1960s.

Language

The Berber language, also called Berber, has over twenty different dialects. Berber is related to Ancient Egyptian but uses the Arabic script. Many Berbers also speak Arabic as well as French or Spanish. Although widely spoken, Berber is not an official language in any

Mountain village

This Berber village rests in a valley of the High Atlas Mountains of central Morocco.

Today, these social divisions are turning into a class system based largely on wealth and prosperity.

Berber women are generally more independent than Arab women. Many trade at the markets and manage their own finances.

MARRIAGE Women arrange marriages and wedding ceremonies. Berber girls tend to marry at the age of fifteen or sixteen. Some of these arranged marriages do not work out, however. If they break up in the first two weeks, the couple can divorce simply and are then free to seek partners of their own choosing.

Culture and religion

RELIGION The majority of Berbers follow Islam, which was introduced by Arab invaders in the seventh century. The Berbers themselves then became active in spreading Islam throughout the rest of northwestern Africa.

ART The only arts practiced that produce works which are recognizably Berber are carried out by women. Irifiyen female artisans are famous for their pottery decorating, for example, while the women of many groups in Morocco weave distinctive rugs.

Rug designs (right)
This rug is typical of those made by the Zemmour, a Berber group in the Middle Atlas Mountains of northwest Morocco. It uses geometric shapes in several colors on a red background. Different groups use particular designs, techniques, and colors for their rugs. Women weave the rugs using sheep's or goats' wool, dyed with natural pigments.

Lucky hand (left)
The symbol of the hand is frequently used in jewelry worn by Berber women. It represents Islam's five fundamental principles, so it is called khamsa *– the Arabic for "five." The khamsa is thought to protect against the "evil eye." The pendants shown here are worn on a chain; one has miniature stylized hands extending from the sides.*

Berber timeline

3000 BCE Berbers settled on North African coast	**c. 85–46** Reign of King Juba I over Numidia	**1147** Almohad dynasty founded	**1990** 50,000 Berbers demonstrate in Algeria after Berber is outlawed
814 Carthage city-state founded	**46** Roman-ruled Carthage divides Numidia	**1150** Almohads take over Almoravid Empire	**1992** Military coup in Algeria
c. 250 Berbers establish Mauretania and two Numidian kingdoms	**640 CE** Arab invasion of North Africa begins; Islam introduced	**1269** End of Almohad Empire	**1994** Berber officially accepted in Algeria and Morocco
203 Berber kingdoms unified	**711** Arabs control North Africa	**1860s** French rule begins in northwest Africa	**1995** Multiparty elections in Algeria
201–148 Reign of King Masinissa over Numidia	**1054** Almoravid dynasty founded	**1920s** Abd al Krim leads wars against colonial powers	**1998** Berbers in Algeria protest when Arabic is made compulsory for all official business
201–46 Numidia encroaches on Carthaginian territory	**1069** Almoravid Empire covers northwestern North Africa	**1956** Moroccan independence	
	1086 Almoravids invade Spain	**1962** Algerian independence	

Beri

Also known as the Kige, Bai or Bari, the Beri are primarily a Sudanese people, though significant numbers also live in Chad, and, to a lesser extent, Uganda and Congo (Dem. Rep.).

The Beri are divided into two main subgroups: the Zaghawa and the Bideyat. There are something like 350,000 Beri, 90 percent of whom belong to the Zaghawa subgroup. The Zaghawa live in Wadai Province of northeastern Chad and Darfur Province of

western Sudan. The Bideyat live farther north in Chad.

Historically, the Beri have long been associated with nomadic lifestyles involving cattle raising and camel herding. Today, however, large numbers are settled farmers or traders. The historic Beri religion was based on the belief in a god called Iru. Since the seventeenth century, increasing numbers have adopted Islam, initially in Sudan, from where it spread to Chad.

Beri-beri *see* **Kanuri**

Berta

The Berta are a subgroup of the Funj (q.v.) people. The Funj live in southern Sudan.

Berti

Closely related to the Beri (q.v.) people, the Berti are also sometimes considered to be a Shilluk (q.v.) people. There are more than 100,000 Berti, the majority of whom live in Sudan's western Darfur Province.

Beta Israel *see* **Falasha**

Bete

The Bete are part of the Kru (q.v.) cluster of peoples. The Kru are one of the largest ethnic groups in Liberia.

Betsileo

The Betsileo are one of the largest ethnic groups in Madagascar and have a population in excess of one million. They are culturally similar to the Merina (q.v.) and inhabit a large area of inland Madagascar to the south of the central Merina. See also **Madagascan peoples**.

Betsimisiraka

The Betsimisiraka are one of Madagascar's largest ethnic groups. There are more than 1.5 million Betsimisiraka, and they inhabit a large area of Madagascar's eastern seaboard. See also **Madagascan peoples**.

Bezanozano

The Bezanozano are one of Madagascar's smaller ethnic groups but they still number more than 100,000. They live in a region of the island bordered by the Merina (q.v.) to the west and the Betsimisiraka to the east. See also **Madagascan peoples**.

Biafada

The Biafada (or Beafada) are one of Guinea-Bissau's larger ethnic groups. They number more than 50,000 and live in the coastal regions of that country.

Bidanis

The Bidanis, or the "White Moors," are one of the two main subgroups of the Moors (q.v.) of Mauritania. They are descended from Berbers (q.v.) and Arabs (q.v.).

Bideyat

The Bideyat are a subgroup of the Beri (q.v.). They live mostly in Chad.

Bini

The Bini were the citizens and founders of the historic Kingdom of Benin. The descendants of the Bini, the Edo (q.v.), still live in southern Nigeria today.

Birifor

The Birifor are a subgroup of the Lobi (q.v.). They mostly live in northwestern Ghana.

Bisharin

The Bisharin are one of the major subgroups of the Beja (q.v.) people. They live mostly in northeastern Sudan.

Bobo

There are more than 200,000 Bobo people living in and around Bobo-Dioulasso in southwestern Burkina Faso and across the border in Mali.

Boers

When the first Dutch settlers began arriving in Southern Africa and setting up farms several hundred years ago, they came to be known as Boers ("boer" is the Dutch for "farmer"). The Boers came to control much of South Africa, establishing many powerful republics in the region, which later became part of South Africa. The modern-day Afrikaner (q.v.) population is descended from the Boers.

Bokora

The Bokora are a subgroup of the Karamojong (q.v.), They live in northeastern Uganda.

Bondei

The Bondei are part of the larger grouping of Shambaa (q.v.) peoples, who inhabit the coastal lowlands of Tanzania. The Bondei are concentrated in the rich plains between the northern coast of Tanzania around Tanga and the Usambara (or Shambaa) Mountains in northeastern Tanzania. The region the Bondei inhabit is known as Bonde. There are more than 100,000 Bondei people living in Tanzania today.

The Bondei probably emerged as a distinct group as recently as the mid-nineteenth century. At that time the Bondei ancestors were ruled by the powerful Shambaa kingdom, but the Shambaa representative in Bonde was becoming increasingly independent. It is thought that the idea of the Bondei as a distinct ethnic group emerged during this period; in fact, this idea was actively encouraged by local settlement leaders in the area who thought that they could lessen the impact of Shambaa rule if they were seen as a united group. During the late nineteenth century, the Bondei declared themselves independent from the Shambaa kingdom, and over the following decades the Bondei have come to be accepted as a separate ethnic group.

Bongo

The Bongo are a subgroup of the Mbenga (q.v.). The Mbenga are one of the major groupings of tropical forest-foragers – the so-called pygmies (q.v.) – of Central Africa. There are roughly 2,000 Bongo living in Congo (Rep.) and Gabon.

Borana

The Borana are one of the nine main subgroups of the Oromo. They live in Ethiopia.

Borgawa *see* Bariba

Borno *see* Kanuri

Borong *see* Brong

Bororo *see* Wodaabe

Bosango *see* Sango

Boubangui *see* Mbochi

Boubouri *see* Adjukru

Boudouma *see* Buduma

Brignan *see* Avikam

British

Thousands of people of British descent live in Africa today. The majority live in former British colonies, such as Nigeria in West Africa and Kenya in East Africa. South Africa has a significant English-speaking population.

Brong

The majority of the 200,000 plus Brong (or Abron, Doma, Borong, or Tchaman) live in Ghana, and a smaller number (less than 100,000) live in the Ivory Coast. The Brong are an Akan (q.v.) people.

Bubis

The Bubis are the original inhabitants of Bioko Island (formerly Fernando Póo), which is now part of Equatorial Guinea. The Bubi are descended from Bantu (q.v.) peoples who probably migrated to the island from nearby Cameroon several centuries ago. The Bubi number more than 15,000, less than 10 percent of Bioko's population. Epidemics in the nineteenth century decimated the Bubi population.

Conveniently situated off the coast of west-central Africa, Bioko was an important staging post in the trade of slaves from West and Central Africa to the Americas. It was "discovered" by the Portuguese in the fifteenth century, and in 1778 the island became a Spanish colony. The Bubis resisted attempts to provide forced labor on the Spanish plantations, however, and Spain began bringing coastal West Africans to the island – the ancestors of the modern-day Fernandino (q.v.) population, who came to dominate Equatorial Guinea's economy and politics after independence.

Like others, the Bubi suffered greatly during the reign of the brutal dictator Macias Nguema in the 1970s. The island became a virtual slave camp, and many Equatorial Guineans fled the country or were killed. Since the end of Nguema's rule, the situation has improved but political activity is still oppressed. Many political parties, such as the Bubi Nationalist Group, founded in 1983 to campaign for Bioko's independence, are still outlawed.

Buduma

The Buduma (or Boudouma), who call themselves the Yedina, occupy the islands of Lake Chad, which is at the "junction" of the West African countries of Chad, Niger, and Nigeria. More than 65,000 Buduma live in Chad and roughly 5000 live in both Niger and Nigeria.

The majority of the Buduma are Muslim, but the Buduma religion, which involves the worship of the god Kumani, is still active.

Situated largely in the south of Chad, the lake region the Buduma inhabit is at times swampy and at times flooded. The Buduma economy focuses on pastoralism (livestock raising) and fishing. When the water level of the lakes is high, grazing land is reduced, and so the size of herds kept by the Buduma is forced to decline. At such times, fishing increases in importance. When the water level is low, the number of cattle kept rises.

Until recently the Buduma led a semi-independent existence out of reach of central government. In the 1990s, however, the region around Lake Chad became heavily involved in civil unrest, with several rebel groups launching attacks in the region. Thousands of people living in southern Chad fled the area in fear of both government and rebel attacks, ending up in neighboring countries such as the Central African Republic.

Bulebule *see* Amba

Busa

The Busa are part of the larger grouping of Bariba (q.v.) people. The Bariba of Nigeria, some 100,000 people living in western regions, are called the Busa.

Bushmen

The San (q.v.), and hence the Khoisan (q.v.), were once widely referred to as the Bushmen. This term, suggesting that they belonged to primitive societies, has largely been dropped now.

Bute *see* Bafou

Buzi *see* Ndau

Bwaka *see* Mbaka

Cape Colored and Cape Malays

Cape Coloreds are people of mixed European, African, and Asian origin from the Cape region of South Africa. Most of the 3.5 million people of mixed race in South Africa and the around 150,000 people of mixed race elsewhere in Southern Africa are of Cape Colored origin. Many South Africans reject the label "Cape Colored," believing the term to be a legacy of apartheid (the racist doctrine of "separate development"). Others feel that the existence of Cape Colored people with a rich cultural and racial heritage is a reality.

Cape Malays are of mixed Malay, Indian, Sinhalese, Arab, Madagascan, and Chinese origin. Most of the 90,000 or so Cape Malays live in or around Cape Town.

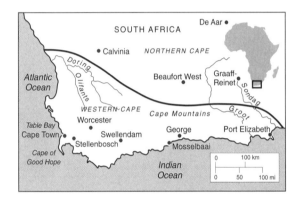

History

In 1652, the Dutch East India Company founded Cape Town as a garrison and supply station for ships sailing between Holland and Asia. Relationships between Dutch settlers and Khoikhoi women were common and many children resulted. During the seventeenth and eighteenth centuries, slaves were introduced into the region from Asia and from other parts of Africa. Interracial marriages and casual sexual encounters were common and the Cape Colored and Cape Malay peoples gradually emerged from this mix. By the late nineteenth century, the Cape Coloreds formed a distinct group.

Cape Colored architecture
An historic Cape Colored rural village in Cape Province. Today, few families still live in traditional whitewashed stone houses such as these; most Cape Coloreds now live in the towns and cities.

Language

Both Cape Coloreds and Cape Malays speak Afrikaans.

Ways of life

The introduction of apartheid in 1948 led to restrictions on South Africa's majority population, including the Cape Coloreds and Cape Malays. Marriage between members of the different "racial" groups was made illegal – extramarital sexual relations were already illegal – and segregation prevented people of different racial origins from living in the same districts. The 1950 Population Registration Act enforced definitions of "race" – based on physical appearance as well as general acceptance and "repute." A person's race then dictated much of what they could do. Classifications were absurd; many families were divided; and many people were evicted from their homes or lost their jobs. Although apartheid has ended, the inequalities it produced remain. Cape Coloreds are found in all occupations, though the legacy of apartheid means many are unskilled or semiskilled workers. The rich farmlands of Western Cape are largely dependent on the labor of poorly paid Cape Coloreds. Cape Malays are renowned as artisans, small traders, and fishermen.

Social structure

POLITICAL STRUCTURE In 1951, the Cape Coloreds' limited voting rights (men only, and subject to property and income qualifications) were removed. In 1983, in an attempt to divide apartheid's opponents, a new constitution was introduced giving people officially classified as "Colored" limited parliamentary representation. The overwhelming majority of these voters boycotted the 1984 and 1989 elections. In 1991, the government repealed all apartheid laws and, in 1994, South Africa's first nonracial elections were held.

Culture and religion

The culture of the Cape Coloreds is in most respects no different from that of Afrikaners of similar social and economic backgrounds.

RELIGION Like Afrikaners, most Cape Coloreds are members of Dutch Reformed churches, though separate wings were created for each racial group. The vast majority of Cape Malays are Muslim.

Cape Malays at prayer
Most Cape Malays are Muslim, their religion being the prime factor that distinguishes them from the Cape Colored population. As required by Islam, Cape Malays typically dress in what they consider to be a "modest" manner, the severity of interpretation a matter of personal choice. Women generally wear long dresses or skirts, long sleeves and a head scarf. Men dress as other urban South Africans though many wear a fez (a brimless felt hat) or a small, white prayer cap.

Cape Colored and Cape Malays timeline			
25,000 BCE Oldest examples of Khoisan rock art in Southern Africa	**1807** British ban slave trade	**1934** South Africa approves independence from Britain	**1983** Separate House of Representation given to Cape Colored voters
c. 400s Some Khoisan begin to keep livestock: Khoikhoi emerge	**1819–1839** Mfecane/Difaqane: period of mass migrations and wars	**1948** Apartheid officially introduced	**1984–1989** Many people refuse to vote in elections for new house
1652 CE Dutch garrison established on the Cape of Good Hope. Dutch and Khoikhoi mix	**1833** British abolish slavery	**1949** Second Immorality Act bans interracial marriages	**1991** Apartheid legislation repealed
	1910 Boers and British form white-ruled Union of South Africa	**1950** Population Registration Act	**1994** First nonracial elections held
1600s–1800s African and Asian slaves brought to Cape; Cape Colored population emerges	**1927** First Immorality Act bans extramarital intercourse between "Europeans" and "natives"	**1951** Colored voting rights removed	**1996** New constitution adopted
1806 British annex Cape Colony		**1961** South Africa becomes a republic; leaves Commonwealth	**1999** Second multiracial elections held

Cape Malays *see* **Cape Colored and Cape Malays**

Chagga

The Chagga live on Mount Kilimanjaro in northern Tanzania – they are virtually the only inhabitants of this famous mountain, one of the highest in the world. There are nearly one million Chagga people in Tanzania. The Chagga language is a Bantu language called Kichagga.

The Chagga's Bantu ancestors probably came to Mount Kilimanjaro at least five or six hundred years ago, establishing several chiefdoms on its slopes. In recent decades, however, many Chagga have moved away from Kilimanjaro to cities.

With land at a premium on the increasingly crowded mountainside, the Chagga developed an intensive system of farming. The Chagga farm millet, corn, beans, cassava, sweet potatoes, yams, sugarcane, coffee, tobacco, pumpkins, and squashes. This variety of crops is often grown on one plot of land at a time, with small plants sown near larger shrubs and trees. Some of the crops are grown as fodder for animals, and fish are often kept in the irrigation ditches. The Chagga are often cited by environmentalists who recommend the adoption of such intercropping techniques, which do not deplete the soil and maintain a biologically-diverse environment.

Chai

The Chai are one of the three closely related groups that make up the Suri (q.v.). The Suri live in Ethiopia and Sudan.

Chakossi *see* **Chokossi**

Chaucho *see* **Temba**

Chewa

Numbering more than two million, the Chewa (or Achewa, Ancheya, or Masheba) are the largest ethnic group in Malawi and one of the largest in Zambia. Some Chewa also live in central Mozambique. They are a Bantu (q.v.) people whose language is called Chichewa.

Chigogo *see* **Gogo**

Chimakonde *see* **Makonde**

Chimaviha *see* **Mavia**

Chimwere *see* **Mwere**

Chisena *see* **Sena**

Chokossi

The Chokossi (Chakossi or Kyokosi) are an Akan (q.v.) people of Togo and Ghana closely related to the Baulé (q.v.). They claim to be descended from Manding (q.v.) ancestors, however, and their language contains many Mande (q.v.) expressions.

Chokwe

The Chokwe (or Jokwe) are one of the principal Angolan ethnic groups and live largely around the headwaters of the Cuango (Kwango in Congo [Dem. Rep.]), Cassai (Kasai in Congo [Dem. Rep.]), and Lwena rivers in northeastern Angola, although a minority live across the border in southern Congo (Dem. Rep.). There are approximately one million Chokwe, three-quarters of whom live in Angola.

History

Chokwe history is closely linked to the Lunda Empire, which dates back to the seventeenth century. At this time, a Lunda chief's son, Mwata Yamvo, emigrated westward with his followers from Lunda territory in present-day southern Congo (Dem. Rep.) into northeastern Angola. Mwata Yamvo was the son of the famous Lunda leader, Kibinda Ilunga, a legendary figure called "The Hunter." By judiciously setting up chiefs who were related to himself and to one another, Mwata Yamvo gained control over the indigenous peoples. Lunda culture, as it blended with that of the indigenous populations, gave rise to a distinctive Chokwe culture, which combined hunting, agriculture, and, later, trade.

By the early nineteenth century, the Chokwe were trading with the Ovimbundu, exchanging wax, ivory, and slaves for Portuguese goods. They traveled in small, seminomadic groups, rather than the larger caravans (companies of travelers) of the Ovimbundu. The Chokwe acquired a reputation for attacking caravans and subjugating local chieftains whose land they had entered. In such cases, they used superior weaponry to overcome their opponents, who often outnumbered them. The Chokwe were governed by the Lunda kings until 1885, when they invaded Lunda territories to the north and succeeded in taking the Lunda capital and establishing their domination over the region west of the Kasai River. Subsequently, they became rubber producers, after which their territorial expansion became rapid.

By the mid-nineteenth century, the Portuguese had expanded inland from the coast to dominate the economic, political, social, and even religious life of the Chokwe. The beginning of the twentieth century saw the Portuguese turn this domination into systematic colonization. In response to forced labor, heavy taxation, discrimination by the Portuguese, and repression of all political protest, the Angolan war of liberation began in 1961. It was fought by the initially Marxist-Leninist

Memorial figure

Dated from before 1850, this carved wooden sculpture is thought to represent a chief's main wife or the queen mother – both women who held important positions at court. As with much Chokwe court art, this figure has elements of naturalism. For example, the hair is real and the hands have been carefully carved. This reflects the fact that nineteenth-century Chokwe aristocracy preferred long fingernails (false ones could be worn) and kept their hands well groomed.

Movimento Popular de Libertação de Angola (MPLA); and the União Nacional para a Independência Total de Angola (UNITA). Angola became independent in 1975.

CIVIL WAR By 1975, however, the MPLA and UNITA were fighting each other in a civil war. MPLA received assistance from Cuba and the USSR, while UNITA received military assistance and foreign arms from the United States and South Africa. By early 1976, the MPLA had defeated UNITA, but the MPLA government remained in conflict with the UNITA guerrilla movement (led by Dr Jonas Savimbi [q.v.]) throughout the 1980s. In 1988, an agreement providing for the withdrawal of South African and Cuban troops was signed in New York. Multiparty elections took place in 1992, and the MPLA leader President dos Santos (q.v.) won a closely fought election battle with Jonas Savimbi. Savimbi and UNITA refused to accept the election results, however, and there was a return to civil war throughout most of 1993 and 1994. Although UNITA and the MPLA government signed a peace agreement (the Lusaka Protocol) in 1994, hostilities continued until 1995 and were resumed in 1998–9.

Language

The Chokwe language is also called Chokwe (or Ciokwe).

Ways of life

The lifestyles of the Chokwe and all other Angolans have been drastically affected by the twenty-year long civil war. Combined with poor transport and marketing facilities, drought, shortages of raw materials, and the concentration of government spending on defense, the development of both agriculture and industry has been severely hampered. As a result, there are serious food shortages and malnutrition is widespread.

HUNTING In the north, hunting has remained an important activity until relatively recently. There was a limit to the number of people that hunting land can support, hence villages were small and widely scattered. Chokwe hunters were renowned for their skill and used a wide range of methods; professional hunters were granted high status in the community. They usually hunted individually, using a rifle or pistol, and small groups of males set traps during the wetter seasons. In the dry season, whole villages sometimes engaged in hunting by burning areas of grassland to flush out small game.

AGRICULTURE To the south, agriculture is more important and villages are more permanent and more densely populated. Fields are cultivated on a rotation system after firing the bush and removing the remaining scrub and trees. Usually men clear the land and women tend the crops. Cassava is the staple food and is ground into flour, which forms an ingredient of a broth to which meat, fish, mushrooms, and vegetables may be added. Cereal crops such as sorghum and millet are grown and stored. The food stores give freedom from immediate material concerns, enabling some of the community to work as artists and craftspeople. The principal domesticated animals are poultry, goats, sheep, pigs, and dogs. Some harvesting of honey is carried out using baskets hung in trees to attract nesting bees.

MINING Angola has valuable diamond deposits – par-

Divination

The basket (below) contains over sixty carved, wooden objects. It is called a ngombo wa tshisuka *and is one of the most important tools of the* diviner, *or* tahi *(left). A tahi is consulted to divine the causes of misfortune, illness, or accident. Each model in the basket has a special name; a fixed symbolic meaning; and represents either a human or an object, animal, plant, or flower. Together, the basket and figures reflect the Chokwe universe. The tahi shakes the basket and reads the positioning of the objects to help his clients find solutions to their problems.*

ticularly in and around the Chokwe and Lunda areas – but extraction and export has been problematic during the civil war hostilities.

Social structure

Historically, Chokwe villages were based upon a group of adult brothers, together with their wives, children, and their sisters' children. A Chokwe village is headed by a chief, who inherits this position providing he has demonstrated suitable leadership qualities. Under the Chokwe matrilineal system, right of succession passes not to a leader's own children, but to his sister's sons. A woman lives with her husband, but her children, when they reach six or thereabouts, often go to live with their uncle on the mother's side. Henceforth, he is responsible for the children's education and welfare. Thus, children belong to their mother's kin group, not their father's.

During the civil war, however, the Chokwe in northeast Angola saw a division of the population into government- and guerrilla-controlled villages – the rebels were attracted by the region's rich mineral deposits, which were used to finance their exploits. These villages often existed side-by-side except that the guerrilla-controlled ones regularly relocated to avoid government takeover.

Culture and religion

RELIGION The Chokwe believe in the existence of a remote supreme being, responsible for creation, called Kalunga or Nzambi. They do not worship this god directly, but do so through mahamba – ancestral

Ndumba Tembo

This portrait of the Chokwe chief Ndumba Tembo was drawn in 1878. The lands governed by Ndumba Tembo in the nineteenth century covered much of present-day central Angola.

Tobacco mortar (right)

This wooden tobacco mortar – used to grind tobacco into snuff (powdered tobacco) – is carved in the shape of a woman. The drum on her head would be used as a snuff container. Elaborate mortars such as this one were produced by the Chokwe as luxury items in the nineteenth century.

Pottery vessel
Water pots that incorporate a human form, such as this example, are made only by men. Although both men and women make pots among the Chokwe, they tend to use different techniques and produce different items.

Mwana pwo mask
The beautiful woman and ideal wife is represented by the costume of mwana pwo, of which the mask is one element. A man wearing mwana pwo instructs boys undergoing initiation into adulthood. Mwana pwo also appear to provide entertainment at festivals where both women and uncircumcised boys can watch.

and nature spirits. Mahamba are represented by small carved statues and by elaborate masks worn by senior village men and women on public and ceremonial occasions.

ART The Chokwe have a rich artistic heritage. Figurative sculptures in both clay and wood represent different categories of supernatural beings or are portraits of ancestors. Incredibly ornate masks are made out of wood, or of resin on a basket frame. The masks often represent male and female ancestors and incorporate animal-like elements. Some of these masks were worn by elders during rites of passage for boys and girls entering adulthood. Often such masks came to symbolize the power and authority of the wearer. For example, the mask worn by a chief's son might evoke the spirit of wealth. When worn during ritual dances, the wearer would receive substantial gifts from the audience as a tribute. The mask could also be used to administer justice, by pointing out a guilty person in the crowd.

From the second half of the eighteenth century, Chokwe art and craft was influenced by the European furniture and other items being carried by trading caravans. Skilled artisans were able to adapt and incorporate foreign motifs into their designs.

Chiefs are often represented seated or playing a musical instrument and their portraits decorate scepters that are among the most remarkable of all African sculptures. The Chokwe people, with their hunting traditions, loved fine weapons made by skillful blacksmiths. Some metal-workers could reproduce – on daggers, swords, or throwing weapons – the fine decorative motifs used by woodcarvers. Chokwe craftspeople are still in great demand. Even everyday objects such as axes, hunting whistles, and drums are often highly embellished and their manufacture is commissioned from well-known artists within the community.

Mbweci staff (above)
Carved, wooden mbweci staff were often used by Chokwe men on journeys. The staff would confer prestige and the female figure would invoke the protection of his ancestors. Many small plaits of hair coated in red clay and oil have been used to construct the elaborate hairstyle. Brass nails and metal wires (representing jewelry) ornament the figure. This staff dates from the end of the nineteenth century.

Cikunza mask (right)
Made from wood, bark, and fibers a cikunza mask like this one would be worn by the man officiating over boys' initiation and circumcision rites. Secluded away from the village for a few months, boys are prepared to enter adulthood by masked men who teach them important social lessons. These masks were intended to be destroyed after use as they were considered too powerful to store.

Ceremonial bench (right)
Over a yard long and with four short legs underneath, this carved wooden board was probably used as a ceremonial bench by a nineteenth-century Chokwe chief. The head's hairstyle reflects Chokwe women's hair fashions in the nineteenth century, and the double circular motifs on either side are very similar to coiled earrings, which were often worn by nineteenth-century women.

Chokwe stool
Stools supported by human figures are an ancient theme in Chokwe art. This style may have been adopted from other people after the Chokwe expanded northward in the 1800s – earlier models do not have the seat resting on the figure's head.

Chokwe timeline	
1600s Mwata Yamvo, a Lunda leader, settles in northeastern Angola	**by 1976** Government formed by MPLA
1800s Chokwe are established as major traders in the region	**1979** Neto dies; José Eduard dos Santos becomes MPLA leader
1830s Chokwe rebellions against Lunda rule	**1991** Cease-fire declared
1885 Chokwe overthrow Lunda and establish control over large areas of present-day Angola and Congo (Dem. Rep.)	**1992** First democratic elections are won by MPLA. Unita refuses to accept election results and civil war breaks out again
1900s Chokwe brought under Portuguese colonial rule	**1994** United Nations-mediated peace treaty signed – the Lusaka Protocol – but hostilities continue
1961 Start of Angolan war of independence against Portuguese colonization	**1995** Savimbi declares war to be at an end and accepts dos Santos as president; hostilities end
1975 Angola gains independence ; civil war is already being fought largely by Movimento Popular de Libertação de Angola (MPLA) led by Agostinho Neto and União Nacional para a Independência Total de Angola (UNITA) led by Dr Jonas Savimbi	**1996** Fragile peace in Angola **1999** Full-scale civil war breaks out again

Chonyi

The Chonyi are one of the nine closely related groups that make up the Mijikenda (q.v.). The Mijikenda mostly inhabit coastal regions of Kenya.

Chope *see* **Shope**

Chuabo *see* **Maganga**

Copts

There are roughly 6,000,000 Copts, who comprise the Christian minority in the predominantly Muslim country of Egypt.

History

Copts are the descendants of Egyptians who kept their Christian faith despite many periods of persecution under the Romans and the influence of Islam after the Arab invasion. The Coptic historical period began around the late 200s when a Copt, Saint Anthony of Egypt (q.v.), founded the early Christian monastic movement. By 642, Muslim Arabs had conquered Egypt, ending the Coptic Period.
RECENT EVENTS The British colonizers of Egypt fostered divisions between Muslims and Christians. Over the years, these divisions have increased to outright persecution and physical attacks, and many Copts have emigrated to Canada, Australia, or the United States.

Language

The Coptic language is a version of Ancient Egyptian enriched with Greek words. It is written in a script derived from the Greek alphabet. Coptic was in fact the last form of Ancient Egyptian to be used. After the Arab conquest of Egypt, the Coptic language gradually gave way to Arabic. By the 1300s, Coptic survived only in the liturgy (services) of the Coptic (Christian) Church. Today, Arabic is used for parts of the Coptic services.

Ways of life

The majority of Copts are farmers, as are their Muslim counterparts. In the past, although Copts were largely excluded from positions of power, they dominated the civil service and were frequently profitable business people. After the monarchy was overthrown in 1952, however, many of their jobs were abolished and much of their property nationalized. Considering that they form a small minority in Egypt, Copts are well represented in the professions, such as law, journalism, and medicine.

Culture and religion

RELIGION Most Copts are members of the Coptic Church, but a minority belong to other churches. Tradition states that Saint Mark brought Christianty to Egypt in c. 60, but Christian communities probably already existed in Egypt by this date. In 451, the Christian Church attempted to standardize its doctrine. The Council of Chalcedon was arranged to carry this out. Coptic Christianity differs from other forms in that it asserts the unity of both the human and the divine in the nature of Christ. This is referred to as the Monophysite doctrine. At the Council of

Key

1 Clergy's seating area
2 Sacristy
3 Altar
4 Haikal
5 Episcopal throne
6 Water tank
7 Pulpit with spiral stairway
8 Steps
9 Baptistery

Plan of a Coptic church

As with most churches, Coptic churches are built on an east-west axis. The nave (central part) is separated from the side aisles by columns. The south aisle is usually reserved for women. A screen called a haikal separates the sanctuary from the choir. The sanctuary is raised above the level of the choir.

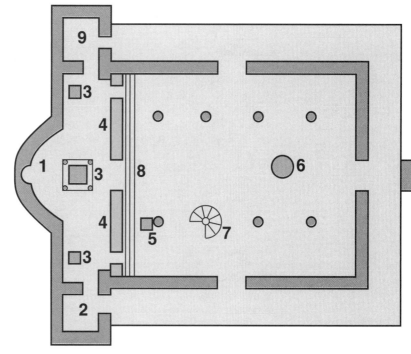

© DIAGRAM

Crux ansata
This Coptic Period limestone panel, from the seventh or eighth century, was probably used as a wall decoration or tombstone. The carved cross is called a crux ansata. *These crosses began to be used from the fifth century onward. The shape is based on the Ancient Egyptian* hieroglyph *(picture symbol) for "life" – the* ankh.

Chalcedon, the church leaders from Constantinople and Rome condemned the Monophysite doctrine and declared that Christ had two separate natures. In response, the Copts established an independent

church. The Coptic Period can therefore alternatively be dated from 451.

ART The early Copts included many fine artists and some of their paintings, sculptures, and textiles have survived. Most of them are on religious themes. Even after the Arab invasion of Egypt, Coptic artists continued to produce carvings, book bindings, and beautifully decorated manuscripts. Muslims often employed Coptic artists to decorate their buildings. In modern Egypt, Coptic art and culture is largely ignored by school curriculums.

Copts timeline			
c. 40 Christianity established	religion of Roman Empire	**1517** Ottoman conquest of Egypt	**1952** Monarchy overthrown
c. 60 Saint Mark visits Egypt	**450s** Byzantine persecution of Copts	**1856** Hamayouni Decree attempts to achieve equality between Muslims and Copts in Egypt	**1961** Nationalization begins
100s Coptic language emerges	**451** Coptic Church established		**1970s** Coptic, Roman Catholic, and Eastern Orthodox churches consider reunion
200s Roman persecution of Copts	**642** Arabs conquer Egypt	**1882** British colonize Egypt	
c. 250–356 Life of Saint Anthony of Egypt (or Memphis or Thebes)	**725–830** Riots against Islamic taxes on non-Muslims	**1920s** Many Copts support the nationalist movement	**1981–1985** Coptic Pope under house arrest; he is accused of trying to be a political leader
313 Edict of Milan legalizes Christianity in Roman Empire	**969** Fatimid rule begins **1200s** Coptic language almost extinct	**1922** Egypt independent as a monarchy	**1990s** Increasing attacks on Copts by radical Islamic fundamentalists
392 Christianity becomes official	**1250** Mamluk rule over Egypt begins	**1934** Laws introduced to hamper the building of churches	

Creoles

In Africa, the Creoles (or Krio) of Sierra Leone are the descendants of former slaves who settled Freetown in the late eighteenth century. Their culture mixes elements of European and African origin, and their language – Creole, or Krio, – has evolved from both English and African languages.

Freetown, on the coast of modern-day Sierra Leone, was established in 1787 by freed slaves from Britain, some of whom had European wives. By 1800 they had been joined by former slaves from the then British

colony of Nova Scotia in Canada as well as Maroons - former slaves from Jamaica who had been deported to Nova Scotia after a successful revolt against their owners 100 years earlier. Later still, the British brought Africans captured from illegal slaving ships to Sierra Leone. Many of these so-called recaptives were of Yoruba (q.v.) descent. By the mid nineteenth century this mixture of settlers and recaptives had blended into the distinct ethnic group known today as the Creoles.

Cushites

The majority of the modern-day population of East Africa is descended from three main African groups: Cushites, Nilotes (q.v.) and Bantu (q.v.) people. The Cushites originated in the Ethiopian highlands. They were the first food producers in East Africa, learning how to grow their own food and keep animals. Over many hundreds of years the Cushites spread out from their original dispersal site to occupy much of northeastern Africa, reaching the Kenyan Highlands by 1000 BCE. Between the fifteenth and eighteenth cen-

turies CE, an important Iron Age site was established by Southern Cushites at Engaruka in northern Tanzania.

Cushitic languages are today spoken in Somalia, Ethiopia, northeastern Kenya, and neighboring regions. The Amhara of Ethiopia and the Oromo (q.v.) of Ethiopia and northeastern Kenya are Cushites, as are the Konso (q.v.) of southern Ethiopia. The Swahili (q.v.) and the Somali (q.v.) also have Cushitic ancestors.

Cushitic *see* Cushite

Dadjo *see* Daju

Dagomba

Numbering more than 400,000, the Dagomba are one of the larger Mole-Dagbane (q.v.) groups. The majority live in northern Ghana and Togo.

Daju

The Daju (or Dadjo) people number more than 180,000 living in the western Sudan and eastern Chad. Some scholars classify the Daju language with that of the Nubian (q.v.) language, though others classify it by itself.

Dan

The Dan (or Yacouba or Gio) are a Manding (q.v.) people of the Ivory Coast. Some Dan also live in Liberia. There are several hundred thousand Dan.

Danakil see **Afar**

Darod

The Darod are one of the main clan-based subgroups of the Somali (q.v.) people. The majority live in northern Somalia. Some also live in southeastern Ethiopia and northern Kenya. There are more than 2 million Darod, and they fall into main subclans and even smaller groupings. In the 1990s in the midst of a civil war, the Darods joined up with the Issaq (q.v.) and declared northern Somaliland independent but received no international recognition of their independence.

Daza

Numbering more than 200,000, the Daza are one of the largest subgroups of the Dazaga (q.v.). The Daza, who are mostly nomadic pastoralists (livestock herders), range over a region that covers much of Chad between the Tibesti Mountains in the north and Lake Chad in the south. Many Daza can also be found in Niger. The Anakaza (q.v.) are a subgroup of the Daza.

Dazaga

A subgroup of the Tebu (q.v.), the Dazaga are themselves further divided into groups such as the Daza (q.v.) and Wajunga (q.v.). There are more than 250,000 Dazaga people living in the desert and semidesert regions of Niger and Chad, and to a lesser extent, Sudan and southern Libya.

De

The De are part of the Kru (q.v.) cluster of peoples. The Kru are one of the largest ethnic groups in Liberia.

Dendi

The Dendi of West Africa number more than 100,000 spread between Benin, Togo, Niger, and Nigeria. They speak a Songhay (q.v.) language and have Mende (q.v.) origins.

Denkyira

The Denkyira (or Kankyira) are one of the larger Akan (q.v.) peoples. They live in southern Ghana and number around 100,000.

Dhopadhola see **Padhola**

Diakkane see **Jahanka**

Dida

The Dida number more than 100,000 people living in south-central Ivory Coast. They are a Kru (q.v.) people.

Diego Garcians see **Ilois of Diego Garcia**

Digil

The Digil are one of the main clan-based subgroups of the Somali (q.v.) people. The majority live in northwestern Somalia.

Digiri

The Digiri are a subgroup of the Okiek of west-central Kenya. The Okiek are, in turn, part of the Kalenjin (q.v.).

Digo

The 70,000 plus Digo are part of the Mijikenda (q.v.) cluster of peoples living in Tanzania near the border with Kenya and along Kenya's coast. They are a Bantu (q.v.) people.

Dindje

The Dindje are a subgroup of the Sara (q.v.) people of Chad. There are around 90,000 Dindje people.

Ancestor mask
This mask from the Dan represents a female ancestor and features a bell suspended from it, for ritual use.

Dinka

The Dinka are a Nilotic people who live in southern Sudan. There are just over one million Dinka in more than twenty different groups, making them the predominant people in southern Sudan.

History

Little is known of Dinka history before 1500, when they are known to have been settled in their present location. **RECENT EVENTS** The north of Sudan and the Sudanese government have long been dominated by Arab culture and politics. Attempts to impose these on the largely non-Muslim, non-Arab south have often lead to conflict. As the largest and most widespread southern Sudanese people, the Dinka have often been at the forefront of these conflicts. In 1978, the Sudanese government began the construction of the Jonglei Canal in the south. The aim of the canal was to conserve water – a great deal is lost through evaporation as the Nile waters pass through the swampy Sudd region. The water saved could be used to irrigate agricultural land reclaimed from the Sudd. The canal was viewed with suspicion by many southerners, especially the Dinka, who saw it as an attempt to convert cattle-herding people like themselves to settled farming, making them easier to control and govern. Furthermore, in 1983, the government divided the south into three regions to break up the power base of the Dinka. Finally, the adoption of Sharia (Islamic holy) law in 1983 led the southern Sudanese to rebel, and civil war broke out.

The southern-based rebel groups draw a lot of their support from the Dinka. The main rebel group was originally divided into two wings: military – the Sudanese People's Liberation Army (SPLA) – and political – the Sudanese People's Liberation Movement (SPLM). In 1988, the Sudanese government was accused by the SPLM and international human rights organizations of attempted genocide (extermination) of the Dinka. Rebel attacks led to work on the Jonglei Canal being suspended in 1984, and work has only

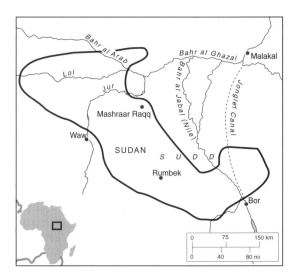

partially been resumed since. By 1991, the SPLA controlled most of the south, but in the same year, it split into different factions. Reports have surfaced of civilians being forcibly conscripted by both the government and rebel groups. Despite several cease-fires, the civil war continues.

Language

The Dinka language is also called Dinka and belongs to the Nilotic language group.

Ways of life

SEMINOMADIC PASTORALISM The vast majority of Dinka practice seminomadic pastoralism, an activity they combine with growing crops. The region inhabited by the Dinka is largely savanna (grassland with scattered trees and shrubs), sloping down to the Sudd – a region of small streams and swamps that is subject to flooding in the rainy season. The year divides into two seasons: the dry season, which stretches from roughly November through April, and the rainy season, which can begin as early as March and last until October. In an apparently inhospitable land, the Dinka's lifestyle has been finely tuned over the years to cope with these changing seasons.

During the rainy season, most Dinka live in permanent settlements. These are built on slightly higher, more-wooded land in the savanna regions to avoid flooding. As the pastures around the villages dry out, the Dinka take their cattle and set up camps near rivers, where the floods have subsided and new grass has sprung up.

During the dry season, the permanent settlements will be virtually deserted by all but elderly people and nursing mothers. Too delicate to survive heavy rains, tobacco is the only crop grown during the dry season. It is mainly grown for sale in the market towns and provides an important source of cash with which to buy goods not produced within the community. Toward the end of the dry season, fishing festivals may be held. Trapped by the receding rivers, large numbers of fish are caught in designated pools that have been left untouched for this purpose.

Sparring
Young Dinka men hone their fighting skills by engaging in mock battles using shields and fighting sticks or spears. Traditionally, these skills are deemed important as they are considered to reflect a man's ability to protect his home and family.

These events attract people from a wide area.

When the first rains come, the Dinka families begin to move back to the permanent settlements, and for the next few weeks they are busy tilling the soil and planting the seed for the next crops. Cereals, for example durra, corn, and millet, and vegetables such as pumpkin and okra, are grown. The main rainy season begins about June, and the rains bring floods with them. A few of the younger herders take the cattle off to drier pastures in the savanna, leaving most of the people to look after the growing crops. When the floods stop, some of the young men go home to help with the harvest, followed a few weeks later by the rest with the cattle.

CATTLE Cattle are central to the Dinka way of life. Owning cattle means wealth. In an environment of scarce resources, the Dinka do not use their animals just for food, which would be wasteful; cattle provide for a wide variety of the Dinka's material needs. Cow's milk is drunk or made into butter which, in turn, can be made into oil for cooking or anointing the skin. Cattle urine is used for washing, dyeing hair, and tanning hides. The dung is used as fuel. The smoke and ash from dung-fires is used as an insect repellent. The ash is also used for body decoration and its fine abrasive quality makes it a good cleaning agent. If an animal dies – usually through old age or accident – every part is put to some use. The skins are made into leather for mats, drums, cloth, and ropes; the meat is eaten; and the horns and bones can be carved into tools or musical instruments.

Not surprisingly, the Dinka endow their cattle with great religious and social significance. Cattle are sacrificed in religious worship and can be used to make payments that settle disputes or seal alliances, or

Pottery
Clay pots are vital for cooking and carrying water and are usually made by women. Coils of clay are built up into the desired shape, then the edges are moistened and smoothed down. Color can be added by rubbing with a colored stone and patterns can be inscribed using a sharp tool. The pot is then fired by placing it overnight in a hole in the ground and covering it with burning straw and dung.

they can be given as bridewealth (a present made by the groom to his new wife's family) to legally confirm a marriage.

Social structure

SOCIAL STRUCTURE One Dinka group may have as many as 30,000 members. Every group has a number of sub-groups, which comprise different extended families. The extended-family unit, or clan, includes all blood relatives and can number in the hundreds. Each of these clans is associated with a particular animal or plant. Clan members respect, and avoid harming, their own clan's particular emblem.

POLITICAL STRUCTURE Each group has a priestly or religious clan, called a bany, whose traditional role is to control and safeguard the land. The head of the bany is known as the beng – "Master of the Fishing Spear." His authority is always based more on persuasion and reputation than force. People will approach him to have their disputes settled and grievances aired. Since 1972, when southern Sudan was granted regional autonomy, the beng of a group has often been elected by the people to be the local political, as well as religious, leader.

Culture and religion

RELIGION Although some Dinka have converted to Christianity or Islam, the Dinka religion is still very

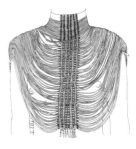

Beaded clothing
Traditionally, unmarried women wear bodices made of thousands of tiny, colored beads. These hang from the neck rather like very wide necklaces. Dinka men may also wear a similar garment: a kind of beaded corset. Beaded clothing is largely reserved for special occasions nowadays; imported or Western-style clothes and fabrics are more often worn on an everyday basis.

Fishing
This Dinka woman is fishing with a specially-designed cane trap. As the rainy season comes to an end, the swamps contract and fish are easily trapped in the shallow waters.

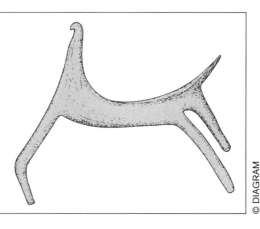

Dinka headrest
The simple form of this wooden headrest enhances the natural shape of the wood. Many Dinka would have at least one of these pieces of furniture. They are used mainly as headrests for sleeping at night and are particularly useful for protecting elaborate hairstyles. Headrests can also be used as stools; it is not considered appropriate, for example, for elderly men to sit directly on the ground.

Hairstyles

This picture shows a hairstyle worn by a young Dinka man, which has an ostrich feather attached to complete the style. The Dinka usually take great care of their hair. It may be cut, shaped, and set in place using cow dung and mud.

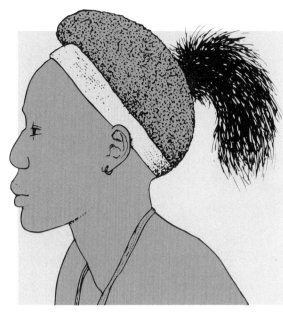

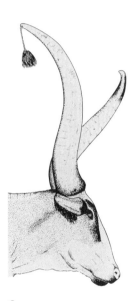

Song ox

Young Dinka men are usually given an ox after their initiation into manhood. The owner will often compose songs praising his ox. It is a Dinka custom to train the horns of these "song oxen" into special shapes and maybe decorate the tips with tassels.

from cattle-dung ash and water. The Dinka also shave, cut, and sculpt their hair into neat designs using cattle dung as a fixing gel; hair may also be dyed a dark orange color using the acidic urine of the cattle. The designs used are constantly developing over time and new ones adopted as each group comes into contact with other groups, gains new members, or undergoes various other changes. Scarification (in which permanent designs are created with scars) is also sometimes used to adorn the body.

much alive. It involves belief in a number of yeeth (divinities or powers). It is not always appropriate to define Dinka gods in a set way. For example, the widely-revered yath (singular of yeeth) Nhialac is several things: the sky; what is in the sky; an entity sometimes called "father" or "creator"; and also a power that can be possessed by any yeeth or even particular men. Another important yath is Deng, who is associated with rain, thunder, and lightning. Garang – associated with the Sun – was the first man, and Abuk – associated with rivers – the first woman. Macardit is the source of death and sterility. Other yeeth include the emblems of clans. New yeeth are adopted as groups come into contact with other Dinka groups.

PERSONAL ART Dinka people, the young in particular, use their own bodies as canvases onto which they create living art. Butter or oil made from milk or the fruit of the shea tree is used to anoint the body. Then friends paint designs onto each other's skin using a paint made

Dinka timeline

c. 1000 Nilotic peoples settled in region to the far southwest of Bahr al Ghazal river	**1956** Sudanese independence
1500s Dinka settled in present location. Different Dinka groups begin to emerge	**1972** End of first Sudanese civil war; south granted regional autonomy
1821 Trade routes opened from north to south; leading to reduced southern population through disease and slavery	**1978** Work on Jonglei Canal begins in southern Sudan
	1983 Sudan adopts Sharia (Islamic holy) law against wishes of mainly non-Muslim south; civil war breaks out again
1840s–1850s Arab slave trade develops in Dinka territory	
1882 Anglo-Egyptian force conquers Sudan; Mahdist campaigns against conquerors begin	**1984** Rebel raids on Jonglei Canal result in suspension of work
	1988 Limited amount of work begins on Jonglei Canal
1898 Anglo-Egyptian force conquers Mahdists; Sudan ruled as a joint British and Egyptian colony	**1990s** Despite many cease-fires, Sudan's civil war continues
1955–1972 First civil war between north and south Sudan	**1998** Sudan's government accepts the principle of secession for southern Sudan

Personal art

This Dinka man and woman have patterns painted onto their faces using ash. The styles, patterns, and designs used for all forms of personal art depend on the taste of the wearer and are influenced by current fashions, which change every few years. Otherwise occupied by the current civil war, many personal art forms are in danger of falling into disuse among the Dinka.

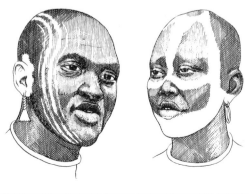

Traditional dry-season home

The traditional Dinka dry-season home is ideally suited to both the Dinka's lifestyle and their environment – which has a few scattered savanna trees but little stone for building. These buildings are made from the plentiful savanna grass, which is dried and attached to a frame of flexible saplings. This type of house is easy to dismantle and carry from camp to village, where more permanent shelters are used.

Dir

The Dir are one of the main clan-based subgroups of the Somali (q.v.) people. The majority live in northwestern Somalia. The Issa (q.v.) of Djibouti are sometimes considered to be a Dir group.

Djeberti *see* Jabarti

Djerma *see* Zerma

Djollof *see* Wolof

Dodo *see* Dodoth

Dodoth

The Dodoth (or Dodo) are Nilotes (q.v.) of Uganda who are part of the Karamojong (q.v.) cluster of peoples. They are concentrated in the north of Uganda in the border regions with Sudan and Kenya.

Dogon

The Dogon of central Mali live in remote, rocky ravines along a 120-mile (190-km) stretch of the Bandiagara Cliffs and on the savannas (grasslands with scattered trees and shrubs) on the plateaus above and below. Although there are fewer than 500,000 Dogon, their culture is significant for many reasons; in particular because they were isolated from neighboring peoples and relatively free of outside influences until quite recently.

History

Very little is known of Dogon history before they came to settle in the Bandiagara region. The Dogon believe that ancient human bones and wooden sculptures found in caves suggest that more than 2,000 years ago the Bandiagara Cliffs were inhabited by a people called the Tellem. Because most of the wood carvings have been dated as no more than 200 years old, however, and because stylistically they resemble modern Dogon work, archeologists believe the sculptures were made by Dogon artisans and that the oldest "Tellem" skeletons probably date from no earlier than the eleventh century.

The Dogon say their ancestors fled from the southwest to the Bandiagara Cliffs from the thirteenth cen-

tury onward to escape conquest by the medieval empires of Ghana, Mali, and Songhay. The isolated and inhospitable terrain also proved to be excellent protection from attacks by neighboring Mossi and Fulani peoples – in particular during the eighteenth- to nineteenth-century period of jihads (Islamic holy wars) against non-Muslims such as the Dogon. The cliffs made access difficult, while the land itself was considered to be of little value by outsiders.

Language

The Dogon language is also called Dogon.

Ways of life

Despite rocky terrain and minimal rainfall, many Dogon are farmers. Terraces have been created on the slopes to enable crops to be grown. Soil, compost, and bird droppings are gathered from cliffside ledges and spread on the terraces. Millet is the main crop, but sorghum, other grains, vegetables, fruit, and cotton are also cultivated. Families keep sheep, goats, and hens,

Cliffside village
This distinctively Dogon village clings to cliffs that can reach as high as 600 ft (180 m) above the plain below.

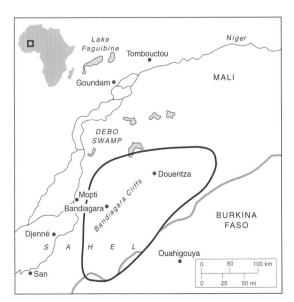

Ginna house (right)
Dogon villages are often clustered around a ginna (or "great house"), which is occupied by the most senior man. The small compartments are used to store religious artefacts.

Granary door (above)
This wooden door from a granary (grain store) is decorated with figures of Dogon women. The zigzag patterns represent the style in which the universe was created as well as the union of man and woman. In recent decades, most such decorative features have been removed from buildings for sale to art collectors or ethnologists.

and where sufficient land is available, cattle and donkeys are raised. Generally, women sow, weed, and harvest grain while the men clear land and fertilize the crops. Water has always been precious, and droughts from the 1960s to the 1980s led to hundreds of deaths and thousands of Dogon left the region. Today, many young men leave their villages to work in the cities of Mali and Ivory Coast, sending most of their wages home to their families in Bandiagara.

Social structure

VILLAGES AND HOUSES The most characteristic Dogon villages are those on the sides of the Bandiagara Cliffs or

beneath them, where the Dogon live in small villages of under 1,000 people. Each village is made up of one or more extended families who trace their descent from a common male ancestor from father to son. These lineages are headed by the oldest man, who lives in the ginna (or "great house"). In villages of only one lineage, this man will also be the village head. Several villages are often grouped around a well or waterhole.

In these villages, the people live in small rectangular mud houses. Tall towers made of rock or mud and with thatched roofs, once used as granaries (grain stores), now provide general storage. Houses and granaries may be joined together with mud walls to form family compounds. The most important public building is the togu na, an open-sided building on the main square, which is used by men for village council meetings.

Dogon social organization and architecture are closely related to Dogon beliefs. The layout of buildings, both individually or collectively, is seen as symbolic of complex aspects of the Dogon religion that may also be expressed by the human form. The Dogon often use the human body as a metaphor for both society and religion. For example, houses and villages are ideally built on a north-south axis to resemble a prostrate being; the togu na represents a man's head; and a house can symbolize the union of man (ceiling) and woman (central room) as well as Heaven (roof) and Earth (floor). The position of buildings is symbolic of how Amma (God) made the world and provides a link between the Dogon and their ancestors.

Culture and religion

RELIGION Today, almost half of the Dogon people are Muslim and a minority are Christian, but even they have not abandoned many of the Dogon religious beliefs and practices. In order to resist outside influences, the Dogon developed an extremely complex view of their environment, based on an intricate web of beliefs and stories, which are most commonly preserved by hogons (Dogon spiritual leaders or priests). For the Dogon, these stories are actual events, not simply symbols of events, and in all aspects of life there is a direct link between the Dogon religion and the physical environment in which they live. Even though Dogon beliefs are not at all secret, most know only a few stories.

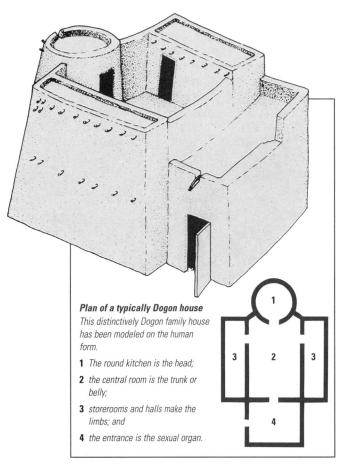

Plan of a typically Dogon house
This distinctively Dogon family house has been modeled on the human form.

1 *The round kitchen is the head;*

2 *the central room is the trunk or belly;*

3 *storerooms and halls make the limbs; and*

4 *the entrance is the sexual organ.*

Granaries (above)
The design of these granaries (grain stores) is inspired by the sheer cliff faces and rocky outcrops of Bandiagara. Few granaries are used to store large amounts of grain now, as most is taken to market.

In one story, the origin of life is symbolized by the smallest cultivated seed, the kize-uzi (fonio grain), which the Dogon call "the little thing." The kize-uzi's life started as a series of seven vibrations or pulses, before it began expanding and revolving into a spiral, creating and forever extending the universe. Looked at from the side, the spiral resembles a zigzag. Spiral or zigzag symbols appear in many areas of Dogon life – for example, as patterns molded or marked on buildings and artwork, and even in the pattern in which grain is planted in fields or houses are arranged in a village. The zigzag has social as well as religious connotations: it can represent the union of man and woman and the harmonious balance of opposites.

ASTRONOMY The Dogon have a remarkably accurate knowledge of the universe, developed separately from that of astronomers elsewhere and handed down from ancient times. For example, the Dogon know of Sirius A – the brightest star in the sky – and also of Sirius B, some 100,000 times less bright and impossible to see with the naked eye. Furthermore, the Dogon know that it takes fifty years for Sirius B (which they call "the smallest thing there is") to orbit Sirius A, and they have inherited from their ancestors a deep understanding of other characteristics of the stars and universe.

CAVES Along the Bandiagara Cliffs are numerous caves, many of which are used by the Dogon as cemeteries. Dogon sculptures (as well as those supposedly made by the "Tellem" people) are found in difficult-to-reach caves, some of which are no more than niches along the sheerest of the cliffsides. Even today, Dogon people keep their most important masks and statues hidden in secret cliffside caves, occasionally removing them for religious ceremonies and festivals. Because of theft by outsiders for sale as works of art, sculptures are often defaced by the Dogon to reduce their value to others and prevent their removal by antique hunters or art dealers.

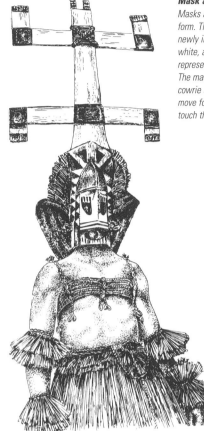

Mask art
Masks are widely considered to be the most important Dogon art form. This kanaga ("Hand of God") mask is usually worn by boys newly initiated into men. It is made from wood and is painted red, white, and black. The mask is topped by a double cross, perhaps to represent a bird or a crocodile, or as a symbol of Heaven and Earth. The mask is surrounded by fiber dyed red and decorated with cowrie shells, and the wearer sports a red-stained skirt. Dancers move forwards and backwards allowing their masks to almost touch the ground.

Rainmaker
This painted wooden figure is one of many ancient works kept in Dogon granaries (grain stores). They are used in rainmaking: the open hand brings the rain and the closed hand stops or prevents it.

Sand pictures
The Dogon have a wide knowledge of astronomy. These pictures drawn in the sand depict:

1 *Saturn's halo;*

2 *the four moons of Jupiter; and*

3 *the orbital path of the star Sirius B.*

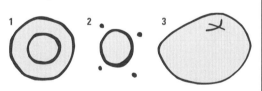

Dogon woman *(above)*
Both Dogon men and women trade at the local markets. Pottery and spinning are largely done by women, while men practice weaving and basketry.

Dogon timeline

1240 End of Dogon vassalage to the Empire of Ghana	**1960s–1980s** Recurring drought causes famine in Sahelian countries	**1984** Mali reenters African Franc Zone and readopts CFA franc as currency
1307–1332 Dogon driven westward to Bandiagara Cliffs by Mossi	**1962** Mali leaves the African Franc Zone and adopts the new Malian franc as currency	**1991** Traoré overthrown in bloodless coup
1359 Mossi invade Empire of Mali	**1968** Lieutenant General Moussa Traoré takes power in bloodless military coup	**1992** Democratic elections end military rule in Mali
c. 1490 Mali's power eclipsed by dominant Songhay Empire		**1994** CFA currency devalued by fifty percent; demonstrations break out as Malians experience economic hardships
1898 French conquest of Soudan	**1977** Modibo Keita's death while in detention leads to widespread popular unrest	
1960 Soudan wins independence from France as Mali		

© DIAGRAM

Doma *see* Brong

Dorobo

Dorobo is a term originally used disparagingly by the Maasai (q.v.) to refer to non-Maasai people. The Okiek (q.v.) are sometimes called the Dorobo.

Duruma

The Duruma are the second-largest of the nine closely related groups that make up the Mijikenda (q.v.). The Mijikenda mostly inhabit coastal regions of Kenya.

Dyula

Dyula are a Mande (q.v.) people of mixed Bambara and Malinke (q.v.) origin whose name literally means "trader" in the Dyula Manding (q.v.) language. The vast majority of the Dyula people are Muslim. The Dyula have long played a dominant role in long-distance trade between West and North Africa, and Dyula traders helped bring the medieval empire of Mali great wealth. Several large towns such as Kong (in the north of modern Ivory Coast) and Bobo-Dioulasso (south-western Burkina Faso) that grew up on major trade routes were largely inhabited by Dyula. Kong was at times an independent kingdom, reaching its height in the eighteenth century. Today, the Dyula are not necessarily traders, and they probably number several hundred thousand spread throughout the West African countries of Mali, Gambia, Burkina Faso, Senegal, and Ivory Coast. Many Dyula live in the towns and cities of these countries.

East African Asians

Asians form a small but economically very important East African minority. Nairobi and Mombasa in Kenya have the largest East African Asian communities, but there are also significant concentrations in Dar es Salaam and Zanzibar in Tanzania, and a growing number are returning to Uganda after an absence of twenty years. The East African Asian population has reduced substantially since independence: in Kenya, the Asian population is around 50,000; in Tanzania, 30,000; and in Uganda, only a few thousand. Emigration has been substantial, with many East African Asians settling in Britain, Canada, or other countries.

History

There has been an Asian presence on the East African coast for many hundreds of years. The region has long been attractive to traders because of its excellent trading prospects. Dhows (cargo-carrying sailboats) plied between India, the Arabian Peninsula, and East Africa, supplying Indian-made textiles and iron goods in exchange for ivory, gold, slaves, and spices.

COLONIALISM The majority of the present-day Asian community dates back to the colonial era and the construction of the East Africa Railway (1896–1902) linking Mombasa with Uganda. Local African labor was either unavailable or was considered unreliable or hostile and so 32,000 laborers were recruited in India. Many of these workers died of tropical diseases, while others returned to India on completion of their contracts. About 7,000 Indians chose to settle in East Africa, however, while retaining close links with their home country. Although some Indians continued to work on the railways, most established

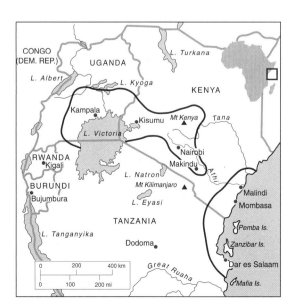

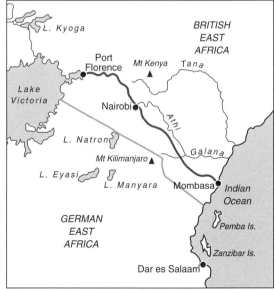

Lunatic Line
Built between 1896 and 1902, the "Lunatic Line"– as it was dubbed by its critics – was built to link Mombasa and Lake Victoria. The British intended to use it to transport troops. Over 30,000 Indian workers came from India to build the railway.

Sikh temple (left)
This Sikh temple at Makindu, like many others, offers free food and lodging to travelers. Visitors are restricted to one night's stay each.

Hindu temple
This Hindu temple in Mombasa was built by volunteers between 1957 and 1960.

themselves as merchants, initially catering to the needs of fellow Indians, but soon expanding their businesses to cater for the African population as well. Hearing of the business opportunities to be found in East Africa, Indian immigrants continued to arrive in the region into the 1920s, by which time Asians, through their trading activities, had done much to integrate even remote areas into the cash economy.

The East African Indian National Congress was formed in 1914 to represent the interests of the Asian community, in particular in demanding equal representation with Europeans on the Legislative Councils, equal economic opportunities (especially in relation to landownership in the highlands of Kenya), and in opposing segregation between Europeans and Asians. Their complaints were principally aimed at the European settler community, whom they far outnumbered. In marked contrast to the Indian community of South Africa and despite the urging of political leaders in India itself, East African Asians rarely took up common cause with the African population toward whom they tended to feel culturally superior.

RECENT EVENTS At independence, Asians were given a choice: they could become citizens of the country in which they lived or they could retain British nationality but without a right of residency in Britain. It was not an easy choice: adopting local citizenship implied loyalty to the new nation, but many Asians felt that their security in Africa was limited and believed that British nationality offered a measure of protection in the event of anti-Asian hostilities. "Africanization" policies of the newly independent states resulted in Asians having to stop doing business in rural areas, but in the cities their skills and economic strength meant that they were not as easily replaced. Nevertheless, many found their shops nationalized or were pressured out of jobs, especially in government. In Kenya, the change happened slowly, thus avoiding disruption, but in Uganda the changes were sudden and brutal. In 1972, Uganda's dictator Idi Amin Dada (q.v.) expelled the entire Asian community of 80,000 from the country, distributing their businesses to his supporters. Although the expulsions were initially widely supported, they had a devastating effect on the Ugandan economy, from which the country is still recovering. In the 1990s, the current government has attempted to encourage the return of Ugandan Asians.

Language

Most East African Asians use Gujarati or Punjabi – languages spoken in western India – in their homes. Most also speak English, and many speak an African language, such as Swahili, as well.

Ways of life

Many East African Asians are in the retail trade, usually owning small shops. They also dominate – in Kenya, and to a lesser extent in Tanzania and Uganda – road transport, the textile and construction industries, hotels, and financial services. Some Asians have entered the profession of law, while others work as artisans or as clerks. In Uganda before 1972, Asians developed agricultural interests, especially in sugar; many have returned since 1991 and are again a major force in this sector.

Indian laborers
These workers are taking a rest from building the "Lunatic Line." The railway was built across hazardous and difficult terrain such as desert, the Great Rift Valley, and tsetse fly-infested land. Over 6,000 people were injured and 2,500 lives lost in the process.

© DIAGRAM

Social structure

Under colonial rule, Asians occupied a middle rung on a three-tiered social and economic hierarchy that placed Europeans at the top and Africans at the bottom. Within their own community, East African Asians have largely retained the basic social structure developed in India. Religious divisions, including the maintenance of the Hindu caste structure, have resulted in a divided community. In general, the Asian community has isolated itself socially from mainstream society and has often been accused of economic exploitation and racism. Sensitive to such accusations, many Asians are active in charitable works, efforts that in the past would have been limited to supporting poorer members of the Asian community but are now extended to a wider population.

Idi Amin (q.v.)
Once the heavyweight boxing champion of Uganda, Idi Amin seized power in 1971 and began a brutal regime in which thousands of opponents were murdered and Ugandan Asians expelled.

Culture and religion

East African Asians were (and still are) a highly visible minority, maintaining Indian styles of dress and cooking, although both have been subject to European and African influences.

RELIGION Most East African Asians are either Hindu or Muslim. Some of those whose families originated in the Punjab are Sikhs, and Zanzibar's few remaining Parsees (Indians originally descended from Persians) are Zoroastrian. Many of the Muslims are Ismailis, a subsect that has as its spiritual leader the Aga Khan, who maintains important business and philanthropic interests in the region, particularly in Kenya.

Street scene
This street scene in Nairobi, Kenya reflects the strong economic presence of Asians in Kenya. The Asians in East Africa have preserved much of their culture, such as their dress. Women still mostly wear Indian saris though many men have adopted Western styles of dress.

East African Asians timeline			
1885–1900 Britain and Germany partition East Africa into colonies	**1964** Tanganyika and Zanzibar unite to form Tanzania	**1972** Ugandan Asian community expelled by Amin; most go to Britain and others to Canada, Norway, or India	**1985** Tanzania abandons socialism
1896–1902 Construction of the East Africa Railway – the "Lunatic Line"	**1965** Each part of Tanzania is allowed only one political party	**1979** Tanzanian forces and Ugandan rebels oust Amin	**1991** Kenya allows for multiparty politics. Uganda invites expelled Asians to return
1914 East African Indian National Congress formed	**1966** Coup by Milton Obote in Uganda	**1981–1986** Ugandan civil war; rebels take power from government	**1993** Anti-Asian attacks in Tanzania
1961 Tanganyikan independence	**1967** Arusha Declaration: Tanzania adopts socialism	**1982** Failed military coup in Kenya results in widespread violence and looting, much of it targeting the Asian community	**1994** Nonparty elections held in Uganda as first step to restoring democracy
1962 Ugandan independence	**1971** In Uganda, Col. Idi Amin Dada seizes power in a military coup; repressive regime installed		**1995** Chaotic first multiparty elections held in Tanzania; new government introduces more liberal economic policies
1963 Kenya and Zanzibar independent			

Ebira

The Ebira (or Igbira) are a Nigerian ethnic group numbering roughly 400,000. They live in western and central regions of Nigeria.

Ebrié

The Ebrié are one of many ethnic groups that make up the so-called Lagoon cluster (q.v.) of peoples living in Ivory Coast. The Ebrié Lagoon is named after them.

Edo

The Edo people of southern Nigeria are the descendants of the Bini, who established the historic Kingdom of Benin – famed worldwide for its beautiful bronze sculptures. The capital of the Kingdom of Benin was Benin City, which still stands on a branch of the Benin River and is the capital of the modern Nigerian province of Edo. More than 2 million people in southern Nigeria speak the Edo language.

Benin City was founded by the Edo sometime before 1300. The Kingdom of Benin reached its height between the fourteenth and seventeenth centuries, amassing wealth from the trade in ivory, pepper, palm oil, and slaves. The kingdom was ruled by an oba, and the Benin division of modern Edo province still boasts a ceremonial oba. Benin City was burnt to the ground in 1897 by the British and more than 2,000 of its bronzes (which are actually brass) were removed. There remains a strong tradition of metalworking among the Edo, with many still practicing the art of lost-wax metal casting that produced the famous Benin bronzes.

Edo Nago see Nagot

Efik

The Efik live in southeastern Nigeria and are closely related to the Anang (q.v.) people. They speak an Ibibio (q.v.) language called Efik-Ibibio.

Ejagham

The Ejagham (or Ekoi) are a large ethnic group of more than 400,000 members based in Cross River State in southeast Nigeria and across the border in Cameroon. They speak a Bantu (q.v.) language and are also closely related to the Efik (q.v.) and Ibibio (q.v.) peoples.

Eket

Eket is the name of an Ibibio (q.v.) language and the people who speak it. The Eket live in southeastern Nigeria.

Ekihaya see Haya

Ekoi see Ejagham

Emafikamuva

Together with the Emakhandzambili (q.v.) and Bemdzabuko (q.v.), the Emafikamuva are one of the three major subgroups of the Swazi (q.v.) of Swaziland and neighboring parts of South Africa. The Emafikamuva are made up of descendants who fled to Swaziland to escape Zulu (q.v.) expansion in southern Africa during the nineteenth century. The Swazi had already settled in the region, so the Emafikamuva are known as the "latecomers" even though they are now largely absorbed into the Swazi culture.

Emakhandzambili

The Emakhandzambili are of Ngoni (q.v.) or Sotho (q.v.) descent. Together with the Emafikamuva (q.v.) and Bembzabuko (q.v.), the Emakhandzambili are one of the three major subgroups of the Swazi (q.v.) of Swaziland and neighboring parts of South Africa. The Emakhandzambili were already living in the region when the Swazi came and founded a kingdom there. Over time they have been absorbed into Swazi culture.

Embu

The Embu live in eastern Kenya and number more than 200,000. They are a Bantu (q.v.) people closely related to the Kikuyu (q.v.) and Meru (q.v.).

Endo

The Endo are one of the several related groups that make up the Kalenjin (q.v.). The Kalenjin are a large ethnic group in western Kenya.

Ennedi

The Ennedi live in the Ennedi Mountains in northeastern Chad and number around 10,000. They are a Muslim people closely related to the Tebu (q.v.).

Esangui

The Esangui are a subgroup of the Fang (q.v.) of Equatorial Guinea. They have dominated that country politically in recent decades, primarily through the Obiang and Nguema families.

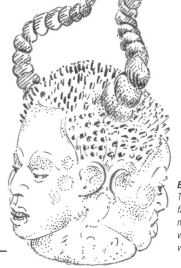

Ekoi society mask
This striking ritual mask has three faces, with antelope-style horns made of wood. The eyes are inlaid with tin, and the faces covered with antelope skin.

Ewe

The Ewe mostly live in lands along the southern end of the border between Ghana and Togo. The Ewe are closely related to the Fon. There are probably over one million Ewe in Togo and over two million in Ghana. There are four main groups: the Ewe "proper," who live in Ghana and southwest Togo; the Anlo Ewe, who live in Ghana west of the River Volta; the Watyi, who live in southeast Togo; and the Mina, a small group living on the Togo coast. A few Ewe also live in Benin.

History

According to Ewe oral history, the Ewe migrated to their present lands from what is now Benin and Nigeria in the mid-1600s. For many years, the coastal Ewe traded with Europeans, at first selling war captives as slaves and – when the slave trade ended – selling raw materials such as copra (the dried "meat" of coconuts) and palm oil.

COLONIALISM In the late 1800s, the western Ewe came under British colonial rule in what was then called the Gold Coast, while the Germans ruled the eastern Ewe in German Togoland. After World War I, Togoland became a joint British and French protectorate (colony). When the Gold Coast was about to become independent as Ghana in the 1950s, some Ewe in Togoland voted to join Ghana. The rest are now in independent Togo.

Language

The Ewe people speak the Ewe language, which has several dialects. The Anlo Ewe dialect has become the main literary language of the Ewe.

Ways of life

FARMING AND FISHING The Ewe are mainly farmers, growing food crops for their own needs, such as cassava, sorghum, corn, millet, yams, and pulses, and cash crops such as onions, shallots, palm oil, and cacao (cocoa-beans). They keep cattle, sheep, and goats. On the coast fishermen make large catches, especially of anchovies. The Ewe fish from canoes or from the shore, using large nets that require fifty men to haul them in. People also catch fish in the rivers and lagoons

that dot the coast.

TEXTILE INDUSTRY Spinning thread and strip-weaving blue and white cloth are ancient crafts among the Ewe. Strips only a few inches wide are woven and then sewn together to make wider fabrics. It is still partly a cottage industry (a small-scale business operated from workers' homes), but in the towns there are now many small textile factories. Blue was for a long time the only dye easily made fast, but since other colors have become available the Ewe have incorporated them into their designs.

TRADE Along with their Fon counterparts, Ewe women have a virtual monopoly over the trading economies of the coastal ports and markets. Acting as both wholesalers and retailers, they buy and sell a wide variety of items from imported cloth to foodstuffs or trade beads.

Social structure

SOCIAL STRUCTURE Ewe society is organized around lineages, or extended families. Members of the same lineage share a common ancestor traced from father to son – usually a grandfather of up to eight generations ago. The head of the lineage is the oldest male. Traditionally, the lineage's ancestral land was considered a gift to unborn descendants and could never be sold. In a system where the lineage group provided for all the needs and welfare of its members, selling land was not wise. The growth of a cash economy, however, and the resulting increased production of cash crops has changed this. In many areas, land is now bought and sold and people depend less on their lineage groups for their livelihoods.

POLITICAL STRUCTURE Lineages are important politically as well as socially. In the past, the head of the founding lineage of a village was considered the leader, or dufia. He had an advisory council of village elders – both male and female – to help him make decisions. In turn, a council of dufias would advise the overall leader of a whole region or dukowo, of which they were ten. These dukowo were politically independent but culturally united.

Tro sculpture
This wooden sculpture is of an unidentified Ewe tro, (spirit or deity). The Ewe religion involves the worship of a supreme god called Mawu. The Ewe believe that Mawu can only be approached through the trowo (the pural of tro). Each tro is worshipped by specific groups, or "cults."

Akple
An Ewe woman prepares a mix of corn and cassava flour to make akple, a staple food eaten with meat or vegetable stew.

Strip-weaving

Many Ewe weavers use hand looms to weave strips of cloth that can be sewn together to make larger pieces of cloth. Each strip is roughly 5 in. (12.5 cm) wide.

The imposition of colonial rule disrupted the political organization of Ewe society. Leaders who had resisted the colonialists were replaced. These new leaders often had their own interests at heart and not those of the group. Furthermore, the Ewe no longer had the right to oust rulers who abused their positions, as they had in the past.

Lineage heads still function politically, but many of their roles are now performed by the government. For example, the dukowo head of the Anlo Ewe, the awoamefia, is the final judge of cases involving customary law. Criminal matters, however, are dealt with by the state judiciary.

Culture and religion

RELIGION Today, nearly half of the Ewe people are Christians. The Ewe religion is still widely practiced, at times in conjunction with Christianity. In fact, new traditions have developed that incorporate the two religions. For example, on the death of a lineage member one soul (the "life-soul") is considered to return to God for judgment. This is according to the Christian tradition. The person's "personality-soul," however, returns to the ancestral lineage in Tisiefa (the "Other World"). This is according to the Ewe religion.

DRUMS AND INSULTS Drumming is at the heart of Ewe festivals. The Ewe call all performances "drums," and their repertory includes dancing, drama, composing and performing poetry, sculpting, and singing. One of the oldest Ewe drums is called kpegisu and was probably originally a war drum. A typical performance starts with a new song. The composer holds a havalu, a session in which he teaches the new song to his fellow drummers. The havalu is followed by a general singing practice for everybody, known as hakpa. A feature of some gatherings is a halo, an exchange of insulting songs between villages.

Twin carving

Twins are considered to be special in many cultures and if one dies, an Ewe mother may bury a carving such as this one with the dead child.

Keta cloth *(above)*

Strip-woven cloth that uses contrasting colors between warp (lengthwise threads) and weft (threads that go across the warp), and usually with inlaid designs, is called keta. Keta shares many similarities with the cloth called kente, which is produced by the Asante people of Ghana.

Keta wrapper

This Ewe man is wearing a wrapper made from keta cloth. Wrappers are wide pieces of cloth made from many strips sewn together. The cloth is wrapped around the body and tucked in at the waist.

Ewe timeline	
c. 1650 Ewe migrate westwards from present-day Nigeria and Benin	**1966** Military rule begins in Ghana
1784 Ewe at war with the Danes settled in forts on coast	**1969–1972** Brief period of civilian rule in Ghana
1807 Britain abolishes slave trade	**1976** In Togo, General Etienne Eyadéma leads military coup
1874 British establish Gold Coast	**1979** In Ghana, Flight Lieutenant Jerry Rawlings forces elections
1884 German Togoland colony established	**1981** Rawlings takes power in military coup in Ghana
1914–1918 World War I. Ewe caught up in fighting between British and Germans	**1991** Widespread civil unrest in Togo; transitional government is set up and opposition parties are unbanned
1954 Togoland Congress founded with the aim of reunifiying Ewe land and people	**1992** Rawlings is elected president in Ghana. 200,000 refugees flee disturbances in Togo; many die during presidential elections; Eyadéma remains as president
1957 Ghana independent	
1960 Togo independent	
1963 Military rule begins in Togo	**1994** Togolese opposition narrowly wins legislative elections

Independence celebrations

This strip is one of a collection woven to celebrate the independence of the Gold Coast as Ghana in 1957. The inlay picture depicts the inkpot and pen used to sign the Instrument of Independence. This representational style is more typical of modern Ewe weaving than the more stylized, traditional designs.

© DIAGRAM

Falasha

The Falasha are mainly situated around the town of Gonder in the Ethiopian Highlands, which surround Lake Tana. They are not the only people in the area, and live scattered among many other ethnic groups in the Tigre and Gonder administrative regions. The Falasha number around 30,000 to 40,000 (roughly half of whom live in Israel).

The word Falasha is probably derived from an ancient Ethiopian word that means "exiles" or "strangers." The Falasha, who are Jewish, refer to themselves as "Beta Israel" ("House of Israel"). Although this community is known by the name of Falasha in international literature – without any derogatory intent – the Falasha themselves consider it an insulting name.

History

The Falasha themselves trace their ancestry to the Jewish bodyguard of Menelik I – the son of King Solomon and the Queen of Sheba – who, legend has it, founded the Ethiopian Solomonic dynasty. Indeed, Greek records mention Jews in Ethiopia as early as 200 BCE and by the 300s CE Judaism was widespread in the area. Other theories suggest that Egyptian or Palestinian Jews escaping religious purges over two thousand years ago spread Judaism to the area; that Jewish traders in the Red Sea converted Agaw people along the Ethiopian coast to Judaism; or even that the Falasha are the lost Old Testament tribe of Dan.

The Falasha were often influential in Ethiopia and had long periods of independence and power. Around 960, led by Queen Judith (or Esther), the Falasha rebelled against the Axumite Kingdom. Under the following Zagwe dynasty, they enjoyed great influence. Under the subsequent Christian Ethiopian Empire established in the thirteenth century, however, they were frequently persecuted. In the sixteenth century, the Emperor Sarsa Dengal (reigned 1563–97) waged a terrible war on the Falasha. His successor, Emperor

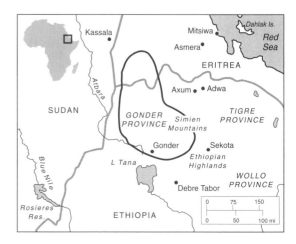

Susneyos, broke their resistance in the massacre of 1616. Since then, the Falasha, who once numbered hundreds of thousands, have declined through persecution, conversion to Christianity, and emigration, to a few thousand.

In the nineteenth century, European missionaries representing themselves as "white Falasha" told the Falasha that the promised Messiah had already lived in Jerusalem, in an attempt to convert them to Christianity. In 1862, many Falasha set out to walk to Israel to see for themselves. Decimated by disease and starvation, many died before the trek was abandoned at Axum.

RECENT EVENTS After years of debate, Israel declared that the Falasha had a right to Israeli citizenship in 1975. As the Ethiopian civil war took hold, the Falasha were among the many thousands of refugees who fled to camps in neighboring Sudan. From here, around 6,000 were able to get to the safety of Israel between 1979 and 1984. As the war worsened, a secret evacuation called "Operation Moses" took place: between 1984 and 1985 over 7,000 Falasha were airlifted to Israel

Falasha priests
These two Falasha priests, or cahenet, are reading a prayer book in a mesgid, or synagogue (Jewish house of worship). Only priests are required to cover their heads. Weekday services are often accompanied by drums and cymbals.

Fasilidas' Castle
The castle of King Fasilida (reigned 1632–67) at Gonder, Ethiopia, which was built in the 1600s with the help of Falasha artisans. Deprived of the right to own land since 1616, many Falasha became craftworkers.

Pottery

Falasha-made pottery is admired by many different people in Ethiopia. Much of this kind of work is carried out by Falasha women, who are also expert weavers of mats. Falasha men are said to be the best blacksmiths in Ethiopia.

from refugee camps in Sudan. In 1991, Israel took control of Addis Ababa airport to allow a further 14,000 Falasha to escape the civil war. Despite the great welcome they initially received, integration has been slow. In 1996, African Jews in Israel were demonstrating on the streets, protesting against being treated as second-class citizens.

Language

In the past, the Falasha spoke dialects of Agaw, which belongs to the Cushitic language group. Since the 1800s, however, the Falasha have adopted the languages of the people they live among and are now more likely to speak Tigrinya in the Tigre region or the national Ethiopian language of Amharic elsewhere. Furthermore, since the 1950s, Hebrew has been taught in Falasha schools.

Ways of life

AGRICULTURE Like their non-Jewish neighbors, most Falasha are farmers and herders. Their staple foods are dairy produce, millet, and fruit. The famine of the 1980s and the recent droughts (water shortages caused by periods of inadequate rainfall) have affected all farming

communities in Ethiopia. The loss of many younger people to Israel has also left some communities without enough able workers. These factors have reduced many Falasha to poverty. During the period of socialism in Ethiopia (1974–91), the Marxist government adopted policies of villagization and reorganized many rural communities into collectives or relocated them elsewhere, sometimes with disastrous results, though some previously landless Falasha benefited.

SHELTER Falasha houses are circular in shape with stone, mud, or timber walls, and thatched roofs. The people live in their own villages, often nearby a river or spring – which in addition to normal uses provides for religious purification rituals – and usually set apart from nearby Christian settlements.

Social organization

As in many Jewish communities, Falasha societies are organized around their religion. Each large village or group of small ones has a kess to lead the community; a cahen (plural cahenet) who conducts all the religious affairs of a community and instructs in the Torah (the first five books of the Old Testament); and a bebtara who helps the cahen by assisting with prayer services. The cahenet are provided for by the community and they are basically its leaders. Each family has its own cahen to give advice on religious matters. Disputes are settled by the village elders who are led by the cahenet.

Culture and religion

RELIGION The vast majority of Falasha are Jewish. They differ from other Jewish communities in that, until relatively recently, they were cut off from developments in Judaism elsewhere and did not know of the Talmud – a collection of writings and instructions on the Jewish way of life based on oral teachings from the time of Moses. Instead, their faith is based largely on the Orit (the Falasha name for the Torah). In many ways, however, the Falasha's form of Judaism is still very similar to that practiced elsewhere: they have equivalents of rabbis (Jewish religious leaders) called kess; the Sabbath (holy day of rest) is observed; boys undergo circumcision; all the festivals mentioned in the Orit are celebrated; and they adhere to the dietary laws as set out in the Orit.

Falasha village

Typical Falasha villages have circular houses with thatched roofs. This style of shelter is the same as that often lived in by other ethnic groups in Ethiopia.

© DIAGRAM

Prayer book
This prayer book is written in Geez, an ancient Ethiopian language little used today and generally understood only by the cahenet (priests). The congregation recite the prayers by heart facing Jerusalem. On the Sabbath (holy day of rest), the Orit *(Torah) is usually read in the local language by the cahen and a sermon is given on matters of faith and on the commandments.*

Certain festivals are unique to the Falasha, such as Sigd, which celebrates the return of the exiles from Babylonia, and there are many fast days followed only by the cahenet. Other unique features include ritual immersion in water for purity and animal sacrifices on special occasions such as Passover, which commemorates the deliverance of ancient Hebrews from slavery in Egypt. Animal sacrifices are becoming less common though. Contact with other Jewish peoples has brought changes to the Falasha faith. Hebrew is increasingly used and many mesgid (houses of worship) now display the Star of David.

Ritual purity and impurity
Traditionally, Falasha women live in the village's "house of malediction" during their menstrual periods, during labor, and for a set period after the birth of a new baby. Before returning home, the women immerse themselves in water to become ritually pure. This practice is dying out, however, as the Falasha learn of different Jewish traditions.

Falasha timeline

200 BCE Greek records mention Jews in Ethiopia	**1500s** Falasha attempt to reassert independence	struggle for independence	**1991** Israel takes control of Addis Ababa airport to fly 14,000 Falasha out to escape civil war. Mengistu loses power
100 CE Judaized peoples in Axumite Kingdom	**1616** Falasha massacred by Ethiopians	**1972–1974** Famine in Tigre and Wollo provinces; great civic unrest	
300s Falasha communities established in Gonder and Simien Mountains	**1790s** Existence of Falasha first known in West	**1974** Military coup overthrows Haile Selassie in Ethiopia	**1993** Eritrea officially independent from Ethiopia
c. 960 Falasha rebel against Axumite Kingdom	**1862** Aborted trek to Israel	**1977** Maj. Mengistu Haile Miriam takes power in Ethiopia.	**1996** Falasha demonstrate against discrimination in Israel
c. 1450 Falasha lands annexed by Ethiopian Empire	**1935–1941** Italian invasion and occupation of Ethiopia	**1980s** Severe *droughts* and famine	
	1961 Eritrean rebels begin armed	**1984–1985** 7,000 refugee Falasha airlifted to Israel from Sudan	

Fali

The Fali are a small ethnic group living in the mountainous regions of northern Cameroon. There are probably not many more than 20,000 Fali people. They are sometimes referred to as the Kirdi (meaning pagans) by their Muslim neighbors, the Fulani (q.v.). The Fali language belongs to the Chad-Adamawa group, but many Fali also speak the Fulani language, Fulfulde.

The Fali religion involves belief in a creator-god, Faw, and the reverence of ancestors, who are approached with prayers and offerings to intercede with Faw on behalf of their living descendants. There is also a mother goddess – Ona, the Earth – and several supernatural beings such as genies, sacred crocodiles, and the black snake, master of darkness. Although increasing numbers of Fali are converting to Islam, though they do not necessarily see holding both sets of beliefs as contradictory.

Fang

The Fang live in an area that straddles southern Cameroon, Equatorial Guinea, and northwest Gabon. There are probably around one million Fang. The largest single group of Fang live in Río Muni, mainland Equatorial Guinea, where they form over eighty percent of the population. Within this province, the Ntumu Fang live north of the Mbini River and the Okak Fang live south of the Mbini.

History

In the early nineteenth century, the Fang gradually migrated southward from the Sanaga River area of central Cameroon to their present location. The Fang were mostly farmers, hunters, and warriors until the arrival of European colonial powers. Trading posts and forts were first established on the Gabonese coast by the French in the early 1800s, and Gabon became part of French Equatorial Africa in 1910. The Fang in what is now Equatorial Guinea came under the control of Spanish colonizers in the late eighteenth century, and the Germans established the protectorate (colony) of Kamerun, which is now Cameroon, in 1884. Although railways, roads, bridges, and hospitals were built, German rule was characterized by harshness, forced

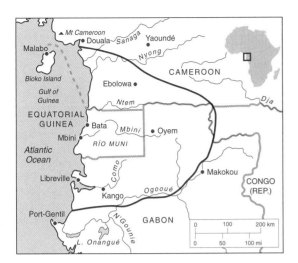

Fang warrior
An early twentieth-century Fang warrior.

the imposition of military rule, positions of power were still dominated by the Esangui clan. Multiparty elections were held in 1993 but were boycotted by most opposition parties in protest against the unfair conditions of entry imposed on candidates – a deposit of thirty million CFA francs was required and exiles were excluded by a ban on people who had not been resident in the country for ten years. Obiang Nguema's regime is dogged by reports of human rights abuses and he has been accused of approving the arrest and torture of his political opponents.

Language
The Fang language is also called Fang. Many Fang also speak Spanish (in Río Muni) or French (in Cameroon and Gabon). Some of the Fang who live on Bioko Island, Equatorial Guinea, speak other local languages as well.

Ways of life
RURAL The majority of the Fang live in rural areas. The environment is dense tropical rainforest – hot, very humid, and with heavy rainfall. Historically, each Fang village cleared land for cultivation, and lived by hunting and subsistence farming. By planting crops that ripened at different periods of the year, the Fang made sure that they never went hungry. In the more remote areas of the rainforest – and the Fang are widely dispersed – this lifestyle has at least partly persisted, but for many Fang today the pattern of life has changed radically.

Large areas of forest have been cleared for timber or for cultivating cash crops, particularly cocoa beans and coffee. In 1940s Río Muni, the Spanish encouraged the small-scale cultivation of coffee but production was devastated during Macías' reign and has only just begun to recover. Livestock raising, always difficult because of the prevalence of the disease-bearing tsetse fly, also suffered during this period and almost disappeared. Recent investment in Equatorial Guinea, however, has encouraged poultry raising and the Río Muni Fang are now well supplied with chicken and eggs. In the 1980s, tsetse-resistant cattle from Gambia, Senegal, and Congo (Dem. Rep.) were introduced to Gabon.
URBAN The way of life for those Fang living in modern environments, for example in the towns and cities of Equatorial Guinea and along the coasts of Cameroon and Gabon, is similar to that of urban dwellers elsewhere. In the later half of the twentieth century many Fang have moved from Río Muni to work in Bioko, the administrative center of Equatorial Guinea. On this island they have joined the civil service and the armed forces in large numbers and now dominate these professions.

Social structure
Until the widespread adoption of Christianity and the introduction of monogamy, the Fang family consisted of a man, his wife or wives, and their children. This extended family constituted the village. Outside the village and family some Fang are organized into clans; as a form of political organization clans have largely been overtaken by the political systems of the countries in which the Fang live. Nevertheless, certain clans (such

labor, and military excesses. During World War I, Britain and France divided Cameroon between them, and in 1920, much of the Fang's territory there became part of the French-controlled territory of Cameroun. The French increased the cultivation of cash crops such as cocoa, palm oil, and timber. This was often achieved at the expense of Africans, including the Fang, who had to seek work on European-owned plantations in order to pay the high taxes or were literally forced to work as conscripts.

Gabon became independent in 1960, Equatorial Guinea in 1968, and the British and French Cameroons were reunited when Cameroon became independent in 1961.
RECENT EVENTS The first president of independent Equatorial Guinea was Francisco Macías Nguema (q.v.), a mainland Fang from the Esangui clan (several families descended from a common ancestor or ancestors). Until his deposition by a military coup in 1979 – led by his nephew Obiang Nguema – Macías headed a reign of terror. A large proportion of the population fled the country during this era, many of them skilled and educated, and the economy was devastated. After

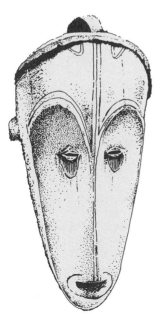

Ngil mask
Connected with the pretwentieth century ngil society, ngil costumes were worn by masters of the society who wielded both political and judicial powers. The mask, which is only part of the whole costume, was a symbol of fear and retribution and its task was to track down sorcerers and criminals. The white color of the mask expresses the power of the spirits of the dead.

Woman and child
This wooden statue dates from the nineteenth century and depicts a woman, maybe the mother, carrying a child on her back – the child figure has been carved separately. The carving style suggests that it was produced by a northern Fang subgroup. The Fang were once renowned for their wood carvings, but commercially-made artifacts have all but wiped out this style of carving. Modern carving is largely done for the tourist trade.

as the Esangui clan in Equatorial Guinea) are still politically important.

In the past, boys were circumcised at elaborate ceremonies; they are still circumcised today, but the operation is usually carried out at the nearest clinic.

MARRIAGE A man was expected to marry outside his village. He had to give the bridewealth, known as a nubsa, to his new wife's family. This became due on the birth of the first child of the marriage. If the wife failed to produce children she was divorced. Despite Christian insistence on monogamy, a man can still have more than one wife if he can afford it.

Reliquary figures
Fang reliquary figures and heads are carved, wooden, guardian statues that sat on top of chests containing ancestral relics (right). The figures, although beautiful, were not considered by the Fang to be as important as the relics they watched over. The Fang were willing to sell them to Europeans, therefore, who were eager to acquire them. Many more of these beautiful sculptures were destroyed by early European missionaries who mistook them for idols or fetishes.

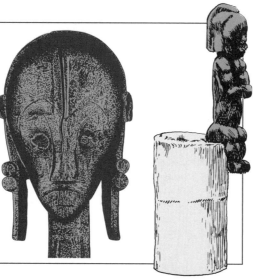

Culture and religion

RELIGION The majority of Fang are Christians. Aspects of the Fang religion still survive, however, often alongside Christianity. Although the Fang believed in one supreme god, Mebere, on a day-to-day basis they were in greater contact with their immediate ancestors through a practice known as bieri. Skulls or relics of male ancestors were kept in bark containers topped with protective wooden statues (reliquary figures). The whole structure would be looked after by the oldest living male. Thousands of the beautiful statues were destroyed by Christian missionaries who mistakenly saw them as idols worshipped by the Fang. The few that survived or were sold to Europeans have become famous in Western art circles for their beauty. Although modern bieri carvings are produced – largely for tourists – they generally do not reach the high standards set in the past.

Since the early 1900s, a politico-religious movement called bwiti has replaced bieri as the main religious force. Bwiti combines aspects of both Christianity and bieri. Originally banned by colonial authorities for its strong nationalist, Africanist influence, bwiti flourished nonetheless. Practitioners meet every week in some localities and enact birth and creation, death and destruction, in dance and song. The aim of the ritual is to encourage "one-heartedness." Singers perform epic songs, mvet, often lasting for several hours. The singers may be accompanied by performers on an instrument also called a mvet – a stringed instrument that is a cross between a zither and a harp – and bells.

Fang timeline

c. 1000 Fang in Sanaga River area	**1920** Fang in Kamerun handed over to French Cameroun colony	up one-party state **1970** Macías sets up one-party state and embarks on reign of terror	**1994** CFA franc devalued by fifty percent: hardship and civil unrest follow in Equatorial Guinea, Gabon, and Cameroon
c. 1473 Portuguese reach Fernando Póo (present-day Bioko Island)	**1960** Gabon and French Cameroun achieve independence	**1979** Coup ousts Macías	**1996** Obiang Nguema is reelected president of Equatorial Guinea amid accusations of vote-rigging
1778 Spanish colonize Fernando Póo	**1961** British Cameroun independent: south as part of Cameroon	**1990** Multiparty elections end one-party rule in Gabon	
1800s Fang migrate southward into present location. French arrive on Gabonese coast	**1968** Equatorial Guinea independent: Macías Nguema, an Esangui Fang, is elected president. Gabon sets	**1993** Multiparty elections in Equatorial Guinea are boycotted by opposition	
1884 German Kamerun formed			

Mother and child
This stylistically beautiful Fante carving features representations of square-shaped scarifications, visible on the mother's cheeks and below her ringed neck.

Fante

Numbering roughly two million, the Fante are one of the larger ethnic groups in Ghana. They are an Akan (q.v.) people, who are closely related to the much larger Akan group, the Asante (q.v.). The Fante, like

Fante drum
This anthropomorphic drum is seated on a lion and - much smaller - an elephant. The lead instrument in an Akan popular band, it would have been used at a variety of ceremonial occasions, although such bands were and are primarily recreational.

other Akan peoples, have largely been Christian since the nineteenth century.

The Fante inhabit a small region of south-central Ghana the southern border of which is formed by the coastline. The coast was once was part of the famed Gold Coast - a region that grew rich from trading in gold, and later slaves. Gold was traded long before contact with the Europeans, but the several Fante states, based as they were near the coast, grew particularly wealthy from trading with Europeans before they were eclipse by the much larger Asante Empire. The Fante were conquered by the Asante by 1816. By the late nineteenth century, Asante power was weakening, and the Fante launched a joint, but unsuccessful, offensive against the Asante with the British in 1863.

Fernandinos

The Fernandinos are the descendants of African settlers brought to the island of Bioko by the Spanish and British. Bioko is now part of Equatorial Guinea.

The island was formerly known as Fernando Po (or Fernando Poó), the name used by its Spanish colonizers. Conveniently situated off the coast of west-central Africa, Bioko was an important staging post in the trade of slaves from West and Central Africa to the Americas. In 1778, the island became a Spanish colony, and the Spanish settlers established plantations growing crops such as cocoa for export. The Bubis (q.v.) – the local African population and the original inhabitants of Bioko – refused to cooperate with the Spanish planters, so Spain imported workers from Liberia, Nigeria, and Sierra Leone. Later, these long-settled immigrants were joined by slaves freed by British anti-slavery patrols. The British leased the island from Spain in the nineteenth century. The present-day Fernandino population, which numbers only a few thousand, are descended from these different incoming groups.

The Fernandinos became an economically and politically important elite in independent Equatorial Guinea, but like others they suffered greatly during the reign of the brutal dictator Macias Nguema, who came from the mainland.

Fingo *see* Mfengu

Fipa

There are probably around 200,000 Fipa people living on the high plateau between Lake Rukwa and Lake Tanganyika in east Tanzania. The name Fipa actually means "people of the escarpment" and was originally used by nineteenth-century traders to refer to the inhabitants of modern Ufipa (the country of the Fipa). The Fipa language, which is also called Fipa, is a Bantu (q.v.) language closely related to that of the Bemba (q.v.) of northern Zambia.

Historically the Fipa were divided into two states – Nkansi and Lyangalile – with related ruling dynasties known as a Twa. History portrays the Fipa states as being wealthy and peaceful societies. Many of the powerful political positions in the Fipa states were open to anybody irrespective of their social position as long as they were able. Only the king and a few other symbolic roles were handed down through particular families.

Fon

The Fon live in the Republic of Benin, the former Kingdom of Dahomey. Culturally, especially in terms of religion, the Fon have much in common with the neighboring Ewe people of Togo and Ghana. Today, there are approximately two million Fon.

History

At its peak the Fon Kingdom of Dahomey had a population of only a quarter of a million people. The concentration of people and the relatively short distances between the main centers of population, however, helped to permit highly centralized rule. Ruled by a strong king and administered by officials in an efficient bureaucracy, the Fon created one of West Africa's most powerful nations, successfully resisting European control until the end of the nineteenth century.

THE RISE OF THE KINGDOM OF DAHOMEY The original inhabitants of what was to become the Kingdom of Dahomey lived in small and scattered groups, with no overall loyalty to a king. Nominally subjects of the Yoruba, individual villages and towns jealously guarded their own independence, but whenever possible sought to extend their influence over weaker neighbors. Up to the beginning of the seventeenth century, the states that were emerging were all small, though some were beginning to gain greater significance.

The foundations of the Fon kingdom were laid in the early seventeenth century, when a group of warriors

© DIAGRAM

Art for art's sake
In Fon society, brass castings of animals and people – such as this figure of a man using a hoe – have long been produced without any religious or ceremonial functions, but purely as ornamental objects of beauty and as symbols of the wealth of their owners. Today, brass casting continues, but mostly for the tourist trade. Other arts for which the Fon are renowned include wood carvings and decorative textiles.

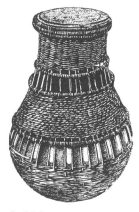

Burial drum
This type of clay and raffia drum, called a kpezi, *would have been part of a Fon funeral ceremony. The dead would have been buried with many pieces of pottery.*

from Allada gradually gained control of much of the interior as far north as where present-day Abomey is located. At Abomey, the first ruler of the new Fon kingdom built his palace on the grave of the local king he defeated, establishing a tradition followed by future kings. The charismatic King Agaja, remembered as a great statesman, reigned from 1708 to 1732 and greatly extended the kingdom.

The Kingdom of Dahomey was one of Africa's few states to maintain an army, which increased from about 3,000 soldiers in the early eighteenth century to 12,000 in the mid-nineteenth century. It included up to 2,500 ferocious female warriors – women dedicated to the personal protection of the king. Arms obtained from European traders enabled the Fon to extend their territories. Controlling the coast allowed the Fon to have greater control over the profitable slave trade and to protect their own people from capture and sale. Fon ports along what was known as the "Slave Coast" became important points on the so-called triangular trading route that linked Europe with Africa and the Americas. In the late eighteenth century, for example, the port of Ouidah was recorded as receiving each year forty to fifty Dutch, English, French, and Portuguese ships importing arms and other goods and exporting slaves.

THE FALL OF THE KINGDOM OF DAHOMEY After the end of the slave trade in the early nineteenth century, palm oil became Dahomey's key export activity. Falling oil prices weakened Dahomey's economy, however, and the French – who had greater military might – seized control of the coast by 1889. In despair the king, Glele, committed suicide and was succeeded by his son

Behanzin. Despite the fierce resistance of King Behanzin and his armies, Dahomey was conquered in 1892, and the French then employed local chiefs to help administer their new territory.

Dahomey became independent in 1960, and in 1975 it changed its name to the Republic of Benin, marking the end of its association with France.

Language
The various Fon dialects belong to the Kwa language group of the Niger-Kordofanian family.

Ways of life
FARMING Historically, the Fon had a wide range of crops, many of which were introduced from the Americas and Asia. Intensive farming remains the primary way of life among the Fon, but cash crops such as palm oil (used for cooking and frying) and cocoa are also grown today. Chickens, sheep, goats, pigs, and cattle are also kept.

HOUSING Traditional housing compounds are wattle-and-daub structures (made of interwoven twigs plastered with mud), with houses arranged around a courtyard in which are placed altars to gods.

Social structure
SOCIAL STRUCTURE The Fon social structure is based on the clan, members of whom are related through their male ancestors and live together in the clan's own compounds within a larger town or village. The children of a marriage are usually considered to "belong" to the father's family and clan. In some cases, however, the children are considered part of their mother's family. This often happens when a man marries a woman without paying her family bridewealth, a payment to seal the alliance.

POLITICAL STRUCTURE In the past, absolute power was invested in the king, but administration was extremely complex. It was organized on strict military lines, often for clear military purposes. For example, agriculture was carefully regulated to control how much grain and other crops would be produced each year and to reserve proportions for the army. The king was treated

Reliefs
A collage of animals and weapons decorate this wooden door from a royal palace in Abomey, the former capital of the Kingdom of Dahomey. The animals shown – the snake and the chameleon – figure in many West African legends.

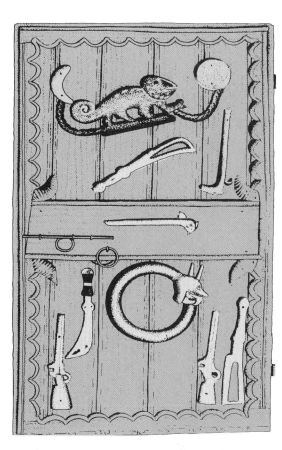

Appliqué cloth
This banner uses brightly colored appliqué (cutout shapes applied to a contrasting background) to depict a lion hunt. This technique has long been used for religious images, banners, and chiefs' headgear. Today, such appliqué work continues as an important art form, with clothes produced for tourists but often also bearing illustrations that feature social commentary.

with great awe, and those approaching him had to lie on the ground and throw dust on themselves as an acceptance of their lowly status. The king would choose one of his sons as heir, with the rest of the royal family kept powerless to reduce chances of a coup.

Local chiefs achieved their positions of power through acts of courage rather than through birth, while the king always appointed commoners as ministers. There was a strict hierarchy of male ministers, all with clearly defined functions, and each had a female equivalent who officially took precedence over him just as, technically, the king was outranked by the queen mother.

Culture and religion

RELIGION Most follow the Fon religion, which closely resembles the Ewe religion, though some Fon (especially along the coast) have adopted Christianity. The Fon creator-god Mawa is usually seen as female, but has both male and female traits. Mawa causes coolness at night and is associated with the Moon, peace, fertility, gentleness, and rain. She gave birth to a son, Lisa, the Sun god who causes the day and its heat and represents strength and endurance. Mawa and Lisa are generally seen as the rulers of all the other gods, who represent earth, sky, thunder, and knowledge, for example. The Fon call their gods vodun (singular vodu).

Fon timeline	
1625 Fon kingdom founded at Abomey	**1972** Major Mathieu Kerekou seizes power in military coup
1708–1732 King Agaja's reign sees Fon expansion to create Dahomey	**1974** Dahomey adopts Marxism-Leninism (communism)
1728–1729 Oyo invades Dahomey and exacts tribute	**1975** Dahomey renamed Benin
1729 Dahomey capital is transferred to Allada	**1989** Benin abanbons Marxism-Leninism
1818–1858 Under King Ghezo, Dahomey begins to free itself from Oyo	**1991** Nicéphore Soglo elected president in first democratic elections
1858–1889 Under King Glele, Dahomey is fully independent again	**1992** Widespread persecution of Kerekou's supporters
1883 French take Porto-Novo	**1994** Widespread unrest and economic hardship after *CFA franc* is devalued by fifty percent
1889 King Behanzin tries to drive French out of Dahomey	
1892 French conquest of Dahomey	**1996** January 10 designated a national holiday in honor of Fon (*Vodoun*) religion
1960 Dahomey wins independence	

King Behanzin as a shark
This painted, wooden figure shows a fusion of man and shark, representing King Behanzin. Fierce animals, most commonly the leopard, are often used as symbols for depicting African rulers.

Foto

The Foto belong to the Bamileke (q.v.) kingdom, or chiefdom, of the same name. The Bamileke are large ethnic group of West Africa.

Fra see Fra-Fra

Fra-Fra

The Fra-Fra (or Fra) are one of the many groups that make up the Mole-Dagbane cluster of peoples. There are well over 300,000 Fra-Fra in northeastern Ghana.

French

There are literally tens of thousands of ethnically French people still in Africa today. The vast majority live in former colonial regions of West and North Africa.

Fula see Fulani

Fulani

The Fulani are one of the largest ethnic groups in West Africa totaling about twenty-three million. They are widely dispersed throughout West Africa and have large groups in Senegal, Gambia, Guinea, Mali, Burkina Faso, Niger, Nigeria, Cameroon, and Chad. Smaller groups live in most other West African states. One group, the Bororo, are found in the semidesert Sahel region of Niger and northern Nigeria. Small numbers of Bororo are also found in Chad and Cameroon.

The Fulani are known by a number of names. They call themselves "Fula." The Hausa people know them as "Fulani" (singular, "Fula"), a name that has been adopted by others. In some French-speaking countries, such as Senegal, they are called "Peul" (singular, "Pullo").

History

The Fulani are descended from both North Africans and sub-Saharan Africans. The earliest Fulani were nomadic cattle herders, who traveled great distances with their herds in search of water and pasture. Although the existence of the Fulani has been known for more than a thousand years, their origins are unknown. One theory is that they originated in East Africa, migrated northward through Sudan and Egypt,

Fulani warriors
Although guns were available in West Africa during the eighteenth-to nineteenth-century period of jihads (Islamic holy wars), the Fulani jihadists disdained to use them, considering them fit only for slaves. The Fulani shown here were part of the cavalry.

© DIAGRAM

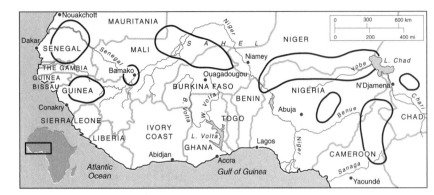

High-class Fulani woman
The huge rings dangling either side of this Malian woman's face are attached to her hair, not her ears, and they are solid gold. She is of the upper classes, and these rings probably represent much of her family's wealth.

Fulani states and migrations
The Fulani have been in West Africa for centuries. They have long been settled in areas such as Futa Toro and Futa Djallon, which at times formed independent states.

then turned westward along the Mediterranean coast to Morocco. It is known, however, that from Morocco, the Fulani moved southward into what is now Mauritania from the 700s. The cradle of the group in West Africa is in northern Senegal, where they settled in Futa Toro, a state founded by the ancestors of today's Tukolor Fulani people. Some Fulani also moved farther southward and eastward, settling in the Futa Djallon region of Guinea and also in northern Nigeria.

In the 1670s, the Fulanis began a series of jihads (Islamic holy wars) against their non-Muslim neighbors, which lasted for almost the next two centuries. During this period Futa Toro, Futa Djallon, Wuli, and Bundu (the latter another Tukolor-founded empire) were established as jihad states. The most significant was the

Sokoto Caliphate founded by a Fulani Muslim scholar named Usman dan Fodio (q.v.). In the late eighteenth century, he rose to power in northern Nigeria, where

Key

1 Fulani migrations 700s–1400s
  ➔ Migration route
  ▨ Empire of Mali c. 1350

2 Islamic (Fulani jihad) states and migrations c. 1650–1800
  ➔ Migration route
  ▨ State c. 1800

3 Fulani jihad states and Tukolor empire 1860
  ▨ Fulani state
  ▨ Jihadist empire of Al Hajj Umar (Tukolor Empire)

4 Fulani states and Tukolor Empire 1885
  ▨ Fulani state
  ▨ Tukolor Empire
  ▦ French colonial expansion

A Futa Toro
B Wuli
C Bundu
D Futa Djallon
E Macina
F Sokoto Caliphate

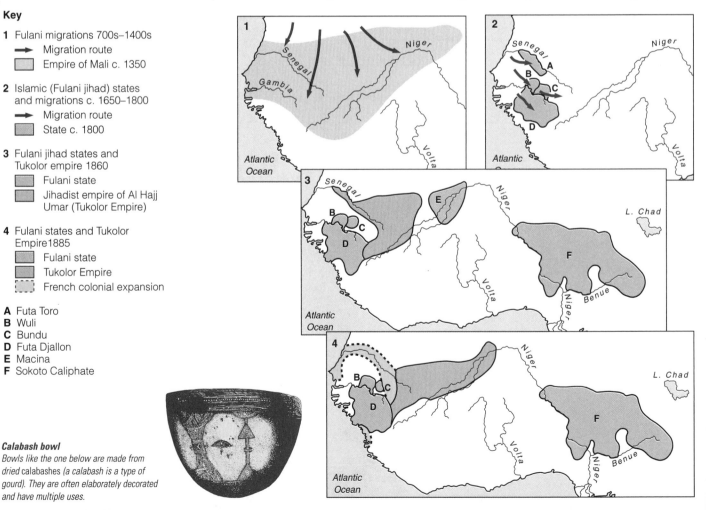

Calabash bowl
Bowls like the one below are made from dried calabashes (a calabash is a type of gourd). They are often elaborately decorated and have multiple uses.

the Fulani shared territory with the Hausas. In 1804 he was elected "Commander of the Believers," and proclaimed a jihad. Within twenty-five years, he had established an Islamic Fulani-Hausa empire – the Sokoto Caliphate – in northern Nigeria and parts of what are now Niger, Benin, and Cameroon. He handed over the government of this empire to his brother and his son, and retired to a simple life of teaching and writing.

As a result of the Fulani conquest of Hausa territory, in northern Nigeria today many Fulani people live in the same villages as Hausa people. There is some intermarriage, and many Fulani living among Hausa have adopted the Hausa language and customs. Although the Fulani are in the minority among the Hausa, historically the Fulani have been the ruling aristocracy.

Language

The Fulani language is called Fulfulde. It belongs to the West Atlantic group of the Niger-Congo language family. A characteristic of Fulfulde is that singular and plural nouns begin with different consonants and have different suffixes, so singular and plural words often appear and sound quite different. There are a number of different dialects of Fulfulde. In northern Nigeria, where the Fulani and the Hausa peoples share territory, about half the Fulani now speak Hausa. A few Fulani have moved east into Sudan, where they are neighbors of Arab cattle herders; these Fulani have adopted Arabic.

Ways of life

There are several groups of Fulani, and this diversity reflects a range of occupations and ways of life. Most Bororo Fulani are seminomadic pastoralists (livestock raisers), living in the savannas (grasslands with scattered trees and shrubs) and the semidesert Sahel with their herds. The Wodaabe are a related Fulani group in northeastern Nigeria numbering only about 45,000; they are also largely cattle-keeping pastoralists. The

Long-horned cattle
The cattle of the pastoral *Fulani* are the long-horned zebu breed. They are hardy animals, able to withstand long marches from one pasture to another and can feed on whatever grazing is seasonally available.

Fulbe n'ai are also pastoralists, but grow crops as well as herd cattle. The Fulbe sire are former pastoralists who have lost their cattle through drought (periods of inadequate rainfall) or disease and have had to settle as farmers or market gardeners; they are usually quite poor and are often disliked by other Fulani groups. The approximately half-a-million Tukolor (or Toucouleur), living mostly in Senegal, are chiefly farmers and fishers. Although they have been linked with the Fulani for several centuries, their origins are separate and some consider the Tukolor a separate ethnic group. Finally, there are the Toroobe, many of whom belong to the professional classes. Toroobe people are often teachers, religious leaders, and local government officials or civil servants, forming a wealthy minority who live among the Hausa in the towns and cities.

NOMADIC PASTORALISM The pastoral Fulani are often nomadic, moving from place to place with their herds of cattle, sheep, or goats in search of water and pasture. Among the pastoralists the Bororo are notable. Their lives are tuned to the seasons. From October to May is the dry season, when the grass withers and the Bororo stay close to deep wells that do not run dry. In late May, the rains come and the climate is wet until September. The grass grows and grazing is plentiful. Many Bororo have a simple life, making temporary shelters of branches and leaves, or carrying portable huts with them. Their material wants are few: ropes, some tools, cooking pots, mats, and blankets. They make butter, using goatskins as churns, and sell milk and butter at markets or exchange them for other foodstuffs and goods.

In the twentieth century, there has been an increasing trend towards sedentary settlement. Government polices – encouraging nomads to settle down in order to make them easier to govern and tax – and modern international boundaries have restricted the activities of nomads. Increasingly frequent droughts and desertification (a type of land degradation) in the fragile Sahel have exacerbated this process. Many Fulani familes are now settled in one place and move their herds from group to group. In fact, the majority of Fulani are now sedentary farmers.

DIVISION OF LABOR In both Wodaabe and Bororo families the women work as hard as the men, if not harder. Their tasks include carrying water from the nearest supply, milking the cows, building and tending the

Bororo nomad
This man is a Bororo Fulani. Most Bororo are pastoralists (livestock raisers) who keep mainly cattle. The lifestyles of many Fulani pastoralists have been drastically altered by the severe droughts (periods of inadequate rainfall) of the 1960s to 1980s. Herds were decimated and many people were forced to sell their animals and migrate to urban areas or refugee camps to avoid starvation.

Milk carrier
A young Fulani woman carries a calabash bowl on her head. It contains milk, which is protected by a smaller, upside-down calabash that floats on the milk's surface.

© DIAGRAM

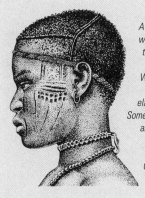

Personal art
A Wodaabe man (left) and a Fulani woman (right) from Benin illustrate the range of personal adornment adopted by the Fulani. Young Wodaabe men paint their faces at certain festivals and wear elaborately embroidered garments. Some Fulani women use facial tattoos and scars as a way of enhancing their beauty and making themselves more attractive, though this practice is becoming less common.

camp fires, and pounding millet into flour to make a kind of porridge.

FARMING The Tukolor, unlike the original Fulani, appear to have been always a settled group, mostly engaged in cultivating field crops and fishing. Muslim since the eleventh century, they migrated in order to spread the Islamic faith, not to seek fresh lands for pasture.

Social structure
Rural households tend to be large and male dominated. A man, his wife or wives, sons, grandsons and their wives and children, make up a typical household. There is a definite class system, with religious leaders holding high status, and artisans and the descendants of former slaves forming the lowest classes. Urban Fulani largely follow the organization of the people who they live among.

MARRIAGE When a Bororo couple have decided on marriage, the man brings a bridewealth – often oxen – to the girl's parents. The animals are then used to provide the wedding feast. The giving of bridewealth seals the alliance and is seen as a token of respect. A Bororo

man may have more than one wife, providing he is rich enough to support them all. Tukolor males follow the Islamic tradition in being permitted to have more than one wife, but few can afford the bridewealth to do this.

Culture and religion
RELIGION Originally, the Fulani had their own religion. Many converted to Islam in the 1300s, however, particularly those in the east. At first, the Fulani of Futa Toro and Futa Djallon retained their old beliefs and persecuted the Muslims. But both these states were converted to Islam in 1776. Today, the majority of the Fulani are Muslims. One of the most devout groups is the Tukolor, who converted to Islam in the eleventh century. By the mid-nineteenth century, the Tukolor had established a large Islamic empire that eventually extended as far north as modern Tombouctou, Mali.

FESTIVALS AND ADORNMENT Among the Bororo, May is the time for festivals and courting. The young men paint their faces to attract the girls. Among the Wodaabe, the men perform certain dances at the annual worso festival, which celebrates marriages and births of the previous year. Two dances dominate the worso – the yaake and the geerewol. During the yaake dance, the men are judged for charm, magnetism, and personality by elders. Dancers apply pale powder to their faces and black kohl to their eyes to accentuate their features. Hairlines are often shaved to heighten the forehead and a painted line may elongate the nose – attributes considered attractive by the Wodaabe. Geerewol dancers dress in tight wrappers and wear strings of beads and feathered turbans. Singing and jumping at an increasing pace, they are judged for their beauty by young, unmarried women. These dances prove the ability of men to attract women, a particularly admired male attribute. Dancers no longer perform when their eldest son is old enough to compete.

Fulani timeline			
700s–1400s Fulani migrate southward and eastward from present-day Morocco and Mauritania	**1775** Second,successful, Fulani jihad launched in Futa Toro	**1830** Sokoto Caliphate reaches greatest extent	**1950–1970s** West African states become independent
1650 Muslims migrate into Futa Toro and Futa Djallon	**1800** Fulani Islamic jihad states of Futa Toro, Futa Djallon, Wuli, and Bundu in existence	**1852** Al Hajj Umar declares jihad in Futa Toro; Tukolor (Fulani) Empire established	**1960s–1980s** Recurring *drought* (period of inadequate rainfall) causes famine in Sahelian countries
1673 Unsuccessful Fulani *jihad* (Islamic holy war) in Futa Toro	**1804–1809** Fulani jihad in Hausaland led by Usman dan Fodio; Sokoto Caliphate established	**1862** Macina conquered by Tukolor Empire	**1994** Widespread unrest and economic hardship in African *Franc Zone* after *CFA franc* is devalued by fifty percent
1725 First successful Fulani jihad launched in Futa Djallon	**1827** Independent Islamic state of Macina established	**1893** French defeat Tukolor Empire	**1999** Nigeria returns to civilian rule
		1903 British defeat conquer the Sokoto Caliphate	

Fulero *see* Furiiru

Fumu
The Fumu are one of the many Teke (q.v.) groups. The Teke live in Gabon, Congo (Rep.), and Congo (Dem. Rep.).

Fung *see* Funj

Funj

The Funj (also spelled Fung) are a mainly Arab (q.v.) but partly Black African people living in the region of southern Sudan between the Blue Nile and White Nile rivers. From the 1500s to the 1800s, the Funj formed the most powerful state in the region, and the present-day Funj people include subgroups such as the Berta, Gule, and Maban, which were once dependent states of the Funj Sultanate.

In the 1400s, Funj herders migrated north from the Blue Nile, and they had occupied the Christian kingdom of Alodia by c. 1500. In the same century, the Funj became Muslims, and their state was ruled by a sultan. Their capital was Sennar, a now-deserted town on the west bank of the Blue Nile. The modern town of Sennar is located about six miles farther south, where it stands near the Sennar Dam across the Blue Nile. Old Sennar lay on an important trade route that ran from Lake Chad in the west to the Red Sea port of Suakin, and the town was also crossed by a north–south trade route. At this commercial crossroads, cloth, dates, and other goods from the north were exchanged with ivory, gold, ebony, and other goods from the south.

Fur

The Fur are a people of northern Sudan who live in the westernmost province of Darfur – the land of the Fur. There are roughly 300,000 Fur in Sudan. Darfur is a highland region dominated by the volcanic mountain slopes of Jabal Marrah at 10,132 ft high. The Fur are concentrated in the mountainous heartland of the province, although many also reside in El Fasher – a town lying to the northeast of the mountainous region that was strategic for controlling passing trade and pilgrimage routes. An important route for West African Muslims journeying to Mecca still passes through Darfur, though the recent civil war in Sudan has seen its use decline. The Fur have been largely Muslim since the seventeenth century.

The Fur have long lived in a centralized state, perhaps as early as 2000 years ago. Darfur became particularly powerful in the 1700s, when it expanded to the south and the east. Much of its power in this era relied on maintaining control over trade routes. Darfur's main "commodity" was slaves, taken from the Bahr al Ghazal region of southern Sudan.

Furiiru

Numbering more than 250,000, the Furiiru (or Kifuliiru or Fulero) live in the eastern highlands of Congo (Dem. Rep.), south of Lake Kivu. They are a Bantu (q.v.) people who can also be found living in Rwanda and Burundi.

Galla *see* Oromo

Gallina *see* Vai

Galoa

The Galoa (or Galwa) are an ethnic group of western Gabon. They number only a few thousand but are economically and politically important.

Galwa *see* Galoa

Gamo *see* Gamu

Gamu

The Gamu are an Omotic (q.v.) people of southern Ethiopia. There are around 400,000 Gamu (or Gamo) people, mostly living in isolated highland communities.

Ganda

The Ganda (or Baganda) people live in a large area of land to the north and west of Lake Victoria in Uganda. The islands in Lake Victoria are inhabited by a people known as the Basese, who are part of the Ganda. There are over three million Ganda people, who form the largest single ethnic grouping in Uganda.

History

There is plenty of information on Ganda history as each clan (extended families who share an ancestor or ancestors) kept its own oral history while court historians preserved royal accounts. The Ganda are descendants of Bantu-speaking people who migrated to East Africa from Central Africa around 1000. Some settled on the northwest corner of Lake Victoria around the Kyadondo region. By the 1300s, this was the heart of a small state, the Buganda Kingdom.

The head of state was the kabaka whose role initially was one of arbiter rather than ruler. His power was limited by that of the batakas, or clan heads. During the eighteenth century, however, successive kabakas skillfully increased their powers at the expense of the batakas. Buganda eventually became a centralized monarchy with the kabaka acting as king.

Despite clashes with the dominant, northerly kingdom of Bunyoro, Buganda increased in size from the sixteenth century onward. By 1870, Buganda was a wealthy and influential nation state with a highly organized system of government led by the kabaka

Bugandan hospitality
In the 1860s, the British explorers John Hanning Speke and James Augustus Grant visited Buganda in their search for the source of the Nile. This picture of the event shows them at the palace of Kabaka Mutesa I. Speke and his men were held as virtual prisoners for six months before Mutesa allowed them to leave.

Ceremonial drum
This ancient drum was beaten by the kabaka.

with help from his Lukiko (council of ministers). A currency of cowrie shells, their value denoted by the holes drilled in the shells so that they could be suspended on strings, was in use. The Basese provided the kabakas with a useful naval capacity, and could sometimes muster fleets of as many as a hundred vessels, each crewed by up to thirty men. This growing economic, political, and military strength had an effect on neighboring areas, particularly on Bunyoro. Buganda supplanted Bunyoro in importance and dominated the region throughout the nineteenth century, helped by several factors. Prime among these was the absence of a Ganda caste system, their military superiority, and their talent for administration.

In 1900, the Buganda Agreement between the British and Bugandan regents (the reigning kabaka was still a boy at the time) made the kingdom a province of the Uganda Protectorate. Its territory was reorganized and numerous counties and parishes were created, each with its own head. In 1955, a second Buganda Agreement made the kabaka a constitutional monarch and the Lukiko became an elected body. As the identity of the wider state of Uganda began to emerge, the solidarity of the Ganda became a block to national unity. Uganda finally became an independent republic in 1962 with Milton Obote (q.v.) as prime minister. Kabaka Mutesa II was made the first president the following year. He was arrested and dismissed in 1966, however, by Obote – an act that led to widespread rioting in Buganda. In 1967, traditional kingdoms were abolished in Uganda. In 1993, however, the Bugandan

monarchy, among others, was restored but with a purely ceremonial and cultural role. Although the monarchy has no real political power, the very fact that it has been restored is, in part, due to its political influence.

Language

The language the Ganda speak is Ganda (or Luganda). This is one of the interlacustrine (between the lakes) branches of the Bantu language group. The Basese speak a dialect of Luganda.

Ways of life

AGRICULTURE The Ganda are mostly agriculturalists. Much of the southern part of their territory is fertile. Because the terrain here is on average more than 3,000 ft (900 m) above sea level, the climate is usually warm but seldom very hot. Rainfall is evenly distributed throughout the year. The staple crops are bananas and plantains, but in modern times the Ganda produce many cash crops. Coffee is particularly successful and, indeed, even before it was cultivated grew in the wild. Other cash crops grown by the Ganda are cotton, sugar cane, corn, rice, and tea. The north and northeast parts of the land are less fertile. Most of the northern border is a region known as a dry zone, and

Mutesa I's tomb
The tall tomb of this Bugandan king is made from long, woven reeds. Mutesa I ruled over Buganda from 1852 until his death in 1884. The kingdom reached its height during this period and, by then, the position of kabaka was one of absolute monarch. Mutesa is renowned for being a particularly cruel ruler. He was succeeded by his son who was young and inexperienced at a time when Buganda needed a decisive ruler.

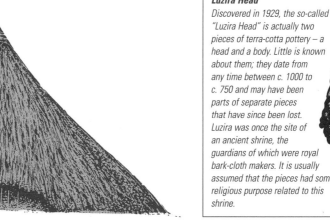

Luzira Head
Discovered in 1929, the so-called "Luzira Head" is actually two pieces of terra-cotta pottery – a head and a body. Little is known about them; they date from any time between c. 1000 to c. 750 and may have been parts of separate pieces that have since been lost. Luzira was once the site of an ancient shrine, the guardians of which were royal bark-cloth makers. It is usually assumed that the pieces had some religious purpose related to this shrine.

in the northeast are the Kyoga Swamps around Lake Kyoga.

INDUSTRY The Ganda are famous in the region for their basket-making, and many of their village houses were built by weaving long reeds. The kabaka's own residence had such walls in excess of 15 ft (5 m) in height. The Ganda were also able to smelt iron using charcoal, building their furnaces with slabs cut from the sides of termite hills. The Basese are renowned fishermen and boat builders.

Social structure

At the time of the Bugandan Kingdom, prestige, wealth, and status could be achieved through military service or service at the court of the kabaka. Talented and ambitious people could, therefore, move upward in Bugandan society. This tradition of advancement through patronage and service is harder to achieve in modern Ugandan society, where education is the key. Nevertheless, the Ganda have an established "middle class" and tend to be among the more prosperous members of Ugandan society. Also, the Ganda people dominate the country's civil service.

Historically, the kabaka guaranteed the rights of all his subjects wherever they resided, land was plentiful, and people were not dependent on their neighbors and families for their status and security. The Ganda argue that this is why it is now customary for men to move from one village to another every few years and not to settle down until middle age. Consequently, Ganda families are largely self-contained units and this is reflected in the villages, which are not particularly close knit.

Culture and religion

RELIGION In recent years, many Ganda have become either Muslim or Christian. They still retain, however, their own systems of belief. The Ganda have one of the most elaborate religions in Africa involving various gods and spirits who are associated with ideas or places such as the forest, a river, or even a particular tree. In the past, each had its own temple, priest, or medium. The most influential of these deities is the great god, Mukasa. The brother of Mukasa, the kindly god, is Kibuka – the war god. Kintu is believed to have been the first man and ancestor; Nambi, daughter of the King of Heaven, became his wife and brought her brother, Death, down to earth.

Kabaka Mutesa II
Kabaka Mutesa II was the first president of the Republic of Uganda and, until 1993, the last king of the Bugandan dynasty. He ruled over Buganda from 1939 to 1967, but the kingdom was never fully independent. It was a province of the British Uganda Protectorate, with some autonomy, and the kabaka kept his status, if not his power, up to 1962. The Bugandan monarchy was restored in 1993 with a purely ceremonial role.

Medicine pot
This large pottery vessel would have once been used for administering medicine, often mixed with beer. Royalty drank from the central spout; ordinary people from the spout on the right; and batakas (chiefs) from the left.

Ganda timeline

c. 1000
Bantu-speakers migrate from Central to East Africa; Ganda settle around northwest Lake Victoria

1500s
Buganda Kingdom expands

c. 1650
Bataka mutiny against authoritarian kabaka

1700s
Kabakas increase power

1800s
Buganda evolves into centralized monarchy

1894
British *protectorate* (colony) over Buganda formed

1900
Buganda is made a semiautonomous province of British Uganda Protectorate

1921
Bataka Association formed to grievances over land allocation under British rule

1955
Kabaka made a constitutional monarch and Lukiko becomes a mainly elected body

1962
Uganda gains independence

1963
Kabaka Mutesa II made first president (nonexecutive) of Ugandan Republic

1966
Coup led by prime minister Milton Obote; Mutesa II flees; Obote becomes president

1967
Buganda Kingdom abolished

1971
Col. Idi Amin Dada seizes power in a military coup; he installs repressive regime

1979
Tanzanian forces and Ugandan rebels oust Amin

1981–1986
Ugandan civil war; rebels led by Yoweri Museveni win power

1993
Bugandan monarchy restored; Ronald Mutebi is kabaka

1994
Nonparty elections held as first step to restoring democracy

1996
Reports of rebel activites in Uganda

1998
Uganda intervenes in civil war in Congo (Dem. Rep.)

Garati
The Garati are one of the three main subgroups of the Konso (q.v.). The Konso live in southern Ethiopia.

Garo
The Garo are a Sadama (q.v.) subgroup. The Sadama are an ethnic group living in Ethiopia.

Gbagyi
The Gbagyi (or Bagyi) are the largest subgroup of the Gbari (q.v.) of Nigeria. They are concentrated in the western half of Nigeria and number around 500,000. They speak a Benue-Congo language.

Gbanda *see* Avikam

Gbari
The Gbari (or Gwari) number more than 500,000 and are concentrated in the west of that country, in particular in Niger State.

Togoland

Cameroon

German colonies

German
East Africa

German South
West Africa

Gbaya see **Baya**

Gcaleka

The Gcaleka are one of the main Xhosa (q.v.) groups. The Xhosa are a large group of peoples united by a common language in South Africa.

Germans

Although Germany did not hold on to its colonies in Africa for long after World War I and II, thousands of people of German descent can be found in Africa, mostly in Germany's former colonies.

Gerse see **Kpelle**

Gewo see **Guere**

Ghandi see **Bandi**

Gikuyu see **Kikuyu**

Gimr

The Gimr are one of the several Tama (q.v.) speaking groups of Sudan and Chad. Arabic is more widely spoke than Tama now by the Gimr, however. The Gimr live largely on the Sudanese side of the Sudan–Chad border, while many others live in western Sudan in Darfur. There are more than 50,000 Gimr people.

Gio see **Dan**

Giriama

Numbering more than 500,000, the Giriama are the largest of the nine closely related groups that make up the Mijikenda (q.v.). The Mijikenda mostly inhabit coastal regions of Kenya.

Gizi see **Kissi**

Gobir see **Gobirwa**

Gobirwa

The Gobirwa (or Gobir) are a subgroup of the Hausa (q.v.) people of southern Niger and northern Nigeria. It is thought that the Gobirwa could have arisen from a mixing of Tebu (q.v.) and Semitic cultures.

Gofa

The Gofa are an Omotic people (q.v.) of southern Ethiopia. There are more than 300,000 Gofa.

Gogo

The Gogo (or Chigogo) number around one million people. They are a Bantu people concentrated in central Tanzania's highlands who have absorbed many aspects of Maasai (q.v.) culture.

Gomei see **Ankwe**

Goula see **Gula**

Gova

The Gova are made up of several small Shona (q.v.) subgroups. They number several thousand people spread along the lower Zambezi River Valley in Mozambique and Zimbabwe.

Grebo

The Grebo are a cluster of peoples that form part of the Kru (q.v.) of Ivory Coast and southeastern Liberia. There are well over 500,000 Grebo.

Griqua

The Griqua are a southern African people descended from Khoikhoi (q.v.), San (q.v.), and European ancestors. The San and Khoikhoi were the first known inhabitants of Southern Africa, and the ancestors of the Khoisan (q.v.). The Khoisan are not Black Africans, but make up a unique "racial" category of their own, once disparagingly referred to as the Bushmen or Hottentots. The Khoisan first emerged in what is now Botswana, from where they spread to what are now Namibia and the Cape of South Africa. After Dutch settlers began arriving in South Africa in the seventeenth century, they forced local Khoisan peoples to work for them. The white settlers developed into the present-day Afrikaner (q.v.) population. Groups such as the Griqua were a result of contact between the Khoisan and European communities. The Griqua adopted many aspects of European culture: they were Christian, wore Western clothing, and spoke Dutch. In the eighteenth century, they migrated north to where the Vaal and Orange rivers meet to escape the hostility of their white neighbors.

Groemai see Ankwe

Grusi

The Grusi (or Nankansi) are a Mole-Dagbane (q.v.) people, in fact the largest such group in northern Ghana and southern Burkina Faso. The Grusi population numbers more than 500,000.

Guere

The Guere (or Wee or Gewo) are part of the Kru (q.v.) cluster of peoples in western Ivory Coast. The Guere in Liberia are known as the Krahn (or Kran). There are about 200,000 people.

Gula

The Gula (or Goula) are the descendants of the founders of the Gula empire, which reached its height before the eighteenth century in north-central Africa. The Gula language was once the lingua franca (common tongue) of the region. Today, the Gula number some 70,000 plus people in the Central African Republic and Chad.

Gulay

The Gulay are the second-largest subgroup of the Sara (q.v.). They live in southern Chad.

Gule

The Gule are a subgroup of the Funj (q.v.) people. The Funj live in southern Sudan.

Gungawa see Reshawa

Gur see Mole-Dagbane

Guro

The Guro (or Kweni) are a Manding (q.v.) people of Ivory Coast. There are more than 200,000 Guro people, most of whom live in western and central regions of the country.

Guruku see Safwa

Gusii

There are more than one million Gusii, or Kisii, living in the western corner of Kenya in a region to the east of Lake Victoria and centered around the town of Kisii, a major urban center in the region. The Gusii language, Ekegusii, is a Bantu (q.v.) language. The Gusii are divided into seven subgroups based around clan groups: Kitutu, North Mugirango, South Mugirango, Majoge, Wanjare, Bassi, and Nyaribari. These were made into administrative districts during the colonial era.

The Kisii highlands were largely uninhabited before 1800, when ancestors of the Luo (q.v.) and Kipsigis (q.v.) began settling the surrounding savanna (grasslands) in large numbers. Inhabitants of the savanna were dislodged, and the Gusii came to settle the Kisii highlands, which at that time were largely covered by forest. Between 1901 and 1908 military expeditions were sent out by British forces to quell the resistance of the Gusii and their neighbors to foreign rule, and the 1960s saw armed conflicts with the Maasai (q.v.) over land.

Gwari see Gbari

Guro Weaving Pulley
Like many Ivory Coast utensils, this carries a carving in which the main human feature is intermingled with animal features, believed to protect the weaver and the materials made.

Elegant mask
The smooth, sloping face and rounded horns are typical of the gracefulness of Guro art.

© DIAGRAM

Habbania

The Habbania are one of the main Baggara (q.v.) subgroups. The Baggara are a Sudanese people of Bedouin (q.v.) and Black African descent.

Hadendowa

Numbering more than 600,000, the Hadendowa are the largest Beja (q.v.) subgroup. They live north of Eritrea, mostly in the Sudanese region that borders the Red Sea and along the seasonal Gash watercourse.

Hadza

The Hadza are a small ethnic group numbering only a few thousand living mostly around Lake Eyasi in northern Tanzania.

Together with the Sandawe, the Hadza (or Hatsa) are perhaps the last-remaining descendants of East Africa's first human inhabitants. Thousands of years ago, before Bantu (q.v.), Cushites (q.v.), and Nilotes (q.v.) peoples settled in the regions, the only human inhabitants of Southern and East Africa were the ancestors of the modern-day Khoisan (q.v.) people. The Khoisan are not Black Africans, but make up a unique "racial" category of their own. They are historically associated with hunter-gatherer lifestyles and distinctive for their short stature and use of languages that contain clicking and popping sounds. Over many hundreds of years, as other groups migrated into the area, most Khoisan people retreated or were absorbed by the incoming communities. The Hadza are sometimes counted among the Khoisan's few direct descendants remaining in East Africa today. Conversely, other experts have questioned this, and place Hadzane (the language of the Hadza) in a different language family from Khoisan, meaning that the Hadza and the Khoisan could be unrelated.

Halaba see Alaba

Hamba see Amba

Harari

The Harari (or Adare or Hareri) once lived almost solely behind the walls of the Ethiopian city of Harer, which lies in the eastern-central region of that country. There are around 40,000 Harari, only a few thousand of which live in Harer. The majority have migrated to other cities, in particular Addis Ababa.

Hareri see Harari

Hatsa see Hadza

Hausa

The Hausa are the most numerous West African ethnic group, and most of them live in a region known as Hausaland. Although mostly in northern Nigeria, Hausaland extends north as far as the Sahara Desert; to Lake Chad in the east; and to the Niger River in the south. Outside of this region, Hausa people can be found throughout Africa working as traders. There are probably about twenty-five million Hausa.

History

The first Hausa settlements were built during the eleventh and twelfth centuries. By about 1350, many of the cities had developed into independent city-states. The major ones were Kano, Katsina, Zamfara, Gobir, Kebbi, and Zazzau (present-day Zaira). Different city-states were dominant during the various periods of Hausa history. Important trade routes had reached Hausaland from the north by the fifteenth century, and it became known for its cloth manufacturing and dyeing.

The greatest upheaval in Hausa history came at the beginning of the nineteenth century. In 1804, the leader of the Islamic Fulani people – the Muslim cleric Usman dan Fodio (q.v.) – declared a jihad (Islamic holy war) against the Hausa rulers. For centuries, the Fulani settlers had coexisted peacefully with the Hausa. Toward the end of the eighteenth century, however, heavy taxes imposed by the Hausa triggered a rebellion that turned into a jihad. It was supported by the rural Hausa, who also suffered under the taxation system. After a four-year struggle, all the Hausa states were conquered, and Fodio established the Fulani-Hausa Sokoto Caliphate. It continued to expand it until the caliphate reached its greatest extent in 1830. The borders of the Sokoto Caliphate remained basically the same until the British conquered the caliphate in 1903. Even today, the ruling class of Hausaland is largely made up of Fulanis.

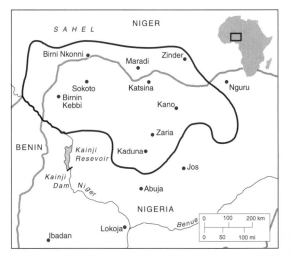

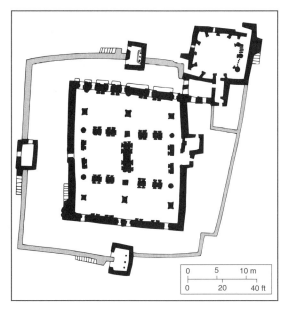

Language

The Hausa speak a language also called Hausa, an Afroasiatic language related to Arabic, Berber, and Hebrew. It is one of the most widely spoken languages in Africa because, in the past, Hausa influence spread far beyond Hausaland thanks to trade. Hausa has been heavily influenced by Arabic. The Hausa script is called Ajemic and uses Arabic characters; the British introduced the Roman script, however, which is now more widely used. Historically, the Hausa script was used for business and government records.

Decorated wall
For centuries Hausa craftsmen have decorated houses inside with painted and molded designs, but more recently they have been applying the same techniques to the exteriors. Here is the external wall of a house in Zaria, Nigeria, decorated with modern motifs: a bicycle and a car.

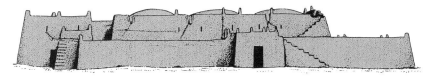

Masallaci Jumaa
The Masallaci Jumaa (Friday Mosque) in Zaria was built in the nineteenth century. It was designed by the Hausa architect Babban Gwani Mikaila for Emir Abdulkarim. This mosque (Muslim house of worship) is a complex of buildings including a central hall of worship, entrance lobbies, and washing chambers surrounded by an external wall.

Ways of life

Most Hausa work on the land, so the pattern of Hausa life is greatly influenced by the changing seasons. The climate in northern Nigeria is an extreme one, with a long, dry season from October to the end of April. This is the main period of harvest. It is also the busiest trading time as most farmers sell at least some of their produce at the local market. The markets vary from weekly to daily events depending on the size of the town or city. Kano, for instance, has a busy market every day.

From February, the weather is hot, dry, and windy. In April and May, a series of violent storms herald the arrival of the rainy season. It is during the rainy season and the months immediately before and after it that the Hausa carry out most work on the land. Cash crops grown include cotton, tobacco, and groundnuts, which are exported and used to make oil and peanut butter. Main food crops include rice, cereals such as millet, sorghum, and corn, and vegetables such as onions, okra, and tomatoes. The richer Hausa own cattle, often looked after by paid herders, and most also keep goats and poultry.

Agricultural work is often carried out within a cooperative system whose basic unit is the gandu. The sons of a family work on the gandu lands of their father in return for seed and equipment. Each son is allocated his own land to work in his own time. The produce grown on it can be used as they wish.

Although the majority of Hausa people are primarily agricultural, many have other skills apart from farming. Hausa women do little farming – they only involve themselves in harvesting. Instead, they are more

Leather bag
The Hausa are famous for their artistry and skill in leatherworking. Items made include saddles and bags. This Hausa-crafted leather bag has been decorated with both appliqué and stitching.

Hausa states
This map shows the regions controlled by the Hausa city-states in the seventeenth century. Each city was independent and self-governing.

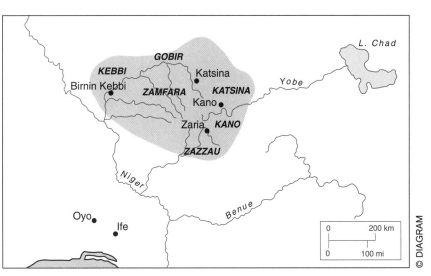

© DIAGRAM

involved in trading; at the market they trade in goods such as medicines, vegetable oils, and cigarettes. Hausa women also weave cloth and make goods for sale such as candy and other foods and cotton blankets, and raise goats and poultry for sale. Hausa men are weavers, dyers, blacksmiths, butchers, leatherworkers, metalworkers, barbers, or tailors as well as farmers; many are also in the Nigerian army.

Markets have their own systems of control. Each market has a headman who is responsible to the village or town leader. He has a number of assistants – often women – who are each concerned with a particular activity, for instance grain-selling or butchery. These assistants not only help the headman but also represent the interests of their own group of traders. In this way, disputes are settled and advice or help is given accordingly.

Social structure

POLITICAL STRUCTURE An emir (Islamic ruler) governs each Hausa state, with a group of his appointed officals who are responsible for collecting taxes and general administration. Unlike the rest of Nigeria, the northern Hausa states follow Sharia (Islamic holy) law.

Culture and religion

Although most Hausa people are rural and live in villages, Hausa society centers on a number of important urban areas – for example, Kano, famous for dyeing fabrics; Katsina, a trading center; and Zaria, once a major provider of slaves. In former centuries, the cities formed self-governing states, often hostile to each other but continuing to trade. The Hausa have always had trade links with Arab and Sudanese merchants, who travel across the great Sahara Desert.

RELIGION Islam was introduced to Hausaland in the 1400s, and now the majority of Hausa people are Muslim.

Koranic board
This wooden board from Hausaland is inscribed with a text from the Islamic holy book, the Koran. Such boards are used in Islamic schools for the teaching of Arabic and learning the Koran.

Calabash bowl
Calabashes are a type of gourd. When grown, they are dried, hollowed out, and used as vessels to store foods and drinks. This calabash has been cut in two to symbolize Heaven (top half) and Earth (bottom half). The patterns have been burnt on using a hot point.

Hausa timeline	
c. 1000s–1100s Hausa communities established in northern Nigeria and southern Niger	**1960** Niger and Nigeria win independence
1350 Hausa city-states emerge	**1967–1970** Biafran (Nigerian Civil) War
1400s Islam is introduced to Hausaland via the empires of Mali and Songhay	**1970s–1980s** Series of failed civilian governments and military coups in Nigeria
1804–1809 Hausa states conquered by Fulani leader Usman dan Fodio; Sokoto Caliphate established	**1974** Oil boom in Nigeria
1830 Sokoto Caliphate at greatest extent	**1975** Capital of Nigeria transferred from Lagos to Abuja
1903 British defeat Sokoto the Caliphate	**1993** In Nigeria, transition from military rule to democratic rule ends when General Sanni Abacha declares himself ruler
1950s Discovery of petroleum desposits in Nigeria	**1999** Civilian rule restored in Nigeria

Hawiye

The Hawiye are one of the main clan-based subgroups of the Somali (q.v.) people. The majority live in and around Mogadishu, the capital of Somalia.

Haya

The Haya (or Ruhaya, Ekihaya, or Ziba) are a large Bantu (q.v.) group of northern Tanzania. Numbering more than one million, they live to the west of Lake Victoria. They formed several powerful kingdoms, all of which were abolished in 1962.

Hehe

The Hehe are a Bantu (q.v.) people of south-central Tanzania. In the nineteenth century the great chief Muyugumba united the various Hehe chiefdoms into one kingdom. The Hehe number more than 600,000.

Herero

In precolonial times, the Herero lived throughout the plateau area of central Namibia, but today they are widely dispersed, concentrated in small areas on the plateau they once dominated. While the overwhelming majority of Herero live in Namibia, there are also smaller numbers in northwest Botswana. The Herero were once one of Namibia's most numerous peoples, but today they number approximately 75,000, about seven percent of the country's population.

History

The Herero and Ovambo share a common early history of migration, probably originating in the region around the great lakes of East and Central Africa. Like the Ovambo, the Herero probably arrived in Namibia in the fifteenth or sixteenth century from what is now Zambia. By the late seventeenth century, the Herero had reached the arid Kaokoveld Plateau, bringing with them their herds of long-horned cattle. By the eigh-

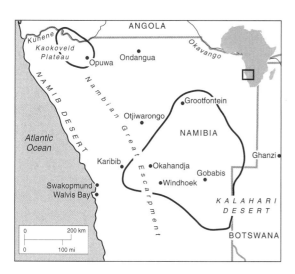

Herero fashions
In the nineteenth century, women converts to Christianity adopted the fashions of the wives of the German missionaries: long dresses with "leg o' mutton sleeves." Even today, Herero women wear this distinctive type of dress. Unlike the dour missionary clothing, however, materials used for Herero dresses are often patterned and very colorful. They are usually worn with a turbanlike headdress.

teenth century, they had moved on south to the superior grazing lands of central Namibia. Unlike the Ovambo, the Herero virtually abandoned agriculture, concentrating almost exclusively on raising cattle.

COLONIALISM In the nineteenth century, European traders, explorers, and missionaries entered Herero territory. In 1884, Germany claimed Namibia (as South West Africa), including the Herero's territory, as a colony. German settlers gradually seized Herero grazing land and property, even confiscating Herero cattle for "trespassing" on their newly acquired lands.

In 1904, the Herero staged a revolt. Their leader, Samuel Maherero, decreed that only German soldiers and male settlers should be attacked – women, missionaries, English, and Afrikaners should be spared. The Herero warriors were no match for German weaponry, however, and Maherero and his followers fled into the Kalahari Desert. The German commander then ordered his forces to exterminate the Herero. In the six months before Germany ordered a halt to the genocide, the Herero were reduced by bullets, poison, thirst, and starvation from a population estimated at 75,000 to 90,000 to less than 20,000. The Herero survivors dispersed, many trekking north and east into desert and semidesert regions of Botswana (then the British colony of Bechuanaland).

APARTHEID The Herero hoped that South Africa's occupation of Namibia following Germany's World War I defeat would lead to positive change, but their position remained largely unaltered. Cattle ownership was again allowed but land rights were not restored. The South Africans introduced a form of apartheid (the racist doctrine of "separate development") that controlled the Herero's places of residence and work. Despite their relatively small numbers, the Herero played an extremely important role in the Namibian struggle for independence from South Africa, contributing several key leaders to SWAPO (South West Africa People's Organization). SWAPO was the country's resistance movement during the struggle for independence and is now its main political party.

Language

The Herero language is called Herero (or Ojitherero); many Herero also speak other Namibian languages.

Ways of life

The 1904–5 massacre had a huge impact on the Herero, greatly altering their ways of life. Those who remained in Namibia were placed in inadequate "native reserves" and their land and cattle distributed to

Milk bottle
This antique milk bottle was made by a Herero artisan from a calabash and strips of leather.

Victims of the Herero massacre
After the 1904–5 uprising, German colonists ruthlessly oppressed the Herero people. Many, such as these, became victims of famine or dehydration after they were driven into desert areas by the Germans.

Herero home
This home has been built in the classic round Herero style. The Herero make these houses from either brick or a mud and dung mixture, but with the arrival of bricks, many modern houses are now square. Aluminum siding is often used as a roof or, if the owner prefers or cannot afford modern materials, grass is made into a thatched roof.

© DIAGRAM

Ovahimba

Although the Ovahimba are a subgroup of the Herero, they are different in many ways. For example, Ovahimba clothing is very different as the women have not adopted the missionary-inspired fashions of the Herero. Instead, they are more likely to wear hide or cloth skirts with a bustlelike effect. The Ovahimba are mostly cattle herders and live on the Kaokoveld Plateau. Most practice seminomadic pastoralism but are increasingly finding it less necessary to migrate as water distribution facilities improve in Namibia. The home shown below, made from a wooden frame coated with mud and cow dung, is ideal for a nomadic existence. As the Ovahimba become more settled, however, more-permanent houses are being built.

German settlers for whom they worked as virtual slaves. Herero refugees arrived in Botswana without cattle and the sacred objects of their ancestors, and survived by hiring themselves out as hands to local, mainly Tswana, cattle herders. Only in the late 1920s did a resurgence of ethnic identity among the Herero in Namibia and Botswana commence, as a result of increases in prosperity and cattle ownership and the rebuilding of family networks. Until independence in 1990, the Herero in South African-controlled Namibia remained restricted to reserves (later, a homeland) or were employed as cattle hands on white-owned farms or as servants or laborers in the towns.

CATTLE Herero life has long been dominated by cattle raising. A man's herd is a measure of his social standing and individuals might own thousands of head of cattle. Most rural labor is devoted to cattle raising and during the frequent droughts huge wells are dug to provide water for the herds. Men are responsible for herding; women are responsible for milking.

Historically, cattle would rarely be eaten unless the animal had died by accident or naturally, but today the Herero raise cattle on a commercial basis for slaughter.

SETTLEMENTS The Herero live in extended family compounds called ozonganda. An ozonganda consists of one or more buildings used for sleeping and storage; a large yard for cooking, eating, and washing; and enclosures for goats and cattle. The extended family living in an ozonganda is headed by a senior male and includes his wife or wives, their children, and wives of their sons and their children. Other relatives including brothers and, especially, unmarried sisters, may also live in the ozonganda. Several ozonganda share the cost and labor of creating a well.

Social structure

Family ancestry is extremely important for the Herero and individuals have a deep knowledge of their family history that stretches back many generations. Each Herero is a member of an oruzo (a line of ancestors traced through male relatives) and a banda (a line of ancestors traced through female relatives). These groups determine social status and inheritance rights.

Culture and religion

RELIGION Most Namibian Herero are Christians. The Herero living in Botswana, however, have not adopted Christianity to any great degree. Meanwhile, their own religion, which was based on the view that cattle were bequeathed to the Herero by their ancestors, has largely died out as cattle are now viewed in more practical and less sacred terms. This has lead to the development of a primarily secular society among the Botswana Herero. The Ovahimba – a small Herero subgroup living on the isolated Kaokoveld Plateau – are considered to retain Herero culture in its most pure form.

Herero timeline			
c. 1500s Herero arrive in Namibia	many Herero are massacred and others flee to Bechuanaland	**1948** Form of *apartheid* introduced	**1989** Apartheid-style legislation repealed in South West Africa
1825–1870 Herero establish supremacy over local Khoisan people	**1910** White-minority ruled Union of South Africa formed	**1960** South West Africa People's Organization (SWAPO) formed	**1990** South West Africa gains independence as Namibia
1884 Germany colonizes Namibia as South West Africa; Christianity introduced to region	**1914–1918** Herero encouraged to revolt during WWII by South Africa	**1966** Botswana independent. Conflict between SWAPO and South African troops begins	**1996** Herero demand compensation from Germany for 1904–5 massacre from Chancellor Kohl on his visit to Namibia
1884–1885 British colonize Botswana as Bechuanaland	**1915** South West Africa occupied by South Africa: Herero restricted to inadequate "native reserves"	**1969** South Africa's occupation of South West Africa declared illegal by United Nations	
1904–1905 Herero uprising against German rule led by Samuel Maherero;	**1920s** Herero nationalism develops		

Hlubi

The Hlubi are one of the main Xhosa (q.v.) groups. The Xhosa are a large group of peoples united by a common language in South Africa.

Hottentot

The name Hottentot was originally used by Dutch settlers in Southern Africa to refer to the Khoikhoi (q.v.) people. The Khoikhoi, like other San (q.v.) people, speak a language that involves the use of clicks and popping sounds. The Dutch named them "the stutterers" for this reason. Hottentot is widely considered to be a derogatory term and has largely fallen out of use now.

Humr

The Humr are one of the main Baggara (q.v.) subgroups. The Baggara are a Sudanese people of Bedouin (q.v.) and Black African descent.

Hurutshe

The Hurutshe are one of the main subdivisions of the Tswana (q.v.) people of southern Africa. Hurutshe peoples can be found living in many parts of Botswana as well as neighboring regions of South Africa.

The Hurutshe, or Barutshe, are one of the many powerful Sotho (q.v.)-Tswana clans (several extended families linked by a common ancestor or ancestors) that emerged after the end of the first millennium. They became a powerful lineage group in the Highveld region of South Africa, controlling the hill country around the head waters of the Eland and Marico rivers.

The Hurutshe capital, Kaditshwena, housed more than 15,000 people.

Most Botswana Hurutshes are descended from people who left the Transvaal region of present-day South Africa in the 1850s. The 1800s were a time of great upheaval in southern Africa, with the rapidly expanding Zulu (q.v.) kingdom causing mass migrations of African populations. More recently, many Hurutshe left South Africa for Botswana during the apartheid era.

Hutu and Tutsi

The Hutu (or Bahutu) and the Tutsi (or Watutsi) are two ethnic groups that make up the majority populations of Burundi and Rwanda. In the past, the Hutu have formed as much as ninety percent of the population of both countries, and the Tutsi nine percent. Minority groups, mostly Twa people, form the rest. Since the fighting that began more than three years ago, however, a great number of Hutu, and some Tutsi, have fled as refugees to neighboring countries – in particular Congo (Dem. Rep.) – severely reducing the numbers of Hutu remaining in their homelands.

Although they are generally considered to be distinct ethnic groups, the history and lives of the Hutu and Tutsi are so intertwined that they are described together here.

History

Ruanda–Urundi The Twa, who are largely hunter-gatherers and potters, were probably the first peoples of Burundi and Rwanda. The Hutu came from the west (modern Congo [Dem. Rep.]) a very long time ago. About 600 years ago, the Tutsi moved in from Ethiopia. They soon dominated the Hutu, who became virtual slaves. The Tutsi founded two kingdoms, known as Ruanda and Urundi. Ruanda was especially powerful. Each kingdom was ruled by a Tutsi king, the mwami. The Tutsi continued to dominate both countries, even after Europeans established colonial rule there. Germany made Ruanda-Urundi a joint territory as part of German East Africa in 1890, but did not exercise much authority over it. Belgium occupied Ruanda-Urundi during World War I, and from 1924 administered it under trust from the League of Nations (later the United Nations).

INDEPENDENCE In 1962, the two countries became independent. Urundi, now called Burundi, remained a monarchy under its Tutsi mwami, Mwambutsa IV. Conflict between the Hutu and the Tutsi followed. In

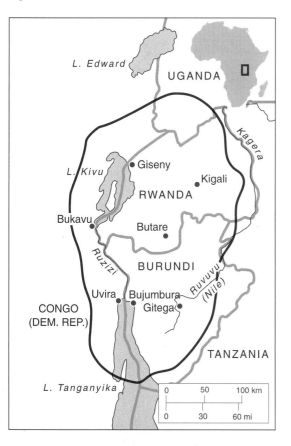

A Tutsi dancer
This Tutsi dancer wears a leopardskin cloak and a headdress and carries a spear. Most dancers now carry javelinlike wands rather than spears. The headdress accentuates the rhythmic movements of the dance.

© DIAGRAM

A Tutsi woman
This aristocratic woman is a Tutsi chief's wife. The Tutsi often cultivate an aristocratic bearing that, historically, helped to separate them from their Hutu subjects more than any real physical difference. Indeed, some regard the diference between Hutu and Tutsi to be one of class, not ethnicity.

1966 the prime minister, Michel Micombero (q.v.), overthrew the monarchy and declared a republic. An unsuccessful Hutu revolt in 1972 resulted in heavy loss of life, mostly among the Hutu. The Tutsi remained in control of the country, despite outbreaks of ethnic warfare that killed tens of thousands of people, especially in 1993. In that year, Burundi's first ever Hutu president was killed, probably in an attempted coup, and over 50,000 people died in the ensuing violence.

Rwanda became an independent republic, with a predominantly Hutu government, in 1962. There was heavy fighting between Hutu and Tutsi in the years before and immediately after independence. The Tutsi sustained the most casualties, and thousands fled to other countries, where many later settled and some became rebels.

RECENT EVENTS Tutsi rebels went on to form the Rwandan Patriotic Front, and although a peace accord between them and the Hutu government was signed in 1993 after three years of conflict, large-scale violence broke out again in 1994, after a plane carrying the presidents of both countries crashed near Rwanda's capital, Kigali, having possibly been hit by gunfire or a rocket. A series of vicious riots and massacres followed, mainly of the Tutsi, resulting in hundreds of thousands dead and more than a million people fleeing to refugee camps in Congo (Dem. Rep.) and other neighboring countries. In 1996, the violence spread to Burundi.

Language
Both Hutu and Tutsi speak a Bantu language, called Rundi (or Kirundi) in Burundi and Rwanda (or Kinyarwanda) in Rwanda. This was originally a Hutu language, which the Tutsi have since adopted.

Ways of life
Hutu Although many Hutu live and work in Rwandan or Burundi towns and cities, the vast majority are farmers. Among them, the Hutu of both sexes have long tilled the soil and grown crops. The men also looked after cattle, often under the supervision of a Tutsi overseer.

The Hutu live in small fenced compounds, each containing several reed and grass structures. One is a kitchen, one a bedroom and sitting room, and a third is for storage. A fourth, among those Hutu who are not

Basketwork
Ornamental baskets and basket trays were made by Tutsi women who were members of the aristocracy. Elegantly patterned and carefully worked, the baskets required the amount of time that only members of a leisured class would have.

Christians, is for the ancestral spirits. Others serve as granaries (storehouses for grain). A group of about twenty compounds makes up a Hutu village.

For years many Hutu, regarded as second-class citizens, have had a largely subsistence diet. It is based on cereals, beans, peas, bananas, and sweet potatoes, with a little goat flesh. When they can, the Hutu eat two solid meals a day of porridge and sweet potatoes. Many dislike sheep flesh and fish. The Hutu make two kinds of beer, one from bananas and one from cassava.

TUTSI In the past, the Tutsi regarded themselves as the only people who ought to own and tend cattle. They expected the Hutu to work for them and do all the dirty jobs such as farming. Today, they work the land like the Hutu, and no longer have exclusive rights to own cattle. Coffee is an important cash crop for both groups, followed by tea. Cattle, goats, and sheep are the main livestock. The Tutsi diet is different from that of the Hutu and in the past was based on curdled milk and butter. A few Tutsi claimed to eat nothing else, but most had one solid meal a day of bananas and beans. Banana beer and mead, made from honey, are drunk.

Social structure
The Tutsi have long considered themselves superior to the Hutu, and until recent years have exclusively formed the ruling classes. The Tutsi, however, allowed some Hutu men to rise to high office. For a long time the Tutsi were the fighting soldiers in any army, with the Hutu providing the supporting services such as servants and carriers. Until modern times, members of each Hutu village or group were "clients" subservient to a Tutsi "patron." Clients were given a cow and in exchange provided beer and agricultural goods to the patron, who protected them against exactions by other Tutsi. This system was called ubuhake.

MARRIAGE The Hutu often marry young (around seventeen for boys, the girls around puberty), usually with local partners. The bridegroom's father has to pay the bridewealth, a gift of cows, goats, and beer given to the bride's family and generally regarded as a token of respect. Both husband and wife are allowed sexual freedom. Hutu men may have more than one wife, each with her own compound. Children are prized, partly because they mean extra pairs of hands to share the work. The Hutu regard twins of different sexes as bad luck. The man owns the labor of his wife or wives and his children if

War orphan
This child is a casualty of the 1990s conflict in Rwanda, and more recently Burundi, between the Tutsi-dominated rebels and the majority Hutu people. Large numbers of Hutu refugees fled to neighboring countries while many Tutsi families found themselves the victims of retaliation.

unmarried. When he dies, the eldest son of his first wife generally succeeds him. Marriage between Hutu and Tutsi sometimes takes place.

Tutsi marriage customs were not unlike those of the Hutu, the groom having to pay the bridewealth. In general, the Tutsi marry among themselves, but they allow some Hutu men to marry Tutsi women. Such a marriage makes the children automatically Tutsi.

Culture and religion

RELIGION Today, more than half the Hutu and Tutsi in both Rwanda and Burundi are Christians, mostly Roman Catholics. Others follow their original beliefs, perhaps in conjunction with Christianity, worshipping a benevolent god called Imana, and acknowledging witches, sorcerers, and the ghosts of the dead. The Hutu take a keen interest in family relationships and remember ancestors, to whom they show respect and make offerings to at the family ancestral shrines, for as many as six generations back.

DRESS In recent years, traditional forms of Hutu dress have tended to die out in favor of "Western" styles and imported fabrics: shorts and shirts for men; skirts and tops for women. Tutsi dress today is also largely "Western" style. Traditional dress is seen now mostly among the Tutsi dancers, who perform largely at ceremonial events.

CRAFTS Hutu crafts include basket-making, carving, and blacksmithing. Both the Tutsi and Hutu make some pottery, but they usually rely on trading agricultural produce for pots with the Twa, or purchase plastic containers. The Tutsi are especially skilled in weaving baskets and in beadwork and also make ornamental screens.

Hutu and Tutsi timeline	
upto 1500s Hutu move from present-day Congo (Dem. Rep.) into present area	**36,000** (mainly Tutsi) Rwandan refugees
1500s Tutsi herders migrate into Hutu and Twa lands from northeast	**1988** 80,000 Hutu refugees from Burundi enter Rwanda
c. 1550s Tutsi found kingdom of Ruanda	**1990** 10,000 Tutsi-dominated guerrillas invade Rwanda; civil war follows
1600s Tutsi kingdom in Urundi	**1992** In Rwanda, 300 Tutsi assassinated; 15,000 forcibly relocated
1897 Urundi under German colonial rule	**1993** In Burundi, 50,000 die in ethnic war. Peace agreed in Rwanda between Tutsi rebels and Hutu government
1899 Ruanda's expansion ended by Germans	
1916–1917 Ruanda-Urundi occupied by Belgium	**1994** Hutu presidents of Rwanda and Burundi die in plane crash, probably assassinated; large-scale massacres in Rwanda and massive refugee crisis follow
1959 Hutu subjects overthrow Ruandan monarchy	
1962 Ruanda wins independence and becomes Rwanda. Urundi wins independence under Tutsi monarchy and becomes Burundi	**1995** Fighting between Hutu and Tutsi intensifies in Burundi
	1996–7 Tutsis in Congo (Dem. Rep.) lead an uprising that brings Laurent Kabila to power
1972 Burundi Hutu revolt against Tutsi elite; over 100,000 Hutu killed in retaliation. Tension between Hutu and Tutsi in Rwanda precedes military coup	**1998** Disatisfied with Kabila, Tutsis are involved in a rebellion in eastern Congo (Dem. Rep.)
1980 Tanzania grants citizenship to	

Hutu knife
This knife has a wooden handle and a metal blade shaped into a flat hook. Such knives are widespread throughout East and Central Africa. They are used mainly by women to knock fruit from trees, but can also serve as weapons if necessary.

Igikubge
A headdress called an igikubge is worn by some Tutsi women of royal ancestry. A leaf is made into a band and decorated with beadwork, including beaded tassels that hang over the wearer's face.

Iambi

The Iambi are a Bantu (q.v.) people living largely in the central highlands of Tanzania. They are closely related to the Iramba (q.v.) and number more than 50,000.

Ibeno

Ibeno is the name of an Ibibio (q.v.) language and the people who speak it. The Ibeno live in southeastern Nigeria.

Ibibio

The Ibibio of the Niger Delta are the largest ethnic group in southeastern Nigeria. There are more than 2 million Ibibio people. The Ibibio language, Efik-Ibibio, is a Kwa (q.v.) language that has six main dialects: Ibibio proper, Efik, Oron, Eket, Anang, and Ibeno. Efik is the most widely spoken dialect – it is used as far away as Cameroon – and it has been established as the literary language of the Ibibio.

Like that of their Igbo (q.v.) neighbors, Ibibio history is characterized by the marked avoidance of central-ized states. Instead, the Ibibio lived in a remarkably open and democratic societies based around dispersed villages with various means of regulating and controlling themselves, such as age sets, councils of elders, and men's and women's societies. Trade was of great importance to the Ibibio lands. Wild palm-oil trees grew in profusion in northern regions, and these were the basis of the region's economy in the nineteenth century after slave trading died out.

Ibolo

The Ibolo are a major Yoruba (q.v.) subgroup. They mostly live in the east of Oyo State, in the southwest of Nigeria, and Kwara State to the north of western Nigeria.

Ichilamba *see* Lamba

Idafan *see* Irigwe

Idoma

The Idoma number more than 400,000 people living in southeastern Nigeria. They are closely related to the Igala (q.v.).

Ibibio figure
A rare carving which represents an ancestor and conveys great authority and dignity

© DIAGRAM

Ife

The Ife are one of the main Yoruba (q.v.) subgroups. While the majority live in Nigeria's southwestern Oyo state, some have migrated to eastern Togo and western Benin.

Igala

With a population of probably more than one million, the Igala are one of Nigeria's larger ethnic groups. The majority of the Igala live in southeastern states such as Benue.

Igbo

Most Igbo live in the forested southeast of Nigeria, to the north of the mangrove forests of the Niger Delta. There up to thirty million Igbo divided into five main groups that differ to varying extents from each other in terms of customs, work, and religion.

History

The Igbo's origins are unknown, but it is believed that they have lived in their present location since at least the ninth century, when the Igbo Ukwu Culture flourished in the southeastern region of modern Nigeria.

In the mid-fifteenth century, Portuguese traders became the first Europeans to visit the region, and in the seventeenth, eighteenth, and nineteenth centuries, tens of thousands of Igbo were captured or bought by Dutch and British traders and sent to the Caribbean and Brazil, where they were sold as slaves. Although the slave trade was made illegal in 1807 by the British, it continued profitably for another fifty years. As the nineteenth century progressed, British traders turned their attention to exploiting the region's raw materials, in particular palm oil, timber, and ivory, relying on local intermediaries to deliver goods to them at the coast. Control of Igbo territory was difficult due to village self-rule, the fact that every grown man had a say in local affairs, and an absence of regional chiefs to make

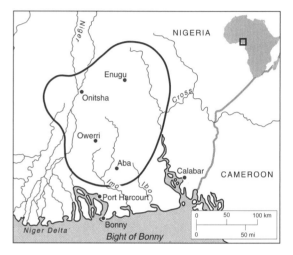

agreements with. Resistance to British rule was fierce, and attacks on traders and soldiers were common.

In 1900, Igbo territory became part of the British protectorate (colony) of Southern Nigeria which, in 1960, formed part of independent Nigeria. After independence, regional rivalries mounted, with Nigeria's political parties representing different ethnic groups. In 1966, an Igbo-led military coup was staged, and many Nigerians resented the large number of Igbo civil servants and army officers who were stationed across the country. In 1967, following riots and the slaughter of thousands of Igbo in the north and west of Nigeria, an independent Igbo state calling itself Biafra, with its capital at Enugu, was declared. The Nigerian government responded by sending the army to put down the rebels, who controlled the country's important oil

Biafran soldier

This Igbo man is a Biafran soldier. Many thousands of Igbo suffered injury and loss when Biafra tried to secede from Nigeria in 1967. The Biafran (Nigerian Civil) War ended unsuccessfully in 1970 after government troops harshly suppressed the rebellion.

Metalwork

Excavations at Igbo Ukwu discovered these ninth-century bronze items – a circular altar stand (below left) with male and female figures on opposite sides and open panels featuring snakes and spiders, and a shell-shaped container (below right), possibly a wine bowl. Metal tools were made for local use or to trade with people on the coast. The Igbo are renowned for their skills in bronze casting and forging, and for the beauty of their work.

Masks

Igbo masks often represent individual spirits such as those linked with aggression and ugliness (the elephant spirit) (below) or beauty and peacefulness (the maiden spirit) (above). Masks are of different sizes, with a community's elders wearing the larger ones to represent powerful spirits, and younger dancers wearing smaller masks for lesser spirits.

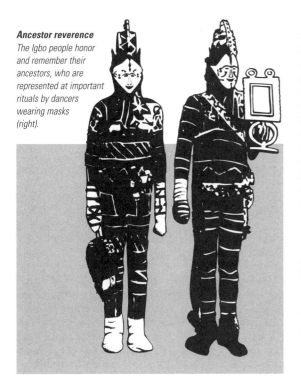

Ancestor reverence
*The Igbo people honor
and remember their
ancestors, who are
represented at important
rituals by dancers
wearing masks
(right).*

Altarpiece
*Pottery altarpieces, such as this
one representing a man with his
wives and attendants, were used
as part of worship for Ifijoku, the
giver and protector of yams. Yam
shrines are dedicated to the Earth
goddess Ala, and the Igbo's most
important festival, the Yam
Festival, is celebrated in her honor.
Yams – a form of sweet potato –
play a central role in the village
economy.*

encouraging individual distinction, rewarded by an increase in social standing. Except in the extreme north and west of Igbo territory where hereditary chiefs govern, rulers of communities owe their positions to age, wealth, and personal achievements.

MEN AND WOMEN Igbo women usually marry outside their villages and normally do not own land. Male children are allotted a portion of their father's land and inherit a share when he dies. This gives men economic and political power within their communities. However, the women run their own affairs by means of their own businesses and political organizations separate from the men's.

In 1929, Igbo women began demonstrating against the British colonial government. They were angry because the British were imposing a male dominated system of control on them, assuming that Igbo women held the same status as their European counterparts – dependent economically and politically on men. This meant that much of the women's state of economic and political independence was being eroded. The demonstrations became more violent as the British ignored their demands, rioting began, and finally open war broke out – the Women's War (1929–30). Since colonial times, the role of women in Igbo society has changed, but Igbo women are still recognized as being economically powerful and are often militant.

Culture and religion

RELIGION Protestant and Catholic missionaries first entered Igbo territory in the mid-nineteenth century, building churches and establishing schools. Many Igbo have since converted to Christianity, but the Igbo religion is still flourishing. It is based on reverence for Ala, generally the Earth goddess, and a number of lesser male and female deities. Some Igbo groups also acknowledge a supreme being, Chukwu the creator of the Universe.

ART The Igbo are especially noted for the diversity of their sculptures. These sculptures are made of many different materials, including bronze, ivory, stone, and wood. Styles vary greatly, a reflection of the Igbo tradition of village autonomy. A variety of elaborate wooden masks are produced and used during initiations, births, weddings, burial rituals, and other celebrations.

reserves. Food supplies ran short, resulting in starvation and Biafran surrender in 1970. The states that form Igbo territory are now incorporated into Nigeria's federal system of government.

Language

The Igbo groups all speak dialects of Igbo, a Kwa language.

Ways of life

FARMING The Igbo village economy is based on agriculture. Due to the density of population, land is fully used. The soil is not very fertile and only a small range of crops are cultivated, including yams and cassava, plus corn and some vegetables and fruit. Igbo men are responsible for growing yams. Women have separate plots where they grow cassava and other crops. In addition to farming their own crops, Igbo women have always played other important economic roles. Women are responsible for the preparation of palm oil (used for cooking and frying), the Igbo's main export product. When the palm oil has been squeezed out of the thick, fibrous outer part of the palm fruit, it belongs to the men, but the kernels of the fruit remain the women's property. The kernels also contain an oil, but it cannot be extracted without heavy milling machinery. The women sell the kernels to oilseed dealers or commercial milling companies. Throughout Nigeria, Igbo women are also famous as traders. Women dominate the markets, a central part of Igbo life. Markets have the multiple roles of encouraging intense individual competition while providing unmarried women with experience of life outside their home villages and giving married women opportunities to socialize with friends.

Social structure

Historically, the Igbo lived in small village settlements, mainly without chiefs. Igbo society is notable for

Igbo timeline

c. 800s Igbo Ukwu Culture in existence	**1929–1930** Igbo Women's War against British colonial rule	military coups in Nigeria
1400–1500 Igbo dominated by historic Kingdom of Benin	**1950s** Discovery of petroleum desposits in Nigeria	**1974** Oil boom in Nigeria
1470 Portuguese reach Niger Delta	**1960** Nigeria wins independence	**1975** Capital of Nigeria transferred from Lagos to Abuja
1807 British abolish the slave trade. Igbo involved in palm oil trade	**1966** Igbo-led military coup staged	**1993** In Nigeria, transition from military rule to democratic rule ends when General Sanni Abacha declares himself ruler
1897 British conquer Igbo	**1967–1970** Igbo attempt to secede from Nigeria; Biafran (Nigerian Civil) War follows	
1900 Igbo lands incorporated into British protectorate (colony) of Southern Nigeria	**1970s–1980s** Series of failed civilian and	**1999** Nigeria returns to civilian rule

Ijebu

The Ijebu are one of the many Yoruba (q.v.) subgroups. They make up a large proportion of Ogun State's population. Ogun State is in the southwest of Nigeria.

Ikikuria *see* Kuria

Ila

The Ila population numbers more than 70,000, and they are often considered a Bantu (q.v.) group. They live primarily in the valley of the Kafue River in southern Zambia.

Ilois of Diego Garcia

Several hundred miles south of the Maldives and east of the Seychelles are found the remote Indian Ocean islands that make up the UK-controlled Chagos Archipelago. One of these islands, Diego Garcia, is now the main US military base in the Indian Ocean. Previously, it was inhabited by the Ilois people, or Diego Garcians.

The Ilois emerged from a mixture of Polynesian, African, and Indian ancestors. Several hundred years ago, the first settlers, who were Malayo-Polynesian migrants, reached the islands by boat; after 1815 African and Indian laborers were brought to the island by the British, who colonized Diego Garcia. These diverse incoming groups developed a distinctive culture and Creole language of their own.

In the 1960s, Britain leased the island to the United States for at least the next 50 years. The Ilois were removed, mostly without consent, from the island to make way for the US defense base. Some Ilois visiting Mauritius were simply not allowed to return home, others were forced off the island after crops were destroyed and food imports cut. Finally, in 1971, the remainder were deported, at first to smaller islands and finally to Mauritius, where today the Ilois number only a few thousand. The UK authorities finally agreed to the Ilois demands for increased compensation in 1982, but payment was delayed, and many Ilois suffered great hardships. (The US has never compensated them for the loss of Diego Garcia.) The Ilois still suffer from high rates of unemployment and poverty.

Imazighen

The Imazighen are a Berber (q.v.) people. They live in central and southeast Morocco. Imazighen can also be used to refer to the Berbers as a whole.

Indian South Africans

There are around one million Indian South Africans, roughly three percent of South Africa's population. Eighty percent of these live in the province of KwaZulu/Natal (especially in and around Durban) with the remainder concentrated in the Johannesburg-Pretoria area. Indian South Africans are completely integrated into national life, unlike in East Africa where Asians' allegiances have often been viewed with suspicion.

History

Indian laborers first came South Africa in 1860 to work on British Natal's sugar plantations, and by 1911, when recruitment was suspended, 152,000 Indians had arrived. Indians were also contracted to work on the railroads, in mines, and on tea plantations, often enduring slavelike conditions. Contracts were for five years, followed by an additional two years. After a further five years as a "free" worker, laborers were given the choice of a free passage to India or of remaining in South Africa with a small land grant. Most of the immigrants were men, but one-third were women – to the objection of many white settlers who argued that the pres-

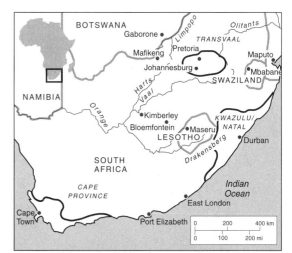

Mohandas Karamchand Gandhi

An Indian lawyer, Gandhi came to South Africa at the end of the nineteenth century and stayed until 1914. By using peaceful means of resistance – such as boycotts and civil disobedience – Gandhi highlighted the often ridiculous and illogical nature of racial laws. His tactics were adopted by many later civil rights movements. Gandhi returned to India in 1914 and led that country's campaign for independence.

Sikh soldier
This late nineteenth-century Sikh soldier was a member of the British colonial armies. His uniform of black, yellow, and white was intended to express racial harmony – though by this time racist polices were in effect in many parts of white-ruled Southern Africa.

ence of women would encourage the creation of a stable Indian community.

Most Indians arrived in South Africa on contracts, but about ten percent went there at their own expense, most of them traders from Gujarat in western India. These often-wealthy immigrants – known as "Passengers" – formed an elite group that campaigned vigorously for political and civil rights, but their economic strength often undermined the few advances ex-indentured (contracted) laborers were making.

In 1893, a young Indian lawyer, Mohandas Karamchand Gandhi, arrived in South Africa to work in Transvaal. It was in South Africa that Gandhi – the future leader of the Indian independence movement – developed and first practiced his philosophy of nonviolent resistance and civil disobedience. Within a few years, Gandhi was regarded as an important leader of Indian South Africans, though he essentially represented the interests of "Passengers."

In 1946, just as Indians were gaining political and economic strength in South Africa, the Asiatic Land Tenure Act was introduced, restricting where they could live and trade. The 1948 electoral victory of the Afrikaner-dominated National Party led to even more restrictions on Indians. Indians – whether born in South Africa or not – were officially regarded as immigrants, "repatriation" was official policy, and Indians' limited parliamentary representation ceased. The following year, rioting by Zulus directed at Indian businesses resulted in 142 deaths, but led to an agreement between Indian and other civil rights movements – the African National Congress and the Transvaal and Natal Indian congresses – to coordi-

nate their resistance to apartheid (the racist doctrine of "separate development").

RECENT EVENTS In 1961, the South African government officially accepted Indians as a permanent part of the country's population. In 1983, in an attempt to divide apartheid's opponents, a new constitution was introduced giving "Colored" people and Indians limited parliamentary representation. In the following year's elections, however, only eighteen percent of Indians voted and the 1989 elections were also boycotted. The abolition of apartheid laws in 1991 led to all adult South Africans being given the right to vote, regardless of race. In 1994, South Africa celebrated its first nonracial elections.

Language

Two-thirds of Indian immigrants to South Africa came from the Tamil- and Telugu-speaking areas of south and east India, while the remainder spoke Hindi, Gujarati, or Urdu. Today, English is the main language of Indian South Africans, though many also speak an Indian language, Zulu, or Afrikaans.

Ways of Life

By the end of the nineteenth century, Indians in South Africa were no longer mainly laborers. Indians had become virtually the sole producers of fruit and vegetables for Natal's rapidly expanding cities; they were also important as artisans and retailers, and many were employed as domestic servants.

Today, less than four percent of Indians are involved in agriculture, mostly as owners of small or medium-sized sugar or market-garden farms. The overwhelming majority of Indian South Africans live in urban areas where they work as artisans, in low-level clerical occupations, in manufacturing industries, or they run their own small businesses. From the late nineteenth century, Indians have been represented in professions such as law, medicine, and education.

EDUCATION Under apartheid, entry to virtually all educational facilities was determined by "race," with separate schools and universities for each officially-designated race. Educational facilities for Indians were not as poor as those for black South Africans, but they were vastly inferior to those enjoyed by whites. In the early 1980s,

Soofie Mosque
This beautiful mosque (Muslim place of worship) is a fine example of Islamic architecture in Southern Africa.

© DIAGRAM

it was estimated that only eight percent of Indian South Africans had completed high school, though the situation is gradually improving. Consequently, there is a considerable gap between educated rich and uneducated poor Indian South Africans. Limited educational opportunities under apartheid and the reservation of many middle-class occupations for whites has meant that an Indian middle class has been slow to develop.

Social structure

Hindu immigrants brought to South Africa the caste system: a strict hierarchy into which a person is born at a certain level that governs marriage, employment, and social status. The vast majority of the indentured laborers were of low caste, however, and very quickly the caste system proved unsustainable in South Africa. Traditional Indian South African family life was based on an extended family system similar to that existing in India. Arranged marriages were the norm and, on marriage, the bride would join the family of her husband and she would come under the authority of her mother-in-law, the female head of household. Since the 1950s, traditional Indian family life has gradually been eroded, social separation of the sexes has largely ceased, and arranged marriages are no longer the norm – social and family life now resemble those of other urban South Africans of similar economic backgrounds.

Culture and religion

RELIGION The majority of Indian South Africans are Hindu, while a minority are Muslim or Christian.

CLOTHING For men, Western styles of dress have become the norm. Young women rarely wear the sari except, perhaps, on formal occasions, though many older women continue to wear them on a day-to-day basis.

Indian South Africans timeline			
1652 Dutch garrison established on the Cape of Good Hope	**1910** Boers and British form white-ruled Union of South Africa	**1949** Rioting South Africans attack Indian businesses	**1983** Separate House of Representation established for Indian voters
1806 British annex Cape Colony	**1911** Recruitment of indentured laborers suspended	**1950** Population Registration Act restricts people to certain jobs and areas according to their officially-designated "race"	**1984–1989** Many people refuse to vote in elections for new house
1843 British annex Natal (present-day KwaZulu/Natal)	**1914** Gandhi leaves South Africa		**1991** End of all apartheid legislation
1860 First indentured (contract) laborers arrive from south Asia	**1934** South Africa approves independence from Britain	**1952** Indian and other antiapartheid movements organize the nonviolent Defiance Campaign	**1994** First nonracial elections held
1893 Mohandas K. Gandhi arrives in South Africa from India	**1946** Asiatic Land Tenure Act	**1961** South Africa accepts Indians as legitimate citizens	**1996** New constitution adopted
	1948 *Apartheid* officially introduced		**1999** Second multiracial elections result in massive victory for the ANC

Indians see Asians of Africa, East African Asians, and Indian South Africans

Iqbailiyen

The Iqbailiyen are a Berber (q.v.) people. They live in Algeria.

Iramba

The Iramba (or Nilamba) are a prominent Bantu (q.v.) people of central and northwestern Tanzania. There are probably more than 450,000 Iramba.

Iraqw

Also known as the Mbulu (or Wambulu), the Iraqw live in northern Tanzania largely in the Mbulu district south of Arusha. The Mbulu district is centered around the town of Mbulu and located on the plateau between lakes Manyara and Eyasi. There are probably more than 350,000 Iraqw people, and they are the largest ethnic group in the Arusha region. The Iraqw language, which is also called Iraqw, is usually classified as Cushitic (q.v.), but this has been disputed.

Beginning in the late nineteenth century, the Iraqw probably expanded outward from their mountainous homeland at the center of the Mbulu plateau. Cattle epidemics and colonial rule had weakened their neighbors, the Maasai (q.v.), allowing the Iraqw to colonize more land. The arts and material culture of the Iraqw have been largely ignored by outsiders even though Iraqw women produce some of the most elaborately decorated items of clothing in East Africa.

Irifiyen

The Irifiyen are a Berber (q.v.) people. They live in northeast Morocco.

Irigwe

The Irigwe are also known as the Idafan, Kwoll, or Miango. Numbering around 40,000, they live in central Nigeria in the Plateau State southeast of Jos, the state capital.

Isala see Sasala

Issa

The Issa are a Somali (q.v.) people who can be found throughout the Horn of Africa in Ethiopia, Djibouti, Eritrea, and Somalia. Numbering around 300,000 in Djibouti and making up at least half of the total population of that country, the Issa are Djibouti's largest ethnic group. The Afar (q.v.) make up the largest portion of the rest of Djibouti's population. Most Issa live in the southern third of Djibouti. There are roughly 250,000 Issa in neighboring regions of northern Ethiopia, including the region of Harer. More than 50,000 Issa live in northern Somalia. Several thousand also live in Eritrea. Since the development of the port of Djibouti in the early 1900s, the Djibouti Issa have been joined by immigrant Issa from Somalia.

Historically the Issa and Afar communities were not particularly divided. From the nineteenth century, however, competing European interests in the region created tensions between the two groups. The French established the French Somaliland colony in the region, and they tended to favor the minority Afar community. In 1967, the colony was renamed the French Territory of the Afars and Issas, some say to emphasize the division. Since independence in 1977, there have been clashes between the Issa, who have dominated the government, and the Afar.

Issaq

The Issaq are one of the main clan-based subgroups of the Somali (q.v.) people. The majority live in northern Somalia and a few live across the border in Ethiopia. There are around 700,000 Issaq.

Italian

Several thousand people of Italian descent live in Africa, primarily in regions that were once Italian colonies. Libya has a substantial Italian community as does the Horn of Africa (Ethiopia, Somalia, and Eritrea).

Iteso

The Iteso people of northern and eastern Uganda and western Kenya are often grouped together with the Karamojong (q.v.), forming the so-called Karamojong-Teso cluster of related peoples. There are something like one million Iteso people, the majority of whom are living in Uganda. The Iteso are a Nilotic (q.v.) people – their language, Teso, belongs to the eastern branch of the Nilotic group of languages.

The Karamojong-Teso people are Plains Nilotes, who emerged as a powerful force in East Africa sometime after 1000 CE and who also include the Maasai (q.v.). During the second millennium BCE the Plains Nilotes began dispersing from the region around Lake Turkana (northeastern Kenya). The Karamojong-Teso moved west toward Mount Elgon (on the present-day Kenya–Uganda border), from where they have since dispersed farther. The Iteso were settled in their present lands by the first half of the 19th century. Like other Nilotes, the Iteso have a history of pastoralism (cattle raising), but they gradually became settled farmers after reaching the fertile lands around Mount Elgon.

Itu

The Itu are one of the nine main subgroups of the Oromo. They live in Ethiopia.

Jaaliyin

The Jaaliyin are an Arab (q.v.) people of southern Sudan who claim direct descent from Prophet Muhammad. There are more than 1.5 million Jaaliyin Arabs in Sudan. Some scholars think that they are Nubians (q.v.) who adopted the Arabic culture and language.

Jabarti

The Jabarti (or Djeberti) number more than 200,000 and speak Tigrinya, the language of the Tigre (q.v.) people. They are a largely Muslim people living in the city of Amhara, Ethiopia, as well as in Eritrea.

Jack-Jacks *see* Alladian

Jahanka

The Jahanka (or Jahanke or Diakkane) number about 50,000 descendants of Soninke (q.v.) ancestors. Most speak Mandinka, however, and not Azer, the Soninke language. The Jahanka live primarily in Senegal and Gambia but also Guinea.

Jahanke *see* Jahanka

Jalof *see* Wolof

Jews of Africa

Judaism, the Jewish religion, originated in the so-called Fertile Crescent at the eastern end of the Mediterranean Sea in the region of present-day Palestine and Israel. Between the sixth and the third centuries BCE, many Jews emigrated from Palestine to Egypt and the region of modern Libya. At that time most Jews were rural farmers, but gradually over the centuries they became increasingly urbanized, with many becoming traders and skilled craft workers. In the late fifteenth century, Jews were being expelled from Spain for refusing to convert to Catholicism, and many settled in North Africa.

The Jewish communities in North Africa, which once numbered more than 500,000, have now declined to only a few thousand. Since 1948 many have left for Israel, and the rise of Arab (q.v.) nationalism has at times made life difficult for Jews who remain in North Africa.

Significant Jewish populations remain in South Africa, however, where they have lived since the earliest days of white settlement. Most came from Britain, Russia, and Germany. Today there are more than 100,000 Jews in South Africa.

The Falasha (q.v.) of Ethiopia, who have now largely emigrated to Israel, were perhaps Africa's most famous Jewish community.

Jibana

The Jibana are one of the nine closely related groups that make up the Mijikenda (q.v.). The Mijikenda mostly inhabit coastal regions of Kenya.

Jie

Like the Dodoth (q.v.), the Jie are part of the Karamojong (q.v.) cluster of peoples. They live in a region of northeastern Uganda that borders Kenya and Sudan and number more than 40,000 people.

Jju *see* Kaje

Jokwe *see* Chokwe

Jula *see* Dyula

Kaana Masala *see* Masalit

Kaba

The Kaba are a subgroup of the Sara. They live in southern Chad.

Kabre

With a population of more than 400,000, the Kabre are a large ethnic group of northern and central Togo.

Kache *see* Kaje

Kagulu *see* Kaguru

Kaguru

The Kaguru (or Kagulu or Sagala) one of the groups that make up the Zaramo (q.v.). They are a Bantu (q.v.) people who number more than 200,000, mostly living in the mountainous coastlands of Tanzania.

Kaje

The Kaje (Jju, Kache, or Baju) are a group of about 300,000 people living primarily in north-central Nigeria. They speak a Benue-Congo language.

Kakwa

The Kakwa (or Kwakwak) are a people of Nilotic (q.v.) origin living mainly in western Uganda (more than 80,000), southern Sudan (about 40,000), and roughly a further 20,000 live in northeastern Congo (Dem. Rep.). Idi Amin Dada was a Kakwa.

Kalanga

The Kalanga are one of the more major Shona (q.v.) subgroups. They live in western Zimbabwe, northeastern Botswana, and Mozambique.

Kaguru pole
Figurative poles and other male symbols were frequently carved with female imagery to create a ritually powerful union of male and female life principles.

Kalenjin

The Kalenjin are made up of several related groups: the Kipsigis (q.v..) the Nandi (q.v.), the Keiyo, the Tugen, the Pokot, the Marakwet, the Endo, the Sabaot, the Terik, and the Okiek. There are more than 2 million Kalenjin people, the vast majority of whom live in western Kenya, and they are that country's fifth largest ethnic group. The Kipsigis are the largest subgroup of the Kalenjin, and the Nandi are the second largest subgroup.

The Kalenjin language is an Eastern Sudanic language and various dialects exist. The most closely-related language to Kalenjin is Maa, the Maasai (q.v.) language.

The ancestors of the Kalenjin were Highland Nilotes (q.v.), who began dispersing from their original cradle-land at the northernmost tip of Lake Turkana in present-day Ethiopia to East Africa during the last millennium BCE. While many of the Highland Nilotes were absorbed by the Bantu (q.v.) societies they encountered, the Kalenjin were the largest of the groups that remained culturally distinct.

Kamadja

The Kamadja are a subgroup of the Daza (q.v.) of Chad. The Kamadja have been linked historically to the Tebu (q.v.), who enslaved many Kamadja. Even today, the Kamadja are often in a semi-servile relationship with the Tebu.

Kambari

The Kambari (or Kamberi) live largely in western Nigeria. They speak a Benue-Congo language and number around one million.

Kambe

The Kambe are one of the nine closely related groups that make up the Mijikenda (q.v). The Mijikenda mostly inhabit coastal regions of Kenya.

Kamberi *see* Kambari

Kami

The Kami are part of the Zaramo (q.v.) cluster of peoples. They are a Bantu (q.v.) people living in the coastal lowlands of Tanzania.

Kana *see* Ogoni

Kanembu

The Kanembu are the descendants of the citizens and founders of the powerful medieval empire of Kanem-Bornu. They can be found in northern Niger and Nigeria as well as on the northern side of Lake Chad in Chad. There are more than 300,000 Kanembu.

Kankyira *see* Denkyira

Kanuri

Also known as the Beri-beri, Borno, or Yerwa, the Kanuri are the dominant ethnic group in Borno Province, northeastern Nigeria. There are well over three million Kanuri in Nigeria and several thousand in bordering regions of Chad, Niger, and Cameroon. The Kanuri language, also called Kanuri, is most widely spoken Central Saharan language.

The Kanuri emerged as a distinct group during the history of the great West African empire of Kanem-Borno. By the 1200s the Kanuri had emerged as a single ethnic group speaking a distinct language out of the various nomadic groups that comprised early Kanem. By that time most Kanuri were also Muslim. In what is probably an oversimplification of the truth, the Kanuri are supposed to be descended from the ruling Sefawa dynasty, while the people they ruled over were the ancestors of the Kanembu (q.v.). The Sefawa claimed descent from a semi-legendary Yemeni leader.

Kanuri girl
This young woman is a member of the largest ethnic group in northeastern Nigeria, whose language had emerged as distinct as early as the thirteenth century.

Kaonde

The Kaonde (Bakahonde, Kawonde, Kaundi, or Kunda) number more than 250,000 living mostly in northwestern Zambia but also in northeastern Congo (Dem. Rep.). They originally came from the Katanga area of Congo (Dem. Rep.) and are related to the Luba (q.v.). They are often also considered, however, to be a subgroup of the Kongo (q.v.).

Kaplelach

The Omotik are a subgroup of the Okiek (q.v.) of west-central Kenya. The Okiek are, in turn, part of the Kalenjin (q.v.). The Kaplelach live on the southern slopes of the Mau Escarpment in western Kenya.

Karamojong

Karamojong is the collective name given to several closely related ethnic groups who live in Karamoja, a semiarid plateau in northeast Uganda on the border with Kenya. The Turkana, who live across the border in Kenya, are sometimes considered one of the Karamojong. The other groups are the Dodoth, Jie, Bokora, Matheniko, and Pian. The Karamojong total a few hundred thousand: the exact number is not known.

History

The Karamojong moved into Karamoja hundreds of years ago. The groups are all Nilotic in origin – some of their ancestors originally came from the Nile River region in present-day southern Sudan. The Karamojong have suffered from a number of severe droughts (periods of inadequate rainfall) and famines since the early 1700s. In the late nineteenth century, drought was accompanied by epidemics, both cattle and human, that devastated the herds and led to the present widespread dispersal of the Karamojong people. Until fairly recently, the Karamojong were isolated and were thus able to maintain their own ways of life, including the cattle rustling that was a major occupation. Raids by one Karamojong group to steal the cattle of another were carried out by warriors armed with spears, who followed various rules of engagement when fighting with another group – in order to limit unnecessary damage and prevent undue conflict. But the British, who administered Karamojong territory earlier this cen-

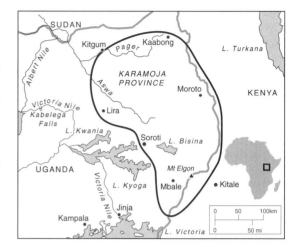

Stool
This low wooden stool was crafted by a Karamojong artisan and was probably intended to be used by a man.

tury, tried to ban the ownership and use of spears. At one time, the administration decided to provide steel plows to encourage the Karamojong to adopt farming and settle in one place – therefore making them easier to control, govern, and tax. The Karamojong accepted them gratefully, but blacksmiths reworked many of the plowshares into new spear blades. This is an example of British attempts to "modernize" (though actually to control) the Karamojong.

RECENT EVENTS Since independence in the 1960s, attempts at control disguised as "modernization" have continued, sometimes by force, and they were especially harsh during the reign of the brutal dictator Idi Amin Dada (q.v., 1971–9), during which 30,000 Karamojong were executed allegedly "for being too primitive." When Amin's troops fled the country in 1979, the Karamojong armed themselves from the abandoned army barracks. The abundance of guns, mostly automatic rifles, disrupted life in Karamoja province in the 1980s, greatly increasing the crime rate. A group of Karamojong elders took matters into their own hands and attempted to curb the rising lawlessness, at first rather brutally. In 1995, government officials, Karamojong elders, and other concerned parties attended a "Peace Forum" to resolve the problem. It was decided to register all weapons in Karamoja and

Karamojong village
This plan shows the composition of a typical Karamojong village.

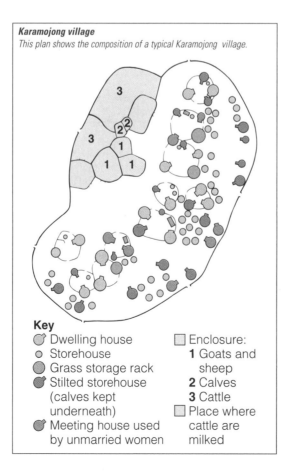

Key
- 🔵 Dwelling house
- • Storehouse
- 🔘 Grass storage rack
- 🔵 Stilted storehouse (calves kept underneath)
- 🔵 Meeting house used by unmarried women

- ⬜ Enclosure:
- **1** Goats and sheep
- **2** Calves
- **3** Cattle
- ⬜ Place where cattle are milked

Women builders
Karamojong women build their own homes. They weave together poles and straw to make a framework, then plaster the walls with mud. Then, they cover each structure with a stepped roof of thatch.

Hairdo extraordinary

Karamojong warriors used to spend a lot of time on elaborate hairstyles, created by a skilled barber. Young warriors had their hair bonded with grease and made into a huge bunlike pile on the back of the head. Older warriors who had passed an initiation ceremony had a more elaborate bun reinforced with colored clay and painted. These styles took many days to complete.

turn the armed men into government-paid, local police forces responsible for policing their own communities under guidance from the elders.

Language

The Karamojong language is a Nilotic language.

Ways of life

PASTORALISM Most Karamojong are cattle-herding pastoralists, who also keep sheep and goats. They also grow crops, which include millet, corn, groundnuts (peanuts), gourds, and marrows. Rainfall is unpredictable, and the crops frequently fail. During the wet season, from late March to September, water is plentiful. During the dry season, from October to early March, water is scarce in the east, and the men must move the cattle to stock camps in the west, near permanent water sources.

DIVISION OF LABOR Among the Karamojong ways of life differ greatly between the sexes. Men between the ages of fifteen and thirty spend most of their time with the herds. They move with the cattle from one grazing ground to another. In the dry season, they may be many miles from home, living in makeshift homes if any.

Karamojong women spend most of their time in or near the stockade. They are expected to do all the hard work around the homestead, including collecting firewood, fetching water, and growing and tending the crops. Day begins with milking the cows and goats. The women shake the milk in gourds until it separates into curds and whey. They mix the whey with grain to make porridge, or drink it as it is. Curds can be used as body lotion. Each woman has her own patch of ground near the settlement. The main crop is sorghum, next to which comes millet. These cereals not only provide grain – which the women grind laboriously

between two stones – but are also fermented to make beer. Each woman builds her own home, plus one used as a kitchen, another for her children, and several on stilts that serve as storehouses.

Social structure

Within Karamojong society there are several systems of classification, most based on different celebrations. One system is the hereditary clan (several extended families related by a common ancestor or ancestors) each of which has its own cattle brand. The Karamojong are also organized by geography into ngitela, areas occupied by people who celebrate social and religious events together. Another is the system of ngikenoi, which means "fireplaces with three stones." These are subsections of Karamojong society whose members gather for certain ceremonies. Festivities related to the seasons and the harvest are celebrated by members of an ekitela. The most common of these festivities is known as an aperit, which means "where people sleep." It is literally a sleep over by elders who gather at a place to eat, drink, and share a pipe.

AGE-SETS Age-sets, groups of men of the same generation, are important elements of Karamojong society. Once they have passed through the male initiation ceremony called the asapan (any time between the ages of eighteen and forty), a man can participate in the assemblies by which many decisions are made. Authority rests with the elders of a group, who make up the most senior age-set.

Women also go through an initiation, called an akiwor ("giving a name for the first time"). This bestows a certain measure of respect on a woman.

MARRIAGE It is usual for Karamojong couples to have long engagements: five years is not uncommon. The reason is the high bridewealth a groom has to pay to the bride's family, which may be as much as fifty heads of cattle and fifty goats. This is not considered to be a payment for his wife, but a token of respect to the family or compensation for the loss of a working member.

Headrest

A headrest was essential for a man to maintain his elaborate hairstyle while sleeping. There are various designs for the headrests; some have two legs, others three.

Water carriers

These young girls are fetching water in large clay pots carried on their heads. This is a daily chore for women and children. They are wearing old-fashioned clothes made from animal skins rather than cloth, which is more often worn nowadays.

Culture and religion

Religion The Karamojong worship one all-powerful god, who they call Akuj. They pray to Akuj regularly, with senior members of the settlement acting as priests. CATTLE The Karamojong regard their cattle as wealth and as objects to be respected. Each boy has an ox named for him, and his attachment to it continues into adulthood. A man takes great care of his name-ox, and may even be heard singing to it. If he should die, the ox is slaughtered. If the ox dies, the name-sharer is distraught.

Karamojong timeline			
1000s–1500s Karamojong ancestors migrate toward Mount Elgon	disperses the people **1900** British-ruled Uganda Protectorate established	**1970** Karamojong refuse to join Ugandan army	**1980s** Armed cattle rustlers disrupt life in Karamojong province
1600s Teso group breaks away	**1916** British control Karamoja region	**1971** Col. Idi Amin Dada seizes power in military coup; during his rule, 30,000 Karamojong are executed "for being too primitive"	**1981–1986** Ugandan civil war; rebels led by Yoweri Museveni win power and install military government
1700s Karamojong settle north of Mount Elgon	**1962** Uganda wins independence; Milton Obote is prime minister		**1994** Nonparty elections held as first step to restoring democracy
1706–1733 Period of *drought* and famine known as the "Nyamdere"	**1966** Political coup against his opponents led by Obote, who becomes president	**1979** Tanzanian forces and Ugandan rebels oust Amin; Karamojong arm themselves from barracks of routed Amin troops	**1995** Karamojong leaders hold "Peace Forum" with officials to resolve arms crisis
1894 An epidemic of cattle diseases decimates Karamojong herds and		**1980** Obote elected president	

Katab

The Katab number more than 30,000 people living in the southern region of Kaduna State in north-central Nigeria. They speak a Benue-Congo language.

Kauma

The Kauma are one of the nine closely related groups that make up the Mijikenda (q.v.). The Mijikenda mostly inhabit coastal regions of Kenya.

Kaundi *see* Kaonde

Kawonde *see* Kaonde

Keiyo

The Keiyo are one of the several related groups that make up the Kalenjin (q.v.). The Kalenjin are a large ethnic group in western Kenya.

Kel Tagelmust *see* Tuareg

Kel Tamacheq *see* Tuareg

Kgafela-Kgatla

The Kgatla (q.v.) are a subgroup of the Tswana (q.v.) people of southern Africa, in particular Botswana and South Africa. The Kgafela-Kgatla are a branch of the Kgatla.

Kgalagadi

The Kgalagadi (or Bakgalagadi) are a large cluster of related peoples in eastern Botswana. Although they speak a Sotho-Tswana (q.v.) language, they are not thought to be a subgroup of the Tswana (q.v.) people.

Kgatla

The Kgatla are one of the major subgroups of the Tswana (q.v.) of Botswana and South Africa. The Kgatla were originally a lineage that controlled the northeast of the central region of Transvaal in South Africa. They were the origin of several powerful offshoots such as the Pedi (q.v.) and Kgafela-Kgatla (q.v.).

Khana *see* Ogoni

Khasonka

The Khasonka are a Manding (q.v.) speaking people. They live along the upper Senegal River in western Mali and number more than 100,000.

Khoikhoi

Khoikhoi is now largely a historical ethnic grouping, its members having been absorbed into the larger Khoisan (q.v.) grouping of eastern Namibia, western and central Botswana, and bordering parts of South Africa. Descendants of Khoikhoi and European parents also helped form the present-day Cape Colored (q.v.) population of South Africa.

Along with the San (q.v.) peoples, the Khoikhoi were the first known inhabitants of Southern Africa. The Khoisan are not Black Africans, but make up a unique "racial" category of their own. The Khoikhoi were San peoples who adopted pastoralism (livestock herding) in favor of a hunter-gathering lifestyle. They first emerged in the dry grasslands of the northern Kalahari desert in what is now Botswana, from where they spread to what are now Namibia and the Cape of South Africa. Over many hundreds of years, these people retreated or were absorbed as other ethnic groups (such as the Bantu, q.v.) migrated into the area and few direct descendants remain. The Khoikhoi were once known as the Hottentots by Dutch settlers – they introduced this disparaging name, which means "the stutterers," after hearing the Khoikhoi speak using clicks and popping sounds as part of their language.

Khoisan

The name "Khoisan" is a linguistic term for the closely-related Khoikhoi and San peoples. The Khoikhoi (now largely a historical grouping) and the San are also known, sometimes disparagingly, as the Hottentots and the Bushmen respectively. In fact, many of the names used to refer to the various Khoisan groups, including "San," are considered insulting by the Khoisan themselves as they are often derogatory labels given them by other peoples. There are less than 100,000 Khoisan: about 50,000 in Botswana (where they are called Basarwa); 33,000 in Namibia; 8,000 in Angola; 4,500 in South Africa; and 2,000 in Zambia and Zimbabwe.

History

Descendants of the first known inhabitants of Southern Africa, the Khoisan probably originated in what is now western Zimbabwe and northern Botswana, where they lived in widely-scattered bands at least 20,000 years ago. Around 2,300 years ago, some Khoisan hunter-gatherers (people who live on food that can be hunted or collected from the wild instead of growing crops or raising livestock) in northern Botswana began to keep livestock. Over the course of generations, these people migrated south, reaching the Cape 2,000 years ago and gradually developing into the pastoralist (livestock-raising) Khoikhoi people. The Khoikhoi first encountered Europeans in the late fifteenth century, when Portuguese mariners visited the Cape. During the course of the sixteenth century, they regularly traded cattle and sheep for iron goods and beads brought by the sailors. In the seventeenth century, Dutch settlers established farms at the Cape and began expanding onto Khoikhoi grazing lands. Without access to land for their livestock, many Khoikhoi became hunter-gatherers or settled on European-owned farms as laborers. The Dutch farmers (Boers) relied heavily on Khoikhoi labor and bound their workers tightly to them using law, coercion, and force. Although technically free, many Khoikhoi had no choice but to work on Boer farms. Now extinct as a separate ethnic group, descendants of Khoikhoi and Europeans helped form the present-day Cape Colored population.

The San faced similar pressures to those experienced by the Khoikhoi. Throughout Southern Africa they were gradually dispossessed of their hunting grounds – first by migrations of Bantu-speaking peoples into Southern Africa and later by European settlers. Small groups of Bantu-speakers began moving into Southern Africa in the early centuries of the first millennium. The San were either displaced by the more-numerous Bantu peoples and forced to retreat to isolated arid regions or were absorbed into the new societies. The Europeans were harsher and many San were killed on sight by the white settlers. By the nineteenth century, only small bands of San remained in South Africa, living in some of the most arid parts of the northwest Cape. Some San succeeded in fleeing to Botswana and Namibia where they joined long-established San communities, but there, too, they found themselves in competition for land with cattle-raising Tswana, Herero, and other peoples.

Ostrich eggshell flask
For thousands of years, ostrich eggshells have been made into flasks and used by the Khoisan to store water and sometimes food. The eggs can be carried or buried in the ground to provide water in the future. This example dates from the twentieth century and has been elaborately engraved. Today, engraved eggshells are produced for the tourist market throughout Southern Africa.

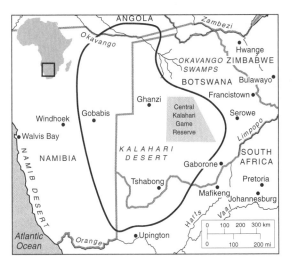

Khoisan woman
The weather-worn face of a Khoisan woman. She is wearing an intricately-beaded headband.

The Coldstream Stone
Painted two thousand years ago by a Khoisan artisan, this quartzite stone was excavated from Coldstream Cave on the southern Cape coast. It was found placed on the shoulder of a skeleton and is thought to have played a role in funerary rites

RECENT EVENTS Many Khoisan were recruited into the Portuguese colonial army in Mozambique and the South African Army in Namibia. After Namibia became independent from South Africa in 1990, however, around 4,000 Khoisan moved to South Africa.

In recent decades, the Botswana government and cattle herders have systematically driven the Khoisan from most of their territories in the Kalahari Desert. The establishment of the Central Kalahari Game Reserve in 1961 helped safeguard the land rights of some of the local Khoisan – the Khwe. Limited provision of facilities in the area, however, has offset the advantages. After surviving drought (inadequate rainfall) in the 1980s, the Khwe now face the threat of relocation. As part of plans to encourage tourism and conserve the environment, the Botswana government announced plans to induce the Khwe to leave the reserve in 1996. Although many are willing to relocate, others are not and they have formed various political groups to put pressure on the government to recognize their rights. The mass relocation has been averted while the government consults with the Khwe.

Language
Khoisan languages are distinguished by their use of various unique "click" or popping sounds made with the tongue on different parts of the mouth – many of which have been incorporated into other African languages.

Ways of life
Historically, the main difference between the Khoikhoi and the San was in their lifestyles – the Khoikhoi were chiefly pastoralists and the San purely hunter-gatherers. Both the Khoikhoi and the San lived a largely nomadic or seminomadic existence, the Khoikhoi herding fat-tailed sheep and long-horned cattle. Those who lived by the coast also gathered shellfish. The Khoisan were

Kung healer
This Khoisan man of the Kung group of northeastern Namibia is healing a pregnant Herero woman. Kung healing involves going into a trancelike state called kia, usually reached by performing a particular dance. This activates num (an energy originally from the gods), which is then used as a healing force. The Kung's reputation for healing is considerable and attracts many clients who nowadays have to pay for the service.

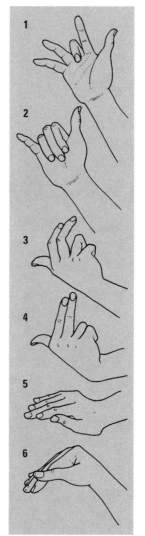

Khoisan rock art *(above)*
The Khoisan are famous for their ancient rock paintings, found in caves and on exposed rock surfaces. Many date from thousands of years ago. This painting is relatively recent (probably from within the last 1,500 years) as the larger people on the right are most likely Bantu-speakers, who did not appear in Southern Africa until the first millennium. It seems the Khoisan (center) have stolen cattle from the herders.

Sign language *(left)*
Hand signals enabled Khoisan hunters to communicate with one another silently while tracking animals.

Key
1 Giraffe
2 Bat-eared fox
3 Sable antelope
4 Eland
5 Tortoise
6 Ostrich

noted for their hunting skills and their tracking ability, a skill that was vital both for locating wildlife and for following animals wounded by poisoned arrows.

Today, dispossessed of their land, few Khoisan are solely hunter-gatherers. Many keep livestock (mostly goats and occasionally cattle) and grow crops such as sorghum, corn, sugar cane, melons, and cowpeas. Many Khoisan still forage for wild nuts and plants – as do poor non-Khoisan people – and hunt for meat, particularly during the dry season, to supplement their diet. Giraffes, antelopes, reptiles, and birds provide most of the meat in the Khoisan diet. Although laws in Botswana have greatly restricted their right to hunt game, many take the risk rather than face hunger. Men are usually responsible for hunting the larger animals and women often do most of the foraging. Division of labor by gender varies from group to group though. In Namibia and Botswana, the Khoisan mainly work as farm laborers or domestic servants and live on the fringes of towns.

Social structure
Historically, the Khoisan lived in bands generally made up of between twenty-five and fifty people related to each other through blood or marriage. Bands had leaders rather than rulers and there was no overall system of government. Discussion and consensus were often the pattern of rule. Food and water were divided according to seniority and property was shared to avoid jealousy.

Most Khoisan now live in mixed settlements that many different ethnic groups call their home. In Botswana, many were forcibly relocated to state-created settlements to make way for cattle herding. Most Khoisan groups have hereditary leadership positions that can be held by a man or a woman. These leaders now have limited official authority but still have some social standing. Hereditary leaders are, however, often elected to state posts such as chairperson of the village development committee or are appointed by local councils to hear minor civil cases.

Culture and religion
RELIGION Khoisan religious beliefs and practices have many features in common between groups but variations exist. The worship of a great and good god (called Nadi in the central Kalahari) is common to many groups. Also, there is sometimes an evil being called Gaua or Gawama, whose mission is to disrupt the good god's work.

Khoisan timeline			
25,000 BCE Oldest examples of Khoisan rock art in Southern Africa	**1713** Foreign epidemic of smallpox devastates Khoikhoi	**1884–1885** British colonize Botswana as Bechuanaland	**1992** "The First People of the Kalahari" (Khwe Khoisan political movement) founded
c. 400s Some Khoisan begin to keep livestock: Khoikhoi emerge	**1774** Dutch begin systematic slaughter of Khoikhoi	**1910** Union of South Africa formed	**1999** A San clan who had been expelled from the Kalahari Gemsbok N.P. receives a grant of 155,000 acres in Northern Cape from the South African government
200s CE Displacement of Khoisan by Bantu-speaking peoples begins	**1799** Last major Khoikhoi revolt	**1963** Central Kalahari Game Reserve established in Botswana	
1652 Dutch settlement of the Cape of Good Hope begins	**1806** British take over Cape	**1966** Botswana independent	
1657–1677 Khoikhoi and Dutch farmers (Boers) fight over land; Khoikhoi pushed out of lands	**1836–1848** Boers on Great Trek with Khoikhoi servants	**1980s** *Droughts* throughout Kalahari	
	1884 Germany colonizes Namibia as South West Africa	**1990** Namibian independence; 4,000 Namibian Khoisan move to South Africa	

Khurutshe
The Khurutshe (or Bakhurutshe) are a subgroup of the Hurutshe (q.v.) of Botswana and South Africa. The Hurutshe are, in turn, a subgroup of the Tswana (q.v.).

Kibera *see* Amba

Kifuliiru *see* Furiiru

Kige *see* Beri

Kikuyu
The Kikuyu, sometimes called the Gikuyu, are the largest ethnic group in Kenya. They total more than 4.5 million and they form around twenty percent of the country's population. Their homeland is sometimes known as Kikuyuland, a highland plateau – part of the lush Great Rift Valley at the foot of Mount Kenya – furrowed by rivers flowing in deep gorges between high ridges. This area has a pleasant climate, with reliable rainfall and moderate temperatures.

History
The origins of the Kikuyu are obscure. Ethnologists believe they came to Kenya from the north and west

and began to settle in Kikuyuland in the 1500s. They were originally hunters and nomadic pastoralists (livestock raisers who migrated with their herds). Their expansion in Kenya continued until the 1800s. They were generally on good terms with their neighbors the Maasai, with whom they traded agricultural produce for hides and livestock.

COLONIALISM The Kikuyu's settled existence was radically disturbed by the European "scramble" for African colonies, which began in the 1880s. A private British company began to set up trading facilities on the coast. In 1895, the British government took over and set up the colony of British East Africa, later called Kenya. The

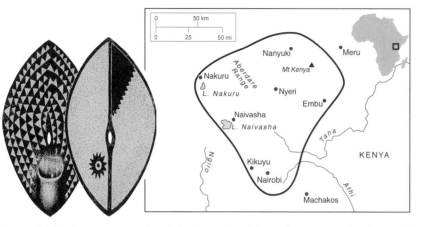

Ceremonial shields
Shields like these were used at initiation ceremonies for different periods in a male's age-set. They were used in dancing, but apparently not in warfare.

British built a railroad from the coast to the shores of Lake Victoria, set up a base at Nairobi, and began to settle in the heart of Kikuyuland. They took over land from the Kikuyu, who were confined to a small reserve, unable to farm on the inadequate land. Many Kikuyu were forced to leave the land and work for the European settlers, or in the factories that sprang up in Nairobi. British officials ruled the colony, and the Kikuyu became third-class citizens (Asians were the middle class). During World War I, many Kikuyu men worked as "carriers" for the British troops. In 1920, the Kikuyu Central Association was established, partly as a response to the discrimination experienced by Kikuyu veterans. In the 1940s, along with other ethnic groups, they began to organize opposition to the colonial power. Many Kikuyu men also served in World War II, fighting against the Germans, and again after the war they were bitter about their treatment. When progress toward independence seemed to be too slow, some Kikuyu organized a society, Mau Mau, which began to commit acts of anticolonial terrorism. Fighting between the Kikuyu and loyalist and British troops continued until 1956, during which 13,000 Africans – mostly Kikuyu – were killed.

INDEPENDENCE Independence was granted in 1963. In elections held that year, the Kenya African National Union (KANU) secured a majority in parliament. KANU was composed largely of Kikuyu and was led by Jomo Kenyatta (q.v.), the country's first president in 1964 – a position he held until his death in 1978. Other ethnic groups formed opposition parties, but the Kikuyu, who were among the best educated people in Kenya, held many of the top posts in government and the civil service. After Kenyatta's death and the succession of vice-president Daniel arap Moi (q.v.) as president, political activity was tightly restricted. Discontent with the one-

party government led by Moi was widespread among the Kikuyu. Moi considered the Kikuyu threatening to his position, and in the 1980s he tried to remove Kikuyu members of his cabinet.

Language
The Kikuyu speak a language also called Kikuyu (or Gikuyu). It is one of the Bantu group of languages, which itself is part of the Benue-Congo language group. Many Kikuyu also speak Swahili (or Kiswahili), which is used as a common language in East Africa and is the national language of Kenya. Many Kikuyu also speak English, the country's official language.

Ways of life
Many Kikuyu have moved away from Kikuyuland to other parts of the country, where they work in a variety of jobs. The Kikuyu have a reputation for having a strong business sense, and many have succeeded as traders and importers and in running industries.
FARMING Those Kikuyu living in rural areas tend to practice farming. Before the arrival of the British, the Kikuyu farmed land until the soil was exhausted, and then moved to a fresh patch. Land was plentiful, and the Kikuyu had no need of crop rotation. Today, they have adopted different farming methods, with most making their living from continuous crop farming. The main crops grown include beans, corn, millet, potatoes, sugarcane, sweet potatoes, and a variety of vegetables. Colonialism introduced the Kikuyu to cash crops such as bananas, coffee, and pyrethrum – used for making insecticides. The Kikuyu also keep bees, goats, and sheep, and a few cattle.

Social structure
SOCIAL STRUCTURE Kikuyu society had a highly organized social structure originally based on nine clans (groups of extended families that share a common ancestor or ancestors); although only remnants remain of this social organization, the emphasis on the family is maintained. In addition, each person belongs to an age-set, called a riika. Which riika a person belongs to depends on the time they first undergo circumcision; this applies to both boys and – more controversially and with more serious, long-lasting consequences – girls.

Mau Mau detention camp prisoners
Prisoners – alleged supporters of the Mau Mau rebellion – were kept in detention camps. Around 80,000 Kikuyu were imprisoned by British security forces in an attempt to crush the Mau Mau rebellion in the early 1950s. Jomo Kenyatta was one of those imprisoned; he served eight-and-a-half years in prison before being released after Kenya won independence in 1963.

Valley view
In the Great Rift Valley, the historic, round, thatched-roof huts of the Kikuyu have largely been replaced by square and rectangular homes with iron roofs.

Ceremonial attire
This Kikuyu man is wearing ceremonial dress. Although modern Western-style clothes are more common nowadays, on special occasions and events some still wear more traditional outfits.

Kikuyu religion is founded on a belief in one all-powerful god called Ngai. According to legend, the Kikuyu are descended from one of Ngai's three sons, Gikuyu, who chose to be a farmer. Gikuyu married a wife provided by Ngai, named Moombi, known as the creator. She bore him nine daughters, each of whom had a family that became a clan, taking their mother's name. This, says tradition, is the origin of the nine main clans of the Kikuyu.

Beads for beauty
A beaded headdress was a popular form of decoration among Kikuyu women before most adopted Western-style clothing.

POLITICAL STRUCTURE In the past, each village was ruled by a council of nine elders. These came from either one of the divisions found in each male age-set: maina or mwangi. The maina and mwangi sub-divisions operate as the political leaders for alternate periods of between twenty and forty years. Every group of nine villages elected a representative to a higher council for an area known as mbari, or sub-clan. Each mbari sent a representative to a district council. The Kikuyu's system of landholding was based on the mbari. The councils acted as courts of law when necessary. The more senior elders served as high priests in the Kikuyu religion.

Culture and religion

RELIGION As a result of missionary activities in the earlier part of the 1900s, many Kikuyu are Christians and they have established their own, independent, churches. A minority still adhere to the Kikuyu religion, perhaps in conjunction with Christianity. The

Kikuyu timeline		
1400s on Eastern Bantu-speakers migrate into region of present-day Kenya	**1952–1956** Terrorism by Mau Mau, a Kikuyu anticolonial society; 50,000 Kikuyu confined in detention camps	**1992** Moi reelected in democratic elections contested as fraudulent by opposition
1500s–1600s Kikuyu settle southeast of Mount Kenya	**1963** Kenya wins independence; Jomo Kenyatta becomes first prime minister and later president	**1993–1994** Kikuyu and Maasai clash in Great Rift Valley area. Many Kikuyu in Rift Valley lose land to Kalenjins; government accused of ethnic cleansing
1700s–1800s Period of expansion and migration	**1978** Kenyatta dies; Daniel arap Moi becomes president	
1895 British take control of Kenya	**1986** "Mwakenya Conspiracy"– mainly Kikuyu political opposition suppressed	**1999** Former Mau Mau guerrillas announce plans to sue the British government for human rights abuses in the 1950s
1920 Kikuyu Central Association (precursor to KANU) formed to fight oppression by British	**1991** Kenya allows for multiparty politics	
1934 British Commission extends Kikuyuland in Nairobi region as compensation for land taken earlier for settlers		

Mount Kenya
Mount Kenya, in the heart of the Kikuyu homeland, is 17,040 ft (5,198 m) high. It is thought to be the home of Ngai, god of the Kikuyu religion, and is called "Keré Nyaga," the "Mountain of Mystery" by the Kikuyu.

© DIAGRAM

Kilanga

The Kilanga are one of the many subgroups of the Bariba (q.v.). Numbering more than 250,000, the Kilanga live in Benin, Togo, and Ghana.

Kilega *see* Lega

Kimatumbi *see* Matumbi

Kipchornwonek

The Kipchornwonek are a subgroup of the Okiek (q.v.) of west-central Kenya. The Okiek are, in turn, part of the Kalenjin (q.v.). The Kipchornwonek live on the southern slopes of the Mau Escarpment in western Kenya.

Kipsigis

The Kipsigis are the largest subgroup of the Kalenjin (q.v.) peoples of Kenya. There are probably more than half a million Kipsigis, most of whom live in the western corner of Kenya, to the east of Lake Victoria, in a region centered around Kericho town. Kipsigis is a tonal Nilotic language, meaning that the pitch (or tone) of spoken words affects their meaning.

The ancestors of the Kipsigis were Highland Nilotes (q.v.), who began dispersing from their original cradle-land at the northernmost tip of Lake Turkana in present day Ethiopia to East Africa during the last millennium BCE. The Kipsigis did not emerge as a distinct ethnic group until sometime after 1000 CE, separating from the Nandi (q.v.) as late as c. 1600–1800. The Kipsigis religion involves belief in a distant sun god, but many are now Christians.

Kirdi

The name Kirdi has long been used to refer to the non-Fulani (q.v.), non-Christian peoples of southwestern Chad in particular and northern Cameroon and southeastern Nigeria as well, including, for example, the Fali (q.v.) of Cameroon. The largely Muslim Sara (q.v.) of southern Chad are, in particular, often referred to as the Kirdi.

Kisi *see* Kissi

Kisii *see* Gusii

Kissi

The Kissi (or Kisi, Gizi, or Kissien) are a largely Christian people of Guinea, where the majority live, Liberia, and Sierra Leone. The more than 500,000 Kissi live in the region where these three countries meet.

Kissien *see* Kissi

Kitutu

The Kitutu are one of the main subdivisions of the Gusii (q.v.). The Gusii are a large ethnic group of western Kenya.

Kola

The Kola are a subgroup of the Mbenga (q.v.). The Mbenga are one of the major groupings of tropical forest-foragers—the so-called pygmies (q.v.)—of Central Africa. There are roughly 20,000 Kola living in Cameroon.

Kololo

The Kololo were a southern African Bantu people who came to prominence in Central Africa under their leader Sebetwane.

The Kololo were a Sotho (q.v.) people who originally came from the west of the Drakensberg Mountains. The expansion of the Zulu (q.v.) kingdom in the early nineteenth century, however, led to a period of great disruption involving mass migrations and conflicts. Known as the Difaqane (to Sotho people) or Mfecane (to Nguni [q.v.] people), this unsettled era led to the Kololo abandoning their home in southern Africa and trekking north and then west into the lands of the Lozi (q.v.) people of present-day Zambia. Led by Sebetwane, the Kololo conquered the Lozi and ruled the Lozi kingdom from about 1840 to 1864. Sebetwane was visited by the missionary explorer Dr. David Livingstone in 1851. The period of Kololo rule was one of peace and unity, and the Lozi adopted the Kololo language. The Lozi still speak Kololo today, and they are sometimes even referred to as the Kololo.

Komba *see* Konkomba

Komono

The Komono are part of the Lobi (q.v.) group of related peoples. They live in Ghana, Ivory Coast, and Burkina Faso.

Konde *see* Makonde

Kongo

Kongo is the name of a former kingdom and the present-day homeland of the Kongo (or Bakongo) people. Numbering about 4,000,000, the Kongo live in an area around the mouth of the Congo River that encompasses the south, the narrowest part of Congo (Dem. Rep,) where it reaches the Atlantic Ocean, and the northern part of Angola.

History

The Kongo Kingdom was founded in the 1300s. The first known king of Kongo was Nimi a Lukeni, the son of the chief of Bungu, north of the Congo River. He led a group of followers to conquer lands south of the river and married the daughter of Kabunga, a Kongo chief. Kabunga had the title of mani (king), which Nimi adopted as his own. From then on the Kongo ruler was known as the Mani-Kongo. The king was the spiritual leader of his people, as well as their ruler and military leader. He had a council of ministers to advise him.

Kongo was already flourishing when Portuguese explorers and traders landed on the coast in 1482. For many years, the Kongo maintained diplomatic ties not only with Portugal but also with the Vatican. The Portuguese gave advice and military help in exchange for exclusive trading rights; the main trade being in slaves for export to the new European settlements in the Americas.

This alliance did not endure, however. The Portuguese fostered Kongo's internal rivalries in their single-minded pursuit of slaves, and following the 1568 invasion of Kongo by the Jaga, from the interior, the Portuguese gradually lost interest. After the Kongo king tried to break Portuguese influence by balancing it with that of the Dutch, the Portuguese decisively defeated his armies at the Battle of Ambuila in 1665. After this

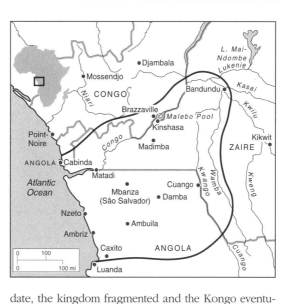

date, the kingdom fragmented and the Kongo eventually came under colonial rule. The Portuguese ruled Angola, the French ruled Congo (Rep.), and present-day Congo (Dem. Rep,) was under Belgian domination. Before becoming a Belgian colony, much of Congo (Dem. Rep.) formed the private colony of the Belgian king Léopold II, as the Congo Free State (1885–1908). His rule was characterized by abuse, brutality, and the committing of atrocities in order to protect and maintain the lucrative rubber trade. The two Congos became independent in 1960 – led by Kongo politicians – and Angola gained independence in 1975.

RECENT EVENTS Since independence, Angola has been devastated by a long-running civil war. A peace accord was signed in 1994, but hostilities continued until 1995 and the peace remained fragile in 1996. From 1964 to 1991, Congo (Rep.) followed Marxist-Leninist policies and has only recently switched to a multiparty system. Political instability has dogged Congo (Dem. Rep,) since independence and, until recently, the country was ruled by President Mobutu Sese Seko (q.v.) as a one-party state. In 1996, the ethnic conflict that has devastated Rwanda and Burundi spread to Congo (Dem. Rep.), leading to Mobutu's overthrow.

Language

The language of the Kongo is also called Kongo (or Kikongo), and has more than fifty dialects. One of these dialects, Kileta, is used as a common language by many Kongo-related peoples who would otherwise use different languages. Many of the Kongo also speak the official language of their country, French in Congo (Rep.) and Congo (Dem. Rep.), and Portuguese in Angola. Lingala is spoken by the Kongo, and many other non-Kongo people, who live in the towns and cities of Congo (Rep.) and Congo (Dem. Rep.).

Ways of life

URBAN The Kongo today are highly urbanized and many live and work in cities such as Kinshasa and Brazzaville, where they are engaged in engineering, construction, and other trades. Most urban Kongo hold a variety of jobs, often in the informal sector (illicit trad-

Kongo crucifix
At least 200 years old, this crucifix is made from bronze, metal, and wood. Kongolese crucifixes helped to spread Christianity in Kongo. Over the years, the Christian message of such crucifixes has been overlaid with interpretations based on the Kongo religion, in which the cross represents the junction between this world and the next.

Tumba
This Kongo tumba (tomb sculpture) probably dates from the 1800s. Tumba were produced at least as early as the 1500s and mostly come from northern Angola. Generally, tumba honor family members. This example may be the tumba of a chief as the figure appears to be chewing a plant stem, which a chief would then have spat out on others during certain rituals.

Pot
This practical and beautiful pot has been made from a yellow clay. While it was still hot from firing, the pot was splashed with a thick and sticky vegetable mixture to give it a distinctive pattern.

ing, for example) in order to earn enough money to live. In Congo (Dem. Rep.) and Congo (Rep.), many Kongo men are employed in the mining sector.

RURAL Outside the towns, the Kongo live in villages of about 300 inhabitants. They build their houses with bricks, either sun-dried or kiln-fired, and roof them with thatch or corrugated iron. Rural people are mainly engaged in arable farming. The main crop is cassava, which is supplemented with eggplants, beans, corn, peanuts, peas, peppers, and rice. Cassava root is turned into flour, from which women prepare a kind of dough called fou-fou. The leaves of the plant are boiled and eaten like spinach. The Kongo cultivate oil palms, which provide cooking oil and wine. Most of the farm work is done by women, except for the heavy tasks such as clearing fresh land. The Kongo keep comparatively few animals, but there are commercially-run ranches where beef cattle are reared to supply the towns. In the country, the Kongo rely on hunting for much of their meat. Men are the hunters, but men and women share in fishing in the rivers. Poor transport facilities handicap the Kongo, especially in Congo (Dem. Rep.), where they rely on local markets to sell surplus produce and to buy other supplies. Without good transport, marketing becomes difficult, especially for people taking their produce into the larger towns. Marketing is mainly controlled by women.

Social structure

POLITICAL STRUCTURE Under Congolese law, the Kongo are supposed to conform to the modern political organization. But many people follow, at least in part, their own traditions. Descent is traced through the female line and local headmen wield limited authority. Chiefs still exist, but they have little authority in either of the Congos. In Angola, where government authority has been weakened by years of civil war, the situation is unclear.

Culture and religion

RELIGION The majority of the Kongo are Christian, mostly Roman Catholics. The Portuguese introduced Christianity (Catholicism) to the Kongo in the sixteenth century. The Kongo nobility became Christians, and eventually many of their people also converted. In 1705, a Kongo prophet called Beatrice Kimpa Vita unsuccessfully attempted to revive the recently decimated Kongo Kingdom. For a few months in 1921,

Simon Kimbangu – another Kongo prophet – preached and healed the sick in the Belgian Congo before being imprisoned for life by the Belgian authorities. Since then, many "Kimbanguist" Christian movements have arisen, including the international Church of Jesus Christ on the Earth, founded by his son Joseph Diangienda. Many Christian churches in Congo (Rep.) trace their origin to Simon Kimbangu.

Nkisi nkondi
Made of wood, iron nails, clay, glass, and mirrors this figure dates from the early twentieth century and is a nkisi nkondi or "power figure." Nails, spikes, or blades would be embedded in the wooden figure to mark an occasion such as the signing of a treaty or to rouse the figure's magical or medicinal properties.

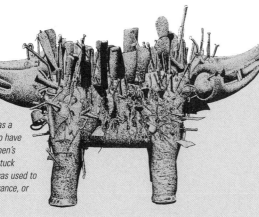

Kozo
This wood and iron nkisi nkondi, or "power figure," probably dates from the nineteenth century. Called Kozo and fashioned as a two-headed dog, this piece is said to have been used in rituals concerning women's affairs. Nails and hoe blades were stuck in the creature's back each time it was used to deal with a particular problem, grievance, or other matter.

Kongo timeline	
1300s Kongo Kingdom founded	**1665** Kongo defeated by Portuguese at Battle of Ambuila: Kongo Kingdom fragments
1482 First contact with Portuguese	**1885–1908** Belgian Congo Free State in present-day Congo (Dem. Rep.)
1491 Kongo king and court convert to Christianity	
1494 Pro- and anti-Portuguese factions develop in Kongo	**1960** Belgian Congo and French Congo both independent as the Republic of Congo
1506 Civil war breaks out: Affonso I succeeds with Portuguese aid	**1964** Former French Congo adopts communism
1520s Kongo is supplying slaves to Portuguese	**1971** Former Belgian Congo renamed Zaire
1545 Succession war follows death of Affonso I	**1975** Angolan independence comes as civil war is being fought
1556 Kongo at war with Portuguese-backed Ndongo to south	**1991** Congo abandons communism
1568 Kongo invaded by Jaga	**1994** Peace accord in Angola, but hostilities continue
1571 Portuguese drive Jaga out; Kongo becomes vassal state of Portugal	**1996** Fragile peace in Angola
1665–1670 Portuguese invade Kongo and establish rule over kingdom	**1999** Civil war resumes in Angola

Konkomba

The Konkomba (or Komba) are a people of northern Togo and Ghana and Burkina Faso. There are at least 70,000 Konkomba.

Kono

The Kono are a West African people closely related to the Manding (q.v.). There are more than 250,000 Kono, and they live in Sierra Leone, Ivory Coast, Guinea, and Liberia. They claim to have originally been Vai (q.v.) people.

Konso

Konso is the name given to three related ethnic groups living in southern Ethiopia – the Garati, the Takadi, and the Turo. These three groups speak very similar dialects of the Konso language, which is an Eastern Cushitic language. The Konso live in a region south of Lake Shamo, in the northern tip of the Great Rift Valley of East Africa. There are probably less than 100,000 Konso in Ethiopia.

The Konso are descended from Cushite (q.v.) ancestors who originated from the Ethiopian highlands. They spread out from their original dispersal site to occupy much of northeastern Africa, reaching the Kenyan Highlands by 1000 BCE. The Konso probably emerged as a separate ethnic group during the last thousand years.

The Konso are concentrated in more than 30 walled towns. Between 10 and 16 feet high, the walls were designed to deter surprise attacks, and the towns are mostly situated on hilltops and other easily defendable sites. The majority of the Konso are farmers, and they practice intensive cultivation of a variety of grain crops, root crops, and vegetables, using terracing to preserve the soil. This involves carving huge "steps" in to the hillside that make the land more suitable to cultivation, trap water, and prevent soil erosion.

Koranko

The Koranko (or Kouranko or Kuranko) are distant relations of the Manding (q.v.) people. They live in many West African countries, particularly in Sierre Leone, Guinea, and Liberia. There are probably around 300,000 Koranko.

Korekore

The Korekore are a subgroup of the Shona (q.v.) of Mozambique and Zimbabwe, where they make up at least fifteen percent of the total Shona population. They are also known as the Northern Shona.

Kota *see* Bakota

Koto *see* Bakota

Kotocoli *see* Temba

Kotoko

The Kotoko are closely related to the Buduma (q.v.). They have a population of around 100,000, the majority of whom live in northeastern Cameroon and the remainder in Chad and Nigeria. The Kotoko state reached its height in the fifteenth century, when it controlled northern Nigeria and parts of Cameroon.

Koulango *see* Kulango

Kouranko *see* Koranko

Kpelle

Also called the Gerse or Kpese, the Kpelle are the largest ethnic group in Liberia, where they number more than 300,000. A substantial number (roughly 100,000) also live in neighboring Guinea. Since 1989, however, many Kpelle have sought refuge from Liberia's civil war in other West African countries. The Kpelle inhabit the rainforested lands of central Liberia, to which they migrated from the savannas (grasslands) south of the Sahara Desert shortly before the end of the sixteenth century. They displaced the original inhabi-tants, the Kwa (q.v.).

The Kpelle language is also called Kpelle, and it is a Mande (q.v.) language. The Kpelle share cultural features with other Mande peoples. Like the Mende (q.v.), for example, most Kpelle belong to either the women's secret society (Sande) or the men's secret society (Poro). These societies are important unifying and con-trolling forces in Kpelle society, they initiate adoles-cents into adulthood, and teach people the "correct" way to behave.

Kpese *see* Kpelle

Krahn *see* Guere

Dance staff
This face is featured on top of a stick used in dancing by the Kru.

Kran Padebu

The Kran Padebu are part of the Kru (q.v.) cluster of peoples. The Kru are one of the largest ethnic groups in Liberia.

Kran *see* Guere

Krio *see* Creoles

Kru

The Kru occupy a region that covers more than half of Liberia – extending from Monrovia on the northern coast to Cape Palmas on the southern coast and reaching roughly 60 miles inland. The Kru are made up of the Kran Padebu, Sakon, Siku, Bassa, De, Grebo, Bete, Krahn, and Kru proper. Together they comprise a quarter of Liberia's population, numbering around 700,000. The Bassa, De, Kru, and Grebo are concentrated on the coast, and members of other groups are mainly inland. The Bete heartland is on the western banks of the Bandama Island. All the Kru groups speak Kru languages, which belong to the Kwa family.

The Kru have long been associated with seafaring and sailing activities, and in the past Kru men would spend much of each year sailing with trading ships around the coast of Africa or farther afield. In recent decades, investment in ports such as Buchanan have detracted from the activities of the Kru coast, which is now one of the most isolated parts of Liberia. Like other Liberians, the Kru have been adversely affected by the Liberian civil war, which began in 1989 and lasted through much of the 1990s.

Kuba

The Kuba (or Bakuba) live in south-central Congo (Dem. Rep.). They include a number of smaller groups such as the Leele and the Njembe. There are probably around 100,000 Kuba.

History

Bantu-speaking peoples had begun settling in the varied habitats of the Congo (Dem. Rep.) Basin in about the third century. In the sixteenth century, one of these groups, the Kuba, moved from the lower part of the Basin to the Kasai region. This move was partly to escape the continuing attacks of the Jaga people and partly to avoid Portuguese influence from the Atlantic coast.

In the seventeenth century, a powerful Kuba state developed under the leadership of the Bushongo group – a name meaning "People of the Throwing Knife." The Bushongo probably gained their initial wealth from fishing, but in the seventeenth century they successfully grew corn and tobacco, adding to their wealth. By the early eighteenth century, a stable

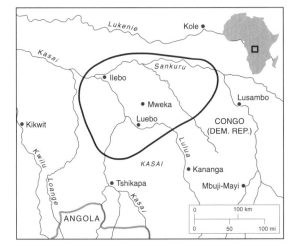

Bushongo government had allowed people to increase their production of agricultural surplus. This burgeoning economy supported a growing number of artisans and aristocrats. Economic growth furthered the development of trade and the Kuba began to export luxury cloth and ivory, and to import slaves, copper, beads, and salt. The Kuba came to control significant trade routes through parts of Central Africa, which remained important until well into colonial times. The kingdom reached its height in the eighteenth century, and remained stable until the late nineteenth century when invasions and upheavals destabilized the area.

The Kuba were incorporated into the private colony of King Leopold II of Belgium in 1885. Like other ethnic groups in the region, the Kuba suffered during Leopold's oppressive Congo Free State regime. International outcry at Leopold's exploitative and brutal regime led to the Belgian government taking over in 1908, resulting in a less oppressive, if nonetheless strongly colonial, period of government. The Belgian Congo, as it was then called, gained independence in 1960 as the Republic of Congo (renamed Zaire in 1971).

RECENT EVENTS The Kuba played an important role in Zairean politics. They formed the state of South Kasai,

Ndop sculpture (above)
Ndop are a series of sculptures made to commemorate dead Kuba kings and to initiate new ones. The identity of the king is revealed by an emblem on the plinth – in this case, a royal drum is used to signify that the statue is of Kata Mbula (reigned 1800–1810).

Royal backrest (left)
Dating from the early nineteenth century, this wooden backrest came from the Kuba capital of Nsheng. It was probably used as a support by the king, who was not supposed to come into contact with the ground.

Ikula knife (above)
In the early 1600s, the peace-loving king Shamba-Bolongongo forbade the use of the shongo knife and introduced the wooden peace knife, ikula. The handle of this ikula knife is inlaid with metal wire.

Mwaash a Mbooy mask
Made from wood, beads, cowrie shells, and fibers, Mwaash a Mbooy masks were used as a tool of royal justice. They were supposed to be able to assess everyone's behavior. When they appeared before their subjects, the whole costume was worn by the king or chief.

which broke away from Zaire for a short period in 1961. Mobutu Sese Seko (q.v.) was the national leader from 1965 and ruled the country as a one-party state until 1997. From 1991 he refused to hand over sovereignty to the National Conference and its Prime Minister, Etienne Tshisekedi. Mobutu and his government were locked in a power struggle with the broad-coalition opposition thereafter. By the mid-1990s, multi-party elections had yet to be held. Since 1992, ethnic Katangans (Lunda people) have been forcing ethnic Kasai mineworkers and their families out of the southern region of Katanga (Shaba) in a wave of violence.

Language
The Kuba languages – of which there are several – are Bantu, most of them belonging to the Bushongo group. Many Kuba also speak French.

Ways of life
The traditional Kuba way of life combines agriculture, hunting, and fishing. By the end of the seventeenth century, cassava had largely replaced yam as the main staple crop. With its higher yield and better storage properties, cassava was a much better hedge against famine. Cassava was one of a number of new crop plants imported from America and grown as cash crops as well as for consumption by the farmers. Other imported crop plants included corn, tobacco, groundnuts, and beans. Today, the staple crops are corn, cassava, millet, groundnuts, and beans, and corn is also exported. Many of the Kuba people live and work in the large towns of their region. Since 1990, however, rampant inflation has forced many people to live a subsistence lifestyle.

Social structure
POLITICAL STRUCTURE In precolonial times, the Kuba kingdom was a federation of chiefdoms, each ruled by a chief and two or three councils that represented the general population and nobles. The ruling Bushongo chief was king by divine right, and his army and a common administration were uniting factors. In practice, the chiefdoms were virtually autonomous. After

Kuba came under Belgian government control in the early twentieth century, the power of the kings again increased for a time as the structure was maintained by the colonial authorities to ease administration. In present-day Congo (Dem. Rep.), traditional political structures are often maintained at a local level as a link between regional and central government.

Culture and religion
RELIGION Throughout the colonial era, although Western values and Christian beliefs were strongly promoted, the Kuba retained many of their own beliefs. There is still some reverence of ancestors, but nature forces dominate the Kuba religion.

ART The Kuba have one of the oldest and most developed cultures in Africa. They are famous for their wooden sculpture, especially their ndop – statues of their kings – which developed as an art form from about the seventeenth century. The Kuba's highly developed sense of history means that the personalities and deeds of about 124 kings are known, though only nineteen ndop have survived. The Kuba were excellent iron forgers as well, and their throwing knife – the shongo – gave its name to the Kuba's ruling group, the Bushongo. The decorative art of the Kuba is remarkably rich and enhances all objects of daily life. Statues, initiation masks, cups, and beautifully embroidered raffia (palm fiber) cloth are especially prized export articles. Many of these items, some statues for example, are purely aesthetic and independent of all forms of worship – rare in Africa. Perhaps the finest objects are the effigy cups, sometimes depicting revered ancestors. According to some, production for the tourist market has served to stagnate rather than enable the development of Kuba artistic expression. Tourists often demand recognizably "tribal" or "traditional" pieces. This demand does not allow carvers to experiment with new forms and ideas – processes that produced much of the so-called traditional art in the first place.

Mortar
In the nineteenth and early twentieth centuries, wooden mortars such as this one – used to grind spices – were status symbols. Designs incorporating human figures were the most valued.

Kot aPe
This picture of the Kuba king Kot aPe was painted by a visiting European. Kot aPe was king at the beginning of the twentieth century.

Friction oracle
Dating from the 1800s, this itoom sculpture was used in divination. A moistened disk would be rubbed on the back while the diviner recited certain phrases. The phrase at which the disk stuck would reveal answers to the client's question.

Kuba timeline

c. 200s Bantu-speaking peoples begin to settle in the Congo (Dem. rep.) Basin	**a few months**	and opposes transitional governments
	1965 Mobutu Sese Seko, army commander, seizes power	**1992** Katangans oust Kasai (including Kuba) mineworkers from the southern region of Shaba (formerly Katanga)
c. 1550 Kuba migrate to Kasai region	**1970** Mobutu elected president	
1885 Congo Free State established	**1971** Congo renamed Zaire	**1995** Outbreak of deadly Ebola virus in Kikwit, southwestern Zaire
1908 Belgian government takes over Free State as the Belgian Congo	**1980s** International criticism of human rights abuses in Zaire and popular unrest mounts	**1997** Laurent Kabila overthrows Mobutu and renames Zaire the Democratic Republic of Congo
1960 Belgian Congo independent as Republic of Congo (Leopoldville)	**1990–1996** Mobutu promises introduction of multiparty politics. Political deadlock follows as Mobutu blocks transition to democracy	
1961 Kuba form the breakaway state of South Kasai, which survives just		

© DIAGRAM

Kukamba see Amba

Kulango

The Kulango (Koulango) are a Mole-Dagbane (q.v.) closely related to the Lobi (q.v.). They live in northeastern Ivory Coast and southwestern Burkina Faso.

Kulya see Kuria

Kunda see Kaonde

Kung

The Kung (or !Kung as it is often written) are a Khoisan (q.v.) people based in the Kalahari Desert of southern Africa, mainly in northeastern Namibia and the Dobe region of northwestern Botswana. The Kung are also known as the Zhu (or Xhu), which derives from their name for themselves – the Zhutwasi, meaning "real people" or just "people." Although they are a relatively small ethnic group and live in a remote region, the Kung have been extensively studied by social scientists, so a large body of knowledge exists about Kung culture. They have a considerable local reputation for healing, and this involves going into a trancelike state called kia, which is usually reached by performing a particular dance.

Like other Khoisan groups, the Kung are not Black African but they are descended from southern Africa's first known human inhabitants. They are historically associated with hunter-gatherer lifestyles and distinctive for their short stature and use languages that contain clicking and popping sounds. Over recent decades, however, the Kung have increasingly been switching to a settled, farming lifestyle, and gathering food and hunting has decreased in importance.

Kuranko see Koranko

Kuri

The Kuri live on the islands and peninsulas of eastern Lake Chad. They speak a Buduma (q.v.) dialect, but share their origins with the Kanembu (q.v.). There are roughly 14,000 Kuri in Chad.

Kuria

The Kuria (or Ikikuria, Tende, or Kulya) number at least 100,000 in western Kenya alone; a further 200,000 live in northwest Tanzania.

Kusu

The Kusu are a Bantu (q.v.) people sometimes thought to be a subgroup of the Mongo (q.v.). They live along the Lomami River in the northeastern region of Congo (Dem. Rep.).

Kutu

The Kutu are one of the many groups that make up the Zaramo (q.v.) of East Africa. They are a Bantu (q.v.) people living in Tanzania's coastal lowlands. There are more than 35,000 Kutu.

Kwaka see Avikam

Kwakwak see Kakwa

Kwena

The Kwena are Sotho-Tswana (q.v.) subgroup, or more exactly clan. The Kwena were the founders of the Kingdom of Lesotho, of which they are still known as the royal clan.

Kweni see Guro

Kwere

The Kwere are one of the many subgroups that make up the Zaramo (q.v.) of East Africa. They are a Bantu (q.v.) people who live in Tanzania's coastal lowlands. There are roughly 80,000 Kwere.

Kwi

The term Kwi is now commonly used to refer to people of Americo-Liberian (q.v.), or part-Americo-Liberian, descent. The Kwi are found in Liberia.

Kwoll see Irigwe

Kyokosi see Chokossi

Labwor

The Labwor are a small group living amidst the Karamojong (q.v.) in northeastern Uganda. They speak a Lwo (q.v.) language.

Lagoon cluster

A complex group of largely Akan (q.v.) speaking peoples that inhabit the southeastern coastal and lagoon regions of the Ivory Coast. They are related linguistically. The Alladian (q.v.), Abbe (q.v.), Abidji (q.v.), Attie (q.v.), and Adjukru (q.v.) are part of this cluster.

Lahou *see* Avikam

Lala

The Lala number more than 170,000 people living largely in central Zambia. They are descended from several ethnic groups and make up one of Zambia's larger Kongo (q.v.) subgroups.

Lali

Although they are of Teke (q.v.) origin, the Lali are part of the Kongo (q.v.) people. They are found in Congo (Rep.), Congo (Dem. Rep.), and Angola. There are more than 500,000 Lali.

Lamba

The Lamba (or Ichilamba) are a people of the Copperbelt (central and northeastern Zambia). Many also live in Congo (Dem. Rep.). There are more than 100,000 Lamba.

Lango

The Lango (or Langi) number more than 700,000 people living in central and northern Uganda. They are perhaps descended from Karamojong (q.v.) ancestors who split away from the main group some 500 years ago. They are the largest non-Bantu (q.v.) population of Uganda.

The Lango are Nilotes (q.v.), belonging to the so-called River-Lake Nilotes, who originated in a region in the south of present-day Sudan. The ancestors of the Lango, a Lwo (q.v.)-speaking people, migrated south probably during the fifteenth century, traveling along the Nile River to the lakes region of central Uganda. They settled in an area inhabited by Ateker-speaking peoples. The present-day Lango people evolved out of the two cultures.

The Lango have often been in conflict with other Ugandans, such as the Ganda (q.v.) and Nyoro (q.v.). A Lango, Milton Obote (q.v.), became the first prime minister of independent Uganda in 1962, but he was overthrown and several turbulent decades followed during which the Lango were often active as guerrilla and opposition movements.

Lango *see* Langi

Lebanese

Many thousands of people of Lebanese descent live in Africa, in particular the West African countries such as Senegal, Mali, and Chad, which used to be French colonies. The Lebanese can often be found in urban areas working as traders.

Lebou *see* Lebu

Lebu

The Lebu (or Lebou) speak a Wolof (q.v.) language but are not a Wolof subgroup. Concentrated in the Cape Verde peninsula of western Senegal, where the capital city Dakar is located, the Lebu are the dominant political and economic group in Senegal.

Lega

The Lega (Kilega, Mwenga, or Rega) are a Bantu (q.v.) people of Congo (Dem. Rep.). They live in the east-central region of that country, to the east of the Lualaba River. There are more than 400,000 Lega.

Lele

The Lele (or Bashilele or Usilele) of Congo (Dem. Rep.) are part of the Kuba (q.v.) group of peoples. They live in the south in the lower Kasai River region and number around 30,000.

Lega mask
The white face looks out from a dark frame, with a beard of animal hair. Unfortunately, the outlawing of Bwami social structure by the colonial authorities in the years after World War Two has led to the decline of Lega art such as this.

© DIAGRAM

Lengola

The Lengola are a subgroup of the Mongo (q.v.) of Central Africa. The Lengola live in central Congo (Dem. Rep.) west of the Lokmani River.

Lete

The Lete are a Tswana (q.v.) people of Nguni (q.v.) origins. The majority live in the southeast of Botswana.

Lia

The Lia are a subgroup of the Mongo (q.v.). They live in a region of Congo (Dem. Rep.) that is concentrated between the Tshuapa and Lomami rivers in the southeast.

Lima

The Lima are a subgroup of the Bemba (q.v.). They number around 45,000 people living largely in central Zambia.

Limba

The Limba (or Yimbe) number more than 600,000, the majority of whom live in northern Sierra Leone. The remainder live either in Freetown in Sierra Leone or in Guinea.

Lisi

The Lisi are a Nilotic (q.v.) people primarily of northern Chad. They number more than 130,000.

Lobale see Lwena

Lobedu

The Lobedu (or Lovedu) are a group of more than 200,000 people living in northern Transvaal in South Africa. They are linguistically related to the Shona (q.v.) and Sotho (q.v.) peoples but their culture resembles that of the Venda (q.v.).

Lobi

The Lobi people live primarily in the southwest of Burkina Faso, northwest Ghana, and northeast Ivory Coast. The Lobi, or Lobi-Dagarti (or Lodagaa) peoples, are actually a cluster of peoples living in these regions of West Africa and who speak a variety of mostly related languages. The Lobi "proper" of Gaoua in southwestern Burkina Faso speak a language called Lobirifor that is similar to Dogon (q.v.), although its classification with Dogon has been disputed. The Birifor, or Lobirifor, are another major subgroup who live to the east of the Lobi proper. The Birifor speak a language called Dagara. There are perhaps just under a million Lobi-Dagarti peoples.

Like the majority of Africans today, the Lobi are mostly farmers, cultivating cereal crops such as sorghum, millet, and maize as well as vegetables such as peppers, beans, and squashes. Historically Lobi women produced gold that was sold to Dyula (q.v.) traders. The Lobi have many expert xylophone players, and differences in xylophone technique are often indications of different ethnic groups within the Lobi cluster.

Janus stool
This ceremonial stool from the Lobi is shaped after a club and features a double-faced head at the top.

Lobi-Dagarti see Lobi

Lobirifor see Birifor

Lodagaa see Lobi

Lokko

The Lokko (or Loko) number more than 100,000 people in Sierra Leone and Guinea. In Sierra Leone, they live in around Port Loko. They are closely related to the Mende (q.v.).

Loko see Lokko

Lokop see Samburu

Lolo see Lomwe

Loma

The Loma (or Toma) are a Manding (q.v.) people of Liberia, where the majority live, Guinea-Bissau, and Guinea. There are more than 100,000 Loma.

Lomongo see Mongo

Lomwe

The Lomwe (or Ngulu, Mihavane, Nguru, or Lolo) are a people of southern Malawi, northern Mozambique, and southern Tanzania. There are more than 2 million Lomwe altogether. They are closely related to the Yao (q.v.).

Loumbou

The Loumbou (or Baloumbou) live in southwest Gabon and Cameroon. They are a Bantu (q.v.) people who number more than 25,000.

Lovale *see* Lwena

Lovedu *see* Lobedu

Lozi

The Lozi (or Barotse) live mainly on the floodplains of the Zambezi River in Western (formerly Barotse) Province of Zambia. The Lozi population of Zambia, including the many smaller ethnic groups that have been absorbed by them (such as the Kwanda and the Makoma), is over 380,000. There are also smaller groups in Mozambique (50,000) and Zimbabwe (over 10,000).

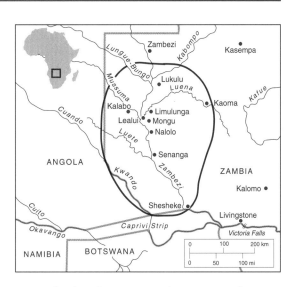

History

The Lozi are descended from the Luyi, a people who migrated from the north to the Zambezi floodplains around the 1600s or earlier. These Luyi migrants were led by a woman, Mwambwa, who was succeeded first by her daughter, Mbuywamwambwa, and then by Mbuywamwambwa's son, Mboo, the first litunga (king) of the Lozi. During Mboo's reign, the Lozi kingdom expanded by conquering and absorbing neighboring peoples. At that time, the kingdom was not so much a centralized state as a collection of semi-independent chiefdoms ruled by Mboo and his relatives. The unification of these chiefdoms into a single kingdom began in the rule of the fourth litunga, Ngalama, in the early 1700s, and was completed by Mulambwa, who ruled from about 1780 to 1830. Mulambwa was able to establish direct rule over the peoples conquered by the Lozi and over the numerous immigrant groups arriving in the kingdom from the north and west.

The most important of these immigrant groups was the Mbunda, who had been driven from their homes in Angola. Mulambwa allowed them to settle in border areas where they could help to defend the kingdom from raids by neighboring peoples such as the Luvale and the Nkoya. As well as helping the Lozi in this way, the Mbunda played a big part in the military and economic development of the kingdom. They brought with them military innovations – such as the bow and arrow and an improved type of battleaxe – new crops including cassava, millet, and yam, as well as medical and artistic skills.

The Lozi prospered under Mulambwa's rule, but after his death the country was torn apart by a civil war between the army of his eldest son, Silumelume, and the supporters of a younger son, Mubukwanu. This war was won by Mubukwanu, supported by the Mbunda, but before he could reunite the kingdom it was attacked and conquered by the Kololo, a Sotho people from Southern Africa. The Kololo ruled the country (and introduced their language) from about 1840 to 1864, when they were defeated by the armies of an exiled Lozi leader, Sipopa. For the next forty years

or so, the kingdom continued to prosper despite a series of leadership disputes, but its power began to wane when treaties agreed with the British in 1890 and 1900 placed it under the control of the Cecil Rhodes' British South Africa Company (BSA).

COLONIALISM The British ruled the Lozi until the 1960s, incorporating the kingdom (as Barotseland) into the colony of Northern Rhodesia in 1924. In 1958, Northern Rhodesia became part of the white-minority ruled Central African Federation (CAF) along with Nyasaland (Malawi) and Southern Rhodesia (Zimbabwe). CAF dissolved in 1963 and Zambia won independence in 1964.

RECENT EVENTS After independence, Zambia was ruled as a one-party state under President Kenneth Kaunda (q.v.) and the United National Independence Party (UNIP). In 1991, Kaunda and UNIP were defeated by Frederick Chiluba and the Movement for Multiparty Democracy (MMD) in the country's first multiparty elections.

Language

During the years of Kololo rule, the Kololo language displaced Luyana, the original language of the Lozi. Kololo is derived from a dialect of Sotho, which is a Bantu language from Southern Africa.

Ways of life

The life of the Lozi in the rural areas is based on subsistence agriculture, in which people grow crops and raise cattle mainly for their own use rather than for sale. Their main crops are millet, cassava, sorghum,

Kneeling statue
This carved wooden figure is a good example of Lozi wood carving. The style shows influences from both Lunda and Chokwe carving in the "wings" coming out from each side of the head.

Wooden spoon
Carved wooden spoon used by the Lozi people.

and corn, plus some vegetables and fruit, and their livestock includes sheep, goats, and poultry as well as some cattle. Additional food is obtained by hunting and fishing.

DIVISION OF LABOR Most of the domestic and light farming work is done by the women, while the men do the heavier farming tasks, tend the livestock, hunt, and fish. Men are also responsible for the skilled ironworking of the Lozi. They dig iron ore from riverbeds and swamps; smelt it into iron; and fashion it into tools, utensils, pots, and other items.

SETTLEMENTS Lozi villages are usually small groups of circular, thatched houses surrounding a central open space, which is often used as a cattle enclosure. On the floodplains of the Zambezi River, the water rises and floods the land every year toward end of the rainy season, in February and March. When this happens, many villages are temporarily abandoned as the inhabitants and their livestock move to higher ground.

Social structure

POLITICAL STRUCTURE In the Lozi kingdom, the power of the ruler passed downward through a hierarchy of junior kings and chiefs to village-headman level. The litunga, based in Lealui in the north of the country, was the overall ruler of the kingdom, but the south of the country was governed by the mulena mukwae, or princess chief, who was based in Nalolo. Various councils and offices provided checks and balances to the power of the litunga. During the years of British rule, the political power of this hierarchy was gradually replaced by a system of districts and provinces ruled by the state government, but the litunga, the mulena mukwae, the royal family, and the chiefs retained their titles and ceremonial roles and the respect of the people, though the powers of the mulena mukwae were eroded to a greater degree. Since independence,

Lozi dancer
This Lozi man is wearing the traditional costume of a dancer. Such dancers still perform at the Kuomboka Festival.

Kuomboka Festival (below right and below left)
When the Zambezi waters begin to rise, animals are sacrificed at all the royal graves and the litunga (king) and his court (below left) leave Lealui on the great royal barge, the nalikwanda (below right). Accompanied by the beating of the royal drums, they travel to the winter capital, Limulunga, on the high land at the edge of the floodplains. During its five-hour journey, the barge is accompanied by thousands of canoes carrying villagers traveling from the floodplains to the higher ground, and its arrival in Limulunga is followed by days of festivities. When the waters begin to recede again, the litunga makes the return journey to Lealui while the people return to their villages and celebrate their homecoming.

the Zambian government has concentrated on creating a national rather than an ethnic identity and any remnants of political power that the king retained have been lost.

MARRIAGE Polygamous marriages, in which men have more than one wife, are common among the Lozi. In such marriages, each of the co-wives usually has her own home, plus a garden and some animals.

Culture and religion

RELIGION Lozi religion includes belief in a supreme god (Nyambe) and the veneration of the spirits of ancestors. The spirits of former rulers are honored in elaborate public rituals at their burial sites, while those of ordinary people are honored by simpler, more private ceremonies.

The two major festivals of the Lozi are centered on the annual rise and fall of the Zambezi River and the move of the king from his home at Lealui on the floodplain to his capital at Limulunga above the floodplain.

Lozi timeline	
c. 1600s Luyi migrate to Zambezi floodplains	including Northern and Southern Rhodesia and Nyasaland (Malawi)
1700s Emergence of Lozi kingdom	**1963** CAF dissolved
c. 1780–c. 1830 Rule of Mulambwa over Lozi: kingdom prospers	**1964** Northern Rhodesia wins independence as Zambia
1830s Civil war after Mulambwa dies	**1965** White-minority declare independence of Southern Rhodesia as Rhodesia
c. 1840–1864 Lozi conquered by Kololo Kololo ousted by Sipopa	**1972** Zambia made a one-party state
1890s Lozi come under control of British South Africa (BSA) Company as Barotseland, part of Northern Rhodesia	**1980** Rhodesia independent with majority rule as Zimbabwe
	1991 First multiparty elections in Zambia
1924 Northern Rhodesia taken over by British government. White settlers take much of Lozi land. Africans moved to inadequate "native reserves"	**1996** Robert Mugabe wins a fourth successive term as president of Zimbabwe
1953 White-minority ruled Central African Federation (CAF) formed	**1999** Zambian high court declares former president Kenneth Kaunda state less

Luba

Luba is the general name for several related ethnic groups living in southeastern Congo (Dem. Rep.). There are three main subgroups: the Luba of Katanga province (previously called Shaba); the Luba Hemba (or Eastern Luba) of northern Katanga and southern Kivu provinces; and the Luba Bambo (or Western Luba) of Kasai province. Altogether, there are between 1,100,000 and 1,500,000 Luba people.

History

Archeological excavations have shown that there has been an uninterrupted culture in the Katanga region from the 700s onward, though the area has undoubtedly been occupied for longer than that. Some authorities think that the idea of government through chiefs originated in this area as early as the eighth century or before. By the 1300s, there were definitely well-established chieftainships in the region. Increasing population levels land shortages set these chieftaincies in conflict with one another and larger, more military groupings evolved as a result. The most important of these was the Luba group, which emerged around the Lake Kisale area.

According to oral traditions, the original rulers of the Luba (then called Kalundwe) were the Songye, who had come from the north. The Songye kongolo (ruler) married the Kalundwe queen and established a new state, which became the Luba kingdom and covered the lands between the Lualaba and Lubilash rivers.

In the 1400s, the Songye rulers of the Luba were displaced by the Kunda from the north. Led by Mbili Kiluhe, the Kunda were at first welcomed by the

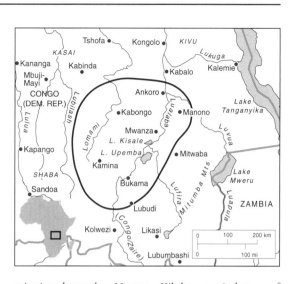

reigning kongolo, Mwana. Kiluhe married two of Mwana's sisters, one of whom gave birth to a son, Kala Ilunga. Kala Ilunga grew up to be a great warrior and he challenged the kongolo for the Luba throne, claiming he was the legitimate ruler through matrilineal descent (descent traced through the mother). The kongolo was eventually defeated and Kala Ilunga founded the Kunda dynasty to rule over Luba and took the title of mulopwe.

By 1550, the Luba kingdom was powerful, with a strong central government. The mulopwe was the head of the government and also the religious leader, believed to have supernatural powers. He had a group of ministers, balopwe, to help him, each with special duties. The sungu was a sort of prime minister who mediated between the people and the mulopwe. The nsikala acted as a temporary ruler when a king died or was unwell. The inabanza had charge of ritual matters concerning the mulopwe's sacred role. This included taking care of the king's sacred spears. Finally, the twite was the army and police commander. All these ministers, and any other chiefs who ruled sections of the Luba, were themselves descendants of Kala Ilunga. In this way, the Luba kept power in the hands of a small aristocracy.

The Kunda dynasty lasted until the arrival, in the 1880s, of the Belgians, who turned what is now Congo (Dem. Rep.) into a private colony called the Congo Free State, owned and ruled by the Belgian king, Léopold II. His rule was characterized by abuses, brutality, and the committing of atrocities in order to protect the lucrative rubber trade. The Luba were engaged in a war of resistance against colonial rule that lasted from 1907 to 1917. The Belgian government took over the country in 1908, as the Belgian Congo, which became independent in 1960 as the Republic of Congo (renamed Zaire in 1971).

RECENT EVENTS In 1960–3, some people in Katanga (Shaba) and Kasai tried to set up independent states. In 1964, Katangan secessionists again rebelled and soon controlled much of the east and northeast of Congo (Dem. Rep.) before being defeated by the army in 1965. The majority of the Luba opposed the breakaway, which was lead by a member of the Lunda royal

Mkisi mihasi
This ivory pendant is a type of mikisi mihasi, which are sculptures named after certain revered ancestors.

Wooden bowstand
Bowstands were never seen in public but were kept by Luba rulers as a symbol of their authority and to commemorate the founder of the Luba dynasty, Mbili Kiluhe – a famous hunter. They often incorporate female figures that represent important women or the king himself – who is thought to return as a woman after he dies.

Luba chief
This present-day Luba chief is holding his staff of office. The geometric patterns on the broad sections serve both to decorate the staff and to empower the owner. They are considered more important than the human figures.

Ancestor statue
Polished, rounded, and beautifully carved, this wooden figure would have been kept inside a room in memory of the dead ancestor it represents.

Luba mask
Like many masks made by the Luba, the purpose of this one is not known. It may have been used in some form of religious or political society ritual, but no details have survived. It is made of painted wood and was probably not worn.

Mboko
The Luba used carved figures like this one in divination. For example, the bowl the woman is holding might be filled with white clay. The clay would be smeared on the body of the diviner to help him divine the cause of a particular problem. This kind of figure is called mboko, *though the diviner who actually used it would call it* kitumpa kya muchi.

family. In fact, the Luba led the wars against the secessionists. Further Katangan rebellions known as the First Katanga War and the Second Katanga War occurred in 1977 and 1978 respectively and there was another rebellion in 1984.

Languages
The Luba language is called Luba (or Tshiluba).

Ways of Life
AGRICULTURE The Luba country is a mixture of tropical rainforest, wooded savanna (open grasslands), and marshland. The rainy season lasts from October to May. In this environment, the Luba are by tradition hunters and farmers practicing slash-and-burn agriculture. Sections of the forest are cleared for agriculture by cutting and burning the vegetation. These are abandoned when the soil becomes exhausted, and the farmers move on to a fresh patch. This allows the fragile tropical soil time to recover after being cultivated. Cassava and corn are the main cereal crops, and farmers grow millet and sorghum for brewing beer. Other crops include a variety of vegetables, plus bananas, mangoes and tobacco. The Luba raise goats, pigs, poultry, and sheep, and breed hunting dogs. They also fish extensively in the rivers and lakes of the area.
TRADE AND INDUSTRY Industrial activities include basket making, blacksmithing, net making, pottery, and woodworking. The Luba also make salt by extracting it from the water in the marshlands. In the past, the Luba were also a caravan-trading people, but rural markets have taken the place of the old trade patterns.

Social structure
The different subgroups of the Luba have their own forms of social structure. The Luba Hemba are matrilineal but the Luba of Katanga and Kasai trace descent mostly through the male line – they are patrilineal. Families group together to form villages, which vary in size from a hundred people or fewer to several thousand. Although the chiefs still have limited autonomy, the Luba are more and more coming under central government control, especially those who live and work in urban centers.

Although monogamy (having only one wife) is the norm, multiple marriages are still common and a man is expected to give a valuable bridewealth to his wife's family. Young people go through initiation ceremonies to mark their transition to adulthood; for young men, this involves circumcision.

Culture and religion
RELIGION Despite the efforts of Christian missionaries, the Luba generally still follow the Luba religion. There is a widespread belief in a supreme being, known as the Great Vidye, who is the creator of everything. Spirits known as mishiki control the supply of game and fish, while other spirits called bavide exert a baleful influence on people, including sorcery. The spirits of the dead, particularly those of ancestors, are thought to exercise a beneficial influence on the living, but some spirits are felt to be malevolent. Specialist witch doctors are called in to combat bad spells. These people also act as medical advisers, because ill-health is though to originate with the spirits. The Luba hold special ceremonies for the accession and funerals of their kings. Other ceremonies cover such activities such as mourning, hunting, and harvest time.
ARTS Luba artists are renowned for their sculpture, masks, and jewelry. They make elaborately-carved figures out of wood, which are finished carefully and highly-polished. Luba masks are probably intended for ceremonial use, particularly in the numerous religious and political societies. The Luba have a well established core of oral literature.

Headrest (right)
Headrests were used by the Luba to protect their elaborate hairdos from being squashed. This example, carved in wood, is supported by two female figures, probably priestesses. Headrests are often seen as the seat of dreams. Dreams are considered to be messages from the other world, so it is appropriate that priestesses – who act as the intermediaries between the two worlds – appear on Luba headrests.

Luba timeline	
700s Shaba region of modern Congo (Dem. Rep.) occupied	**1965** Mobutu Sese Seko seizes power in Congo. Katangans defeated
1300s Luba chieftainships well-established under Songye	**1970** Mobutu elected president
1400s Songye displaced by Kunda	**1971** Congo renamed Zaire
1550 Luba kingdom a powerful centralized state	**1977** First Shaba War in Zaire
1885 Belgian king's Congo Free State is established (Zaire)	**1978** Second Shaba War in Zaire
1907–1917 Luba wage resistance war against Belgian colonizers	**1990–1996** Mobutu promises introduction of multiparty politics. Political deadlock follows as Mobutu blocks transition to democracy
1908 Belgian government takes over Free State as Belgian Congo	**1995** Outbreak of deadly Ebola virus in Kikwit, southwestern Zaire
1960 Belgian Congo independent as Republic of Congo	**1996–7** Civil war leads to the overthrow of President Mobutu and the renaming of the country to Democratic Republic of Congo; Shaba reverts to its former name, Katanga
1960–1965 Wars to suppress Katangan rebellions are led by Luba	

Luena *see* **Lwena**

Lugbara

The Lugbara live in the region in east-central Africa from where the great rivers of Africa – the Nile and the Congo rivers – begin their journeys to the sea. The majority of the Lugbara live in northwestern Uganda, much of the remainder inhabit northeastern Congo (Dem. Rep.). The Lugbara speak a variety of Eastern Sudanic languages, which belong to the Nilo-Saharan family of languages. The Lugbara languages are distantly related to the Azande (q.v.) and Mangbetu (q.v.) languages.

In the 1950s the Lugbara numbered around 250,000 people. In the late 1970s and early '80s the Lugbara suffered near genocide (extinction) since they were persecuted under the regime of Milton Obote (q.v.) – after being treated favorably by the country's previous leader, the brutal dictator Idi Amin (q.v.), who came from the Lugbara region. As a result, the Lugbara number a great many fewer than they did in the mid twentieth century.

Lugulu *see* **Luguru**

Luguru

The Luguru (or Lugulu) are a Bantu (q.v.) people who live in and around the Uluguru Mountains of central coastal Tanzania. They are closely related to the Zaramo (q.v.) and number more than 400,000.

Luhya *see* **Luyia**

Lukenyi *see* **Soga**

Lunda

The name "Lunda" covers scores of groups that once lived within the precolonial Lunda Empire of Central Africa. Altogether, these groups total around 1,500,000 people. Approximately half of these live in southern Congo (Dem. Rep.), around a third in eastern Angola, and the rest in northern and western Zambia.

History

The Lunda are descended from Bantu-speaking peoples who settled in Central Africa in the early centuries of the Common Era. By the 1500s, the Lunda occupied small separate territories in what is now southern Congo (Dem. Rep.). Around 1600, Kibinda Ilunga (probably a relation of a sixteenth-century Luba king) married the Lunda's senior chief – a woman called Lueji – and became paramount chief. Kibinda's son (by another wife), Lusengi, introduced Luba methods of

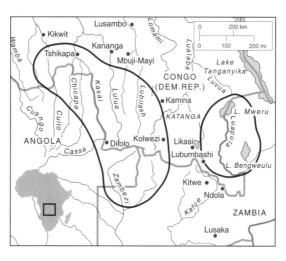

Lunda sculpture
This carved wooden figure has been attributed to the Lunda. Lunda artisans largely produce baskets, masks, and – historically – chiefs' regalia. Many have praised the sensitivity of their work, but others call them poor imitations of Chokwe and Luba work. One expert even claims the Lunda made no ceremonial sculpture of their own but obtained it from the Chokwe readymade, along with the actual ceremonies.

Kazembe IV
A Portuguese portrait of Kibangu Keleka (reigned c. 1805 to c. 1850) the fourth Kazembe. He rightly saw the Portuguese as a threat to his kingdom.

government. Lusengi's son Naweji, began conquering new lands, thus laying the foundation of the Lunda Empire. By 1700, the Lunda Empire had a capital, Mussumba; a king bearing the title Mwata Yamvo; and a tax-gathering system run by provincial administrators. These changes coincided with a local growth in trade. Central African commodities such as copper, honey, ivory, and slaves became increasingly sought after by European and Arab traders based on Africa's west and east coasts. Profiting from their own strategic location, the Lunda charged passing merchant's transit taxes or bartered food and goods with them for guns and other manufactured goods.

Partly to extend their hold on trade and partly to avoid paying tribute to the Mwata Yamvo, some Lunda groups migrated west, south, and east in the seventeenth and eighteenth centuries. These Lunda migrants set up kingdoms in what are now Angola and Zambia. The most important of these was the Kazembe kingdom in present-day Zambia. The building of this kingdom began in the late seventeenth century when the

Kibinda Ilunga
The founder of the Lunda nation, Kibinda Ilunga, is revered by all Lunda people and many who came under their influence such as the Chokwe, who produced this sculpture. Hundreds of statues of this heroic figure have been produced over the years. Kibinda was a legendary hunter and introduced new hunting methods, metal weapons, and charms. Later statues of Kibinda show him holding a rifle to symbolize his hunting prowess.

Coiled basket
Woven from coiled plant fibers, this basket dates from the beginning of the twentieth century. It was probably used in the preparation of food.

Mwata Yamvo, Muteba, rewarded the loyalty of one of his citizens by giving the man's son, Ngonda Bilonda, the title Mwata Kazembe and by putting him charge of the eastward expansion. Bilonda's successor, Kanyembo (Kazembe II), became ruler of the lands east of the Lualaba River, and he and his successors completed the expansion into present-day Zambia. Kazembe prospered through trade and tribute and by 1800 its capital controlled many of trade routes that crossed the continent.

In the nineteenth century, however, disagreements weakened Lunda rule and in the 1880s the empire broke up under pressure from the Chokwe, a people it had once controlled. Then the European nations of Belgium, Britain, and Portugal colonized Lunda lands. The Portuguese ruled Angola, the British ruled Zambia as Northern Rhodesia (annexing Kazembe in 1899), and Congo came under Belgian domination. Before becoming a Belgian colony, much of present-day Congo (Dem. Rep.) formed the private colony of the Belgian king, Léopold II as the Congo Free State (1885–1908). His rule was characterized by abuses, brutality, and the committing of atrocities in order to protect and maintain the lucrative rubber trade. Congo became independent in 1960, Zambia in 1964, and Angola gained independence in 1975.

RECENT EVENTS Ethnic tensions in Congo (Dem. Rep.) have led to many rebellions particularly in the north of Katanga (formerly Shaba) province in southern Congo (Rep.), the Lunda heartland. Katanga was only finally defeated by the army in 1965. The secessionist leader Moïse Tshombe (q.v.), a member of the Lunda royal family, was subsequently made interim prime minister. Despite winning a majority of seats in the elections, a political deadlock ensued that was only broken when Mobutu Sese Seko (q.v.) took power in a military coup. Until 1997, the country was ruled by President Mobutu as a one-party state. Further Katangan rebellions known as the First Katanga War and the Second Katanga War occurred in 1977 and 1978 respectively and there was another in 1984. They were harshly put down by government troops, usually with Western backing. In 1993, the governor, Gabriel Kumwanza, declared the province independent as Katanga. Kumwanza was arrested in 1995 after arms, allegedly for use in a Katangan rebellion, were found at his home. Clashes between his supporters and government troops were defused by his release.

Language

People living in the old Lunda Empire heartland speak Lunda. Those who migrated to Angola and Zambia have tended to adopt Angolan or Zambian languages.

Ways of life

AGRICULTURE Most Lunda people live in rural villages carved out of the woodland, grassland, or scrub that cover the land. Many villagers practice shifting cultivation – land is cleared and tended for a few years and then, before overuse exhausts the soil, they move their village and its croplands somewhere else. The main food crops grown are cassava, bananas, corn, and yams. Women grow millet and sorghum, largely to brew beer from. Cassava, corn, pineapples, and sun-

flower seeds are also grown as cash crops. Most communities keep livestock, chiefly chickens, goats, pigs, and sheep, with smaller numbers of cattle. Trapping forest animals and gathering edible fungi, fruits, and honey adds variety to the diet.

Fishing provides another source of protein, and since the mid-1980s, fish farming has become increasingly popular.

TRADE During the colonial era, the Lunda's trading activities were widely curtailed and they consequently lost much of their economic wealth. Many Lunda now benefit from cross-border trade that takes advantage of different price structures in Angola, Congo (Dem. Rep.), and Zambia. Dried fish and meat are exchanged for salt, clothes, sugar cooking oil, and household utensils.

Social structure

SOCIAL STRUCTURE Each individual fits into a complex system of social relationships. Besides belonging to his or her family and village, a person may be a member of a particular religious group, social club, or political group. In Lunda society, people feel free to marry who they will and many marry someone from another culture. Descent is traced through the mother's side, but personal relationships may often be stronger than family ties, although these do provide a network for support if needed. Far-flung maternal relatives meet up at weddings and funerals, and inherited goods and status pass on through the maternal line. The mother supervises her own unmarried daughters and young sons, although there are close bonds between grandparents and their grandchildren. A woman's sons, and their wives and children, typically form the basis of a village.

POLITICAL STRUCTURE The Lunda are just one of many peoples under the central control of the governments of the three countries they now inhabit. The Zambian and

Mythical tree
According to legend, the first Lunda man, Mbar, planted this tree at the site where he lived with his wife Musang. Mbar told his son, Mwaku, that when the tree sprouted Mwaku would know that Mbar was always by his side.

Congo (Dem. Rep.) governments still recognize traditional leaders, who are incorporated into national structures at a local level. Village headmen superintend local affairs and help to settle minor disputes, while senior headmen and chiefs oversee larger areas. Both political and social structures have been disrupted by the civil war in Angola, leaving the Lunda in that country with very little stability.

Culture and religion

RELIGION Many Lunda have converted to Christianity in the twentieth century. The Lunda have long held a belief in a supreme creator god called Nzambi, who was reinterpreted as the Christian God by European missionaries. Nevertheless, many Lunda still hold that ancestors' spirits have the power to bless and punish them, and they fear the malign effects of witchcraft.

Lunda timeline

c. 1500 Lunda settle in southern Zaire	**1889** Kazembe annexed by British	**1970** Mobutu elected president	**1990–1996** Mobutu promises introduction of multiparty politics. Political deadlock follows as Mobutu blocks transition to democracy
1600s Lunda chiefdoms unite	**1908** Belgian government takes over Free State as Belgian Congo	**1971** Former Belgian Congo is renamed Zaire	
1700s Centralized Lunda Empire exists	**1960–1963** Belgian Congo independent as Republic of Congo. Katangan rebellion in south (Shaba)	**1972** Zambia made a one-party state	**1991** End of one-party rule in Zambia
by 1800 Kazembe kingdom is center of transcontinental trade routes		**1975** Angola independent as civil war is being fought	**1994** Peace accord in Angola
1880s Lunda Empire breaks up	**1964** Zambia independent. Katangan rebellion in Congo (Zaire)	**1977** First Shaba War in Zaire	**1995** Outbreak of deadly Ebola virus in Kikwit, southwestern Zaire
1885 Chokwe overthrow Lunda. Belgian king's Congo Free State is established (Congo [Dem. Rep.]	**1965** Mobutu Sese Seko seizes power and reunites Congo (Zaire)	**1978** Second Shaba War in Zaire	**1996–7** Civil war occurs and Laurent Kabila seizes power and renames the country

Luo

More than 3 million Luo people live in the western corner of Kenya, mainly in the Nyanza region. Several hundred thousand live in neighboring parts of Kenya and Tanzania.

The Luo claim descent from a mythical ancestor called Ramogi. The Luo are actually a Nilotes (q.v.), belonging to the so-called River-Lake Nilotes, who originated in a region in the south of present-day Sudan. The ancestors of the Luo, a Lwo (q.v.)-speaking people, migrated south probably between the fifteenth and eighteenth centuries, traveling along the Nile River to the lakes region of Kenya and Tanzania. The Luo arrived in Nyanza in four separate clan groups: the Jok group arrived in the sixteenth century, the Jokowiny and the Jokomolo in the early seventeenth century, and the non-Lwo Abasuba in the eighteenth and nineteenth centuries. Although the Luo are mainly Christian, elements of the Luo religion, such as the reverence of ancestors, still remain.

Lusoga *see* Soga

Luvale *see* Lwena

Luyana

The Luyana are a subgroup of the Lozi (q.v.). They live in Botswana, Angola, and Zambia.

Luyia

The Luyia are also known as the Luhya or Abaluyia, the latter especially in Kenya. The Luyia homeland in eastern Uganda and southwestern Kenya is located in the region between the northern shores of Lake Victoria and Mount Elgon to the north. The Luyia region was split in half in 1902 when the British colonial rulers established the boundary between present-day Uganda and Kenya. The Luyia are the second largest ethnic group in Kenya, and they probably number nearly 4 million in that country alone. A smaller, but still substantial number (more than one million) live in Uganda.

The Luyia have a variety of origins. They are descended from Kalenjin (q.v.), Bantu (q.v.), and Maasai (q.v.) ancestors who probably merged sometime in the seventeenth century. The dominant influence was Bantu, and indeed the Luyia language, LuLuyia, is a Bantu language. Luluyia has been spoken in the region for more than 500 years. Different Luyia subnations exist that speak different dialects of Luluyia though most are mutually understandable.

Lwena

The Lwena (Lovale, Luvale, Lobale, or Luena) claim descent from the Lunda (q.v.) of Central Africa. There are around 600,000 Lwena people, mostly living in northern and western Zambia. Others, however, live in Angola and the south of Congo (Dem. Rep.).

Lwo

The Lwo people make up a large family of related ethnic groups largely in East Africa that includes the Alur (q.v.), Lango (q.v.), Luo (q.v.), Nyoro, and Acholi (q.v.). Lwo is a linguistic and cultural grouping within the larger umbrella group of River-Lake Nilotes (q.v.). Centuries ago the River-Lake Nilotes migrated south from their cradleland in southern Sudan, along the Nile to the lakes region of Uganda. The Lwo adapted to and absorbed parts of the cultures they met with on their migrations, at the same time transmitting elements of their own – notably their language. Today Lwo languages are widely spoken, both by people of Lwo descent and by those of other origins who adopted the language. The Luo are descended from Lwo people who settled in Kenya and Tanzania. The Shilluk (q.v.) and the Anuak (q.v.) of southern Sudan and western Ethiopia are descended from Lwo ancestors who first migrated south then returned north.

Ma

The Ma (or Mano) are a Manding (q.v.)-speaking people. The majority of the 100,000 plus Ma live in Liberia, but many also live in Guinea-Bissau and Guinea.

Maale

The Maale live in Ethiopia, mostly along the southern fringe of the central Ethiopian Highlands. There are around 30,000 Maale.

Maasai

The Maasai are a collection of groups who live mostly in the grasslands of the Great Rift Valley that straddle the border of Kenya and Tanzania. The cattle-herding Maasai are often regarded as the Maasai "proper." Other Maasai groups include the Samburu of Kenya and the Arusha of Tanzania. There are over 250,000 Maasai.

History

The Maasai are Plains Nilotes (people originally from the southwestern fringe of the Ethiopian Highlands who migrated to the plains of East Africa). The ancestors of the Maasai initially settled to the east of the Great Rift Valley between mounts Kilimanjaro and Kenya. From the 1600s, the Maasai "proper" migrated southward while the Samburu turned east and settled in the mountains.

The 1700s were a period of increasing power and geographical expansion for the Maasai. Despite their relatively small numbers, by the early 1800s they dominated the region between Mount Elgon and Mount Kenya in the north and Dodoma, now the capital of Tanzania, in the south. As a rule they were not conquerors, but conflict with their neighbors or other Maasai groups began when they raided cattle or defended their own herds.

The nineteenth century was a period of increas-

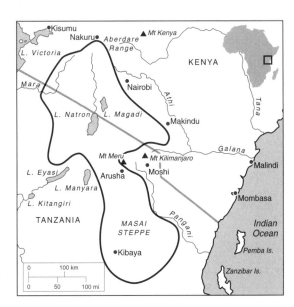

ingly frequent civil war among the Maasai. In particular, the Maasai "proper" – united for the first time under one leader, the laibon (prophet) Mbatiany – were in conflict with the Laikipiak, an agricultural Maasai group. This was followed by rinderpest (a cattle disease), smallpox, and cholera epidemics and famine during the 1880s and 1890s, which impoverished or killed thousands of Maasai. These disasters sparked further civil wars. This troubled period of Maasai history coincided with the British and German partition of East Africa. Maasai lands in British East Africa were taken over by European settlers and the Maasai were restricted to reserves.

Language

The Maasai speak a Nilotic language called Maa.

Ways of life

SEMINOMADIC PASTORALISM The majority of Maasai are seminomadic pastoralists (livestock raisers who move seasonally with their herds to make the best use of available water and pasture), herding mostly cattle and keeping a few sheep and goats. A minority, such as the

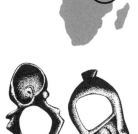

Giraffe-bone mortars
The pelvic bones of a giraffe have been used to make these mortars, used by laibons (healers and prophets) to grind medicine in. The Maasai have long been sculpting surrealistic artifacts based on the natural shapes of animals' bones. These mortars have been shaped to resemble elders' ears.

Battle dress
This line-up of moran shows them in full battledress. The feathered headdresses made it difficult for enemies to count their numbers. The Maasai frequently won their battles as they were well prepared both physically and psychologically. Their reputation for belligerence and ferocity, however, was largely fostered by Arab slave traders to scare competitors off inland trade routes.

Maasai moran
Moran (the youngest age-set) sometimes wear their hair in thin braids. Painstakingly done by a friend, the braids are extended by interweaving them with string caked with ocher (a yellow or reddish-brown clay).

Arusha, are farmers. Boys take the cattle out to graze by day and herd them back inside the village enclosure at night. Each family has its own cattle, but they are managed as part of a larger village herd. During the dry season, the Maasai men drive the cattle to distant water holes, making temporary camps until the rains come.

The Maasai's pastoral way of life is under threat as their right to graze cattle over land historically dominated by the Maasai is being eroded. This process began under colonialism when white settlers were given Maasai lands to farm and group ranches were set up to bring the Maasai into the money economy – a process continued after independence under pressure from the World Bank. Under the independent Kenyan government, the Maasai ranches were divided into individual farms and a lot of land was sold to big landowners or allocated to well-connected non-Maasai people. In Tanzania during the socialist era of the 1970s and 1980s, a process called villagization placed dispersed populations such as the Maasai into settled villages. Fortunately, however, politicians are beginning to realize the efficiency of traditional herd management techniques and now try to combine them with new developments, for instance in veterinary care, instead of trying to eradicate them.

Another threat to Maasai grazing lands has resulted from the loss of wildlife. Widely-roaming elephant and giraffe populations once helped maintain grasslands by grazing them, preventing the formation of dense scrub

(or bush, dense vegetation of scraggly trees and shrubs). The boom in big-game hunting, which began during the colonial era and was succeeded by poaching, has allowed large tracts of grassland to convert to scrub, which cannot support cattle. One unique solution to this problem, adopted in particular by the Samburu, has been to change to camel herding. Camels are hardy animals that can feed from scrub; they can go for long periods without water; and the milk they produce is more nutritious, more plentiful, and lasts longer than cow's milk. They are also popular with tourists.

INDUSTRY Historically, few Maasai engaged in industry. Although some Maasai families have long been blacksmiths, they are despised by others and not allowed to intermarry. As their seminomadic lifestyle is curtailed, however, many Maasai have left the pastoral economy and sought employment in urban areas working in hotels and lodges or as security guards.

TOURISM The Maasai, who are sought out by visitors, have been greatly affected by tourism; some villages earn a considerable part of their income from sightseeing tours. These tourists expect the Maasai to appear "traditionally authentic," however, and this has to be balanced with the need to adapt to the changing economic climate. Much of the revenue earned through tourism does not reach the Maasai; a lot of the crafts marketed as Maasai are in fact neither manufactured nor sold by them. Some Samburu, however, organize camel safaris.

HOUSING During the dry season, Maasai men live in temporary camps. During the rainy season, they live in homesteads called enkang. These are usually built on high ground by women from cattle manure, mud, and grass. They are relatively permanent and are rebuilt every five to ten years. From time to time, the site of the village is moved. As the Maasai become more settled, however, enkang are increasingly being used as year-round homes. To cope with the greater demands on their homes, Maasai women have adopted new

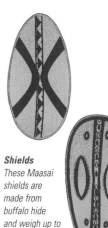

Shields
These Maasai shields are made from buffalo hide and weigh up to 50 lb (23 kg) each. They carry designs called sirata that indicate the age-group and family of the shield's owner. In battle, such shields would be carried with an 8 ft (2.5 m) long spear, but it is now illegal to carry a spear in Kenya.

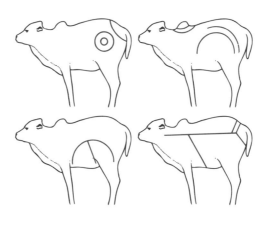

Cattle branding
Until recently, the Maasai would brand their herds. These marks identified the owners of the cattle. This practice has died out, however, as the Maasai now often sell the hides and can get a better price for unmarked ones.

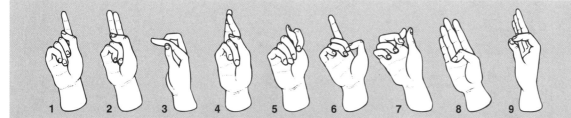

Numbering system
Hand signals are a common Maasai method of indicating numbers, and are still used today.

1 2 3 4 5 6 7 8 9

Maasai girl
This young Maasai girl is wearing beaded necklaces, earrings, and a beaded headband. Beadwork is a major art form in Africa and Maasai jewelry reflects this. Some Maasai girls do not consider themselves fully dressed without their jewelry.

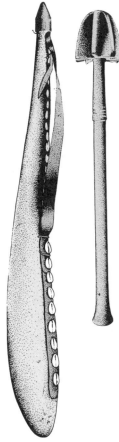

Calabash *(above left)*
This bottle is made from a long calabash (gourd). It has been decorated with leather and cowrie shells. Such bottles were once in common use among the Maasai. Now, they are more likely to be found in museums.

Wooden stick *(above right)*
A wooden stirring stick used in making butter from milk.

Orinkas
Orinkas are ceremonial clubs that men would carry to age-group meetings. In the past, age-group leaders carried ivory or rhinoceros horn orinkas, but the use of these materials is now illegal.

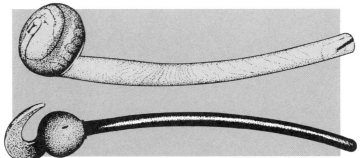

building techniques. Houses are often improved by adding a ferro-cement coating to the roof (a thin, watertight layer) and gutters to channel off rainwater into a container. Also, changes in the Maasai diet that have entailed more cooking have, in turn, led to the addition of chimneys.

DIET The Maasai diet was once based on milk, mixed with cattle blood at times of scarcity. Young men were supposed to stick strictly to a milk, blood, and meat diet; others could eat butter and honey. Only male elders could drink mead made from honey. If cows' milk was scarce, women could drink the milk of goats. Men were supposed to drink only cows' milk.

The Maasai diet is now no longer restricted to milk, meat, and blood. In fact, milk with blood is rarely drunk today. Instead, the Maasai supplement their diet with tea, sugar, vegetables, and grains such as corn. Cattle, goats, and sheep are traded for these items.

CLOTHING Until recently, the Maasai usually wore clothes made from calfskin or buffalo hide. Women would wear long skirtlike robes and men shorter tunics. Greased with cow fat, such garments provided protection from both Sun and rain, were hard wearing, easily available, and did not need to be washed with water. As imported fabrics and Western clothes become the norm, however, greater pressure is put on limited water resources as these textiles need to be washed with water when soiled.

Social structure

AGE-GRADES Maasai society is organized into male age-grades (basically, the social hierarchy). Every man belongs to a particular age-set (a group of males who were initiated at the same time) and moves with this same set up through the various age-grades.

For their initiation into manhood, young men around the age of sixteen live in camps called manyattas away from the village. Here, they are taught about herd management, religion, politics, and the skills of social life. After they have undergone circumcision they join the youngest age-grade of moran, often translated as "warriors." Moran did act in the past as the Maasai army, but fighting is not their main function. The moran are usually responsible for the herds when they are far from the village during the dry season and provide a source of labor for specific tasks. Since the 1960s, many moran now complete their education after circumcision. The Maasai trace their history by referring to the time when particular age-sets were serving as moran.

After a period of between seven and fifteen years, all existing moran are upgraded to the status of elders. As elders they have the right to chew tobacco, take snuff, and settle, but at this stage they have little influence. The most recent age-set to become elders is called ilterekeyani. There are two more grades of elder: senior and retired. Senior elders take decisions on such matters as disputes, allocation of pasture lands, and, in the modern world, development projects. Retired elders are still very influential and can act as patrons of men in younger age-sets.

COUNCILS Each age-set holds council meetings chaired

Maasai woman
Coiled-wire earrings, necklace, and armbands indicate that this woman is married and a mother.

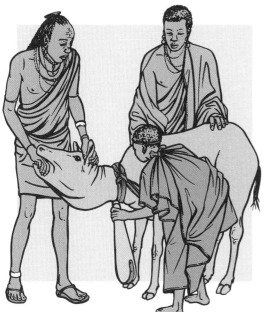

Bleeding cattle
Cattle are very important to the Maasai and are only killed on special occasions. Instead, their milk provides the staple food. At times of scarcity in particular, this milk would be mixed with blood from the cow to make it go further. The animal's jugular would be pierced, the blood caught, and then the wound would be stopped with mud or dung leaving the animal none the worse.

The Maasai have great respect for their laibons, who are prophets, leaders of rituals, and healers. Their major function was once to advise the moran on advantageous times for raiding or war, and to bless their ceremonies. Laibons would also announce major prophecies from a trancelike state. In the present, laibons admit that their prophetic abilities are on the wane but they claim still to be able to divine the sources of personal misfortune; therefore, they now deal on an individual basis with clients who have problems such as infertility or bad luck rather than advise the whole community or foretell the future.

DANCING In a traditional Maasai dance, the performing moran would jump up and down, without using their arms, and grunt as they touched the ground. Moran would perform this dance in unison, keeping perfect time, and watched by other Maasai.

Maasai shield
Made from, cowhide and wood, its design is the badge of the clan to which its owner belonged.

by a nominee known as the olaiguenani. Every man can have his say and decisions are taken by consensus. If an issue affects other age-sets, then olaiguenani from the relevant groups meet. They cannot take decisions without referring back to their age-set though and they also consult with the women.

Culture and religion

RELIGION The Maasai worship one god, Ngai, the husband of the Moon. He is thought to dwell above Mount Kilimanjaro, Tanzania – Africa's highest mountain. Legend says that in the beginning Ngai created the Maasai and then created all cattle for them. In the past, this was used to justify raiding a neighbor's cattle. Now, disputes over cattle are more likely to be settled by negotiation than raiding.

Maasai timeline		
1600s Maasai migrate southward from Rift Valley	**1904–1908** Maasai lands in British East Africa settled by Europeans	**1967** Arusha Declaration; Tanzania adopts socialism
1700–1800 Period of expansion and increasing power	**1961** Tanganyika wins independence	**1985** Tanzania abandons socialism
1880s–1890s Rinderpest (a cattle disease), cholera and smallpox epidemics spark famine	**1963** Kenya wins independence	**1991** Kenya allows for multiparty politics
1885–1895 Britain and Germany partition East Africa	**1964** Tanganyika and Zanzibar unite to form Tanzania	**1993** Maasai and Kikuyu clash in Kenya's Rift Valley
	1965 Each part of Tanzania is allowed only one political party	**1995** Chaotic first multipartly elections held in Tanzania

Maba

Most of the more than 200,000 Maba live in eastern Chad but around 20,000 live in Sudan. They speak a Nilo-Saharan language called Bora Mabang.

Maban

The Maban are a subgroup of the Funj (q.v.) people. The Funj live in southern Sudan.

Mabiha *see* Mavia

Macha

The Macha are one of the nine main subgroups of the Oromo (q.v.). They live in Ethiopia.

Machinga

The Machinga are widely considered to be a subgroup of the Yao (q.v.). They number around 35,000 people living in Tanzania.

Maconde *see* Makonde

 © DIAGRAM

Madagascan Peoples

Madagascar is a large island – the fourth largest in the world – in the Indian Ocean off the southeast coast of Africa. It has a population of over thirteen million, made up of eighteen principal ethnic groups plus minority groups of Europeans (mainly French nationals), Comorans (from the nearby Comoros Islands), Indians, Pakistanis, and Chinese.

The Madagascan peoples can be divided into two main groups: those of Indonesian descent, who live mainly in the central and south-central highlands of the interior, and those of Black African descent, who inhabit the coastal regions and are sometimes known collectively as the Côtiers (the coastal people).

The most important of the highland peoples are the Merina, who make up about twenty-seven percent of the island's thirteen million population, and the Betsileo (thirteen percent of the population). The major coastal peoples include the Betsimisaraka, the Antandroy, and the Sakalava. These peoples represent about fifteen, eight, and six percent of the total population respectively. The Merina, Betsimisaraka, and Betsileo each number over one million people.

History

The first people to settle in Madagascar were of Malayo-Polynesian origin. They arrived on the island from Indonesia between 2,000 and 1,500 years ago, and over the following centuries they were joined by waves of immigrants from Africa, Asia, Arabia, and Europe.

THREE GREAT KINGDOMS Madagascar's history is dominated by three large, powerful kingdoms, formed by the unification of smaller states. The first of these was the Sakalava kingdom – established along the west coast in the late sixteenth century. By the middle of the eighteenth century it controlled nearly half the island, but began to fragment after the death of its last ruler, Queen Ravahiny, in 1808. The second had its origins in

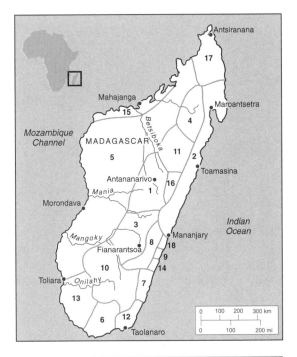

Mother and child
This Malagasy woman is carrying her baby in a makeshift pocket of her lamba – a wraparound dress. The lamba is a very traditional style of clothing and was once worn by people of all the principal ethnic groups of Madagascar. Today, the lamba is rarely worn.

The peoples of Madagascar
The map on the right shows the locations of the eighteen principal ethnic groups of Madagascar, who are listed below in order of decreasing size.

1 Merina	**7** Antaisaka	**13** Mahafaly
2 Betsimisaraka	**8** Tanala	**14** Antaifasy
3 Betsileo	**9** Antaimoro	**15** Makoa
4 Tsimihety	**10** Bara	**16** Bezanozano
5 Sakalava	**11** Sihanaka	**17** Antankarana
6 Antandroy	**12** Antanosy	**18** Antambahoaka

King Radama I
Son and successor of Andrianampoinimerina, Radama I ruled over the Merina kingdom from 1810 until his death in 1828. He extended Merina control over most of the island. Radama was succeeded by his wife, Queen Ranavalona, who continued the subjugation of the island.

the Tsitambala confederation, a seventeenth-century alliance of chiefdoms along the east coast. This confederation was taken over and expanded in the early eighteenth century by Ratsimilaho, an English-educated son of an English pirate, who created from it the Betsimisaraka kingdom. The third great kingdom emerged in the central highlands during the fifteenth century, when the Merina settled there and subjugated the original inhabitants, the Vazimba. The Merina kingdom grew and prospered and, after the fall of the Betsimisaraka kingdom in 1791 and the Sakalava kingdom in 1822, it controlled most of the island.

COLONIALISM European contact with the island began with the arrival of a Portuguese fleet in 1500. For the next three hundred years, the Portuguese, British, Dutch, and French tried to set up colonies on the island. These early colonies were repeatedly destroyed by the islanders, but they tolerated small bases that were set up in the late seventeenth century by pirates from Europe and the American colonies, who preyed on shipping in the Indian Ocean.

During the first half of the nineteenth century, the Merina ruler King Radama I opened up Madagascar to outside influences, particularly French and British. In 1817, the British acknowledged him as king of all Madagascar, and British and other European advisors

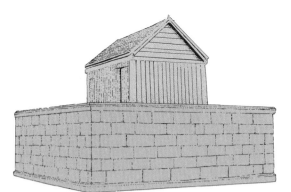

Tomb
This tomb of a noble family consists of a burial vault with a prayer house on top. Tombs can be seen dotted all over Madagascar's countryside. Originally a Merina custom, many peoples now build tombs for their dead. Often the focus of ceremonies and festivals, ancestral tombs signify a person's place in society and their rights to land – without a tomb a person is a nobody. Since World War II, tombs have been built with cement-finished sides and painted designs. The cost of this, however, has lead to a revival of more-traditional, affordable forms.

began helping him establish schools, industries, and a professional army and set up Christian churches. These policies were reversed when Radama died, in 1828, and was succeeded by his wife, Queen Ranavalona I. She forced most of the Europeans from the country and closed the schools and churches, but the French and British began to return after her death in 1861.

Over the next thirty years, France, Britain, and the Merina argued over which of them should control the island, and there was war between the Merina and the French from 1883 to 1885. In 1890, Britain agreed to let France have Madagascar in return for control of Egypt and Zanzibar, and the country was declared a French protectorate (colony) in 1895. This was opposed by the queen, Ranavalona II, and by the people, so the French imposed their rule by force.

INDEPENDENCE Madagascar remained a French colony until 1960, when it regained its independence under its first president, Philibert Tsiranana (q.v.). French influence remained strong under Tsiranana's right-wing rule, but ended when he was forced to resign after an

anti-government uprising in 1972. The army commander, General Gabriel Ramanantsoa (q.v.), then took control of the government and closed the French military bases on the island. Ramanantsoa was forced out in 1975, but his successor, Colonel Richard Ratsimandrava, was shot dead within a week of seizing power by an army group who staged a military takeover. In turn, this group was defeated by another military faction and Didier Ratsiraka (q.v.), formerly the country's foreign minister, became president and set the country on a socialist path. The country, which since 1958 had been known as the Malagasy Republic, was renamed the Democratic Republic of Madagascar.
RECENT EVENTS Demonstrations, a general strike, and pressure from France in 1991 and 1992 forced presidential elections in which Ratsiraka was defeated by Professor Albert Zafy, leader of the opposition alliance Forces Vives. However, in presidential elections in 1996 Albert Zafy was defeated and Didier Ratsiraka again became president, winning fifty per cent of the votes cast.

Languages
The official languages of Madagascar are Malagasy and French, but less than thirty percent of the population can speak French – outside of the cities, most people speak only Malagasy. The different ethnic groups speak various dialects of the Malagasy language, which is a member of the Western Austronesian language family. Standard Malagasy (the "official" form) is used to bridge the gap between dialects; it is based on the Merina dialect and written in the Roman alphabet.

The minority populations such as the Indians, Europeans, Chinese, and Arabs speak either an Indian or European language, Chinese, or Arabic respectively – usually in addition to Malagasy.

Ways of life
agriculture Outside of the main towns and cities, the way of life is mostly agricultural and so is heavily influenced by climate and geography. In the hot and humid tropical climate of the north and east, important crops include coffee, vanilla, cloves, fruit, and sugar cane. The hot coastal plains of the west and southwest are

Wooden figure
Mystery surrounds this nineteenth-century wooden sculpture. The top half of a post, it may have been used as a tomb sculpture (by the Mahafaly) or as a hazomanga (a village ritual post) by the Sakalava. It has been attributed to many different Malagasy peoples at one time or another. This sculpture was a source of inspiration for the American sculptor Sir Jacob Epstein.

Bamboo (right)
This woman is carrying two large bamboo poles. On the east coast of Madagascar the climate is very hot and damp. These are ideal conditions for growing bamboo, which has a great variety of uses.

Betsimisaraka house
This Betsimisaraka house has been built with bamboo and has a thatched roof.

Antanosy granary (above)
This raised wooden structure would have been used by the Antanosy as a granary (a place to store grain). Wooden disks on the supporting pillars stop rats destroying the stores.

© DIAGRAM

Wooden spoon
Throughout Madagascar, sculpted wooden spoons are used for serving rice on special occasions. This spoon has been attributed to the Sakalava people.

Mahafaly tomb sculpture
This wooden sculpted pole was produced for the tomb of a Mahafaly of some standing. Known as aloalo, up to thirty of such poles can appear on on the top of one tomb. More recent aloalo often incorporate figures such as airplanes and buses above the semicircular and circular shapes, which are thought to represent the Moon and half-Moon. The sculptures are both commemorative of the deceased and symbolic of the link that ancestors provide between the dead and the living.

Betsileo hairstyle
This Betsileo woman has her hair braided and looped into an attractive arrangement. Hairstyles vary according to the current fashions.

drier than the north and east, and their main products are rice, cotton, tobacco, and cassava. Livestock is raised in the arid south of the country, the temperate highland regions of the interior, and on the coastal plains. Cattle are often regarded as indicators of wealth and not as sources of income. The highlands are important rice-growing areas but have been badly affected by soil erosion and deforestation. Fishing is important in many areas, both along the coast and in the numerous rivers and lakes.

Most farmers practice subsistence agriculture, in which people grow food for their own consumption, but some crops, such as tobacco, coffee, and vanilla, are grown to be sold for cash. The work involved is usually divided between men and women. For example, men typically prepare the ground for planting, build the houses and cattle pens, hunt, and fish. Women usually tend the crops, grow herbs and vegetables, and do domestic tasks such as cooking and laundry.

TRADE AND INDUSTRY Only a relatively small proportion of people are involved in industry, and the majority of these work in food processing plants. Textiles, brewing, and paper and soap production are other important sectors. Sea fishing, by coastal fisherman, is in the process of being industrialized. The Indian population largely dominates the jewelry and textile trades. On the east coast, the Chinese community is largely engaged in small-scale banking and the trading of agricultural products. Others work in tourism – Madagascar's many unique plants and animals and diversity of environments attract a considerable number of tourists to the island.

Social structure

SOCIAL STRUCTURE Family and clan relationships are very important in Madagascan society. The members of a clan trace their origins back to a common and revered ancestor. Marriage customs vary from one ethnic group to another. Although most marriages are between one man and one woman, the customs of some people allow a man to have more than one wife, while others allow a woman to have more than one husband.

POLITICAL STRUCTURE Politically, Madagascar is divided into six provinces and each of these is further divided into administrative districts down to village level. A typical village is governed by its male and female elders led by the senior male.

Culture and religion

RELIGION About fifty percent of the population of Madagascar follow the Malagasy religion, which is based on reverence for spirits and ancestors. This is expressed in

regular ceremonies centered on the ancestral tombs, which are built and maintained with great care. These ceremonies help people to maintain a feeling of identity with each other and with their past, and, whenever possible, the dead are always buried in their ancestral tombs. Often, aspects of the Malagasy religion (such as ancestor reverence) are practiced in conjunction with Christianity or Islam.

Christianity was brought to Madagascar by European missionaries during the nineteenth century and today about forty percent of the population are Christian. The Christians in the interior of the country, where the British had most influence, are mainly Protestant. Those in the coastal regions, where French influence was stronger, are mostly Catholic.

The third major religion of Madagascar is Islam. This is followed by around ten percent of the population, and was brought to the island by Arab, East African, and Comoran traders who began to trade there in the ninth century. These traders, who were mostly Sunni Muslims, also brought with them a tradition of divination, or prophecy, called sikidy. Although the majority of Madagascar's Muslims belong to the Sunni branch of Islam, there are also a number of Shiite and Ismaili Muslims on the island, most of whom are of Indian or Pakistani origin.

Mpsikidy
Among the Sakalava, there are religious practitioners called mpsikidy. These are basically diviners who diagnose and attempt to heal particular ills or foretell the future. In this example, a mpisikidy is using seeds to tell his client's future. The seeds are shuffled into sixteen small piles and the arrangements of shapes formed are then interpreted by the diviner.

Madagascan Peoples timeline			
upto 1000 Indonesians arrive on island of Madagascar	**1700s** Betsimisaraka kingdom emerges from Tsitambala confederation	island unification and opening up to foreign influences begins	**1958** Semiautonomous Malagasy Republic established
1400 Muslim trading colonies and kingdoms established	**1791** Fall of Betsimisaraka kingdom	**1822** Sakalava kingdom collapses	**1960** Malagasy Republic independent
1500s Sakalava kingdom established	**1797** Unified Merina kingdom in existence	**1883–1885** Franco-Merina War over control of island	**1975** Malagasy renamed Madagascar
1600s Tsitambala confederation	**1810–1828** Reign of Merina king Radama I,	**1895** French rule begins	**1993** Free elections end eighteen years of dictatorship

Madi

The Madi (or Maditi) live mostly in northwestern Uganda but some also live in southern Sudan. Of the around 250,000 Madi, more than 200,000 live in Uganda. They are sometimes classified as a Lugbara (q.v.) subgroup.

Maditi *see* Madi

Madjigodjia

The Madjigodjia are one the major subgroups of the Buduma (q.v.). They have a population of around 10,000, who live in southern Chad's lake region.

Madjingaye

The Madjingaye are a subgroup of the Sara (q.v.) of Chad. They number around 100,000 people.

Maganga

The Maganga (or Chuabo) are a subgroup of the Chewa (q.v.) of Malawi, Zambia, and Mozambique. They have a population of more than 300,000 people.

Mahafaly

The Mahafaly are one of Madagascar's ethnic groups. They live in the southwest of the island and number around 150,000. See also **Madagascan peoples**.

Mahi

The Mahi are closely related to the Ewe (q.v.) and are considered to be a Fon (q.v.) subgroup. The more than 100,000 Mahi live mostly in Togo but a minority live in northern Benin.

Maibuloa

The Maibuloa are one of the major Buduma (q.v.) subgroups. They number more than 17,000, living primarily in southern Chad.

Maiombe *see* Mayombe

Maji

The Maji are often thought to be related to the Sadama (q.v.).The more than 20,000 Maji live in southwest Ethiopia near the border with Sudan.

Majoge

The Majoge are one of the main subdivisions of the Gusii (q.v.). The Gusii are a large ethnic group of western Kenya.

Makonde

The Makonde (or Maconde, Chimakonde, Konde, or Matambwe) are a large ethnic group of southeastern Tanzania. They are closely related to the Makua (q.v.) and are sometimes classified as a subgroup of the Yao (q.v.). There are roughly 1.5 million Makonde. The distinctive Makonde carvings have been widely copied by carvers throughout the region, largely to supply tourist and foreign markets.

Makua *see* Makua-Lomwe

Makua-Lomwe

The various ethnic groups that make up the Makua-Lomwe peoples account for roughly 40 percent of Mozambique's total population. There are around six million Makua-Lomwe. They are concentrated along the lower Zambezi River Valley in the center of Mozambique, in the northernmost provinces of Niassa and Cabo Delgado, and along parts of the northeast coast of the Indian Ocean.

The Makua proper make up the bulk of the Makua-Lomwe peoples, and most live north of the Ligonha River and along the coast. The majority of the Lomwe live south of Ligonha and inland from the coast.

Attempts to balance the power of different ethnic groups have been made in Mozambique. Nevertheless southerners, such as the Tsonga (q.v.), have tended to benefit from better educational opportunities than northerners, and as a result the government is largely drawn from southern and central groups.

Maligo

The Maligo are a Khoisan (q.v.) people living in the far south of Angola. They are a small ethnic group, numbering only a few thousand.

Malinke *see* Bambara and Malinke

Makonde mask
This Makonde face mask from southern Tanzania features rabbit-like ears and a "beard" made from vegetable fibre.

Mamprusi

The Mamprusi are one of the several ethnic groups that make up the Mossi (q.v.) people. The Mamprusi inhabit a region in northern Ghana bounded on the north by the White Volta River. The Mamprusi language, Mampruli, is one of many Moré (or Molé) languages spoken in Ghana and Burkina Faso. There are probably around 200,000 Mamprusi people in northern Ghana. Although they do not make up the majority of that region's population, they are its largest ethnic group.

The Mamprusi probably emerged as a distinct group in the fifteenth century, when a cavalry group from northern Ghana rode north in search of land. These people established the seven main Mossi kingdoms, one of which was Mamprusi. Historically, the king had an important religious as well as political role, but this role has diminished somewhat in the late twentieth century as more and more Mamprusi convert to Islam.

Mamvu

The Mamvu are concentrated in Mozambique and Congo (Dem. Rep.). They are a Bantu (q.v.) people who number more than 50,000.

Manala

The Manala are one of the main Ndebele (q.v.) groups. The Ndebele live in South Africa.

Manasir

The Manasir are descended from Nubian (q.v.) and Arab (q.v.) ancestors. They number more than one million people, mostly living in north-central Sudan.

Mande

The Mande people make up a large family of related ethnic groups that includes the Bambara (q.v.), Dyula (q.v.), Malinke (q.v.), Soninke (q.v.), Susu (q.v.), and Mende (q.v.) peoples.

The Mande homeland is centered on the border between present-day Mali and Guinea. Historically, the Mande were politically important since Mande-speakers were the founders of two of West Africa's most important states: the Empire of Ghana, founded by the Soninke, and the Empire of Mali, founded by the Malinke (neither empire should be confused with the present-day country of the same name). The domi-

nance and large size of these empires is in part responsible for the prevalence of Mande-speaking societies in West Africa. Furthermore, a wave of Mande-speaking migrants spread across West Africa in the fifteenth century when the Empire of Mali was in decline.

Mande languages include Manding, which is spoken throughout much of West Africa in, for example, Guinea, Burkina Faso, Gambia, Senegal, Mali, Ivory Coast, and Guinea Bissau. The Mande language group belongs to the Niger-Congo subfamily of the Niger-Kordofanian family.

Dan ceremonial spoon
The Dan people are descended from the Manding, rulers of the vast medieval empire of Mali, which rose to prominence in the thirteenth century.

Mandija

The Mandija are a subgroup of the Baya (q.v.) of the Central African Republic. They number more than 150,000.

Manding

The Manding (or Mandinka or Mandingo) is a group of peoples related by language who are spread throughout much of West Africa, and in particular in Guinea, Guinea-Bissau, Mali, Senegal, Niger, and Gambia. There are well over 13 million Manding people in Africa. The Bambara (q.v.), Malinke (q.v.), Susu (q.v.), Mende (q.v), Kpelle (q.v.), Dan (q.v.) and Dyula (q.v.) are all Manding peoples. Many other West African groups are closely related to the Manding. The Manding lan-

guages belong to the wider grouping of Mande (q.v.) languages.

All Manding peoples originated from a mountainous region of the same name that sits astride the border of Mali and Guinea – the base of the vast medieval Empire of Mali, which rose to prominence in the thirteenth century. All Manding peoples share a common origin forged by the Islamic Empire of Mali, and the majority have been Muslim for centuries.

Mandingo see Manding

Mandinka see Manding

Mandyako see Manjaco

Manga

The Manga of Niger, Nigeria, and Chad number around 200,000 people. They speak a Kanuri (q.v.) language.

Mandingo sword
The brass handle matches the brass end of its sheath.

Mangbetu

The Mangbetu of northeastern Congo (Dem. Rep.) probably number around three-quarters of a million people. The Mangbetu language is known as Mangebtu or Kere, and it belongs to the Central Sudanic subfamily of the Nilo-Saharan family. Mangbetu is distantly related to the Lugbara (q.v.) language.

The Mangbetu are unique in having created one of the few centralized political systems in Central Africa. The Mangbetu kingdom was founded in the first half of the nineteenth century by a leader called Nabiembali, who extended Mangbetu control over non-Mangbetu speakers for the first time. By the second half of the nineteenth century, the court of the Mangbetu king, Mbunza, was famed as a center for the arts and performance. Mbunza was probably the most powerful of a number of Mangbetu kingdoms.

It is a custom for Mangbetu villagers to decorate the outside of their houses with murals, and the beautiful Mangbetu villages were much visited and photographed by Western travelers in the early years of the twentieth century.

Beer mug
Mangutu pottery often features a stylized head such as this, elongated to show tribal hairstyle.

Mangutu

The Mangutu are closely related to the Mamvu (q.v.). They number more than 60,000 people, the majority of whom live in northeastern Congo (Dem. Rep.), though some also live in northwestern Uganda and southern Sudan.

Manhica

The Manhica (or Manyica) are a subgroup of the Shona (q.v.). They live in Mozambique and Zimbabwe.

Manigiri

The Manigiri are a subgroup of the Yoruba (q.v.). They live in Benin and Togo.

Manja

The Manja are descended from Baya (q.v.) ancestors who broke away from the main group. The majority live in the center of the Central African Republic.

Manjaco

The Manjaco (Mandyako or Manjago) live in Senegal, Guinea-Bissau, and Gambia. Their population is more than 100,000 people.

Manjago *see* Manjaco

Mano *see* Ma

Manyica *see* Manhica

Mao

The Mao are Nilotes (q.v.) from Ethiopia. There are more than 20,000 Mao, the majority of whom are seminomadic or nomadic pastoralists.

Marait *see* Marari

Marakwet

The Marakwet are one of the several related groups that make up the Kalenjin (q.v.). The Kalenjin are a large ethnic group in western Kenya.

Marari

The Marari (or Mararit or Marait) number around 20,000 people, and they are closely related to the Abu Sharib (q.v.). The Marari speak a Tama (q.v.) language and live on and around the border between Sudan and Chad, mostly in Chad.

Mararit *see* Marari

Marave *see* Maravi

Maravi

The Maravi (Marave) number roughly 300,000 people. The majority live in northern Mozambique, where they migrated to from the Congo (Rep.) several hundred years ago.

Marya

The Marya are one of central Eritrea's main ethnic groups. They number more than 25,000 people.

Masai *see* Maasai

Masalit

The Masalit (of Kaana Masala) mostly live in Darfur Province in western Sudan and a minority live farther west in Chad. There are more than 350,000 Masalit.

Masheba *see* Chewa

Massa

The Massa (or Banana or Walia) live in northern Cameroon and southern Chad. There are more than 150,000 Massa.

Matabele *see* Ndebele and Matabele

Matakam

The Matakam live in northern Cameroon and northern Nigeria. They number more than 200,000.

Matambwe *see* Makonde

Matheniko

The Matheniko are a subgroup of the Karamojong (q.v.). They live in northeastern Uganda.

Matumbi

The Matumbi (or Kimatumbi) are a Bantu people who live on the Tanzanian–Mozambique border, mostly in Tanzania. They number more than 70,000.

Mavia

The Mavia (or Mawia, Mabiha, or Chimaviha) are a subgroup of the Makonde (q.v.). They live in northern Mozambique and southern Tanzania, mostly in Mozambique. There are around 70,000 Mavia.

Mawia *see* Mavia

Mayombe

The Mayombe (or Maiombe) are a subgroup of the Kongo (q.v.). They live in Cabinda, the northern extension of Angola, and in Congo (Dem. Rep.).

Mbai *see* Mbaye

Mbaka

The Mbaka (or Bwaka or Ngbaka) number more than 200,000 people. They live in the Central African Republic and Congo (Dem. Rep.). Jean-Bedel Bokassa was a Mbaka.

Mbaka-Mandija

The Mbaka-Mandija have relatively recently emerged as a separate ethnic group from the intermingling of Baya (q.v.) and Mbaka (q.v.) people. They live in the Central African Republic.

Mbala

The Mbala are a Bantu (q.v.) people who live in the south of Congo (Dem. Rep.). The majority live in and around Kikwit on the Kwilu River. The Mbala language is related to that of the Kongo (q.v.).

Mbay

The Mbay (or Mbai) are a subgroup of the Sara (q.v.), and they are probably of Nilotic (q.v.) origin. They number more than 60,000 people living largely in southern Chad.

Mbeere

The Mbeere live in south-central Kenya in the plains below the town of Embu on the slopes of Mount Kenya roughly 100 miles northeast of the capital, Nairobi. The Mbeere are a Bantu (q.v.) people – their language, which is called Kimbeere, belongs to the Bantu subgroup of the Benue-Congo group. There are probably less than 200,000 Mbeere living in Kenya. The Mbeere are sometimes classified as a subgroup of the Kikuyu (q.v.), who are also a Bantu-speaking people. Also like the Kikuyu, the Mbeere believe in a high-god called Ngai, who is said to live at the top of nearby Mount Kenya. In the twentieth century, however, many Kikuyu have converted to Christianity.

It is not known when the Mbeere settled in their present area, but they were well established in that region by the mid-nineteenth century.

Mbenga *see* Mbuti, Twa, and Mbenga

Mbila *see* Safwa

Mbochi

The Mbochi (or Mboshi or Boubangui) number more than 250,000. They live in central Congo (Rep.), the west of Congo (Dem. Rep.), and eastern Gabon.

Mbole

The Mbole are a subgroup of the Mongo (q.v.) of Central Africa. The Mbole live in central Congo (Dem. Rep.) west of the Lokmani River.

Mboshi *see* Mbochi

Mbugwe

The Mbugwe live in central Tanzania to the east and south of Lake Manyara. They are a Bantu (q.v.) people.

Mbulu *see* Iraqw

Mbun

The Mbun are a historically important Bantu (q.v.) people of Central Africa. They once dominated the Adamawa Highlands region of present-day Cameroon. They now live in southern Chad, northern Cameroon, and the west of the Central African Republic. The Mbun number around 800,000.

Mbundu

With a population well in excess of 2.5 million, the Mbundu account for about one quarter of Angola's total population. They inhabit north-central Angola, including Luanda – the capital. The Mbundu language, Kimbundu, is a Bantu (q.v.) language.

Toward the end of the fifteenth century, the Mbundu founded the Ndongo kingdom. The ruler of Ndongo was known as the the Ngola. In the seventeenth century, the Ndongo Kingdom was ruled by Nzinga Nbandi, or Anna Nzinga (q.v., 1623–63). This famous African queen was a leader of anti-colonial resistance. In the mid-twentieth century, the Mbundu were central in the battle to expel the Portuguese. The MPLA (Movimento Popular de Libertação de Angola) drew much of its support from the Mbundu. When independence was achieved in 1975, however, the country was plunged into civil war. Although peace was made in the 1990s and the MPLA won parliamentary and presidential elections, rebel groups remain in control large areas of Angola, and civil war resumed in 1999 after an uneasy peace from 1996.

Mbunga

The Mbunga number roughly 30,000 people. They are a Bantu (q.v.) people and live mostly in Tanzania.

Mbute *see* Vute

Mbuti, Twa, and Mbenga

Mbuti, Twa, and Mbenga are the three major groupings of the tropical forest-forager peoples (forest-dwelling people who live mainly by hunting and gathering) of Central Africa. These people are scattered across nine countries from the Atlantic coast in the west to Uganda in the east.

The Mbuti, of whom there are about 35,000, live in the Ituri Forest of northeast Congo (Dem. Rep.). About 100,000 Twa live in the area around Lake Tumba in western Congo (Dem. Rep.) and there are a further 30,000 in the high forests along the borders of Congo (Dem. Rep.), Uganda, Rwanda, and Burundi.

The Mbenga peoples – the Aka, Baka, Bongo, and Kola – number about 45,000. There are about 20,000 Aka, who live in northern Congo (Rep.) and the south of the Central African Republic. Some 20,000 Baka live in southeast Cameroon, northwest Congo (Rep.), and northern Gabon. There are about 2,000 Bongo in western Congo (Rep.) and southern Gabon. The Kola number around 3,000 and live in southwest Cameroon.

History

The origins of tropical forest-foragers – sometimes derogatorily referred to as "pygmies" because of their short stature – are obscure, but they have been living in the dense tropical rainforests, forests, marshes, and sometimes the savannas (grasslands with scattered trees and shrubs) of Central Africa for thousands of years. They were probably the region's first inhabitants and were known to the Ancient Egyptians nearly five thousand years ago. Until comparatively recently, the outside world – apart from their closest neighbors – knew very little about them. About two thousand years ago, Sudanic and Bantu-speaking peoples from the north, east, and southeast began to settle and farm on the fringes of the rainforests. These settlers cleared large areas of forest for their farmland, but found the forest itself hostile and threatening. In contrast, the forest dwellers felt safe in the forest and were threatened by its destruction.

The settlers and the forest people developed a rela-

Twa pottery
These small Twa pots, ingondo, date from 1940s Rwanda and were intended to contain love charms. Women would wear them tied around the waist to ensure their husbands' affections. For generations, the Twa in Rwanda have been dominated by the non-Twa population. Largely employed as potters, their market was ruined by the introduction of plastic and metal containers.

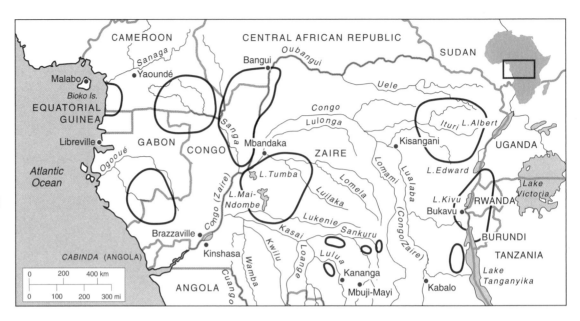

Pongo
Made by a woman from the Ituri Forest in Congo (Dem. Rep.), this bark-cloth pongo has been patterned with designs in natural dyes. Much of Ituri expressive culture is dominated by women and forager art has a great influence on painting in surrounding regions.

Hunting
This man has just fired an arrow into the treetops. The arrowhead is treated with poison made from a forest plant. Prey grazed by such an arrow become slow and weak and the hunter would track them until the animal is dead or trapped. Typical animals hunted in this fashion include antelopes, monkeys, and even elephants.

tionship that was generally of benefit to both groups. The individual groups of forest people allied themselves with neighboring settlers; adopted their languages; and supplied them with forest products, such as game, nuts, and wild honey in exchange for corn, bananas, rice, metal, and other village products. By providing the villagers with the forest products that they needed, the forest-dwellers ensured that the villagers did not need to enter the forest themselves thus preserving their environment. This mutual arrangement still survives, but in many parts of Central Africa has been under increasing threat since the late nineteenth century.

COLONIALISM This threat began with the colonization of Central Africa by European powers, especially France and Belgium. In the late nineteenth and early twentieth centuries, the colonial governments began forcing villagers to grow crops, such as rubber, for export. In turn, the hard-pressed villagers needed their forest neighbors' labor to produce food crops. At the same time, large areas of the forest were taken over by trading companies and the forest people were made to supply them with valuable products such as ivory and antelope skins. As a result, many of the forest people became dependent on villagers.

For a while, this suited the colonial governments but policies changed in the 1930s and attempts were made to govern the forest peoples directly and "free" them from the domination of the villagers – in reality, an attempt to make them dependent on the state instead.

RECENT EVENTS In the twentieth century, Mbuti, Twa, and Mbenga groups have all been affected by deforestation, government policies, and regional conflicts. In the early 1990s, the Twa of Rwanda have been caught up in the violence between the principal Hutu and Tutsi ethnic groups. Over 3,000 were probably killed in the genocide of 1994 and nearly 10,000 are now refugees, mostly living in refugee camps in Congo (Dem. Rep.).

Language
There is no common tropical forest-forager language as most groups speak the language of their nearest neighbors. The Mbuti and Twa peoples are Bantu speakers, and the languages of the Mbenga peoples are Bantu or Ubanguian. Two other Central African forest peoples, the Asua and Efe, speak a Sudanic language.

Ways of life
HUNTING AND GATHERING Specialists at extracting resources from the forest, the ways of life of the Mbuti and other forest peoples is usually a seminomadic existence, based on hunting game and gathering forest products such as fruit, nuts, and wild honey. Communities live in forest camps for several months a year. To set up a camp, a group clears a patch of undergrowth and builds small, conical huts made of bent branches covered in leaves and furnished with benches and beds made of sticks. When the camp has been built, the group spends part of each day gather-

Chair
Made from wood, vines, and fiber this chair exemplifies the wide range of uses that forest-foragers can use forest products for.

Forest home
This shelter has a frame made from saplings that has been covered in leaves and ferns to provide a canopy. Such shelters are usually temporary as camps often move on and reorganize elsewhere in order not to exhaust one area of game.

ing food and hunting game, such as antelope and monkeys, with bows and arrows, spears, or nets. The rest of their time is spent on activities such as making and repairing weapons; weaving baskets; making cloth out of beaten tree bark; and on communal entertainment such as storytelling, singing, and dancing. When food becomes scarce in the area, the group moves on to another site.

In the present-day, none of the forest-forager communities live in isolation. Forest products are traded with settled, farming communities for food products such as cassava and corn or for goods such as iron tools, tobacco, salt, and clothes. Time has to be spent near a village so that these exchanges can be carried out. Many also provide labor for the villagers, by working in gardens for instance. To outsiders it has often appeared that the forest-foragers are the servants of the villagers, but their ability to live in the forest keeps them independent.

DEFORESTATION Since the colonial era, vast areas of rainforest have been cleared for timber or to make way for cattle ranching or plantations of tea, coffee, rubber, cotton, and other cash crops. This large-scale destruction of the Twa and Mbenga lands has led to huge changes in their lifestyles – the Mbuti lands in the Ituri Forest have largely been spared so far as they lack the "high-grade" timbers in demand in Europe. As a result of these changes, many people can no longer follow their hunting-gathering way of life and have become an impoverished rural labor force. Since the Gishwati Forest was virtually all cut down for tea plantations and pasture in the 1980s, for example, the Impunyu Twa of Rwanda have largely abandoned hunting and gathering and are now mostly employed as domestic servants or landless laborers or have to beg to survive.

NATIONAL PARKS Even forest conservation measures, such as the establishment of national parks, have caused problems for tropical forest-foragers as most were created without consultation of the indigenous peoples of the forest. Conservation laws introduced to Rwanda in 1973 have made hunting and gathering virtually illegal. Most national parks restrict or prohibit the access of people to forests, forcing them to live on the fringes of the settled community. One exception is the Okapi National Park in Congo (Dem. Rep.) where many Mbuti who were originally excluded are now employed as trackers.

SEDENTARY LIFESTYLES Many groups now follow a sedentary (settled) lifestyle. In an often misguided attempt to "integrate" them into national life, forest dwellers have been encouraged to abandon the forest and farm since the colonial era. Some communities have therefore been sedentary farmers for generations and most now incorporate at least some form of cultivation into their lifestyle. The Bongo of southwest Congo (Rep.), for example, raise chickens for local markets and supply firewood, no longer relying on hunting and gathering.

DIET Recent research suggests that groups who continue their hunting and gathering way of life actually tend to be better nourished than other African peoples. Economic and political pressures mean that many rely on agricultural produce for most of their food though.

Foraging

This young girl is collecting ferns to build a shelter with. Tropical forest-forager groups gather more than food from the forest. Forest products provide shelter, fuel, medicines, tools, musical instruments, and clothing made from bark-cloth – the main type of attire until recent decades.

Knifes

Few forager groups actually work with metal. Instead, forest products are exchanged with villagers for knives such as these. The one on the left was originally a spear but has been converted into a knife, probably by its Mbuti owner. The wooden-handled knife on the right was used by the Ituri but its style suggests that it originates from Uganda.

Social structure

SOCIAL STRUCTURE While living in the forest, the Mbuti, Twa, and Mbenga peoples live in bands of between seven to thirty households. These communities are renowned for their egalitarianism as their social organization is based on cooperation, equality, and sharing. Decisions affecting the group are taken collectively and food that is collected is distributed equally throughout the group. Conflicts and disputes are resolved using humor and ritual rather than confrontation. If any members of the group are unhappy with decisions or wish to leave, then they can set up their own community. As a result, groups are fluid and people move freely between one group and another – to visit relatives or to stay for good.

Often specific bands of forest foragers have historical ties with a certain group of villagers. The commercial exploitation of forests has not only affected peoples' way of life, however, but also their social structures. These reciprocal relationships between foragers and villagers, now forced to compete for land and revenue from the destruction of forests, have broken down in many cases and resulted in outright exploitation or discrimination to the disadvantage of the more vulnerable forest-foragers.

POLITICAL STRUCTURE By taking care of tax returns and other official matters on their behalf, villagers have often established themselves as intermediaries with officialdom for the forest-dwellers. This can work against the interests of the people, as they are left unable to easily get hold of official documents needed to prove their citizenship and exercise their political rights. One of the greatest threats to the independence of these people is the fact that none of the countries in which they live recognize that they have any legal rights to the land they inhabit. The Mbuti, Twa, and Mbenga peoples are therefore often politically marginalized and discriminated against. To counteract this, some Twa people have set up political and cultural organizations in the 1990s: the Association pour le Promotion des Batwa (APB), is one such group.

DIVISION OF LABOR Responsibilities are decided according to age and gender. Each age group – children, young

Shield

This wooden shield was made by a Rwandan Twa artisan.

people, adults, and the elderly – has its own duties and responsibilities. Hunting is basically a male activity, but women and children help by driving the game toward the hunters; women also do most of the food gathering.

Culture and religion

RELIGION Religions vary between the various groups, but most involve a recognition of the central role that the forest plays in the communities' survival. Many forest people believe in a spirit world inhabited by the souls of the dead and presided over by the spirit of the forest itself. To them, the forest is a living being that is to be loved and respected and most of their rituals are concerned with honoring it and the food that it provides. All groups have healers and their own hunting rituals as well as ceremonies concerning the collection of honey. There are cultural and religious prohibitions against overhunting.

Mbuti, Twa and Mbenga timeline			
c. 3000 BCE Ancient Egyptians in contact with rainforest peoples	**1885** Belgian king's Congo Free State is established	Congo. Gabon independent. French Cameroun independent as Cameroon	ethnic groups **1990–1996** Mobutu promises introduction of multiparty politics. Political deadlock follows as Mobutu blocks transition to democracy
c. 200s Bantu-speakers begin to arrive	**1908** Belgian government takes over Free State as Belgian Congo	**1961** British Cameroon independent; south as part of Cameroon	
500s CE First recorded sightings of rainforest peoples	**1916** Kamerun occupied by Britain and France	**1971** Former Belgian Congo renamed Zaire by Mobutu Sese Seko	**1996–7** Mobutu is overthrown following a civil war; Zaire is renamed Congo (Dem. Rep.)
1884 German colony of Kamerun established	**1960** Belgian Congo and French Congo independent, both as Republic of	**1994** Twa in Rwanda caught up in genocide between Hutu and Tutsi	

Mbwera *see* **Shirazi**

Meidob

The Meidob (or Tiddi) live in the Meidob Hills in Sudan's western Darfur Province. They claim to descend from Nubian (q.v.) ancestors and number around 50,000.

Mende

Most Mende live in central and southeast Sierra Leone and they are that nation's largest single ethnic group. A few also live in western Liberia. There are presently more than one million Mende people.

History

During the thirteenth and fourteenth centuries, the ancestors of the Mende lived around the upper stretches of the Niger and Senegal rivers, in what is now Guinea. These lands formed part of the medieval Empire of Mali. Mali was declining in the fifteenth century when the Mende probably moved slowly south as part of a wave of Mande-speaking migrants that spread across West Africa.

According to Mende oral history, in the beginning of the sixteenth century a group of Manding (another Mande language) speakers called the Mani were exiled from the Empire of Mali. Under their queen, Mansarico, they traveled southwest, finally settling in the Cape Mount area of modern Liberia around 1540. From there, the Mani conquered much of present-day Sierra Leone, establishing many subkingdoms. The resulting peoples of mixed Mani and local descent formed new ethnic groups, the largest of which was the Mende.

In the early eighteenth century, the Mende began migrating west of the Sewa river. They gained control of the southern half of modern Sierra Leone by the early nineteenth century. By 1896, however, they were conquered by the British. The Mende people were among the most active in the fight for independence from colonial rule. Sierre Leone became independent in 1961, with Dr Milton Margai (q.v.), a Mende, as head of state.

Nomori
This soap-stone nomori *figurine was probably used by a Mende farmer to protect his rice fields. It may originally have been carved to mark a grave or as part of an ancestor cult. Nomori figurines have no set form and can vary in style widely.*

RECENT EVENTS In the 1990s, both Sierra Leone and Liberia have been hit by civil wars. In 1991, rebels launched an attack on Sierra Leone and the country was ripped apart by fighting between government and rebel troops. The aims of the rebels were to expel foreigners from the country and to take control of the rich diamond-mining regions. The people most affected by the conflict were ordinary civilians. Many Mende suffered through loss of employment and land, and many were victims of brutality meted out by both the government and rebel troops. The fighting was ended by a cease-fire in 1996.

Liberia has been torn apart by recurring fighting between various rebel groups since 1989. Thousands

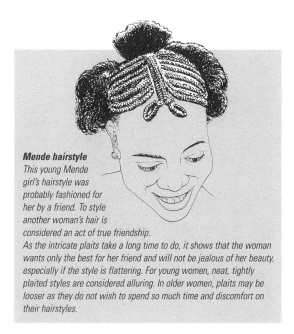

Mende hairstyle
This young Mende girl's hairstyle was probably fashioned for her by a friend. To style another woman's hair is considered an act of true friendship.
As the intricate plaits take a long time to do, it shows that the woman wants only the best for her friend and will not be jealous of her beauty, especially if the style is flattering. For young women, neat, tightly plaited styles are considered alluring. In older women, plaits may be looser as they do not wish to spend so much time and discomfort on their hairstyles.

have fled the country since this date and the conflict still continues today.

Language
The Mende language, also called Mende, belongs to the Mande language group.

Ways of life
FARMING The majority of the Mende people live in rural areas and make their living from the land. Rice, cassava, and yams are important food crops. The Mende also produce crops to sell, especially coffee, cocoa, ginger, kola nuts, groundnuts (peanuts), and cassava. Most rice is grown on upland farms by a system called shifting cultivation. This involves clearing patches of forests, growing crops on the cleared land for a few years, and then moving on to let the soil recover fertility. An increasing population and the growing levels of urbanization, however, have pushed farmers into using more intensive methods of cultivation. Since 1923, they have been encouraged to reclaim and farm swamp lands.
MINING Diamonds have been Sierre Leone's most important export since the 1930s. Originally, diamond mining was monopolized by a government-run company. Widespread diamond smuggling and illicit mining in the 1950s forced the government to allow the licensing of independent diggers. Today, many Mende men work as diamond diggers, either independently or as part of a gang employed by a company.

Social structure
The basic economic and social unit in Mende society is the mawe. Simply put, this is a farming household. It comprises one or more older men and their wives; their children; wives and husbands of these children; and

any grandchildren. Although the senior male is head of the household, the functioning of the mawe is controlled by the women. The senior wife organizes the farm work, which is done by both men and women. She also has her own plot of land on which she can grow cash crops. Senior wives are therefore largely responsible for the wealth and prosperity of a mawe.
"SECRET" SOCIETIES Most Mende belong to one or more hale ("secret" societies). These act as unifying and controlling forces in Mende society. Hale lay down various rules, sanction acceptable forms of behavior, prohibit unacceptable behavior, and generally provide cultural and social unity to the Mende. Hale are both religious and political organizations. The officials serve as contacts with spirits who affect human affairs while, in the past, chiefs depended for their authority on support from the men's hale, Poro. Historically, these societies were very important as the Mende were rarely under the rule of any particular nation or state.

The most important hale are the men's society Poro, and the women's society Sande. At puberty, almost all boys and girls join one or the other. Initiation into Poro and Sande takes place in secret. Initiates are taken to a camp in the forest where they live in seclusion for weeks. Sande and Poro mostly teach Mende ideals of manhood and womanhood, though Poro also settles disputes and regulates trading.

Other secret societies include the Humui, Njayei, and Kpa. The Humui regulates sexual behavior; the Njayei uses herbs and other substances to cure madness, which is attributed to breaching this society's taboos; and Kpa apprentices learn to use herbs to treat minor ailments.

Recently, the activities of secret societies have been

Mende attire
This man is wearing the attire of a Mende chief. The shirt has been woven from locally grown cotton and richly embroidered; thread for weaving is more likely to be imported than locally produced today.

Minsereh figure *(above)*
Carved wooden female figures such as this are used for divination and healing. They are called minsereh *and some are over 3 ft (1 m) tall. Female diviners of the Yassi society (hale) often use them to practice the art of spiritual healing.*

Mende script *(below)*
The Mende language uses the Roman alphabet today, but in the past it was written in its own script.

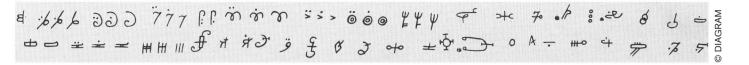

drastically affected by foreign ideas and by changes in Sierre Leonean society. Many of the rites are no longer performed in larger urban areas. In such areas, it would be impossible to ensure that everyone in the vicinity followed the necessary prohibitions on behavior while the events took place; people no longer observe taboos as they once did. In cities, initiation into Poro now involves simply paying the society's membership fees. Sande no longer circumcises girls and has incorporated prenatal and postnatal education, as well as medical developments into its initiates' lessons. Newly initiated girls return smartly dressed in modern adult clothes.

Culture and religion

RELIGION The majority of the Mende profess either Christianity or Islam. The Mende religion is still widely followed, even by converts to these world religions. The Mende religion involves belief in a supreme god, Ngewo, who created everything; belief in an afterlife; various nature spirits associated with such things as forests and rivers; spirits linked to particular hale; and the reverance of ancestor spirits.

CEREMONIES AND RITUALS Masked members of the Poro and Sande societies represent spirits at ceremonies. These are held to mark events such as the coming out of a group of initiates or, in the past, to make crops grow. Dancing and singing play an important part of Sande initiations, at the climax of which a woman disguised as a spirit whips away witches and unfriendly spirits. Today, these dances are largely performed to entertain.

Sande masquerades
The major character at a Sande masquerade is Sowo – the spirit of Sande. Only a senior Sande official who is an expert dancer wears the wooden mask and raffia-covered cloth costume of Sowo. Sowo-wui are the wooden heads that complete Sowo costumes. Each sowo-wui is unique. The Mende do not view these masks as separate entities. They have to be lightweight and are worn on top of the head like helmets. They depict the Mende ideal of feminine beauty, with delicate features, high foreheads, and elaborate coiffures. Rolls at the base of the mask represent a ringed neck – the height of beauty. The mask is stained a deep black color, as the Mende prize very black skin. Palm oil rubbed into the wood makes it resemble glossy skin.

Mende timeline

1235–c. 1500 Empire of Mali: Mende ancestors part of empire	**1808** British rule established in Freetown (Sierra Leone)	**1967–1969** Period of military rule in Sierra Leone	**1992** Military coup in Sierra Leone
1400s Mende begin moving southwest into present-day Sierra Leone and Liberia, conquering local peoples	**1847** Liberia established by freed American slaves	**1980–1985** Period of military rule in Liberia	**1995** Short-lived peace accord signed in Liberia
c. 1500 Mani people exiled from Mali	**1896** A British protectorate (colony) declared over Sierra Leone.	**1989** Civil war erupts in Liberia	**1997** Miltary group seizes power in Sierra Leone; former warlord Charles Taylor is elected president of Liberia.
c. 1540 Mende ancestors settled in Cape Mount area (Liberia)	**1898** Mende revolt sparked by the "hut tax"; revolt suppressed	**1990** Assassination of Liberian president Samuel Doe; civil war escalates	**1998** Civilian government is restored in Sierra Leone.
1800s Christianity spreads in Sierra Leone	**1961** Sierra Leone independent	**1991** Sierre Leonean rebels invade from Liberia; civil war breaks out	

Merina

The Merina are one of Madagascar's most important ethnic groups. Numbering around 3 million, the Merina are the largest ethnic group on the island, where they are concentrated in the center. They have long dominated the country's politics and founded the Merina kingdom in the fifteenth century. See also **Madagascan peoples**.

Meru

The Meru live in northern Tanzania and across the border in southern Kenya. They are a Bantu (q.v.) people and number more than 700,000.

Merule *see* **Murle**

Messiriya

The Messiriya are one of the main Baggara (q.v.) subgroups. The Baggara are a Sudanese people of Bedouin (q.v.) and Black African descent.

Metoko

The Metoko are a subgroup of the Mongo (q.v.) of Central Africa. The Metoko live in central Congo (Dem. Rep.) west of the Lokmani River.

Mfengu

The Mfengu (or Fingo) are a Xhosa (q.v.)-speaking people. They live in the Transkei and Ciskei regions on the eastern seaboard of South Africa and number more than one million.

Miango see Irigwe

Mihavane see Lomwe

Mijikenda

The Mijikenda inhabit the coast of Kenya; historically they were concentrated between the towns of Kilifi and Vanga. The Mijikenda are made up of nine closely-related groups: the Chonyi, the Digo, the Duruma, the Giriama, the Jibana, the Kambe, the Kauma, the Rabai, and the Ribe. The nine Mijikenda groups speak different dialects of the same, Mijikenda, language. There are roughly one million Mijkenda; the Giriama are the largest group followed by the Duruma.

The Mijikenda are a Bantu (q.v.) people who probably migrated into East Africa from the Katanga region in modern-day Congo (Dem. Rep.) of Central Africa sometime early in the first millennium. The Mijikenda are also known as the Nyika—a name for the dry, waterless regions they had to cross to reach the coast. In the early seventeenth century oral history relates how several Mijikenda groups, including many Giriama, migrated south from the northern Kenyan coast around Lamu as a result of pressure from the Somalis (q.v.) and Oromo (q.v.). The Giriama built a fortress on top of a hill near Kilifi, roughly a hundred miles south.

Mikhifore

The Mikhifore are related to the Malinke (q.v.) and speak a Manding (q.v.) language. They number around 230,000 people living in Sierra Leone, Liberia, and Guinea.

Mileri

The Mileri are a Tama (q.v.)-speaking people of Sudan and Chad. The majority of the 9,000 Mileri live in Sudan, however.

Mima

The Mima number around 30,000 living in southern and western Sudan, largely living in the urban areas. They are closely related to the Mimi (q.v.) of Chad.

Mimi

The Mimi number around 35,000 people living in eastern Chad. They are closely related to the Mima (q.v.) of Sudan.

Mina

The Mina (or Popo) are a small but socially important ethnic group in both Togo and Benin. The more than 150,000 Mina are concentrated in the south of these two countries. They are part of the Ewe (q.v.) cluster of peoples.

Minianka

The Minianka are a northerly subgroup of the Senufo (q.v.). They have only recently been absorbed into that group. There are around 250,000 Minianka living largely in the north of Ivory Coast and the south of Mali and Burkina Faso.

Mirifab

The Mirifab have both Arab (q.v.) and Nubian (q.v.) ancestors. They number more than one million people, the majority of whom live in north-central Sudan.

Mobeur

The Mobeur number around 50,000, and they are partly descended from the Kanembu (q.v.). They live in eastern Niger and northeastern Nigeria.

Mole-Dagbane

The Mole-Dagbane (Gur or Voltaic) peoples of West Africa are united by related languages. There are more than nine million Mole-Dagbane people, and they include the Mossi (q.v.), Mamprusi (q.v.), and Grusi (q.v.).

Mom see Bamum

Mongo

The Mongo (or Lomongo) people inhabit the Congo Basin in central Congo (Dem. Rep.). They include a number of smaller groups such as the Mbole, Ntomba, Metoko, Lengola, and the Tetela. There are probably less than half a million Mongo people.

History

Bantu speakers began to settle in the Congo Basin during the first centuries of the Common Era and gradually displaced and absorbed the local tropical forest-foragers. These settlers and the indigenous peoples are ancestors of the present-day Mongo population. Initially, they engaged in fishing, hunting, and yam farming, but by 1000, bananas had become the staple crop. Over the years, new areas of forest were cleared for settlement and agriculture, populations increased, and surplus labor was freed to engage in specialized arts and crafts activities. By the nineteenth century, many villages engaged in craft production such as pottery-making, ironworking, and the construction of dugout canoes. Agriculture assumed greater importance and was integrated with trapping, hunting, gathering, and fishing. The balance of these activities depended on local environmental conditions.

In the mid-nineteenth century, the increased European demand for ivory stimulated Mongo traders to buy ivory from specialized elephant hunters, in particular from Twa hunters. The Mongo traded crops such as cassava, tobacco, and corn; crafts such as raffia (palm fiber) production, pottery, and basketry; and specialized products such as knives, iron, salt, and dugout canoes with neighboring peoples and European traders. In exchange, they received other regionally-produced crafts, pieces of copper or brass, and European-manufactured goods. The village elders, and the village chief himself, exercised strong control over local trade and, together with the traders themselves, they were able to amass power and fortune as a result.

COLONIALISM Following King Leopold II of Belgium's establishment of the Congo Free State (his own personal colony) in 1885, the Mongo peoples endured a period of harsh exploitation under the new regime. Leopold's rule was characterized by abuse, brutality, and the committing of atrocities in order to protect and maintain the lucrative rubber trade. Some communities waged war against the white rubber agents or opted for migration. The leaders of rebellious communities were punished or humiliated if caught. International outcry led to the Belgian government taking over in 1908, which resulted in a less oppressive, if nonetheless strongly colonial, period of government until independence in 1960.

RECENT EVENTS Mobutu Sese Seko (q.v.) came to power after a military coup in 1965 and was elected president in 1970. During the 1970s, he promulgated a strong national identity; European place names were Africanized and the country was renamed Zaire. During the 1980s, Mobutu came under growing international criticism at human rights abuses in Zaire, then a one-party state. Mounting tensions led to Mobutu calling a National Conference in 1991 to draft a multiparty constitution. Mobutu refused, however, to grant

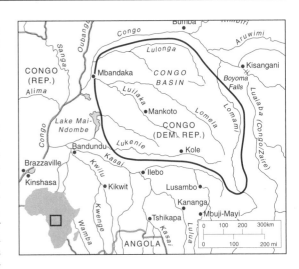

sovereignty to the National Conference. Civil war broke out in the east in 1996 and, in 1997, Mobutu was overthrown by a rebel force led by Laurent Kabila (q.v.). Kabila promptly renamed the country the Democratic Republic of Congo.

Language

The Mongo language is also called Mongo.

Ways of life

In the face of political uncertainty and social unrest, many Mongo communities continue to engage in a part hunter-gatherer, part agricultural way of life. A wide range of produce is gathered from the rainforest: fruits, vegetables, palm kernels (seeds), mushrooms, snails, and edible insects, as well as roots and vegetation used for beverages, spices, and medicines. Shifting cultivation – in which newly-cleared areas of vegetation are cultivated for three to five years before being left to revert to natural vegetation – is still commonly practiced. Cassava and bananas, for example, are often grown in this manner. Oil palms are harvested in partially cleared terrain and provide a range of products: fruits for oils in cooking and cosmetic products; fronds

Ironwork
The Mongo are famous for their ironwork, in particular statues, weapons, and jewelry. Both the necklace (above) and the knife (below) were made from iron by Mongo artisans. The knife has a wooden handle.

Mbole mask
Produced by the Mbole subgroup, only six of these wooden masks are known to exist.

for housing and craft production; and sap, which is fermented to make wine.

CASH CROPS Corn, groundnuts (peanuts), and beans were introduced as cash crops by Portuguese colonists in the late sixteenth century. The Mongo people were responsive to trading opportunities and they adapted their subsistence activities accordingly. Present-day cash crops include coffee, palm products, rubber, cotton, sugar, tea, and cocoa, many of which are grown on large plantations.

division of labor Much of the farming and gathering is done by women, who also engage in seasonal fishing. The more prestigious activities of hunting larger forest animals and trapping smaller ones are generally carried out by men. As agriculture has become an increasingly important subsistence activity in the twentieth century, the relative workload of women has increased.

Social structure

SOCIAL STRUCTURE Despite aggressive colonization and the subsequent creation of a national identity, many distinctive aspects of Mongo culture have survived in the wider Zairean community. Mongo society is centered on the household. Each household has twenty to forty members and is led by a senior male elder, commonly referred to as tata (father).

POLITICAL STRUCTURE Several households in the same area generally form a village of 100 to 400 people led by a village chief, the bokulaka, and a council comprising the compound elders. In the past, high status was conferred by birthright or in response to good leadership skills and recognition of the individual's and family's economic power and influence. At times of instability – when communities were threatened by war, for example – villages would form coalitions, with decisions at the district level being made by a loose collection of village chiefs, prominent male elders, and religious practitioners.

MEN AND WOMEN Women in Mongo society were given much less power and authority than men. Women did not play a part in decision-making at the community level and, within the household, they had to defer to men. In general, they received harsher penalties than men if found guilty of certain crimes such as adultery.

Culture and religion

RELIGION Although many Mongo have converted to Christianity, a significant number of Mongo beliefs and practices have survived. Belief in witchcraft is strong and the veneration of ancestors, which played a central role in the Mongo religion, is still widely practiced.

oral literature The Mongo oral tradition is very rich, with poems and songs that celebrate community life and provide guidance on how to live in harmony with community members. Folk tales, which were usually centered on a piece of wisdom, were an essential part of a child's education as were proverbs. These proverbs dealt with all aspects of life, especially promoting the importance of the family, respect for authority, and the mutual obligations of members of a community. Hunting and trapping feature strongly in many local proverbs and fables, and in rituals and ceremonies, indicating the high esteem and importance of these activities.

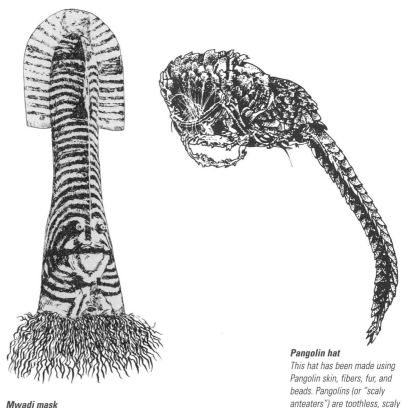

Mwadi mask
This mwadi mask was produced by the Tetela people, a Mongo subgroup. The mask was part of a costume worn by dancers who performed at funerals and marital celebrations. It is made from wood and raffia and has been painted with natural pigments. It would have been worn with a raffia (palm fiber) costume.

Pangolin hat
This hat has been made using Pangolin skin, fibers, fur, and beads. Pangolins (or "scaly anteaters") are toothless, scaly mammals that eat termites and ants. Pangolins have rich symbolic associations and they can represent both mammals and reptiles.

Mongo timeline	
200s Bantu-speaking people begin to settle in the Congo Basin	**1980s** Popular unrest mounts in Zaire and international criticism of human rights abuses is voiced
1500s Portuguese begin settling on the Angolan coast and start trading with the Mongo peoples via intermediaries such as the Ovimbundu	**1991** Mobutu calls a National Conference to draft a multiparty constitution to ease tensions
1885 Belgian king's Congo Free State is officially established	**1992** National Conference establishes High Council of the Republic (HCR), which elects Etienne Tshisekedi prime minister
1908 Belgian government takes over Free State as Belgian Congo	**1994** Mobutu dissolves HCR and new transitional government (HCR-PT) is established. Kengo wa Dondo elected prime minister
1960 Belgian Congo gains independence as Congo	
1965 Mobutu Sese Seko seizes power in military coup	**1995** HCR-PT votes to extend transition period by two years
1970 Mobutu is elected president	**1996–7** Civil war leads to the overthrow of Mobutu; his successor Laurent Kabila renames the country the Democratic Republic of Congo
1971 Congo renamed Zaire	

Male figurine
Over 5 ft (1.5 m) tall, this wooden sculpture depicts a man standing with his arms raised. It has been attributed to the Lengola – a subgroup of the Mongo who live in northeastern Congo (Dem. Rep.). Very little is known regarding the use of Lengola figurines.

© DIAGRAM

Moor

The name "Moor" has been applied to many different peoples over the centuries. For years it was used to describe the people of Morocco and also the Muslims from North Africa who conquered large parts of Spain in the Middle Ages. Today, it generally refers to the people who make up seventy percent of the population of Mauritania. It also applies to a few of the people of Western Sahara, which has been occupied by Morocco – and, for a while, Mauritania – since 1975.

There are probably about 1,500,000 Moors. There are two main Moor groups: the Bidanis, or "White Moors," who are of Berber-Arab origin; and the Sudanis, or "Black Moors," who are largely of Black African origin and are related to the Fulani, Soninke, Tukolor, Wolof, and other peoples.

History

The original ancestors of today's Moors are said to have moved into what is now Mauritania in the eleventh century, with the spread of the Berber Almoravids led by Abu Bakr. Others followed in subsequent centuries.

The Moors fall into several subgroups. Two of the most important are the Hassani and Zawiya, both Bidani. The Hassani descend from a group of Arab people who settled in Mauritania from the fifteenth century onward. Moorish history holds that the division into Hassani and Zawiya occurred as a result of the Cherr Baba War between the Berbers and the Arabs in 1644–74.

RECENT CONFLICTS There have long been rivalries between the majority Moor population and the minority Black African population of Mauritania. Since the 1980s, this animosity has often turned into open conflict; there have been many instances of violence. The government troops' support of the Moors in these conflicts has led to the death of hundreds of Black African Mauritanians.

Language

The language of almost all the Moors is Arabic. French is also widely spoken in Mauritania – a relic of colonial days. A few Moors speak Berber languages.

Ways of life

About sixty percent of Moors live in rural areas, and the rest in towns. Industrialization and urbanization are attracting many people away from their nomadic

Clothing
A man typically wears a long robe, with baggy trousers and a shirt underneath, and covers his head with a turban. In cold weather, he may add a cloak made of wool or sheepskin. A woman typically wears baggy trousers and a long tunic, with a shawl to cover her head when needed. Moorish women rarely veil their faces. Blue is a popular color for the clothing of both sexes.

Gourd harp
These stringed musical instruments are made from gourds. The design is very old, similar ones were used in Ancient Egypt. Historically, the dominant Moor groups retained musicians to sing their praises and entertain them.

ways of life, in which they travel over a large area with their herds of animals in search of water and pasture. Many people now work in the copper and iron mines concentrated in the northwest of the country. Young Moors from all ranks study at the University of Nouakchott, Mauritania's capital, or at other universities in Africa or abroad.

NOMADISM Most of Mauritania is desert, unsuitable for agriculture. For this reason, many Moors are nomads. Cattle are the mainstay of the nomads, but they also keep flocks of sheep and goats, besides camels, donkeys, and horses. Most of the cattle are in the southern part of the country, where the Sahara Desert gives way to the semidesert region of the Sahel. During the wet season, the cattle herders roam the Sahel, moving to pastures along the banks of the Senegal River during the dry season. Camels, goats, and sheep are herded in the desert.

FARMING Settled farmers live in the southern region, where they grow corn, dates, melons, millet, pulses, rice, sorghum, and vegetables and raise chickens. Many farmers also live in the scattered oases (fertile pockets in the desert), where there is enough water for agriculture.

DIVISION OF LABOR Men do most of the herding and heavy agricultural work. Women make goods from leather and weave cloth, including the fabric of tents. Among the nomads, it is the women who set up the tents and take them down again.

DROUGHT AND DESERTIFICATION During the 1960s and 1980s, droughts (periods of inadequate rainfall) struck Mauritania; the country was devastated and the nomadic Moors, in particular, were badly affected. Cropping on the flood plains of the Senegal River was impossible because it failed to flood; over a million cattle were lost; and death rates for vulnerable people rose. Refugees flocked to urban areas in search of emergency food supplies, putting great strain on the resources of these areas.

Over the years, patches of the fragile Sahelian lands have been turning into desert, threatening the farming and grazing lands of the Moors. This process of desertification has been worsened by drought and also threatens the ability of rural people to make a living from the land. Drought and desertification have caused not only great immediate distress but also disrupted the nomadic pattern so severely that many will probably not return to that lifestyle. For example, in 1963, eighty-three percent of the population was nomadic, but by 1980 this figure was only twenty-five percent. Drought and desertification have also caused the remaining nomadic Moors to alter their habits. For instance, they may stay in one place for longer if they know there is a water supply available. This has put many cattle herders into conflict with the settled farming populations. In fact, in recent decades there have been many instances of violent conflict between the Moor and non-Moor populations.

Social structure

There are many clans (groups of several extended families who share a common ancestor or ancestors) within the subgroups and a strong class structure exists. The highest class is that of the nobles. Some subgroups serve the nobles, and slavery was not abolished in Mauritania until 1980. Below the nobles come smiths, wandering entertainers, and the imraguen, or fishermen, on the coast. Each subgroup has its own code of laws and has civilian and religious leaders who inherit their positions from their fathers. Some Moors are marabouts, or holy men. A few families are considered

Wooden bowl
The Moors use wood for many items, including dishes. This type of bowl is used for heating milk. Hot stones are placed inside, with the milk, and the taste of burning milk is thought to keep away evil spirits.

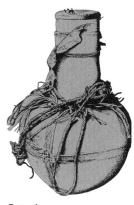

Butter jar
This jar, made of leather and rope, would have been used by Moorish nomads to carry butter. Butter is an important food item, but is also used as a cosmetic.

particularly holy because they are claim descent from of the Prophet Muhammad. In the past, the Bidanis were considered superior to the Sudanis, though a Sudani of noble birth could outrank an ordinary Bidani – the division was based on class not color.

MARRIAGE People tend to marry within their clans. One man may have several wives, but men generally only marry a new wife after divorcing the previous one, rarely keeping more than one or two wives at a time.

Culture and religion

RELIGION The vast majority of Moors are Muslim.

Moors timeline			
c. 1070 Moors arrive in West Africa with invading Almoravids	**1960** Maurtianian independence	**1974** Mainly foreign-controlled iron mines are nationalized	**1984** Lieutenant Colonel Ould Taya takes power in military coup
c. 1400s Trade with Europeans begins	**1960s** Discovery of iron ore and copper deposits in Mauritania	**1976** Mauritania and Morocco invade Western Sahara	**1990s** Islamicization policy favored instead of Arabicization – to ease ethnic tension
1644–1674 Cherr Baba War; Hassani and Zawiya Moors emerge	**1960s–1980s** Recurring droughts cause famine in Sahelian countries	**1978** Ould Daddah overthrown	**1992** Ould Taya elected President
1700s–1800s Moors involved in flourishing gum arabic trade	**1964** Mauritania declared a one-party state	**1979** Mauritania renounces claim to Western Sahara	**1994** Government cracks down on radical Islamic groups
1903 Mauritania becomes a French colony	**1966** Arabicization campaign; violence erupts between Moors and other peoples	**1980** Civilian government formed. Slavery abolished	**late 1990s** UN attempts to hold a referendum on Sahara's future fail through lack of agreement on a voters' registers
1959 Moktar Ould Daddah elected prime minister of Mauritania			

Wooden pole
Carved wooden poles are used to hang leather bags, dishes, and cooking utensils inside tents. The bottom of the poles are sharpened so that they can be pushed into the ground and made to stand upright.

Mossi

Mossi as a term refers to a number of different ethnic groups who have similar cultures and lifestyles but maintain some distinct ethnic identity. The Yarse, for instance, are one group within Mossi society. Together, the groups that make up Mossi society represent half the population of Burkina Faso.

There are about four million Mossi. Most live in Burkina Faso, but some 500,000 Mossi have emigrated to live and work in cities or on plantations in Ghana, Ivory Coast, and France.

History

Mossi oral history states that Mossi society originated in the fifteenth century when a cavalry group from northern Ghana rode north in search of land. The invaders conquered the various farming peoples who inhabited the valley of the White Volta River and set-

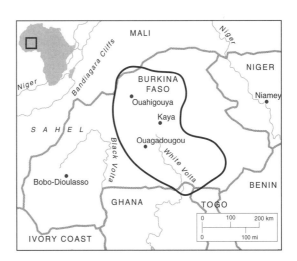

© DIAGRAM

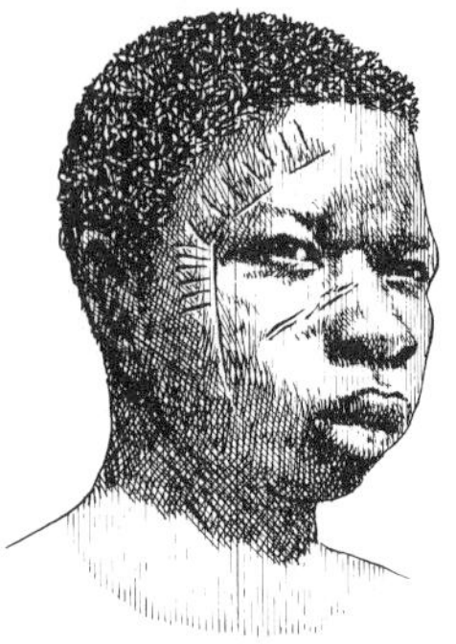

Mossi boy *(left)*
This young Mossi boy has facial scars that, in the past, marked someone who could not be taken as a slave.

Mogho naba *(right)*
A mogho naba (center) *surrounded by his chiefs (naba). The mogho naba was the supreme ruler of the Mossi, and the role is still important today, though less powerful than in the past. He rules from the court of Ouagadougou, now the capital of Burkina Faso.*

tled among them. Some of the peoples in the area fled to locations where the invaders' horses could not follow, such as to Mali's isolated Bandiagara Cliffs where the Dogon people sought refuge. Other peoples, however, remained behind in the newly created kingdoms, which included Ouagadougou, Ouahigouya (or Yatenga), Dagomba, and Namumba and became part of a new society known as the Mossi.

The conquerors became the ruling class and were called the nakomsé ("the right and power to rule"). The defeated farmers became the commoners and were called nyonyosé – "the ancient ones" or "children of the earth," references to their origins as the original inhabitants of Mossi territory. The nakomsé generally respected the nyonyosé, maintaining preexisting clans (several extended families who share a common ancestor or ancestors) and assimilating many of their traditions into the new society. This reduced the likelihood of revolt and explains the cultural variations that are still found in Mossi society. Today, there continues to be a distinction between nakomsé and nyonyosé in terms of power relationships, but these have been lessened by intermarriage.

COLONIALISM In 1897, France gained control of Mossi territory: Mossi myth explains that they were conquered not because they were weaker than the French, but because the ruler of Ouagadougou had ignored the warnings of the gods. French direct influence over the Mossi remained limited, however, because the conquerors did not consider the area to be economically important. France's administrative hold over the Mossi remained weak, and it was subject to frequent revolts over such issues as the imposition of taxes, forced labor, and military conscription. When Burkina Faso (then known as Upper Volta) gained its independence from France in 1960, its first president, Maurice Yameogo (q.v.), was a Mossi.

Language

The Mossi language, called Moré (or Moore or Molé), is one of the Niger-Congo family of languages.

Ways of life

In the seventeenth and eighteenth centuries, large towns and markets developed through which goods such as salt and dried fish were imported and cotton

Masks
Mossi masks are varied in appearance. They can be over 6 ft (180 cm) high.

This mask (left) has an antelope figure as the face, and a human figure makes up the mask's superstructure, which is many times the height of the facial covering.

This wooden mask (right) may represent an albino. The ridge extending from the mask's forehead is carved to resemble a rooster's comb.

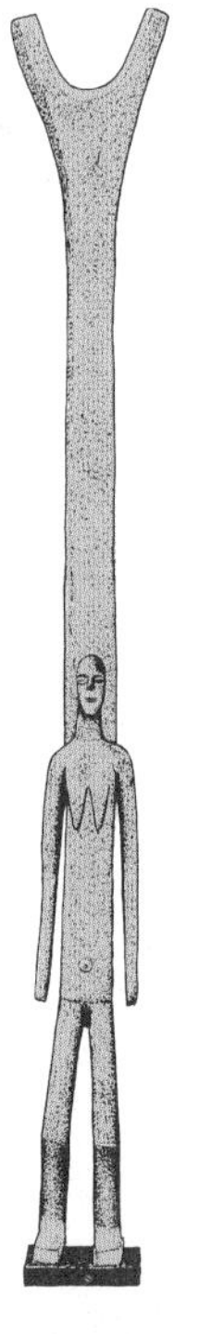

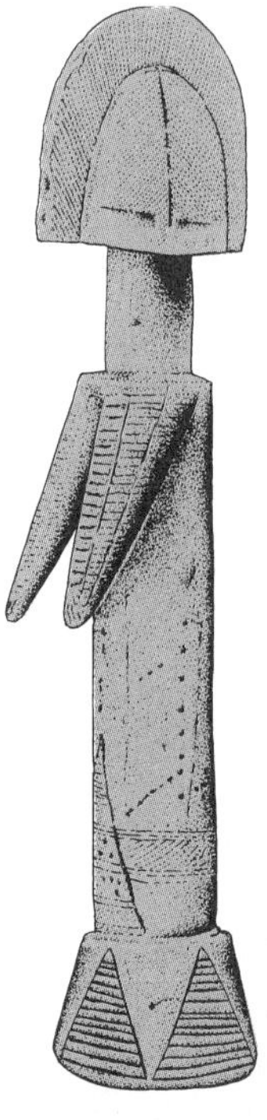

Shelter post *(right)*
Forked support posts like the one shown held up shelters that provided shade for community meetings, which were presided over by Mossi chiefs. Few decorated posts – this one shows a figure of a woman – are in use today.

Doll *(far right)*
Dolls are produced in different shapes and sizes and represent different Mossi clans or regions. Sometimes they are used as fertility symbols – they may be carried on the back by a woman having problems conceiving. More often, dolls are used as children's toys for use in role play, as in many other cultures.

Diviner
A Mossi diviner seeks guidance in sand patterns. As in other cultures, the diviner is a sort of oracle, interpreting messages concerning major life decisions using various divination methods.

Calabash balafon
In a balafon – a type of xylophone common throughout Africa – the wooden keys are attached to calabashes of different sizes, providing a range of sounds. The Mossi, in common with other African peoples, use calabashes for many instruments. A technique unique to the Mossi is to fill a large calabash bowl with water, place a smaller calabash bowl, upside down, on the water, and strike the floating calabash.

Social structure
Mossi society is based on extended families, each of which typically consists of the head of the family, his wife, their children and grandchildren, and other close relatives. These extended families are grouped together into clans. The members of a clan have the same surname and claim descent from a common ancestor, and each clan is symbolically represented by an animal.

Culture and religion
RELIGION Muslim traders from the north helped to introduce Islam to West Africa in the early years of the second millenium. Since this date, most have converted to Islam, nevertheless many Mossi people have remained faithful to the Mossi religion, which is based on the devotion to ancestors and spirits.

WEAVING Since the integration of weavers of Mande origin into Mossi society in c. 1600, the Mossi have been renowned for their cotton and silk weaving. Some Mossi groups tell a creation myth that recalls how the founding ancestor was a weaver who descended to earth on the threads from his loom.

Weaving is done by men during the dry season, but women usually dye the woven strips in pits filled with indigo (deep blue) dye. Some of the resulting blue-and-white strips are combined to form a larger cloth. Despite competition from industrial textile mills, this traditional cloth is still highly sought after and is passed down through the generations in families.

MASKS The Mossi are well known for their masks, used in celebrations. In the past, only the nyonyosé used masks, typically painted intense shades of red, white, black, and sometimes brown. Masks are owned by individual families or clans and are passed down through generations. The masks can be used to invoke protection and serve as a direct means of communication with the owners' ancestors and celebrate individual and group identity. In some regions, women and children are prohibited from viewing mask appearances, while in others both men and women, old and young, participate in performances.

Mossi masks, which are usually tall, are often carved from the soft, fine-grained, and very lightweight wood of the ceiba tree. Ceiba wood is very susceptible to insect damage, however, and every year, after the harvest but before the dry season, all the masks in a village are soaked in a river or a swamp to kill any insects and to remove the paint applied to the masks the previous year.

cloth, livestock, and surplus grain exported. This led to specializations within Mossi society and the creation of specialized occupational groups such as blacksmiths and weavers. These were once associated with separate ethnic groups; the Yarse, for example, were largely weavers and traders. But these distinctions were flexible, so that a person could change from one group to another throughout a lifetime.

Most Mossi, however, live in rural areas and are subsistence farmers, producing cereals, yams, and legumes, and providing for themselves off the land. Poor soil and an increasing population, however, have made it more difficult to grow enough crops. For this reason, over the years Mossi farmers have shifted their farms, leading to a continuous shifting of the population. This has further contributed to the diversity of Mossi society.

Mossi timeline

late 1400s White Volta area invaded by horsemen from Ghana; Mossi society founded. Ouagadougou Kingdom founded by Naba Oubri	**1591** Mossi defeated by Moroccan invaders	**1919** Upper Volta declared a separate colonial territory under France	**1984** Upper Volta renamed Burkina Faso
	1744–1745 Asante Empire occupies Dagomba, a Mossi kingdom	**1960** Independence from French rule	**1991** Elections held and Captain Blaise Compaoré, former coup leader, is elected unopposed
mid-1500s Ouahigouya (or Yatenga) kingdom founded by Naba Yadega	**1897** France takes control of Ouagadougou	**1969–1974** Prolonged *drought* causes crisis among Burkina Faso farmers, including Mossi	**1998** Campaoré is re-elected president

Mouroum
The Mouroum are a subgroup of the Sara (q.v.). They number almost 70,000 people, living in Chad.

Mpondo

The Mpondo are a large ethnic group living in South Africa. There are around two million Mpondo people, primarily living in the Transkei region, which lies between the Drakensberg Mountains and the Indian Ocean coast in southeastern South Africa. They are spread along the northeastern, coastal region of Transkei, roughly from Port St Johns to the border with the KwaZulu/Natal Province to the north.

The Mpondo are Xhosa (q.v.)-speaking people, and they share a common origin with the Thembu (q.v.) and Xhosa proper. Like other Nguni (q.v.) Bantu people, the Mpondo ancestors were established in South Africa by at least the sixteenth century. By the eighteenth century, the Mpondo were living in large clan-based chieftaincies east of the Kei River. The present-day Mpondo are still divided into clans (the members of which claim descent from a common ancestor or ancestors).

Mpongwe

The Mpongwe are a small ethnic group (not more than 5,000 people) in Gabon. They have been highly influential in that country, however, dominating the teaching and business professions.

Mumuye

The Mumuye are a Bantu (q.v.) people of Nigeria. They live in and around the Jos Plateau in north-central Nigeria. There are more than 400,000 Mumuye.

Murle

The Murle (or Ajibba, Beri, or Merule) number some 60,000 people in Sudan. Originally from Ethiopia, the Murle only number a few thousand in that country today.

Mwela *see* **Mwere**

Mwenga *see* **Lega**

Mwera *see* **Mwere**

Mwere

The Mwere (or Mwera, Mwela, or Chimwere) are a people of southeastern Tanzania. They number around 300,000 and are sometimes considered to be a subgroup of the Yao (q.v.).

Nagot

The Nagot (or Edo Nago) are a Yoruba (q.v.) people. They live in southern Nigeria and number more than 50,000.

Nama

The Nama are a Khoisan (q.v.) people originally of Namibia and more recently Botswana. Many fled to Botswana from Namibia in the early 1900s, escaping the anti-German rebellion. There are more than 50,000 Nama.

Namchi

The Namchi are closely related to the Baya (q.v.) and Mbun (q.v.) people of Central Africa. They live in the west of the Central African Republic and the east of Cameroon.

Namnam

The Namnam are a Mole-Dagbane (q.v.) people. The majority of the more than 35,000 Namnam live in eastern Ghana.

Namwanga

The Namwanga number more than 80,000 people. They live in the far northeast of Zambia. Many of the Namwanga are Jehovah's Witnesses.

Nandi

The Nandi are one of the largest of the several related groups that make up the Kalenjin (q.v.). There are very roughly 500,000 Nandi people in western Kenya.

The ancestors of the Kalenjin were Highland Nilotes (q.v.), who began dispersing from their original cradleland at the northernmost tip of Lake Turkana in present-day Ethiopia to East Africa during the last millennium BCE. The separate Kalenjin groups such as the Nandi emerged as the Highland Nilotes spread out over the region and mixed with people already living there. The Nandi did not emerge as a distinct ethnic group until sometime after 1000 CE, separating from the Kipsigis (q.v.) as late as c. 1600–1800. While both Nandi and Kipsigis are very similar Kalenjin languages, they are distinguishable by small differences in sounds and terms used, comparable to the difference between American and British English.

Nanerge

The Nanerge are part of the Senufo (q.v.) group of people. Closely related to the Minianka (q.v.), they are concentrated around the border between Mali and southwestern Burkina-Faso.

Nankansi *see* **Grusi**

Nar

The Nar are a subgroup of the Sara (q.v.). The majority live in southern Chad.

Nbule *see* **Bafou**

Ndau

The Ndau (or Buzi or Vandau) are a subgroup of the Shona (q.v.). They number more than 400,000 living in southeastern Zimbabwe and Mozambique.

Ndebele and Matabele

The Ndebele live in the Transvaal province of South Africa. They are commonly divided into two separate groups: the Northern Ndebele and the Southern Ndebele. The Southern Ndebele are subdivided into two main branches: the Ndzundza and the Manala, which take their names from early leaders. The Northern Ndebele have been absorbed into the Sotho population and are no longer considered a distinct ethnic group.

The Matabele live in a region of southern Zimbabwe called Matabeleland. They are sometimes, confusingly, called Ndebele as well – the Ndebele and Matabele both refer to themselves as amaNdebele. The histories and cultures of the Ndebele and the Matabele are closely connected and the two groups are often treated as branches of the same, Ndebele, people. The Ndebele number about 500,000 and the Matabele about 4,000,000.

History

NDEBELE The Ndebele story begins with the Nguni, a Bantu-speaking people who arrived in Southern Africa around the 200s. The Ndebele of today are one of many ethnic groups descended from the original Nguni settlers. ("Ndebele" is the Sotho name for "Nguni.") History suggests that they probably split off some time in the late 1500s under a chief named Musi. Early on, the Ndebele split into two groups – Northern and Southern – most of whom migrated from present-day KwaZulu/Natal northward to modern Transvaal, where the Northern Ndebele gradually became absorbed by their Sotho neighbors. In the 1700s, the Southern Ndebele fragmented into different groups. Two branches survived this fragmentation into the present day: a smaller group, led by Manala, and a larger group, led by Ndzundza.

The Ndzundza Ndebele reached a height of prosperity in the mid-nineteenth century under the rule of King Mabhogo, but they were finally conquered by the Boers' South African Republic (Transvaal) in 1883. All the Ndzundza lands were confiscated and the people forced to work for the Boers (Afrikaner farmers) virtually as slaves. After the Union of South Africa was created in 1910, the Ndebele came under white-minority rule.

MATABELE The Matabele are also descended from early Nguni settlers, but did not emerge as an independent people until the nineteenth century. In the early 1800s,

Ndebele woman (below)
This Ndebele woman is wearing a beaded apron and a blanket. Many women wear copper, brass, or beaded necklaces, rings, and leg rings. Ndebele women are more likely to be seen wearing traditional-style clothes than Ndebele men.

Mapoto (right)
This beaded apron is called a mapoto and would have been

worn by a married woman. It dates from the mid-1900s and would be considered old-fashioned by the Ndebele today. Modern beadwork clothes use a variety of colors, often on a white background. The

designs reflect current fashions and incorporate modern motifs. Originally, the beads used were glass and were sewn onto leather; today, canvas bases, plastic beads, and fabric braids are also used.

© DIAGRAM

Beadwork doll
Ndebele women produce a great variety of beaded items, including bottles, gourds, dolls – such as the one above – and clothing.

Beaded hoops
Beaded hoops are often worn by married women on their legs, necks, and arms. They are made from bundles of dried grass shaped into circles, bound tightly, and then encrusted with beads and other decorative items such as the brass buttons this woman has used. Since the 1920s, neck hoops have grown in size and can now be up to 8 in. (20 cm) wide.

South Africa was dominated by the Zulu led by Shaka (q.v.). His lieutenant was Mzilikazi (q.v.), one of the Khumalo, an Ndebele group who had not migrated to the Transvaal but remained in present-day KwaZulu/Natal. In 1823, Mzilikazi rebelled against Shaka during the violent Mfecane/Difaqane era and led the Khumalo northward to safety. Mzilikazi settled north of the Vaal River and established a powerful (Ndebele) kingdom near present-day Pretoria. This kingdom was attacked repeatedly by Zulu, Griqua, and Kora people and finally by Boers on the Great Trek. In 1837, Mzilikazi led his people to a new settlement that he called Bulawayo ("Great Place"), which is where they came to be known as the Matabele.

The Matabele came into conflict with the British in the late 1800s when the British South Africa Company, headed by the imperialist Cecil Rhodes, occupied most of the region. In 1890, the Matabele found themselves the second-largest ethnic group in a British-dominated territory called Southern Rhodesia, for Rhodes.

RECENT EVENTS In 1973, under apartheid (the racist doctrine of "separate development") the Ndebele were given a homeland called KwaNdebele, which was in lands completely strange to them. Great conflict arose in the 1980s between the government-appointed regime of the homeland and the supporters of the Ndebele monarch: 160 died; 300 were detained; and hundreds simply disappeared. The homelands were abolished, in 1994, following the ending of apartheid legislation in 1991.

Meanwhile, the Matabele experienced years of oppression at the hands of the white-minority governments of Southern Rhodesia and Rhodesia. After a prolonged guerrilla war, majority rule was introduced with the birth of the independent state of Zimbabwe in 1980. Even after independence, the Matabele suffered the effects of a power struggle between the leaders of two former rebel groups: Robert Mugabe (q.v.) – the new prime minister – and Joshua Nkomo (q.v.), whose opposition party drew most of its support from Matabeleland. Government reprisals against dissidents in Matabeleland were harsh and culminated in a very brutal massacre in 1987. An amnesty declared in 1988 has eased the situation.

Language
The language of both the Ndebele and the Matabele is called Ndebele (or isiNdebele).

Ways of Life
The ways of life of both the Ndebele and the Matabele people are still greatly affected by the legacy of white-

Ndebele children
Among the Ndebele of Zimbabwe and South Africa, it is customary to decorate a home with designs of the kind seen behind these children.

minority rule. In South Africa and Rhodesia, the best farming land was allocated to whites and, despite land redistribution plans in independent Zimbabwe and the end of apartheid in South Africa, the situation has not improved greatly. Most Matabele households rely on food-crop farming augmented by the sale of cash crops and surplus produce; on casual employment; money sent by family members working as migrant laborers; and wages from working as farm laborers. Today, the majority of Ndebele work for wages in a variety of jobs including farm labor, but some with access to land still farm. Even today, some Ndebele farm laborers work under the same conditions as they did in the 1880s for the Boers and still do not receive any wages. The main food crops grown are corn, wheat, millet, and sorghum as well as, in South Africa, pumpkins, beans, and potatoes. In Zimbabwe, the main cash crops are cotton, tobacco, and sugar. Matabele farmers in Zimbabwe are still recovering from the effects of the 1991–2 drought.

Social structure
SOCIAL STRUCTURE Families are based on men as heads of households and in the country three generations often share the same home or live close together. Because so many Ndebele women, as well as men, go to distant parts to work, grandparents frequently bring up the children. Inheritance of property generally passes to the youngest son. A man may still have more than one wife, though having only one wife is the general rule in South Africa. A woman, however, can have only one husband.

POLITICAL STRUCTURE Historically, the Ndebele and Matabele were ruled by kings and paramount chiefs, and vestiges of this system remain today. Chiefs retain some authority, but they have to work within the modern systems of government in both countries. Justice was administered by a group's local court, and some disputes are still settled in this way.

Mural art
The walls of this house have been decorated with murals. Ndebele women have become famous for the geometric designs with which they paint their houses. The custom probably originated in the eighteenth century but has undergone an explosion in popularity since the 1940s. Initially, paints were made from clay, ash, and dung and natural pigments were used to create earthy colors – still seen in some rural areas. Today, brightly-colored, commercially-produced paints are used. Earlier designs incorporated mainly chevron and triangular shapes. More recent designs also incorporate shapes of airplanes, lightbulbs, and other modern influences on Ndebele life. Some women are privately commissioned to paint on canvas or to decorate shopping centers and even cars.

Culture and religion

RELIGION **T**he majority of Ndebele are Christians, most have converted since the emergence of the many independent African-run Christian churches. Certain features of the Ndebele religion are still widely followed. The most important of these, is belief in amaNdlozi, the revered ancestors of the family who are also believed to be spirit guardians. The Ndebele also maintain their beliefs in healing through spiritual forces. This is carried out by sangomas (diviners), who may be men or women, and nyangas (essentially herbalists), who are always men.

Ndebele and Matabele timeline			
200s Bantu-speaking peoples begin to arrive in Southern Africa	**1837** Mizilikazi and followers move north	South Africa created **1923** British government takes control of Southern Rhodesia; white immigration encouraged	Zimbabwe; one-party state emerges **1982** Antigovernment terrorism and violence in Matabeleland
1500s Ndebele groups emerge	**c. 1840** Mabhogo's reign over Ndzundza Ndebele begins	**1948** Apartheid begins in South Africa	**1991** Zimbabwean single–party system abandoned. Apartheid officially ends in South Africa
1700s Southern Ndebele fragment	**1883** Ndebele conquered by Boers	**1965** Illegal white-minority rule established in Southern Rhodesia as Rhodesia	**1994** First nonracial elections are held in South Africa
1819–1839 Mfecane/Difaqane: period of mass migrations and wars	**1890** British South Africa Company colonizes Southern Rhodesia	**1967–1975** Period of guerrilla warfare against white Rhodesians	**1999** Mugabe is re-elected president of Zimbabwe
1820s Mizilikazi founds Ndebele state	**1896** Shona and Matabele at war with British colonizers	**1980** Rhodesia independent as	
1836–1848 Great Trek brings Boers into conflict with people inland	**1910** White-minority ruled Union of		

Ndembu

The Ndembu are one of the many groups that make up the Lunda (q.v.) people. The precolonial Lunda Empire brought together a variety of Central African peoples, who, like the Ndembu, are often just referred to as the Lunda. While living in the northwest of modern-day Zambia, the Ndembu inhabit the southern regions of the historic Lunda Empire, the heartland of which was in what is now southern Congo (Dem. Rep.). For this reason the Ndembu are also known as the Southern Lunda. There are probably around 50,000 Ndembu people in Zambia.

The Ndembu separated from the Northern Lunda in the eighteenth century, leaving the lands of the Lunda Empire and migrating south. During the nineteenth century the Ndembu were regularly raided, and many were enslaved by Chokwe (q.v.) and Ovimbundu (q.v.) slave traders. A small Ndembu community was established in Angola in the early twentieth century when some crossed the border to escape taxation by the colonial British.

Ndundza

The Ndundza are one of the main Ndebele (q.v.) groups. The Ndebele live in South Africa.

Ndwandwe

The Ndwande are a Nguni (q.v.) people of South Africa and Swaziland. They once had a powerful kingdom in southern Africa under their leader Zwide in the early nineteenth century.

Ngama

The Ngama are a subgroup of the Sara (q.v.). They have a population of nearly 50,000 and live in southern Chad.

Ngambay

The Ngambay are a subgroup of the Sara (q.v.). There are more than 450,000 Ngambay.

Ngan *see* Beng

Ngbaka *see* Mbaka

Ngichoro

The Ngichoro are one of the two main subgroups of the Turkana (q.v.). The Turkana live in northwest Kenya.

Ngimonia

The Ngimonia are one of the two main subgroups of the Turkana (q.v.). The Turkana live in northwest Kenya.

Ngizm

The Ngizm are a subgroup of the Kanuri (q.v.). They live in northeastern Nigeria.

Ngonde

There are probably around 300,000 Ngonde in Malawi. The Ngonde are closely related to the Nyakyusa (q.v.) of southwestern Tanzania. The Ngonde inhabit the lands at the northern end of Malawi, just across the border and the Songwe River from the Nyakyusa. The Ngonde and the Nyakyusa languages are closely related Bantu (q.v.) languages.

The Ngonde's home on the side of Lake Malawi was an important crossroads of historical trade networks, allowing the Ngonde to profit from the lucrative ivory trade but suffer from the raids of slave traders. A powerful Ngonde kingdom (or chiefdom) arose in the nineteenth century, stimulated by the trade in ivory and slaves. This coincided with one of the most violent periods in Ngonde history – a Swahili slaver set up business in Ngonde country, initially with Ngonde consent, but Ngonde villages were attacked by the Swahilis and many people captured or killed.

Ngoni

Many East Africans are descended from Nguni (q.v.) refugees who fled from the violence of the Mfecane in the mid-1800s – they are known as Ngoni (q.v.) peoples. The Mfecane (the Nguni word for "crushing") is used to refer to the period (1819–39) of mass migrations and wars in the southeastern half of Southern Africa. The Mfecane was triggered by the rise of the Zulu kingdom under Shaka (q.v.). In Mozambique, the Ngoni refugees adopted Zulu battle tactics and raided the local Tsonga (q.v.) and Portuguese trading settlements on the coast, dominating the region by the 1830s. Led by Shaka's former general Soshangane, the Ngoni established a powerful military empire called Gaza. Gaza was a major obstacle to the Europeans trying to colonize Mozambique in the 1890s. Ngoni states were also established in Central Africa by Ngoni refugees. These were eventually absorbed into local groups, forming centralized chieftaincies.

Ngqika

The Ngqika are one of the main Xhosa (q.v.) groups. The Xhosa are a large group of peoples united by a common language in South Africa.

Nguin see **Beng**

Ngulu see **Lomwe**

Nguni

There are two major Black African cultural and linguistic groupings in southern Africa: the Nguni and the Sotho–Tswana (q.v.). Both share a common origin centuries ago in eastern Nigeria along with other Bantu (q.v.) speakers. The Nguni arrived in Southern Africa around the 200s CE, and it is possibly from the Tsonga (q.v.) of Mozambique that the earliest Nguni trace their origins. In southern Africa, the Nguni are concentrated in the southeast of the region, mostly between the Drakensberg Mountains and the sea. The larger Nguni groups in this area include the Zulu (q.v.), Swazi (q.v.), and the Xhosa. Other groups, such as the Ndebele (q.v.) and Matabele (q.v.), live in regions farther north, pushed north by the Mfecane. Many East Africans are descended from Nguni refugees who fled from the violence of the Mfecane in the mid-1800s – they are known as Ngoni (q.v.) peoples. The Mfecane (the Nguni word for "crushing") is used to refer to the period (1819–39) of mass migrations and wars in the south-eastern half of Southern Africa. The Mfecane was triggered by the rise of the Zulu kingdom under Shaka (q.v.).

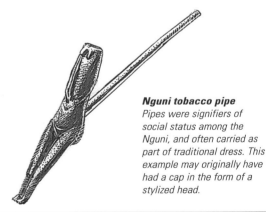

Nguni tobacco pipe
Pipes were signifiers of social status among the Nguni, and often carried as part of traditional dress. This example may originally have had a cap in the form of a stylized head.

Nguru see **Lomwe**

Nguru

The Nguru are part of the Zaramo (q.v.), a Bantu (q.v.) people of East Africa. The Nguru number more than 150,000 and live mostly in the mountainous highlands of coastal Tanzania.

Nikki

The Nikki are part of the Bariba (q.v.). They number more than 500,000 living in Benin.

Nilamba see **Iramba**

Nilotes

The majority of the modern-day population of East Africa is descended from three main African groups: Cushites, Nilotes (q.v.) and Bantu (q.v.) people. In turn, the Nilotes are divided into three main groups: Highland, Plains, and River-Lake. All three groups share a common homeland in the southwestern borders of the Ethiopian Highlands in the Nile River region of southern Sudan. This migration, which was gradual and occurred over several centuries, was perhaps triggered by overpopulation, the need to find more land to graze cattle on, or pressure from other ethnic groups.

Between 1000 BCE and 1500 CE the Highland and Plains Nilotes migrated into the highlands and plains of Kenya and Tanzania. The River-Lake Nilotes, however, followed the Nile Valley and settled in the lakes region of northern Uganda.

The Plains Nilotes emerged as a new and powerful force in East Africa during the second millennium CE. The Maasai (q.v.), Turkana (q.v.), Karamojong (q.v.), and Iteso (q.v.) people are Plains Nilotes. The Kipsigis (q.v.), Nandi (q.v.), and other Kalenjin (q.v.) peoples are Highland Nilotes. Lwo (q.v.)-speaking peoples such as the Alur (q.v.) and the Anuak (q.v.) are descended from River-Lake Nilotes.

Nilotic *see* Nilotes

Nladja-Wron *see* Alladian

Nono

The Nono are closely related to the Manding (q.v.) people. There are more than 20,000 Nono living in Mali.

North Mugirango

The North Mugirango are one of the main subdivisions of the Gusii (q.v.). The Gusii are a large ethnic group of western Kenya.

Nsenga

The Nsenga are closely related to the Bemba (q.v.). Living in eastern Zambia and across the border in Mozambique are more than 300,000 Nsenga.

Ntomba

The Ntomba are a subgroup of the Mongo (q.v.) of Central Africa. The Ntomba live in central Congo (Dem. Rep.) along the Maringa River.

Ntumu

The Ntumu are a Fang (q.v.) subgroup living in Equatorial Guinea, Cameroon, and Gabon. There are more than 200,000 Ntumu.

Nuba

The Nuba live in the Nuba Hills of Kordofan province, southern Sudan. This region lies west of the White Nile River and south of Khartoum, the Sudanese capital. There are more than 500,000 Nuba, and they fall into more than sixty groups and many more subgroups. (The Nuba should not be confused with the Nubians, who originate from the region now covered by Lake Nasser.)

History

Although very little is known about Nuba history until the Arab invasion of North Africa in the seventh century, it seems they have lived in their present location for centuries. Three hundred years before the Arab invasion, references had already been made to the presence of people called the "Black Noba," who were probably ancestors of the modern Nuba. Some Nuba groups claim to have always lived in the Nuba Hills. Since the eighteenth century, others have moved up into the inaccessible hills in retreat from Baggara raids or, in the late nineteenth century, Mahdist troops.

RECENT EVENTS During the lengthy Sudanese civil war between the Islamic north and the mainly non-Muslim

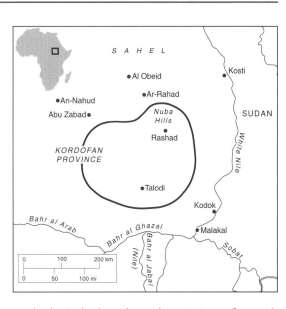

south, the Nuba have been drawn into conflicts with their Islamic neighbors, the Baggara. The government has armed the Baggara, which has resulted in thousands of Nuba being killed. Many thousands more have

Cicatrix
Some Nuba men and women have elaborate patterns on their faces and bodies, produced by scar tissue called cicatrix.

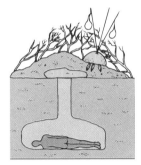

Nuba grave
Traditionally, the Nuba bury their dead in individual tombs. A hole is dug with a very narrow entrance and the body is laid on its side, facing east with its head pointing north. A mound of earth covers a stone over the entrance, and objects such as water-filled gourds and cattle horns are placed on the mound to help the deceased in the afterlife.

Dung bowls
These bowls were made by Nuba artisans from animal dung and water, which have been made into a paste and molded by hand. The patterns are similar to those used to decorate Nuba homes. Vessels like this may have been used in wedding ceremonies and were part of a girl's collection of items with which she would enter marriage.

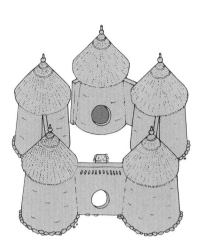

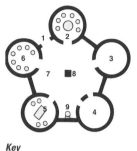

Traditional Nuba architecture
Structures called tukls – with thatched, cone-shaped roofs – are traditional Nuba buildings. Each tukl is connected by mud walls with several others, and the tukls surround a courtyard to form an individual family's complex. Several of these complexes clustered together form a community. The ongoing civil war, forcible relocations, and the development of new building techniques have made these distinctly Nuba buildings less common.

Key
1 Entrance **2** Granary **3** Sleeping tukl **4** Shelter for animals
5 Grinding stone **6** Storage tukl
7 Courtyard **8** Cooking area
9 Shower

been deported from the hills to government-run "peace villages," where they are under pressure to convert to Islam or to join the government troops fighting the southern rebels. Reports of rebel groups forcibly conscripting civilians have also surfaced.

Language
The Nuba speak over fifty different languages of the Koalib, Tegali, Talodi, Tumtum, and Katla groups of the Niger-Kordofanian language family.

Ways of life
Most Nuba are farmers and live in permanent settlements. They cultivate the land with spadelike hoes, and terrace and irrigate their fields. Common crops are millet, sorghum, and corn. Other crops include cotton, gourds, melons, okra, onions, cucumbers, peppers, and sesame. The Nuba also keep cattle and goats, which provide milk, and chickens, donkeys, horses, and sheep. Except in the few Muslim subgroups, many Nuba also raise pigs.

Normally, men work on the land and milk the cattle and goats, while women look after the chickens and pigs and gather wild foods such as nuts. Women also work in the fields to help with harvesting.

In the 1970s, oil companies began drilling in the oil-rich south of Sudan. Many Nuba men were employed by the companies. Since the outbreak of the civil war, however, exploitation has largely ceased and job opportunities in the industry have dried up.

HOMES The traditional Nuba home is a cylindrical mud structure with a cone-shaped thatched roof. Entrances are generally keyhole shaped. Home to a family may consist of five of these grouped around a courtyard. In towns scattered around the Nuba Hills, where many of the administrative centers are, the Nuba work and live in flat-roofed buildings of brick or stone.

Social structure
Nuba society has been drastically affected by the decade-long civil war. Many people have been killed during the conflict and a large proportion of Nuba men and boys have been forcibly conscripted into either the rebel armies or government troops. With many Nuba living in the so-called "peace villages" or in refugee camps in neighboring countries such as Congo (Dem. Rep.) and the Central African Republic, Nuba social structures, which differ from group to group but are generally based around clans (several extended families linked by a common ancestor or ancestors, in this case often a woman) are gradually being dismantled.

Culture and religion
RELIGION The majority of the Nuba follow the Nuba religion, which differs in nature from group to group. A minority of Nuba are Christians, however, and an even smaller proportion are Muslims.
PERSONAL ART The Nuba are famous for their elaborate forms of personal art, which involve scarring and painting their bodies. The patterns used to decorate the skin are rich in symbolism. Both men and women have this decorative scarring, but for women it denotes important milestones, and the scarring process continues for many years. The skin is cut in patterns and then rubbed with ash, saliva, or sesame oil. The first scarring is done in childhood or at the start of puberty, and the final scarring takes place after a woman has weaned her first child. The scars fade with age and become less prominent. As the Nuba are otherwise occupied by the current civil war, however, many personal art forms are in danger of falling into disuse.

Wrestling
Wrestling is a popular sport and is taken very seriously. Bouts can be fierce, but end when one wrestler pins his opponent's shoulders to the ground. In more peaceful times, huge crowds attended matches and skillful wrestlers could draw people from miles around; many wrestlers became celebrities whose fame was widespread.

WRESTLING A popular social activity among the Nuba is wrestling. Boys begin their training at the age of thirteen or fourteen. From that time onward, a boy ideally spends at least half his time at a camp where he learns and practices wrestling. As he progresses, he passes through four grades. Each grade has a belt or sash. White is the lowest grade; the belts of higher grades are made of colored cloth or goatskin, with a cow's tail as a badge of rank. The most accomplished wrestlers adorn their belts with brass bells. A wrestler paints his body with patterns in yellow or white. He also shaves his head and smears it with ashes mixed with milk. Nowadays, however, few can spare time for wrestling in the midst of a civil war.

Nuba timeline			
300s "Black Noba," probable ancestors of present-day Nuba, recorded in southern Sudan	**1882** Anglo-Egyptian forces conquer Sudan; Mahdi begins campaigns; more Nuba retreat into hills	**1975** Chevron begins drilling for oil in southern Sudan	**1990s** Famine hits Nuba Hills. Reports of "ethnic cleansing" of the Nuba by Baggara militias
640 Arabs begin conquest of North Africa; Islam introduced	**1898** Anglo-Egyptian force conquers Mahdist State	**1983** Sudan adopts Sharia (Islamic holy) law against wishes of mainly non-Muslim south; civil war breaks out again	**1992** Relocation camps for Nuba, so-called "peace villages," set up by government
1700s Arab slave raids against the Nuba. Baggara raids begin; more Nuba retreat into hills	**1955** First civil war between south and north Sudan begins	**1983– 1996** Many Nuba join Sudanese People's Liberation Army (SPLA), a southern-based rebel group	
1821 Trade routes opened from north to south Sudan – as a result, southern population is reduced by disease and slave trading	**1956** Sudanese independence **1972** South granted regional autonomy; first civil war ends	**1986** Chevron pulls out of Sudan	

Nubians

Nearly 3,000 years ago in what is now southern Egypt and northern Sudan, the Kingdom of Nubia became independent from ancient Egypt, from which it lay upriver along the Nile. For a while, the Nubians even controled ancient Egypt. Until recently, descendants of the historical Nubians still lived in this region. The 1960s saw the building of the Aswan High Dam on the Nile River, and more than 100,000 Nubians were relocated to elsewhere in Egypt and Sudan after much of Nubia was flooded. The region is now covered by Lake Nasser. UNESCO launched a massive campaign to save the historical treasures of Nubia, which include temples (Abu Simbel, for example), statues, fine pottery, and tombs full of gold and silver jewelry, bronze work, and other treasures. While greatly influenced by its powerful northern neighbor, Nubian culture was distinctly African in its origin and expression.

Nuer

The Nuer are a Nilotic people who live in southern Sudan. The Nuer are closely related to the Dinka, another Nilotic group. There are about 300,000 Nuer.

History

Along with other Nilotic peoples, the Nuer originated in a region to the southwest of their present location. Over the years, they migrated to their present location. This gradual process of migration was forced to halt when the British and Egyptians conquered Sudan in 1898. After Sudan achieved independence, an ongoing civil war tore the country apart; many Nuer temporarily fled to neighboring countries, and their herds were drastically reduced. This civil war ended in 1972, after the south, an area populated by many different ethnic groups, was given regional autonomy.

RECENT EVENTS In 1983, the Sudanese government adopted Sharia (Islamic holy) law, and triggered another civil war between the Muslim north and the largely non-Muslim south. By the 1990s, the main rebel groups had split into many different, often warring, factions. The Nuer-dominated South Sudan Independence Movement (SSIM) is often in conflict with the mainly-Dinka Sudanese People's Liberation Army (SPLA). Despite many cease-fires, the civil war still continues in Sudan today. Attacks on civilians are common and

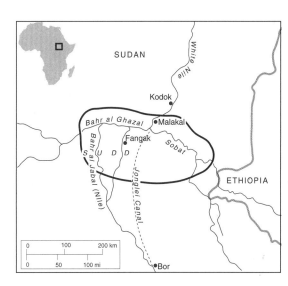

Nuer civilians have been forcibly conscripted into both rebel and government troops.

Clay oxen (right)
These ox figures, made from clay with tassels hanging from their horns, symbolize the important role cattle have in Nuer culture.

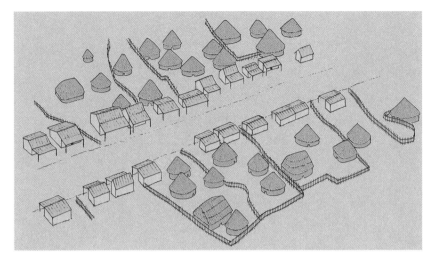

Nuer village
This Nuer village combines modern, metal-roofed brick buildings with old-fashioned, traditional mud houses that have thatched roofs.

Scarification
People of both sexes decorate their faces and bodies with scarring, though this traditional custom is becoming less common. The six lines on the man's forehead would have been made after his initiation into manhood – they are considered to be a mark of Nuer identity.

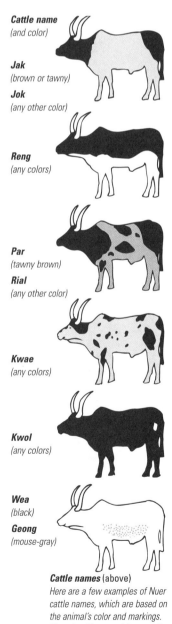

Cattle name
(and color)

Jak
(brown or tawny)

Jok
(any other color)

Reng
(any colors)

Par
(tawny brown)

Rial
(any other color)

Kwae
(any colors)

Kwol
(any colors)

Wea
(black)

Geong
(mouse-gray)

Cattle names (above)
Here are a few examples of Nuer cattle names, which are based on the animal's color and markings. There is a Nuer word for any of the many possible variations.

Language

The Nuer language is also called Nuer and belongs to the Nilotic language group.

Ways of life

SEMINOMADIC PASTORALISM The vast majority of Nuer are seminomadic pastoralists who rear cattle, an activity they combine with growing crops. The Nuer live in a region that is largely savanna (grasslands with scattered tree and shrubs), but some of their land is in the Sudd – a seasonally swampy region. During the rainy season, from May to December, the pastures around the rivers flood and become uninhabitable swamps. This is the time when the Nuer move to settlements on higher ground. During this season, the women cultivate crops such as peanuts, millet, and corn, while the men graze their herds nearby. As the swamps dry out during the dry season, from January to May, the Nuer men and their herds follow the receding rivers to new pastures.

In the 1970s, drilling for oil by the US company Chevron brought trucks and bulldozers to Nuer territory. Many Nuer took work on oil rigs. Production was stopped indefinitely in 1986, however, after several Chevron employees were kidnapped and murdered by rebels. Although the lifestyle of many Nuer was altered from seminomadic pastoralism to wage-labor, the work brought in much-needed cash for families and villages.

CATTLE Cattle are central to the Nuer way of life and are rarely killed for their meat alone. Cows are important as they provide milk; the Nuer milk-based diet is supplemented by some fishing and hunting. Cattle are important in many other ways. The prestige of the head of the household is determined by the size of the herd owned by the family. Cattle are sometimes sacrificed in religious rituals, and they are presented by the groom to his bride's family upon marriage. Young men often take a name based on the color of their favorite bull.

Because of their major role in Nuer culture, cattle are often the source of conflict; a cow owned by one man might eat the crops of another, for instance. They are also often the means of resolving conflicts, however, and not just those caused by cattle. Serious disputes are referred to the kuuarmuon (the chief and local magistrate) who determines the appropriate compensation, which is often a payment of cattle.

Social structure

SOCIAL ORGANIZATION The Nuer are organized into many clans, which are extended families that share a common founding ancestor or ancestors. Territory and other resources are divided by clans. Members of a particular clan do not marry one another.

MARRIAGE Upon marriage, the Nuer, like many African people, practice a system called bridewealth, which involves a gift – usually cattle – given by the bridegroom to the bride's family. An ideal arrangement might be a gift of forty cows to be given to the father of the bride-to-be; these would then be distributed to the bride's relatives. Few can afford this amount while they are at war, however. Bridewealth does not represent payment for the woman, but compensation for her family's loss of a working member and is considered a token of respect. Marriages are only considered legal once the bridewealth has been received in full.

Children are important in that they link the families of their mother and father. This is believed to reduce the potential conflicts between families because they share an interest in the child's well-being. In Nuer eyes a marriage is not finalized until the woman has given birth to at least two children. This, combined with the fact that it may take many years to complete the bridewealth, makes Nuer marriages a lengthy process.

Nuer couples can divorce, but bridewealth complicates this if there are children. With no children, the bride's family returns all the bridewealth, and the couple is free to divorce and remarry. If the couple has had only one child, the husband can ask for the bridewealth to be returned, but some will be retained by the bride's family in exchange for the one child, who remains part of the husband's family. If more children are born, the bride's family will be justified in retaining more or all of the bridewealth, making divorce an expensive option for the husband.

Culture and religion

RELIGION Although some Nuer have converted to Christianity, the vast majority follow the Nuer religion, which is centered around a creator-god called Kowth. The Nuer pray to Kowth for health and good fortune and offer sacrifices of cattle. There is no organized hierarchy of religious officials, though some people act as diviners and healers. According to Nuer religion, the first Nuer, Dja-gay, came out of a hole in the ground.

Nuer timeline

c. 1000 Nilotic peoples settled in region to the far southwest of Bahr al Ghazal river	**1840s–1850s** Arab slave trade develops in Nuer territory; Nuer are targeted by slave raiders	**1956** Sudanese independence	**1986** Chevron pulls out of Sudan
c. 1700s Nuer people begin to migrate eastward	**c. 1850** Active period of eastward Nuer migrations begin	**1972** End of first Sudanese civil war; south granted regional autonomy	**1990s** Despite many cease-fires, the civil war continues
1821 Trade routes opened from north to south Sudan, leading to a reduced southern population through disease and slave trading	**1898** Britain and Egypt colonize Sudan. Boundaries between Nuer and Dinka fixed	**1975** Chevron begins drilling for oil in southern Sudan	**1996** Rebel groups warn foreign oil companies not to return to southern Sudan after reports of planned investment
	1955–1972 First Sudanese civil war between north and south	**1983** Sudan adopts Sharia (Islamic holy) law against wishes of mainly non-Muslim south; civil war breaks out again	**1999** Sudan's government concedes the principle of secession for southern Sudan

Nupe

The Nupe number more than 500,000 people living in Nigeria. Their language is related to that of the Yoruba (q.v.) and the Igbo (q.v.). The Nupe live in west-central Nigeria.

Nyakyusa

The Nyakyusa inhabit the lands at the northern end of Lake Malawi in the southwest of Tanzania, just across the border and the Songwe River from the Ngonde. There are probably more than 600,000 Nyakyusa in Tanzania.

The Nyakyusa are closely related to the Ngonde (q.v.) of northeastern Malawi. The Nyakyusa and the Ngonde languages are closely related Bantu (q.v.) languages. The Ngonde-Nyakyusa peoples originally came from Bukinga (meaning the land of the Kinga people) in the Livingstone Mountains, which run along the northeastern edge of Lake Malawi in present-day Tanzania. The Nyakyusa chiefs claimed descent from the Kinga, while the "commoners" were supposed to have descended from local people conquered by the Kinga leaders.

The Nyakyusa and Ngonde were famous for their age-system of social organization, which has not been practiced, however, since the 1950s by the Nyakyusa. Different generations lived in separate "age villages." Every 30 or 35 years there was a ceremony in which fathers handed over power, land, and goods to their son's generation and became priests. The last such ceremony held by the Ngonde was in 1913.

Nyamwezi

The Nyamwezi live in west-central Tanzania where they are one of about 120 ethnic groups. There are between 1,000,000 and 1,500,000 Nyamwezi if not more. Their name, originally "Wanyamwezi" meaning "People of the Moon," was given because they came from the west, where the new Moon is first seen. Their homeland is known as Unyamwezi.

History

Oral history holds that the region of Unyamwezi was uninhabited until the seventeenth century. Then, chiefly families began to arrive from various directions. The earliest records are from the late 1600s, and concern the Galagansa, a western group. The Nyamwezi formed a number of semi-independent, self-governing units called ntemi (chiefdoms). A few powerful ntemi such as the Ha, Zinza, and Ngoni dominated the others.

By about 1800, traders from these groups were visiting the east coast – whose inhabitants gave them the name Wanyamwezi. The Nyamwezi gained a considerable reputation as pioneers of long-distance trade in East and Central Africa by organizing trading caravans. The principal trade was in iron – made and worked by the northern Nyamwezi – and salt. Later, copper and ivory, became the main commodities. There was also some slave trading. During the 1800s, the Nyamwezi

Gift figure
This wooden figure dates from the nineteenth century and was probably made by a Nyamwezi carver who accompanied an ivory-trading expedition to the island of Bukerebe in southeast Lake Victoria. It was presented by the traders to the Kerebe chief. The making and giving of such figures helped the traders enhance their standing with powerful chiefs.

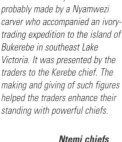

Ntemi chiefs
These two men were the chiefs of Kahima and Karitu chiefdoms in 1959. They are shown wearing their ceremonial robes, which are rarely seen today.

Staff (below)
This carved, wooden staff is 3ft (1m) long and would have been used as a status symbol by a ntemi (chief). It is simple and elegant in design and, like a lot of African art, both functional and aesthetic.

bought guns and some groups established standing armies. There were several wars among the chiefdoms, and also armed conflict with the Arab traders from the coast.

In the nineteenth century, a ntemi chief named Mirambo managed to establish his dominance over several chiefdoms. Mirambo's short-lived empire came into conflict with Arab traders but broke up soon after his death in 1884. During the 1890s, German colonists took control of mainland Tanzania, which they ruled as German East Africa. Britain took over after World War I. In 1951, the British evicted 3,000 Africans from their land to make way for white farmers.

RECENT EVENTS Tanganyika became independent in 1961 and, on union with the island of Zanzibar in 1964, became Tanzania. In 1965, the two parts of Tanzania were allowed only one political party each and two years later the country adopted a policy of socialism and self-reliance set out under the Arusha Declaration. Attempts to reorganize Tanzanian society along socialist lines had limited success but great impact on all Tanzanians including the Nyamwezi. Agriculture, in particular, was widely affected by villagization policies – the creation of new rural villages (ujamma), collectives, and large farming cooperatives. Although the planned improvements in agricultural production were never realized, social benefits in the area of health and education were achieved. After the retirement, in 1985, of President Julius Nyerere (q.v.) – who oversaw the socialist era – the worsening economic crisis led to the

abandonment of socialism. More pragmatic policies introduced since have helped the economy to recover.

Language
The Nyamwezi speak a language called Nyamezi (or Kinyamwezi). In addition, many Nyamwezi speak Swahili (or Kiswahili) and, or, English.

Ways of life
AGRICULTURE Many Nyamwezi live and work outside their homeland where they are engaged in various professions. Nevertheless, for the majority, growing crops and raising animals is their livelihood. The territory of the Nyamwezi is undulating country, some of it forested or dry grassland, which is unsuitable for agriculture or grazing. There is a dry season lasting from May to October, and a wet season from November to April. Farming is mostly confined to the wet season. The Nyamwezi still cultivate some of their land with hand hoes, but plows drawn by oxen or tractors are becoming more common. Cereal crops include corn, millet, sorghum, and rice. Other food crops include beans, cassava, mushrooms, onions, groundnuts (peanuts), spinach, and tomatoes. Fruit crops include bananas and oranges. The major cash crops are cotton, sunflowers, rice, and tobacco. The Nyamwezi raise large numbers of cattle, and also keep, goats, sheep, and chickens.

TRADE Athough most people are dependent on agriculture, trading is still important. During the colo-

Female figure (left)
The lack of feet on this carved, wooden figure suggests that it was formerly part of another piece, an altar perhaps. The figure is female and may have been used to represent the nurturing qualities of the person represented, probably a chief.

Houses (right)
In the rural villages, traditional Nyamwezi houses are circular, with an internal cylinder that provides an interior room. The walls are trellislike structures, plastered from the inside with mud. This steep, conical roof is thatched. Today, some homes are rectangular and have metal sheeting on top.

nial era, Nyamwezi trading caravans to the coast ceased. Instead, the Nyamwezi were often engaged as porters. Many also came to be employed as migrant laborers and this is still true today. For many years, the independent Tanzanian government discouraged private trade as part of its socialist stance. More recently, private businesses have been encouraged and many Nyamwezi are now involved in trade again.

DIET The basic food is bugalli, a form of porridge made from grains and eaten with meat and vegetables. The Nyamwezi make beer from corn or sorghum, and also drink coffee and tea.

Social structure

Nyamwezi society is very open and well adapted to absorbing newcomers – including those from other ethnic groups. People who are not Nyamwezi but live among them are encouraged to follow their own ways of life and not to conform necessarily to Nyamwezi traditions. This cosmopolitan outlook on life could, in part, be thanks to their long history of trade and traveling for commercial reasons. As a result, many people regard themselves as Nyamwezi though their ancestors had no connection with any of the original groups. The political functions of the chiefs have now been abolished, but they still retain their social status.

Culture and religion

RELIGION A few Nyamwezi have converted to Christianity or Islam but neither of these religions have flourished among the Nyamwezi. Many still follow the Nyamwezi religion. Generally, the Nyamwezi believe in a supreme god, variously refered to as Likube (High God), Limatunda (the creator), Limi (the Sun), or Liwelelo (the Universe). This god is rarely worshipped directly. Ancestor reverence is the main component of the religion that is practiced daily. The ancestors of each family are thought to affect the lives of their descendants. Chiefs' ancestors, however, have a more widespread influence over all the inhabitants of their former domains. People make offerings, mostly of grain but occasionally of sheep or goats, to show respect to their ancestors, having first invoked the help of Likube.

There are also spirits who are believed to influence the lives of people and specific societies or cults are devoted to them. The Baswezi society, for example, recruits people who have been attacked or possessed by the Swezi spirit. Many people believe in bulogi (witchcraft) and attribute misfortunes or illness to its practice. Religious practitioners or diviners called mfumu are often consulted during trouble or illness;

they interpret the belief system for their clients and use several methods to divine the forces active in a person's life and to arrive at remedies. Most mfumu act as medical consultants, using herbal medicines. The Nyamwezi are equally happy to make use of modern hospitals and medical facilities.

Chief's stool (above)
One of the most famous pieces of Nyamwezi art, this high-backed stool is typical of those made for chiefs. It was made for the chief of Buruku in the nineteenth century and has a human figure on the backrest. The three legs are carved in the characteristic, curved Nyamwezi style.

Dancer (above left)
Music and dancing are major Nyamwezi art forms. This man is wearing a traditional dancer's outfit. Long-familiar songs are sung at dances and weddings but new songs are always being composed.

Nyamwezi timeline

1600s Nyamwezi settle in present-day are of west-central Tanzania	**1961** Tanganyika wins independence
1800s Nyamwezi develop trade links with east coast	**1964** Tanganyika and Zanzibar unite to form Tanzania
1860–1870 Mirambo controls Ugowa and begins empire building	**1965** Each part of Tanzania is allowed only one political party
1871–1875 Mirambo frequently at war with Arabs from coast	**1967** Arusha Declaration; Tanzania adopts socialism
1884 Death of Mirambo; empire begins to disintegrate	**1985** Tanzania abandons socialism
1885 German Protectorate includes Unyamwezi	**1992** Tanzania introduces multiparty politics
1898 First "hut-tax" collected by Germans	**1995** Chaotic first democratic elections held in Tanzania
1920 Britain administers Germany's East African colonies	**1996** Thousands of refugees fleeing fighting in Burundi enter Tanzania. War crimes tribunal set up in Tanzania to deal with Rwandan and Burundi war criminals
1951 3,000 Africans evicted to make way for white farmers	

Nyankore

The Nyankore are a Bantu (q.v.) people of East Africa who number than more than one million living in southwestern Uganda. They were the founders of Uganda's historic Ankole Kingdom, which was abolished in 1966 along with the Nyoro (q.v.), Toro (q.v.), and Ganda (q.v.) kingdoms.

Nyaribari

The Nyaribari are one of the main subdivisions of the Gusii (q.v.). The Gusii are a large ethnic group of western Kenya.

Nyika see Mijikenda

Nyoro

The Nyoro (or Banyoro) people live in the lakes region of northwestern Uganda. The main area they inhabit is bounded on its western side by Lake Albert and on the north and northeast by the Victoria Nile River and by the Muzizi River in the southeast. The southern borders are less clearly defined. There are over 250,000 Nyoro.

History

BUNYORO Nyoro history is centered around that of the medieval empire of Bunyoro-Kitara and later the Bunyoro Kingdom. Oral history attributes the founding of the first Bunyoro-Kitara Empire to the mythical Abatembuzi (or Tembuzi) people. They were succeeded by the Bachwezi (or Chwezi) dynasty (c. 1350 – c. 1500) about whom little is certain except that they were a immigrant, cattle-herding people. The Bachwezi established a centralized monarchy over the local Bantu peoples. They had a hierarchy of officials and also maintained an army. After the death of the last Bachwezi bakama (king), Wamara, the Bunyoro-Kitara Empire broke up into several separate states, one of which was Bunyoro. The Babito dynasty took control of Bunyoro around the start of the sixteenth century. The Babito were originally Lwo-speaking River-Lake Nilotes – peoples who migrated from the Nile River in present-day southern Sudan to the lakes region of modern Uganda. Under their first omukama (ruler), Mpuga Rukidi, the Babito took over the country from the Bachwezi but kept many of the previous dynasty's rituals and customs. Raids against neighboring peoples expanded Bunyoro. By 1870, it extended to the north and east of the Nile and to the west of Lake Victoria.

Bunyoro was governed as a loose federation of saza (provinces) each under a chief appointed by the

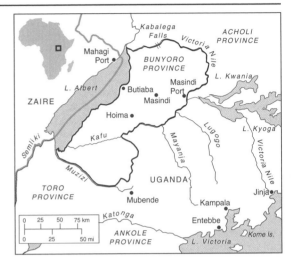

omukama. These saza were semi-independent and some on the edges of Bunyoro territory broke away to form independent states. During the long reign of Omukama Kyebambe Nyamutukura III (1786–1835), for instance, four of his sons turned against him. One of them, Kaboyo Omuhanwa, took the saza of Toro and established his own kingdom. Toro then became one of the border regions in dispute between the various Nyoro factions.

Omukama Kabalega (reigned 1870–98) tried to unite Bunyoro once again and regain the ascendancy it had lost on the rise of Buganda, a kingdom to the southeast. Kabalega created the Abarusura, a standing army of 20,000 men in ten divisions, each with its own commander. One division went to the capital Masindi to maintain law and order, under Kabalega's greatest general, Rwabudongo. Omukama Kabalega defeated the British in 1872 at the battle of Baligota Isansa, when they tried to set up an Egyptian protectorate (colony) in the northern part of Bunyoro. Kabalega later led a guerrilla war against the British for seven years until he was deported by them to the Seychelles in 1897. Toro and Bunyoro had already been made British protectorates in 1896. In 1900, they became part of the British Uganda Protectorate.

RECENT EVENTS In 1962, Uganda gained its independence. In 1967, President Milton Obote (q.v.) abolished all of Uganda's kingdoms, including Bunyoro. From 1971 to 1979, Uganda was dictated to by its military ruler Colonel Idi Amin Dada (q.v.). After he was ousted in 1979 by joint Tanzanian and Ugandan forces, the country was torn apart by civil war. After the end of this war in 1986, Uganda came under military rule until 1994. In 1993, Uganda's monarchies were restored but with ceremonial and cultural roles only. Solomon Gafabusa Iguru was crowned as Omukama of Bunyoro in 1994.

Language

The Nyoro speak a language also called Nyoro, which belongs to the Bantu group of languages.

Ways of life

AGRICULTURE Most Nyoro are farmers, living in scattered settlements, rather than villages. The most common

Trumpeter
The Nyoro leader's retinue always included special trumpeters, who performed at biennial festivals held to celebrate and renew the kingship. The trumpets are made from a gourd, covered with hide, and decorated with cowrie shells.

Bunyoro-Kitara Empire
This map shows the empire of Bunyoro-Kitara in the early sixteenth century, shortly before its disintegration. Bunyoro was the most important kingdom that emerged from its breakup. Although Bunyoro was influential and powerful, it never matched the Bunyoro-Kitara Empire in size.

Bachwezi defenses
The Bachwezi dynasty constructed large earthworks for defensive reasons. This example at Biggo in Bwera district, Uganda, lies on a tributary of the River Katonga and must have had a role in defending the southern border of Bunyoro-Kitara. It is a system of trenches and ditches that extends over 6.5 miles (10.5 km) and would have protected large herds of cattle. It also has a royal enclosure, or orirembo.

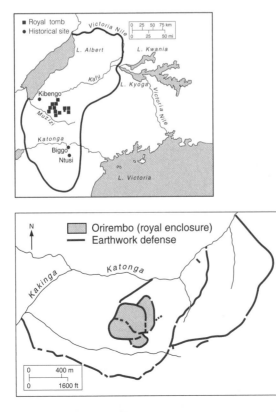

cash crops are coffee, cotton, and tobacco. Bananas, usually beer-making varieties from which mwenge is brewed, are also used. The staple food is finger millet, although vegetables like sweet potatoes, cassava, peas, and beans are also grown. Corn cultivation is rapidly expanding both as a food and a cash crop. In precolonial times, the Nyoro were cattle farmers, but the herds were ravaged by the wars and rinderpest (a cattle disease) epidemics of the nineteenth century. Now the tsetse fly – which carries both cattle and human diseases – prevents large herds from being kept in modern Uganda. Instead, most farmers keep a few goats or sheep and chickens.

INDUSTRY Before Amin's era, Uganda had one of the richest economies in tropical Africa. Political insecurity, the expulsion of Ugandan Asians (who owned many businesses), hasty nationalization, and the civil war devastated Ugandan industries. This has affected the Nyoro as much as any other people in Uganda, despite improvements since the late 1980s, though locally based industries such as salt-making and blacksmithing have survived. Salt-making has been carried out by the Nyoro since the time of the Bunyoro Kingdom. Iron ore is plentiful and the Nyoro have long been skilled blacksmiths. In 1990, Uganda and Congo (Dem. Rep.) agreed jointly to exploit petroleum reserves beneath Lake Albert. This will undoubtedly have an impact on the Nyoro, who live on the east of the lake.

Social organization

In the past, Nyoro people were divided into three main subgroups based on ethnic origin: the Babito (who took over Buganda from the Bachwezi), who always produced the hereditary omukama; the aristocratic,

Milk pot
This pot, made from clay and burnished with graphite, was made at the beginning of the twentieth century. It would have been used to contain milk. Such pottery was reserved for the royal family and nobility. Normally, women would make pots, but royal pots are always made by men. The sling is made from fiber and allows the pot to be hung on a pole, usually in a line with others.

cattle-owning Bahima pastoralists (livestock raisers); and the Bairu cultivators, the largest group. While the Bairu are indigenous to the region, the Babito and the Bahima originally arrived as invaders. Intermarriage and mixing over the years, however, has blurred any ethnic basis for distinction between the three groups. Today, the divisions are more a matter of class than ethnicity or occupation – if they are considered at all. The Babito were originally Lwo-speaking peoples while the Bairu spoke a Bantu language. All Nyoro now speak the same language.

Culture and religion

RELIGION The Nyoro are predominantly Christian, though a few are Muslims. Many Nyoro still follow the Nyoro religion, inherited from the Bachwezi Empire in which the rulers were viewed as hero-gods. Even after the Bachwezi dynasty ended, senior mediums of the Bachwezi gods passed on advice to the omukama on how to maintain his personal fertility, achieve success in warfare, and promote the fruitfulness of the land. As well as being thought of as the ancient rulers of the kingdom, the Bachwezi gods are each associated with a place, event, element, or idea. For example, Mugizi, is the god of Lake Albert; Nduala, the god of pestilence; Muhingo, the god of war; and Kaikara the harvest goddess.

Omukama
This picture, from 1936, shows the Bunyoro omukama (king), Sir Tito Winyi Gafabusa. Seated on the royal stool, he is wearing ceremonial robes and a crown reserved for certain court appearances. The Bunyoro Kingdom was abolished in 1967 but was restored in 1993. Sir Tito died before this in 1971.

Nyoro timeline	
1000s–1300s Bantu–speakers migrate to lakes region of present-day northwest Uganda	**1962** Uganda wins independence; Milton Obote is Prime Minister
c. 1350–c. 1500 Bachwezi dynasty rules over Bunyoro-Kitara Empire	**1966** Coup led by Milton Obote
c. 1500 Babito rule begins in Bunyoro	**1967** Bunyoro and Toro abolished
c. 1550 Bunyoro Kingdom at greatest extent	**1971** Colonel Idi Amin Dada seizes power in military coup; he installs repressive regime
c. 1830 Babito prince founds independent Toro Kingdom	**1979** Tanzanian forces and Ugandan rebels oust Amin
1859–1870 Bunyoro-Toro civil war	**1980** Milton Obote elected President
1870–1898 Reign of Omukama (King) Kabalega	**1981–1986** Ugandan civil war; rebels led by Yoweri Museveni win power
1872 Battle of Baligota Isansa	**1993** Buganda and Toro restored
1896 Bunyoro and Toro made British protectorates (colonies)	**1994** Nonparty elections held as first step to restoring democracy though political parties were banned
1900 Uganda Protectorate established; Bunyoro and Toro Kingdoms included	

Royal appearance
An omukama of Bunyoro is pictured outside his palace accompanied by his royal retinue.

© DIAGRAM

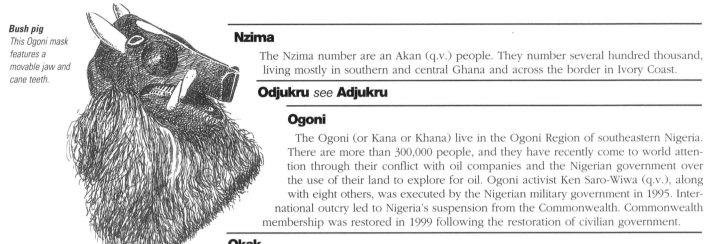

Bush pig
This Ogoni mask features a movable jaw and cane teeth.

Nzima

The Nzima number are an Akan (q.v.) people. They number several hundred thousand, living mostly in southern and central Ghana and across the border in Ivory Coast.

Odjukru *see* Adjukru

Ogoni

The Ogoni (or Kana or Khana) live in the Ogoni Region of southeastern Nigeria. There are more than 300,000 people, and they have recently come to world attention through their conflict with oil companies and the Nigerian government over the use of their land to explore for oil. Ogoni activist Ken Saro-Wiwa (q.v.), along with eight others, was executed by the Nigerian military government in 1995. International outcry led to Nigeria's suspension from the Commonwealth. Commonwealth membership was restored in 1999 following the restoration of civilian government.

Okak

The Okak are a subgroup of the Fang (q.v.) of Central Africa. They live in Equatorial Guinea, Cameroon, and Gabon.

Okiek

The majority of the Okiek people inhabit the highlands of west-central Kenya though smaller groups live across the border in Tanzania. They are sometimes also called the Athi or Dorobo, but these are confusing terms originally used by the Maasai (q.v.) to refer to many different non-Maasai groups. There are more than 20 different Okiek groups, including the Akie of northeastern Tanzania, the Digiri and Omotik of savanna (grassland) regions of west-central Kenya, and the Kaplelach and Kipchornwonek, who live on the southern slopes of the Mau Escarpment in western Kenya. There are probably around 100,000 Okiek people living in Kenya and Tanzania put together.

The ancestors of the Okiek were the Kalenjin, High-land Nilotes (q.v.) who began dispersing from their original cradleland at the northernmost tip of Lake Turkana in present-day Ethiopia to East Africa during the last millennium BCE. The separate Kalenjin groups such as the Okiek emerged as the Highland Nilotes spread out over the region and mixed with people already living there. Although Nilotic peoples are historically associated with cattle herding, the Okieks have historically been hunters and gatherers of forest regions. As a result, the Okiek, who are in a minority, have been considered inferior by their cattle-herding neighbors. Modern-day Okiek people farm, keep livestock, gather honey, and work in towns; hunting and gathering are now supplementary activities.

Omotic

Omotic peoples account for well over 1.5 million people divided into eighty different ethnic groups. They are ranged from the lakes region of East Africa to southern Ethiopia.

Omotik

The Omotik are a subgroup of the Okiek (q.v.)of west-central Kenya. The Okiek are, in turn, part of the Kalenjin (q.v.).

Oquies *see* Akwamu

Oring

The Oring number more than 400,000. They live in Cross Rivers State, southeastern Nigeria, and farther east into western Cameroon. They speak a Bantu (q.v.) language.

Oromo

The Oromo are a large ethnic group living in Ethiopia. Other African peoples call them Galla, a name the Oromo themselves dislike. Their territory, Oromia, covers southeastern Ethiopia and part of northern Kenya. It is almost as large as Texas in the United States and was once an independent country.

Estimates of the total number of Oromo vary between 2,500,000 and 25,000,000. They probably make up roughly half of the population of Ethiopia. There are nine main subgroups. They are the Arusi, Bararetta, Borana, Itu, Macha, Randili, Tulama, Walega, and Wollo. Altogether, there are about 200 different subgroups.

History

The Oromo are a Cushitic people. The Cushites originated in the Ethiopian Highlands and were the first food producers in East Africa. Historians think that the ancestors of the Oromo lived in Ethiopia at least 5,000 years ago. From the highlands of Ethiopia the Cushites gradually expanded to occupy most of northeast Africa, slowly migrating south and east to their present homeland. They began expanding northward in the 1500s, and by 1563 they controlled about one-third of Ethiopia. Sometime after 1600 they began raiding southward, and by 1699 they had reached Malindi, Kenya. In 1788 one of their chiefs, Ali, founded the

Kingdom of Begemder in central and northwest Ethiopia. Other Oromo chiefs founded kingdoms in the early 1800s. Oromo chiefs served as ministers in the Ethiopian government, which they dominated.

In 1853 Kassa, a former bandit, overthrew Ras Ali of Begemder and married the successor to the Begemder throne. In 1855, he made himself emperor of Ethiopia, with the title of Tewodros (or Theodore) II. Later he was overthrown by a British expeditionary force. In 1880, Menelik II (q.v.), the Amhara ruler of the Ethiopian province of Shoa, began to overrun Oromia. He became emperor of Ethiopia in 1889, and by 1900 had completely conquered Oromia. Menelik made the Oromo into slaves, and he and Queen Taitu personally owned 70,000 of them. The unfortunate Oromo fared little better under the last Ethiopian emperor, Haile Selassie I (q.v., reigned 1930–74), or under the Italians, who occupied the country from 1935 to 1941. Thousands of Oromo died in the civil war that racked Ethiopia from the 1960s to 1991. In this war, the Oromo and other ethnic groups strove to win independence. By 1993, only the Eritreans had attained it. Since 1995, the Oromo have been increasingly victimized with Oromia virtually under army occupation and many Oromo have become victims of summary rape, torture, or execution at the hands of government troops.

Language
The Oromo language is also called Oromo, and is one of the Cushitic language group.

Ways of life
The Oromo were originally a cattle-herding people, moving from place to place. Many, particularly in the lowlands of the south, are still pastoralists. They keep cattle, sheep, and goats, with donkeys as beasts of burden. Some groups have horses and camels, and one small group keeps pigs. They do no hunting or fishing, and milk, meat, and butter are the main items of their diet. In the highlands they are sedentary farmers, growing cereals and coffee as well as keeping animals, including chickens and goats.

DIVISION OF LABOUR Work is divided between the sexes: men tend to do all the herding, while women do the milking and look after the plants. The Oromo

cultivate the soil with plows, drawn by pairs of oxen.
CLOTHING Clothing varies from one subgroup to another. In isolated areas traditional dress predominates. This includes, for men, a waya, a togalike garment, or a short kilt, and, for women, leather skirts, often with a cotton top. Men generally wear their hair short, while women have many elaborate hairstyles.

Social structure
In their days of independence, the Oromo were governed under a democratic system called the gadaa. The leaders were elected by adult males who had attained certain grades in the gadaa system. There were eleven of these grades, the first three being for boys. The sixth grade, also called gadaa, was that of the ruling class. Its members held office for only eight years. After that they became advisers for three grades, totaling twenty-four years. At the final grade they were retired. The system provided training so that when men entered the gadaa grade they were fully equipped to run their local government. The gadaa system has been in existence for more than five centuries. Under the republican government of Ethiopia, the system has declined and many of its attributes are banned, though in principle it still exists.

Culture and religion
The Oromo have a rich culture, which is slowly being eroded by their position within Ethiopia. They had their own calendar, based on a lunar month of twenty-nine days. The Oromian year is 354 days long, so their calendar is out of step with the Sun. Each day of the month has its own name, but as there are only twenty-seven names, each month begins on a different day. In many parts of Oromia, the Oromo calendar has given way to the Muslim calendar.

RELIGION Most Oromo follow either Islam or Christianity, and some still practice the Oromo religion, which features one supreme god, Waqaayo, plus a great many ayanas, or saints. Religious leaders are known as quallus, and their office is hereditary. There are also female religious leaders, qalittis. Some Muslim and Christian Oromo follow the Oromo religion at the same time. Islamicization was made easier by the Oromo's eagerness to resist the domination of the Amhara, who are predominantly Christian.

Market day
An Oromo woman, wearing a colorful headscarf, sells coffee beans at an open-air market. Her silver jewelry incorporates Austrian Maria Theresa dollars. These were once used as a trading currency in Ethiopia.

Oromo granary
This granary (storehouse for grain) is made from woven sticks and has a conical thatched roof. Oromo houses and other buildings vary from one subgroup to another.

Goatskin containers (left)
This Oromo woman is filling a container called a gerber with water. Gerbers are made from whole goatskins; the leg, tail, and neck openings have been tied shut.

© DIAGRAM

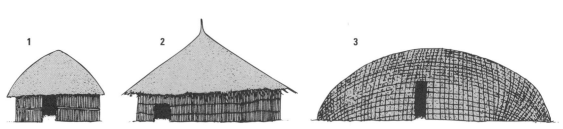

1   2   3

Traditional architecture
Different types of house are generally associated with different Oromo subgroups. **1** *Beco house* **2** *Shoa house* **3** *Arusi house*

Elaboration includes adding verandas, providing a shady, porchlike area. Inside, they are divided into several compartments.

The Oromo believe in life after death. They used to hold a special prayer ceremony before the annual harvest, but the republican government of Ethiopia has made the ceremony illegal. The Oromo religion and its practices have survived mainly in southern Ethiopia. These practices include ceremonies to honor or celebrate birth, circumcision, marriage, and death.

ARTS AND CRAFTS Oromo blacksmiths make tools, spears, and other objects from iron. Goldsmiths make ornamental work such as bracelets from gold, which is panned in Oromia, and from silver. The silver is imported, mainly in the form of Maria Theresa dollars. These old Austrian coins were used as currency in East Africa for many years, and were still being minted in the twentieth century – always dated 1780. Oromo woodworkers fashion tools and plows, spears and bows, and simple tables. They make small barrels that are hung in trees as beehives. Some honey barrels are made of reeds. Weavers make plain cloth on simple looms.

Holy tomb
The Oromo make frequent pilgrimages to the shrines or tombs of saints and holy figures. This is the tomb of an ancient miracle-worker called Sheikh Hussein and it is visited by people hoping to benefit from its healing powers. The tomb has been covered with colorful cloths to mark a celebration.

Oromo timeline		
1500s "Great Migration" into highlands of Ethiopia	**1935–1941** Ethiopia invaded and occupied by Italy	**1991** Mengistu loses power; OLF part of new government; end of civil war and Eritrean liberation from Ethiopia follows
1600s–1700s Oromo begin to expand southward and settle	**1961** Ethiopian civil war begins	**1992** OLF leaves government after dispute; renews rebellion; 20,000 Oromo detained
1788 Begemder Kingdom founded	**1974** Military coup overthrows Haile Selassie I; Ethiopia declared a socialist state	
1825–1850 Sudanese slave trade flourishing in Oromia	**1975** Oromo Liberation Front (OLF) formed; active near Kenyan and Sudanese borders	**1994** Ethiopia organized into nine states based on ethnicity; Oromo state formed
1850s–1890s Oromo monarchies in southwest Ethiopia	**1977** Maj. Mengistu Haile Mariam takes power in Ethiopia	**1995** Small OLF bands still active. Dr Negasso Gidado elected Ethiopian president. 280 Oromo rebels on trial. Persecution of Oromo peoples continues
1853 Begemder king overthrown		
1889–1896 Oromo influence in decline in East Africa	**1980s** Severe droughts cause famine throughout decade. OLF support increases	

Oron

Oron is the name of an Ibibio (q.v.) language and the people who speak it. The Oron live in southeastern Nigeria.

Otman

The Otman are an Amarar (q.v.) subgroup. The Amarar are, in turn, a subgroup of the Beja (q.v.). They are a Cushitic (q.v.) people who number around 100,000. The majority live in a large area bordered on the east by the Sudanese Red Sea coast.

Ouagadougou

The Ouagadougou (or Wagadugu) area a part of the Mossi (q.v.). They live in and around the city of Ouagadougou in central Burkina-Faso. There are more than one million Ouagadougou.

Ouara *see* Wara Wara

Ouassoulounke

The Ouassoulounke (or Wassalunka) are a Manding (q.v.) people. They live in the Wasulu region of southwestern Mali.

Ouatchi

The Ouatchi are a Ewe (q.v.) people. They number more than 250,000 people living mostly in southern Togo but also in Benin.

Ovahimba

The Ovahimba are a subgroup of the Herero (q.v.). The majority live in northeastern Namibia.

Ovambo

The Ovambo are concentrated on the high, flat, stoneless plains between the Kunene (Cunene) and Okavango (Cubango) Rivers in the far north of Namibia and the far south of Angola. The 150,000 Angolan Ovambo are one of that country's smaller ethnic groups, but the half million Namibian Ovambo constitute almost half of Namibia's population. Many Ovambo have migrated to live elsewhere in Namibia where they work, either on a permanent or temporary basis, on farms, in mines, and as civil servants. Due to the policy of apartheid ("separate development") and South Africa's policy of "divide and rule," many people have come to reject being labeled "Ovambo," instead preferring to be identified simply as "Namibian."

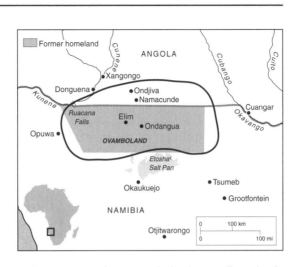

History

It is believed that the Ovambo migrated to their present homeland from the northeast – in the area of present-day Zambia – sometime around the fifteenth or sixteenth centuries. The Ovambo have a close cultural and historical relationship with the Herero who live farther south: legend states that the two peoples are descended from brothers who parted when they reached the present home of the Ovambo – Ovamboland.

COLONIALISM In 1884, Namibia became a colony of Germany, but because of difficulties in controlling the smaller Herero and Nama population to the south, the Germans never took much interest in the areas of Ovambo territory under their jurisdiction. In 1915, Namibia (as South West Africa) – and with it much of Ovamboland – came under South African administration. The South Africans took more interest in Ovamboland, and in the 1920s and 1930s they crushed numerous Ovambo rebellions. The Portuguese had occupied the Angolan coast since the late fifteenth century, but until they ruthlessly asserted their claims to part of southern Angola in the early twentieth century they took little interest in the isolated Ovamboland.

APARTHEID South Africa's policy of apartheid, introduced in 1948, was also forced on Namibia. In 1973, Ovamboland was declared "independent" by South Africa. This independence was rejected by the overwhelming majority of Ovambo and by the international community. An assembly of mainly South African-appointed chiefs was created. The Chief Minister, Filemon Elifas, was assassinated in 1975 for his brutal reign of fear, which was backed by the South African army and

police. Absences from Ovamboland were allowed only with a work permit – and then without any accompanying family members. Frustration with this system and with the lack of opportunities in Ovamboland, resulting from overpopulation and overgrazing, led to the development of an Ovambo workers' movement.

INDEPENDENCE In 1960, the South West Africa People's Organization (SWAPO) emerged from the opposition to South African rule. After more than twenty years of armed struggle, SWAPO led Namibia to independence in 1990. Although SWAPO has been accused by its opposition of being dominated by Ovambo, it upholds strong nontribal and nonracial principles. Ovambo, however, do make up almost half Namibia's population and Ovamboland was in the frontline of the guerrilla war, so it is not surprising that many of the organization's members and leaders are Ovambo.

Language

The Ovambo are a Bantu-speaking people whose main language is Ovambo, also called Ambo. There are linguistic differences between Ovambo subgroups, but their dialects are easily mutually intelligible.

Ways of life

AGRICULTURE The northern part of Ovamboland is open wooded grassland and the south is more arid grassland. It is subject to two to three months a year of heavy rain that causes widespread flooding of the silt-covered plain, followed by nine or ten months of drought. To adapt to these harsh conditions, the Ovambo have taken advantage of what resources are available. Culti-

Fishing

Fish are an important part of the Ovambo diet – often eaten dried, powdered, and mixed with durra (sorghum) as flavoring. These women are catching fish trapped in the shallows with shikuki – reed baskets that have an opening in the top so that when a fish is trapped inside, the fisherwoman can put her hand in to remove the fish.

Ovambo village (left)
Stockades of tall poles surround this settlement and create pathways inside that join the compounds together. The open central area is used as a gathering place. This small village contains only around twenty homes.

© DIAGRAM

vation is largely the preserve of women. The staple crop is millet, pounded into flour and eaten in the form of a dry porridge, while corn is produced for making beer. Beans, sweet potatoes, groundnuts (peanuts), melons, and pumpkins are also cultivated. Men tend the livestock: cattle and goats are raised, but, due to flooding, local grazing conditions are not as favorable as they are to the south in Herero territory.

MIGRANT LABOR Since the late nineteenth century, Ovambo men have traveled south to work in Namibia's mines or on the railroads, while many women have left Ovamboland to work as domestic servants.

HOUSING Most Ovambo live in compounds (a linked group of houses) completely encircled by a fence. Husbands, wives, young men and women, and visitors all live in separate buildings. Encircling the compound is a cattle enclosure, which also includes safe storage areas for grain and other goods.

Social structure

A special feature of Ovambo society is its matrilineal succession (descent is traced from mother to daughter). Children are inherited from their mother or their maternal aunts and uncles. Only mothers are considered to be the immediate relations of their children as suggested by the Ovambo proverb "The family does not come from the penis"; the closest relative a father had was his own sister. A husband, wife, their children, and any elders, make up the basic family unit, but the maternal uncle is regarded as the family leader and so he is accorded great respect.

Despite this matrilineal inheritance, official positions are the preserve of men. Social status depends on a man's ancestry, age, and number of cattle. Historically, the ruling elite had the means to survive extended periods of drought and build up grain stocks as well as distribute aid to the poor, thereby earning prestige.

Culture and religion

RELIGION The Finnish Missionary Society has had a continuous presence in Ovamboland since 1870 and its missionaries have established schools, clinics, and churches. The first baptisms took place in 1883. Most Ovambo are now members of the Lutheran Ovambokavango Church; a minority in Namibia are Anglicans and, in Angola, a minority are Catholics.

ARTS AND CRAFTS The western Ovambo groups have developed a reputation for their skills in copper and ironworking, making practical implements such as knives and hoes. As there are no iron or copper deposits in Ovamboland, it is assumed that the Ovambo knew the art of smelting iron before they settled in their present lands. Apart from metalworking, other major handicrafts include pottery and basketry.

Omakipa (left)
These ivory clasp-buttons date from the 1930s. Perforations at the back allow the buttons to be attached to belts, strands of beads, or straps that are worn loose. It is an Ovambo custom for a bridegroom to give omakipa to his bride on their wedding day. After marriage, the husband would add to his wife's collection, which she would wear on special occasions. Today, buttons such as these are more likely to be family heirlooms than wedding gifts. Omakipa like these are no longer made as it is now illegal to hunt elephants for ivory.

Ovambo timeline	
c. 1500s Ovambo arrive in Namibia	South West Africa declared illegal by United Nations
1500s Portuguese establish colony in present-day Angola	**1973** "Independent" Ovamboland homeland created in South West Africa
1884 Germany colonizes Namibia as South West Africa; Christianity introduced to the region	**1974** Portuguese revolution; Angola promised independence
1915 German South West Africa occupied by South Africa	**1975** Civil war breaks out in Angola. Autocratic Ovamboland ruler Filemon Elifas assassinated
1920s–1930s Numerous Ovambo rebellions quashed by South Africa	**1989** Apartheid legislation repealed in South West Africa
1948 Form of apartheid introduced to South West Africa	**1990** Namibia independent. Peace accord in Angola
1950s–1960s Main Angolan independence movements formed	**1992** Civil war in Angola resumes
1960 South West Africa People's Organization (SWAPO) founded	**1994** Stretch of Namibian-Angolan border closed
1966 Conflict between SWAPO and South African troops begins	**1995** Fragile peace in Angola
1969 South Africa's occupation of	**1999** Civil war resumes in Angola

Subterranean potter
Working underground to ensure that the pots dry evenly, this woman is preparing her pots to be fired.

Ovimbundu

The Ovimbundu (or Umbundu) form the largest ethnic group in Angola. Concentrated around the Benguela Highlands of central Angola, they number approximately three and a half million.

History

The Ovimbundu emerged as a distinct group in the sixteenth and seventeenth centuries. They arose from the merging of two ethnic groups: the Jaga, a Lunda people from northeast Angola, who invaded central and western Angola and settled with the indigenous populations – the second group. The Ovimbundu were firmly established by the 1770s, with royal families providing both political and ritual leadership through the king and his counselors. Originally, they incorporated many of the warrior traditions of the Lunda, but these were diluted as the Ovimbundu became primarily a trading people.

The economic history of the Ovimbundu is largely a record of violent contact with, and then commercial exploitation by, Portuguese colonists. This began in about 1600. The slave trade remained an important element of the Ovimbundu economy right up until the early twentieth century, during which time over three million slaves had been exported, mainly to Brazil.

The geographic location of the Ovimbundu kingdoms – between the coast and the peoples of the interior – promoted a rich trading economy in the nineteenth century with the Ovimbundu acting as middlemen. By the mid-nineteenth century, Ovimbundu trading caravans (companies of travelers) were journeying across the continent dealing in slaves, ivory, wax, and rubber. They were soon numbered among the greatest traders of Africa, with caravans sometimes comprising thousands of people. The height of the Ovimbundu economy was reached between c. 1874 and 1900, when high-grade rubber became almost the sole export from the coastal port of Benguela. Increased competition with rubber from West Africa, Asia, and South America led to a huge fall in the price paid for Angolan rubber, which was classified as third-grade. Coupled with continuing injustices and exploitation by the Portuguese, this decline triggered the Bailundo War of 1902 and 1903.

COLONIALISM The Portuguese occupation in subsequent years and the collapse of Ovimbundu caravan trading by 1911 resulted in widespread famine. In response to forced labor, heavy taxation, discrimination by the Portuguese, and repression of all political protest, the Angolan war of liberation began in 1961. Initially, it was fought by the Marxist-Leninist Movimento Popular Libertação de Angola (MPLA) and the Frente Nacional de Libertação de Angola (FNLA). The MPLA received backing from Cuba and the USSR. In 1967, when União Nacional para a Independência Total de Angola (UNITA) was formed, a lot of its support was drawn from the rural Ovimbundu.

CIVIL WAR Angola became independent in 1975, by which time the MPLA and UNITA were fighting each other in a civil war. UNITA received military assistance and arms from the United States and South Africa. By early 1976, the MPLA had taken control of most of Angola and formed the government, but it remained in conflict with the UNITA guerrilla movement, led by Dr Jonas Savimbi (q.v.), throughout the 1980s. Multiparty elections took place in 1992, which the MPLA leader José Eduardo dos Santos won (q.v.). Savimbi refused to accept the election results, however, and there was a return to civil war. Although UNITA and the MPLA government signed a treaty (the Lusaka Protocol) in 1994, hostilities continued until 1995. In 1996, the peace remained fragile and civil war broke out again in 1999.

Language

The Ovimbundu language is called Umbundu.

Ways of life

The lifestyles of the Ovimbundu, and all other Angolans, have been drastically affected by the twenty-year long civil war. Combined with poor transport and marketing facilities, drought (inadequate rainfall), shortages of raw materials, and the concentration of government spending on defense, the development of both agriculture and industry have been severely hampered. As a result, there are serious food shortages and malnutrition is widespread. The presence of an estimated nine million landmines left over from the civil war, not only endangers the lives of civilians but has left much fertile land uncultivated.

Although many Ovimbundu live and work in Angola's towns and cities, during the war there was a general population shift from cities to rural areas. Many urban Ovimbundu have fled to the rural communities of central Angola to avoid persecution. The civil war has created a huge population of internally displaced people (internal refugees). In rural areas, the Ovimbundu have become concentrated in villages fortified against attacks by antigovernment rebels and government troops.

AGRICULTURE Most Ovimbundu make their living as farmers. Cassava is the staple food crop. Cash crops include corn, palm oil, palm kernels (seeds), cotton, coffee, bananas, and sisal (a fiber crop). Farming and cattle-rearing are the mainstays of many communities – the Ovimbundu highland areas are relatively free of the tsetse fly (a disease-bearing fly), which prevents animal husbandry in much of Angola.

Wooden staff
The rise of powerful Angolan chieftainships in the sixteenth and seventeenth centuries concentrated artists on producing prestige items. Ovimbundu staffs in particular were produced in large numbers. Many Ovimbundu men carried staffs as walking aids, but the quality of the carving in this example suggests it was owned by a wealthy or noble man and its primary function was probably as a status symbol.

Protective objects
These three items belonged to an early twentieth-century Ovimbundu chief. The necklace is made from cloth, beads, and animal horn and was worn around the neck to prevent bronchitis. The rattle, made from wood and seeds, was probably used to awaken spirits. The cloth bag contains substances to use against enemies.

Social structure

From the seventeenth until the nineteenth centuries, Ovimbundu society adapted itself to a cattle-rearing and crop-farming economy that was heavily involved in trade. During this time, a double-descent kinship system helped maintain social cohesion. In this system, each individual belonged to both a local patrilineal group (descendants of a common male ancestor traced through male relatives) and a more dispersed matrilineal grouping (descendants of a common female ancestor traced through female relatives). Membership of the patrilineal group gave an individual claims to land and residence rights, while membership of the matrilineal group conferred the right to inherit movable property. Matrilineal kin also provided financial resources for trading enterprises and so underpinned the Ovimbundu economy. This dual system helped to separate village and chiefdom concerns from the inheritance of wealth gained from trade.

The economic and cultural domination of the Ovimbundu by the Portuguese, combined with the decline of the Ovimbundu trading economy, has eroded much of this system of social organization. In modern Ovimbundu society, the nuclear family of husband, wife, and children is now the basic social unit and there is little distinction between matrilineal and patrilineal kin.

Culture and religion

RELIGION Over half of Ovimbundu people are Christian. Of these, over three-quarters are Catholic. Ovimbundu religious beliefs are also still widely held. The Ovimbundu religion involves the belief that the chief and certain family members – especially his principal wife (inakulu) – are imbued with certain powers. Through rituals and ceremonies, the chief and his family exercise power over the fertility of people, animals, and plants.
ART Much of Ovimbundu art is associated with the cult of the sacred chief and royal family, the carvings on wooden statues, staffs, and musical instruments particularly reflect this.

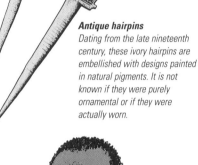

Antique hairpins
Dating from the late nineteenth century, these ivory hairpins are embellished with designs painted in natural pigments. It is not known if they were purely ornamental or if they were actually worn.

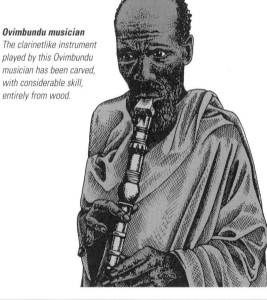

Ovimbundu musician
The clarinetlike instrument played by this Ovimbundu musician has been carved, with considerable skill, entirely from wood.

Ovimbundu timeline			
c. 1500s Portuguese begin settling on Angolan coast and start trading with the Ovimbundu peoples	**1961** Start of Angolan War of Independence fought by the MPLA and the FNLA	**by 1976** Government formed by MPLA	**1994** Lusaka Protocol signed, but hostilities continue
c. 1580 The Jaga Lunda people settle in the highlands of Angola	**1967** Jonas Savimbi forms UNITA, which recruits from Ovimbundu	**1988** South African and Cuban forces begin to leave Angola	**1995** Savimbi recognizes MPLA leader José Eduardo dos Santos as president and declares war to be at an end
1902–1903 Bailundo War fought against Portuguese colonization	**1975** Angola gains independence ; civil war is already being fought by Soviet- and Cuban-backed MPLA and US- and South African-backed UNITA	**1991** Peace agreement signed by Unita rebels and government	**1996** Fragile peace in Angola
1911 "Year of the Great Hunger": the last Ovimbundu trading caravans do not return and many die from hunger		**1992** First democratic elections are won by MPLA. Unita refuses to accept election results and civil war breaks out again	**1999** UN peace-keeping mission withdraws as civil war resumes in Angola

Oyo

The Oyo are a major Yoruba (q.v.) subgroup. The majority live in Oyo State, western Nigeria.

Padhola

The Padhola (Adhola or Dhopadhola) number more than 200,000 people living in the northeast of Congo (Dem. Rep.) and the west fo Uganda. They are a Nilotic (q.v.) people sometimes argued to be part of the Luo (q.v.) cluster.

Pare

The Pare are part of the larger grouping of Shambaa (q.v.) peoples, who inhabit the coastal lowlands of Tanzania. The Pare heartland includes the Pare Mountains in the northeastern corner of Tanzania.

The Shambaa are descended from both Bantu (q.v.) and Cushitic (q.v.) ancestors who migrated into East Africa hundreds of years ago. The first Bantu-speaking settlers reached the Pare region some time before the sixteenth century. From the 1700s on, there was a steady movement of Bantu speakers into the Pare region, where they intermingled with other groups and eventually organized themselves into lineage (family-based) groups. The northern Pare state of Gwena, ruled by the Wasuya lineage, was a stable and well organized union that survived well into the nineteenth century. The leader, or Mangi Mrwe, ruled with the help of chila (councils), wanjama (ministers), and local chiefs (wamangi).

Pazande *see* Azande

Pedi

The Pedi are a Sotho people who emerged as a distinct ethnic subgroup under the influence of the Bapedi Empire. Today the Pedi inhabit a region called Sekhukhuneland that is centered around the Olifants River in the northeastern tip of South Africa.

The Pedi are a Bantu (q.v.) people whose ancestors had settled their present lands by about 1000 CE. By about 1400 the main Sotho clans had emerged, including the Pedi. During the seventeenth century the Pedi clan became dominant among the Northern Sotho and established the Bapedi Empire. Bapedi lasted for over 200 years and expanded the Pedi clan into a wider political and then ethnic grouping made of people who joined or were conquered by the Bapedi Empire. In the nineteenth century, Bapedi became a popular destination for Africans seeking to escape the harsh labor laws of the newly-formed white-ruled South African Republic. In the 1860s open war broke out between the Boers (q.v.) and the Pedi, led by their king Sekhukhuni. The Boers were defeated, but three years later the British defeated the Pedi with the help of the Swazi (q.v.).

Pende

The Pende inhabit a region in Congo (Dem. Rep.) between the Kasai and Lutshima rivers in the southwest of the country. The Pende are divided into two main subgroups: the eastern Pende (or Pende-Kasai) and the western Pende. The two groups differ linguistically, culturally, and economically from each other. For example, the eastern Pende are not as economically developed as the western Pende. The two groups are separated physically by the Loange River, and there are a great many more western than eastern Pende. There are roughly 900,000 Pende in Congo (Rep.).

The Pende probably originated from northern Angola, but fled to their present region to escape slave raids by the Chokwe (q.v.).

The Pende religion involves a belief in Nzambi, who created the universe, but is not often directly worshiped. The reverence shown to ancestors is a more immediate aspect of the Pende religion.

Peul *see* Fulani

Pian

The Pian are a subgroup of the Karamojong (q.v.). They live in northeastern Uganda.

Pogoro

The Pogoro (or Pogulu) are a Bantu (q.v.) people of East Africa. The majority of the around 200,000 Pogoro live in Tanzania.

Pogulu *see* Pogoro

Pokomo

There are more than 60,000 Pokomo people, who are of both Bantu (q.v.) and Oromo (q.v.) descent. They live along the banks of the Tana River in Kenya.

Pokot

The Pokot inhabit a region that extends from the lands around Lake Baringo in western Kenya in the east to the plains of eastern Uganda in the west. The Pokot are one of the several related groups that make up the Kalenjin (q.v.). Numbering more than 250,000, the Pokot make up roughly 10–15 per cent of the Kalenjin-speaking people. The Pokot have also been known as the Suk, a term first used derisively by the Maasai (q.v.) and adopted by the European colonizers of East Africa.

The ancestors of the Kalenjin were Highland Nilotes (q.v.), who began dispersing from their original cradleland at the northernmost tip of Lake Turkana in present-day Ethiopia to East Africa during the last millennium BCE. The separate Kalenjin groups such as the Pokot emerged as the Highland Nilotes spread out over the region and mixed with people already living there. In the case of the Pokot, the Karamojong (q.v.) and Iteso (q.v.) people were of particular influence on the development of Pokot culture.

Pombo

The Pombo are a subgroup of the Kongo (q.v.). They live in northwestern Angola and southeastern Congo (Dem. Rep.). They are a Bantu (q.v.) people who number more than 50,000.

Popo *see* Mina

Portuguese

Many thousands of people of Portuguese descent live in Africa. They are concentrated in the former Portuguese colonies, such as Angola, Mozambique, and Guinea-Bissau.

Pounou *see* Bapounou

Pullo *see* Fulani

Forest dwellers
This group of Pygmies lives by hunting and gathering wild fruits, insects and roots in Congo (Dem. Rep.).

Pygmies

The term pygmy has been used, mostly in the past, to refer to a member of the tropical-forest forager groups such as the Mbuti, Twa, and Mbenga (q.v.) of Central Africa. These people are not Black Africans and generally are of short stature, hence the name pygmy.

Qimant

The Qimant are closely related to the Agaw (q.v.). There are more then 20,000 Qimant, mostly living in western Ethiopia.

Rabai

The Rabai are one of the nine closely related groups that make up the Mijikenda (q.v). The Mijikenda mostly inhabit coastal regions of Kenya.

Randili

The Randili are one of the nine main subgroups of the Oromo (q.v.). They live in Ethiopia.

Rangi

The Rangi are a Bantu (q.v.) people of East Africa. There are more than 250,000 Rangi living in central Tanzania.

Rapulana

The Rapulana are one of the four main subgroups of the Rolong (q.v.). The Rolong are a Tswana (q.v.) people of Southern Africa.

Ratlou

The Ratlou are one of the four main subgroups of the Rolong (q.v.). The Rolong are a Tswana (q.v.) people of Southern Africa.

Rega *see* Lega

Reizegat

The Reizegat are one of the main Baggara (q.v.) subgroups. The Baggara are a Sudanese people of Bedouin (q.v.) and Black African descent.

Rendille

The Rendille are a Cushitic (q.v.) people closely related to the Somali (q.v.). They number around 25,000 people living in northern Kenya.

Reshawa

The Reshawa (or Gungawa, Bareshe, or Reshe) live along and on the islands of the Niger River in northwestern Nigeria. The Reshawa number about 30,000.

Reshe *see* Reshawa

Ribe

The Ribe are one of the nine closely related groups that make up the Mijikenda (q.v.). The Mijikenda mostly inhabit coastal regions of Kenya.

Rolong

The Rolong are one of the main subdivisions of the Tswana (q.v.) people of southern Africa. Rolong peoples can be found living in many parts of Botswana as well as neighboring regions of South Africa.

The Rolong claim descent from a founding ancestor called Marolong, who is thought to have lived around 1300 ce. They are one of the many powerful Sotho (q.v.)-Tswana clans (several extended families linked by a common ancestor or ancestors) that emerged after the end of the first millennium. The Rolong became one of the most powerful of the western clans, dominating a region that extended from the Kalahari Desert in the north to the Vaal River in the south. They kept large herds of cattle and controlled access to local sources of iron ore. By the eighteenth century, the Rolong had established a powerful kingdom, the most famous ruler of which was Tau, who is still remembered as a great military leader. The four main subdivisions of the Rolong – the Ratlou, Tshidi, Rapulana, and Seleka – each claim descent from one of Tau's four sons. The Thlaping are a Rolong people who separated from the main group during Tau's reign and established a powerful independent state.

Ronga

The Ronga are a subgroup of the Central African Tonga (q.v.) people. They are concentrated in southern Mozambique.

Rongo

The Rongo are sometimes considered to be a part of the Sukuma (q.v.) people. They number more than 100,000 people living in Tanzania.

Rozvi

The Rozvi (or Rozwi) are a subgroup of the Shona (q.v.) of Zimbabwe. The Rozvi founded a powerful empire, the Rozvi Empire, or Changamire State, which dominated the region in the late seventeenth and eighteenth century. It was destroyed by Nguni (q.v.) invasions in the early nineteenth century.

Rozwi see Rozvi

Rufiji

The Rufiji are a Bantu (q.v.) people of East Africa. They number more than 150,000 people, living between the Rufiji and Kilombero rivers.

Ruhaya see Haya

Rukuba

The Rukubu, or Bache as they sometimes call themselves, make up a small ethnic group living on the highlands around the town of Jos in central Nigeria. There are around 20,000 Rukuba people, and their language (also called Rukuba) is not often understood by non-Rukubas. Rukuba is a Bantu language.

In the eighteenth century or earlier, the Rukuba migrated from Ugba, more than 37 miles in the north to their present location on the Jos Plateau. There they set up several chiefdoms centered around separate villages. Rukuba society as a whole is made up of a federation of such chiefdoms. Historically, the chief held a semi-religious position, and if things were going badly, he would be held to blame and deposed.

Marriage in Rukuba society is unusual in that a Rukuba woman can marry more than once, and she is considered to be married to all her husbands even though she will live with only one at a time. A man might have more than one wife living with him at any time. Any children belong to the husband the mother claims is the father.

Sabaot

The Sabaot are a subgroup of the Kalenjin (q.v.) people. There are more than 75,000 Sabaot people, the majority of whom live in the western highlands of Kenya.

Sadama

The Sadama (or Sadamo) are a Cushitic (q.v.) people who live in a region of southwest Ethiopia near Lake Abaya. There are probably more than 1.5 million Sadama people. They are closely related to the Oromo (q.v.) people. There are two main Sadama subgroups: the Yamarico and the Aleta, who live south of the Gidabo River. Each group claims descent from a different ancestor. As well as these lineage-based divisions, there are other subgroups that are largely based on the region a group inhabits or the religion its members follow.

The majority of the Sadama practice the Sadama religion, which involves a belief in a creator-god called Magano and the showing of reverence to ancestors. Many followers are also Christian. About 10 percent of the Sadama are Muslim, and the members of the Tambo, Garo, and Alaba subgroups mostly follow Islam. In recent decades a new religion called Wando Magano has fast been gaining converts. It brings together elements of the Sadama religion, Christianity, and Islam.

© DIAGRAM

Sadamo *see* **Sadama**

Safwa

The Safwa (Guruku or Mbila) are a Tanzanian people. They number more than 150,000.

Sagala *see* **Kaguru**

Sagara

The Sagara (or Saghala) are a part of the Zaramo (q.v.). They number more than 80,000 people living in the coastal lowlands of Tanzania.

Saghala *see* **Sagara**

Saharawis

The inhabitants of the coastal deserts of what is now Western Sahara are collectively referred to as the Saharawis, or Western Saharans. The Saharawis are Moors (q.v.) of mixed Berber (q.v.), Arab (q.v.), and Black African descent. They speak a dialect of Arabic known as Hassaniya. The Saharawis were once a nomadic people, but since the 1950s the majority have settled in the towns and villages and become farmers or traders. Today, many of the approximately 150,000 Saharawis live in refugee camps in Algeria.

During the European scramble for Africa at the end of the nineteenth century, the Spanish ended up with Western Sahara under its supposed control. The Spanish were not much interested in the area itself; they wanted it mostly so that they could protect the Canary Islands off its shores in the Atlantic Ocean. Much of the desert regions remained out of their control well into the twentieth century, and the area became a refuge for people fighting the French expansion into Mauritania and Morocco. When Spain withdrew from the area in 1976, it was divided up between Mauritania and Morocco. Mauritania withdrew from the Western Sahara three years later, however, and Morocco annexed the entire territory. The Saharawis embarked on a long campaign of resistance against Moroccan rule, forming the rebel Polisario movement in 1973. A U.N.-backed referendum will be held in July 2000 on whether or not the Western Sahara will become an independent state.

Saho

The Saho (Shiho or Shoho) are a group made up by different peoples, including the Afar (q.v.), Tigre (q.v.), and Arab (q.v.) speakers, who are united by the Saho language. The majority live in coastal northern Ethiopia and coastal Eritrea. There are more than 120,000 Saho.

Sahwi *see* **Sefwi**

Sakalava

The Sakalava are one of Madagascar's larger ethnic groups. They number more than 600,000. See also **Madagascan peoples**.

Sakon

The Sakon are part of the Kru (q.v.) cluster of peoples. The Kru are one of the largest ethnic groups in Liberia.

Samburu

The Samburu (or Lokop or Sampur) are a Maasai (q.v.) people of Kenya. They number more than 80,000.

Samo

The Samo (q.v.) people are closely related to the Manding (q.v.). They number more than 70,000 people living in northwestern Burkina Faso.

Sampur *see* **Samburu**

San

Along with the historical Khoikhoi people, San-speaking peoples make up the Khoisan (q.v.) grouping of eastern Namibia, western and central Botswana, and bordering parts of South Africa. Distinct San groups include the Kung of northeastern Namibia and the Khwe who live in the central Kalahari Desert in Botswana.

The San were the first known inhabitants of Southern Africa, where they lived in widely scattered bands at least 20,000 years ago. Many beautiful rock paintings in the region have provided important clue to their history. The Khoisan are not Black Africans, but make up a unique "racial" category of their own. Historically, the San were predominantly hunter-gatherers. The Khoikhoi were San peoples who adopted pastoralism (livestock herding) in favor of a hunter-gathering lifestyle. Over many hundreds of years, these people retreated or were absorbed as other ethnic groups (such as the Bantu, q.v.) migrated into the area and few direct descendants remain. The San were once referred to as Bushmen, an offensive term that has now fallen largely out of use.

Sandawe

The Sandawe live in the northern regions of Tanzania's central highlands. The districts they inhabit include Mbulu, Singida, Iramba, and Kondoa, which cover the plateau south of lakes Eyasi and Manyara in northern Tanzania. There are well over 50,000 Sandawe people.

Together with the Hadza, the Sandawe are perhaps the last-remaining descendants of East Africa's first human inhabitants. The original human inhabitants of Southern and East Africa were the ancestors of the modern-day Khoisan (q.v.) people. The Khoisan are not Black Africans, but make up a unique "racial" category of their own. They are historically associated with hunter-gatherer lifestyles and distinctive for their short stature and use languages that contain clicking and popping sounds. Over many hundreds of years, as other groups migrated into the area, most Khoisan people retreated or were absorbed by the incoming communities. The Sandawe and sometimes the Hadza are counted as the Khoisan's only direct descendants remaining in East Africa today.

Sanga see Sango

Sango

The Sango (or Sanga or Bosango) live in a region that includes the Central African Republic (CAR), Congo (Rep.), Congo (Dem. Rep.), and Chad. Sanga is the national language of CAR, and the Sango number more than 70,000.

Sapei see Sebei

Sar

The Sar are a subgroup of the Sara. They live in southern Chad.

Sara

The name Sara refers to the non-Muslim people of southern Chad who speak similar languages. There are around 2 million Sara people in Chad, where they form the largest ethnic grouping. It is often used by outsiders to refer to several groups as one unit when they are, in fact, distinct ethnic groups themselves. The main peoples that make up the Sara are the Kaba, Nar, Sar, Gulay, Ngambay, and Mbay. The largest Sara subgroup is the Ngambay, followed by the Gulay and then the Sar. The Sara language group is a Central Sudanic Nilo-Saharan language

The Sara are also called the Kirdi – a name used by Muslims to refer to non Muslims   originally by people such as the Bagirmi (q.v.), who frequently raided the Sara for slaves in the nineteenth century. The balance of power was tipped after the colonial era, however, which transformed Sara society. Being settled farmers living in the more fertile south of Chad, the Sara bore the brunt of colonial policies – the introduction of a cash economy and forced labor, for example, but they also had greater education opportunities. As a result, in present-day Chad, most government and other official posts are filled by southerners such as the Sara. The religious, economic, and social differences between northerners and southerners have led to tensions and, at times, war between northerners and southerners.

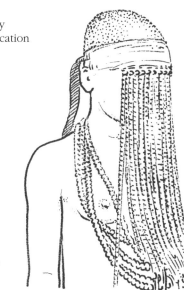

Girl in a veil
This ritual beaded veil is worn by members of the Sara people of southern Chad, who were frequently raided for slaves in the nineteenth century but are now socially ascendant, leading to tensions between northerners and southerners in the country.

Sasala

The Sasala (Isala or Sisala) are a people of northern Ghana. There are more than 100,000 Sasala.

Sebei

The Sebei (or Sapei) live on the northeastern slopes of Mount Elgon, Uganda. They are a Kalenjin (q.v.) people and are related to the Maasai (q.v.).

Sefwi

The Sefwi (or Sahwi) are closely related to the Anyi (q.v.) and Baulé (q.v.) people. They number around 200,000 people primarily living in western Ghana.

Seleka

The Seleka are one of the four main subgroups of the Rolong (q.v.). The Rolong are a Tswana (q.v.) people of Southern Africa.

Sena

The Sena (or Chisena) are a large ethnic group living in the border region of Malawi and Mozambique. There are more than one million Sena.

Funeral drum
Known as a Plievo, this drum comes from the Senufo and was used at burials. Among the powerful symbols on its body are slave shackles.

Senufo

The Senufo are one of the larger ethnic groups of West Africa. Numbering more than three million, they can be found living in region bordered by the Bani River to the north, the Bagoe Rivertothewest,and the Black Volta River to the east. This places them in the countries of Mali, Burkina Faso, and Ivory Coast. Various Senufo subgroups exist, such as the Fodonon of Lataha, Kulebele, and Tyebara of Korhogo. The vast majority of Senufo people are what is known as Southern Senufo, nearly a quarter of whom are Muslim.

Like the Mende (q.v.) of Sierra Leone and Liberia, in the past many Senufo men belonged to the Poro secret society. The organization of these groups differed from village to village, but they all aimed to teach boys becoming men how to behave. Poro were powerful regulatory forces in society. They laid down rules, sanctioned acceptable behavior, punished or prohibited unacceptable behavior, and generally provided social and cultural unity to the Senufo. In recent decades, however, more and more Senufo are adopting Islam, and the influence of the Poro societies has diminished.

Senufo statue
This carving from the Ivory Coast may be associated with the rituals of the Poro secret society, a once-powerful regulatory force which is giving way to Islam among the Senufo.

Serer

Reaching more than one million people, the Serer are one of Senegal's largest ethnic groups. They inhabit the rolling plains of Cayor, Baol, and the town of Nioro du Rip, mostly in the regions to the south and west of Dakar, the capital city. Smaller numbers of Serer people live in Gambia and Guinea-Bissau. The majority of the Serer are farmers, cultivating groundnuts and millet. The Serer language is closely related to that of the Temne (q.v.) and Wolof (q.v.) peoples as well as Fulfulde, which is spoken by the Fulani (q.v.).

Together with the Wolof, the Serer were the primary inhabitants of the Wolof Kingdom, and later empire, which became powerful in the fifteenth century. The Wolof introduced the Serer to Islam, which was at first violently resisted. Since the nineteenth century, however, Islam has spread increasingly rapidly among the Serer. By the early 1990s, more than 80 percent of the Serer were Muslim.

Shambaa

The Shambaa are a cluster of closely-related ethnic groups, including the Shambala, the Pare (q.v.), and the Bondei (q.v), who inhabit the coastal lowlands of Tanzania. There are more than 400,000 Shambaa, the majority of whom are Muslim.

Although they are what is known as an Eastern Bantu (q.v.) people, the Shambaa are descended from both Bantu and Cushitic (q.v.) ancestors. Early in the first millennium, Bantu speakers migrating into East Africa from Central Africa mingled with Cushitic peoples who had already moved into that region. Interaction between the two cultures led to the development of the Shambaa and other groups such as the Kikuyu (q.v.). At first the Shambaa's ancestors lived in widespread, independent settlements. After experiencing Maasai (q.v.) raids in the early eighteenth century, however, the different family-based groups began to form closer political unions. Under Mbegha, who perhaps came from areas in western and central Tanzania that had already established chieftaincies, the Shambaa began to develop a powerful centralized state. Ruled by a group known as the Kilindi, the Shambaa kingdom reached its height in the nineteenth century under the famous Kimweri ye Nyumbai.

Shambala

The Shambala are a subgroup of the Shambaa (q.v.). The Shambaa inhabit the coastal lowlands of Tanzania.

Shamya *see* Sinyar

Shanga *see* Shangawa

Shangawa

The Shangawa (or Shanga) live in and around the islands and Niger River near the Nigerian city of Shanga in the northwest of the country. They were once part of the Songhay (q.v.) empire and number more than 40,000 today.

Sherbro

The Sherbro (or Southern Bullom) number more than 170,000, the majority of whom live along the coast of Sierra Leone. The Sherbro are increasingly being absorbed by the Mende (q.v.).

Shiho *see* Saho

Shikongo

The Shikongo (or Bashikongo) are part of the Kongo (q.v.) peoples. They number more than 50,000 and live in coastal regions of northwestern Angola and the southeast of Congo (Dem. Rep.).

Shilluk

The Shilluk are Nilotes (q.v.) people who live in southern Sudan, along the banks of the White Nile River. There are roughly 120,000 Shilluk.

History

According to Shilluk history, their Nilotic ancestors began to migrate into their present-day location roughly four hundred years ago. Much of Shilluk history is preserved orally, through legends and stories, and goes back hundreds of years.

RECENT EVENTS With its ethnic and religious diversity, Sudan has suffered internal conflict for many years. Like the Sudanese Dinka, Nuer, Nuba, and many other southern groups, the Shilluk are non-Muslim minorities in a country in which Muslim Arabs from the north dominate the government. In 1983, the imposition of Sharia (Islamic holy) law triggered the outbreak of civil war between north and south Sudan.

In 1989, at least seven hundred Shilluk – mostly farmhands working roughly 100 miles (160 km) north of Kodok on the White Nile – were massacred by an Arab militia that had been armed by the government.

Language

The Shilluk speak a Nilotic language, which is also called Shilluk. Recently, Arabic has been imposed in schools and government-controlled areas.

Ways of life

The majority of Shilluk are pastoralists who combine the herding of cattle, sheep, and goats with growing crops. Beans, corn, millet, sesame, and pumpkins are common food crops and tobacco is grown both to use and to sell. Living along the banks of the White Nile River, fishing is an important activity for the Shilluk and fish are an important supplement to the diet. Shilluk fishermen intensively exploit the Nile waters for fish, which are caught with nets or specially designed fishing spears. Infrequent hunting parties are arranged by Shilluk men, though only smaller mammals – certain antelopes and gazelles, for example – are caught. In the past, hippopotamuses were hunted by the Shilluk, but they are now protected by law.

Social structure

SOCIAL STRUCTURE The Shilluk are divided into about one hundred clans or groups, each with a common

ancestor or ancestors. The clans are scattered throughout various villages. Each village has an original or founding family called a diel.

POLITICAL STRUCTURE Each village has a chief, who is usually a member of the diel, subject to approval by the Shilluk king, or reth. The shilluk reth is a living symbol of Shilluk history and culture and is thought to be possessed by the spirit of Nyikang – the first Shilluk king and Shilluk culture hero. Nyikang is closely associated with the Shilluk religion. The reth is, therefore, sometimes described as a divine king. Indeed, the reth's role is more religious than political. He is the central figure who unites the Shilluk into a people. His subjects believe he is the reincarnation of the legendary Nyikang and that his good health ensures their prosperity. The reth resides at Kodok, formerly known as Fashoda. Since 1956, the reth has had the status of magistrate within the Sudanese judiciary.

Many traditions surround the ceremony of electing a new reth. The new ruler must be the son of any former king who can win the support of the people. The successful candidate is chosen by the two paramount chiefs. An electoral college of fourteen other chiefs has to approve their choice. There follow ceremonies at which effigies of Nyikang and his son Dak are paraded. Finally, the new king is enthroned, when it is believed that the spirit of Nyikang enters him.

Animal pipe
Decorative pipes are one of the few artworks made by the Shilluk. This one, in the form of an animal, is made from clay and bamboo and decorated with beads and paints.

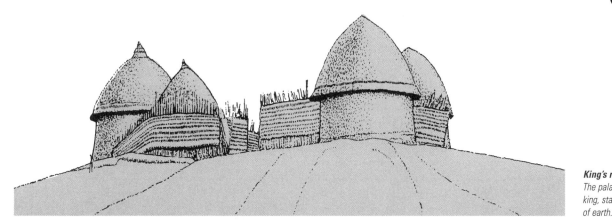

King's residence
The palace of the Shilluk reth, or king, stands on an artificial mound of earth.

© DIAGRAM

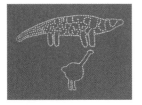

Shrine painting
This picture of a crocodile and ostrich is painted onto the wall of a shrine dedicated to the legendary founder of the Shilluk people – Nyikang. The crocodile is an important figure in the Shilluk religion. Some legends say that Nyikang's mother was a crocodile, or at least part crocodile, and the Shilluk make offerings to her at riverbanks.

Shilluk man
The Shilluk are a Nilotic people. This is a cultural and linguistic grouping that also includes the Dinka and Nuer. Nilotic people are often tall in stature. Shilluk men average between 6 and 7 ft (1.8–2.1 m) tall.

Culture and religion

RELIGION Although a tiny minority of Shilluk people have converted to Islam, the vast majority adhere to the Shilluk religion. The Shilluk religion is centered around a creator-god known as Juok. Nyikang is considered to be the intermediary between an individual and Juok. Whereas Nyikang founded the Shilluk people, it was Juok who created the world and who continues to maintain it. Also, whereas Nyikang is represented by a human – the reth – Juok is not.

The Shilluk have a wealth of stories about Nyikang. According to one legend, Nyikang came from the south sometime in the 1500s accompanied by his warrior son, Dak, and their followers. Using his powers, Nyikang helped his followers cross the crocodile-infested waters of the White Nile. Another legend says that Nyikang's mother was a crocodile, which may explain his power over these guardians of the river. Nyikang's mother is associated with rivers and river creatures, and offerings are left for her on riverbanks. In another legend, Nyikang fought with the Sun, which had gained possession of one of his cows, and drove it back into the sky. When the rains come at the end of the dry season, Nyikang is said to be overcoming the Sun and bringing much-needed water to the thirsty land.

Headrest
Headrests, such as the one shown here, are carved from wood, often in the shapes of animals or birds. The Shilluk believe the headrest was invented by Nyikang, their founder. They were generally used by Shilluk men while they slept so that their hair, which in the past was often elaborately styled, would not be ruined.

Wrist club
In the past, Shilluk men would wear a wrist club, like the one shown, for life. After a boy had been initiated into manhood, the blacksmith would fix one of these metal bracelets onto his wrist.

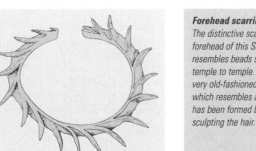

Forehead scarring
The distinctive scarring on the forehead of this Shilluk man resembles beads stretching from temple to temple. He sports a very old-fashioned hairstyle, which resembles a helmet and has been formed by training and sculpting the hair.

Shilluk timeline

c. 1000 Nilotic peoples are known to be settled in region to the far southwest of the Bahr al Ghazal river	**1821** Trade routes opened from north to south Sudan, leading to a reduced southern population through disease and slave trading	**1955–1972** First Sudanese civil war between north and south	**1989** Over seven hundred Shilluk massacred at Jebelein
c. 1500s Nilotic ancestors of Shilluk migrate into present location along banks of White Nile	**1840s–1850s** Arab slave trade at height in Shilluk territory; Shilluk are targeted by slave raiders	**1956** Sudanese independence **1972** End of first Sudanese civil war; south granted regional autonomy	**1990s** Despite many cease-fires, the civil war in Sudan continues. Reports of forcible conscriptions into both the rebel and government troops surface
1684 Shilluk attacks on Arab settlements	**1898** Britain and Egypt jointly colonize Sudan	**1983** Sudan adopts Sharia (Islamic holy) law against wishes of mainly non-Muslim south; civil war breaks out again	**1998** Sudan's government concedes, in principle, the right of southern Sudan to secede

Shirazi

The Shirazi (or Mbwera) are descended from Persian, Arab (q.v.), and African ancestors. They inhabit the islands off the northeast coast of Tanzania and number around 300,000.

Shoho *see* Saho

Shona

The lands of the Shona people cover most of Zimbabwe and extend into Mozambique; there are also Shona populations in South Africa, Botswana, and Zambia. They are the dominant ethnic group in Zimbabwe, where the Shona population of over eight million makes up about seventy percent of the total. Around 500,000 Shona people live outside Zimbabwe, mainly in neighboring countries.

History

The Shona are descended from Iron-Age, Bantu-speaking farmers who settled on the Zimbabwe plateau in around 200. Little is known of these early settlers except that they worked with iron. From about the tenth century, however, the Shona civilization that had developed in the area became adept at working with gold and copper, both of which were found on the

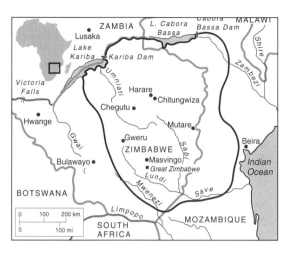

Birds of God
Made from soapstone, these strange, stylized bird figures with animal-like legs were found at Great Zimbabwe. They are thought to be symbolic of long-dead Shona chiefs who represented a link between the heavens and the Earth. Some people doubt they are birds, but prefer to think of them as forgotten mythological beasts.

plateau, and traded those metals with coastal cities. The people who ruled this trade became the wealthy elite, the graves of whom were found to contain gold ornaments and imported beads and cloth.

ZIMBABWES From around the late 1100s, the Shona began to construct impressive dry-wall enclosures (built without mortar) serving as palaces and called zimbabwes (literally, "stone houses"). This building system was perfected at the site of Great Zimbabwe (south of modern Masvingo) from the 1300s onward. Great Zimbabwe had been abandoned as a palace by the Shona kings by the end of the fifteenth century, but it continued as a religious and ceremonial site. The capital was moved north to the area around the Zambezi River. This marked the beginning of a new Shona dynasty, the Mwene Mutapas. The first Mwene Mutapa was Nyatsimba Mutota, who conquered territory from the Kalahari Desert to the Indian Ocean. After the death in 1480 of his successor, Matope, the kingdom split, the southern part being dominated by the Rozvi peoples, a Shona subgroup.

When the Rozvi Empire finally collapsed in the early nineteenth century, over a hundred small Shona

states took its place. Many of these were disrupted after 1820 as a result of the wave of emigration emanating from Shaka's (q.v.) Zulu Mfecane expansion. This brought the Matabele people into southern Zimbabwe. It was the Matabele who gave these many groups the name "Shona." Previously, each group was known by its own name, even though they were all Shona-speaking peoples.

COLONIALISM After 1850, most of the area was colonized by the British and renamed Southern Rhodesia, for the British imperialist and colonial administrator Cecil Rhodes. In 1965, the white population declared independence from British rule as Rhodesia. After a prolonged civil war, full independence and majority rule were negotiated in 1980.

Language
The Shona language is also called Shona and is one of the most important of the Bantu languages. It is spoken not only by the Shona but also, as a second language, by many other people in Southern Africa. Many Shona also speak English – a legacy of colonialism.

Ways of life
AGRICULTURE The majority of the Shona people earn their living from agriculture. The staple food crop is corn and other cereal crops grown include wheat, millet, sorghum, and barley. Other important food crops include vegetables, fruit, cassava, and soybeans. Sugar, cotton, and tobacco are the main cash crops. The Shona also raise cattle, goats, sheep, pigs, and poultry.

During the colonial period and the following era of white rule, the most fertile farming land in present-day Zimbabwe was taken by white settlers. As a result, many Shona lost their land. Even today, despite official land resettlement schemes, the Shona suffer the legacy of these policies. Land shortages combined with recurring drought (inadequate rainfall) mean that few are able to support themselves by agriculture alone. Instead, they have to supplement their income by working in nearby towns.

INDUSTRY In Zimbabwe, many Shona work in mining where over forty different minerals are exploited. Gold is the most important mineral and has been mined by the Shona for many hundreds of years. Other important minerals mined are nickel, coal, copper, and iron.

Social structure
Before colonialism, Shona society was organized into chiefdoms, each led by a hereditary chief. This man would be responsible for land distribution and would judge disputes. Historical records report that most societies were basically egalitarian and chiefs were not markedly more wealthy than their subjects. The authority of the chiefs is still recognized, but they no longer have any real political power. Instead, they now perform the more socially oriented function of maintaining and preserving Shona culture and values.

MARRIAGE Most Shona have only one marriage partner. An important part of marriage arrangements is the bridewealth, which is given by the groom to the bride's family. Previously this sum was in cattle but it is now more likely to be cash. Alternatively, some sort of ser-

Nyatsimba Mutota
Mutota was the founder of the Mwene Mutapa dynasty and ruled from c. 1440 to c. 1450. During this period, he abandoned Great Zimbabwe and took the capital north to the Zambezi River, from where the expansion of Shona territory and influence continued.

Shona headrest
Dating from the late nineteenth or early twentieth century, the design of this wooden headrest combines concentric circles and triangles – motifs that are said to be a typically Shona. Headrests were once used solely by mature men, who until the end of the nineteenth century commonly wore their hair in elaborate styles. Today, few headrests are used, though some diviners use them as symbolic links with the spirit world.

Soapstone figurine
This soapstone figurine was found at Great Zimbabwe. It has a pointed end that could have been used to stand it upright in a stone or clay base. Little is known of its use, though it may have had a religious role.

vice can be provided instead of cash. The families of well-educated girls normally demand a higher amount. If a couple divorces, a negotiable proportion of the original bridewealth has to be repaid.

Culture and religion

RELIGION With colonialism came Christian missionaries. Although they made little headway at first, over a quarter of all Shona are Christians today. The majority are members of independent churches established, attended, and controlled largely by Africans, not by Europeans. Also, the Shona religion is still widely followed and remains a vital force in Shona society.

The Shona religion involves the recognition of a supreme god, referred to in historical documents as Murungu but more commonly called Mwari today. A major part of the Shona religion involves ancestral spirit cults. The spirit of an ordinary person is known as a mudzimu while that of someone more influential as mhondoro. Mhondoro spirits provide the link between mortals and Mwari. When they possess a medium they can intercede with Mwari on behalf of the people, on ethical as well as practical matters such as predicting rainfall. Harmful spirits called ngozi are thought to cause evil and they can be the spirits of people who were murdered. N'anga are religious and medical practitioners who both heal illnesses with herbs and diagnose evil forces at work through various means of divination.

The incoming religion of Christianity and the already present Shona religion have each altered in response to the presence of the other. Many of the independent churches incorporate so-called "tradi-

tional" beliefs about healing into their form of Christianity, so that the Holy Spirit is believed to heal through possession; in turn, the Shona religion has developed a "traditional" creation story that was not in existence before colonialism.

Shona pottery
This Shona pot, from Zambia, was made in the 1960s. From early times, pottery has been an important part of Shona culture. In the kitchen buildings of many ancient zimbabwes (stone houses), stepped platforms can be seen on which women displayed their pots. The pots were highly valued and their display celebrated the household, marriage, and the woman's central role in these institutions. Even today, such platforms can be found in old-fashioned Shona homes.

Shona timeline	
200s Bantu-speaking peoples begin to arrive in Southern Africa	**1896** Shona and Matabele at war with British colonizers
900s Bambandyanalo/Mapungubwe trading center on Limpopo River	**1923** British government takes control of Southern Rhodesia; white immigration encouraged
1000s Major Iron-Age settlement, Leopard Kopje, built	**1965** Illegal white-minority rule established in Southern Rhodesia as Rhodesia
1100–1300 Bambandyanalo/Mapungubwe at height	**1967–1975** Guerrilla war fought against white Rhodesians
1100s Great Zimbabwe building begins	**1980** End of white-minority rule in Rhodesia, which is renamed Zimbabwe
1300s–1400s Great Zimbabwe reaches height; wealth boosted by gold trade	**1987** Prime-minister Robert Mugabe becomes President
1480 Mutapa Empire breaks up; Rozvi dynasty emerges	**1991** Zimbabwean single-party system abandoned
by 1500 Great Zimbabwe abandoned; Shona civilization moves north to create Mutapa Empire	**1990s** Drought hits Zimbabwe
1700s Rozvi Empire fragments	**1994** Government corruption scandal
1890 Cecil Rhodes' British South Africa Company establishes colony of Southern Rhodesia	**1996** Mugabe re-elected President

Great Zimbabwe: the outer wall
This is the outer wall of Great Zimbabwe, the largest of the Shona zimbabwes (stone houses). The function of its meandering stone walls was largely symbolic – to separate ordinary citizens from nobility.

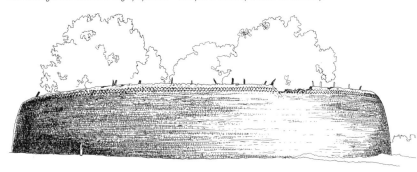

Shope

The Shope (or Chope) live in southern Mozambique, a country where they are considered to be among the earliest known inhabitants. There are more than 600,000 Shope.

Sia

The Sia are closely-related to the Manding (q.v.). They number around 150,000 people living in Mali and Burkina Faso.

Sihanaka

The Sihanaka are a Madagascan people (q.v.) who live inland in the northern half of the island. They number roughly 200,000.

Siku

The Siku are part of the Kru (q.v.) cluster of peoples. The Kru are one of the largest ethnic groups in Liberia.

Sinyar

The Sinyar (or Shamya) live on and either side of the border between Sudan and Chad. They number more than 30,000.

Sisala *see* Sasala

Sisi

The Sisi are one of the many Teke (q.v.) groups. The Teke live in Gabon, Congo (Rep.), and Congo (Dem. Rep.).

Soga

The Soga (or Basoga, Lukenyi or Lusoga) live in southeastern Uganda, where they are one of the larger ethnic groups. They have a population that exceeds one million.

Solongo

The Solongo (or Basolongo) are one of the larger Kongo (q.v.) subgroups. They live in northwestern Angola and southwestern Congo (Dem. Rep.) and number more than 100,000.

Somalis

There are over seven million Somalis, most of whom live in Somalia, where they make up approximately seventy-five percent of the population. In addition, two million Somalis live in eastern Ethiopia, 100,000 in Djibouti, and 240,000 in northeast Kenya. Political turbulence in the 1980s and 1990s has caused thousands of Somalis to seek refuge in neighboring countries as well as outside Africa, especially in Yemen, Saudi Arabia, Italy, and Britain.

History

The Somalis' origins are uncertain, but by 1000 what is now Somalia was home to Cushitic people who had migrated from the Ethiopian Highlands. These people developed close contacts with Arabs and Persians who had settled on the coast. Through marriage and cultural and commercial ties the Somali people gradually emerged from these different groups. Between the eleventh and thirteenth centuries, the Somalis converted to Islam. During this period, their influential clans (several extended families who claim descent from a common ancestor or ancestors) originated – the founding fathers of which, according to tradition, were related to the Prophet Muhammad and came from Arabia. By 1500, Somalis were raiding eastern Ethiopia (where they pushed the Oromo people out of the

Ogaden region) and were expanding their territory southward. The Somalis gradually consolidated their position, but in the late nineteenth century, Britain, France, Italy, and Ethiopia divided Somali territory into separate colonies.

RECENT EVENTS In 1960, British (northern) and Italian (southern) Somaliland united to form the independent state of Somalia. After independence, rivalry between northern and southern Somalia mounted, and the government was accused of corruption. In 1969 the army, led by Major General Muhammad Siad Barre (q.v.), staged a coup and abolished the elected parliament. For the next two decades, Somalia was under Barre's personal control.

Due to Somalia's strategic importance, Barre obtained foreign economic and military support, first from the former Soviet Union (USSR) and later from the United States (US). The weapons that these superpowers poured into the region enabled Somalia and Ethiopia to enter into disastrous wars with each other in 1964 and again in 1977, helped create a "gun culture" in the country, and provided Barre with the means to brutally persecute rival clans.

In the late 1980s, there emerged organized opposition to Barre and, with the end of the Cold War, the US ceased to support him. In January 1991, Mogadishu fell to rebel forces and, in May, the northern area declared independence as the "Somaliland Republic." Somalia's civil and political institutions collapsed, with opposition leaders unable to exert control. Into this power vacuum stepped armed factions, loosely allied to a clan or sub-

Camels
Camels are vital in the Somalis' semidesert environment as they can survive for long periods without water. Camels have long been used to transport both possessions and goods. The camels are Arabian dromedaries (single-humped).

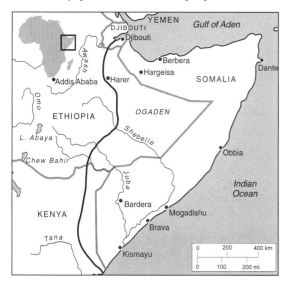

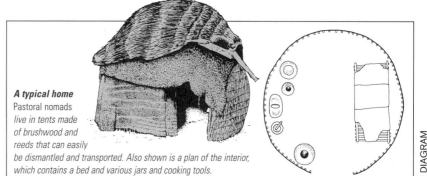

A typical home
Pastoral nomads *live in tents made of brushwood and reeds that can easily be dismantled and transported. Also shown is a plan of the interior, which contains a bed and various jars and cooking tools.*

Education
Schooling among rural Somalis tends to be for boys. This student is studying Arabic at an Islamic school that teaches about the Arabic language and Islam.

Milk pot
A Somali artisan made this wooden pot for holding milk. The surface has been stained black and then a decorative pattern has been carved, revealing the light wood beneath.

Off to market
A Somali woman going to market. Women carry their wares on their heads, with more bulky items on the backs of donkeys. This lady is carrying a marrow.

clan. The breakdown of Somalia led to widespread famine and, with food deliveries from abroad interrupted by armed gangs, the United Nations attempted unsuccessfully to impose order between 1992 and 1995. By 1996, a fragile peace had returned to Somalia, but the country still remains divided today.

Backed by the Somali government, Ethiopian Somalis have been agitating for union with Somalia for many years. Rebel groups were particularly active from the 1960s until the mid-1980s. Ethiopia's new constitution, introduced in 1994, however, established a separate Somali state within the republic. This has helped to ease the situation somewhat. Kenyan Somalis have often found themselves used as political pawns between the Kenyan and Somali governments. The situation briefly improved after Barre renounced his claim to northeastern Kenya in 1981. In 1989, however, the Kenyans accused Somalis of poaching elephants, and many thousands were evicted from around game parks while others had their Kenyan nationality questioned.

Language
The Somali language is also called Somali. Somali has been heavily influenced by Arabic, but has been written in the Roman script since 1972.

Ways of life
Somalia's contrasting climate and terrain have led to the development of many different ways of life. The north and centre is mostly semidesert and dry grassland, with little rainfall and without permanent rivers. Here crops are grown only in the highlands, with wells providing a year-round water supply. The south is largely low-lying and fertile, and is watered by the Juba and Shebelle rivers.

NOMADIC PASTORALISM Most Somalis are nomadic pastoralists, who herd goats, sheep, cattle, and camels, with herd management based on migrating between water holes and pastures. Camels, which provide milk and meat as well as serving as a means of transportation, are especially suited to dry areas since they can survive for many days without water.

Nomad encampments are typically occupied by between five and ten families (that generally consist of a man, his wives and children, and elderly or unmarried relatives) who live in tents or temporary houses, which are surrounded by a stockade, made of thorn branches, where goats and sheep are kept at night. These animals are tended by women and children. Camels, kept outside the stockade area, are herded and milked only by men.

FARMING In the south, between the Shebelle and Juba rivers, are farmers who grow bananas, citrus fruits, corn, cotton, millet, sorghum, and sugar cane. Historically, nomadic Somalis regarded these people as inferior and not true Somalis. In recent years, many have had their land confiscated by more powerful, armed groups.

Social structure
CLANS The Somalis are divided into six major clans or qabiil: the Daarood, Hawiye, Issaq, Dir, Digil, and the Rahanwayn. In turn, these are divided into numerous subclans. Northern Somalia is dominated by the Samaale group, which comprises the Daarood, Dir, Hawiye, and the Issaq clans. They are mostly pastoral nomads. The Sab group, consisting of the Digil and Rahanwayn clans, dominates the south, and its members are generally farmers. Organization into clans has enabled the region's scarce resources to be shared peaceably, with disputes over water and pastures mediated by clan leaders. At times, however, the clan system can be extremely fragile as allegiances between subclans often shift.

MARRIAGE It is customary for marriages to be contracted between men and women of different clans, thereby extending clan alliances. Although women are able to count on the protection of both their parents' and their husbands' clans, during times of conflict they have had to choose between allegiance to one clan or the other. Nevertheless, even at the height of the civil war, this dual position has enabled women to serve as important channels of communication between warring clans, since their status has permitted them to travel between clans.

Culture and religion
RELIGION The vast majority of Somalis are Muslims.
POETRY There is a long tradition of Somali epic poetry, which has always been transmitted orally. Poems are frequently complex and draw upon history, a poet's personal experience, politics, or debate. Poets recite or chant their poems at both formal and informal occasions.

Somali timeline	
900s Arab trading post at Mogadishu	**1977** Djibouti wins independence. Maj. Mengistu Haile Mariam takes power in Ethiopia.
900s–1500s Somalis disperse around present area of occupation and convert to Islam	**1980s** rought and famine in Ethiopia
1500s–1800s Somali migrants settle in Ogaden region of Ethiopia	**1981** Rebel Somali National Movement (SNM) formed in Somalia
1884–1886 Italians, British, and French divide Somali lands	**1988–1992** Civil war and drought cause severe famine in Somalia
1900s–1920s Somalis revolt against British, Ethiopian, and Italian colonists	**1989** Kenyan Somalis victimized
1960 Somalia wins independence	**1991** Mengistu loses power in Ethiopia. Civil war begins after Barre ousted in Somalia; northern Somalia declares "independence"
1963 Ethiopian Somalis begin revolt	
1964 Somalia at war with Ethiopia	**1992–1995** US-led United Nations forces deployed to ensure the distribution of humanitarian aid in Somalia
1969 Muhammad Siad Barre leads military coup in Somalia	
1974 Military coup overthrows Haile Selassie in Ethiopia	**1995** Gen. Muhammed Farrah Aideed declares himself "president" of Somalia
1975–1980s Somalia organizes and funds Somali rebel groups in Ethiopia	**1996** Aideed is killed; his son, Hussein Muhammad Aideed succeeds

Somba

The Somba (or Tamberma) number well over 300,000 living in northwestern Benin and neighboring parts of Togo. They are sometimes classified as a Ewe (q.v.) people; their language is a part of the Mole-Dagbane group.

Songhay

The Songhay people emerged as a distinct ethnic group under the influence of the historic Songhay Empire, which was one of the most powerful precolonial West African states. Roughly 800,000 Songhay people live in eastern Mali and perhaps an equal number live in western Niger, where they are one of the largest ethnic groups, and a minority live in northern Benin. Their language, also called Songhay, is used by traders over a large area of West Africa. The Songhay language is a Nilo-Saharan language. The Songhay religion has been Islam for many centuries.

The Songhay state was founded in c. 750 on the Niger River on an important trade route. The capital was on the Niger River at Gao, which is still a major Malian city today. From c. 1240 to the 1340s Songhay was part of the Empire of Mali, but under Sunni Ali (1464–92) Songhay became the most powerful empire in West Africa, absorbing much of Mali's lands. Askia Muhammad (1493–1528) extended the boundaries of Songhay to their utmost, and Songhay remained powerful until it was conquered by the Moroccans in 1591.

Songye

The Songye are a subgroup of the Luba (q.v.) peoples of Central Africa. There are approaching two million Songye people in Congo (Dem. Rep.). The Songye inhabit a region in the southeast of that country, concentrated around the town of Kabinda and dispersed mainly between the Lubufu and Lomami rivers. Separate Songye subgroups, such as the Bangu-Bangus, exist.

According to oral histories, the Songye were the founders of the powerful Luba kingdom, which covered the lands between the Lubilash and Lualaba rivers. The Songye are said to have migrated into this region from the north led by their kongolo (king), and they settled on the Lubilash River. The first kongolo married the queen of the local people, the Kalundwe, founding the Luba kingdom. The Luba kingdom reached its height under Songye rulers, but they were displaced by the Kunda (who also migrated into the region from the north) some time in the fifteenth century.

Songe shield
The purpose of this shield is uncertain, but was probably as a sign of rank. The face is typical of a Songe mask.

Soninke

The Soninke are a large ethnic group of well over two million people who are widespread in many countries of West Africa. The largest Soninke communities can be found in Mali, Burkina Faso, and Ivory Coast, and smaller numbers live in Guinea-Bissau, Senegal, Gambia, Guinea, and Mauritania. Many Soninke can also be found as far afield as France, working as migrant laborers. The Soninke language belongs to the Mande (q.v.) language group, but most Soninke speak the language of the people they live among instead of Soninke (or Azer).

The Soninke people were the citizens of the historic state of Ghana, which lay to the north of the Senegal and Niger rivers in what is now western Mali and southern Mauritania. The Soninke eventually overthrew the Maga, the people who founded the state. By the 1200s, Ghana had grown powerful from the trade in gold mined by the Soninke, and salt, and it controlled the West African ends of the trans-Saharan trade routes.

Soso see Susu

Sotho

The Sotho (or Basotho) are one of the principal Bantu-speaking peoples of Southern Africa. There are about 2.5 million Northern Sotho who live in northern and eastern Transvaal, a province of South Africa. A further two million Southern Sotho live in the Orange Free State – also part of South Africa – and in the independent Kingdom of Lesotho.

History

The Bantu-speaking ancestors of the Sotho originated in present-day eastern Nigeria. There, over 2,000 years ago, they developed a way of life based on farming and ironworking. These people gradually spread southward and by about 1000 they had settled on the Highveld – the high arid plains to the west of the Drakensberg Mountains – and in the valleys of the Orange, Vaal, and Tugela rivers. They slowly absorbed the existing population, the Khoisan, adopting many aspects of their culture including elements of their languages and many of their musical instruments. By about 1400, the Sotho had established their main clans (several families who share the same ancestor or ancestors). Each clan adopted an animal, such as a wildcat, porcupine, or a crocodile as its symbol, or totem. Groups of these clans

Moshoeshoe I
In the 1820s, Moshoeshoe I (q.v.), the son of a Sotho chief, founded a wealthy mountain kingdom – the Basuto (Lesotho) Kingdom – that was protected from the Zulu Mfecane/ Difaqane.

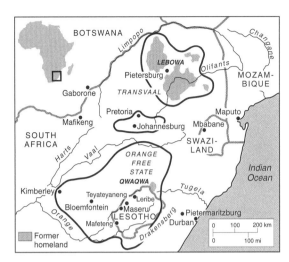

Initiation costume
As part of an initiation ritual, this girl is wearing a straw mask that covers her face. Historically, Sotho boys and girls both underwent initiation rites at special lodges or schools to mark their transition to adulthood; the boys in the winter months and the girls in summer. Some Sotho boys and girls still undergo initiation.

a number of separate regions within Transvaal, collectively known as the Lebowa homeland.

In the south, the only people to resist the Mfecane were some members of the Kwena (Crocodile) clan, led by their chief Moshoeshoe I (q.v.), who was able to unify the Southern Sotho clans and establish the Basuto Kingdom. After losing about two-thirds of his country's arable land to the Afrikaners' newly-formed Orange Free State, Moshoeshoe requested British protection. In 1868, the country became the British protectorate of Basutoland, which remained a British colony until it gained independence in 1966 as Lesotho.

RECENT EVENTS The abolition of apartheid laws, in 1991, has given all South African citizens equal rights. In 1994, the Land Rights Bill – designed to help people in South Africa regain land lost since 1913 because of unjust laws – was introduced.

In Lesotho in 1994, King Letsie III (q.v.) and some sections of the military tried to take power, unsuccessfully, from the democratically-elected government, which was led by Dr Ntsu Mokhehle (q.v.). King Letsie abdicated and the former king – Letsie's father, Moshoeshoe II (q.v.) – was restored to the throne in 1995. After Moshoeshoe's death in 1996, however, Letsie became king again.

Language

Northern Sotho (or Sesotho sa Leboa) is spoken in South Africa and the closely-related Sesotho in Lesotho.

Ways of life

The Sotho have a long history of agriculture. Until the late nineteenth century, they accumulated wealth in the form of cattle and exported grain to other parts of Southern Africa. But since then, a large proportion of the able-bodied men have become migrant laborers who leave their homes to work in the gold, diamond, and coal mines and other industries of South Africa. In the rural areas, the women they leave behind have to raise the children and tend the farms, often single-handed. They raise cattle, sheep, goats, and pigs; corn, sorghum, wheat, and vegetables are grown, but farming is hampered by overgrazing and soil erosion. Most

eventually came together to form the three major divisions of the Sotho people: the Northern Sotho, the Southern Sotho, and the Tswana (or Western Sotho). The Tswana are now generally viewed as a separate ethnic group from the other Sotho peoples.

During the seventeenth century, the Pedi group of clans became dominant among the Northern Sotho and established the Bapedi Empire, which lasted for over 200 years. During the same period, the Southern Sotho were living in an age of relative peace and prosperity. This was to last until the 1820s, when the lives of all the Sotho peoples were disrupted by the Mfecane/Difaqane – two decades of invasion, warfare, and famine triggered by the Zulu upheavals east of the Drakensberg Mountains. After the Mfecane, the Bapedi lands were taken over by Afrikaners, or Boers. This region (now Transvaal) eventually became part of South Africa. The introduction of apartheid (the racist doctrine of "separate development") in 1948 made the Northern Sotho third-class citizens in their own land. In 1959, the South African government attempted to divide the black population from the whites by creating homelands or Bantustans in which black people were forced to live. The Northern Sotho were allocated

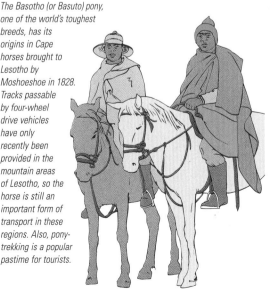

Basotho ponies
The Basotho (or Basuto) pony, one of the world's toughest breeds, has its origins in Cape horses brought to Lesotho by Moshoeshoe in 1828. Tracks passable by four-wheel drive vehicles have only recently been provided in the mountain areas of Lesotho, so the horse is still an important form of transport in these regions. Also, pony-trekking is a popular pastime for tourists.

Sotho beadwork
This unusual doll is a fine example of Sotho beadwork. It has been made using wood, glass beads, and a metal button.

Sotho compound
In the past, most Sotho families would live in a compound of linked circular houses with stone or wicker walls and conical thatched roofs. Nowadays, housing is less predictable and different materials and designs are also likely to be used. Unlike in South Africa where apartheid policies dictated the housing facilities of the Sotho (which were generally poor), settlements such as this can more often be found in Lesotho.

depend on the money sent back to them by the men.

Many people have left the land to live in the lowland towns that serve as temporary homes for migrant workers on their way to and from the mining and industrial areas of South Africa. Typical of these "camp towns" are those along the northwestern and western borders of Lesotho, including Teyateyaneng, Leribe, Mafeteng, and the capital, Maseru.

Social structure

SOCIAL STRUCTURE The main social levels of Sotho society are clan-groups, individual clans, lineages, and families. The members of each clan share a common name referring to the originator or founding father of that clan. Within each clan are lineages (extended families descended from a common ancestor). Several lineages comprise a clan. The lineages are divided into families and groups of families live together in villages.

POLITICAL STRUCTURE The Sotho are now ruled by democratic central government structures and so the traditional hierarchy of chiefs has lost much of its power, but it still survives as a social force. At the top of the hierarchy is the paramount chief or king, and below him are the chiefs, subchiefs, and headmen. Chiefs exercise their powers in consultation with all the adult males of their areas, and reach their decisions at pitsos (public meetings) held in their kgotlas (courts or meeting places).

Culture and religion

RELIGION The majority of Sotho are now Christians, but many still follow the Sotho religion, which they share with the Tswana. The souls of the dead are believed to have the power to influence the lives of the living and the Sotho make offerings to these badimo to thank them for their help or to ask them for assistance.

The Sotho also have professional alternative medical practitioners who employ a wide range of herbal medicines and rituals to cure diseases, bring good luck and fertility, and protect people from misfortune. In South Africa, the health authorities have come to recognize the value of these health workers. Instead of trying to obliterate such practices, which were scorned under apartheid, the government has tried to incorporate them into the official health system at the community level. Workshops and courses are provided to give them a wider healthcare education.

ORAL LITERATURE The Sotho have a rich culture of poetry, song, dance, and storytelling. This includes lithoko, or praise poems; lifela, songs describing the life of migrant laborers; and tumellano, in which groups of people sing together in harmony.

Sotho pipe
Finely carved and made from wood, tobacco pipes like this one were once normally used by both men and women. The quality, style, and size of a pipe indicated the social status of its owner. Pipes were handed down from one generation to the next.

Sotho timeline

200s Bantu-speaking peoples begin to arrive in Southern Africa	**1851–1852** Sotho-British wars I and II: British withdraw from Sotho land	**1907** Nationalist movements emerge; Progressive Association formed	African-backed) follows and 60 ANC members are expelled
by 1400 Emergence of Sotho *clans*	**1855** Height of Basuto Kingdom	**1913** South African Sotho restricted to inadequate "native reserves"	**1991** Military coup in Lesotho
1600s–1800s Bapedi Empire of Northern Sotho Pedi clan	**1858** Basuto at war with Boers	**1966** Basuto independent as Lesotho (a constitutional monarchy)	**1993** Elections end military rule
1819–1839 *Mfecane/Difaqane*: period of mass migrations and wars: Boers colonize Northern Sotho	**1860–1867** Sotho and Venda drive Boers south of Olifants River	**1979** King bans opposition parties	**1995** Letsie III abdicates and Moshoeshoe II becomes king
1824 Moshoeshoe founds Basuto	**1865–1868** Basuto at war with Boers; Basuto made a British colony	**1986** South Africa blockades Lesotho after king refuses to expel African National Congress (ANC) activists; military coup (probably South	**1996** Death of Moshoeshoe II. He is succeeded by Letsie III
	1880–1881 "Gun War": Sotho rebel when British try to disarm them		**1998** Army revolt causes chaos; South Africa sends troops to restore order

Sotho–Tswana complex

A large proportion of Southern Africa's population is made up of people or Sotho (q.v.) or Tswana (q.v.) descent. These two closely-related groups share a common origin in the early Iron Age population of South Africa. By the fifteenth century large numbers of Sotho-Tswana settlements extended over much of what is now the highveld of northern South Africa. BY the sixteenth century a large number of Sotho-Tswana states had emerged, and these and their dominant lineage groups developed into the different Sotho and Tswana groups and subgroups recognized today.

South Mugirango

The South Mugirango are one of the main subdivisions of the Gusii (q.v.). The Gusii are a large ethnic group of western Kenya.

Southern Bullom *see* Sherbro

Sudanis

The Sudanis, or the "Black Moors," are one of the two main subgroups of the Moors (q.v.) of Mauritania. They are descended from Black African peoples such as the Fulani (q.v.), Soninke (q.v.), Tukolor (q.v.), and Wolof (q.v.).

Suk *see* Potok

Suku

The Suku inhabit a region in southwestern Congo (Dem. Rep.) called Kwango for the Kwango River, which runs through it before becoming the Cuango in Angola. There are very roughly 200,000 Suku people. The Suku language, also called Suku, is a Central Bantu language closely related to Kongo (q.v.).

In the seventeenth century, the Lunda (q.v.) Empire was conquering lands in the southwest of modern-day Congo (Rep.), and refugees from the Lunda invasions established the Suku kingdom. The king was known as the Yaka of MiniKongo, and hence the Suku were once known as the Yaka of Minikongo to differentiate them from the Yaka proper, who inhabit lands to the south of the Suku. In the nineteenth century the Suku profited as intermediaries of the trade in oil, raffia, cloth, beads, and guns. The carving up of Africa by European colonialists, however, brought an end to this trade and Sukuland became an economic backwater.

Sukuma

The Sukuma are closely related to the Nyamwezi (q.v.) people. The Sukuma live in lands to the north of the Nyamwezi in west-central Tanzania, covering the regions of Shinyanga and Mwanza (on the southern shores of Lake Victoria). In fact, "sukuma" literally means "north" in the Nyamwezi-Sukuma language. The languages Sukuma and Nyamwezi are sometimes considered to be two closely-related Bantu (q.v.) languages, but they are really several different dialects of the same language. Despite their many similarities and ties the Sukuma and Nyamwezi are two distinct ethnic groups. There are well over three million Sukuma people in Tanzania, if not more.

Like other Bantu peoples of what is now western and central Tanzania, the Sukuma formed semi-independent, self-governing units called ntemi. The ntemi system of political organization was in use by the Sukuma and Nyamwezi people by the fourteenth century, and it was adopted by other peoples in the region who came into contact with them.

Suri

The Suri (or Surma) inhabit a region that straddles the border between southwestern Ethiopia and Sudan. There are three Suri subgroups: the Bale and the closely related Chai and Tirma. The Chai and Tirma dwell in the lowlands of southwestern Ethiopia on the southern edge of the Ethiopian Highlands. The majority of the Bale live across the border in southeastern Sudan. There are probably not more than 50,000 Suri peoples altogether, the majority of whom live in Ethiopia. The Suri speak Surmic languages, which belong to the Eastern Sudanic branch of the Nilo-Saharan family of languages.

The majority of the Suri are cattle-raising pastoralists. After experiencing civil conflict in both Sudan and Ethiopia, Suri herders can often be found protecting their herds with automatic rifles. Guns were easily available from the rebel Sudanese People Liberation Army, and the Suri have now virtually formed a self-governing region of their own. The Chai and Tirma live in a semi-arid region, and were badly affected by drought and famine in the mid-1980s, as were many Ethiopians.

Surma *see* Suri

Susu

The Susu, or Soso, are a Manding (q.v.) people of West Africa. The Susu language is a Mande (q.v.) language, which is part of the Niger-Congo sub-family of African languages. It is the common tongue used by the many ethnic groups living in southern Guinea. There are around 1.5 million Susu people, the vast majority of whom live in Guinea, where they are very influential. The remainder of the Susu can be found in northwestern Sierra Leone and Guinea-Bissau.

All Manding peoples originated from a mountainous region of the same name that sits astride the border of Mali and Guinea. Before the thirteenth century, the area was ruled by a Susu leader called Sumunguru. In 1235, however, Sumunguru was defeated by Sundiata (q.v.) – the famous Malinke leader who founded the vast medieval Empire of Mali. For much of the following two centuries the Susu numbered among the many people ruled over by Mali. After Mali began to disintegrate in the fifteenth century, however, the Susu left their homeland, migrating west to the Futa Djallon plateau of Guinea. From there they have continued to spread westward. The majority of the Susu have been Muslims since the seventeenth century.

Swahili

The Swahili people live in the coastal regions and on the small offshore islands of Kenya and Tanzania. Their name is derived from an Arabic word and means "coast dwellers." There are between 200,000 and 400,000 Swahili people.

History

The Swahili people are of mixed Black African, Arab, and Persian descent. The coastal Black Africans were mainly Bantu and Cushitic groups who had migrated into the area from the northwest, and some Bantu from the south, before 1000. After the Bantu people, came the Arabs and Persians from southwest Asia. Most were attracted by the trade in ivory, skins, and slaves, though some were seeking refuge from political or religious persecution. By the start of the first millennium, there were Arab settlements in Mogadishu, Lamu, Malindi, Zanzibar, and Kilwa. Some of the settlements were

ruled by Arabs and others by Africans. Around 1200, Persians from Shiraz established the Shirazi dynasty on the Banadir coast around Mogadishu.

GOLDEN AGE Swahili culture emerged from the intermingling – mainly through marriage and trade – of these Arab, African, and Persian groups. By the 1100s at the latest, the Swahilis had emerged as a distinct people. They had a number of small kingdoms based on trading cities up and down the coast. One of the most important was Kilwa. Here, gold, gum, ivory, slaves, and lumber from inland were traded for cotton, glass, porcelain, and pottery, supplied by Arabian, Chinese, and Indian merchants. Kilwa was just one of about forty such ports along the East African coast, and on the islands of Pemba and Zanzibar, which are now part of Tanzania. The ruins of their stone buildings and palaces still survive.

FOREIGN DOMINATION This golden age of Swahili culture came to an abrupt end when Portuguese adventurers arrived on the coast, at first in 1498. By 1509, the Swahili had lost their independence to the Portuguese. In the seventeenth century, Omani Arab traders began to settle on the East African coast, driving out the Portuguese. They controlled most of the region by 1699 and between 1822 and 1837 the coast was ruled over as part of the Omani Empire. During this period, the Omani sultan, Seyyid Said, transferred his capital from Muscat in Oman to the island of Zanzibar, in order to gain control of the trade routes. Zanzibar dominated

East African trade and became an international trading depot during the nineteenth century. Of particular importance in its prosperity was the slave trade. This was stimulated by the development of Arab plantations of cloves and coconuts on the East African coast and its islands, and French sugar plantations on islands in the Indian Ocean. Caravans began to be sent to the interior of East Africa as far south as present-day Malawi to collect slaves and many Arab and Swahili traders made their fortunes in this destructive trade. By the 1860s, 70,000 people a year were being sold as slaves at the Zanzibar slave market. Zanzibar declined with the abolition of the slave trade and the advent of German and British colonists.

RECENT EVENTS By 1900, Britain and Germany had taken control of Zanzibar and the mainland regions covered by the modern states of Kenya and Tanzania. Kenya, Tanganyika, and Zanzibar became independent in the early 1960s. In 1964, Tanganyika and Zanzibar united to form Tanzania.

Language

The Swahili language is called Swahili (or Kiswahili), and it belongs to the Bantu group of languages. Swahili contains about 20,000 Arabic words and has borrowed others from English, Persian, Portuguese, Urdu, and Gujarati. Swahili is not confined to the Swahili and it is widely spoken by many other people – about 30,000,000 altogether. Swahili is the official language of Tanzania and one of the national languages of Kenya and Uganda, it is spoken by some people in Djibouti, Somalia, Mozambique, and Madagascar, and a dialect is the main language in the Comoros Islands, which lie in the Indian Ocean between Madagascar and Mozambique. Those people (about 1,000,000) who have Swahili as their mother tongue are called Waswahili, but they are not necessarily ethnic Swahili. Pidginized versions of Swahili are spoken in some parts of East Africa. A pidgin language is a grammatically simple one that combines elements of one or more languages. Pidgin Swahili is used as a common language by people of different nationalities, particularly in trade. An attempt was begun in 1925 to standardize Swahili. The Germans, who ruled what is now Tanzania, helped to spread the Swahili language by using it in their administration.

Ways of Life

The Swahili live in mixed societies alongside other ethnic groups. The coastal area where they mostly live is a narrow strip of fertile land, which gives way inland to a region of dry plains. Dotted along the coast are

A gift to a Chinese emperor
This Chinese painting on silk shows the giraffe sent by the Swahili ruler of Malindi to the Ming Emperor of China, Ch'eng Tsu, in 1414. The emperor received a second giraffe from Malindi three years later.

Carved doors
This carved door was made by a Swahili craftsman around the beginning of the twentieth century. Its structure – two panels that open inward from the central bar – is typical. The quality and size of such external doors served as an indicator of the household's wealth and status. The carving of doors reached a zenith in the eighteenth century when it was boosted by the wealth of Zanzibar. The carving on this door is relatively simple compared to that on some of the doors that belonged to the Zanzibari elite.

An ancient board game
Mankala is a game that has been played for at least 7,000 years and versions of it can be found throughout Africa as well as the rest of the world. This board was made by a Swahili craftsman in Tanzania. The object of the game is to capture the opponent's seeds. Players move seeds around a board, which is carved with a series of cups. It is a highly skilled game requiring a keen mathematical mind.

Printed khanga cloth
A khanga cloth is a large rectangle of cotton, printed with a border and a central design that usually incorporates a Swahili proverb. These were originally block-printed by hand – a technique introduced by the Omani Arabs. In recent times, khanga cloths are more likely to have been mass produced at a modern textile factory.

Lamu horn
This Swahili man from Lamu is blowing a brass horn called a siwa. Used to announce ceremonies and religious events, this siwa was made in the eighteenth century by the lost-wax casting method.

Grandee's chair
Chairs such as this one were used in many Swahili royal courts from the 1300s to the 1800s. Elaborately carved in ebony and inlaid with ivory, the chair was a symbol of power and would be offered as a sign of respect to visiting notables.

Precious comb
This comb is one of six designed for a sultan of Zanzibar by a Swahili craftsman in the nineteenth century. It is made from silver and gold and is decorative as well as functional.

many small islands also occupied by the Swahili.

URBAN The Swahili are essentially seen as town dwellers although this was probably more true of the past than the present. Typically, Swahili houses were built of stone or coral and their inhabitants had a high standard of living, with plumbing, elaborate furniture, and many imported luxury goods. Town houses are now more likely to be made of wattle-and-daub and thatched with palm leaves. In these houses live various tradesmen, such as carpenters, leatherworkers, and builders. The Swahili no longer dominate trade in East Africa; in fact retailing is often viewed as an occupation beneath the Swahili.

RURAL Outside the towns there are strings of small villages, where farming and fishing communities live in wattle-and-daub or coral houses thatched with palm leaves. Land owning and farming are occupations that are given a relatively high status by the Swahili. Farmers mostly grow coconuts, millet, rice, sorghum, fruits, and vegetables. Fishing is also an important way of making a living for many. Women fisherfolk wade into the shallow waters of the Indian Ocean with nets to catch fish, which they carry home in baskets balanced on their heads. Fishermen sail further out to sea to the grounds where fish are plentiful.

Social organization

Unlike some African ethnic groups, the Swahili are not a completely distinct people. Having emerged over the years from the mixing of separate cultures, it can be difficult to determine which people are "true Swahili" and which are marginal peoples. The Swahili themselves give higher status to families who can claim to be "true Swahili" descended from the earliest settlers. In the past, such older and respected families were distinctive in that they controlled life in the towns; lived in the wealthiest section; were adept at Swahili verse; and dressed in the Arab-influenced fashions. Clothing today still shows Arab influence. For example, many women wear black robes, cover their heads, and veil their faces. Although, most women work as hard as the men, wealthier women stay at home and do not work. This is considered to be a symbol of status.

Culture and religion

RELIGION Swahili culture is based on their religion, which is Islam. Here, the Arab element in Swahili ancestry is paramount. The many mosques (Muslim houses of worship), and the ruins of many ancient ones, bear witness to the importance of religion in Swahili life.

Bao kiswahili
These Swahili men are playing a game called bao kiswahili. It is an East African version mankala.

LITERATURE The Swahili have a long history of literacy and literature. Although the Roman script is often used today, Swahili has been written for centuries in the Arabic script. There is a long tradition of elaborate poetry and written verse chronicles. The earliest known poem is the Hamziya, which survives in a manuscript of 1652. A group of poems in a manuscript of 1728 was probably written a century earlier. Early prose has survived in the form of a letter written in 1772. There are also many historical Swahili chronicles of particular kingdoms, for example, the Chronicle of Pate and the Chronicle of Kilwa. A Swahili history of Mombasa was translated into Arabic in 1824.

Painted hands
It is customary for Swahili women to paint their hands and feet with henna for their wedding day, and also on other special occasions. Henna is a kind of vegetable paste that is applied on the skin in the desired patterns and left to dry. When it is removed, the skin beneath the henna has been stained a reddish brown.

Swahili timeline	
1000 BCE – 1000 CE Bantu and Cushitic peoples migrate into East Africa	**1822–1837** East African coast under rule of the sultan of Oman
900s Arab trading posts established at Mogadishu and Kilwa	**1832** Zanzibar made Omani capital
by 1100s A distinct Swahili culture exists	**1840–1880s** Height of Swahili/Arab slave trade in East Africa
c. 1150 Mombasa and Malindi founded	**by 1900** Most Swahili under either German or British rule
c. 1200 Persian Shirazi dynasty founded near Mogadishu	**1961–1963** Kenya, Tanganyika, and Zanzibar win independence
1200s Mogadishu the preeminent port	**1964** Tanganyika and Zanzibar unite to form Tanzania
c. 1400 Kilwa most important trading center on east coast	**1965** Each part of Tanzania is allowed only one political party
c. 1270 Kilwa starts minting coins	**1967** Arusha Declaration: Tanzania adopts socialism
c. 1470 Mombasa begins period of growth; Kilwa declines	**1985** Tanzania abandons socialism
1498 Vasco da Gama in East Africa	**1991** Kenya allows multiparty politics
1502–1509 Portuguese conquer East African coast to control trade	**1993** Tension between Muslims and Christians in Tanzania
1699 Omani Arab traders control much of coast	**1995** Chaotic first multiparty elections held in Tanzania

Swazi

The Swazi comprise over ninety percent of the 906,000 inhabitants of Swaziland, an independent kingdom located between South Africa and Mozambique. Many more Swazi live in the neighboring areas of South Africa (largely in the former homeland of KaNgwane) and Mozambique.

History

The Swazi are descended from a group of Bantu-speaking peoples called the Nguni who migrated from present-day eastern Nigeria to what is now Mozambique before the late fifteenth century. Dlamini I was their leader, and his descendants became the Swazi kings. About 1750 Ngwane II, the earliest king commemorated in Swazi ritual, led his people into Swaziland. At this time, both the kingdom and people were known as Ngwane.

SWAZI KINGDOM In 1839, Mswati I (q.v.) succeeded to the Ngwane throne at the age of thirteen, so his mother, Thandile, ruled as regent until he came of age in 1845. Thandile set the foundations for the success of Mswati's reign by centralizing the kingdom and introducing age-regiments (groups who could be called upon for work or warfare) and establishing royal villages around the country to control them. The previous king, Sobhuza I (reigned c. 1815–39), and the powerful Mswati I (reigned 1839–65) extended their territory and effectively forged Swaziland by fusing local peoples and refugees from the Zulu Mfecane into a nation powerful enough to resist Zulu pressure. Swazi means "the people of Mswati," and, since the nineteenth century, this name has been given to both the people and the nation previously known as Ngwane.

Toward the Boers, the Swazi kings pursued friendly policies in the later nineteenth century; by granting them concessions, however, the Swazi lost their land, resources, and finally their independence on becoming a British colony, administered by the Boers, in 1894.

RECENT EVENTS Swaziland became independent as a constitutional monarchy in 1968. In 1973, Sobhuza II (q.v., reigned 1921–82) suspended the constitution, banned political parties, and assumed absolute power. Since then, opposition to the loss of democracy has grown. Several protest movements emerged in the early 1990s but, despite various government inquiries and reports, no real changes have been made. In 1995, some dissatisfied extremists began a campaign of arson and bomb attacks on official targets.

Language

The Swazi language is Swazi (or Swati or siSwazi).

Ways of life

AGRICULTURE The majority of Swazi are farmers. Over fifty percent of land in Swaziland is owned by the monarchy, managed by local headmen, and granted to small-scale farmers to work. The main food crops grown are corn, sorghum, sweet potatoes, groundnuts (peanuts), and beans. Cash crops include, cotton, rice, tobacco, citrus fruits, vegetables, and sugar. Cattle, goats, sheep, and chickens are kept.

ECONOMY One-third of all adults work for wages in the

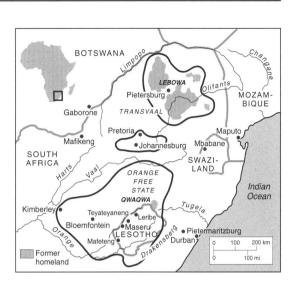

private sector of the economy. Manufacturing industries employ many people in the processing of agricultural products. Tourism and forestry also provide jobs.

Increasingly, men move away temporarily to find paid work elsewhere in the mines of Swaziland or South Africa. The drift of workers to towns and cities and the growth of large-scale commercial farming of citrus fruits, pineapples, and sugar cane are creating new patterns of living.

DIVISION OF LABOR Men generally plow fields and sow seeds while women tend and harvest crops. Because many men work as migrant laborers, however, the division of labor is not strict as the work often has to be done by whoever is available – generally the women.

Social structure

SOCIAL ORGANIZATION The basic social unit is the indlu (a husband and wife and their children). Several indlu make up a umuti. Each umuti has as its head an umnumzana, who is usually male, but with so many men working away from home it is often a woman. The umnumzana settles disputes, allocates land, and organizes workers. The members of an umuti share agricultural tasks. The clan (several families who share a common ancestor or ancestors) is the broadest unit.

MARRIAGE People belong to the same clan as their father

Swazi initiate
The hairstyle worn by this young Swazi man – shaggy and dyed blond – suggests that he is undergoing initiation into adulthood.

Founder of the Swazi kingdom
Shown here with Swazi chiefs in full ceremonial dress is King Mswati I (reigned 1839–65). Skillfully using both warfare and diplomacy, Mswati forged a powerful kingdom at a time when the region was under threat from Boer, British, Portuguese, and Zulu aggressors.

© DIAGRAM

Swazi dress
This woman is wearing a brightly-colored body wrap called an emahiya, a garment worn by both men and women. Other traditional styles of dress, such as those using animal skins, have largely been replaced by Western-style clothing – except on ceremonial occasions. The emahiya still survives, however, as the design lends itself well to modern methods of mass production.

Umhlanga
Dressed as Swazi warriors, these men are ritually paying court to girls as part of the Umhlanga, or Reed Dance. Each September in Swaziland, unmarried girls perform the Umhlanga to pay homage to the queen mother. Wearing necklaces, bead skirts, bracelets, and anklets they perform a dance as they bring reeds from different parts of the country to raise symbolic screens around the queen mother's cattle enclosure.

and must marry outside it. Ideally, a man marries a woman from his paternal grandmother's clan. Marriage can be arranged by the parents of the bride and bridegroom but "love" matches are just as common. The groom's family gives the bride's family cattle, cash, or both. Some men have more than one wife but as many Swazi are Christian this is not common.

POLITICAL STRUCTURE In Swaziland, the king and his mother have supreme legislative, executive, and judicial powers, which are exercised through a framework of local and political officials and organizations. The king inherits the throne from his father, a member of the powerful Nkosi Dlamini clan. If the last king had many sons by different wives, a family council chooses the new king by taking into account factors such as his mother's rank and his own age and character. Until this crown prince's coming of age – marked by his first marriage – his mother acts as queen regent and she remains influential even after her son is installed as king. The king is given the title Ngwenyama (Lion) and his mother is known as Ndlovukazi (Lady Elephant).

A prime minister and cabinet ministers, approved by the king, head the government departments, which run the country on a day-to-day basis. Since 1978, the non-party parliament has been elected indirectly through tinkhundla (local authorities based on chieftaincies) – in a system that preserves the king's powers.

Culture and religion

RELIGION Over half of the Swazi are Christians and the Swazi religion is still widely practiced. It involves belief

Headrest
Carved in the distinctive Swazi "grooved" style, this wooden headrest is both functional and aesthetic.

in a creator god, Mkhulumnqande, and in ancestors' spirits who can either help or punish their living relatives and so merit respect and appeasement. Many Swazi seek help from religious practitioners who use herbal cures; from diviners who use bones, cards, or other devices to diagnose the causes of ailments; and from Christian faith healers. Specialist diviners "smell out" witches who are believed to harm people or their possessions. In Swaziland today, most of these practitioners are officially registered, belong to trade organizations, and many also have set fees.

FESTIVALS Famous Swazi cultural institutions include sibhaca dancing and the annual Umhlanga, or Ree Dance. Sibhaca dancers are teams of men performing vigorous, rhythmic dances in colorful skirts, with their wrists and ankles decorated with cowtails. Dancing also plays a part in the Incwala, or First Fruits Festival, a three-week-long period when king and nation reaffirm their relationship. This festival was introduced by Queen Regent Thandile in the nineteenth century to unify the kingdom and raise the king's standing.

Swazi timeline		
200s Bantu-speaking peoples begin to arrive in Southern Africa	**1836–1848** Great Trek brings Boers into conflict with people inland	**1968** Swaziland independent as a semiconstitutional monarchy
300s–400s Bantu-speakers reach modern Transvaal (South Africa)	**1839–1865** Reign of Mswati I over Ngwane; Swazi kingdom founded	**1973** Swazi king dissolves parliament
c. 1750 Swazi king, Ngwane II, alive	**1879** British and Swazi defeat Pedi	**1978** New constitution approves king's absolute hold on power
by 1800 Ngwane kingdom one of most powerful in region (present-day KwaZulu/Natal in South Africa)	**1894** Swaziland made a British colony (administered by the Boer's Transvaal republic until 1902)	**1991** Apartheid legislation repealed
c. 1815–1839 Reign of King Sobhuza I over Ngwane kingdom	**1910** White-minority ruled Union of South Africa created	**1994** First nonracial elections are held in South Africa
1816 Ngwane driven north by Ndwandwe kingdom	**1913** Swazi in South Africa restricted to inadequate "native reserves"	**late 1990s** Pro-democracy demonstrations in Swaziland continue as political parties remain banned
1819–1839 *Mfecane/Difaqane*: period of mass migrations and wars	**1948** *Apartheid* begun in South Africa	

Taita

The Taita are a cluster of Bantu (q.v.) people in East Africa. They mostly live in the Taita Hills of southwest Kenya near the border with Tanzania. There are more than 150,000 Taita.

Takadi

The Takadi are one of the three main subgroups of the Konso (q.v.). The Konso live in southern Ethiopia.

Talensi

The Talensi are a Mole-Dagbane (q.v.) people of northeast Ghana. They number around 300,000.

Tama

The Tama are a cluster of ethnic groups linked by the Tama language. They are concentrated on and around the border between Sudan and Chad. There are more than 300,000 Tama-speaking peoples, including the Tama proper, Marari (q.v.), Abu Sharib (q.v.), Gimr (q.v.), and Mileri (q.v.). Increasingly, however, Tama is being replaced by Arabic.

Tamberma see Somba

Tambo

The Tambo are a Sadama (q.v.) subgroup. The Sadama are an ethnic group living in Ethiopia.

Tanala

The Tanala are a Madagascan people (q.v.). living in the southern half of the island inland from the eastern seaboard. They number more than 400,000.

Tandroy see Antandroy

Taqali

The Taqali are a Nuba (q.v.) people of southern Sudan. There are more than 180,000 Taqali.

Tchaman see Brong

Tebou see Tebu

Tebu

The Tebu (Tebou,Toubou, or Tibbu) live in the desert and semidesert regions of Niger, Sudan, and northern Chad. There are more than 200,000 Tebu, and most live in Chad. The Teda (q.v.) are a Tebu people.

Teda

The majority of the Teda inhabit the mountainous plateaus of the Tibesti Mountains in northwestern Chad, where Chad's highest point can be found: Emi Koussi (11,237 ft). Some also live in Niger or in desert oases across the border in southern Libya. There are probably not more than 40,000 Teda people altogether. The Teda language, Tedaga, is a Nilo-Saharan language.

The majority of Chad's population live in the grasslands of the south; the Teda are one of the several minority groups that do not. The region they live in is arid since it is part of the Sahara Desert. Unlike their southern neighbors (the Sara (q.v.), for example), the Teda are mostly nomadic and seminomadic farmers and livestock raisers. The Teda, like other northerners, are Islamic. The religious, economic, and social differences between northerners and southerners have led to tensions and, at times, war between northerners and the state. In Chad, most government and other official posts are filled by southerners.

Teke

The Teke (or Bateke) live on a plateau bordering the Congo (Zaire) River in an area that straddles Gabon, Congo (Rep.), and Congo (Dem. Rep.); the vast majority live in Congo (Rep.). The Teke comprise many smaller groups such as the Fumu and Sisi. The Teke probably number about 500,000 people, most of whom live in the Congo (Rep.).

History

The Teke are a Bantu-speaking people, one of many groups descended from those that settled in the varied habitats of the Congo Basin in the early centuries of the first millennium. By the fifteenth century, the Teke were long-established in the middle reaches of the Congo (Zaire) River in an area around its confluence with the Kasai River. From the fifteenth century onward, they developed to become a powerful river-trading people. In the fifteenth and sixteenth centuries, the Teke waged war with the Kongo to the southwest and, by the mid-fifteenth century, the Teke were trading in slaves and tobacco. The Teke kingdom had, by the early eighteenth century, grown very large and powerful through trade and military conquest. It extended on both sides of the Congo (Zaire) River from Malebo Pool (formerly Stanley Pool) northward to the area around Bolobo. By the late eighteenth century,

however, the Teke had lost some of this territory to neighboring groups. During the nineteenth century, there were many skirmishes between the Teke and the Bobangi upriver. The Bobangi set up villages closer and closer to Malebo Pool and began raiding Teke villages for slaves. Following a series of local battles, the Teke agreed to let the Bobangi trade at the pool but did not allow them to found villages.

COLONIALISM In 1880, Pierre Savorgnan de Brazza – a French citizen – started a trading station, which later became the town of Brazzaville, near Malebo Pool. De Brazza met the great Teke king, Ilo Makoko, and negotiated with him for the region to become a French colony. In 1882, the Teke kingdom was ceded to the Middle Congo colony (part of French Equatorial Africa), of which de Brazza was the commissioner general. In the late nineteenth and early twentieth centuries, the French operated a harsh, violent, and oppressive regime and Ilo Makoko's successor tried unsuccessfully to revolt against the colonialists in 1898. Over three-quarters of the Teke were killed in reprisals. Independence was finally won in 1960 as part of the Congo (Rep.).

RECENT EVENTS In Congo (Rep.), following industrial unrest, a communist state was established in 1964 with a centrally-planned economy. In the 1970s, tensions between the country's ethnic groups led to political unrest and military coups. In 1990, Congo (Rep.) became a multiparty democracy. Elections were held in 1993, but the elected president was overthrown in 1997 by former president Denis Sassou-Nguesso (q.v.).

Language
The Teke speak various dialects of the Teke language. Some Congolese Teke also speak French.

Ways of life
The Teke were originally farmers, hunters, and fishing people of the Congo River. In the late eighteenth and early nineteenth century, Teke culture underwent fundamental changes: much of what had been local produce – ironware, raffia cloth and salt – was now replaced by produce imported from the coast such as iron, cloth, pottery, shells, and copper rings; the crafts of smelting iron, carving canoes, and making fine

potteryware were largely lost; and guns replaced the bow and arrow for use in hunting and in warfare. Slaves became the main source of revenue to pay for these items. The Teke received slaves from upriver and passed them on by a variety of routes to points along the coast. The name Teke actually denotes their occupation as traders, as "teke" literally means "to buy."

Many Teke now form part of a trained and skilled workforce in industrial centers such as those in and around Brazzaville, the capital of Congo (Rep.). Subsistence agriculture is still carried out in rural areas, however, and is often supplemented by fishing, hunting, and gathering.

Social structure
POLITICAL STRUCTURE In precolonial times, the Teke's basic political unit was the chiefdom, composed of a scattered group of villages. Any holder of a political office had to be a member of the Teke aristocracy – either father or mother had to be of noble blood. Villages were relatively unstable because ambitious young men would aspire to leave the community and set up their own village a short distance away. Villages are now grouped together under a district chief with a local notable at the head of each village.

SOCIAL STRUCTURE Villages were often small, ranging from a nuclear family to up to forty individuals. Each of the villages was under a chief, who was normally related to all his villagers. The maternal family and its close connections formed the village community. Chieftainship, as with other political offices, was hereditary; son usually succeeded father.

Culture and religion
RELIGION The Teke religion is based on belief in the existence of an invisible world ruled over by the creator god, Nziam. Dead people are believed to be reborn into this world. Various spirits, often representing natural forces, act as mediators between the two worlds. People in the world of the living can communicate with these spirits through prayer or ritual. These prayers can be facilitated by items that are assumed to contain a nature spirit or the spirit of a deceased person. Such items are often kept in a container attached to a wooden statue.

Teke chief
This Teke chief is wearing traditional attire. His arms, chest, and face are made-up with white clay and his headdress is made from parakeet and cock feathers. His multilayered necklace is made from the teeth of meat-eating animals such as panthers and small blue, glass beads, once used as a form of currency.

Kidumu mask
This kidumu mask is worn by Tsaayi (eastern Teke) dancers at funerals and celebrations. Kidumu masks are usually colored black, red, and white and are generally symmetrical in design. Violent oppression by French troops during the early twentieth century wiped out three-quarters of the Teke people. As a result, their cultural heritage was nearly lost. Some of the artistic activities of the Tsaayi have been revived since the late 1960s, however, for example in the design and production of kidumu masks.

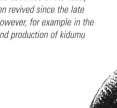

Teke nobleman
The rounded bunlike structure on top of this man's head indicates that he is of noble rank. This style is known as imwu.

Hatchet
Made from wood and sheets of copper, this hatchet would have been used as a symbol of a chief's authority. The blade juts out from the mouth of a beautifully carved head and the copper on the handle has been embossed with geometric designs.

Teke sculpture
These Teke statues have very characteristic features: proudly standing figures, rigid and symmetrical, with facial tattooing as incised vertical or oblique parallel lines on their cheeks. These figures have holes in their abdomens in which magical substances would be placed. These are believed to energize the power of the statue and enable it to perform specific functions such as to ward off disease or protect children.

Teke timeline

c. 200s Bantu-speaking peoples begin to settle in the Congo Basin	become a French colony (Middle Congo). Belgian king's Congo Free State established (in Zaire)	Congo (Zaire) **1967** Omar Bongo becomes president of Gabon. He is accused of favoring his own, Teke, ethnic group by the opposition	**1991** Congo abandons communism and legalizes opposition parties
1400s–1500s Teke, a slave-trading people, at war with neighboring Kongo	**1908** Belgian government takes over Free State as the Belgian Congo		**1994** *CFA franc* devalued by fifty percent causing hardship and unrest in Congo and Gabon
1600s Teke kingdom reaches height	**1960** French and Belgian Congo independence, both as Republic of Congo. Gabon independent	**1971** Former Belgian Congo is renamed Zaire	**1996** Civil unrest mounts in Zaire
1700s Teke become important traders		**1980s** International criticism of human rights abuses and popular unrest mounts in Zaire	**1997** Elected government in the Republic of Congo is overthrown; Mobutu is overthrown in Zaire which is renamed the Democratic Republic of Congo
1800s Skirmishes between Teke and neighboring Bobangi	**1964** Former French Congo – known as Congo (Brazzaville) – adopts communism		
1885 Kingdoms of Teke and Loango	**1965** Mobutu Sese Seko takes power in	**1990** Mobutu promises introduction of multiparty system	

Tekna

The Tekna are a Berber (q.v.) people who live throughout North Africa, especially in southern Morocco but also Algeria and Mali. They are primarily a nomadic people.

Tekrur *see* **Tukolor**

Tem *see* **Temba**

Temba

The Temba (or Kotocoli, Tem, or Chaucho) number more than 300,000 people living largely in Ghana and Togo. They speak the Tem language and are largely Muslim.

Temne

The Temne, or Timmannee, are the second largest ethnic groups in Sierra Leone. They live in a region of the northwest in the coastal hinterland around Port Loko. The Mende (q.v.) – Sierra Leone's largest ethnic group – live in lands to the south of the Temne. About one-third of all Sierra Leoneans are Temne: just under two million people.

Historically, the Temne were ruled by local chiefs, and played an important role in the trade with Europeans on the coast at least 500 years ago. In the late eighteenth century free blacks and former slaves from Britain and Canada settled on the coast of what is now Sierra Leone, and the Temne were hostile to the colonists and invaded the colony, nearly destroying it. The British then established a colony in the region, and large numbers of freed slaves, the ancestors of the modern-day Creoles (q.v.), were settled in the region, and expeditions were launched against the Temne. Since 1991 the Temne and others in the country have been involved in a civil war.

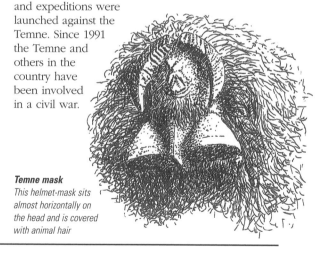

Temne mask
This helmet-mask sits almost horizontally on the head and is covered with animal hair

Tende *see* **Kuria**

Tera

The Tera are a Kanuri (q.v.) people living in northeastern Nigeria. There are around 50,000 Tera.

Terik

The Terik are one of the several related groups that make up the Kalenjin (q.v.). The Kalenjin are a large ethnic group in western Kenya.

Teso *see* **Iteso**

Tetela

The Tetela are a subgroup of the Mongo (q.v.) of Central Africa. The Tetela live in south-central Congo (Dem. Rep.).

Tew *see* **Tumbuka**

Ritual possession
These seated female figures are prized among the Temne, kept privately by senior members of the Bondo secret society and only produced in public for the initiation ceremonies of girls into adulthood.

Thembu

The Thembu are a large ethnic group living South Africa. There are several thousand Thembu people, primarily living in the Transkei and Ciskei regions, which lie on southeastern seaboard of South Africa, to the east and south of Lesotho.

The Thembu are a Xhosa (q.v.)-speaking people, who originally consisted of the Mpondo (q.v.), Thembu, and Xhosa proper. These three groups all claim to have originated in a cradleland at the headwaters of the Dedesi River. Their customs and beliefs are similar as well as their languages, which are all dialects of Isixhosa. Today, the Thembu still comprise one of the main Xhosa-speaking groups. By the eighteenth century, the Thembu were living in large clan-based chieftaincies east of the Kei River.

Nelson Mandela (q.v.), the first of South Africa's presidents to be brought to power by truly multi-racial elections, is a Thembu. Like many South Africans who suffered under South Africa's racist apartheid system of government (which denied and accorded rights based on "tribal" or racial origin), Mandela says that he is not a "tribalist," but a South African first and foremost.

Thlaping

The Thlaping, a Southern African ethnic group, are descended from Rolong (q.v.) ancestors. They separated from the main Rolong group in the eighteenth century.

Tibbu see Tebu

Tiddi see Meidob

Tigray see Tigre

Tigre

The Tigre, or Tigrinya, are one of the largest ethnic groups in Eritrea, where the population is fairly evenly divided between Tigrinya-speaking Christians and Muslim communities. In Ethiopia, the Tigre are the largest ethnic group in the province of Tigre, which lies in the northernmost part of the country and once housed the capital of the ancient Axumite Kingdom. There are more than 2,000,000 Tigrinya-speakers divided between Eritrea and Ethiopia. Tigrinya is a Semitic language related to Amharic and the ancient Geez language. Although only around 7 percent of the Ethiopian population are Tigre, they have long been an important political force in that country.

The Tigre share an imperial heritage with the Amhara (q.v.) – members of both groups provided emperors for the throne of the Ethiopian Empire. The last Tigre emperor was Yohannes IV who reigned in the second half of the nineteenth century. In more recent decades the Tigre were active in Eritrea's struggle for independence and Ethiopia's fight to establish democracy during the reign of the dictator Mengistu (q.v.). The Tigre People's Liberation Front was formed in 1975, and it became a leader among the various Ethiopian and Ertitrean liberation movements.

Tigrinya see Tigre

Tikar

The Tikar are a Cameroonian people who are part of the Bamileke (q.v.). They live in the western highlands of the country and number more than 600,000.

Timmannee see Temne

Tirma

The Tirma are one of the three closely related groups that make up the Suri (q.v.). The Suri live in Ethiopia and Sudan.

Tiv

The Tiv occupy an area that stretches from the foothills of the Adamawa Mountains along the Cameroon–Nigeria border in the southeast to the Jos Plateau, central Nigeria, in the north. There are well over one million Tiv in Nigeria.

Oral history states that the Tiv originate from the highlands of northern Cameroon. Like many other African societies, the Ibibio (q.v) and Igbo (q.v), for example, historically the Tiv lived in noncentralized (acephalous) societies. This meant that they had no acknowledged ruler. The basis of Tiv society was lineage (the greater, extended family a person belonged to). The Tiv did not live in villages but family groups, with related groups positioned near to each other. Law and order was maintained largely by discussion and the following of customary mores. To settle a dispute, each side would pick a leader; the two leaders would then argue it out.

Toka

The Toka are a Tonga (q.v.) subgroup. They number more than 20,000 people living in southern Zambia.

Toma see Loma

Tombuca *see* Tumbuka

Tonga

The Tonga live in a region called Butonga that spreads from the Southern Province of Zambia southeastward across the border to the middle of the Zambezi plain in northern Zimbabwe. There are about a million Tonga, the majority of whom live in Zambia, where they form roughly ten percent of the population.

History

Archeologists have discovered remains that suggest the Tonga have been in their present location for about a thousand years. The early Tonga were farmers and fishermen who raised cattle and goats. Bones found in waste dumps show that they also hunted antelopes. The Scottish explorer David Livingstone visited Butonga in the 1850s and found the Tonga living in small, scattered settlements. In the earlier 1800s they had been subjected to raids from other groups, including the Lozi, Kololo, and Matabele, who had taken many of their cattle. The Tonga were not a warlike people, although they had weapons such as spears and clubs. They had a simple system for dealing with raids: they hid grain in their long hair, so that if they had to flee to fresh territory they had the means of planting fresh crops and beginning again.

In the 1890s Cecil Rhodes' British South Africa Company (BSA) occupied Southern Rhodesia (present-day Zimbabwe) and Northern Rhodesia (present-day Zambia). White settlers consequently took over much of Butonga. In the 1920s, the company handed its Rhodesian lands over to British government rule. Under colonial rule, the Tonga were grouped into three small "native reserves," leaving

Tonga drums
Drums are important for ceremonial, ritual, and social occasions. The Gwembe Tonga, in particular, pride themselves on their drumming teams. There are two main types of Tonga drum: mankuntu (cylindrical drums that vary in pitch) and badima (pedestal-based funeral drums that come in seven sizes). Others include masabe and musimbo.

Key
1 Masabe   **3** Musimbo
2 Mankuntu   **4** Badima

the better land for the white settlers. The first group was the Plateau Tonga in Northern Rhodesia. The Toka Tonga of Kalomo and Livingstone districts were allocated land with poor soils, while the Gwembe Tonga were in the more isolated locality of the Zambezi Valley. Unable to survive solely by farming in the inadequate reserves, the Toka and the Gwembe Tonga were forced to work mainly as migrant laborers for the whites – in particular, in the copper mines of the Copperbelt in north-central Zambia.

RECENT EVENTS In the late 1950s, the building of the Kariba Dam on the Zambezi River displaced over 50,000 Gwembe Tonga. They were forcibly evicted to new homes in the hills above Lake Kariba or to the more arid lands below the dam where rainfall is irregular. Conditions changed for the Tonga after Zambia, in 1964, and Zimbabwe, in 1980, finally became independent as they were no longer restricted to these native reserves. Between 1972 and 1991, Zambia was governed as a one-party state under Kenneth Kaunda (q.v.), whose government has since been accused of carrying out torture and human rights abuses in a network of secret tunnels beneath the presidential residence.

Language

The main language of the Tonga is Tonga (or Citonga), of which there are several dialects. The dialect used by the Plateau Tonga is the one most often used in schools. Tonga literature is usually written in English.

Ways of life

RURAL Butonga is plateau country, intersected by the Zambezi River and Lake Kariba and Kariba Dam. The rainy season lasts from November through March, while from April through to early August the weather is cold and dry. Hot weather starts in late August. Rainfall is unreliable and droughts are common. In this environment, many Tonga are subsistence farmers, working on their own plots of land and growing food for their own needs. The main crop is maize and other crops include groundnuts (peanuts), millet, sorghum, and vegetables. The chief cash crop is cotton. Plateau

Gwembe Tonga woman
Pictured in 1950 before the mass relocation of thousands of Gwembe Tonga, this woman typifies Tonga attire of the era. Noses pierced with bones or grass are very rarely seen today.

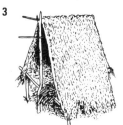

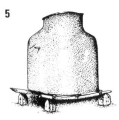

farmers include many who have substantial holdings and large herds of cattle. Some of these wealthier farmers have tractors, which they hire out to neighbors. Others, including small-scale farmers, work on the land of rich farmers. As the Zambian government allocates large areas of land to multinational businesses, a landless rural class is developing.

URBAN Since the 1940s, many Tonga in Zambia have migrated to urban areas in search of employment. Although the Tonga are predominantly rural, around forty percent live in urban areas where they are mostly engaged in commercial and service industries. "Traditional" crafts such as blacksmithing, carpentry, pottery, and basket-weaving have been revived in the last few decades. The high cost of transportation and the rising costs of imports have reversed the trend for factory-made foreign goods.

DIVISION OF LABOR Men are usually responsible for building houses, herding cattle, and hunting. Women do most of the other farm work, make pots and baskets, and are largely responsible for childcare. Women also dominate trading at local markets. Increasingly they do paid work as domestic servants or shop assistants, and many hold professional jobs. Both men and women work in various trades and craft professions, which include car repairs, brick making, tailoring, and needlework.

Social structure

The Tonga are divided into clans (several families who claim descent from a common ancestor or ancestors). The family, headed by the husband, is the core of the social structure, but descent is traced through the female line.

MARRIAGE Increasing numbers of families are headed by single mothers. This may be because under customary law a divorced wife does not receive an equal share of the assets (those built up jointly by both husband and wife usually go to the man) and if the wife is widowed she does not inherit anything (the husband's maternal family does). Civil courts, however, often try to ensure that women and their children are treated fairly.

Culture and religion

RELIGION Large numbers of Tonga are Christians and many combine this with features of the Tonga religion. The Tonga religion involves belief in a creator god called Leza, who is now often identified as the Christian God. The Tonga have a great veneration for the spirits of the dead and make offerings to their ancestors, or mizimo. Basango are spirits who have a wider influence than mizimo and are thought to affect whole neighborhoods not just families. Mizimo and basango

are consulted on family and communal matters by mediums. Masabe are invasive spirits who are thought to attack people. Both men and women can be possessed by masabe and, after recovery, they may go on to help others similarly afflicted. New masabe have emerged to represent the particular ills of the twentieth century. Christian Tonga call these spirits demons.

Tonga timeline	
1000s Tonga settled in present location	**1963** CAF dissolved
1850s Tonga visited by explorer/ missionary David Livingstone	**1964** Northern Rhodesia independent as Zambia; nationalist leader Kenneth Kaunda is president
1890s Tonga come under control of British South Africa (BSA) Company as part of Northern and Southern Rhodesia	**1965** White-minority declare illegal independence of Southern Rhodesia as Rhodesia
1923–1924 BSA hands over Rhodesias to British government. White settlers take much of Tonga land. Tonga divided into three inadequate "native reserves"	**1972** Zambia made a one-party state **1980** Rhodesia independent with majority rule as Zimbabwe; Prime Minister Robert Mugabe develops a one-party system
1940s Tonga begin to migrate to urban areas in search of employment	**1991** End of one-party rule in both Zambia and Zimbabwe. Kaunda looses presidency of Zambia
1950s Many Tonga displaced by building of the Kariba Dam on the Zambezi River	**1991–1992** Drought hits Tonga in Zimbabwe
1953 White-minority ruled Central African Federation (CAF) formed including Rhodesia colonies	**1996** Mugabe reelected president of Zimbabwe for a second time

Mbanje smoking
Although increasingly uncommon, some Tonga women still smoke long calabash pipes called mbanje. Tobacco was once a major domestic crop but is less important in modern Tongan agriculture. The mbanje used by men tended to be smaller and made from clay.

Key for structures

1 Stilt-house with platform.
2 A day shelter for garden or village use.
3 A garden shelter on a low platform.
4 A groundnut (peanut) store.
5 A bottle-type *granary* (grain store) made from mud and grass and with no roof.
6 A butala granary: mud and grass grain store.
7 A butala granary with a thatched roof.

Toposa

The Toposa are a Nilotic (q.v.) people of southern Sudan and parts of Ethiopia. There are more than 90,000 Toposa in Sudan and about 10,000 in Ethiopia.

Toro

The Toro are a Bantu (q.v.) people of western Uganda. They share a common origin with the Nyoro (q.v.) people of the lakes region of western Uganda. There are at least 500,000 Toro people, and most live in the western corner of Uganda. The region they inhabit lies south of Lake Albert along Uganda's western border with Congo (Dem. Rep.). The majority of the Toro are Christians, many of whom still also follow the Toro religion. A very small minority are Muslim.

The Nyoro people had established a powerful kingdom – Bunyoro-Kitara – in the region by the fourteenth century CE Bunyoro was a federation of provinces called a saza. In the first half of the nineteenth century,

the Toro saza became an independent kingdom in its own right under the rule of the first Toro omukama (king), Kaboya, who was the rebellious son of the Bunyoro omukama. After Kaboyo's death in the 1850s, however, Toro nearly lost its new-found independence. When British forces overthrew the Bunyoro omukama, however, Toro independence was restored. In 1966, all the Ugandan kingdoms, including Toro, were abolished by the Ugandan government, and it was not until 1993 that the Toro kingdom was restored. It functions largely as a cultural institution, however, and the omukama has limited political powers.

Torodo see Tukolor

Toubou see Tebu

Toucouleur see Tukolor

Tshidi

The Tshidi are one of the four main subgroups of the Rolong (q.v.). The Rolong are a Tswana (q.v.) people of Southern Africa.

Tsimihety

The Tsimihety are one of the more numerous Madagascan peoples (q.v.). They number more than 700,000 living in an inland region in the northern end of the island. The Tsimihety claim to be descended from the Sihanaka (q.v.).

Tsonga

Numbering around two million, the Tsonga are one of the largest ethnic groups in Mozambique. At least another one million live in the northern Transvaal region of Southern Africa. The Tsonga have been living in this region for several hundred years and were settled there before the sixteenth century. The Nguni (q.v.) peoples of Southern Africa are probably descended from the Tsonga (q.v) of Mozambique.

In southern Mozambique around what is now the bay of Maputo, the Tsonga established kingdoms whose wealth was based on agriculture and trade. After the Portuguese introduced corn into the region in the sixteenth or seventeenth century, food production

and population expanded. Europeans visiting the coast also provided opportunities for trade in ivory and copper. Other Africans captured by the Tsonga in battle were sold as slaves to the Europeans. Such trade played a part in the emergence of three powerful Tsonga kingdoms: Nyaka, Tembe, and Maputo, which successively dominated the region from the 1500s to the 1700s. In 1800s, however, Ngoni (q.v) refugees fleeing a turbulent era of southern Africa's history came to dominate the region. As a result, the Tsonga came under a Zulu (q.v.) cultural influence, adopting cattle as a central aspect of their economy as well as the Zulu language.

Tswana

The Tswana (or Batswana or Western Sotho) are one of the principal Bantu-speaking peoples of Southern Africa. The Tswana number about three million and live in a region stretching southeast from the Okavango Swamps to the Limpopo River, and southwest from there to the Kuruman River area. This region includes eastern and northwestern Botswana, and the former Tswana homeland of Bophuthatswana, which consisted of a number of separate blocks of territory in South Africa.

History

The Tswana are descended from Bantu-speaking peoples who migrated southward from present-day eastern

Nigeria. They reached the eastern part of their present lands some time between 300 and 400. From there, groups spread slowly westward over the following two centuries and set up new territories and settlements. The Tswana originally emerged as a separate group from within the Sotho group of people sometime before the 1400s. Over many years, groups of Sotho clans (several families linked by a common ancestor or ancestors) came together to form the three major divisions of the Sotho people: the Northern Sotho, the Southern Sotho, and the Tswana (or Western Sotho) – who are now often viewed as a separate group.

The first half of the nineteenth century was a period of turmoil for the Tswana. They had to endure a series

Tswana architecture

In the past, most Tswana houses were circular, with mud or stone walls and a thatched roof supported on rafters. Today, many Tswana houses are rectangular, however, and made of brick. In fact, a great diversity of housing styles is reflected by modern Tswana homes.

Beer brewing

This Tswana woman is brewing beer, a profitable cottage industry (largely performed at home using nonmechanized means of production) in Botswana and South Africa.

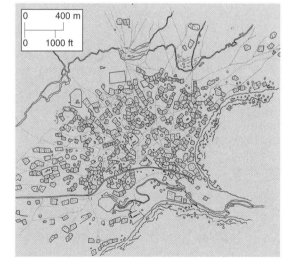

Tswana village

In this plan of a Tswana village in Botswana, a mixture of modern and old-fashioned influences can be seen. Alongside a school, clinic, shops, and restaurants are compounds arranged in crescent shapes: according to Tswana custom, male relatives live in neighboring compounds arranged in a crescent shape around the family kgotla (meeting place). The main village kgotla is headed by the chief. In modern-day Botswana, chiefs are now elected and paid a salary. Although they have lost much of their power, chiefs are still seen as leaders and deal with many local disputes at the village kgotla.

of civil wars followed by the Mfecane/Difaqane – a period of devastating invasions by neighboring peoples fleeing the Zulu expansion. The Tswana's first contact with Europeans came in 1801, when a small group of explorers reached the southernmost Tswana settlements. These events were followed by occupation and rule by the Afrikaners, or Boers, and the British under whom Tswana lands were divided between South Africa and the British protectorate (colony) of Bechuanaland, which became independent in 1966 as Botswana. The country's first president, from 1966 until his death in 1980, was Sir Seretse Khama (q.v.).

In South Africa, the Tswana were reduced to third-class status by the government's policy of apartheid ("separate development") and were required to live in the Bophuthatswana homeland, but allowed to work as migrant laborers elsewhere in South Africa.

RECENT EVENTS The Tswana in South Africa have benefited from the abolition of the apartheid laws in the early 1990s, which has given all South Africans equal rights. In Botswana, Sir Ketumile Masire (q.v.) was re-elected as president for a third five-year term in 1994.

Language

The Tswana language is called Setswana.

Ways of life

SETTLEMENTS Tswana villages can be very large with populations of up to 25,000 people. A typical Tswana compound is built in a large yard, usually enclosed by a fence or hedge and containing a garden area plus one or more large trees, for shade. Within the yard, two or more houses providing dwelling and storage space for the family stand in or next to the lolwapa, a low-walled courtyard that is the heart of the compound.

AGRICULTURE As well as its compound, each Tswana family has houses on its farming and cattle-grazing lands, which may be some distance from the village. During the farming season, from November to June, most people in the villages leave for these outlying areas to plow their land, plant and harvest crops, and tend their cattle, goats, and sheep. In Botswana, cattle make up eighty-five percent of total agricultural output and meat products are a major export.

INDUSTRY Away from the land, many Tswana men have found work in the mines and industries of South Africa, or in the rapidly-expanding mining industries of Botswana and Zimbabwe.

DIVISION OF LABOR The farming work and other tasks are divided between men, women, and children. The men herd and milk the livestock, do the heavier building work, and hunt wild game. They also help with the plowing, but that is often left to the women. The women also tend and harvest the crops – which include sorghum, corn, millet, vegetables, and fruit – and do the cooking and other household jobs. With many men working away from home as migrant laborers, however, it increasingly falls to the women to perform most agricultural work. The children usually help by collecting water and firewood.

Tswana warriors

Pictured in the nineteenth century (a time of great turmoil for the Tswana), the Tswana warrior in front is carrying a distinctively-shaped shield.

Social structure

AGE-REGIMENTS In the past, everyone joined an age-regiment after initiation into adulthood. These provided a pool of labor for large-scale activities such as rounding up cattle or building compounds and, in the case of the men, they also comprised the army when needed. During the colonial era, many male age-regiments fought for the British army abroad while others were forced to provide labor for tasks such as building roads. In the modern era, the tasks that an age-regiment can be called on to perform are defined in law. Also, every Tswana is no longer a member of an age-regiment. The role of these institutions has largely been replaced by the existence of social clubs, voluntary associations, churches, and other groups that cross divisions based on ethnicity, age, and class.

MARRIAGE Although marriages between cousins are encouraged in Tswana society – as they help to keep wealth and property within family groups and strengthen the bonds of kinship between them – most marriages are between people from different family groups. A man may have more than one wife and marriages are usually arranged by the family group or relatives of the bride and groom.

Culture and religion

RELIGION The first Christian missionaries arrived in Tswana lands in 1816. Most Tswana are now Christians, yet their own religion, based on ancestor reverence, still survives and is widely followed. Like Christianity, it is based on the belief that people have immortal souls and that the world was created by a supreme being, called Molimo. The Tswana believe that the souls of the dead have the power to influence the lives of the living and make offerings to them to thank them for their help or to ask them for assistance. They also have an enduring belief in the power of magic and its practitioners.

The Tswana used to perform rainmaking ceremonies at the beginning of the farming season. Although these ceremonies have fallen into disuse, many Christian churches now hold prayer days for rain.

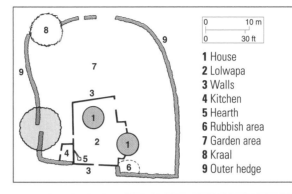

0 ____ 10 m	
0 ____ 30 ft	

1 House
2 Lolwapa
3 Walls
4 Kitchen
5 Hearth
6 Rubbish area
7 Garden area
8 Kraal
9 Outer hedge

Tswana compound
The layout of a typical Tswana compound. The main yard is surrounded by a hedge and incorporates a cattle enclosure. The walled inner courtyard, the lolwapa, contains one house and has another opening onto it.

Tswana timeline

200s Bantu-speaking peoples begin to arrive in Southern Africa	**1836–1848** Great Trek brings Boers into conflict with people inland	**1970** Bophuthatswana, Tswana homeland, created by South African government; many Tswana forcibly relocated to this homeland in following years
300s–400s antu-speakers reach present-day Transvaal (South Africa)	**1884–1885** Bechuanaland, British colony, established over Tswana	
650–1300 "Toutswe tradition" in Botswana: large, cattle-owning communities	**1910** Boers and British form white-ruled Union of South Africa	**1980** Death of Seretse Khama
by 1400 Tswana emerge from Sotho	**1913** Tswana in South Africa restricted to "native reserves"	**1991** Apartheid legislation repealed
1801 First contact with Europeans	**1948** Apartheid officially begins in South Africa	**1992** Botswana government in corruption scandal
1816 First Christian mission		**1994** First nonracial elections are held in South Africa
1819–1839 Mfecane/Difaqane: period of mass migrations and wars	**1966** Bechuanaland independent as Botswana; Tswana leader Seretse Khama is president	**1996** South Africa adopts new constitution

Tuareg

The Tuareg (or Kel Tamacheq or Kel Tagelmust) are Berber in origin. Most live in and around the Sahara Desert from Algeria and Libya in the north to northern Nigeria and Mali in the south. This area covers a variety of terrains including desert and semidesert, mountainous regions in southern Algeria, and savanna (grasslands with scattered tress and shrubs). The southern part of Tuareg territory is in the Sahel – a strip of semidesert south of the Sahara – and in the savannas to its south. The vast majority of the Tuareg inhabit the Sahel. There are probably between one and three million Tuareg.

History

About 5,000 years ago, the Berber ancestors of the Tuareg lived along the North African coast of the Mediterranean, probably in present-day Libya. Since the seventh-century Arab invasion of North Africa, the Tuareg have traveled southward in a series of migrations. A proud and independent people, they fought with Arab, Turkish, and European invaders over the years. Arabs had conquered all of North Africa by 711, however, and the Tuareg were driven south into the desert.

In the fifteenth century, the Sultanate of Aïr emerged as a centralized Tuareg state with its capital at Agades (modern Agadez) in present-day Niger. Aïr's wealth was based on control of the trans-Saharan trade routes. Great Tuareg trading caravans (companies of travelers)

Tree of Ténéré
In the desert in Niger, this tree is the only one for six hundred miles and is used by desert travelers such as the Tuareg as a reference point.

© DIAGRAM

Camel caravan
A Tuareg camel caravan (company of travelers) crossing the vast expanse of the Sahara Desert.

Tuareg drummer
Women are generally the musicians among the Tuareg. This Tuareg woman is using a hollowed-out gourd placed upside down in a wooden bowl as a drum.

Tuareg weaponry
Historical Tuareg weapons exhibit a blend of styles from African to Arabic and even European. The European influence is a possible result of the crusades of the eleventh to thirteenth centuries, or may derive from captured pirate weaponry that made its way south to the Sahara. The blades of this sword and dagger were forged from metal and the hilts covered in leather.

1 Dagger with sheathed tip, which would have been worn on the arm.
2 Sword with leather carrying sheath.

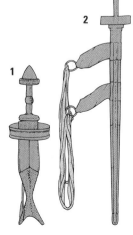

crossed the Sahara bringing gold, ivory, ostrich feathers, and slaves from West Africa to the Mediterranean coast. Southbound caravans carried salt and Arab and European goods to West Africa. Agades was part of the Songhay Empire from 1501–32 and was tributary to the Kanem-Borno Empire from 1532 until the 1600s. After attacking Borno, Aïr greatly expanded its territory at the expense of neighboring states during the seventeenth and eighteenth centuries. In the 1800s, the Sultanate of Aïr reached its greatest extent and Agades became an important political center in the region. By 1870, however, Agades had ceased to be of political importance and by 1900 Aïr had become part of the French West Africa colony.

COLONIALISM In 1917, a Tuareg rebellion against French rule was harshly suppressed. Many were killed and others (around 30,000) fled to northern Nigeria. By the 1960s, North and West Africa were independent from colonial rule, but the Tuareg found themselves divided up between various different nations that had no relevance to their history, lifestyle, or social and political structures.

RECENT EVENTS Sahelian droughts (periods of inadequate rainfall) have been increasingly frequent since the 1960s. They have forced many Tuareg to migrate northward to Algeria and Libya. Returning Tuareg refugees have come into conflict with the Malian and Niger governments in particular. A Tuareg uprising in Niger in 1992 sparked a conflict that lasted until a peace accord was signed in 1994. A similar Tuareg uprising in Mali has led to thousands of Tuareg refugees fleeing to neighboring countries. The conflict worsened before peace was reached in mid 1995.

Language
The Tuareg speak a Berber language called Tamacheq. It has four main dialects, which are largely mutually intelligible. The Tuareg often call themselves "Kel Tamacheq" – "People of the Tamacheq Language." Many Tuareg also speak Songhay, Hausa, or French. Tamacheq is written in a script called Tifnagh.

Ways of life
NOMADIC PASTORALISM Precolonial Tuareg were largely nomadic pastoralists (livestock herders who travel with their herds in search of pasture and water) who kept

large herds of cattle, camels, sheep, and goats. The Tuareg would migrate with their herds of animals, moving from one water hole or pasture to another. Oases (fertile pockets in the desert) provided resting places and water. Surplus produce could be exchanged at oases for products such as dates and millet grown by the resident cultivators.

Many Tuareg are still nomadic, but colonial and government policies, drought, and pressure on the land from an increasing population have changed the way of life of many. Colonial governments limited each group of nomads to specific areas and the new national boundaries that were imposed further restricted nomadic activities. Since the colonial era, the improvement of existing wells and the provision of new ones has had side effects. Combined with improved veterinary care, permanent water holes have allowed herds to increase dramatically in size and overgrazing has seriously damaged pasturelands. Attempting to control the Tuareg, governments have often pursued policies that encourage them to settle and practice farming. Until recently, the Algerian government even had a policy of forced sedentarization, which grouped the Tuareg in agricultural cooperatives.

A severe drought struck the Sahelian lands in 1968–74 and again in 1984–5, permanently changing the Tuareg lifestyle. Thousands of people and whole herds of cattle died, while others were forced to sell their herds and thousands more moved south to Niger and Nigeria. Although many returned to nomadic pastoralism – with greatly depleted herds – others did not. As a result, many Tuareg are now settled farmers or seasonal laborers in the ports and docks of North and West Africa.

TRADE Most Tuareg engaged in trading across the Sahara as well as nomadic pastoralism in the precolonial era. Trade was deeply affected by the arrival of the French, however. Trans-Saharan trading was largely curtailed by the imposition of customs duties and competition from new coastal trading centers. Only the salt trade remained active. International trade has partly replaced the trans-Saharan trade but it is not as lucrative. Using their camels to travel cross-country in long caravans, the Tuareg take advantage of price differences between countries to make a profit. Potash, which is used in fertilizers and soaps, is taken from Bilma in eastern Niger to Katsina in northern Nigeria, for example.

The tagelmust
This Tuareg man is wearing the tagelmust, a long cloth that is wrapped around to cover the head and sometimes the face. The tagelmust is of great importance to all Tuareg men; traditionally, it is rarely removed and should always be worn in the presence of non-Tuaregs. One of the names the Tuareg call themselves is "Kel Tagelmust," which means "People of the Tagelmust."

Tifnagh
The Tuareg script is called Tifnagh and is related to an ancient Libyan script. Inscriptions in Tifnagh have been found on rocks in the Sahara. These inscriptions often record early events in Tuareg history.

Tent

This nomadic tent is made from cloth suspended on wooden poles. Many Tuareg now use plastic sheeting for their tents. A tent is usually made by elderly female relatives and owned by a married woman. Mud or stone permanent houses, however, are built and owned by men. As the nomadic Tuareg are increasingly being forced to settle down, the property balance between men and women is changing as tents – owned by women – are gradually being replaced by permanent houses, which are owned by men.

CAMELS Although trucks now cross the Sahara, most Tuareg still rely on camels for transportation as they can go places where no wheeled vehicle can. The camel has large eyes, protected by long eyelashes and heavy eyebrows. Its long legs end in cushionlike feet that act on the loose sand like snowshoes on snow. Camels can travel for days with little food and for weeks without water. A camel can eat almost any kind of plant, no matter how thorny. The camel's strength and endurance have earned it the name "ship of the desert."

The Tuareg take great care of their camels, making sure that they get enough rest and are unloaded when they stop. Typically, the animal's burden includes: trade goods, tents, blankets, provisions, and pots and pans.

Social structure

POLITICAL STRUCTURE In the past, the Tuareg were divided into seven main groupings or confederations: the Kel Ahaggar, Kel Ajjer, Kel Adrar, Kel Aïr, Kel Geres, Aullemmeden Kel Dennek, and the Aullemmeden Kel Ataram. The Kel Ahaggar and the Kel Ajjer of southern Algeria are known as the Northern Tuareg. The other groups, who live mostly in the Sahel, are known as the Southern Tuareg. Each confederation was led by an amenokal (king). These confederations have been disempowered since the colonial era; each amenokal now provides a link with the relevant central government.

SOCIAL STRUCTURE There are three main Tuareg social classes. At the top are the imajeghen (nobles) one of whom is elected as the amenokal of each confederation. The imajeghen were decimated by French reprisals after the rebellion of 1917 and today form less than one percent of the total Tuareg population. After the nobles come the imghad – the ordinary people. The third main group is the iklan, descendants of Black

Africans who were once Tuareg slaves. Postcolonial governments have largely eradicated slavery, however, and many iklan are now farmers, herders, artisans, blacksmiths, or laborers.

Women and men have equal status and husbands and wives may both own property. Women join in the decision-making processes of the group and both men and women tend to be equally well educated. Usually, the men tend the animals, while the women look after the children, prepare food, and milk the animals.

Culture and religion

RELIGION The vast majority of Tuareg are Muslims – Islam was introduced to North Africa by Muslim Arabs in the seventh century. Most Tuareg groups have ineslemen or marabouts (a religious class that was introduced after the adoption of Islam). Ineslemen act as teachers, counselors, and mediators in local disputes.

DRESS The Tuareg are sometimes known as the "People of the Black Veil" because the men shield their faces with a tagelmust (a long strip of cloth). The tagelmust can be as much as 20 ft (6 m) long. The cloth is, in fact, not black but dark blue. In the past, the veil was made from strips of Sudanese indigo (deep blue) cotton, but today this material is expensive and cheaper imported fabrics are used instead. Sudanese cotton is still used for special garments though. Some of the blue dye of this fabric would come off on the faces of the wearers, giving the Tuareg their other nickname of "Blue Men." Women usually go unveiled but often wear a headcloth.

Tuareg bedstead

Made from wood and decorated with silver, copper, and bronze, this twentieth-century bedstead harks back to the design of Ancient Egyptian beds. Indeed, the ancestors of the Tuareg were already settled in North Africa when Ancient Egypt was flourishing thousands of years ago.

Cross of Agades

Tuareg silversmiths are famous for a particular pendant known as the Cross of Agades (or Agadez), which cames in various designs. Once regarded as being endowed with powers to protect and heal, these crosses are now seen as symbols of wealth. They are made using the "lost-wax" method – the mold in which the cross is cast is formed around a wax cross, which is then melted away. Designs based on the Cross of Agadez are often repeated on Tuareg leatherwork, such as saddles.

Tuareg timeline	
3000 BCE Berber ancestors of Tuareg settled on the Mediterranean coast of North Africa	**1899** First French military expedition against the Tuareg
c. 100 Camels are introduced to North Africa	**1900** Aïr part of French West Africa
640 CE Arab invasion and conquest of North Africa begins	**1917** Tuareg rebel against French
	1954 Algerian war of independence
711 Arabs control North Africa	**1960** Niger and Mali independent
1400s Sultanate of Aïr established	**1962** Algerian independence
1500s Aïr loses its independence to Songhay Empire then to Kanem-Borno Empire	**1990s** Tuareg uprisings in both Niger and Mali
1600s Aïr independent again	**1994** Tuareg rebels sign peace accord in Niger
1800 Aïr reaches greatest extent	**1995** Tuareg end uprising in Mali

Meeting of elders

A meeting of Tuareg elders in an ancient graveyard in the Sahara. The Tuareg believe such graves to be those of legendary giants. This belief lends decisions made at these graveyards great significance.

Tuareg saddle

The saddle on this camel is recognizably Tuareg as it has the uniquely Tuareg cross shape – the Cross of Agades (or Agadez) – rising from its pommel.

Tugen

The Tugen are a subgroup of the Kalenjin (q.v.) of Kenya. They number more than 200,000 people living in the hills above the Kerio River.

Tukolor

There are around one million Tukolor people spread throughout West Africa but particularly concentrated in the north of Senegal near the border with Mauritania, and several thousand live in Guinea. Originally a Fulani (q.v.) people, modern-day Tukolors (Toucouleurs, Tekrurs, or Torodos) are descended from Fulani, Moors (q.v.), Soninke (q.v.), and other ancestors. Although most Fulani groups are nomadic, the Tukolor have long been settled farmers. The Tukolor Fulani people founded the state of Tekrur in what is now Senegal several hundred years ago. The Tukolor are said to be the first large group of West Africans to adopt Islam as their religion. The Tukolor were very active in the Islamicization of West Africa, through both jihad (holy war) and simple contact. The best-known Tukolor in the spread of Islam was Al Hajj Umar, who established the powerful Tukolor empire in West Africa in the nineteenth century.

Tukulor see Tukolor

Tulama

The Tulama are one of the nine main subgroups of the Oromo (q.v.). They live in Ethiopia.

Tumbuka

The Tumbuka (or Tew or Tombuca) are related to the Tonga (q.v.). They number well over one million and can be found in northern Malawi and northeastern Zambia.

Tunjur

The Tunjur are a relatively small ethnic group today, but they had established a powerful kingdom by the sixteenth century in what is now Sudan. Numbering around 10,000, the present-day Tunjur live in Darfur, western Sudan, and across the border in Chad.

Tupur

The Tupur number around 160,000, the majority of whom live in northern Cameroon. Significant numbers also live in southwestern Chad and southeastern Nigeria, however.

Turka

The Turka are a subgroup of the Senufo (q.v.). The more than 150,000 Turka live in northern Ivory Coast, southern Mali, and southwestern Burkina Faso.

Turkana

The Turkana inhabit the semidesert regions of northwestern Kenya. The region they occupy is bordered to the east by the western shores of Lake Turkana and to the west by the Rift Valley. Turkana District is now an official administrative region of Kenya. The Ngimonia and the Ngichoro are the two main divisions of the Turkana people. There are well over 200,000 Turkana people in Kenya.

The Turkana are sometimes considered to be part of the Karamojong cluster of peoples. The Karamojong live across the border in northeastern Uganda, and the Turkana and Karamojong speak closely-related Nilotic languages. They also share a common ancestry, descending from Nilotes (q.v.) who originated several millennia ago on the southwestern fringe of the Ethiopian Highlands. The Turkana are Plains Nilotes, who emerged as a new and powerful force in East Africa during the second millennium CE.

Like many other Nilotic peoples, the Turkana have a history of pastoralism (livestock raising), and many are still herders today. The Turkana adapted to their arid environment and variable climate by herding a variety of animals and by moving frequently to find new pastures and water.

Turo

The Turo are one of the three main subgroups of the Konso (q.v.). The Konso live in southern Ethiopia.

Turu

The Turu are a Bantu (q.v.) of central Tanzania. There are more than 500,000 Turu people.

Tutsi see Hutu and Tutsi

Twa see Mbuti, Twa, and Mbenga

Twi

Twi is used to refer to the Akan (q.v.) language. The Asante (q.v.) Fante (q.v.) speak Twi languages.

Udok *see* **Uduk**

Uduk

The Uduk (or Udok) live mostly in eastern Sudan but also across the border in western Ethiopia. They number more than 10,000.

Umbundu *see* **Ovimbundu**

Unga

The Unga are a subgroup of the Bemba (q.v.) of Zambia. There are more than 20,000 Unga, mostly living near Lake Bangweulu in the northeast of Zambia.

Upila

The Upila are a subgroup of the Edo (q.v.). They number about 25,000 living in south-central Nigeria north of Benin City.

Urhobo

The Urhobo are closely related to the Edo (q.v.). The more than 600,000 Urhobo mostly live in southeastern Nigeria.

Usilele *see* **Lele**

Vai

The Vai (or Gallina, Vei, or Vey) are of Manding (q.v.) origin and are closely related to the Kono (q.v.). They can be found in Liberia, Guinea, and Sierra Leone. There are more than 150,000 Vai.

Vandau *see* **Ndau**

Vei *see* **Vai**

Venda

The Venda (or Vhavenda: "the People of Venda") live in the province of Transvaal in northeastern South Africa just south of the border with Zimbabwe. Their region is also known as Venda. The Venda comprise more than 520,000 people of various subgroups (Vhasenzi, Vhalemba, Vhatavhatsindi, and Vhangona, for example). Each subgroup has its own customs and further subdivisions, yet most share the same language and culture that distinguishes them from Southern Africa's other Bantu-speaking peoples.

History

The Venda migrated from East Africa's great lakes region to the north in several waves. The first arrivals, the Vhangona, reached the Limpopo River by the 1100s. A Venda group led by Thoho ya Ndou was the first to cross the Limpopo and enter the northern region

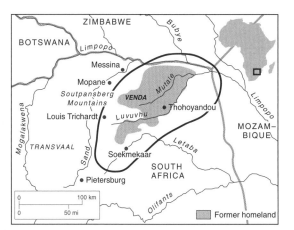

of present-day Transvaal, most likely in the 1600s. Large, powerful bows probably gave the Venda a military edge over the previous inhabitants and for a time they controlled much of eastern Southern Africa. Rivalries between Thoho ya Ndou's descendants lost the Venda their supremacy, however, and kept them divided into a number of chiefdoms. During a Swazi invasion in 1839, the decentralized structure of the state and its mountain refuges helped save the Venda from being wiped out. Later that century, though, they suffered from famines and wars of succession.

In the 1840s, Afrikaners established the Soutpansberg republic in Venda. At first it was basically a hunting settlement, employing Venda men to hunt for ivory but the Boers (Afrikaner farmers) established a large army to carry out slave-raids on Venda villages. The Venda rose in rebellion and by 1867 had ousted all the white settlers from their land. Gradually, however, Boer commandos isolated and defeated the Venda chiefdoms one by one. An onslaught in 1898 finally drove the remaining Venda north of the Limpopo River and the Venda lands were incorporated into the Boers' South African Republic (later, Transvaal).

RECENT EVENTS In 1910, the British colonies and the Boer republics were united as the white-minority ruled Union of South Africa. Racist policies increasingly began to be used to oppress the Venda, along with all other black South Africans, and the Venda were restricted to three small "native reserves." After the 1948 election, apartheid (the racist doctrine of "separate development") came into being In 1973, the government turned the reserves into a "self-governing" homeland, which was given "independence" in 1979.

Divining bowl
This ndilo (divining bowl) is made from wood, bone, and fiber and dates from the 1800s. It was used at the courts of Venda chiefs to identify witches. The images carved on the rim represent different Venda subgroups. If any of these was touched by a seed floating in the bowl, then it would indicate the presence of a witch in that group.

© DIAGRAM

Girl drumming

Many Venda girls are accomplished drummers. The python dance of the domba (female initiation society), for example, is accompanied by drumming performed by girls.

Venda potter

This Venda woman is fashioning a pot. Pieces of the pods of certain plants are used to shape and smooth the pots, which are then usually fired in a pit.

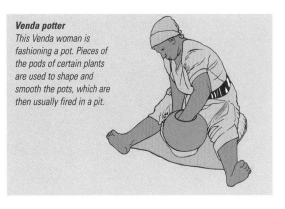

This independence was fictional, however, and never recognized outside of South Africa. After the end of white-minority rule in 1994, South Africa reabsorbed the homelands.

Language

The Venda language is Luvenda (or Tshivenda).

Ways of life

AGRICULTURE Most Venda inhabit the well-watered land between the Soutpansberg Mountains and the Letaba River to the southeast. A large tract north of the mountains is drier, more subject to drought, less fertile, and more sparsely peopled. The majority of the Venda live in sizable farming villages of stone or thatched homes surrounded by fences or walls and sited on hillsides. The region allocated to the Venda by the apartheid system was insufficient for the population and never received adequate investment. Consequently, cropland is in short supply and is shrinking further as the population rises, and soil erosion is a problem. The Venda chiefly grow crops to eat, yet most of their food has to be imported from other parts of South Africa. Dryland food crops include corn, millet, sorghum, and peanuts. On the region's much smaller area of irrigated land, people grow corn, wheat, sweet potatoes, beans, peas, vegetables, and citrus fruits. Cash crops include sisal (a fiber crop), tea, coffee, sugar cane, tobacco, and cotton. Nearly nine-tenths of the land is suitable only for grazing. The Venda raise a few cattle and also sheep, goats, and chickens.

INDUSTRY Lack of investment in Venda during the apartheid years has meant that the region has poor infrastructure and therefore few large industries. Also, businesses were previously encouraged to set up on the edge of homelands – in order to take advantage of the cheap labor force – but not inside. As a result, more than one in ten of the population commutes to work in mines and factories outside Venda. Nevertheless, there is some forestry and freshwater fish farming within

Matano figures

Made from clay or wood, matano figures are used to illustrate the stories and milayo (aphorisms) that are part of the teaching process of girls undergoing initiation. Until recently, mutano figures were kept at the chief's capital for use in the initiation schools. Today, these figures are more likely to be hired each time from the carver. These four figures were carved by Nelson Mukhuba and represent the four stages of a woman's life: childhood; graduation from domba (the female initiation society); marriage and motherhood; and old age.

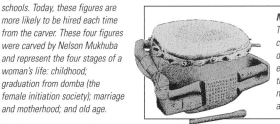

Ngoma drum

This ngoma drum is only used in the courts of Venda headmen. Ngoma drums are hemispherical and usually elaborately decorated. Legend holds that the first Venda leaders had a ngoma drum, the sound of which alone could defeat their enemies.

Venda. Mines yield some copper and graphite, and quarries produce sandstone. Various small-scale industries include ceramics, woodcrafts, and sawmilling.

Social structure

SOCIAL STRUCTURE The basic social unit consists of a husband (generally the head of the family), his wife or wives, and their children. Each extended family involves two sets of relationships, based on male and female lines of descent. The male line includes a father, his brothers and sisters, and his and his brothers' children. The female line includes a wife, her brothers and sisters, and her and her sisters' children. This female line is especially important on religious occasions. Lineages that share a common ancestor or ancestors are grouped into clans, whose members generally do not intermarry.

POLITICAL STRUCTURE Historically, large Venda chiefdoms ruled over, or strongly influenced, smaller ones. Within his area, each chief had the role of lawmaking and other powers, but certain officials and relatives played important roles too. A council advised him on royal village affairs such as ceremonies and public works. A private council of influential men advised him on local affairs, including items he planned to bring up at the next meeting of the council – a body that could freely criticize any of the chief's decisions.

Apartheid established a framework of so-called "traditional" chiefs to administer the Venda homeland. These chiefs were at first appointed by the government but provisions were later made for limited voting rights within the Venda homeland. This established a falsely traditional political structure as it was dependent not on Venda culture but the approval of the white-minority South African regime, even after the Venda were given their "independence" in 1979. Since the dismantlement of apartheid, the Venda can vote for representatives to the national government and the homeland government has been abolished.

Culture and religion

RELIGION The majority of Venda are Christians, yet traces of the Venda religion linger. The Venda believe witches are women unaware of their terrible influence, and they try to remove this by "good" magic or detecting the witches and driving them out. The Venda also consult diviners who try to foretell the future from the patterns produced by seeds and other ingredients placed in a bowl.

INITIATION At puberty, girls enter a vast building and undergo the six-day vhusha initiation process. This includes learning the evils of premarital sex and adultery. Later, they attend a school known as the domba to learn the duties expected of wives and mothers. The process can last from three months to a year. Its special features include the python dance, which is performed by a chain of chanting girls, each holding the forearms of the girl in front. For boys entering adulthood, murundu (a circumcision ceremony), has largely replaced older initiation rituals.

LITERATURE The Venda have a rich store of songs, poems, riddles, legends, and myths, which have all been passed on by mouth from one generation to the next.

Venda timeline

by 1100s
First Venda group, Vhangona, reach north of Limpopo River after migrating from great lakes region of East Africa

1600s
Venda led by Thoho ya Ndou cross Limpopo and arrive in present-day Transvaal

1819–1839
Mfecane/Difaqane: period of mass migrations and wars

1836–1848
Great Trek brings Boers into conflict with people inland

1840s
Boer republic of Soutpansberg established on Venda lands

1858–1864
Soutpansberg incorporated into Boer's Transvaal republic

1860–1867
Venda drive Boers out of their lands north of Olifants River

1898
Venda conquered by Transvaal

1910
British Natal and Cape colonies and Boer's Orange Free State and Transvaal republics unite to form

the white-minority ruled Union of South Africa

1913
Venda restricted to inadequate "native reserves"

1948
Apartheid officially begins

1973
Venda homeland created from "native reserves"

1979
Venda homeland given artificial "independence," which is not recognized outside of South Africa

1991
Apartheid legislation repealed

1994
First nonracial elections won by African National Congress (ANC) led by Nelson Mandela. Homelands are reabsorbed

1996
New constitution is adopted

1999
ANC wins huge majority in national elections

Python dance
For three months or more, Venda girls undergo a process of initiation called domba. A highlight of domba is the python dance, which is regularly performed by the initiates. The dance involves moving close together in a snakelike fashion.

Vey *see* Vai

Vhalemba

The Vhalemba are one of the many subgroups of the Venda (q.v.). The Venda live in the province of Transvaal in northeastern South Africa.

Vhangona

The Vhangona are one of the many subgroups of the Venda (q.v.). The Venda live in the province of Transvaal in northeastern South Africa.

Vhasenzi

The Vhasenzi are one of the many subgroups of the Venda (q.v.). The Venda live in the province of Transvaal in northeastern South Africa.

Vhatavhatsindi

The Vhatavhatsindi are one of the many subgroups of the Venda (q.v.). The Venda live in the province of Transvaal in northeastern South Africa.

Vhavenda *see* Venda

Vidunda

The Vidunda are part of the Zaramo (q.v.). They are a Bantu (q.v.) people and number more than 30,000. The majority live in the mountainous highlands of coastal Tanzania.

Vili

The Vili are a subgroup of the Kongo (q.v.). The majority live in southwestern Gabon and neighboring parts of Congo (Rep.).

Voltaic *see* Mole-Dagbane

Voutere *see* Bafou

Vute *see* Bafou

Vute

The Vute (or Mbute) are closely related to the Baya (q.v.) and Mbun (q.v.) peoples. They number around 35,000, the majority of whom live in Cameroon.

Wagadugu *see* Ouagadougou

Wagga *see* Waja

Waja

The Waja (or Wagga or Wuya) live in northeastern Nigeria, Niger, and northern Benin. There are about 30,000 Waja.

Wajunga

The Wajunga are a subgroup of the Dazaga (q.v.). They live to the east of the Tibesti Mountains in northwestern Chad.

Wala

The Wala are a Mole-Dagbane (q.v.) people. They number more than 120,000 people living largely in northern Ghana and Togo.

Walega

The Walega are one of the nine main subgroups of the Oromo (q.v.). They live in Ethiopia.

Walia *see* Massa

Wambulu *see* Iraqw

Wangara *see* Dyula

Wanjare

The Wanjare are one of the main subdivisions of the Gusii (q.v.). The Gusii are a large ethnic group of western Kenya.

Wanyamwezi *see* Nyamwezi

Wara

The Wara Wara (or Ouara) are part of the Senufo (q.v.). They are a small ethnic group living in southwestern Burkina Faso.

Warsha *see* Wassa

Wassa

The Wassa (or Warsha) are an Akan (q.v.) people. They live in western Ghana and eastern Ivory Coast. There are more than 200,000 Wassa.

Wassalunka *see* Ouassoulounke

Watyi

The Watyi are one of the main subdivisions of the Ewe (q.v.). They live in the southeast of Togo.

Wee *see* Guere

Welamo

The Welamo are an Omotic (q.v.) people of Ethiopia. There are more than 500,000 Welamo.

Western Saharans *see* Saharawis

Western Sotho *see* Tswana

Westerners *see* Anglophones of Cameroon

Widekum

The Widekum are a Bamileke (q.v.) people. They live in the western highlands of Cameroon and have a population of more than 200,000.

Wodaabe

The Wodaabe (or Bororo) are a Fulani (q.v.) people of West Africa. Sometimes referred to as the cattle Fulani (as opposed to the settled groups such as the Tukolor q.v.), the Wodaabe are a largely nomadic people who travel in the semidesert Sahel regions on the southern border of the Sahara Desert. Nomads travel with their herds of animals in search of water and fresh pasture. There are more than 100,000 Wodaabe, and they range over broad stretches of northern Nigeria and southern Niger. Their nomadic activities have been greatly restricted in recent years, however, by drought and government intervention. Huge numbers of cattle died, and many people were forced to sell their animals and migrate to urban areas or refugee camps to avoid starvation.

The Wodaabe men are famous for their concern with personal appearance. At certain festivals they paint their faces to accentuate their good features and wear elaborately embroidered clothing. Each woman then chooses the man she finds most attractive.

Wollo

The Wollo are one of the nine main subgroups of the Oromo. They live in Ethiopia.

Wolof

The Wolof (or Jalof, Djollof, or Yolof) figure among the largest ethnic groups in two West African countries, Senegal and Gambia, where they are concentrated in the northwest of the Senegambia region between the Senegal and Gambia rivers. There are well over two million Wolof, and their language (also called Wolof) is the lingua franca (common tongue) of Gambia and Senegal. The Wolof language is related to Serer (q.v.) and Fulfulde, which is spoken by the Fulani (q.v.).

Positioned with the Sahara desert to the north and the Atlantic to the west, the Wolof became powerful from involvement in both the Atlantic and Saharan trades. By the end of the fifteenth century, the Wolof Kingdom had become an empire with much of modern-day Senegal under its control. The empire was divided into five kingdoms: Djollof, which was inland, and Walo, Cayior, Baol, Sine, and Saloum on the coast. Each burba, or king, was elected, and sixteenth-century Portuguese travelers recorded that the Burba Djollof had a more than 100,000-strong army.

Wute see Bafou

Wuya see Waja

Xesibe

The Xesibe are a subgroup of the Xhosa (q.v.). They live in the northeastern corner of Transkei, which is on the eastern seaboard of South Africa.

Xhosa

The Xhosa live mostly in rural areas of southeastern South Africa. The overwhelming majority of the black population of Cape Town, Port Elizabeth, and East London are Xhosa and there are also very large Xhosa populations in the Johannesburg area. There are over six million Xhosa, who belong to a diversity of groups, the main ones being the Mpondo, Thembu, Hlubi, Ngqika, and Gcaleka. Together, they are sometimes referred to as Southern Nguni peoples.

History

The Xhosa are descended from Bantu-speaking peoples from present-day eastern Nigeria who arrived in Southern Africa around the 200s. The Xhosa are one of many ethnic groups who emerged from the Nguni Bantu-speaking peoples. They originally consisted of three main groups: the Mpondo, the Thembu, and the Xhosa. These groups share the same language and hold the belief that their cultures originate from the same source. Over the course of many centuries, internal friction, migration, and contact with the Khoisan-speaking peoples created subdivisions within the original Xhosa groups, which fragmented into numerous clans (extended families or several families who share a common ancestor or ancestors). Sons of chiefs established new chiefdoms of their own and this was the main way in which the Xhosa gradually expanded their territory. Eventually, they occupied an area along the eastern coast that reached roughly from the Groot-Vis River to present-day KwaZulu/Natal and spread inland to the Drakensberg Mountains. The various Xhosa groups remained linked through marriage and political and military alliances.

Between 1779 and 1878 there was a series of nine frontier wars – the Cape-Xhosa wars between the Xhosa and the Boers (Afrikaners) and British of the Cape Colony. In addition, in the early 1800s many Xhosa fled from the northeast of their territory (in what is now KwaZulu/Natal) to escape the armies of the great Zulu leader Shaka (q.v.). The Xhosa suffered their most traumatic blow in the "cattle-killings" of 1856–7. A young girl called Nongqawuse – said to be possessed by the spirits of the ancestors – had a vision that the white invaders would be swept into the sea, that great Xhosa chiefs would return from the dead, and the land would be filled with cattle and crops. For this to happen, Nongqawuse said, all existing cattle and food supplies must first be destroyed. Coming at a time of great conflict for the Xhosa, many people saw this as a way out of the turmoil. Despite the slaughter of 200,000 cattle, however, the prophecy was not fulfilled and only hunger, death, and poverty resulted. Survivors of this desperate act of resistance were compelled to seek work on the invaders' farms and the Xhosa were finally defeated in 1878.

RECENT EVENTS Under apartheid (the racist doctrine of "separate development"), the South African government created homelands for the country's black population. The Xhosa homelands of Ciskei and Transkei were later declared "independent" by the government, which then withdrew South African citizenship from all Xhosa. After South Africa's first nonracial elections in 1994, Ciskei and Transkei were reabsorbed into South Africa.

Pipe
This long pipe has been made using wood, thread, and glass and seed beads and has a metal bowl. Beadwork continues to be an important Xhosa craft though much of the output is produced for sale to tourists.

Map labels: BOTSWANA, Gaborone, Pretoria, Mafikeng, Johannesburg, Mbabane, Olifants, SWAZILAND, Harts, Vaal, KWAZULU/NATAL, NAMIBIA, Kimberley, Bloemfontein, Maseru, Durban, Orange, LESOTHO, Drakensberg, SOUTH AFRICA, Umtata, Great Kei, Umzimvubu, Groot-Vis, Bisho, East London, Cape Town, Port Elizabeth, Indian Ocean

0 100 200 300 km
0 100 200 mi

▨ Former homeland

Xhosa headdress
This woman has painted her face with ocher (a reddish-brown clay) and wears a headdress of a type often described as "traditional." In fact, fabric headdresses have only been worn since the arrival of mass-produced cloth. Fashion dictates the large size.

© DIAGRAM

Xhosa initiate
This boy's headdress of lamb's wool and feathers physically sets him apart from others and prepares him for his initiation into manhood. Initiation instills in Xhosa boys the values and moral views of their society.

Snuff box
Made from clay and hide scrapings mixed with blood, this snuff (powdered tobacco) box has symbolic protective qualities. This distinctive style of snuff container has historically been associated with the Xhosa people.

Language
The Xhosa language is Xhosa (or isiXhosa), which is one of the Bantu languages. Along with Zulu, it is one of the most widely spoken South African languages.

Ways of life
Until most of their land was taken by Europeans, the Xhosa were a cattle-raising people whose herds represented wealth and social stability. Although cattle continues to be important in rural areas, few Xhosa survive purely from the land (which tends to be of poor quality). Instead, most rural Xhosa rely on family members working in the cities to send money home.

Under apartheid, Black Africans were unable to live within city boundaries and instead were confined to government-built townships, usually located considerable distances from places of work and with their residency dependent on continuous employment. With the end of apartheid, there are no longer restrictions on where people may live, but living conditions remain fundamentally unchanged. In common with the black urban population as a whole, most Xhosa are employed in manufacturing industries, mining, and domestic service.

Social structure
POLITICAL STRUCTURE Historically, the Xhosa's allegiance was to their clan, led by an inkosi (chief) whose status was gained through his mother. Inkosi were obliged to be hospitable and generous – "inkosi" actually means "thank-you" – and their powers were limited by public opinion and counselors. Within the homelands, so-called "traditional" forms of government were encouraged by the South African government. In fact, these so-called "traditional" forms of government were not like the Xhosa's own system of government since they had none of the power balances the Xhosa's own system incorporated. The use of ethnicity and "tradition" in this way during apartheid has led many to regard them as inappropriate – President Nelson Mandela (q.v., a Thembu), for instance, states that he is

not a "tribalist" but a South African. After the homelands were reincorporated into South Africa, in 1994, their governments were abolished and replaced by national government structures.

SOCIAL STRUCTURE During the course of the early twentieth century, an urban elite developed that became increasingly distanced socially and culturally from the rural Xhosa. The urban Xhosa were commonly called "School" Xhosa and the rural "Red" Xhosa – named for the fashion of using red ocher (a yellow or reddish-brown clay) as a body decoration. The conservative Red Xhosa kept Xhosa beliefs and traditions while the School Xhosa adopted new customs and Christianity. Despite considerable changes in rural areas in recent decades and rural-urban migration, these divisions remain, though they are now less marked.

MARRIAGE Although the majority of Xhosa are Christians, many still retain certain Xhosa customs concerned with marriage. Lobola (or bridewealth – gifts given by the groom's family to the bride's family) is still given even by Christians. The function of lobola is to legitimize the marriage and any children born to the couple.

Culture and religion
RELIGION The sufferings that followed the cattle-killings of the mid-nineteenth century caused many Xhosa to lose faith in the power of their own beliefs and turn to Christianity, which is now the Xhosa's main religion.

LITERATURE The Xhosa have a long history of literature. Earlier forms are mostly oral and include praise poems, folk tales, and prophecies – many of which have now been written down. This tradition has continued into the present and there are several important Xhosa writers, such as the novelist and playwright John Knox Bokwe and the novelist Sinxo.

Mother and child
This Xhosa woman is grinding grain while her baby sleeps on her back.

Xhosa timeline		
200s Bantu-speaking peoples begin to arrive in Southern Africa	**1834–1835** Cape-Xhosa War VI: British annex Xhosa lands	**1913** Xhosa restricted to inadequate "native reserves"
300s–400s Bantu-speakers reach present-day KwaZulu/Natal	**1836** British return Xhosa lands	**1948** Apartheid in South Africa
1799–1803 Cape-Xhosa wars I, II, and III: Xhosa-Boer frontier wars	**1846–1847** Cape-Xhosa War VII: British annex Xhosa lands as far east as Great Kei River	**after 1959** Transkei and Ciskei Xhosa homelands created
1811–1812 Cape-Xhosa War IV: British drive many Xhosa east of Groot-Vis River	**1850–1853** Cape-Xhosa War VIII: Xhosa rebel against British	**1976** Transkei "independent"
1818–1819 Cape-Xhosa War V: British drive remaining Xhosa east of Groot-Vis River	**1856–1857** Xhosa sacrifice 200,000 cattle in accordance with prophecy	**1981** Ciskei "independent"
1819–1839 Mfecane/Difaqane: period of mass migrations and wars	**1877–1878** Cape-Xhosa War IX: final defeat of Xhosa by British	**1991** Apartheid legislation repealed
	1910 British and Boers form white-ruled Union of South Africa	**1994** First nonracial elections
		1996 New constitution is adopted
		1999 The ANC win the second multiracial elections

Xhosa homesteads
Built on higher ground to keep fertile lowlands free for farming, these Xhosa homesteads have lime-washed walls. Xhosa homes in remote rural areas tend to be strung out along ridges rather than concentrated in villages.

Xhu *see* **Kung**

Yacouba *see* **Dan**

Yaka of Minikongo *see* **Suku**

Yakö *see* **Yakurr**

Yakurr

The Yakurr, or Yakö, live in the so-called Cross River region of southeastern Nigeria, northeast of the Niger Delta. The Yakurr territory lies roughly 60 miles inland from Calabar on the coast. The biggest town in the region is Obubra, which lies on the Cross River. The Yakurr speak a language called Kö, which is a Bantu (q.v.) language.

There are probably less than 50,000 Yakurr in Nigeria. The land they inhabit was once densely forested, and although a lot of this forest remains, large areas have been cut down to provide land for farming and firewood.

Yakurr oral history states that fairly recently, perhaps as late as the early nineteenth century, they migrated north into their present lands from the Oban Hills to the southeast, just north of Calabar. They established five main towns in the region of considerable size. The Yakurr are not truly urbanized, however, as the majority are farmers.

Fetish figure
This statue would have had powerful properties for the Yaka.

Yalunka

The Yalunka are a Manding (q.v.) people. The more than 100,000 Yalunka live in northeastern Sierra Leone and across the border in Guinea.

Yamarico

The Yamarico are one of the two main Sadama (q.v.) subgroups. The Sadama live in Ethiopia.

Yao

The Yao are a large ethnic group of East and Central Africa. Numbering more than one million, Yao people can be found in Malawi, Tanzania, and Mozambique. They are not to be confused with another group also called Yao (or Pila-Pila) who live in Benin, West Africa. The Makua (q.v.) of Tanzania and Mozambique are closely related to the Yao, with whom they are sometimes grouped as part of the larger Yao cluster of peoples.

The Yao are a Bantu (q.v.) people, whose ancestors originated from the Niger-Congo region of West-Central Africa more than 2000 years ago. The Malawian Yao population dates from the 1850s, when groups of Yao people from the north of present-day Mozambique began migrating into the region. One group, the Amchinga, settled at the southeastern corner of Lake Malawi in the 1860s. During the 1870s, Makanjila founded a powerful Yao kingdom in the area. Other, smaller kingdoms (or chiefdoms) were established by other Yao leaders. The Yao states were important in East African trade between the coast and interior, dominating the trade in slaves and ivory around the Lake Malawi region. During this era the Yao came under the cultural influence of the Swahili (q.v.) people, adopting the Muslim religion, learning Arabic, and wearing Arabic clothes.

Yao dancers
The Yao gained economically from the ivory and slave trades but have since been influenced by Swahili culture.

Yarse

The Yarse are one of the many separate ethnic groups that make up the Mossi (q.v.). The Mossi live in Burkina Faso.

Yatenga

The Yatenga are a Mole-Dagbane (q.v.) people. They live in northwestern Burkina Faso and neighboring parts of Mali. Tere are more than 800,000 Yatenga.

Yedina *see* **Buduma**

Yergam *see* **Yergan**

Yergan

The Yergan (or Yergam) are a Bantu (q.v.) people of Nigeria. With a population of around 140,000, the Yergan live in central Nigeria's Plateau State.

Yerwa *see* **Kanuri**

Yimbe *see* **Limba**

Yolof *see* **Wolof**

Yombe

The Yombe are a subgroup of the Kongo (q.v.). Their homelands are the Yombe Mountain region of Congo (Rep.). There are more than 30,000 Yombe.

Yoruba

The Yoruba mainly live in the southwest of Nigeria, in eastern Benin, and in parts of Togo. There are approximately twelve million Yoruba.

History

Through their myths, the Yoruba believe that they have lived in their present homeland for thousands of years. The kingdom of Ife is accepted as the birthplace of the Yoruba as a separate people. The town of Ife is considered to be the Yoruba spiritual capital, perhaps having emerged in the seventh or eighth century. The Yoruba's traditional ruling families are able to trace their ancestors back to the twelfth century.

From Ife new Yoruba kingdoms were later established, the most powerful being Oyo in the grasslands to the north. Oyo grew into a great empire, controlling the trade routes linking the sea with the north. In the eighteenth century, the Oyo Empire was torn apart by civil war, collapsing completely in the 1830s. After the demise of Oyo, Ibadan became the most powerful Yoruba town, eventually controlling a large empire. European slave traders benefited from Yoruba divisions, with rival kings capturing and selling large numbers of their enemies into slavery for transportation to the Americas. Even today clear elements of Yoruba culture survive in the Americas, in particular in Brazil.

COLONIALISM As the nineteenth century progressed, more and more British traders, missionaries, soldiers, and government officials entered Yoruba territory, making agreements with local kings or forcefully stripping power from those who resisted, often destroying and looting their towns. By 1897, the British had established control over the Yoruba and the region was incorporated into the protectorate (colony) of Southern Nigeria in 1900.

RECENT EVENTS The Yoruba played an important role in Nigeria's gaining independence in 1960; since then they have continued to be of major importance in political life.

Language

In the past, the Yoruba spoke a number of dialects of Kwa, a branch of the Niger-Congo family of languages. Over the past hundred years, however, a common version of their language has developed called Yoruba. There is a rich heritage of literature and poetry written in Yoruba; the playwright Duro Lapido is one example of a well-known writer in the Yoruba language.

Ways of life

Town kingdoms Although an agricultural people, the Yoruba have always lived in towns – Ibadan was the largest city south of the Sahara in precolonial Africa. In a typical Yoruba town the majorty are farmers and a few are artisans or traders. Farms can be up to 20 miles (8 km) from town and produce a wide range of crops including yams, cassava, and cocoa.

Historically, Yoruba towns were enclosed by a high

Clothing
This Yoruba woman from Nigeria ia wearing a brightly colored outfit made from a combination of locally produced cloth and imported waxed cotton.

Door panel
Intricately carved with tiny figures, this door panel is in the Nigerian Museum in Lagos.

Gelede dancer
Once intended to appease local witches, gelede dances are still held at regular intervals, but now largely to entertain. The Yoruba have many masquerades, which involve elaborately costumed characters such as this one.

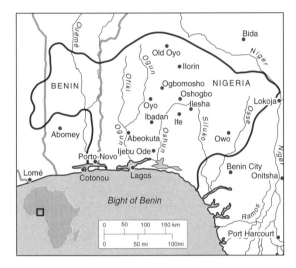

wall with the palace of the oba (king) marking the central point. In front of the palace was the central market and around the palace were grouped the interconnecting courtyards, houses, and rooms that formed the compounds where other families lived. The compounds could be huge, often housing more than a thousand people. In modern times, compounds have largely been replaced by two-story houses, and many oba have built luxurious palaces.

Social structure

POLITICAL STRUCTURE The position of oba is held by a descendant of the town's founder, passing in turn to princes from several ruling houses. Decision-making powers, however, were held by a council of chiefs, made up of representatives of the town's families. Chiefs would meet every day in a palace courtyard, sending their decisions to the oba for formal approval. This form of government made it possible to unite the people of each town together. This system, however, meant that it was extremely difficult to unite with neighboring towns making resistance to colonial rule difficult.

Culture and religion

POLITICAL Today, over half of the Yoruba are Muslim or Christian. Even so, the Yoruba religion remains important to Yoruba life and culture, although some of the

Obas
In the past, much ceremony surrounded obas (kings), who spent most of their time hidden from view. They appeared in public only at important events and even then surrounded by attendants and totally veiled by a crown and robe made of thousands of coral beads.

purest forms are found not in Nigeria but amongst the descendants of former Yoruba slaves living in Brazil. Yoruba religion centres on a supreme god, Olodumare (the owner of Heaven), but few temples or shrines are erected in his honor. This is because he is considered detached from everyday life so lesser deities are more likely to be approached to deal with specific situations. These deities or spirits can act as intermediaries between Olodumare and his followers; called orisa, they concern themselves with the affairs of the Earth. Each orisa has its own cult, priests, temples, and shrines. Orisa have two roles, to protect and provide for the individual cult member and to provide a particular service to all members of the community. There are hundreds of orisa, some considered more important than others. Obatala is the most important of the orisa as the chief representative of Olodumare on Earth. Obatala was taught to create the human form into which Olodumare then put life. Esu is the messenger of good and evil and the main link between Heaven and Earth. Esu, often described as the "trickster god," tells Olodumare of the activities of the other orisa and of people. Sango is associated with thunderstorms and the anger of Olodumare. Yemoja is a female orisa, associated with water, rivers, lakes, and streams. Olokun is an orisa who lives in the sea, controlling its anger and sharing its riches. Over time, orisas can acquire new associations. For example, Ogun, the god associated with iron and other metals and metalwork,

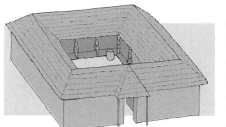

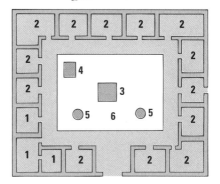

is often shown respect by taxi drivers, who have singled him out for to provide protection while they drive their vehicles – as cars are made from metal.

Respect for ancestors forms a major part of the Yoruba religion. Dances and dramas are performed to praise the dead and promote the well-being of the community.

Yoruba compound

Extended families live together in compounds, which comprise several buildings surrounding one or more courtyards. In the past, common construction materials were mud for the thick walls, wood for beams and posts, and straw and palm leaves for the thatched roofs, which together helped to keep the buildings cool. Today, however, concrete and metal sheeting are more often used in building.

1 Rooms for the head of the compound.
2 Isolated rooms for the wives or for the family's married male children and their wives.
3 Shrine
4 Storehouse
5 Dye pit
6 Courtyard

Sango staff
Yoruba religion and art are closely intertwined. During a festival, a Sango priest would probably rest this beautiful wooden staff on his shoulder.

Sango shrine figure
Recognizable for the double ax-head shape at the top, carvings such as this one would appear on an altar devoted to the orisa (god) Sango. Associated with thunder, storms, and rain, Sango priests are sometimes approached to act as rainmakers.

Yoruba timeline

600s on Emergence of Ife Kingdom	**1862** Ibadan Empire established in Nigeria and becomes most powerful in region	**1967–1970** Biafran (Nigerian Civil) War between Yoruba and northern Nigerians against eastern (mainly Igbo) secessionists	Lagos to Abuja **1993** In Nigeria, transition from military rule to democratic rule ends when General Sanni Abacha declares himself ruler
1300s Bronze and terra-cotta sculpture produced in Ife. Oyo state founded	**1897** British conquest of Yorubaland completed	**1970s–1980s** Series of failed civilian governments and military coups in Nigeria	**1999** Nigeria returns to civilian rule with Olesegun Obasanjo, a Yoruba, as president
1510 Start of Atlantic slave trade	**1950s** Discovery of pertroleum desposits in Nigeria	**1974** Oil boom in Nigeria	
1789 Oyo Empire reaches greatest extent	**1960** Nigeria wins independence	**1975** Capital of Nigeria transferred from	
1836 Oyo dominated by Sokoto Caliphate: Oyo dissolves			

Zaghawa

The Zaghawa are the largest subgroup of the Beri (q.v.). They live in Chad and Sudan.

Zande *see* **Azande**

Zaramo

The Zaramo occupy a 100-mile-wide "strip" of Tanzanian coastline centered around Tanzania's biggest city, Dar es Salaam. This strip extends from Kisiju, roughly 50 miles south of Dar es Salaam, to Bagamoyo, roughly 50 miles north of Dar es Salaam. The Zaramo language is called Kizaramo, and most also speak Swahili (q.v.), East Africa's common language.

More than 200 years ago, the Zaramo migrated into their present lands. They share a common ancestry with the Luguru of the Uluguru Mountains

about 125 miles west of Dar es Salaam. The name Luguru simply means "people of the mountains," and when these people migrated eastwards, they developed into new ethnic groups. Kizarama and the Luguru language have only slight differences.

Today, the majority of Zaramo are Muslims, but as recently as 100 years ago they were worshiping a god called Kolelo. The Zaramo traveled west to pray to Kolelo at a cave in the Uluguru Mountains.

Throwing knife
These knives were a common feature of tribal conflict. This one was made by the Zaghawa in Darfur.

Zarma *see* **Zerma**

Zerma

After the Hausa, the Zerma (or Zarma or Djerma) are the largest ethnic group in Niger. They are closely related to the Songhay people of Niger and Mali, and the two groups speak different dialects of the Songhay language. Although Songhay has been classified as a Nilo-Saharan language, it is not obviously related to any other known language. Together the Zerma and Songhay account for around 20 percent of Niger's population, with the Zerma numbering more than one 800,000.

The Zerma are spread across a region in western Niger that is bordered by the Niger River in the east and extends west to a seasonally dry river, the Dallol Maouri, in the east. Many Zerma can be found living in the large towns of western Niger such as the capital, Niamey. The Zerma are thought to have originated from the swampy inland delta of the Niger River, near Lake Debo in modern-day Mali. They were part of western Songhay – the medieval empire founded by the Songhay people in c. 750 on the Niger River, an important trade route. The Zerma began migrating southward in the fifteenth century, reaching their present lands in the seventeenth and eighteenth centuries.

Zezuru

The Zezuru are a Shona (q.v.) subgroup. They make up one-quarter of the Shona population in Zimbabwe. They are also known as the Central Shona.

Zhu *see* Kung

Zhutwasi *see* Kung

Ziba *see* Haya

Zigalu

The Zigalu are part of the Zaramo (q.v.). They are a Bantu (q.v.) people living in Tanzania's coastal lowlands.

Zombo

The Zombo are a subgroup of the Kongo (q.v.).They live in Angola and Congo (Dem. Rep.).

Zulu

There are about seven million Zulu, most of whom live in the province of KwaZulu/Natal on the east coast of South Africa. The Zulu emerged from the Nguni group of Bantu-speaking peoples and have close cultural and linguistic links with other Nguni peoples such as the Xhosa and the Swazi. "Zulu" originally referred to the people descended from a man of the same name, but it came to refer to a much broader population after the Mfecane/Difaqane.

History

Mfecane/Difaqane Before 1816, the Zulu chiefdoms belonged to the Mthethwa kingdom, which was ruled by Dingiswayo (q.v.). When Dingiswayo died, his Zulu general Shaka (q.v.) took over. With military skill and ruthlessness, Shaka founded the Zulu kingdom and launched the Mfecane – a series of wars and migrations triggered by the rapid expansion of the Zulu nation. This wave of conflict, which lasted from 1819 to 1839, left an estimated five million people dead and made the region vulnerable to takeover by white settlers.

After 1836, the Zulu came into conflict with the growing number of white settlers, first the Afrikaners, or Boers, and later the British. In 1879 at Isandhlwana, a massive onslaught of Zulu warriors defeated the British, who retaliated later that year and defeated the 40,000-strong Zulu army led by Cetshwayo at Ulundi. **RECENT EVENTS** In the twentieth century, the Zulu's lives have been dominated by the South African policy of apartheid (the racist doctrine of "separate development"), which discriminated against black people in every area of life.

A homeland, consisting of only a portion of the orig-inal Zululand, was set up for the Zulu in the 1970s. This homeland, called KwaZulu, was in the region of the modern KwaZulu/Natal province of South Africa. Following the end of apartheid in the early 1990s, the Zulu have become a powerful political force. Their Inkatha Freedom Party (IFP), led by Chief Mangosuthu Gatsha Buthelezi (q.v.), has claimed that the ruling African National Congress (ANC) does not represent their interests, and there have been many violent clashes between Inkatha and ANC supporters.

Language

The Zulu language is also called Zulu (or isiZulu). Zulu has some 19,000 words and one of the most complex grammars in the world. Many Dutch and English words have been incorporated into Zulu.

Embedded-wire art
Barely 3 in. (7.5 cm) in diameter, this snuff (powdered tobacco) container has been crafted using wire embedded into a gourd to form geometric patterns. This technique has transformed the container from a purely practical object into one of great appeal.

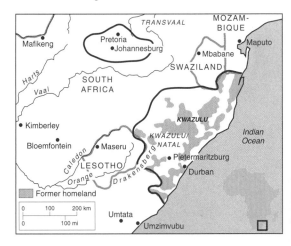

Ways of life

AGRICULTURE Although many men have left Zululand to work as laborers in South Africa's mines and industries, farming is still the backbone of the Zulu economy. The soil is generally poor and suffers from increasing erosion, in spite of this the Zulu are able to grow crops such as millet, corn, sweet potatoes, and vegetables and to raise cattle, sheep, and goats.

INDUSTRY Like many other peoples of Southern Africa, the Zulu have a long tradition of metalworking and use their skills to manufacture axes, hoes, spears, and other tools and weapons. Their ceramics are all well-made, simple, and practical and have few decorative additions. Many Zulu are skilled woodworkers and makers of baskets and beadwork artifacts.

Social structure

The Zulu have a complex social organization that has survived the pressures of modern life relatively intact. It is based on the imzi, or homestead, a group of circular thatched houses (or, increasingly, brick-built houses) enclosed by a fence. A number of imzi, spaced at intervals of half a mile to a mile apart, make up a ward, or village. Each imzi is occupied by an elder or imzi head and his extended family, and the other imzi in the ward are usually occupied by related families.

From ward level, the social structure extends upward through district head and clan chief levels to the ultimate head of the Zulu nation, the king. The present king is Zwelethini Goodwill Ka-Cyprian Bhekezulu. The position of the king is one of solely cultural and social importance, however, as the Zulu are governed by the Republic of South Africa.

MARRIAGE A man may have more than one wife, but no marriage is considered legitimate until the husband has given lobola (or bridewealth), usually a gift of cattle, to the bride's family to compensate them for their loss. Marriage between members of the same clan (several families who share descent from a common ancestor or ancestors) is discouraged.

Culture and religion

RELIGION Christianity is widespread among the Zulu. There are many independent churches with Zulu clergy as well as Anglican and Catholic churches. Zionist Spirit churches that stress faith healing are also popular. During the apartheid era, people were denied a political voice and this, in part, explains the vibrancy of many churches as they often provided the only forum for people to air their complaints. Christianity coexists with the Zulu religion, which is still widely followed. The Zulu religion is mostly concerned with the reverence of ancestors. Ancestors are believed to directly influence their living descendants so respect must be shown to them. Healing methods as practiced by religious practitioners of the Zulu religion (diviners, or sangomas, for example) also survive, alongside modern clinics and hospitals, and are used to alleviate diseases thought to arise from defective personal relationships or from supernatural causes. Many of these healers work within the official healthcare system at the local level.

Figurines
These two figurines are probably Zulu as they are sporting typically Zulu (if old-fashioned) hairstyles: the man (right) a headring and the woman (left) a circular tuft of hair.

Zulu homestead
In the past, Zulu homes comprised two concentric fences, with houses in the outer ring and cattle and goods in the inner one. Brick is now preferred and land is in too short supply to build such extensive homesteads. Although a few such villages have been preserved (or created) for tourists to see, they have been compared to human zoos.

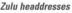

Battle formation
As founder of the Zulu kingdom, Shaka devised an ingenious battle formation that helped the Zulus gain military supremacy. It involved four battalions of warriors: the central group would attack the enemy; the side battalions would encircle the enemy; and the last group were the reserves. The warriors would be lined up with their shields touching their neighbors.

Zulu headrest
In the past, Zulu headrests were carved from a single piece of wood. They all had concave strips on top, supported by blocks or feet. Headrests could also be used as stools.

Zulu headdresses
Zulu women are famous for their beadwork, which has become an art-form in itself, as the elaborate headdress on the right shows. Beads were once made from bone, ivory, clay, shells, wood, or iron. Today, however, the tiny colorful beads are mass produced in plastic, allowing women to spend more time on design than bead production.

Zulu weapons
Most of these highly-effective weapons were developed during Shaka's reign and they ensured Zulu supremacy in battle.

1 A shield made from wood and animal skin.
2 An iron-bladed throwing spear.
3 A hardwood knobkerrie (or iwisa) sometimes thrown as a weapon.

© DIAGRAM

Zulu timeline			
200s Bantu-speaking peoples begin to arrive in Southern Africa	**1828** Shaka assassinated, Dingane succeeds him as Zulu leader	**1885–1887** Zululand divided between British Zululand and Transvaal	**1970s** KwaZulu homeland created
300s–400s Bantu-speakers reach present-day Kwazulu/Natal	**1838** Zulu defeated by Boers at the Battle of Blood River	**1910** White-minority ruled Union of South Africa created	**1975** Inkatha reconvened
1787 Birth of Shaka	**1840** After defeating Dingane, Mpande becomes Zulu leader	**1913** Zulu restricted to inadequate "native reserves"	**1980s–1990s** Fighting between Inkatha and ANC supporters
1816 Shaka becomes Zulu leader	**1872** Cetshwayo becomes Zulu king	**1920** Zululand joined to South Africa	**1991** Apartheid legislation repealed
1818–1819 Zulu-Ndwandwe War establishes Zulu supremacy	**1879** British conquer Zulu	**1928** Inkatha, Zulu nationalist movement, founded	**1994** First nonracial elections
1819–1839 Mfecane/Difaqane: period of mass migrations and wars	**1883–1884** Zulu Civil War after British partition Zululand	**1948** Apartheid in South Africa	**1999** ANC wins large majority in South African elections; the Inkatha Freedom Party comes third with 8% of the vote

SECTION 2

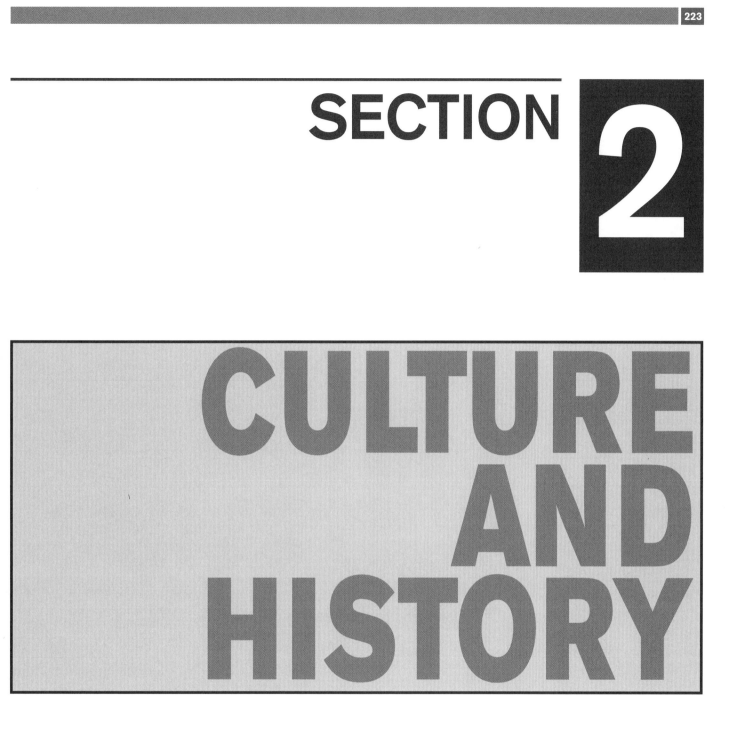

CULTURE AND HISTORY

Pictorial history of North Africa

Key

————— Trade route

Tangier Modern town or city

1 This twelfth-century picture depicts a Moorish naval invasion of Spain. Between the 700s and the 1200s, Muslims from North Africa invaded and conquered southern Spain, where they were known as the "Moors."

2 The Great Synagogue of Tunis, which was built six hundred years ago. Until the mid-twentieth century, many Jewish people lived in North Africa.

3 An eighteenth-century North African Sufi lodge, which would have housed students, guests, and pilgrims. Sufi lodges such as this one were active in spreading Islam throughout North Africa, in particular during the 1700s and 1800s.

4 A camel caravan (company of travelers) crossing the Sahara Desert. Ever since camels were introduced to North Africa about 2,000 years ago, caravans of pack-carrying animals have crisscrossed the desert along well-worn routes.

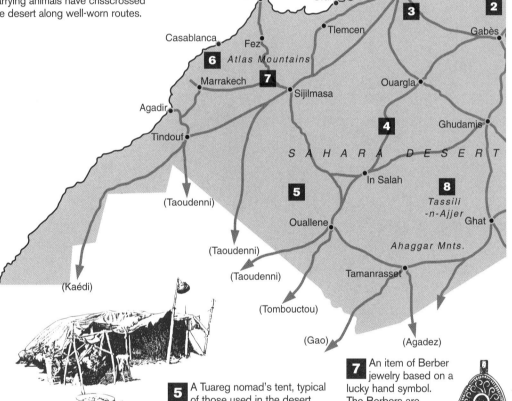

5 A Tuareg nomad's tent, typical of those used in the desert and semidesert regions. In the 1900s, colonial and government policies, war, civil strife, and increasingly frequent droughts have all combined to threaten the nomadic way of life.

6 A gravestone of an Arab sultan of Morocco dating from the thirteenth century. In 640, Arabs first invaded North Africa from Arabia in southwest Asia; by 711 they had conquered the whole region. The Arabs brought with them their religion, Islam, and their language, Arabic, which now dominate North African culture.

7 An item of Berber jewelry based on a lucky hand symbol. The Berbers are the earliest known inhabitants of North Africa; they were settled on the Mediterranean coast by 3000 BCE.

8 Paintings on the rocks of Tassili-n-Ajjer, Algeria, depict life in the Sahara thousands of years ago, when the desert had rivers, lakes, and a wealth of plant and animal life.

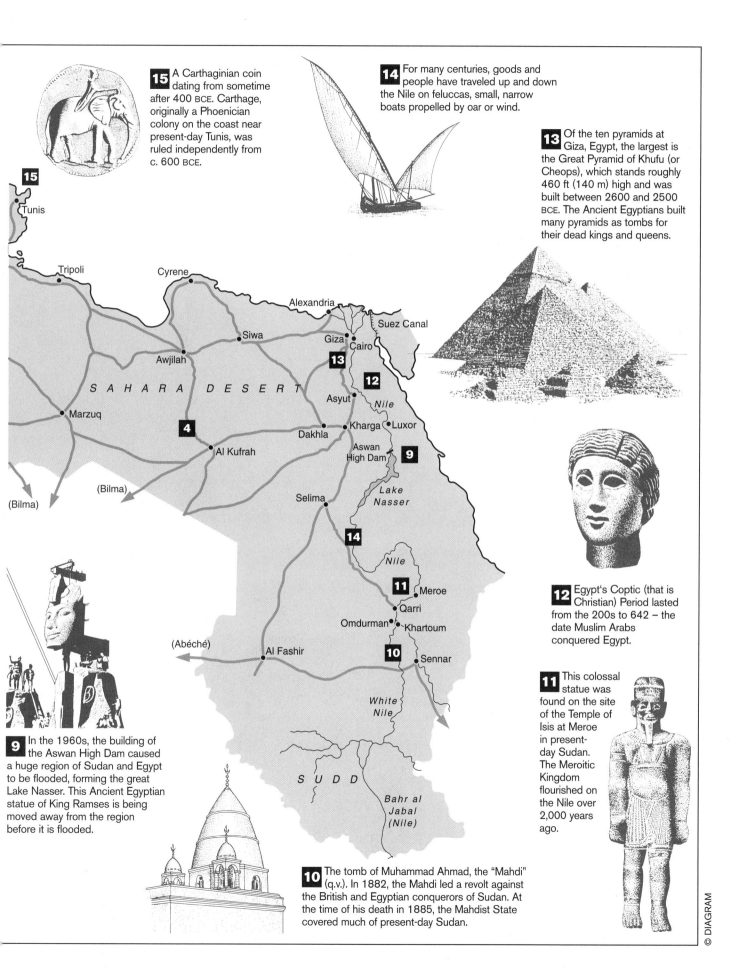

15 A Carthaginian coin dating from sometime after 400 BCE. Carthage, originally a Phoenician colony on the coast near present-day Tunis, was ruled independently from c. 600 BCE.

14 For many centuries, goods and people have traveled up and down the Nile on feluccas, small, narrow boats propelled by oar or wind.

13 Of the ten pyramids at Giza, Egypt, the largest is the Great Pyramid of Khufu (or Cheops), which stands roughly 460 ft (140 m) high and was built between 2600 and 2500 BCE. The Ancient Egyptians built many pyramids as tombs for their dead kings and queens.

12 Egypt's Coptic (that is Christian) Period lasted from the 200s to 642 – the date Muslim Arabs conquered Egypt.

11 This colossal statue was found on the site of the Temple of Isis at Meroe in present-day Sudan. The Meroitic Kingdom flourished on the Nile over 2,000 years ago.

9 In the 1960s, the building of the Aswan High Dam caused a huge region of Sudan and Egypt to be flooded, forming the great Lake Nasser. This Ancient Egyptian statue of King Ramses is being moved away from the region before it is flooded.

10 The tomb of Muhammad Ahmad, the "Mahdi" (q.v.). In 1882, the Mahdi led a revolt against the British and Egyptian conquerors of Sudan. At the time of his death in 1885, the Mahdist State covered much of present-day Sudan.

Tunis
Tripoli
Cyrene
Alexandria
Siwa
Suez Canal
Giza
Cairo
Awjilah
SAHARA DESERT
Asyut
Nile
Marzuq
Kharga Luxor
Dakhla
Al Kufrah
Aswan High Dam
(Bilma)
(Bilma)
(Bilma)
Selima
Lake Nasser
Nile
Meroe
Qarri
Omdurman Khartoum
(Abéché)
Al Fashir
Sennar
White Nile
SUDD
Bahr al Jabal (Nile)

© DIAGRAM

Distribution of major Northern peoples

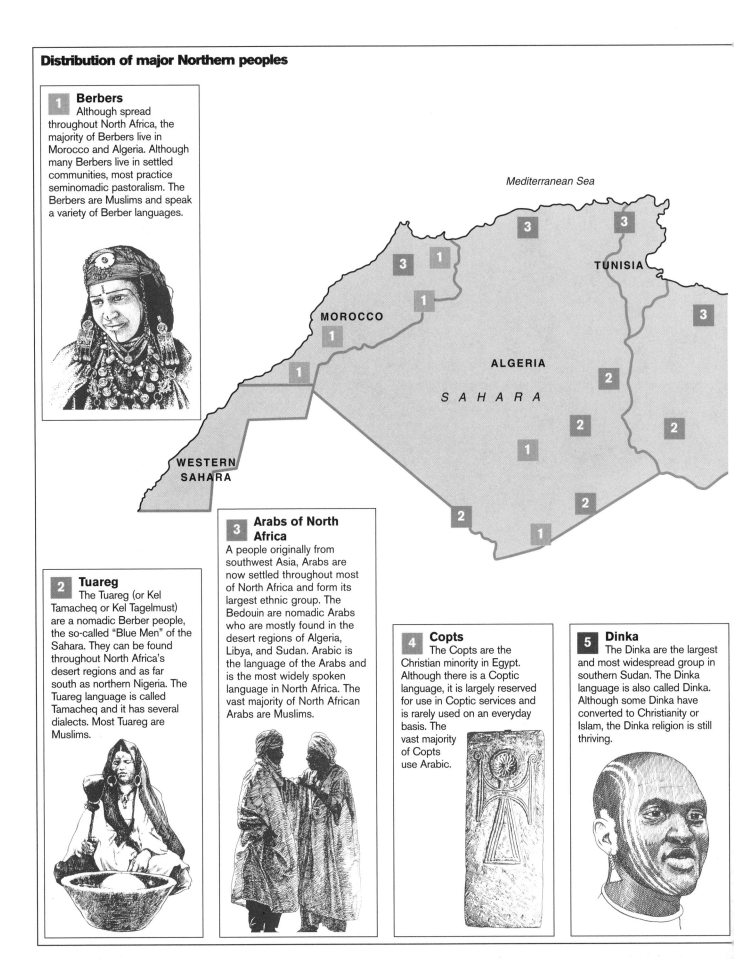

1 Berbers
Although spread throughout North Africa, the majority of Berbers live in Morocco and Algeria. Although many Berbers live in settled communities, most practice seminomadic pastoralism. The Berbers are Muslims and speak a variety of Berber languages.

Mediterranean Sea

TUNISIA

MOROCCO

ALGERIA

S A H A R A

WESTERN SAHARA

3 Arabs of North Africa
A people originally from southwest Asia, Arabs are now settled throughout most of North Africa and form its largest ethnic group. The Bedouin are nomadic Arabs who are mostly found in the desert regions of Algeria, Libya, and Sudan. Arabic is the language of the Arabs and is the most widely spoken language in North Africa. The vast majority of North African Arabs are Muslims.

2 Tuareg
The Tuareg (or Kel Tamacheq or Kel Tagelmust) are a nomadic Berber people, the so-called "Blue Men" of the Sahara. They can be found throughout North Africa's desert regions and as far south as northern Nigeria. The Tuareg language is called Tamacheq and it has several dialects. Most Tuareg are Muslims.

4 Copts
The Copts are the Christian minority in Egypt. Although there is a Coptic language, it is largely reserved for use in Coptic services and is rarely used on an everyday basis. The vast majority of Copts use Arabic.

5 Dinka
The Dinka are the largest and most widespread group in southern Sudan. The Dinka language is also called Dinka. Although some Dinka have converted to Christianity or Islam, the Dinka religion is still thriving.

10 Beja

The Beja are groups of people who live in northeastern Sudan and Eritrea. Some Beja groups practice nomadic pastoralism, while others live in settled communities. At one time Christian, most Beja people are now Muslims. The Beja language is also called Beja, but many Beja people speak either Arabic or Tigrinya, depending on where they live.

9 Shilluk

The Shilluk live along the banks of the White Nile River in southern Sudan. Most Shilluk people follow the Shilluk religion. The Shilluk language is also called Shilluk.

8 Nuba

The Nuba live in the Nuba Hills of southern Sudan. The Nuba speak a variety of Kordofanian languages. Although a minority of Nuba have converted to Islam or Christianity, the majority follow the Nuba religion.

7 Nuer

The Nuer live in southern Sudan. Most Nuer people follow the Nuer religion and speak the Nuer language, which is also called Nuer. The Nuer are closely related to the Dinka.

6 Baggara

The Baggara (or Baqqara) are a largely nomadic people who live in western and central Sudan. The Baggara are descended from Bedouin Arabs and Black Africans. The majority of Baggara are Muslims and most use the Arabic language.

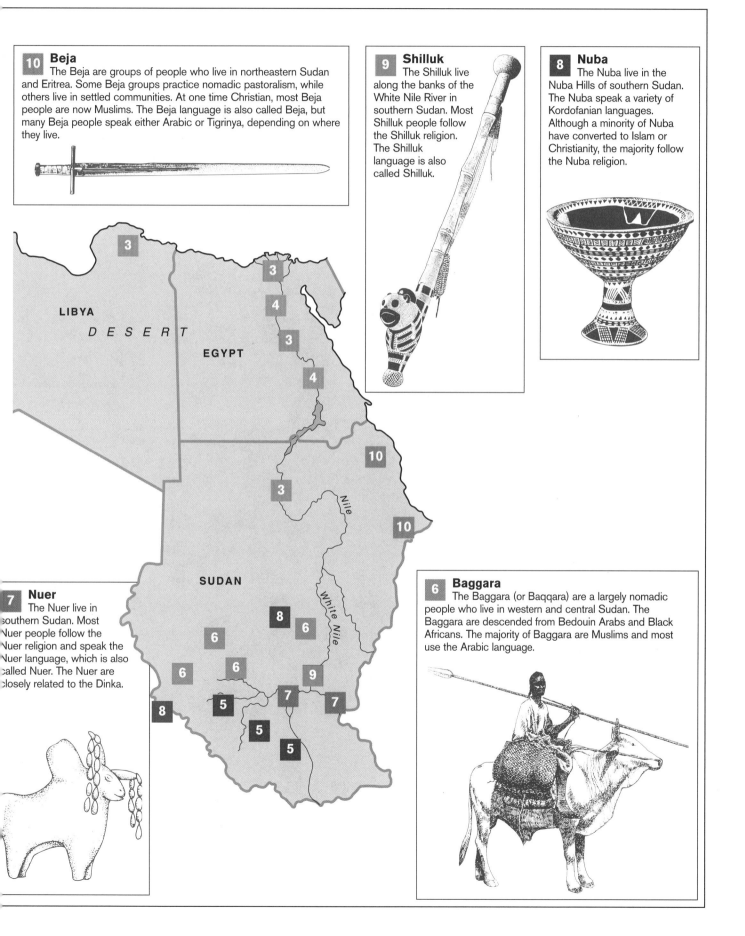

LIBYA

DESERT

EGYPT

SUDAN

Nile

White Nile

Pictorial history of East Africa

1 A nineteenth-century Nyamwezi carving (right) given as a gift to encourage trade. The Nyamwezi people were pioneers of East and Central African trade.

2 Above is a prayer book written in Geez – an ancient Ethiopian language rarely spoken today.

3 This historic painting captures the Ethiopian defeat of Italian forces at the Battle of Adowa (modern Adwa) in 1896.

5 Many kingdoms flourished between lakes Victoria and Albert. One of the most important of these was the Kingdom of Bunyoro, which was established in the sixteenth century. The Bunyoro king (right) is still an important figure in modern Ugandan society, though his role is largely ceremonial.

4 This child (left) has been orphaned by the recent conflicts between the Hutu and Tutsi in Rwanda and Burundi.

6 Another kingdom that flourished between lakes Victoria and Albert is the Bugandan Kingdom, which was established over five hundred years ago and still exists today as part of Uganda. The Bugandans were visited by the explorers Speke and Grant, shown here at the king's palace (left).

7 Since the colonial era, cash cropping has increased dramatically in East Africa. The most common cash crops are tea, shown being picked (left), and coffee.

8 East Africa was one of the first homes of early humankind. This artist's impression (right) is of Australopithecus afarensis, a 3-million-year-old skeleton that was found in Ethiopia.

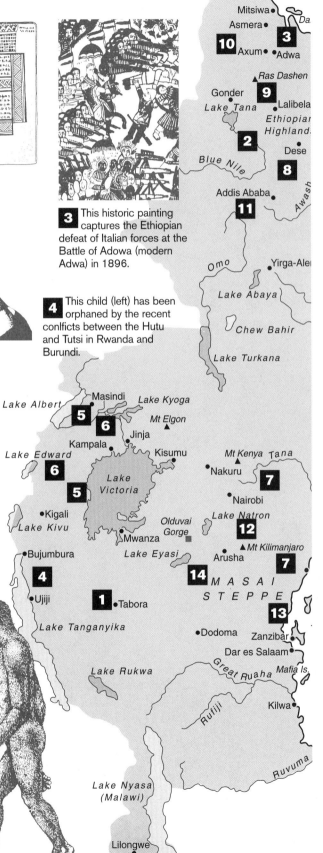

Mitsiwa
Asmera
Da

10 Axum Adwa **3**

Ras Dashen ▲

Gonder **9**
Lake Tana Lalibela
Ethiopian
Highland.
2 Dese
Blue Nile **8**

Addis Ababa
11
Awash

Omo Yirga-Ale

Lake Abaya

Chew Bahir

Lake Turkana

Lake Albert
Masindi Lake Kyoga
5 Mt Elgon ▲
6 Jinja
Kampala Kisumu Mt Kenya Tana
Lake Edward ▲
6 Nakuru **7**
5 Lake
Victoria Nairobi
Kigali Lake Natron
Lake Kivu Olduvai **12**
Mwanza Gorge Mt Kilimanjaro ▲
Bujumbura Lake Eyasi Arusha
4 **14** M A S A I
Ujiji **1** Tabora S T E P P E
7
13
Dodoma Zanzibar
Lake Tanganyika Dar es Salaam
Mafia Is.

Great Ruaha
Lake Rukwa
Kilwa
Rufiji

Ruvuma

Lake Nyasa
(Malawi)

Lilongwe

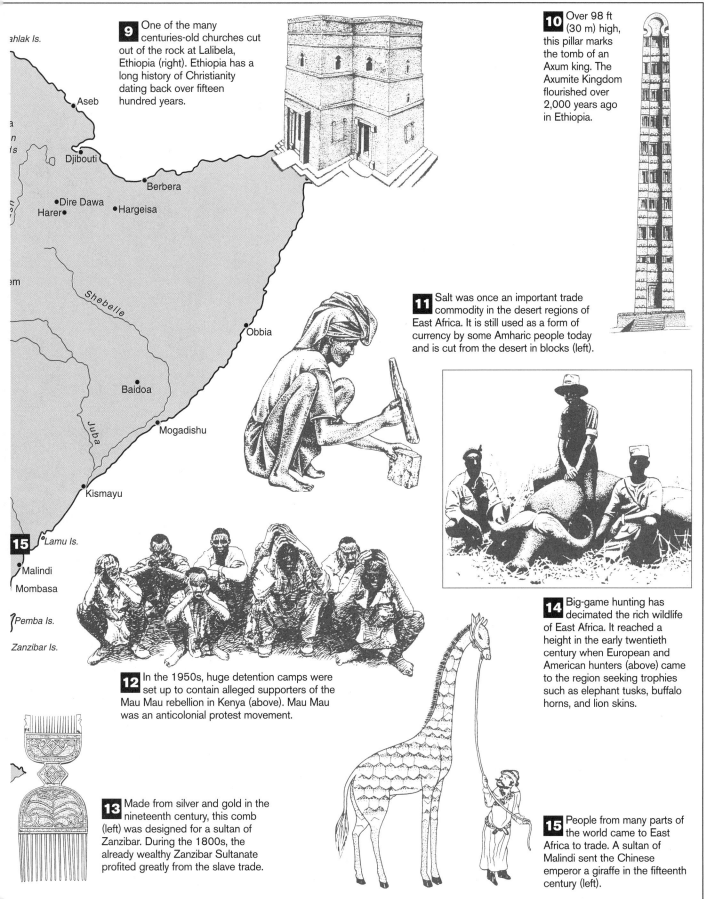

9 One of the many centuries-old churches cut out of the rock at Lalibela, Ethiopia (right). Ethiopia has a long history of Christianity dating back over fifteen hundred years.

10 Over 98 ft (30 m) high, this pillar marks the tomb of an Axum king. The Axumite Kingdom flourished over 2,000 years ago in Ethiopia.

11 Salt was once an important trade commodity in the desert regions of East Africa. It is still used as a form of currency by some Amharic people today and is cut from the desert in blocks (left).

12 In the 1950s, huge detention camps were set up to contain alleged supporters of the Mau Mau rebellion in Kenya (above). Mau Mau was an anticolonial protest movement.

13 Made from silver and gold in the nineteenth century, this comb (left) was designed for a sultan of Zanzibar. During the 1800s, the already wealthy Zanzibar Sultanate profited greatly from the slave trade.

14 Big-game hunting has decimated the rich wildlife of East Africa. It reached a height in the early twentieth century when European and American hunters (above) came to the region seeking trophies such as elephant tusks, buffalo horns, and lion skins.

15 People from many parts of the world came to East Africa to trade. A sultan of Malindi sent the Chinese emperor a giraffe in the fifteenth century (left).

Map labels: ahlak Is., Aseb, Djibouti, Berbera, Dire Dawa, Harer, Hargeisa, Shebelle, Obbia, Baidoa, Juba, Mogadishu, Kismayu, Lamu Is., Malindi, Mombasa, Pemba Is., Zanzibar Is.

© DIAGRAM

Distribution of major Eastern peoples

1 Falasha
The Falasha (or Beta Israel) live in the highlands of northern Ethiopia, although many have recently emigrated to Israel. Most Falasha speak either Tigrinya or Amharic – depending on where they live in Ethiopia – or, more recently, Hebrew. The Falasha are a Jewish people but have only been in contact with world Judaism for the last hundred years.

3 Afar
The Afar (or Danakil) live in the desert regions of Ethiopia, Eritrea, and Djibouti. The majority of the Afar are nomadic pastoralists. Historically, the Afar formed various sultanates but are now almost semiautonomous. The Afar are Muslims and speak a language also called Afar.

2 Amhara
The Amhara live mostly in the highlands of northern Ethiopia. Although the Amhara only form around one-third of Ethiopia's population, they dominate the country's political and economic life, both now and historically under the Ethiopian Empire. Amharic is the language of the Amhara. The majority of the Amhara are Christians and Christianity has played a major role in Amhara culture for many centuries.

ሳ፡ወእጠየተፋታሪ፡ወደቢ ሲ፡ሶበ፡ታተርብ፡ቶርኮከ። ፺ በ፡ምሥየፅ፡ወተዘኩር ከ፡በሀየ፡ከ∞ዮ፡ህየ፡እኂ ከ፡ዘየጊይስከ፡ላ∞ጌ፡ህየ ተርበናቲከ፡ወተዐረት፡ም ስለ፡እኌከ፡ወየእዚፈ፡እ ንከ፡እሬኢ፡ብዙጎን፡ይትም ጠ፡ሥገሁ፡ለእንገዚእ፡ ከርስቶስ፡፡እ∞፡እንከ፡ተ በወሐ፡ለሐየር፡እንዘ፡ይተ ሳወ፡በዝጎቺ፡ላዓየ፡ዘእ ሳዮ፡ሕገ፡ይገብሩ፡ከ∞ዘ፡ ስበ፡በጽሐ፡ጸ∞፡ፋሊከ ወእ∞ፋተወ፡ይኌጸሩ፡ጸ ∞፡በዓሳተ፡ዘእንበለ፡እኂ ጹሐ፡ኔፋ፡ስ፡ወሥገ፡ወስ ምየዓፈ፡ዘጎቺ፡ይተ∞ጠ ∞፡ እምሥወጢራተ፡ተጀሳቱ፡

4 Oromo
The Oromo (or Galla) live in southeastern Ethiopia and northern Kenya. In the past, they formed many Muslim kingdoms. The Oromo language is also called Oromo. Most Oromo follow either Islam or Christianity, and a minority still practice the Oromo religion.

5 Somalis
The majority of Somalis live in Somalia. Others form considerable minorities in Ethiopia and northern Kenya and a few also live in Djibouti. The Somalis have a distinctive social structure organized around clans. They speak a language also called Somali. The vast majority of Somalis are Muslims.

6 Karamojong
The Karamojong live in northeastern Uganda. They are a seminomadic, pastoral people to whom cattle are very important. The different Karamojong groups speak various dialects of the Karamojong language. Few Karamojong have converted to Christianity or Islam; their own religion is most frequently followed.

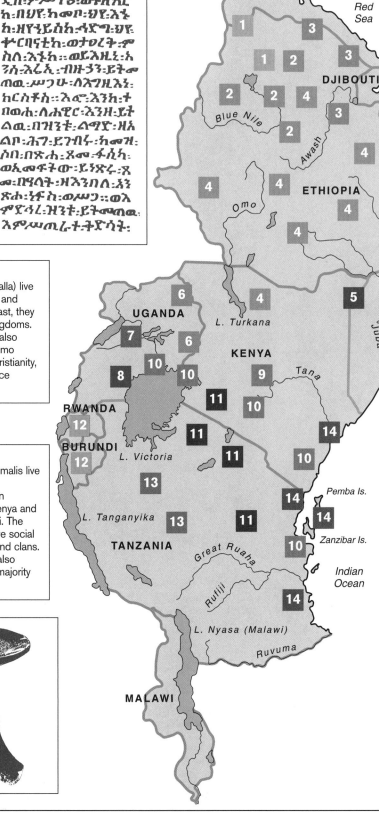

8 Ganda

The Ganda (or Baganda) live mostly in the northwestern lakes region of Uganda. They established a highly centralized monarchy under the Buganda Kingdom, which is now part of modern Uganda. The Ganda language is also called Ganda. Relatively recently, many Ganda have become Christian or Muslim, but the Ganda religion is itself still widely practiced.

9 Kikuyu

The Kikuyu (or Gikuyu) are the largest ethnic group in Kenya. The Kikuyu were often at the forefront of resistance to British rule during the colonial era. The Kikuyu language is also called Kikuyu. Many Kikuyu are Christians and have established their own, independent, churches. A few follow the Kikuyu religion.

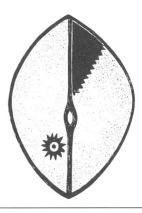

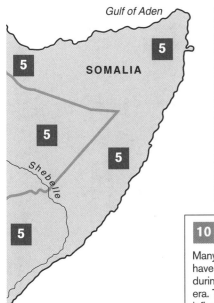

Gulf of Aden

SOMALIA

5 5 5 5 5 5

Shebelle

7 Nyoro

The Nyoro (or Banyoro) are from the northwestern lakes region of Uganda. They once formed the Bunyoro-Kitara Empire and later the Bunyoro Kingdom, now part of Uganda. The Nyoro speak a language that is also called Nyoro. Most Nyoro are either Christian or Muslim, but the Nyoro religion is still followed.

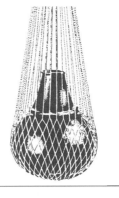

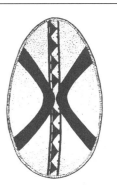

10 East African Asians

Many Asians, largely from India, have settled in East Africa during and since the colonial era. They form a small, but influential, minority in Kenya, Tanzania, and Uganda. East African Asians speak a variety of Indian languages, in particular Gujarati or Punjabi. Many also speak an African language such as Swahili and, or, English. Most East African Asians are either Hindu or Muslim though a minority follow the Zoroastrian religion.

11 Maasai

The Maasai live in a region that spans the border of Kenya and Tanzania. They are largely nomadic pastoralists who herd cattle but are increasingly becoming settled and sometimes practice agriculture. The Maasai speak a language called Maa. The Maasai have mostly resisted conversion to Islam or Christianity and largely follow their own religion.

12 Hutu and Tutsi

The Hutu and Tutsi make up the bulk of the populations of Rwanda and Burundi. Their culture and history are closely related and interwoven. Historically, the Tutsi dominated the Hutu but more recently there have been many, often violent, reversals of the balance of power. Both peoples speak the same language, called Rundi in Burundi and Rwanda in Rwanda. The majority of Hutu and Tutsi are Christians, but the indigenous religion still has many followers.

13 Nyamwezi

The Nyamwezi live in west-central Tanzania. They speak dialects of the Nyamwezi language. In the past, the Nyamwezi were pioneers of long-distance trade in East and Central Africa. Although a few Nyamwezi are Muslim or Christian, the majority follow the Nyamwezi religion.

14 Swahili

The Swahili live along the coast of Kenya and Tanzania and on offshore islands such as Pemba and Zanzibar. Swahilis are of mixed Black African, Arab, and Persian descent. The Swahili have a long history of international trading, and, as a result of this, the Swahili language is widely used throughout East Africa as a common or trading language. The vast majority of Swahili people are Muslim.

Pictorial history of West Africa

Key

───── Trade route

● Modern town or city

■ Slave port

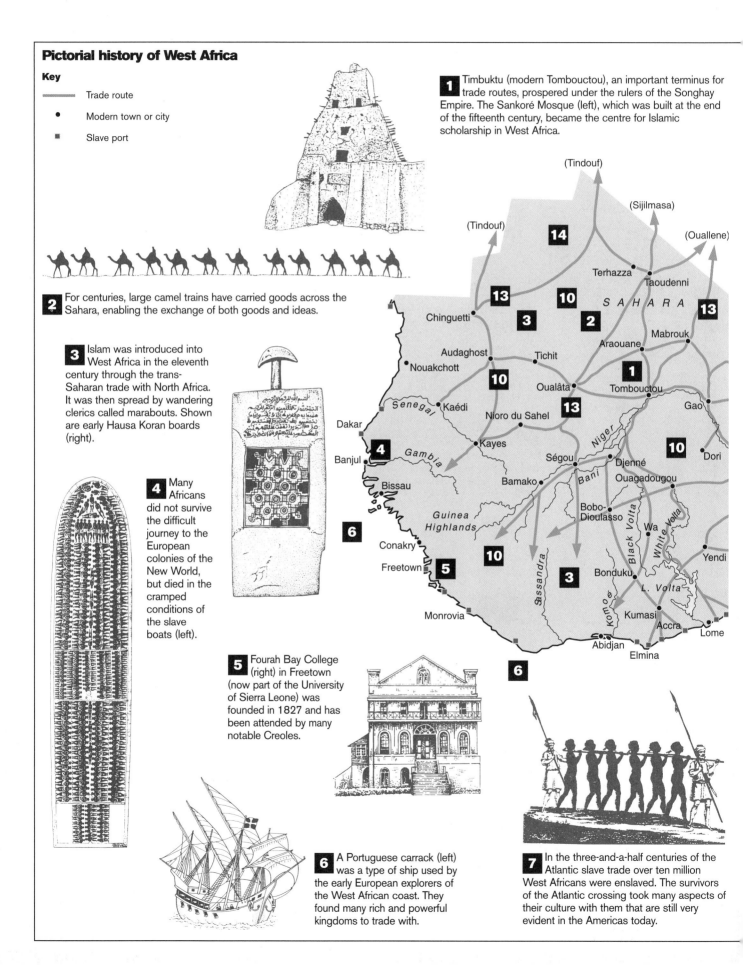

1 Timbuktu (modern Tombouctou), an important terminus for trade routes, prospered under the rulers of the Songhay Empire. The Sankoré Mosque (left), which was built at the end of the fifteenth century, became the centre for Islamic scholarship in West Africa.

2 For centuries, large camel trains have carried goods across the Sahara, enabling the exchange of both goods and ideas.

3 Islam was introduced into West Africa in the eleventh century through the trans-Saharan trade with North Africa. It was then spread by wandering clerics called marabouts. Shown are early Hausa Koran boards (right).

4 Many Africans did not survive the difficult journey to the European colonies of the New World, but died in the cramped conditions of the slave boats (left).

5 Fourah Bay College (right) in Freetown (now part of the University of Sierra Leone) was founded in 1827 and has been attended by many notable Creoles.

6 A Portuguese carrack (left) was a type of ship used by the early European explorers of the West African coast. They found many rich and powerful kingdoms to trade with.

7 In the three-and-a-half centuries of the Atlantic slave trade over ten million West Africans were enslaved. The survivors of the Atlantic crossing took many aspects of their culture with them that are still very evident in the Americas today.

8 The Masallaci Jumaa (Friday Mosque) in Zaria, Nigeria, was designed in the nineteenth century by Hausa architect Babban Gwani Mikaila for the Hausa emir, Abdulkarim.

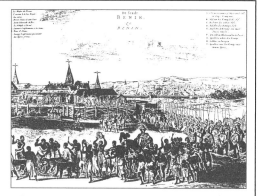

9 Benin City was the capital of the historic Kingdom of Benin. For centuries the city thrived until sacked by the British in 1897, when many of the famous Benin works of art were carried off.

10 Ivory, along with gold, was the major West African commodity before the advent of the slave trade. Shown is an ivory amulet.

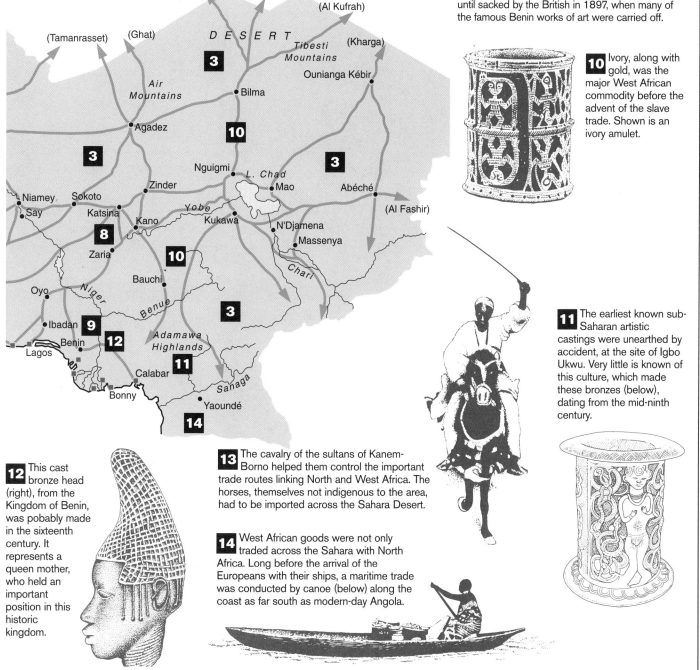

11 The earliest known sub-Saharan artistic castings were unearthed by accident, at the site of Igbo Ukwu. Very little is known of this culture, which made these bronzes (below), dating from the mid-ninth century.

12 This cast bronze head (right), from the Kingdom of Benin, was pobably made in the sixteenth century. It represents a queen mother, who held an important position in this historic kingdom.

13 The cavalry of the sultans of Kanem-Borno helped them control the important trade routes linking North and West Africa. The horses, themselves not indigenous to the area, had to be imported across the Sahara Desert.

14 West African goods were not only traded across the Sahara with North Africa. Long before the arrival of the Europeans with their ships, a maritime trade was conducted by canoe (below) along the coast as far south as modern-day Angola.

© DIAGRAM

Distribution of major Western peoples

1 Moors
The Moors are the largest ethnic group in Mauritania. They are of mixed Berber, Arab, and Black African descent. Most Moors speak Arabic, though a minority speak Berber languages. Historically, the Moors were a nomadic people. In recent years, however, many have become settled. The vast majority of Moors are Muslims and follow the Islamic religion.

2 Bambara and Malinke
The Bambara and Malinke are both Manding (or Mandinka or Mandingo) peoples. They speak different dialects of the Manding language. Manding peoples are widely spread throughout Mali and neighboring countries. The majority are Muslims. The medieval Empire of Mali was founded by the Malinke people.

3 Mende
The Mende live mostly in Sierra Leone and are the largest single ethnic group in that country. They speak a language also called Mende. Mende society is distinctive for the importance given to various hale (secret societies). Until quite recently, knowledge of the workings and functions of these hale was kept secret from outsiders.

4 Dogon
The Dogon live in central Mali. The Dogon language is also called Dogon. The Dogon have become famous for their knowledge of astronomy, in particular, of the "Dog Stars," Sirius A and Sirius B. Throughout their history, the Dogon have actively resisted the adoption of Islam or Christianity and most still practice the Dogon religion.

5 Fulani

The Fulani (or Fulbe or Peul) are one of the most widespread ethnic groups of West Africa: Fulani people can be found in most West African countries. The Fulani speak a language called Fulfulde. Some of the Fulani are nomadic whilst others live in settled communities. The Fulani are Muslims and were important in the spread of Islam throughout West Africa. They launched many jihads (Islamic holy wars) from the 1700s to 1800s to convert non-Muslims to Islam.

6 Mossi
The Mossi live mostly in Burkina Faso and they speak a language called Moré. The majority of Mossi people follow the Mossi religion. The Mossi are well known for their beautiful masks, which are used in celebrations and at festivals.

9 Fon

The Fon live mostly in south-central Benin. The speak a language called Twi. From the seventeenth century to the end of the nineteenth century, the Fon Kingdom of Dahomey flourished. The Fon religion involves the worship of gods called vodu – of which "voodoo" is a Western corruption.

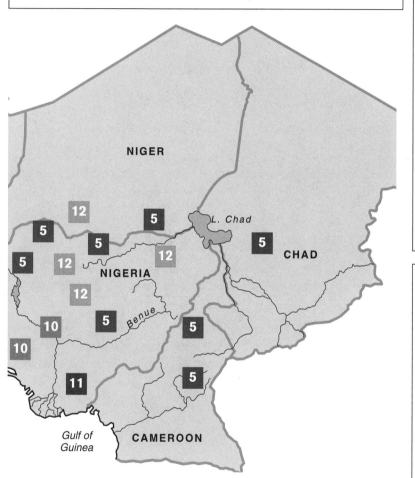

NIGER

L. Chad

CHAD

NIGERIA

Benue

CAMEROON

Gulf of Guinea

11 Igbo

The Igbo live mostly in southeastern Nigeria. The five main Igbo groups all speak dialects of the Kwa language. Igbo society is characterized by the avoidance of centralized political systems and, instead, status is accorded by individual merit and achievement. Since the nineteenth century, many Igbo have converted to Christianity. The Igbo religion, however, is still widely practiced.

10 Yoruba

The Yoruba live mostly in southwestern Nigeria and they speak a language also called Yoruba. The Yoruba people have a long history of urbanization and had many town kingdoms, dating from before colonial times. Although many Yorubas are either Muslim or Christian, the Yoruba religion is still flourishing.

12 Hausa

Although the majority of Hausa people live in northern Nigeria, the base of the historic Hausa city-states, there are others living in southern Niger and northern Benin. The Hausa speak a language also called Hausa. The Hausa people have a long history of involvement in trade. Consequently, the Hausa language is used widely throughout West Africa as a trading language. The vast majority of Hausa people are Muslim.

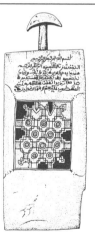

7 Asante

The Asante (or Ashanti) live in south-central Ghana. They are the largest ethnic group in Ghana and once formed their own Empire – the Asante Empire, the base of which (the Asante Kingdom) is now part of modern Ghana. The Asante speak a dialect of Twi called Asante. Most are either Christian or Muslim.

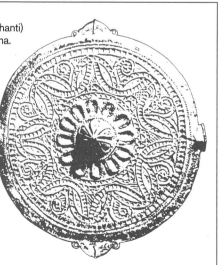

8 Ewe

The Ewe live in lands that sit astride the southern half of the border between Ghana and Togo. They speak various dialects of the Ewe language. The Ewe are famous for their strip-weaving skills and produce cloth for many people in West Africa. Although many Ewe people are Christian, the Ewe religion is still widely practiced.

© DIAGRAM

Pictorial history of Central Africa

1 Many Africans fought in the armies of the European Colonial powers during World War II. These men (right) fought for the Belgian colonial army.

2 Nzinga Nbandi (or Anna Nzinga [q.v.]) queen of the Ndongo Kingdom (1623–63) and leader of anticolonial resistance is shown above negotiating with the Portuguese. They have refused her a seat, so she is using one of her attendants as a chair.

3 This nineteenth-century woodcarving from Angola gives a sharp commentary on how Africans viewed Europeans. A trader is shown holding a glass and a bottle of gin, while a barrel of alcohol is balanced on his hat.

4 After its adoption by the court in the late 1400s, Christianity gradually spread throughout the Kongo Kingdom. The advance of Christianity was helped by the use of Kongolese-made crucifixes such as this 200-year-old one

5 This sixteenth-century engraving (below) shows Mbanza, the capital of the Kongo Kingdom from the 1300s. Following the invasions of the Jaga people in the 1500s the city was destroyed, but a small village still remains today.

BANSA ville de São SALVADOR
Hauel Stade van der Stad
C O N G O
BANSA or formerly the chief City of ye Kingdom of Congo.

DE RIVIERE LELUNDA

6 This nineteenth-century sculpture shows Kibinda Ilunga, "the Great Hunter" revered by many Central African peoples. Originally a minor Luba prince, he took new hunting techniques to the Lunda at the start of the seventeenth century, united their chiefdoms, and founded the Lunda nation, which later became an empire.

Bangui

Malabo
Bioko Is.
(Fernando Póo)

Libreville

8   **2**   **7**

8

1

7

Brazzaville

Pointe-Noíre
(Loango)

Kinshasa
(Leopoldville)

L. Mai-
Ndombe

7

Cabinda
Mpinda

Boma

5

Kasongo-Lunda

Mbanza
(Sâo Salvador)

4

Ambriz

Luanda

6

Kasanje

3

Huambo
(Nova Lisboa)

Benguela

7

Moçâmedes

Ogooué   *Sanga*   *Oubangui*   *Congo*   *Congo*   *Kasai*   *Kwilu*   *Cuango*   *Cuanza*   *Cunene*   *Cubango*   *Cuito*

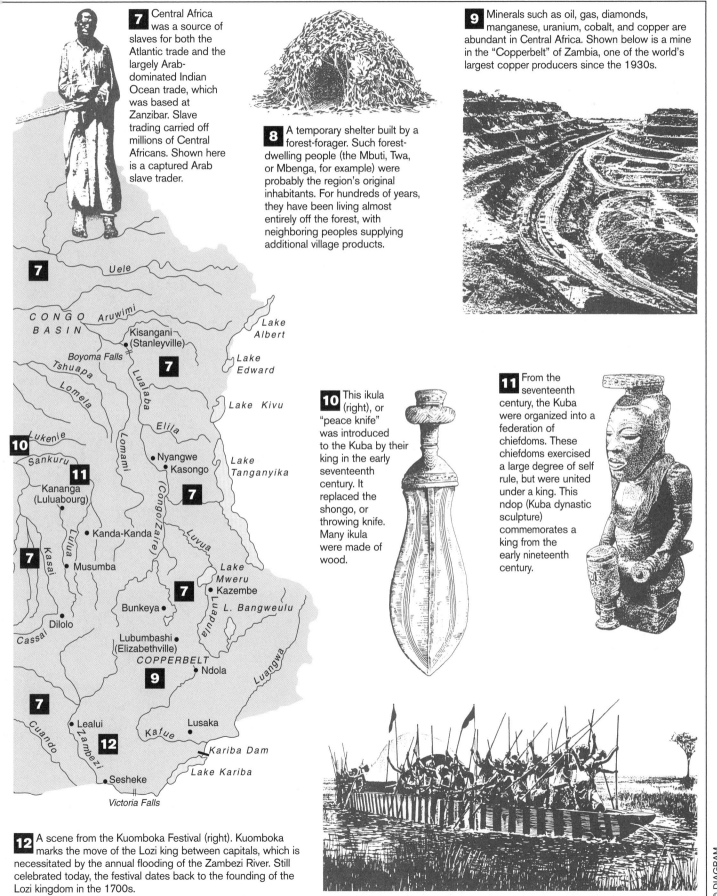

7 Central Africa was a source of slaves for both the Atlantic trade and the largely Arab-dominated Indian Ocean trade, which was based at Zanzibar. Slave trading carried off millions of Central Africans. Shown here is a captured Arab slave trader.

8 A temporary shelter built by a forest-forager. Such forest-dwelling people (the Mbuti, Twa, or Mbenga, for example) were probably the region's original inhabitants. For hundreds of years, they have been living almost entirely off the forest, with neighboring peoples supplying additional village products.

9 Minerals such as oil, gas, diamonds, manganese, uranium, cobalt, and copper are abundant in Central Africa. Shown below is a mine in the "Copperbelt" of Zambia, one of the world's largest copper producers since the 1930s.

10 This ikula (right), or "peace knife" was introduced to the Kuba by their king in the early seventeenth century. It replaced the shongo, or throwing knife. Many ikula were made of wood.

11 From the seventeenth century, the Kuba were organized into a federation of chiefdoms. These chiefdoms exercised a large degree of self rule, but were united under a king. This ndop (Kuba dynastic sculpture) commemorates a king from the early nineteenth century.

12 A scene from the Kuomboka Festival (right). Kuomboka marks the move of the Lozi king between capitals, which is necessitated by the annual flooding of the Zambezi River. Still celebrated today, the festival dates back to the founding of the Lozi kingdom in the 1700s.

© DIAGRAM

Distribution of Central peoples

1 Baya
The Baya (or Gbaya) are the second largest ethnic group in the Central African Republic, where they live in the northeast. The Baya language is also called Baya. Many Baya are Christians although elements of the Baya religion still survive.

2 Fang
The Fang live in southern Cameroon, Equatorial Guinea, and northwest Gabon. The Fang language is also called Fang. Many Fang are Christians while others follow the Fang religion. Fang art became famous in the West after its "discovery" by artists such as Pablo Picasso, on whom it had a great impact.

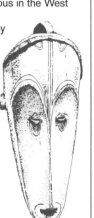

3 Mbuti, Twa, and Mbenga
The Mbuti, Twa, and Mbenga are the three major groupings of tropical forest-foragers – people living in the tropical rainforests who are usually hunter-gatherers. These people speak various languages depending on where they live, and the religion of each group also varies. Although often treated as second-class citizens, tropical forest-forager communities are renowned for their egalitarian social structures and environmentally sustainable use of the Central African rainforests.

4 Teke
The Teke (or Bateke) live mostly along the Congo River in an area that straddles Congo (Rep.), Congo (Dem. Rep.) and Gabon. They were the founders of a kingdom that grew rich through control of the trade on that river. The Teke speak various dialects of the Teke language. Most Teke people follow the Teke religion.

5 Kongo
The Kongo (or Bakongo) live mostly around the mouth of the Congo River in Congo (Rep.), Congo (Dem. Rep.) and Angola. The Kongo founded one of the most important Central African kingdoms, the Kongo Kingdom. The Kongo kings adopted Christianity in the sixteenth century and, over the years, the religion has spread to other levels. The Kongo language is also called Kongo.

6 Ovimbundu
The Ovimbundu (or Umbundu) are the largest ethnic group in Angola. The Ovimbundu language is Umbundu. The majority of Ovimbundu people are Catholics and Ovimbundu religious beliefs are still widely held. The Ovimbundu have been caught up in the Angolan civil war for the last two decades.

7 Chokwe
The Chokwe (or Jokwe) are one of the main Angolan ethnic groups. They mostly live in the northeast of Angola. The Chokwe language is also called Chokwe. The majority of Chokwe follow the Chokwe religion. The Chokwe have been embroiled in the twenty-year Angolan civil war until very recently.

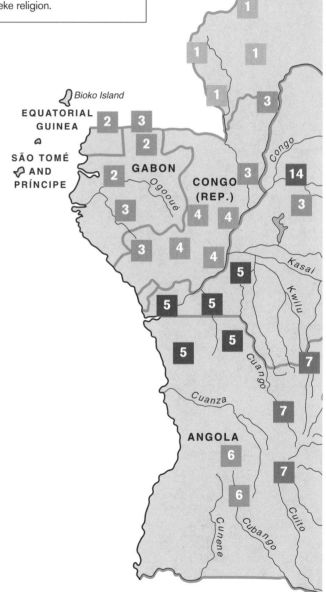

Bioko Island

EQUATORIAL GUINEA

SÃO TOMÉ AND PRÍNCIPE

GABON

Ogooué

CONGO (REP.)

Congo

Kasai

Kwilu

Cuango

Cuanza

ANGOLA

Cunene

Cubango

Cuito

15 Azande
The Azande are a group of people who live in the northeast of the Central African Republic. Some also live in neighboring regions of Sudan, Congo (Dem. Rep.), and Congo (Rep.). The Azande language is also called Azande. The majority of Azande people follow the Azande religion.

13 Kuba
The Kuba live in south-central Congo (Dem. Rep.). The Kuba developed a powerful trading kingdom in the seventeenth century. The Kuba speak various Kuba languages and largely follow the Kuba religion. The Kuba are famous for their ndop (dynastic statues), which feature past kings.

14 Mongo
The Mongo (or Lomongo) people mostly inhabit the Congo Basin in central Congo (Dem. Rep.). Until the colonial era, the Mongo were wealthy traders. The Mongo language is also called Mongo. Although many Mongo people are Christians, a significant number of Mongo beliefs and practices are still adhered to.

12 Luba
The Luba ethnic group comprises three main subgroups who live largely in southeastern Congo (Dem. Rep.), where they once established a powerful, centralized kingdom. The Luba are closely related to the Lunda people. The Luba language is also called Luba and the vast majority of Luba people follow the Luba religion.

9 Tonga
The Tonga live mostly in southern Zambia and northern Zimbabwe. The region in which they live is known as Butonga. Many Tonga were displaced by the building of the Kariba Dam on the Zambezi River. The language of the Tonga is Tonga. Most Tonga are Christians and many combine this with elements of the Tonga religion.

11 Lunda
The Lunda group includes a variety of peoples who came under the control of the historical Lunda Empire, which covered much of southern Congo (Dem. Rep.), western Zambia, and eastern Angola. Most of the Lunda population still live in these regions today. The Lunda language is also called Lunda. Many Lunda are Christians and aspects of the Lunda religion are still widely practiced.

10 Bemba
The majority of the Bemba inhabit the northern regions of Zambia and a minority live in neighboring countries such as Congo (Dem. Rep.). The Bemba kingdom was founded by the legendary Chitimukulu. The Bemba language is also called Bemba and is used by many non-Bemba people. While many Bemba are Christians, the Bemba religion still has an impact on religious practice.

8 Lozi
The Lozi (or Barotse) live in Zambia in the Western (formerly Barotse) Province. The language mostly used by the Lozi is Kololo. The majority of Lozi people follow the Lozi religion.

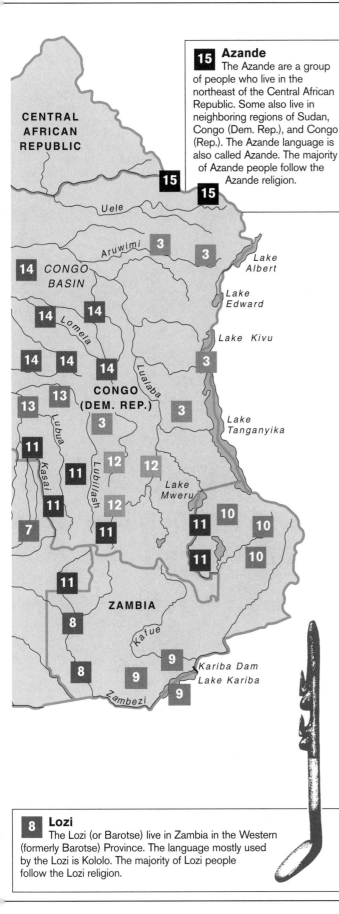

Pictorial history of South Africa

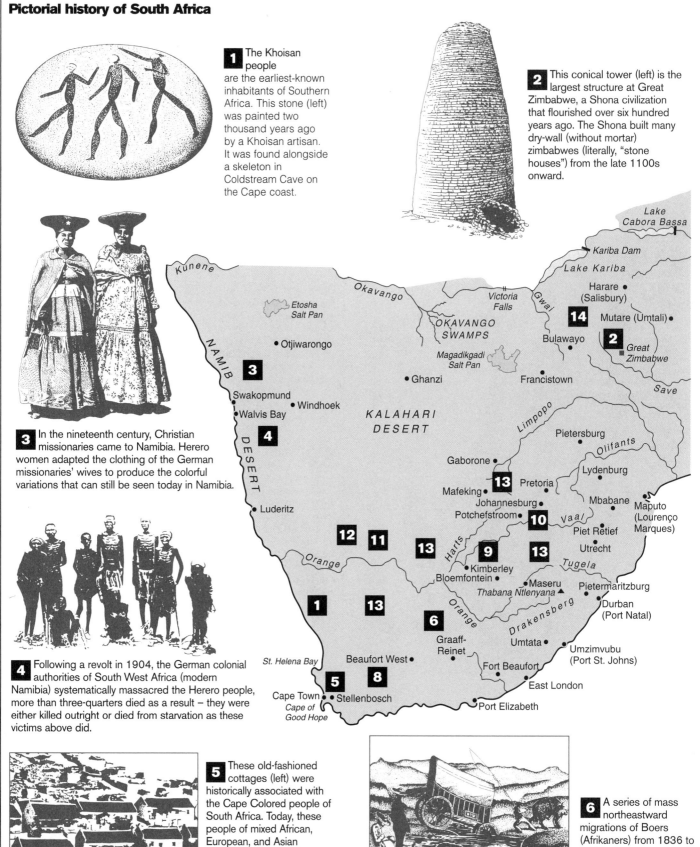

1 The Khoisan people are the earliest-known inhabitants of Southern Africa. This stone (left) was painted two thousand years ago by a Khoisan artisan. It was found alongside a skeleton in Coldstream Cave on the Cape coast.

2 This conical tower (left) is the largest structure at Great Zimbabwe, a Shona civilization that flourished over six hundred years ago. The Shona built many dry-wall (without mortar) zimbabwes (literally, "stone houses") from the late 1100s onward.

3 In the nineteenth century, Christian missionaries came to Namibia. Herero women adapted the clothing of the German missionaries' wives to produce the colorful variations that can still be seen today in Namibia.

4 Following a revolt in 1904, the German colonial authorities of South West Africa (modern Namibia) systematically massacred the Herero people, more than three-quarters died as a result – they were either killed outright or died from starvation as these victims above did.

5 These old-fashioned cottages (left) were historically associated with the Cape Colored people of South Africa. Today, these people of mixed African, European, and Asian descent live, fully integrated, in the modern towns and cities of the Cape region.

6 A series of mass northeastward migrations of Boers (Afrikaners) from 1836 to 1848 came to be called the Great Trek and its participants Voortrekkers.

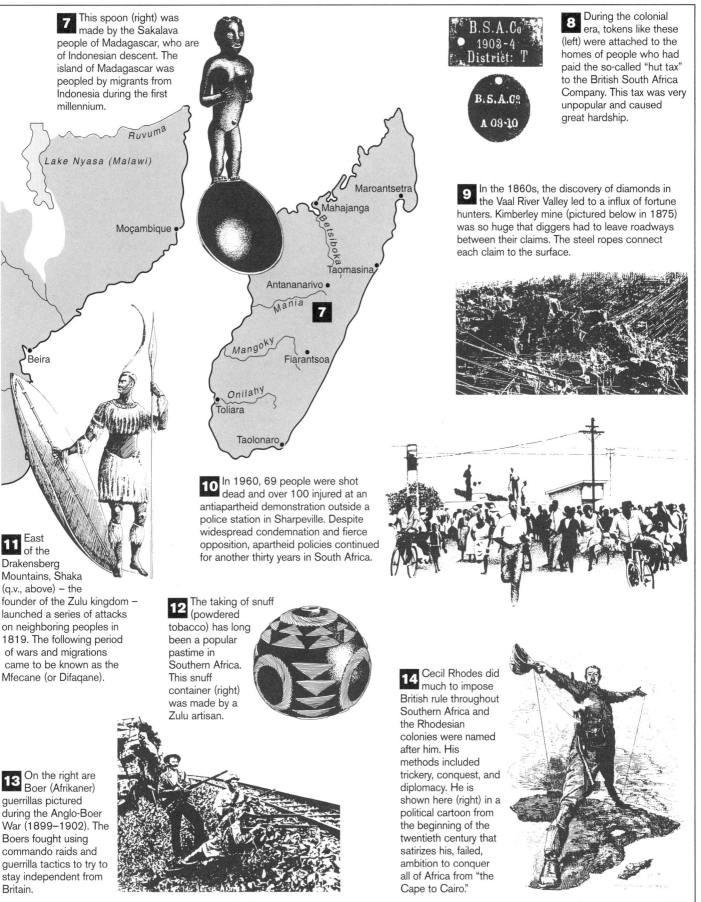

7 This spoon (right) was made by the Sakalava people of Madagascar, who are of Indonesian descent. The island of Madagascar was peopled by migrants from Indonesia during the first millennium.

8 During the colonial era, tokens like these (left) were attached to the homes of people who had paid the so-called "hut tax" to the British South Africa Company. This tax was very unpopular and caused great hardship.

B.S.A.Co 1903-4 District: T

B.S.A.Co A 09-10

9 In the 1860s, the discovery of diamonds in the Vaal River Valley led to a influx of fortune hunters. Kimberley mine (pictured below in 1875) was so huge that diggers had to leave roadways between their claims. The steel ropes connect each claim to the surface.

Ruvuma
Lake Nyasa (Malawi)
Moçambique
Maroantsetra
Mahajanga
Betsiboka
Taomasina
Antananarivo
Mania
7
Mangoky
Fiarantsoa
Beira
Onilahy
Toliara
Taolonaro

10 In 1960, 69 people were shot dead and over 100 injured at an antiapartheid demonstration outside a police station in Sharpeville. Despite widespread condemnation and fierce opposition, apartheid policies continued for another thirty years in South Africa.

11 East of the Drakensberg Mountains, Shaka (q.v., above) – the founder of the Zulu kingdom – launched a series of attacks on neighboring peoples in 1819. The following period of wars and migrations came to be known as the Mfecane (or Difaqane).

12 The taking of snuff (powdered tobacco) has long been a popular pastime in Southern Africa. This snuff container (right) was made by a Zulu artisan.

14 Cecil Rhodes did much to impose British rule throughout Southern Africa and the Rhodesian colonies were named after him. His methods included trickery, conquest, and diplomacy. He is shown here (right) in a political cartoon from the beginning of the twentieth century that satirizes his, failed, ambition to conquer all of Africa from "the Cape to Cairo."

13 On the right are Boer (Afrikaner) guerrillas pictured during the Anglo-Boer War (1899–1902). The Boers fought using commando raids and guerrilla tactics to try to stay independent from Britain.

© DIAGRAM

Distribution of major Southern peoples

1 Ovambo
The Ovambo live on the plains that straddle the border between Angola and Namibia. They form the largest single ethnic group in Namibia. The Ovambo language is also called Ovambo. The vast majority of Ovambo are Christians.

2 Herero
Most Herero live in Namibia but a few are also in Botswana, where many settled after a brutal German massacre at the beginning of the twentieth century. The Herero language is also called Herero. The vast majority of Herero are Christians and the women are recognizable for their "leg o' mutton" dresses, which were adapted from nineteenth-century German missionary fashions.

3 Khoisan
The Khoisan live mainly in the arid regions of Botswana and Namibia and a few have recently moved to South Africa. The Khoisan are the earliest-known inhabitants of Southern Africa and have lived in the region for thousands of years. The Khoisan speak various Khoisan languages and mostly follow their own religions.

4 Tswana
The Tswana (or Batswana) are the main ethnic group in Botswana and from a significant minority in South Africa. They are closely related to the Sotho people. The Tswana language is Setswana. Most Tswana people are Christians, yet the Tswana religion is still widely followed.

5 Afrikaners
The Afrikaners live mainly in South Africa though significant numbers can be found in Namibia. The Afrikaners are descended from Dutch farmers (Boers), who settled on the Cape of Good Hope in the seventeenth century, and local African populations. The Afrikaner language is called Afrikaans – a descendant of Dutch. The vast majority of Afrikaners are Christians.

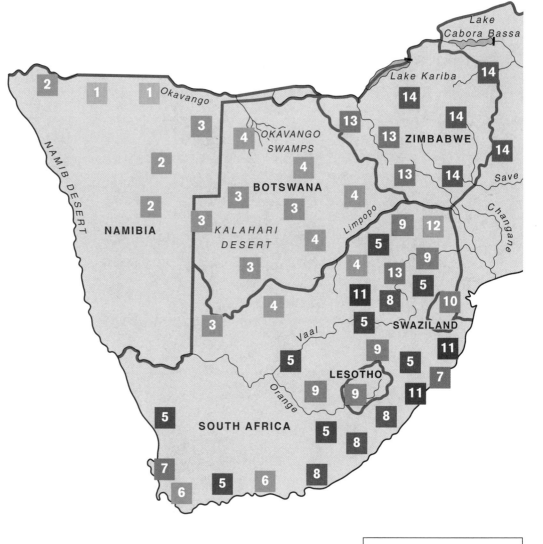

6 Cape Coloreds and Cape Malays
The Cape Coloreds and the Cape Malays live mainly around the Cape region of South Africa. They are descended from European, Asian, and African ancestors. The major difference between the two groups is religion: most Cape Coloreds are Christian and the vast majority of Cape Malays are Muslim. Both groups speak Afrikaans. Some reject the classification of Cape Coloreds as a separate ethnic group believing it to be a legacy of apartheid (South Africa's racist doctrine of "separate development").

7 Indian South Africans
Indians first came to South Africa as contracted laborers; they were followed by businessmen and traders. Today, they form a small but economically influential minority in the republic. Indian South Africans speak a variety of Indian languages. The vast majority are either Muslim or Hindu.

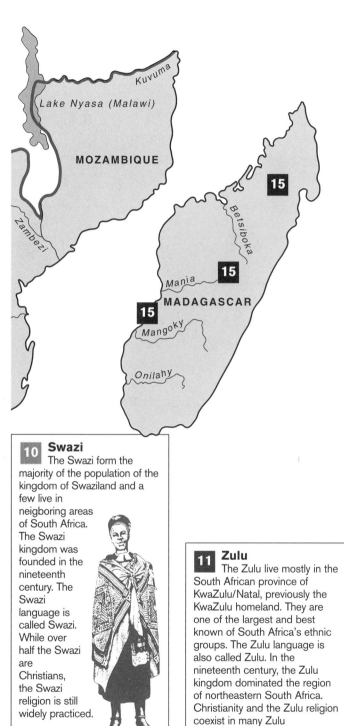

15 Madagascan peoples
Madagascans are descended from Asian, African, and Arab immigrants to the island. Indonesians were the first to arrive – in the first millennium. There are eighteen principal ethnic groups on the island. Many kingdoms flourished on Madagascar but the most powerful was the nineteenth-century Merina kingdom. Many dialects of Malagasy are spoken on Madagascar and many religions followed, though over a quarter of the population are Christian.

14 Shona
The Shona are the largest ethnic group in Zimbabwe. They have a long history of centralized civilization and were responsible for the building of Great Zimbabwe, the ruins of which mystified historians for years – they could not accept that an indigenous African society created them. The language of the Shona is also called Shona. Although the majority of Shona are Christians, the Shona religion is still strong.

13 Ndebele and Matabele
The Ndebele and the Matabele are sometimes both referred to as Ndebele people. The Ndebele live in South Africa and the Matabele in Zimbabwe. The Matable are an Ndebele group who migrated north from present-day South Africa to modern Zimbabawe in the previous century. Ndebele women are famous for their beadwork and mural art. Both groups speak Ndebele and the vast majority are Christians.

12 Venda
The Venda live in the far northeast of South Africa. Their initiation rites for girls, which involve the famous python dance, attract much attention. The Venda language is Luvenda and the majority of Venda are Christians.

9 Sotho
The Sotho form the majority of the population of the Lesotho Kingdom and a few also live in neighboring regions of South Africa. The Lesotho Kingdom was established in the early nineteenth century. The Sotho languages are called Northern Sotho and Sesotho. The majority of Sotho are Christians, yet many still follow the Sotho religion.

10 Swazi
The Swazi form the majority of the population of the kingdom of Swaziland and a few live in neigboring areas of South Africa. The Swazi kingdom was founded in the nineteenth century. The Swazi language is called Swazi. While over half the Swazi are Christians, the Swazi religion is still widely practiced.

11 Zulu
The Zulu live mostly in the South African province of KwaZulu/Natal, previously the KwaZulu homeland. They are one of the largest and best known of South Africa's ethnic groups. The Zulu language is also called Zulu. In the nineteenth century, the Zulu kingdom dominated the region of northeastern South Africa. Christianity and the Zulu religion coexist in many Zulu communities.

8 Xhosa
The Xhosa live in the southeastern regions of South Africa. During the eighteenth and nineteenth centuries, they fought a long campaign of resistance to British and Boer expansion. The Xhosa language is also called Xhosa and the vast majority are Christians, though aspects of the Xhosa religion still remain.

In about 2600 BCE, King Huni begins construction of the first "true" – smooth-sided – Egyptian pyramid, at Maidum. It is completed by Huni's successor, King Snofru.

An ancient oil lamp from Nubia. Nubian kingdoms flourished along the Nile River in present-day Sudan over two thousand years ago.

North Africa

to 1000 BCE

c. 4500	Predynastic Egypt emerges (Nile River)
c. 4000	Predynastic Nubia emerges (Egypt/Sudan)
c. 3200	Nubian Kingdom of Kush emerges (Egypt/Sudan)
c. 3100	Egyptian dynasty established
c. 3000	Berbers settled on coastal region (from Morocco to Egypt)
c. 2560	Great Pyramid of Khufu (Cheops) and Sphinx built (Egypt)
c. 1500	Kush conquered by Egypt
c. 1300	Temples of Ramses II and Nefertari built (Egypt)

1001 BCE – 1 CE

c. 920	Kingdom of Nubia emerges (Egypt/Sudan)
814	City-state of Carthage founded (near Tunis)
750	Greek Empire extends to North African coast (Libya)
671	Assyrian (Iraqi) rule begins in Egypt
651	Assyrian rule ends in Egypt
525	Persia (Iran) conquers Egypt
332	Macedonian (Greek) rule in Egypt
304	Ptolemaic dynasty founded by Ptolemy (Egypt)
c. 300s	Kingdom of Nubia transfers capital to Meroe (Sudan)
264–146	Three Punic Wars between Rome and Carthage
c. 250	Three Berber kingdoms established on northwest coast
146	Romans destroy Carthage
100	Camels introduced to North Africa
30	Ptolemaic Empire conquered by Romans

1–1000

285	Romans abandon much of African empire on northwest coast
324	Meroitic Kingdom conquered by Axumite Kingdom
429	Vandals (Europeans) begin conquest of north coast
533	Vandals conquered by Byzantine (East Roman) Empire
640	Arabs begin conquest of North Africa; Islam introduced
711	Arabs control all of North Africa
789	Independent Arab dynasties begin to emerge
969	Fatimid dynasty reunites North Africa under Arab rule

1001–1500

1054	Berber Almoravid dynasty founded (Western Sahara)
1069	Almoravids conquer Morocco
1147	Berber Almohad dynasty founded (Western Sahara)
1150	Almoravid Empire collapses; succeeded by Almohads
1169	Collapse of Fatimid Empire
1269	Collapse of Almohad Empire
1250	Mamluk rule in Egypt begins; Egypt becomes center of eastern Arab world
1400s	Funj herders migrate north from the Blue Nile (Sudan)

1501–1700

1505	Funj Kingdom founded (Sudan)
1517	Mamluks conquered by Ottoman (Turkish) Empire
1551	Ottomans conquer Tripoli (Libya)
1574	Ottomans control most of North Africa except Morocco
c. 1600	Darfur established (Sudan)
1670	Alawid rule begins (Morocco)
1700s	Funj Kingdom at greatest extent

1701–1900

1750	Darfur expands to south and east

Cleopatra (q.v.), who rules Egypt from 47–30 BCE, is the last of the Ptolemaic dynasty. The Ptolemies were of Macedonian (Greek) origin and ruled Egypt from 304 through 30 BCE.

Between 1086 and 1106, the Islamic Almoravid Empire of North Africa conquers southern Spain.

Muhammad Ali (q.v.), pasha (military leader) of Egypt from 1805–48, acts as an independent ruler retaining only nominal allegiance to the Ottoman Sultan.

1798	Napoleon, Emperor of France, conquers Egypt
1801	Ottoman and British forces take Egypt from France
1805	Egypt independent
1821	Egyptians destroy Funj Kingdom
1842	French rule begins in Algeria
1874	Egypt annexes Darfur
1881	French rule begins in Tunisia
1882	British rule begins in Egypt; Anglo-Egyptian force conquers Sudan; Mahdi begins campaigns
1885	Spanish Río de Oro colony established (Western Sahara)
1869	Suez Canal opened (Egypt)
1889	Mahdist State reaches greatest extent
1898	Anglo-Egyptian forces conquer Mahdists. Darfur independent

Muhammad Ahmad (q.v.) – the "Mahdi" – and his forces create a powerful Islamic state by 1885 in what is now Sudan.

1901–1950

1911	Italy conquers Libya
1912	French rule begins in Morocco
1914	All North Africa under foreign rule
1914–1918	World War I; Egypt used as a British military base; parts of Egypt and Sudan ceded to Italian Libya
1916	Anglo-Egyptian Sudan absorbs Darfur
1925	Huge irrigated farming project begun in Gezira (Sudan)
1939–1945	World War II; many major battles fought in North Africa; Allied forces take Libya from Italy
1945	The Arab League, an organization of Arab states, is founded

Gamal Abd an-Nasser (q.v.) takes power in Egypt in 1954. His nationalization of the Suez Canal in 1956 leads to French, British, and Israeli forces invading the country.

1951–1960

1951	Libya declared an independent monarchy under King Idris I
1952	Military coup in Egypt ousts king
1953	Egypt's king deposed by military
1954	Military coup in Egypt; Gamal Abd an-Nasser becomes head of state
1955	Civil war in Sudan between northerners and southerners
1956	French and Spanish Morocco unified; Alawid dynasty in power
1956–1957	Israel, France, and Britain invade Egypt during Suez Crisis
1960	Organization of Petroleum Exporting Countries (OPEC) forms to unite oil exporters

King Idris I (q.v.) becomes the first leader of independent Libya in 1951.

The Egyptian army is heavily defeated in the Yom Kippur War against Israel in 1973.

1961–1970

1960s	Aswan High Dam built in Egypt, creating the huge Lake Nasser
1961	Libya starts exporting oil
1963	Organization of African Unity (OAU) founded
1965	Military coup in Algeria led by Colonel Houari Boumedienne
1967	Six-Day War between Egypt and Israel
1969	Military coup in Libya led by Colonel Muammar al Qaddafi. Military coup in Sudan
1970	Nasser dies; succeeded by Colonel Anwar Sadat

Egypt's nationalization of the Suez Canal is orchestrated by the recently-appointed head of state, Gamal Abd an-Nasser in 1956. Ships are sunk to blockade the canal and despite French, British, and Israeli military intervention, Egypt keeps control of the canal.

1971–1980

1971	Libya begins to nationalize foreign oil company holdings
1972	End of first Sudanese civil war; south granted regional autonomy
1973	Yom Kippur War between Egypt and Israel
1975	Western Sahara ceded to Morocco and Mauritania by Spain
1976	Libya involved in unsuccessful coup attempt in Sudan. Western Saharan guerrillas launch anti-Moroccan offensive. Multiparty elections in Egypt
1977	Four-day war between Libya and Egypt
1978	Death of Boumedienne. Strikes and protests turn into large-scale rioting in Tunisia
1979	Camp David talks end state of war between Egypt and Israel
1980	Libyan troops sent to Chad

Anwar Sadat (q.v.), Egyptian president, makes peace with Israel at the Camp David talks in 1979; he is assassinated in 1981.

Muammar al Qaddafi (q.v.), Libyan leader since 1969, has proved to be a controversial figure in international politics.

© DIAGRAM

1981–1990

1981	Casablanca Massacre in Morocco. Sadat is assassinated; Hosni Mubarak succeeds him
1983	Sudan adopts Sharia (Islamic holy) law against wishes of non-Muslim south; civil war breaks out
1984	First free elections in Egypt
1985	OAU admits Western Saharan representatives; Morocco leaves OAU. Military coup in Sudan
1986	US bombs Tripoli, Libya. Elections end military rule in Sudan
1988–1989	Economic hardship causes civil unrest to escalate in Algeria
1989	Libyan military aircraft shot down by US. Opposition parties legalized in Algeria. Multiparty elections in Tunisia. Military coup in Sudan. Union of Arab Maghreb (UAM) founded
1990	Famine in Sudan threatens 8,000,000 people. 50,000 Berbers demonstrate in Algeria after Berber language is outlawed

In 1986, nearly one hundred years after the Mahdi is defeated by Anglo-Egyptian forces, one of his descendants, Sadiq al Mahdi, becomes prime minister of Sudan.

1991–

1991	US and British courts blame Libya for terrorist attacks on civilian airplanes. Ruling party in Algeria refuses to allow second round of legislative elections to be held after losing to radical Front d'Islamic Salvation (FIS) in the first; FIS is banned. Ceasefire declared in Western Sahara
1992	UN's demand that Libya turns over suspected terrorists is refused; sanctions are imposed. Rioting in Algeria and president is assassinated; military coup
1993	Islamic militants in Egypt clash with security forces and attack foreign tourists
1994	Libya and Chad sign agreement that ends twenty-year border dispute. Algeria's military rulers install Liamine Zeroual as president
1995	Zeroual elected president in multiparty elections; Islamic militants continue terror campaign in Algeria and plant bombs in France. Mubarak cracks down on Islamic militants. Government and rebels declare cease-fires in Sudan
1996	Unrest continues in Algeria. Anti-Qaddafi protestors shot dead in Libya
1998	Sudan's government offers to hold a referendum on the future of the south
1999	Libya seeks to end its pariah status by handing over the two suspects responsible for the Pan Am bombing over Lockerbie in 1986 for trial in a Scottish court on Dutch soil; civil war continues in Algeria, but newly elected president Abdelaziz Bouteflika offers compromises in government policy to end the conflict; in Morocco, Hassan II dies and is succeeded as king by his son Sidi Mohamed

Muslims at prayer in a North African town. Radical Islamic fundamentalism is growing increasingly popular in the 1990s. Radical Muslim groups in Algeria and Egypt, in particular, are employing terrorist tactics and attacking foreigners to further their causes.

Fearing the popularity of radical Islamic fundamentalists, the Algerian government cancels the second round of multiparty elections in 1991. Rioting follows and radical Muslim fundamentalists battle with pro-government death squads.

East Africa

to 1000 CE

1000 BCE	Cushitic peoples reach Kenyan Highlands after migrating from the Ethiopian Highlands
500 BCE – 300 CE	Bantu-speaking people migrate into East Africa, bringing with them iron-working and hoe cultivation
200	Greek records mention Jews in Ethiopia
c. 100	Axumite Kingdom established in Ethiopia
300s	Axumites issue gold coinage
320	Ezana first Christian king of Axum
640 on	Rise of Islam; decline of Axumite Kingdom begins
800s	Muslim Arabs settle Horn of Africa
900s	Islamic Somali nomads begin to expand southward; Arab trading posts at Mogadishu (Somalia) and Kilwa (Tanzania) established

1001–1300

1117	Zagwe dynasty begins rule (Ethiopia)
c. 1150	Probable founding date for both Mombasa and Malindi (Kenya) as trade and export centers on coast

In the first millennium, early Axumite sculptors produce stone statues such as this one, probably for religious purposes.

Sailing boats called dhows enable the Arabs to travel from southwest Asia, using the monsoon winds, to trade in East Africa and elsewhere. Some of these traders settle in the region as early as the tenth century.

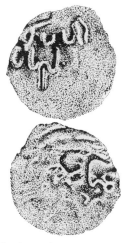

Two fourteenth-century copper coins inscribed with the name of a sultan of Kilwa.

1200s	Mogadishu the preeminent port
1268	Zagwe dynasty overthrown; Amharic Solomonic dynasty begins rule (Ethiopia)
1285	Muslim Afar unified under the state of Ifat; at war with Ethiopia
1300–1400s	Kilwa most important trading port on east coast

1301–1500

c. 1320	Under Sultan Sulaiman II, Kilwa conquers Mafia Islands (Zanzibar)
c. 1350– c. 1500	Bachwezi dynasty rules over Bunyoro-Kitara (Uganda) and Nyoro religion develops
1415	Ifat conquered by Ethiopia; Ifat state succeeded by Adal
c. 1470	Mombasa begins period of growth; decline of Kilwa follows
1498	Portuguese sailor Vasco da Gama visits cities on East African coast
c. 1500	Buganda expands (Uganda); Babito rule over Bunyoro begins
1502–1509	Portuguese conquer East African coast to gain control of trade
1526	Adal declares a jihad (Islamic holy war) on Christian Ethiopia
1543	Ethiopia conquers Adal
c. 1550s	Bunyoro Kingdom at greatest extent. Tutsi people found kingdom of Ruanda (Rwanda)

1501–1700

1580	Portugal united with Spain
1600s	Tutsi kingdom in Urundi (Burundi) established
1640	Portugal independent again
1652	Omani Arab traders begin to settle on East African coast
1699	Omanis control much of coast
1700s	Ethiopia splits into feudal states

1701–1850

1756	Seychelles made French territory
1794	Seychelles captured by British
1800s	Buganda supplants Bunyoro as most important regional kingdom
1814	Seychelles made British colony and base of antislavery patrols
1822–1837	East African coast under rule of Sultan of Oman
c. 1830	Babito prince of Bunyoro founds independent Toro Kingdom (Uganda)
1832	Zanzibar made capital of Oman
c. 1835	Slave caravans begin to visit interior of East Africa
c. 1840	Arrival of Ngoni, Bantu-speaking people from Southern Africa, fleeing Zulu attacks
1840s–1880s	Height of Swahili/Arab slave trade in East Africa
1850s	Oromo begin to establish Muslim kingdoms (southwest Ethiopia)

1851–1900

1859–1870	Bunyoro and Toro kingdoms at war
1855–1930	Series of attempts to resurrect Ethiopian Empire
1856	Zanzibar becomes an independent sultanate
1873	Zanzibar slave market closes
1884	French Somaliland (Djibouti) and British Somaliland (Somalia) established as colonies
1886	Anglo-German agreement defines European "spheres of influence" in East Africa and the boundaries of Sultanate of Zanzibar. Italian Somaliland (Somalia) established
1891	British declare a protectorate (colony) over Nyasaland (Malawi)
1895	British and Germans complete partition of Sultanate of Zanzibar. British take control of Kenya
1896	Italians defeated by Ethiopians at battle of Adowa; Ethiopia conquers Oromo kingdoms. Bunyoro and Toro kingdoms made British protectorates
1897	Urundi under German rule
1900	Buganda made a part of the British protectorate of Uganda

During the golden age of Swahili culture (c. 1200–1500), metalworkers melt copper in clay pots such as these.

The Gereza (fortress) on Kilwa is built by the Portuguese in the sixteenth century. The Portuguese arrival on East Africa's Indian Ocean coast brings an end to the Swahili and Arab dominance of trade.

The 1896 Battle of Adowa (modern Adwa), in which the Ethiopian forces under Emperor Menelik II (q.v.) defeat the Italians.

The Zanzibar slave market in 1872. Although slavery is not new to the region, in the nineteenth century it reaches an unprecedented level.

© DIAGRAM

During World War I in German East Africa, many Africans fight in the colonial armies. This Swahili sculpture portrays one of these "askari" soldiers.

This detention camp is set up at Nyeri, in Kenya, by the British in the 1950s and detains people suspected of involvement in the anticolonial Mau Mau uprising.

1901–1950

1914–1918	Many Africans fight in East Africa during WWI for Britain, Belgium, or Germany; colonies suffer and Germans lose territories
1916	Ruanda and Urundi occupied by Belgium
1930	Haile Selassie I becomes Emperor of Ethiopia
1935–1941	Italian forces invade and occupy Ethiopia
1939–1945	Many East Africans fight for Allies in India and Burma during WWII

1951–1970

1952	Eritrea federated to Ethiopia
1952–1956	Mau Mau rebellion in Kenya fights against British rule
1959	Hutu overthrow Tutsi monarchy in Ruanda
1961	Eritrean rebels begin armed struggle for independence
1963	Dr Hastings Banda becomes prime minister in Malawi
1964	Tanganyika and Zanzibar unite to form Tanzania
1965	Tutsi purge Hutu from army and bureaucracy in Rwanda
1966	Military coup in Burundi. Political coup in Uganda; prime minister Milton Obote becomes president
1967	Uganda abolishes traditional kingdoms. French Somaliland becomes the French Territory of the Afars and the Issas
1969	Peaceful coup in Somalia led by Maj. Gen. Muhammad Siad Barre

In 1971, Colonel Idi Amin Dada (q.v.) takes power in Uganda. Initially he is popular, but then creates a repressive regime under which many thousands are executed.

1971–1980

1971	Col. Idi Amin Dada seizes power in Uganda. Banda becomes president in Malawi
1972	Hutu people in Burundi revolt against Tutsi elite; civil war breaks out; over 100,000 Hutu killed. 80,000 Asians expelled from Uganda by Amin
1973	Military coup in Rwanda
1974	Haile Selassie I overthrown by army in Ethiopia; socialism adopted by military government
1976	Peaceful coup in Burundi
1977	Military coup in Seychelles. Maj. Mengistu Haile Mariam takes power in Ethiopia and launches "red terror" campaign. Conflict between Somalia and Ethiopia over Ogaden region
1978	Amin invades Tanzania
1979	Amin ousted by Ugandan and Tanzanian forces. Seychelles made a one-party state
1980s	Ethiopia and Somalia hold talks to end conflict over Ogaden region. Severe famine in Ethiopia

Haile Selassie I (q.v.) becomes Emperor of Ethiopia in 1930 and rules until 1974. During his long reign he achieves a great deal, but becomes unpopular when he begins to ignore problems at home while concentrating on foreign affairs.

1981–1990

1981	Somali National Movement (SNM) begins guerilla activities. Djibouti becomes a one-party state. Failed coup attempt in Seychelles
1981–1986	Ugandan civil war; rebels led by Yoweri Museveni win power
1984–1985	"Operation Moses" 7,000 refugee Falasha airlifted from Sudan to Israel
1985	Military coup in Uganda
1986	Rebels oust military in Uganda
1987	Military coup in Burundi; clashes between Hutu and Tutsi. Ethiopian and Somalian forces clash. Failed coup in Seychelles
1988	Fighting breaks out between Somali government and seccessionist SNM forces in former British Somaliland
1990	Prodemocracy and antigovernment riots in Kenya

1991–

1991	Afar guerillas in Djibouti demand multiparty politics. Mengistu loses control of Ethiopia; end of civil war: Eritrean liberation. Multiparty politics allowed in Kenya. Civil war in Somalia after Barre is ousted by rebel clan groups; former British Somaliland declares independence as Somaliland Republic. Ugandan Asians invited to return
1992	Tutsi are massacred in Rwanda. First multiparty elections held in Djibouti. Civil war in Somalia leads to famine; UN and US intervene. Multiparty politics introduced in Tanzania

This is the insignia of the Eritrean Popular (or People's) Liberation Front (EPLF). The EPLF launches a rebel movement fighting for Eritrean independence from Ethiopia in the 1960s. In 1991, they achieve their goal when Eritrea is liberated from Ethiopia.

Julius Nyerere (q.v.), a leading campaigner for independence from colonial rule, is the president of Tanzania from 1964 until 1985. He introduces policies of socialism and self-reliance to Tanzania between the 1960s and the 1980s.

1993	Burundi Hutu president killed – probably assassinated. Ertirea officially independent. Ugandan monarchies restored; nonparty elections held. Fighting between UN troops and Somali rebels. Multiparty elections in Seychelles
1994	Afar rebels end insurrection in Djibouti. Rwandan and Burundi Hutu presidents assassinated; in Rwanda, the Hutu army attacks Tutsi and moderate Hutu; over 500,000 people are massacred in three months. Short-lived cease-fire in Somalia; UN begins to withdraw. Ethiopian war crimes trial begins work
1995	Ethnic violence between Hutu and Tutsi spreads to Burundi. Ugandan and Sudanese troops clash in Sudan. Massacre at Hutu refugee camp in Rwanda. Aideed declares himself "president" of Somalia, but effective power remains with the clan leaders
1996	Rwandan war crimes tribunal set up. Violence escalates in Burundi; Rwandan Hutu refugees forcibly repatriated; military coup in Burundi, neighboring countries impose economic sanctions
1998	War breaks out along the disputed borders between Ethiopia and Eritrea
1999	Warfare resumes along the Ethiopian-Eritrean border; Ethiopian troops enter Somalia to halt the import of Eritrean arms for the Oromo Liberation Front

In 1996, Burundi's Hutu president, Sylvestre Ntibantunganyu, accompanied by Tutsi soldiers, attends the funeral of 320 victims massacred by suspected Hutu rebels at a refugee camp in Burundi. Soon after this Ntibantanganyu is deposed by a coup led by former president Pierre Buyoya.

During Somalia's long civil war, arms pour in from both the former USSR and US, creating a culture of violence in which even children are involved.

West

to 1000 CE

500 BCE	Nok Culture in existence (Nigeria)
C. 1 CE	Start of dispersal of Bantu peoples
200	Nok Culture ends
300	Empire of Ghana emerges (Mali)
c. 700s	Igbo Ukwu Culture in existence (Nigeria)
c. 750	Kingdom of Kangaba, from which the Empire of Mali emerges, is founded (Mali). Songhay state emerges (Mali)
c. 800	Kingdom of Kanem emerges (Lake Chad region)
800s	Takrur founded (Senegal)

1001–1500

1050	Islam introduced to West Africa
c. 1150	Empire of Ghana at its height
1200s	Kingdom of Benin emerges (Nigeria). Mossi states begin to be established (Ghana)
1230	Kanem at its height
1235	Empire of Mali founded (Mali)
c. 1240	Mali absorbs Ghana and Songhay
c. 1250	Takrur absorbed by Mali
1300	Yoruba state of Oyo is established (Nigeria)
c. 1325	Empire of Mali at its height
1340s	Songhay independent from Mali
c. 1350	Hausa city-states emerge (Nigeria)
1386	State of Borno established (Lake Chad region)
1400s	Wolof Empire founded (Senegal)
1443	Portuguese establish first fort on coast (Mauritania)
c. 1490	Mali eclipsed by Songhay Empire

1501–1700

1510	Start of Atlantic slave trade
c. 1515	Songhay at its height
1526	Borno controls Kanem
c. 1550	Wolof Empire dissolved. Mali ceases to exsist
1587	Portuguese take control of Cape Verde Islands
1590	Songhay defeated by Moroccans
1591	Kanem-Borno at greatest extent

During the period 1500 to 1800 – the "Era of Firearms and the Slave Trade" in West Africa – the Portuguese introduce firearms to the coastal states of West Africa. This Benin "bronze" depicts a Portuguese soldier with his gun.

The artistic achievements of the Nok Culture (c. 500 BCE – 200 CE) include superb terra-cotta sulptures such as this head.

In the ninth century, the Igbo Ukwu Culture of Nigeria produces fine bronze artifacts, such as this bowl and stand.

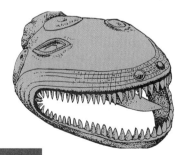

The Kingdom of Benin flourishes in what is now Nigeria from around the 1200s to 1897. This eighteenth-century Benin "bronze" (actually brass) is of a python's head.

1625	Dahomey (Benin) established
1631	England establishes first post on Gold Coast (coastal Ghana)
c. 1640	Fante states emerge (Ghana)
c. 1650	Sultanate of Wadai founded (Chad)
1670s	Asante clans unify (Ghana)

1701–1850

1700	Kingdom of Kong emerges (Ivory Coast)
1727	Dahomey at greatest extent
1740	State of Segu (Mali) founded
1748	Dahomey conquered by Oyo
1789	Oyo at greatest extent
1809	Hausa states defeated by Fulani jihad (holy war). Sokoto Caliphate founded by Fulani (Nigeria)
1816	Fante defeated by Asante
1818	Dahomey breaks away from Oyo
1824–1874	Four major Anglo-Asante wars leave Asante Empire in disarray
1830	Sokoto reaches greatest extent
1836	Oyo dissolves. Ibadan Empire emerges
1847	Liberia established by freed American slaves
1850s	Wadai at greatest extent

1851–1900

1852	Tukolor Empire established (Mali)
1870s–1880s	Second Mandinka Empire established (Senegal) as successor to Empire of Mali
1879	Rabih b. Fadl Allah begins to build empire (Chad/Nigeria)
c. 1880	European imperialist "Scramble for Africa" begins
1892	Dahomey conquered by French
1893	Kanem-Borno defeated by Rabih. French defeat Tukolor Empire
1895	France forms federation of colonies that becomes French West Africa. Kong Kingdom defeated by Mandinkas
1896	Asante made a British colony
1897	Benin Kingdom and Ibadan Empire conquered by British
1898	Second Mandinka Empire conquered by the French

1901–1950

1901	French defeat Empire of Rabih and Mossi states
1902	Asante annexed to Gold Coast
1903	Sokoto conquered by British.
1903	Mauritania becomes a French protectorate (colony)
1909	Wadai defeated by French
1914	All West Africa, except Liberia, under European domination
1914–1918	West African troops fight on both sides in World War I. Germany defeated in Togoland & Kameruns military campaigns
1916	German colonies of Togoland & Kameruns occupied by Britain and France
1939–1945	West African troops fight on Allied side in World War II

1951–1970

1957	Gold Coast renamed Ghana
1960	Soudan renamed Mali
1963	Military coups in Dahomey and Togo. Organization of African Unity founded (OAU)
1966	Popular uprising in Upper Volta topples president; military rule is installed. Military coups in Ghana and Nigeria. Antigovernment guerrilla activity begins in Chad
1967	Military coups in Dahomey, Sierra Leone, and Togo. Twelve-state structure introduced in Nigeria; Biafran (Nigerian Civil) War begins
1968	End of military rule in Dahomey. Military coup in Mali

Ahmadu is the caliph (ruler) of the Tukolor Caliphate from 1862 to 1893 and spends much of his long reign resisting French colonialists.

The Asante Empire (1670s–1896) produces many of these gold-weights, actually brass weights that were used to weigh gold dust.

Captured Africans after a battle against the French army during the European colonial "Scramble for Africa," which escalates after the 1884 Berlin Conference.

In Nigeria, a brutal civil war begins in 1967 when the southeastern region, calling itself Biafra, declares independence.

The Organization of African Unity (OAU) is founded in 1963. This stamp marks the OAU summit conference held in Ghana in 1965.

The civil war in Chad begins in 1979. These casualties are awaiting evacuation.

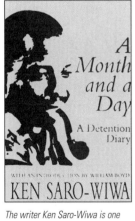

Master Sergeant Samuel Doe (q.v.) takes power after a military coup in Liberia in 1980. His assassination in 1990 leads to the escalation of Liberia's civil war.

1969	Return to civilian rule in Ghana and Sierra Leone. Military coup in Benin
1970	Biafran secessionists defeated. Civilian rule returns in Upper Volta

1971–1980

1972	Military coups in both Dahomey and Ghana
1974	Military coups in Niger and Upper Volta. Dahomey adopts Marxism-Leninism. Oil boom in Nigeria
1975	Dahomey renamed Benin. Mauritania at war with Western Saharan guerrillas. Military coups in Chad and Nigeria
1976	Launch of Economic Community of West African States (ECOWAS). Military coup in Togo
1977	Nigeria hosts international Black Festival of Arts
1978	End of military rule in Upper Volta. Military coup in Mauritania
1979	Return to civilian rule in Benin and Nigeria. Military coup in Ghana forces elections. Civil war breaks out in Chad. End of Mauritanian-Western Saharan conflict as Mauritania withdraws
1980	Uranium boom in Niger. Military coups in Liberia, Upper Volta, and Guinea-Bissau. Libyan troops invade Chad

1981–1990

1981	Military coup in Ghana
1982	Oil production begins in Benin. Military coup in Upper Volta. Senegal and Gambia unite to form Senegambia Confederation
1983	Military coups in Upper Volta and Nigeria
1984	Military coups in Guinea and Mauritania. Upper Volta renamed Burkina Faso
1985	Military coup in Nigeria. Elections end military rule in Liberia
1986	Volcanic eruption in Cameroon. Nigerian writer Wole Soyinka wins Nobel Prize for Literature
1987	Military coup in Burkina Faso
1989	Senegambia dissolved. Civil war erupts in Liberia. Benin abandons Marxism-Leninism
1990	Government overthrown by rebels in Chad. Popular pressure leads to first multiparty elections in Ivory Coast. President Samuel Doe of Liberia assassinated; civil war escalates. End of one-party politics in Cameroon. Tuareg uprising in Niger begins

1991–

1991	First free elections in Benin. End of military rule in Burkina Faso. Military coup in Mali. Legalization of opposition parties follows widespread popular unrest in Togo. Multiparty elections end one-party rule in Cape Verde. Rebels launch antigovernment offensive in Sierra Leone sparking a bloody civil war
1992	Multiparty politics introduced in Guinea. Elections end military rule in Mali, Mauritania, and Ghana. Military coup in Sierra Leone.
1993	Elections end military rule in Niger. Military coup in Nigeria annulls recent elections
1994	African Franc Zone currency (CFA) devalued by fifty percent; Franc Zone countries experience economic hardship; strikes and protests are widespread. Military coup in Gambia. First multiparty elections in Guinea-Bissau. Tuareg sign peace accord with Niger government. Elections in Togo won by opposistion
1995	Military government in Nigeria executes nine Ogoni dissidents to international condemnation; Nigeria's membership of the Commonwealth is suspended. Rebel groups in Liberia sign peace agreement. Ethnic fighting in north Ghana. Tuareg uprising ended in Mali by peace initiative
1996	Military coup in Nigeria. Renewed fighting in Liberia; refugee crisis follows as thousands attempt to flee country in passing ships. Cape Verde and Guniea-Bissau join the Community of Portuguese-Speaking Countries. Rebels and government agree cease-fire in Sierra Leone
1997–1999	Civil wars occur in Guinea-Bissau, Liberia and Sierra Leone; civilian government is restored in Nigeria in May 1999

Nigerian officers at the staff college in Jaji. Officers from this college are often involved in the many coups that Nigeria has had since independence in 1960.

Ex-president of the Ivory Coast, Félix Houphouët-Boigny, commisions the building of the Basilica of Our Lady of Peace, which is built between 1987 and 1989 and is the largest church in the world.

The writer Ken Saro-Wiwa is one of nine Ogoni activists executed by the Nigerian government in 1995. These executions lead to the suspension of Nigeria's membership of the Commonwealth.

After months of pressure from the International Monetary Fund (IMF) and France, these nine West African countries are forced to devalue their currency – the CFA franc – by fifty percent. This causes great economic hardship and widespread civil unrest in the African Franc Zone.

© DIAGRAM

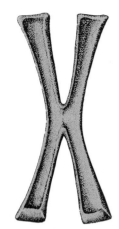

A copper ingot (metal bar) from Ingombe Ilede, a major trading center at the confluence of the Zambezi and Kafue rivers. Used as a form of currency, this X-shaped ingot is over 1 ft (30 cm) in length. At its height (1300s–1400s), Ingombe Ilede plays an important role in transcontinental trade. It has links with both Great Zimbabwe (in present-day Zimbabwe) and the trading cities on the east coast.

Central

up to 1000 CE

c. 3000 bce	Ancient Egyptians in contact with Central African rainforest peoples
100s ce	Bantu-speaking people begin to arrive in Central Africa
c. 300s	Iron-making begins in Central Africa
c. 850	At Ingombe Ilede (Zambia) first burials of chiefs with gold items

1001–1500

1300s	Founding of Kongo Kingdom on Congo River (Angola/Congo [Dem. Rep.])
1300s–1400s	Ingombe Ilede is a major Central African trading link with east coast
1400s	Ndongo Kingdom established to south of Kongo (Angola)
1482	Portuguese reach Congo (Dem. Rep.) estuary and visit Kongo
1484	Kongo introduced to Christianity
1491	Kongo king (Nzinga Kuwu) and court convert to Christianity
1494	Pro- and anti-Portuguese factions develop within Kongo Kingdom
1500s	Ingombe Ilede abandoned

1501–1600

1506	Civil war breaks out in Kongo; Affonso I succeeds as king with Portuguese support; Affonso attempts to westernize Kongo
1520s	Kongo is supplying slaves to the Portuguese colony of São Tomé
1543	Affonso dies; succession war follows in Kongo
1548	Jesuit (Catholic) missionaries arrive in Kongo
1550	Centralized Luba kingdom in existence (Congo [Dem. Rep.])
1556	War breaks out between Kongo and Portuguese-backed Ndongo to south; Ndongo ngola (ruler) is victorious; Portuguese slave trade with Ndongo expands
1560–1880	Slave trade flourishes on Central African coast; over three million people taken as slaves from area
1561–1567	Civil war in Kongo over succession, won by Bernado
1568	Jaga from interior invade Kongo
1571	Portuguese drive Jaga from Kongo; Kongo made a Portuguese vassal
1576	Independent Portuguese fort established at Luanda (Angola); it becomes a major slave depot
1592	Portuguese unsuccessfully attempt to impose complete colonial rule on Luanda

1601–1850

1619	Portuguese and Jaga ruthlessly conquer Ndongo Kingdom
1623	Nzinga Nbandi (Anna) becomes Ndongo queen and leads Ndongo against Portuguese
1641	Dutch take Luanda from Portuguese; Nzinga chases Portuguese from Angola
1648	Angolans and Dutch defeated by Brazilian landowner Salvador de Sa
c. 1650	Bemba kingdom founded (Zambia)
1665–1670	Portuguese invade Kongo and establish rule over Kongo
1700s	Emergence of Lozi kingdom (Zambia). Centralized Lunda Empire exists (Congo [Dem. Rep.])
c. 1770	Umbundu kingdoms established (Angola)
by 1800	Kazembe (Zambia) controls transcontinental trade routes
1836	Portuguese outlaw slave trade
c. 1840–1864	Kololo dynasty rules over Lozi kingdom

1851–1900

1852–1873	David Livingstone explores Central and East Africa opening up the region to European colonization

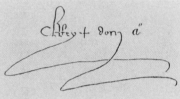

The signature of the Kongo king Affonso I (reigned 1506–43). A convert to Catholicism and initially pro-Portuguese, Affonso becomes disillusioned with his European allies when they continue to enslave Kongo citizens despite appeals to stop the slave trade in his kingdom.

A bust of Antonio Nigrita who died in Rome, Italy, in 1608. This bust was sculpted by Francesco Caporale. Nigrita was the Kongo Kingdom's ambassador to Rome.

In the nineteenth century, Scottish explorer and missionary, David Livingstone encourages the expansion of Christianity and trade with Europe in East and Central Africa hoping that it will bring the slave trade to an end. Sekeletu, the Kololo ruler of the Lozi kingdom, was keen to establish external trade relations so he gave Livingstone a great deal of assistance – such as porters, guides, and supplies – for his travels.

1858	Portuguese abolish slavery
1880s	Lunda Empire breaks up
1885	Belgian king. Leopold II, officially establishes his own personal colony – Congo Free State (Congo [Dem. Rep.])
1890	Barotseland Treaty delivers Lozi kingdom to British South Africa Co. (BSA) as Barotseland, part of BSA's colony of Northern Rhodesia
1897–1900	Bemba conquered by BSA; they become part of Northern Rhodesia
1899	Kazembe conquered by British

1901–1950

1902–1903	Bailundo War against Portuguese colonization of Angola
1908	Belgian government takes over Congo Free State as a colony called Belgian Congo
1920s–1930s	Copper mining develops in Northern Rhodesian Copperbelt
1923–1924	BSA hands over Southern and Northern Rhodesia to British government; Africans in Rhodesias begin to be forced into reserves and whites encouraged to settle
1939–1940	African mineworkers strike for better pay in Northern Rhodesia
1946	The Federation of Welfare Societies, a nationalist movement, is formed in Northern Rhodesia
1950s	Kariba Dam built on Zambezi River displacing thousands of people

1951–1970

1953	Northern Rhodesia (Zambia), Southern Rhodesia (Zimbabwe), and Nyasaland (Malawi) join to form white-minority ruled Central African Federation (CAF)
1957	Oil discovered in Congo
1958	Zambia Africa National Congress (ZANC) formed with Kenneth Kaunda as president
1959	Kaunda imprisoned
1960	Provinces of South Kasai and Katanga (now Shaba) announce secession from Congo (Dem. Rep.); civil war breaks out; military coup follows. Kaunda is released
1961	Angolan independence war starts. Congo (Dem. Rep.)'s parliament is reconvened
1962	One-party state set up in Central African Republic (CAR)
1963	Congo (Rep.) president resigns after popular unrest; one-party state established. Government forces reunite Congo (Dem. Rep.). CAF dissolved
1964	Military coup in Gabon; President Léon M'ba reinstalled by French. Kaunda elected president of Zambia. Rebellions in Congo (Dem. Rep.)
1965	Mobutu Sese Seko takes power in Congo (Dem. Rep.) and bans all political parties. Jean-Bédel Bokassa takes power in CAR after military coup
1968	One-party state declared in Gabon. Macías Nguema elected president of Equatorial Guinea. Military coup in Congo (Rep.)
1970	Macías establishes one-party state in Equatorial Guinea and embarks on a ten-year reign of terror. Mobutu establishes one-party state in Congo (Dem. Rep.)

1971–1980

1971	Former Belgian Congo renamed Zaire as part of Mobutu's "authenticity" drive to remove foreign influences from Congo (Dem. Rep.)
1972	Zambia made a one-party state. Bokassa declares himself "president-for-life" in CAR
1975	Civil war erupts in Angola between Soviet- and Cuban-backed Movimento Popular de Libertação de Angola (MPLA), South African- and US-backed União Nacional para a Independência Total de Angola (Unita), and the Frente Nacional de Libertação de Angola (FNLA). MPLA forms government

In 1960, Moïse Tshombe (q.v.) declares mineral-rich Katanga (Shaba) independent from Congo (Dem. Rep.). The rebellion collapses in 1963 when Tshombe flees the country, but is followed by another in 1964–5.

Kenneth Kaunda (q.v.), a leader of the fight against colonial rule, becomes first president of newly-independent Zambia (formerly the British colony of Northern Rhodesia) in 1964.

In the 1920s and 1930s, copper mining booms in the Copperbelt in the north of Northern Rhodesia (present-day Zambia). Largely worked by African miners but owned by white settlers, most of the profits of this lucrative industry go overseas. Forced to live in inadequate "native reserves," mining is one of the few ways to make a living not denied to Africans. As a result, the copper industry drains labor away from rural areas leading to food shortages and the disruption of whole communities.

Kariba Dam is built in the 1950s at a cost of many millions of dollars. Thousands of Zambians are moved to make way for the dam, built to supply hydroelectric power.

© DIAGRAM

In 1976, President-for-life Jean-Bédel Bokassa (q.v.) declares himself "Emperor" and renames the Central African Republic the "Central African Empire." A lavish coronation ceremony follows in 1977, reputed to cost over US$20 million, which includes substantial gifts from France and diamond-mining companies operating in the country.

Mobutu Sese Seko, president of Zaire was widely criticized for his autocratic regime and refusal to relinquish power. Although in 1990 he announced his intention to turn Zaire (Congo [Dem. Rep.]) into a multiparty democracy, he refused to hand over power to any of the transitional governments established subsequently.

Roughly 27,000 years ago, Khoisan rock art (opposite) is created throughout Southern Africa at around 15,000 different sites. The paintings often vividly depict hunting scenes, as shown in this example far right.

1976	Bokassa makes himself "emperor." MPLA destroys FNLA; conflict with Unita rebels continues
1977	Martial law in Congo (Rep.) after president is assassinated. First Shaba War in Zaire (Congo [Dem. Rep.]) as Katanga attempts to secede; Moroccan and French troops help quell uprising
1978	Second Shaba War – another unsuccessful Katangan rebellion
1979	South Africa and Rhodesia (Zimbabwe) escalate military action in Angola. Bokassa ousted from CAR with help from French; multiparty politics are adopted. In Equatorial Guinea, Macías is ousted after a military coup led by Obiang Nguema; he is executed and military rule is established

1981–1990

1981	CAR's president transfers power to a military government
1983–1984	Acute drought hits São Tomé and Príncipe
1985	Equatorial Guinea adopts African Franc Zone currency, the CFA
1986	Bokassa sentenced to death in CAR (this is later commuted to life imprisonment)
1988	South African and Cuban forces begin to withdraw from Angola
1990	Elections end one-party rule in Gabon. Mobutu announces plans to make Zaire (Congo [Dem. Rep.]) a multiparty democracy; several people reported to have been killed by troops at antigovernment demonstrations around the country

1991–

1991	Opposition parties legalized in Congo (Rep.) and CAR. Multiparty elections in Zambia and São Tomé and Príncipe. Mobutu calls a National Conference to draft a multiparty constitution for Zaire (Congo [Dem. Rep.]); rioting follows as transition to democracy is frustrated
1992	Elections in Angola won by MPLA; Unita does not accept results and resumes civil war. Zairean National Conference dissolves itself and establishes High Council of the Republic (HCR), which declares Etienne Tshisekedi head of Zaire's transitional government – Mobutu is still president
1993	United Nations (UN) imposes sanctions against Unita. Results of presidential elections in Gabon not accepted by opposition. Troops riot in Zaire after being paid with worthless 5 million Zaire banknotes. CAR holds multiparty elections; Bokassa is released early from jail in CAR
1994	MPLA and Unita sign peace treaty, but hostilities continue. CFA devalued by fifty percent: Congo (Rep.), Equatorial Guinea, Gabon, and CAR suffer from economic hardship and social unrest. Over two million refugees fleeing conflict in Rwanda enter Congo (Dem. Rep.).
1995	Commission reports on human rights abuses in Zambia during Kaunda's presidency. Outbreak of deadly Ebola virus in Kikwit, Congo (Dem. Rep.). Fragile peace achieved in Angola
1996	Angola and São Tomé and Príncipe join the new Community of Portuguese-speaking Countries. Bokassa dies. Rwandan-backed Congo (Dem. Rep.) Tutsi take up arms against government
1997	Rebel army led by Laurent Kabila overthrows Mobutu in Zaire; after taking power, Kabila renames Zaire the Democratic Republic of Congo
1998	Civil war breaks out again in Congo (Dem. Rep.); Rwanda and Uganda support the rebels, while Angola, Chad, Namibia, and Zimbabwe send troops to support Kabila's government forces
1999	Civil war breaks out again in Angola; negotiations for a ceasefire continue in Congo (Dem. Rep.)

Soldiers from the União Nacional para a Independência Total de Angola (Unita), a United States- and South African-backed rebel movement in Angola. In 1995, Dr Jonas Savimbi, the leader of Unita, agrees to accept José Eduardo dos Santos – the leader of Movimento Popular de Libertação de Angola (MPLA) – as president of Angola, officially bringing to an end the twenty-year civil war.

The insignia of the MPLA (right).

Southern

to 999 BC

25,000 BCE	Oldest examples of Khoisan rock art in Southern Africa
200s CE	Bantu-speaking peoples begin to arrive in Southern Africa
300s–400s	Bantu-speakers reach north and southeast of modern South Africa
600s	Indonesians in Madagascar

650–1300	Large, cattle-owning, Iron-Age "Toutswe tradition" communities in existence (Botswana)
900s	Bambandyanalo/Mapungubwe trading center on Limpopo River flourishes
1000s	Bantu-speakers migrate from mainland to Madagascar. Major Iron-Age settlement, Leopard Kopje, built (Zimbabwe)

1001–1500

1100s	Great Zimbabwe civilization develops (Zimbabwe)
1100–1300	Bambandyanalo/Mapungubwe at height of prosperity
1300s–1400s	Great Zimbabwe building and trading at height. Muslim trading colonies and kingdoms established on Madagascar
by 1500	Great Zimbabwe site abandoned; civilization moves north and Mutapa Empire established
1500s–1700s	Successive Tsonga kingdoms, Nyaka, Tembe, and Maputo flourish (Mozambique)

1501–1800

1506	Portuguese dominate gold trade
1511	Portuguese discover the uninhabited island of Mauritius
1590s	Dutch trading ships begin to stop for supplies at Cape (South Africa). Dutch occupy Mauritius
1652	Dutch East India Company sets up a supply station on Cape
1657	Some Dutch East India Company soldiers are freed to become full-time farmers (Boers) on Cape
1657–1677	Khoikhoi and Boers fight over land; Khoikhoi defeated
1710	Dutch abandon Mauritius
1715	French occupy Mauritius
1795–1799	Unsuccessful Boer rebellions against Cape authority
1799–1878	A series of nine Cape-Xhosa wars between Xhosa and Boers and, later, Xhosa and British: Xhosa are eventually defeated by British
by 1797	Merina kingdom on Madagascar

1801–1830

1806	British take Cape from Dutch
1806	Cape and Mauritius become British colonies
1806	British capture Mauritius
1815	Nguni kingdoms of Ndwandwe (ruled by Zwide), Ngwane (ruled by Sobhuza I), and Mthethwa (ruled by Dingiswayo) dominate region east of Drakensberg Mts
1816	Shaka becomes Zulu leader (South Africa)
1818–1819	Zulu-Ndwandwe war establishes Zulu supremacy in the region
1819–1839	Mfecane/Difaqane period of mass migrations and wars (South Africa)
1820	5,000 British emigrate to Cape
1820s	Mzilikazi founds Ndebele kingdom on Highveld (South Africa)
1824	Moshoeshoe founds Basuto Kingdom (Lesotho)
1830s	Ngoni state of Gaza emerges (Mozambique)

1831–1850

1831	Sotho defeat invading Ndebele
1836–1848	Great Trek brings Boers into conflict with people on Highveld
1836	Voortrekkers battle with Ndebele
1837	Boers drive Ndebele from Highveld; Ndebele migrate north to reform kingdom (Zimbabwe – where they become Matabele)
1838	Zulu defeated by Boers at Battle of Blood River
1839	Boer republic of Natalia created
1841	Mayotte (one of the Comoros Islands) becomes a French colony
1843	Natalia seized by British; colony of Natal established

In 1488, the Portuguese sailor Bartholomeu Dias and his crew are the first Europeans to round the Cape of Good Hope, which Dias named the Cape of Storms. King John of Portugal later renamed it the Cape of Good Hope because its discovery indicated that a sea route to India would soon be found.

A gold rhinoceros from the ancient trading center of Mapungubwe on the Limpopo River. Unfortunately, the delicacy of the sheet metal from which such items are made means that few examples will survive until the present day.

A nineteenth-century Xhosa warrior. The Xhosa are the first Bantu-speaking people to come into conflict with the white settlers (the Boers and the British) from the Cape. During the 1770s, the Boers begin to encroach onto Xhosa territory and a series of Cape-Xhosa wars follow that span the next century.

During the Mfecane/Difaqane (1819–39), Zulu warriors such as these form the spearhead of Shaka's (q.v.) attacks on neighboring peoples. The rise of the Zulu kingdom has a huge impact on the whole of Southern Africa.

1839–1865	Reign of Mswati I over Ngwane: creation of powerful Swazi nation
1848	British annex lands on Highveld

1851–1880

1851–1852	Sotho-British wars I and II; British withdraw from Highveld
1852	South African Republic (Transvaal) created by Boers
1854	Orange Free State (OFS) created by Boers
1855	Basuto Kingdom reaches height
1858	OFS-Sotho War I sets boundaries
1858–1864	War between Boer republics; Transvaal unites with others
1860–1867	Venda and Sotho drive Boers out from lands north of Olifants River
1865–1868	OFS-Sotho War II; Basuto made into British colony of Basutoland
1867	First diamond found in Vaal Valley
1868	Gold rush in Tati Valley
1871	British annex diamond fields; De Beers and Kimberley mines grow
1876	Transvaal-Pedi War
1877	British annex Transvaal
1879	British defeat Pedi – with help of Swazi – and Zulu
1880	De Beers Mining Co. formed
1880–1881	"Gun War": Sotho rebel when British try to disarm them
1880–1881	Transvaal Boers rebel against British rule; British withdraw

1881–1900

1883	Franco-Merina War (Madagascar)
1883–1884	Zulu Civil War after British partition Zululand
1883–1902	Paul Kruger is president of Transvaal Republic
1884–1885	Bechuanaland, British colony, established over Tswana. Comoros made a French colony
1884	Germans colonize South West Africa (Namibia)
1885–1887	Zululand divided between British Zululand and Transvaal
1886	Gold rush on Witwatersrand; Johannesburg founded
1889	De Beers' monopoly over African diamond mining is complete
1890	British South Africa Company colonizes Southern Rhodesia
1894	Swaziland made a British colony
1895	French colonize Madagascar
1899–1902	Anglo-Boer War; Boers defeated by British

1901–1950

1904–1905	Herero uprising brutally suppressed in South West Africa
1910	White-ruled Union of South Africa unites British Cape and Natal colonies and Boer republics
1912	Afrikaner-based National Party and South African Native National Congress (SANNC) formed
1914–1918	World War I, German colonies transferred to South Africa
1920	Zululand joins South Africa
1923	SANNC becomes African National Congress (ANC)
1928	Inkatha, Zulu nationalist movement, founded
1939–1945	World War II; manufacturing industries expand in South Africa
1944	ANC Youth League formed
1948	Apartheid begins in South Africa

1951–1970

1952	Antiapartheid Defiance Campaign in South Africa
1953	Southern and Northern Rhodesia and Nyasaland form white-ruled Central African Federation (CAF)

The discovery of gold in Southern Africa in the late 1800s causes a huge gold rush and eventually leads to the establishment of colonial rule. This Krugerrand, a South African coin, contains 1 oz (28 g) of pure gold.

In 1905, the world's largest uncut diamond, the "Cullinan" is found in Transvaal. The "Star of Africa" stone (above) that is cut from it in 1908 is then incorporated into the British crown jewels.

This banknote is issued by the British while under seige at Mafeking (present-day Mafikeng) during the Anglo-Boer War (1899–1902). This war introduces new tactics, such as trench warfare, commando raids, and the use of concentration camps, which come to be features of many twentieth-century wars.

The old flag of South Africa features the flags of Britain and the Boer republics, which united with the British colonies in 1910 to form the Union of South Africa. In 1934, South Africa approves independence from Britain and leaves the Commonwealth in 1961, but this flag is kept until 1994.

The insignia of the South West Africa People's Organization (SWAPO). This organization led the resistance against South Africa's illegal occupation of Namibia.

This silk screen poster is made in 1986. Between 1948 and 1991 opposition to apartheid takes many forms. In particular, much of South African art highlights the inequalities and injustices of apartheid.

In 1994, former prime minister of KwaZulu homeland and leader of Inkatha, Chief Mangosthutu Gatsha Buthelezi (q.v.) becomes Minister for Home Affairs in South Africa's first democratically elected government.

1960 South West Africa People's Organization (SWAPO) founded

1962 Formation of Frente de Libertação de Moçambique (Frelimo). Zimbabwe African People's Union (ZAPU) formed (S. Rhodesia)

1963 Zimbabwe African National Union (ZANU) formed. CAF dissolves

1964 Nelson Mandela imprisoned

1965 Illegal white-minority regime established in Northern Rhodesia, which becomes Rhodesia

1966 SWAPO rebels begin operations against South African forces. Basutoland renamed Lesotho. Bechuanaland renamed Botswana

1967–1975 Period of guerrilla warfare against white Rhodesians.

1969 United Nations declares South Africa's occupation of South West Africa illegal

1971–1990

1972 Military take over in Madagascar

1973 Swaziland bans political parties and king assumes absolute power

1975 Inkatha reconvened. Frelimo forms government in newly-independent Mozambique and Resistência Nacional

Mocambicana (Renamo) rebels begin civil war

1976 Rioting in South Africa dealt with harshly by government. ZAPU and ZANU merge to form Patriotic Front (PF) resistance movement

1978 Mercenaries oust Comoros' president. South Africa bombs SWAPO refugee camp

1979 Lesotho bans opposition parties

1980 End of white-minority rule in Rhodesia; African government renames Rhodesia Zimbabwe

1986 South Africa blockades Lesotho; military coup in Lesotho. South Africa declares state of emergency after escalating troubles in townships

1990 In South Africa, Nelson Mandela is released; ANC ends armed struggle; talks with government begin; state of emergency ended

1991–

1991 One-party system abandoned in Zimbabwe. Official end of apartheid. Military coup in Lesotho

1993 Elections end dictatorship in Madagascar. Lesotho returns to civilian rule after elections

1994 ANC wins first nonracial elections in South Africa; Nelson Mandela is first black president. South Africa returns Walvis Bay to Namibia

1995 Letsie III abdicates and Moshoeshoe II, his father, becomes Lesotho's king. Former apartheid leaders in court for hit-squad murders. Military coup in Comoros. All Africa Games are held in Zimbabwe

1996 Floods in KwaZulu/Natal kill 100. South Africa wins African Nations Football Cup. Marathon runner Josia Thugwane becomes first black South African to win an Olympic gold medal. Mozambique joins the Community of Portuguese-speaking Countries. Moshoeshoe II killed in a car crash. Opening of Truth and Reconciliation Commission in South Africa, which attempts to heal divisions of apartheid era

1997 The islands of Anjouan and Moheli announce their secession from the Comoros

1999 Following elections in South Africa, Mandela retires and is succeeded as president by Thabo Mbeki

These white women are being taught to shoot during the outbreak of guerrilla war in Rhodesia. Ian Smith's illegal Unilateral Declaration of Independence (UDI) in 1965 sets up a white-minority government and is strongly opposed by the majority of the population, many of whom take up arms against the regime. These women, however, are prepared to fight to protect themselves and Smith's regime.

Apartheid, in effect from 1948 to 1991 in South Africa, uses force and official classifications of "race" and ethnicity to oppress the majority of the population. Separate houses of representation are created for "Colored" and Indian voters in 1983, but in a ratio that keeps the balance of power in the hands of the whites. Many people choose not to vote, as the author of this graffiti in Johannesburg demands.

© DIAGRAM

Colonial occupation and independence

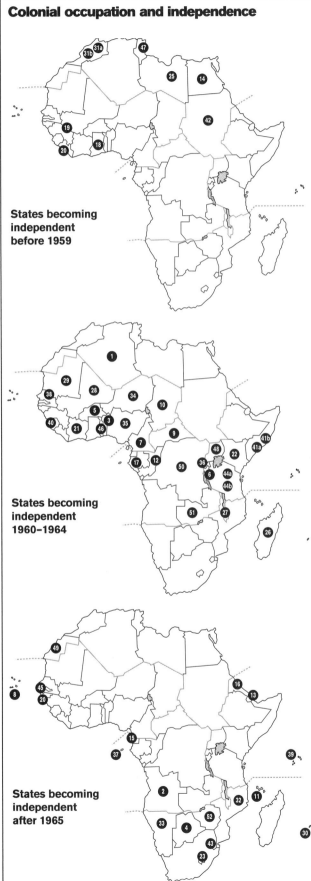

States becoming independent before 1959

States becoming independent 1960–1964

States becoming independent after 1965

	Country
1	Algeria
2	Angola
3	Benin (as Dahomey)
4	Botswana (as Bechuanaland)
5	Burkina Faso (as Upper Volta)
6	Burundi (as part of Ruanda-Urundi)
7	Cameroon
8	Cape Verde
9	Central African Republic (as Oubangui-Chari, part of French Equatorial Africa)
10	Chad (as part of French Equatorial Africa)
11	Comoros
12	Congo (as Middle, or French, Congo, part of French Equatorial Africa)
13	Djibouti (as French Somaliland then French Territory of the Afars and the Issas)
14	Egypt
15	Equatorial Guinea Bioko Island (as Fernando Póo)
16	Eritrea
17	Gabon (as part of French Equatorial Africa)
18	Ghana (as Gold Coast)
19	Guinea (as French Guinea)
20	Guinea-Bissau (as Portuguese Guinea)
21	Ivory Coast (as part of French West Africa)
22	Kenya
23	Lesotho (as Basutoland)
24	Liberia
25	Libya
26	Madagascar
27	Malawi (as Nyasaland)
28	Mali (as Soudan)
29	Mauritania (as part of French West Africa)
30	Mauritius
31a	Morocco: (French)
31b	Morocco: (Spanish)
32	Mozambique
33	Namibia (as South West Africa)
34	Niger (as part of French West Africa)
35	Nigeria
36	Rwanda (as part of Ruanda-Urundi)
37	São Tomé and Príncipe
38	Senegal (as part of French West Africa)
39	Seychelles
40	Sierra Leone
41a	Somalia (As British Somaliland)
41b	Somalia (As Italian Somaliland)
42	Sudan
43	Swaziland
44a	Tanzania (as Tanganyika)
44b	Tanzania (Zanzibar)
45	The Gambia
46	Togo (as Togoland)
47	Tunisia
48	Uganda (as Uganda Protectorate)
49	Western Sahara (as Río de Oro)
50	Zaire (as the Congo Free State, then as the Belgian Congo, now Congo [Dem. Rep.])
51	Zambia (as Northern Rhodesia)
52	Zimbabwe (as Southern Rhodesia then Rhodesia)

Independence	Occupied*	Colonial powers
July 3, 1962	1842	France
November 11, 1975	1670	Portugal
August 1, 1960	1892	France
September 30, 1966	1885	Britain
August 5, 1960	1892	France
July 1, 1962	1890	Germany 1890–1919; Belgium 1919–1962
January 1, 1960	1884	Germany 1884–1919; France and Britain divided and took control of Cameroon after Germany's defeat in WWI
July 5, 1975	1587	Portugal
August 13, 1960	1894	France
August 11, 1960	1900	France
July 6, 1975	1843	France
August 15, 1960	1885	France
June 27, 1977	1884	France
February 28, 1922	1798–1801 1882	France Britain
October 12, 1968	1845 (mainland) 1493 1778	Spain Portugal Spain
May 24, 1993	1889	Italy 1889–1941; Britain 1941–1952; ruled by Ethiopia 1952–1993
August 17, 1960	1839	France
March 6, 1957	1896	Britain
October 2, 1958	1898	France
September 10, 1974	1880	Portugal
August 7, 1960	1914	France
December 12, 1963	1895	Britain
October 4, 1966	1868	Britain
		Liberia has been independent since its establishment in 1847
December 24, 1951	1911	Italy
June 26, 1960	1895	France
July 6, 1964	1891	Britain
June 20, 1960	1898	France
November 28, 1960	1903	France
March 12, 1968	1715	France 1715–1810; Britain 1810–1968
March 2, 1956 April 7, 1956	1912 1912	France Spain
June 25, 1975	1505	Portugal
March 21, 1990	1884	Germany 1884–1919; occupied by South
August 3, 1960	1908	France
October 1, 1960	1880	Britain
July 1, 1962	1890	Germany 1890–1919; Belgium 1919–1962
July 12, 1975	1493	Portugal
June 20, 1960	1890	France
June 29, 1976	1742	France 1742–1814; Britain 1814–1976
April 27, 1961	1787	Britain
June 26, 1960 July 1, 1960	1884 1886	Britain Italy 1886–1941; 1950–1960; Britain 1941–1950
January 1, 1956	1898	Under joint British and Egyptian rule
September 6, 1968	1894	Britain (administered by the Boer's South African Republic 1894–1902)
December 9, 1961 December 10, 1963	1885 1890	Germany 1885–1920; Britain 1920–1961 Britain
February 18, 1965	1816	Britain
April 27, 1960	1884	Germany 1884–1919; France 1919–1960
March 20, 1956	1881	France
October 9, 1962	1888	Britain
(ceded to Morocco and Mauritania in 1975)	1885	Spain
June 30, 1960	1876	Belgium
October 24, 1964	1890	Britain
18 April, 1980	1890	Britain

© DIAGRAM

* The years given for the beginning of colonial occupation of the modern-day nation states are those by which a significant area of coastal and hinterland territory had been effectively occupied by a colonial power.

Ancient Egypt

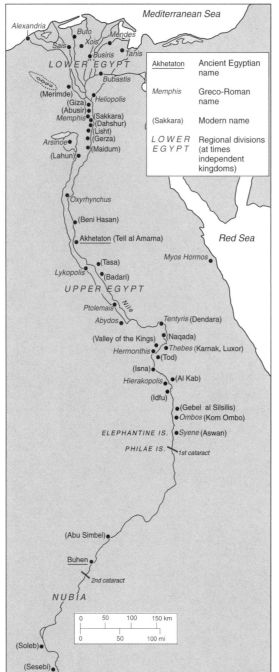

Egypt has one of the world's oldest civilizations and has been in existence since c. 4500 BCE. The dynastic Egypt of the pharaohs (kings) emerged in c. 3100 BCE. At its greatest extent (in the 1400s BCE), the Kingdom of Egypt reached as far as present-day Syria. For one hundred years from c. 1670 BCE, Egypt was ruled by "Hyksos" – literally "foreigners." After the end of the Twentieth Dynasty in c. 1070 BCE, a period of decline set in. Various nations invaded Egypt, which then fell under their control: Nubians (Sudanese) from the 700s; Assyrians from 671; Persians from 525; and Macedonians (Greeks) under Alexander the Great from 332. After the death of Alexander, one of his generals, Ptolemy, claimed Egypt. His successors were known as the Ptolemies. They ruled Egypt until 30 BCE when it became part of the Roman Empire. Arabs from southwest Asia conquered Egypt in 642 CE and converted most of its people to Islam. Since this time, Egypt has been dominated by the language and culture of the Arabs.

The gift of the Nile

Egyptian civilization arose in, and continues to be based around, the Nile Valley. Every year, beginning around July, the river flooded. When the floods retreated, around September, they left a deposit of rich, black, fertile soil along each bank about 6 miles (10 km) wide. Here, the Ancient Egyptians grew their crops. In an otherwise arid environment, the Nile provided water for irrigation as well as fertile soil. In ancient times, the river was the main transport route and most of Ancient Egypt's population lived in the Nile Valley. For these reasons, Ancient Egypt has been described as "the gift of the Nile."

Daily life in Ancient Egypt

Egyptian society had three main classes: upper, middle, and lower. The upper class comprised the royal family, religious and government officials, army officers, doctors, and wealthy landowners. Merchants, artisans, and manufacturers made up the middle class. There were many skilled workers such as architects, engineers, teachers, accountants, stonemasons, and carpenters. The majority of people, however, were of the lower class – laborers who mostly worked on farms owned by the upper classes. The main crops grown were wheat and barley, which were often given as wages to the workers. Other crops included vegetables and fruit. Bread made from wheat was the staple food and beer

Greatest extent
The Kingdom of Egypt at its greatest extent in the 1400s BCE.

Gateway to Horus
At Idfu in Upper Egypt, this massive pylon (gateway) guards the entrance to the Temple of Horus, which was built 2,300 years ago.

Ancient sites
This map shows the major sites of Ancient Egypt from c. 3100 to 332 BCE.

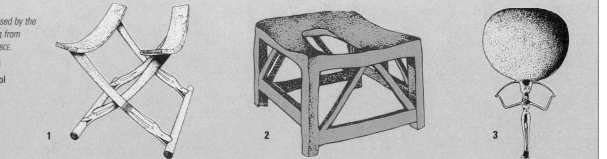

Ancient artifacts
Some everyday objects used by the Ancient Egyptians, dating from between 1500 and 1000 BCE.

1 Wooden folding stool
2 Wooden lavatory stool
3 Hand mirror

made from barley the main drink. Flax was grown to make linen. Farmlands were irrigated with water taken from canals. Antelopes, cattle, goats, sheep, donkeys, and pigs were raised. Egyptians also kept dogs and cats, and at one time hyenas.

The Ancient Egyptians made many long-lasting contributions to worldwide civilization. They established the first national government, built many great cities, and devised a 365-day calendar.

Ancient Egyptian religion

Ancient Egyptians believed in an afterlife and many gods and goddesses who ruled over different aspects of the world. The most important of these was the Sun god Re, who could grant good harvests, and the creator-god Ptah. The fertiltiy goddess Isis, wife and sister of Osiris (judge of the dead), was the mother of Horus, the lord of Heaven. The pharaohs were believed to be incarnations of Horus. Every city and town also had its own particular god or goddess. The people of Thebes, for instance, worshipped a Sun god called Amon. Over time, Amon became identified with Re and was known as Amon-Re.

Amon-Re   Re   Ptah

Osiris   Isis   Horus

Egyptian deities
These pictures of Ancient Egyptian deities have been executed in a typically stylized fashion. Some are portrayed as having human bodies with animal heads, which reflect the different natures of the deities and helped make identification easier.

Hieroglyphic writing

Ancient Egyptians used picture symbols called hieroglyphs to represent ideas and sounds. They were used from c. 3000 BCE until after 300 CE when a new alphabet was introduced. Over 700 symbols were used. Hieroglyphs were most often used for religious and royal inscriptions in stone. Usually, trained scribes carved or wrote using hieroglyphs. As the demand for written records and communications grew, there was a need to simplify the process. The invention of paper made from papyrus (reedlike plants), pens made from sharpened reeds, and ink made by mixing soot and water, enabled writing to become more commonplace. Simplified forms of hieroglyphs developed called hieratic and demotic, which were suitable for writing quickly on papyrus.

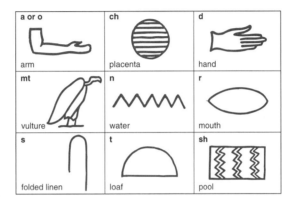

a or o	ch	d
arm	placenta	hand
mt	**n**	**r**
vulture	water	mouth
s	**t**	**sh**
folded linen	loaf	pool

The Age of Pyramids

The Egyptian pyramids are tombs that were built for royals and nobles. They are the oldest and largest stone structures in the world. Imhotep, a great architect, built the first – the Step Pyramid – for King Zoser in c. 2650 BCE. The following 500 years are known as the "Age of Pyramids" because many of the most magnificent pyramids were built during this time. Royalty and nobles spent fortunes building these elaborate tombs, which were stocked with everything a person could wish for in the afterlife. Many skilled craftsmen were employed to decorate and furnish the tombs. As thieves robbed many of the pyramids in ancient times, tombs were increasingly built in secret underground locations, such as the Valley of the Kings near Thebes, and without a pyramid to attract looters.

Mummies
The Ancient Egyptians preserved dead bodies so that people could use their own bodies in the afterlife. This involved removing and preserving the internal organs; filling the empty cavities; embalming the body; and finally wrapping it in linen bandages. This mummified form (above, left) would be placed in a wooden or stone coffin (above, right), which would have been ornately decorated if the deceased was wealthy or royal.

Cattle inspection
This ancient wall painting from a tomb shows a herder having his cattle counted and recorded.

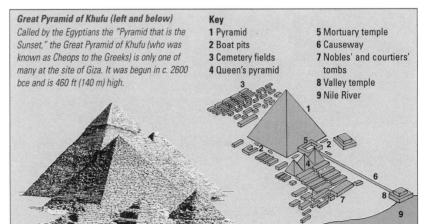

Great Pyramid of Khufu (left and below)
Called by the Egyptians the "Pyramid that is the Sunset," the Great Pyramid of Khufu (who was known as Cheops to the Greeks) is only one of many at the site of Giza. It was begun in c. 2600 bce and is 460 ft (140 m) high.

Key
1 Pyramid
2 Boat pits
3 Cemetery fields
4 Queen's pyramid
5 Mortuary temple
6 Causeway
7 Nobles' and courtiers' tombs
8 Valley temple
9 Nile River

© DIAGRAM

J. B. M. Hertzog
A Boer general in the Anglo-Boer War (1899–1902), Barry Hertzog was prime minister from 1924 to 1939. Hertzog created the Ministry of Native – later, Bantu – Affairs in 1910 and founded the Afrikaner-based National Party in 1912, two institutions that were central to apartheid.

Dr Daniel François Malan *(q.v.)*
Malan was prime minister from 1948 to 1954. He was a fierce Afrikaner nationalist and his cabinet was the first to consist entirely of Afrikaners and to use only Afrikaans. Malan promoted Afrikaner interests above those of anyone else.

The architect of apartheid
Under Malan, apartheid was largely a vote-winning slogan. It was Dr Hendrik Verwoerd (q.v.) – Minister of Native Affairs from 1950 to 1958 and prime minister from 1958 to 1966 – who actually introduced the policies needed to make apartheid a reality. Verwoerd tried to justify apartheid by describing it as "separate development of the races." He was assassinated in 1966.

Apartheid

Apartheid (the Afrikaans word for "apartness") was the name given to South Africa's policy of racial segregation, discrimination, and white domination that was in force from 1948 to 1991.

The roots of apartheid

By the time apartheid was officially introduced, racist policies had been practiced for over three hundred years in South Africa. The Dutch who settled on the Cape in the seventeenth century soon established semislave relationships with the local Khoikhoi population – whose way of life became dependent on Afrikaner (the name the Dutch settlers later adopted) employment. The Boers (the Dutch word for farmers) then began to import slaves from other parts of Africa and elsewhere to provide cheap labor for building and farming work.

In the nineteenth century, Britain took Cape Colony from the Dutch. In 1807, they outlawed slave trading – though slaves could still be kept legally – and, in 1820, about 4,000 Britons settled in the Cape. Unable to purchase slaves legally and with no free labor available, the new settlers set about wresting the Afrikaners' slaves from them by decreeing that nobody, of whatever color, could be forced into service. This was followed by the abolition of slavery throughout the British Empire in 1833. Combined with other changes, this threatened to destroy the Afrikaners' lifestyle, and, in 1836, they began to trek to the interior of Africa where they planned to live unhampered by British bureaucrats. The Afrikaner republics that were set up en route of this Great Trek had as the bases of their constitutions the right of Afrikaner self-determination and the "right" to rule the "natives."

After the discovery of huge diamond and gold reserves, the British set about conquering the whole of present-day South Africa. The Afrikaners were defeated by the British during the Anglo-Boer War (1899–1902). A liberal backlash in Britain over the cruel measures used to win the war, however, set the agenda for Anglo-Boer conciliation. In 1910, the British colonies and the Afrikaner republics (most of which had been given their independence back in 1907) united to form the white-ruled Union of South Africa. Louis Botha, an Afrikaner, was the first prime minister.

Over the years, the Afrikaners – who were mainly farmers or, later, part of the underclass of urban workers – came to resent the British, who dominated the lucrative mining industry, skilled professions, the military, and the civil service. Indeed, the strident Afrikaner nationalist sentiment that emerged had developed largely as a result of British imperialism and domination. This nationalism was turned on the black population in force after the National Party (NP) – formed in 1912 to further Afrikaner interests – came to power in 1924. This does not mean, however, that English-speaking South Africans were not in collusion with the Afrikaners in the creation of apartheid.

The 1948 election

The NP merged, in 1934, with another party to form the United Party, which addressed the interests of both English-speakers and Afrikaners. The remnants of the

NP were resurrected by the Broederbond (an influential, secret nationalist Afrikaner society) and other Afrikaner extremists led by Dr Daniel François Malan. This "purified" National Party came to power in 1948 promising to create apartheid. Malan promised to send all black people to reserves, run a white-only economy, and "to save civilization from black hordes" – a task he claimed to be ordained by God. This message appealed to many white industrial workers who feared competition from the black majority for their jobs. Apartheid was also welcomed by the mine owners and white farmers as it allowed them to maintain the profitable – for them – status quo. In order to provide themselves with cheap labor, mine owners had long been employing black workers and installing them in cramped, single-sex barracks.

Apartheid in practice

Apartheid was different from the racial segregation practiced historically in South Africa because it was enshrined in, and enforced by, the law. Under J. B. M. Hertzog the Ministry of Native – later, Bantu – Affairs (created in 1910) began drafting some of the laws and policies that formed the bones of apartheid. Although many racist policies were in place before 1948, after this date they were extended and enforced to a greater extent.

DISENFRANCHISEMENT At the heart of apartheid was the denial of voting rights to all but the white population. Like other policies, disenfranchisement had a long history. The first Afrikaner republics of the 1800s had only allowed Afrikaner men to vote. Also, the British passed a law to deny black people the right to vote outside the Cape. Within the Cape, few could meet the strict educational and financial requirements needed to qualify. Indian and "Colored" voters were given separate houses of representation in 1983, but in a ratio that ensured continued white domination. In protest, many did not exercise their right to vote.

RELOCATION Relocation policies aimed to limit the number of black people staying overnight in "white" towns and to segregate people within urban areas. After the 1913 Native Land Act, black South Africans were allowed to buy or rent land only in "native reserves." Over sixty percent of the population was restricted to living in only 7.3 percent of the land (later increased to 13 percent). Denied access to land, black

Segregation of amenities
After the Defiance Campaign of civil disobedience in 1952, the government introduced the Separate Amenities Act. Separate facilities had to be provided for different races and this included public benches, beaches, and even stairways. The bill also stated that the facilities did not have to be of an equal standard.

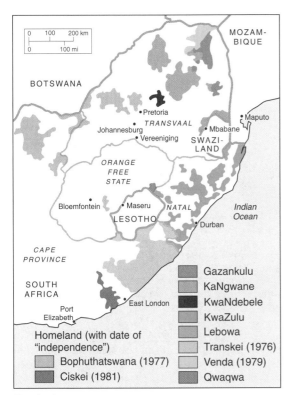

Homelands

At first self-governing – as long as the Minister of Bantu Affairs approved – many homelands were given their "independence" after 1970. This independence was not recognized anywhere but inside South Africa as it was simply an excuse for the government not to concern itself with the provision of facilities. More importantly, the inhabitants of homelands could be denied any rights in the rest of South Africa as they were now "foreign" nationals. Homelands were wholly dependent on external areas for work: industries were encouraged to set up on the edge of homelands but not inside. Most homeland leaders – with the exception of Chief Buthelezi, Prime Minister of KwaZulu – were supporters of apartheid.

South Africans had to work for the white population, who needed their labor on farms, in towns, and down the mines. The 1948 Group Areas Act created separate residential and business areas for each officially-designated race into which people could be forcibly moved.

HOMELANDS By the 1960s, it was obvious that the reserves were unviable; they were overpopulated and under-resourced, and starvation was widespread. Nevertheless, in 1959 the 260 reserves were organized into several homelands or Bantustans. Despite segregationist policies, sixty percent of the black population lived in "white" areas in 1948. Between 1960 and 1983, however, over three million people were evicted to live in the homelands.

COLOR BARS Color bars prevented the majority of South Africans from doing many things, such as working as skilled professionals. Unofficial color bars had long been in existence in the mining industry, for example. White workers filled supervisory and skilled positions while black workers were left to do the lower-paid manual jobs. When the mines tried to promote black workers to supervisory positions in 1922 – simply to save money on wages – strikes and demonstrations by white miners nearly caused a civil war. Two years later the NP came to power with the support of the white-only trade unions and immediately legalized color bars.

BANTU EDUCATION In 1955, the Bantu Education Act was passed. After this date, many students were denied the right to a high-standard academic education. Instead, a poor-quality education was provided as approved by the Department of Native (Bantu) Affairs. Schools that refused to conform were closed down and reluctant teachers sacked.

POPULATION REGISTRATION Act Under this act, every South African was required to register and be classified by "race," which would then be stamped in his or her identity pass. This would then be used to determine, for example, where people could live, what job they could do, and who they could marry.

PASS LAWS The first pass law – the Hottentot Code – was introduced by the British to the Cape Colony in 1809. It required that all Khoikhoi have a fixed place of abode and a pass with an employer's stamp if they needed to travel. This law forced the Khoikhoi to work for the Afrikaners in order to get a pass. Although repealed a few years later – in order to create a mobile supply of workers for the British settlers – it was the first of many similar laws. Pass laws gave the authorities power to restrict people's access to towns, send others back to homelands, and ensured the supply of labor to the white population.

Front-line states

Wealthy and heavily armed, South Africa was able to dominate neighboring countries – the front-line states in the fight against apartheid – in order to protect its own policies. Intimidation, sabotage, military action, and subversion were all used to destabilize the regimes that South Africa found threatening and prop up those that supported it – the illegal white-minority regime in Rhodesia (present-day Zimbabwe), for example. Using the excuse of trying to eliminate its enemies' guerrilla bases, South Africa invaded many front-line states. Angola was invaded, bombed, and – along with Mozambique – subjected to a prolonged civil war due, in part, to South Africa's funding of rebel groups. Other East and Central African countries suffered from these problems through the influx of refugees from war zones. Namibia was illegally occupied by South Africa (as South West Africa) until 1990 and a form of apartheid was introduced. South Africa easily pressured Lesotho and Swaziland, which are economically reliant on the goodwill of South Africa, into supportive roles. Border blockades were often used to force Lesotho's policies into line.

Opposition to apartheid

Opposition to apartheid was widespread, involved people of all colors, and took many forms. The first organized resistance was led by Mohandas Karamchand Gandhi, an Indian lawyer, who came to Natal in 1893 and stayed until 1914. Using nonviolent methods and recourse to the law, Gandhi was an inspiration to later movements. The South African Native National Congress – it became the African National Congress (ANC) in 1923 – was formed in 1912. Its first leaders – John L. Dube, president, and Sol Plaatje, secretary – attempted to effect changes by appealing to Britain and challenging unjust laws in court. The government's stubborn refusal to reform, however, led to

Pass laws

During apartheid, pass laws were used to enforce racial segregation. Every black person had to carry a pass – with an employer's stamp if they were in a "white" town. Police could stop people at any time to check their passes.

Treason Trial

The 1956 "Treason Trial" of 156 people involved in the 1952 Defiance Campaign – including Nelson Mandela (q.v.) – lasted until 1961. All charges were eventually dismissed as the defendants' nonviolent principles did not substantiate the government's claim that they had incited violence. The trial attracted worldwide attention, which enabled the International Defense and Aid Fund to be established to fund antiapartheid activities.

Sharpeville massacre

In 1960, a demonstration organized by the newly-formed Pan-Africanist Congress (PAC) outside a police station in Sharpeville was fired on by the police. Sixty-nine people were killed – most were shot in the back – and over one hundred were injured.

Patrolling the townships *(above)*
Regular patrols by armed police made townships seem like war zones. Many people were moved to these government-built townships out of sight of the "white" cities. Roads wide enough for a tank to turn around were built and an empty space left around the edge of the township – wider than the range of a rifle – so that troops could easily contain any uprising.

the development of more militant methods. The ANC really became a mass movement only in 1944 with the founding of the ANC Youth League by Anton Lembede. His colleagues included Nelson Mandela (q.v.), Walter Sisulu (q.v.), and Oliver Tambo (q.v.).

One of the first examples of successful mass political mobilization was the Defiance Campaign of 1952. With Indian and other groups and using trained volunteers, the ANC orchestrated local defiances of unjust laws all over the country. The campaign was called off after outbreaks of violence occurred. Reprisals by the government were often severe. Police powers were increased to deal with the growing unrest caused by apartheid. Torture and informers were widely used and many died in police custody. More "humane" methods included the banning and restraining orders put on political activists in order to halt their activities.

In 1961, as president of the ANC, Tambo left South Africa to open overseas offices of the ANC. From Lusaka, Zambia, he organized guerrilla forays into South Africa and raised funds. In the same year, Mandela formed the Umkonto we Sizwe (Spear of the Nation) movement, which was to perform sabotage on economically important facilities – but to avoid harming people – in order to pressure the government into talks. The initial result was that Mandela and Sisulu, among others, were imprisoned for life in 1964.

Huge uprisings led by the schoolchildren of Soweto (the southwestern townships of Johannesburg) followed the announcement, in 1976, that Bantu education would be in Afrikaans. Protests escalated and strikes brought Johannesburg to a standstill. Police response was harsh, and by the end of the year over five hundred people, including many children, had been killed.

Most opposition leaders were committed to nonviolent methods (Desmond Tutu [q.v.] won the Nobel Peace Prize for his nonviolent campaigning) but this was sometimes ignored by others. Apartheid policies of segregation, not only by race but also by ethnic group, inevitably led to outbreaks of what came to be called "black-on-black" violence – though many incidents were no doubt incited by government agents. Although Chief Buthelezi's (q.v.) Zulu Inkatha move-

Steve Biko (q.v.)

Medical student Steve Biko was the leading thinker of the Black Consciousness movement, which emerged in the1970s. He believed that oppression had caused many to feel that they really were inferior to whites and argued that pride in being black should be cultivated instead. Biko was arrested in 1977 and killed while in police custody.

ment (originally formed in 1928 and reconvened in 1975) and Mandela's Umkonto were mutually supportive, their members often clashed.

The fall of apartheid

Deaf to moral arguments, economic reasons for the government to end apartheid brought matters to a crisis point. Even before the 1948 elections, serious drawbacks to segregationist policies had become obvious. The government soon discovered that labor provided by the excluded majority was vital for the fastest-growing sector of the economy: manufacturing industries. This labor force also needed to be well-educated and mobile enough to be efficient – impossible within apartheid. Employers, especially in the construction sector, often had to ignore color bars just to fill vacancies. After the Sharpeville massacre in 1960 and the 1970s Soweto uprisings, foreign investment halted, capital flowed out of the country, house prices and the share market slumped, and businesses collapsed. In many ways, apartheid did not make sound economic sense. Pressure at home and from abroad was also making the system increasingly unworkable. As increasing numbers of African and Asian countries joined the United Nations, calls for sanctions against South Africa grew. Antiapartheid movements had been arguing for sanctions for years and, in 1985, many international banks paid heed. Loans were not renewed and the promise of future ones withdrawn. In 1990, Mandela was released from prison and, in 1991, all apartheid legislation was repealed. Finally, in 1994, the first nonracial elections were held in South Africa and Mandela was elected president. The inequalities that apartheid created over many years will not disappear overnight though.

1994 elections

South Africa's first nonracial elections were held in 1994 and Nelson Mandela, as leader of the ANC, was elected president.

Benin

Historic Benin was a city-state, and later a kingdom, in what is now southeastern Nigeria. (The present independent country of Benin – known as Dahomey until 1975 – lies to the west of Nigeria and has no direct connection with this Benin.) The capital of the old empire was Benin City, which still stands on a branch of the Benin River and is the capital of the modern Nigerian province of Edo (another name for Benin and its inhabitants).

The king of Benin had the title of oba. He was an absolute monarch, but he had many religious duties and left the actual government to his ministers. The first known oba was a Yoruba prince from Ife called Oran-miyan, who became ruler in about 1176, though local dynasties existed before this date. About forty obas have held office since Oranmiyan, though the power of the current oba is limited to local government.

People and trade

The Kingdom of Benin reached its greatest extent in the two hundred years beginning in the mid-1400s. It reached as far west as modern Lagos, where Benin set up a ruling dynasty. The people of Benin were the Bini, who spoke a language also called Bini. They were farmers, hunters, and warriors. Their artists made fine sculptures in metal and terra cotta. The most important works of art were made of brass, though they are often called Benin "bronzes," and include plaques, statues, busts, masks, and jewelry.

Benin became wealthy through trade with other African peoples, mostly in such goods as copper, foodstuffs, ivory, and salt. The first Europeans to visit Benin were Portuguese explorers, who reached the coast in 1485. They have left the earliest descriptions of Benin City and its people. For several years the Portuguese traded with Benin, mostly buying peppers and slaves. Benin wanted firearms, which the Portuguese refused to supply. The rulers of Benin decided not to continue to sell slaves, and trade with Europe languished for about two hundred years. In the late 1800s, the Bini resumed selling slaves to European dealers.

The old city

A Flemish writer describing the city in the 1600s said it was large and prosperous. It was about 5 or 6 miles (8–9 km) around, protected by a high wall – except where it was defended by marshes or impenetrable vegetation. The streets were broad and the royal headquarters contained a number of magnificent buildings. The British took over the Kingdom of Benin in 1897 and made it part of the protectorate (colony) of Southern Nigeria. In the same year, British forces stormed Benin City and burned part of it as punishment for the massacre of an unarmed trade mission. Many brass, copper, and ivory works of art were seized and sent to London. The descendants of the Bini still flourish in and around Benin City. The language is spoken by more than two million people in southwestern Nigeria, who are now mostly known as the Edo.

Religious beliefs

The people of Benin had many gods, some regarded as beneficial and some not. Osanobua, the creator, and

Queen Mother
This brass bust of a queen mother is thought to date from the 1500s. The title of queen mother was introduced by Oba Esigie, whose reign began about 1504. He wanted to honor his own mother.

Kingdom of Benin
The historic Kingdom of Benin was in what is now southeastern Nigeria.

his son Olokun were gods who brought prosperity and long life. Ogun was the god of farmers, hunters, and metalworkers. Ohgiuwu, the bringer of death, and Esu, the trickster, were other gods. The Bini believed that every human had a spirit of destiny, called an Ehi, which the soul created before birth in conversation with Osanobua. The religion of old Benin is very similar to that practiced by the present-day Yoruba people.

View of Benin City
This seventeenth-century illustration shows the bustle of Benin City.

The "Leopard of the Town"
This brass plaque was made during the 1500s. It shows an oba (king) with his tame leopard cub, a symbol of kingship in Benin. The oba was sometimes called the "Leopard of the Town." The second figure may have been the oba's wife.

Ivory sistrum
This elaborately carved ivory artifact is from the sixteenth century. It is a sistrum, a rattlelike musical instrument with bells inside.

© DIAGRAM

Figure of a woman
This brass figure from Benin was made sometime in the 1700s and is one of the famed Benin "bronzes."

Birthplace of humanity

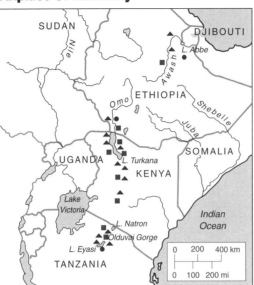

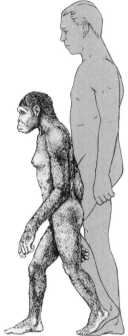

Australopithecus afarensis
This artist's reconstruction compares afarensis with, in the background, a modern male human.

Lucy (above)
This skeleton, nicknamed "Lucy," is of the genus Australopithecus afarensis and was found in 1974 in northern Ethiopia.

Over one hundred years ago, the naturalist Charles Darwin suggested that humans originated in Africa. We now know that this is probably true; scientific discoveries since the 1950s have shown, in fact, that the earliest human beings and their immediate ancestors most likely evolved in East Africa. The oldest known fossils of human ancestors have been discovered in Ethiopia, Kenya, and Tanzania. These precursors of present-day human beings are collectively called "hominids," from the Latin word "homo," meaning "man." Scientists group humans, apes, monkeys, and several other animals, such as lemurs, together as primates. They believe the primates all had a common ancestor, which lived in East Africa more than five million years ago.

The earliest hominids

Fossilized bones of several specimens of the earliest known hominid were discovered in eastern Ethiopia by American anthropologists in 1992–94. This creature has been named Australopithecus ramidus (ramidus means "root" in the language of the Afar who live in the area; Australopithecus means "southern ape"). This species lived about 4.4 million years ago, 500,000 years before the previously known earliest hominid. Several species of australopithecines have been found, some in East Africa and some in southern Africa. Before ramidus the oldest known hominid was Australopithecus afarensis ("southern ape of Afar"). In 1974, a partial afarensis skeleton, three-million-years old, was found in northern Ethiopia (in the Afar region) and was nicknamed "Lucy." Both ramidus and afarensis were lightly built and only about 4 ft (1.3 m) tall. So was the next oldest species, Australopithecus africanus, which probably lived from three million to one million years ago. A later species, boisei, was discovered in East Africa in 1959; it was named after a British industrialist, Charles Boise, who funded East African fossil hunts.

The first humans

After the australopithecines, all our supposed ancestors are grouped in the scientific genus Homo. The first

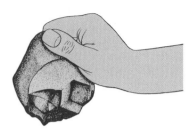

known species of Homo was habilis, or "handyman." Habilis remains were discovered in Tanzania in 1961, and it probably lived about two million years ago. It is thought that the earliest known toolkit, containing pebbles chipped into tool-like shapes, was made by habilis; these and other artifacts from what is known as the Oldowan Culture have been found in the Olduvai Gorge in Tanzania. Habilis is also believed to have built shelters to live in and hunted for food. Evidence of early campsites suggests that the earliest human settlements might have been at Olduvai Gorge. The remains of very early fences and even a stone circle that was probably the foundation for a hut have been found, making it, at nearly two-million-years old, the oldest known human-built structure.

The next hominid was Homo erectus, "upright man." Its earliest fossil was found near the western shore of Lake Turkana in Kenya, and is 1.6-million-years old. Homo erectus spread from East Africa over Europe and Asia, and persisted until about 200,000 years ago. Modern humans belong to the species Homo sapiens sapiens, which appeared sometime between 400,000 and 300,000 years ago in Africa, Europe, and Asia, and are almost certainly descended from erectus.

Fossil hunters

Much of the research into early humans in East Africa was carried out by Anglo-Kenyan anthropologists of the Leakey family – Louis and Mary Leakey (q.v.) and their sons Richard (q.v.) and Jonathan – and their Kenyan co-workers, including Bernard Ngeneo and Kimoya Kimeu, who made some of the most important finds. One of Kimeu's most important discoveries was a Homo erectus skeleton, 1.5-million-years old, found in 1984 near Lake Turkana in northern Kenya.

Olduvai Gorge
Olduvai Gorge, in northern Tanzania, is a deep cleft in the ground in the Great Rift Valley. Its cliffs are 330 ft (130 m) high and expose deposits ranging in age from 10,000 to 2,000,000 years old. Stone tools made by members of the Oldowan Culture 2.5 million years ago, have been found in Olduvai Gorge.

Carthage

According to legend, Dido, queen of the Phoenician city of Tyre, founded Carthage. She fled to North Africa with a small band of warriors after her brother murdered her husband. Dido asked the Berber inhabitants of the region for a plot of land on which to build a city; she was offered as much as could be surrounded by a bull's hide. She ordered the hide to be cut into thin strips, which laid end to end surrounded a large block of land.

Phoenicia was an ancient region of city-states in the coastal regions of present-day Syria and Lebanon. For hundreds of years, the trading ships of the Phoenicians dominated the waters of the Mediterranean Sea. In the course of trade they founded a number of colonies, the greatest of which was Carthage, founded in 814 BCE. Carthage stood on a promontory on the shores of the Gulf of Tunis, close to the modern city of Tunis. The sea defended Carthage on three sides. On the landward side, the Carthaginians built a huge wall, 30 ft (9 m) thick and more than 50 ft (15 m) high. Quarters for thousands of soldiers, horses, and 300 elephants were built nearby. Carthage replaced an older Phoenician settlement called Utica, which was about 15 miles (24 km) to the northwest. Carthage was probably independent from about 600 BCE.

Carthage had two excellent harbors and a large fleet of vessels. The oblong outer harbor was for merchant shipping. A narrow channel led to the circular inner harbor, which had berths for 220 warships. Trade with sub-Saharan Africa and across the Mediterranean Sea were the bases of Carthage's wealth and power. Dates and animal skins from the Sahara; ivory, slaves, and gold from West Africa; grain and copper from Sardinia; silver from Spain; tin from Britain; and grains, wine, glassware, and textiles from Carthage itself were traded.

Daily life

People lived in houses with many floors that stood on very narrow streets; whole families often slept in just one room. At ground level were open-fronted shops. Sanitation was basic and the city suffered from repeated epidemics. Wealthy Carthaginians lived on estates outside the city, surrounded by orchards, farms, and Berber villages.

Carthaginian farmers concentrated on the intensive cultivation of almonds, figs, grapes, olives, pears, and pomegranates. Berber farmers supplied staple foods such as cereals and vegetables. Cattle, goats, horses, poultry, bees, and sheep were kept. Transportation was provided by mules and donkeys.

Carthaginian men wore long gowns with sleeves, and turbans or conical caps. Their hair was cut short and they had long pointed beards. Women wore long gowns and veils over their heads. Both men and women wore jewelry, including nose rings, and often used perfume. Carthaginian craftsmen and artists were greatly influenced by Greece in their work. Typically, though, Carthaginian statues had heavier, more robust forms than the finer Greek ones. Many artifacts and statues were imported from Greece or made by resident Greek artists. Carthage had an extensive library, most of which was destroyed by the invading Romans – except for an encyclopedia of farming techniques.

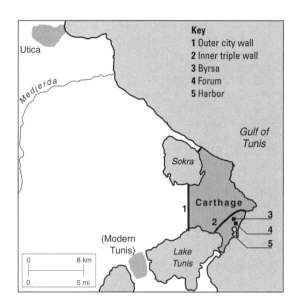

Key
1 Outer city wall
2 Inner triple wall
3 Byrsa
4 Forum
5 Harbor

Coinage
An African elephant appears on this Carthaginian coin. Carthage did not have its own curreny until c. 400 BCE. The Carthaginians managed to tame elephants and Hannibal used them in the invasion of Italy during the Second Punic War (218–201 BCE).

Carthaginian religion

The Carthaginians worshipped Phoenician deities – the Sun god Baal-Moloch and the Moon goddess Astarte. They renamed them Baal-Haman and Tanit-Pene-Baal, meaning "Tanit the Face of Baal." Priests served Baal-Haman and priestesses served Tanit. The Carthaginians mostly buried their dead and practiced embalming – archeologists have found many preserved bodies. Like the Egyptians, the Carthaginians made and buried grave goods for the afterlife. Most of these were terra-cotta models.

Decline of Carthage

For a long time, the local Berbers of Numidia were friendly to the Carthaginians, but eventually they turned against them under the leadership of King Masinissa (reigned 201–148 BCE). This conflict – when combined with a series of wars against the Romans, (the three Punic Wars, 264–146 BCE) – wore out the strength of Carthage. In 146 BCE, the Roman general Scipio Aemilianus captured the city and destroyed it. The Romans later built a new city of Carthage, but on a different site.

Statues
These terra-cotta heads show typical Carthiginian styles of dress. The man has a long beard but no mustache and the woman wears a long headdress. Both women and men often wore nose rings, as these heads show.

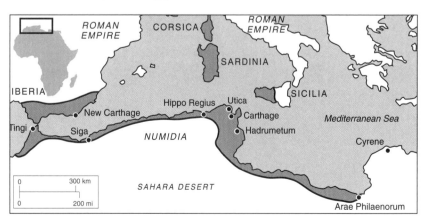

Hannibal's empire
Thanks to the military skills of the great Carthaginian general Hannibal (who lived 247–183 BCE), Carthage came to control most of the North African coast, parts of Spain and Sicily, and Corsica and Sardinia. It was their island possesions that brought Carthage into conflict with the Romans and led to the three Punic Wars.

© DIAGRAM

Ethiopian crosses
Ethiopian crosses vary greatly in design but all are usually intricately worked. The cross shown is a processional cross and would be mounted on the end of a tall, wooden staff. Such crosses have been made in Ethiopia since the twelfth century. In Ethiopia, crosses are associated with the resurrection as well as the crucifixion of Christ.

Christianity in Ethiopia

About half the people of two East African countries, Ethiopia and Eritrea, are Christians, and the story of their religion begins almost 2,000 years ago. According to tradition, Saint Mark the Evangelist was preaching Christianity in Alexandria, Egypt, not many years after the crucifixion of Jesus. The Christian Church in Alexandria regards him as its founder. A series of Christian Churches spread southward from Alexandria along the Nile River Valley, and by the 300s had reached Axum, the capital of an ancient Ethiopian kingdom. The Nile Valley Churches perished, except for the Egyptian Coptic Church, but Ethiopian Christianity survived and, isolated in a mountainous terrain, even withstood the influx of Muslims into East Africa in the 800s.

Lalibela

The heart of East African Christianity is Lalibela, which lies in rough country less than 100 miles (160 km) east of Lake Tana. Under its old name of Roha, it was the capital city of the Zagwe dynasty, which ruled in northern Ethiopia in the Middle Ages. Tradition has it that in the late 1300s a prince was born there and christened Lalibela, and the place is now named for him. When Lalibela became king, he set about constructing eleven churches in the town. The churches are cut into the solid, red volcanic rock in three groups. Four of the churches are huge blocks of stone cut and carved into buildings and set amid deep trenches. The other seven are more closely

attached to the cliffs in which they are cut. A network of artificial caves and tunnels connects the churches, which are served by about a thousand priests and a community of nuns.

Despite the legend of Lalibela, some experts believe at least some of the churches were begun well before his time, possibly even before the arrival of Christianity in Ethiopia. One church is known to be older: it is the Church of Mekina Medahane Alem, which was built in the conventional way inside a vast cave 300 years before Lalibela. The town of Lalibela today is hardly more than a village, but it is a place of pilgrimage at Genna (Christmas) and Timkat (Epiphany – the revelation and baptism of Christ).

Christian art

Ethiopian Christian art is based on the cross, of which there are many elaborate designs. Craftsmen in the Axumite Kingdom made early crosses of gold or iron. When the center of government and Christianity moved to Lalibela, copper became the preferred metal. Later crosses, not made in Lalibela, are of wood or brass. The designs of crosses may have been copied from those of the Coptic Church of Egypt, with which the Ethiopian Church has links, and are of several types. Tall crosses are carried in processions; pilgrims carry crosses on staves on their shoulders; men and children wear neck crosses, while women wear theirs lower as pendants; priests have hand crosses for blessing the faithful. Cross symbols are also used in manuscripts as paragraph signs. Manuscript copies of the Gospels were made from the 1200s onward in Ethiopia, mostly on parchment and often richly decorated.

Illuminated manuscript
These pages from an illuminated manuscript of the Four Gospels were made in the 1600s. Christ and the Four Evangelists are shown on the left-hand page. The text is written in Geez, an ancient Ethiopian language, and was probably originally translated from Greek.

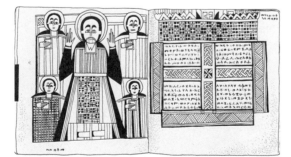

Cut from the living rock
Beta Ghiorghis, which means the "House of Saint George," is one of the eleven churches in Lalibela. It is cross shaped, and cut out of the solid rock. It is more than 40 ft (12 m) high. Legend says that St George himself supervised its construction, and the hoofprints of his horse are held to be still visible in the ditch around the church.

Pilgrim's prayers (below)
The pilgrim carries a carved wooden cross and a wooden staff. The staff represents the rod with which Moses struck a rock in the wilderness and brought forth water. He is reading from the most popular Ethiopian prayer book, the Psalms of David.

Colonists in Sierra Leone and Liberia

The slave trade indirectly led to the establishment of new communities on the West African coast: Freetown, now the capital of Sierra Leone, and Monrovia, now the capital of Liberia. Both were peopled by former slaves and their descendants who had been forcibly transported from their homes in West Africa to Britain and the Americas. They were established by abolitionists in Britain and the United States (US), both as a way to atone for the horrors of the slave trade and to resolve what was a growing social problem regarding the undefined role of former slaves.

Freetown: a community of "recaptives"

Freetown was established in the late eighteenth century by an English humanitarian group, the Sierra Leone Company. It was settled by freed slaves from Britain (some of the men accompanied by their white English wives), who were joined by freed slaves from Nova Scotia, including Maroons – former slaves from Jamaica who had been deported to Nova Scotia after an initially successful revolt against their owners – and by former slaves who had sided with the British in the American War of Independence in exchange for their freedom.

The new settlers of Freetown were not well received by the African population. The local Temne people would not give up land to the colonists, and in 1789 the Temne nearly destroyed Freetown. In 1807 Sierra Leone was made a British colony, and the population increased with more people freed from slave ships by British antislavery activists.

Most of these settlers – also called "recaptives" and the descendants of whom are today called "Creoles" – were converted to Christianity and educated in English traditions. But many, especially those who were Yoruba, also retained their African culture and language, resulting in the mix of English and African languages that are known as Creole languages. Some also returned to their homelands: Samuel Ajayi Crowther (q.v.), a Yoruba Creole and the first black bishop of the Anglican Church, returned to his native Nigeria and became a well-known historian and writer on the Yoruba language.

In the late nineteenth century, the Creoles – who had become the educated elite of Sierra Leone –

were replaced in positions of power by white Europeans. Nevertheless, they continued to have a major influence on the development of the country, and in particular on the rise of African nationalism. They were at the forefront of the independence movement that began in the 1930s.

Monrovia: "asylum from degradation"

Monrovia was founded in 1847 by a white philanthropic group called the American Colonization Society, though settlers had already been arriving in the region since the 1820s. Named after James Monroe, US president at the time, it was a settlement for freed slaves from the US. The Americans were also joined by thousands of Africans who were freed by US patrol vessels trying to interrupt the slave trade. These liberated slaves – the "Congoes," as they came to be called – were soon absorbed into what became the Americo-Liberian community.

The attitude of the newcomers toward the region's inhabitants differed little from that of white settlers toward Africans in other parts of the continent. The Americo-Liberians were determined to retain American culture and so-called "civilized" standards and resisted integration with the "tribals" – the name they gave to the indigenous population.

The Americo-Liberians and their descendants were always a minority but, until the 1980s, they were Liberia's elite, providing most of the country's presidents. Also, the professions of law and the senior ranks of the civil service were dominated by Americo-Liberians, who shunned agriculture, seeing it as a reminder of their slave origins.

Americo-Liberians were devout Christians – most were members of the long-established American Episcopal, Baptist, or Methodist churches – and placed great importance in symbols of Western culture so as to distance themselves from what they saw as "barbarous" Africa. They built houses in the style of the American South and dressed in formal European clothing (including top hats and tailcoats on state occasions), which was inappropriate in the tropics. Their children were usually sent abroad to complete their studies, often to the US.

It was common practice for Americo-Liberians to bring African children into their homes, raise them as Christians, and teach them English. Following the custom of white Southern US plantation owners, Americo-Liberian men often kept "tribal" wives in addition to having a wife from their own social background. Children of such unions were often adopted by the Americo-Liberian family, contributing to the gradual merging of Americo-Liberians with indigenous peoples that exists today.

Creole college
Fourah Bay College (now part of Sierra Leone University) was founded in 1827. It was attended by many notable Creoles.

President's residence
The style of the American South was visible in Americo-Liberian architecture, such as the president's official residence

Declaration of Independence
(excerpts below)
Liberia's Declaration of Independence written in 1847 when the Republic of Liberia was established, explains why Americans settled in Africa and expresses the aspirations that they had brought with them.

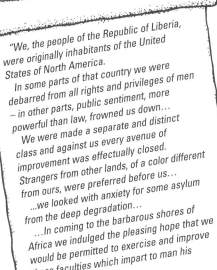

"We, the people of the Republic of Liberia, were originally inhabitants of the United States of North America.
In some parts of that country we were debarred from all rights and privileges of men – in other parts, public sentiment, more powerful than law, frowned us down...
We were made a separate and distinct class and against us every avenue of improvement was effectually closed.
Strangers from other lands, of a color different from ours, were preferred before us...
...we looked with anxiety for some asylum from the deep degradation...
...In coming to the barbarous shores of Africa we indulged the pleasing hope that we would be permitted to exercise and improve those faculties which impart to man his dignity..."

© DIAGRAM

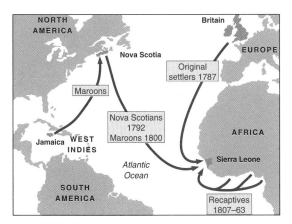

Paths to Sierra Leone
Freed slaves came from Jamaica, via Nova Scotia, and from Britain to settle Freetown in the eighteenth century.

Former empires

Three empires in turn dominated West Africa from the 300s to the late 1500s: Ghana, Mali, and Songhay. A fourth empire, that of Kanem-Borno, lay farther east. Ghana and Mali are known as the Empire of Ghana and the Empire of Mali to distinguish them from the present-day states with the same names. For more than a thousand years, these empires flourished and grew wealthy by trading in gold and salt. Most of what we know about them comes from West African oral history and accounts written by travelers and traders from North Africa, such as the Arab geographer Al Bakri in the 1060s and the Moroccan explorer Ibn Battuta, who visited Songhay and Mali in the 1300s.

Empire of Ghana

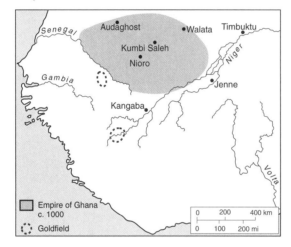

Empire of Ghana
c. 1000
Goldfield

The Soninke people were the citizens of historic Ghana. They are a present-day people and speak a language also called Soninke, which belongs to the Mande language group. Present-day Soninke people live in Senegal. A Berber family, the Maga, were probably the founders of Ghana in c. 300. The empire was called Wagadu by its people. In the 500s, the Soninke overthrew the Maga. The despotic king of this empire was called the ghana (war-chief), and other peoples began to use the title of the ruler as the name of the empire.

Ghana lay to the north of the Senegal and Niger rivers, in what is now western Mali and southern Mauritania. Its capital, Kumbi Saleh, lay southwest of Timbuktu (modern Tombouctou). It was a twin city. One part was a stone-built Muslim town, with a dozen mosques (Muslim houses of worship) and 20,000 inhabitants. This was the commercial center, where Berber traders brought fabrics, manufactured goods, and food to exchange for gold and salt. It also became a center for the spread of Islam, which was introduced in the 1050s. The other part of the town was where the ghana lived, and he made sure that Soninke religion and ways of life prevailed there.

Medieval Ghana's sources of power and prosperity were the gold and salt trades. For much of its timespan, the state controlled the West African ends of the trans-Saharan trade routes. Some of Ghana's gold came from goldfields to the south, outside the empire's nominal borders, but the Soninke themselves mined most of it. Ghana remained powerful until 1076, when Islamic

invaders from the north overran it. It regained its independence after about ten years, and until the 1200s, was the richest country in West Africa. The king kept a large standing army with archers and cavalry to protect it. After 1200, invasions by the Susu people greatly weakened the empire. Ghana lingered on until 1240 when it was taken over by the Empire of Mali.

Empire of Mali

Medieval Mali was based on the smaller Kingdom of Kangaba, which was close to and dominated by historic Ghana. Kangaba was founded in c. 750 by the Mande-speaking Malinke people. In 1224, the Susu – a people now living in Guinea and Sierra Leone – overran Ghana, and six years later they invaded Kangaba. The invaders put to death all of the ruling family of Kangaba except for one crippled prince, Sundiata (q.v.), who they thought would not be a threat. This was their mistake. Sundiata was a great hunter and a good soldier; he became known as the "Lion of Mali." Sundiata built up his forces, and in 1235 defeated the Susu. By 1240, he had also conquered what was left of the Empire of Ghana, and the Empire of Mali came into existence.

The empire gradually expanded, and by the 1330s it extended to the Atlantic coast covering present-day Senegal, Gambia, Guinea-Bissau, most of modern Mali, parts of Mauritania, and even southern Algeria. It controlled three major trading points, Niani on the upper Niger River (now known only as ruins); Jenne (modern Djenné in Mali); and the legendary, desert-city of Timbuktu. The major sources of Mali's wealth were control of both the gold-trade routes and the goldfields of Bambuk, Bure, and others on the Volta River and in the forests of modern Ghana.

The last, and most, powerful ruler of medieval Mali was Mansa Musa (q.v.). A devout Muslim, he went on pilgrimage to Mecca in 1324, taking with him a huge quantity of gold. He stopped in Egypt on the way and gave away and spent so much gold that its price fell sharply, with disastrous effects on Egypt's currency.

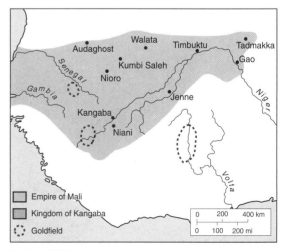

Empire of Mali
Kingdom of Kangaba
Goldfield

Empire of Mali
This is a map of Mali in c. 1335, two years before the death of its most powerful ruler, Mansa Musa. By this time, Mali had reached its greatest extent.

Empire of Ghana
This map of the Empire of Ghana shows its territories in c. 1000, toward the end of its era of power. Kumbi Saleh was the capital and Walata, Timbuktu, and Audaghost were major trading centers.

Mansa Musa on his throne
The first European map of West Africa was drawn in 1375 and depicts the Malian king, Mansa Musa. Mali's fame had obviously spread far around the world. Musa is holding up a large gold nugget as if to trade with the Arab merchant who is riding on a camel toward him.

Great Mosque of Djenné

This mosque in Djenné built earlier this century, stands on the same site as the original mosque built when the city was part of medieval Mali in the thirteenth century.

After he died thirteen years later, the Empire of Mali began to disintegrate. By c. 1490, Mali was no longer politically important and by c. 1550 it had been completely absorbed by the Songhay Empire.

Songhay Empire

Songhay was originally a small state founded by the Songhay people in c. 750. It lay on the Niger River across an important trade route, with its capital at Gao. About 1240, the Mali empire absorbed Songhay, but it regained its freedom by the 1340s. Songhay rose to greatness during the 28-year reign of Sunni Ali (q.v.). He began by seizing Timbuktu from the Tuareg, who had wrested it from Mali. Four years later he captured Jenne. By the time of his death in 1492, Sunni Ali had made Songhay the most powerful empire in West Africa. Songhay reached the height of its power during the reign of Askia Muhammad (q.v., 1493–1528). He was a devout Muslim, and he organized his large empire into provinces, each with a governor. Through military might and religious zeal, Songhay remained powerful until 1591, when Moroccans conquered it. In 1618, the Moroccans set up a puppet state, governed by the rulers of Timbuktu. This state lasted until 1787, when the Tuareg conquered it. Today, about 800,000 Songhay people still live in southern Mali. Their language, also called Songhay, is used by traders over a large area of West Africa.

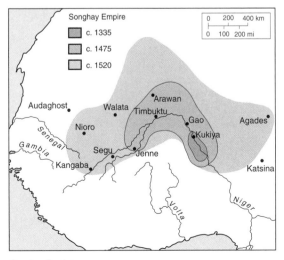

Songhay Empire

Above is a map of Songhay in c. 1515, during the reign of Askia Muhammad. Under this king, Songhay reached the height of its power and took over much of historic Mali's former territories.

Kanem-Borno

The empire of Kanem-Borno lay to the northeast of Lake Chad. According to tradition, an Arab leader, Dugu, founded Kanem in c. 800. His descendants ruled the land until 1846. Their dynasty was known as the Sefawa, after Dugu's grandfather, Sayf b. Dhi Yazan – a hero credited with freeing the Yemeni in southwest Asia from foreign rule. The people they ruled over in Africa were the Kanembu, an originally nomadic ethnic group who spoke a language called Kanuri. Their descendants live in Chad, Niger, and Nigeria today.

Kanem became a wealthy empire because of its control of trade routes. It exported ivory, slaves, and gold and imported salt, copper, tools, and horses. By 1150, Kanem was an Islamic state. During the 1200s, it expanded to the north and west and by 1230 Kanem had reached its greatest extent.

Borno was at first a province of Kanem, but in the 1300s nomadic invaders forced the Sefawa to flee from Kanem to Borno, southwest of Lake Chad, and Borno was established in 1386. By the 1500s, Borno had become the dominant power, and Kanem became a province of Borno in 1526. The empire of Kanem-Borno became a center of Islamic civilization. After the collapse of Songhay in 1591, Kanem-Borno became the most powerful empire in sub-Saharan Africa. From 1671, however, the empire began to decline. Much territory was lost in the 1700s and 1800s to the Tuareg people in the north and the Fulani people in the south. Kanem-Borno lasted until it was invaded by the Darfurian slave trader Rabih b. Fadl Allah between 1892 and 1893.

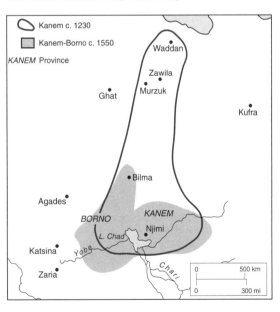

Borno royal procession

A nineteenth-century engraving depicting the processsion of a sultan of Borno through one of the regional capitals.

Sankoré Mosque

The Sankoré Mosque in Tombouctou was built by the Muslim kings of Mali. It became the center of Islamic worship during the era of the Songhay Empire, and West Africa's first university was established within its walls. It is built of mud bricks and is the oldest surviving mosque in West Africa.

Tomb of a mighty ruler

The tomb of Askia Muhammad of Songhay still survives. This is a view of the exterior.

Kanem-Borno

Left is a map showing the empire of Kanem in c. 1230 and Kanem-Borno in c. 1550. In 1230, Borno was still just a province of Kanem, which had reached its greatest extent. After being ousted from Kanem, by 1550 the rulers had regained a lot of their old territories from their new base in Borno. The Kanem-Borno Empire reached its height after the collapse of Songhay in 1591.

Jewish communities

Although there are only a few thousand Jews in North Africa today, until the foundation of Israel in 1948 and the rise of Arab nationalism in the 1950s and 1960s, the Jewish population numbered over 500,000. There were communities throughout North Africa, the majority of whom lived in the region's main towns and cities. Over the past few decades, the Jewish communities of Egypt, Libya, and Algeria have virtually ceased to exist, but a few small communities remain in Tunisia and Morocco.

History of settlement in North Africa

Between the sixth and third centuries BCE, many Jews emigrated from Palestine to Egypt and the region of present-day Libya. Their settlement was encouraged by the Egyptians to populate and defend border regions. Communities were established elsewhere in North Africa, with Jewish traders reaching Morocco by the second century BCE. Following a failed Jewish revolt against Roman rule of Egypt in 115–17 CE, the Egyptian Jewish community was destroyed and Jews were not to return for several centuries. Elsewhere, Jews participated in resistance to the Muslim Arab invasion of North Africa in the seventh century with, for example, Berber converts to Judaism achieving a number of victories in Algeria.

By 711, Arabs had conquered all of North Africa, and Jewish immigrants from southwest Asia soon followed the Arabs into Africa. In Egypt, a Jewish presence was reestablished, and by the twelfth century Egypt's Jewish population numbered between twelve and twenty thousand. Although the Arabs often pressured Jews to convert to Islam, most Jewish communities resisted Islamicization. New arrivals from southwest Asia strengthened Jewish communities and kept them in touch with religious developments elsewhere.

In 1492, Jews who refused to convert to Catholicism were expelled from Spain and in 1496 from Portugal. Morocco and Algeria were important destinations for those expelled, but Spanish Jews also settled in towns and cities elsewhere in North Africa. The Spanish Jews maintained a separate existence from the local Arabic-speaking Jewish communities, preserving their language (Ladino – a medieval form of Spanish using the Hebrew script) and religious rituals until modern times.

Under Muslim rule, the treatment of Jews varied. Although under some rulers Jews were much respected, only in the thirteenth century was Judaism officially tolerated. Following the Ottoman (Turkish) takeover of Egypt in 1517 and the extension of its empire across North Africa, discrimination was often harsh. Although the Ottomans continued to encourage Spanish Jews to settle in North Africa, they were confined to ghettos and limited to practicing a few occupations. Nevertheless, the treatment of Jews in North Africa was generally no worse – and sometimes better – than that experienced by Jews in Europe at the time.

In the nineteenth century, much of North Africa came under European influence or control. This brought great changes to the position of the Jewish communities and opportunities for Jews to improve their economic status. Many Jews identified closely with French culture, and Algerian Jews were given automatic citizenship by the French, an act resented by the Muslims, who were not given this status. Jews from other parts of the Ottoman Empire, North Africa, Italy, and Eastern Europe migrated to Egypt – attracted by the tolerant environment – to escape persecution or for economic reasons.

Berber Jews

It is believed that some of the survivors of the Jewish revolt against the Romans (115–17), and Jews who fled later waves of persecution, found refuge among Berbers in western Libya and in the mountains and desert regions of Morocco and Algeria. Many of the Berbers with whom they settled converted to Judaism. Although most Berbers had adopted Islam by the twelfth century, small isolated groups of Jewish Berbers continued to live in the High Atlas Mountains on the edge of the Sahara until the early twentieth century.

Typical occupations

North African Jews generally lived in urban ghettos and were small-scale merchants or itinerant peddlers. Many were poor artisans, often acquiring their professional skills – in particular tailoring, leatherwork and metalwork, and filigreeing silver and gold jewelry – on a hereditary basis. In some areas, Jews dominated the wine trade, an activity prohibited to Muslims, cultivating vineyards and operating wine presses. This is the case even today on the Tunisian island of Djerba. A small Jewish elite also existed, basing their wealth on foreign trade and moneylending.

A Jewish family from Fez
Dressed in traditional costume, this Jewish family lived in Fez, Morocco, in the 1920s. Fez is one of North Africa's great commercial centers and was developed in part by Jewish traders. During the tenth and eleventh centuries, the city became a center of Jewish learning, attracting great rabbis, poets, and scholars from Spain. In modern times, the community has been much reduced by migration to Casablanca and abroad.

African refuge
During the European Middle Ages, the increase of Christian intolerance toward Judaism led to a period of Jewish expulsion. Between 1492 and 1497, many Jews from Spain, Portugal, Sardinia, and Sicily settled in the towns and cities of North Africa.

The Great Synagogue of Tunis
Built six centuries ago, this synagogue (Jewish house of worship) is in the Jewish quarter and is the oldest in Tunis. Following the exodus of most of Tunisia's Jews after 1948, Tunis and the small island of Djerba off the Tunisian coast have the only two remaining sizable Jewish communities left in Tunisia.

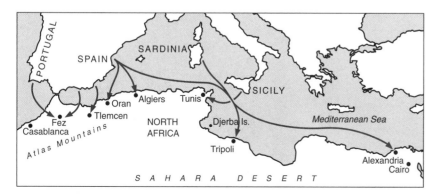

In the nineteenth century, occupational restrictions imposed on Jews were abolished, enabling them to become teachers, doctors, lawyers, and even politicians, and enabling merchants to expand into foreign trade and banking. Despite the position of Algerian Jews as French citizens and the newly acquired wealth and influence of some, it was not the Muslims who were most hostile to Jewish advances. It was the European settlers who most resented the competition from Jewish traders.

Departure from North Africa

The creation of Israel and the rise of Arab nationalism had a devastating effect on Jewish communities, which increasingly came under attack. During the Arab-Israeli War in 1948, hundreds of Egyptian Jews were arrested and their businesses seized. Bombings in Jewish areas of Cairo and Alexandria killed and injured hundreds of people. As a result, some 25,000 of Egypt's 70,000 Jews emigrated between 1948 and 1950. Most Jews, however, wanted to stay in Egypt, but nationalist measures threatened their schools, businesses, and jobs, leading to the emigration of virtually all Egyptian Jews within twenty years.

Elsewhere, Jews met with similar fates, most dramatically in Algeria, where in the early 1960s Jews found their loyalties tested in the violent war of independence against the French. Within a few years of Algeria's independence in 1962, almost the entire Jewish population of 140,000 had emigrated.

Only in Morocco and Tunisia do Jewish communities remain, though much reduced in number. From a Jewish population of 270,000 in 1948 there remain only about 18,000 Jews in Morocco, while in Tunisia the population fell from 105,000 to just 3,000. In Morocco, the majority live in Casablanca, though some remain in other ancient Jewish centers.

The Jews of North Africa are now widely scattered, living mainly in France, but also in Israel, Canada, and elsewhere. Wherever they settled, however, separate community institutions and synagogues were established, preserving in exile aspects of the North African Jewish tradition.

An example of a typical girl's dress
This Jewish girl, from south of the Atlas Mountains in Morocco, is wearing the traditional, everyday clothing of the 1930s. She is wearing an izar (a long, striped garment, usually red or white) that hangs down to her feet and is worn over a colored blouse called a derra.

An example of a typical boy's dress
This Jewish schoolboy is from one of the last Jewish communities of the southern Atlas Mountains in Morocco. He is wearing the traditional male costume of the 1920s and 1930s, including the akhnif (a long, beautifully embroidered cape).

Metalwork
Most North African Jews were artisans who made high-quality goods. These examples are from nineteenth-century Morocco.

1 Mortar and pestle made from brass and used for making cosmetics and medicines.

2 A hand indicator (or yad), made from molded and chiseled brass, for use while reciting from the Torah (the first five books of the Old Testament) – reciting the words from memory and touching the parchment are forbidden.

1

2

Exodus
In the twentieth century, the majority of Jewish people in North Africa have emigrated to France, Canada, or Israel. The figures on the map show the numbers of Jewish people who have left each country since the mid-twentieth century. Many had suffered persecution and resentment from other North African people.

MOROCCO
252,000

TUNISIA
102,000   Djerba Is.

Mediterranean Sea

ISRAEL

ALGERIA
140,000

LIBYA
35,000

EGYPT
70,000

Red Sea

Key

NOBATIA	Kingdom
(Abu Simbel)	Modern city or town
●	Historical site
▨	Kush (1750 –1500 BCE)

Nubian crown
This silver and gold crown was found on the head of a Nubian king in a tomb at Ballana. It is identical to those worn by the royalty of Meroe, as depicted in ancient reliefs found in Sudan.

Nubia

The historical region of Nubia covered parts of present-day southern Egypt and northern Sudan, extending southward along the Nile from its first cataract (unnavigable stretch) almost as far as present-day Khartoum, the Sudanese capital.

Nubian civilizations

Several civilizations emerged in Nubia. The oldest known – and the oldest in sub-Saharan Africa – is the Kingdom of Kush, which began to emerge as early as 3200 BCE. Around 2400 BCE, Kush entered its period of expansion. Nine hundred years later, however, the Kingdom of Kush was conquered by Ancient Egypt. Pictures and statues of Nubians have been found in Ancient Egyptian tombs.

Around 920 BCE, a dynasty of Nubian kings in Napata began to govern, as the Kingdom of Nubia, independently from Egypt. Under King Piankhy (reigned 751–712 BCE), Egypt was conquered and Nubia reached its territorial zenith. These gains began to be lost to invading Assyrians during the reign of Taharqa (683–663 BCE). In 671 BCE, the Nubians lost control of most of Egypt including Memphis, the capital, and by 657 BCE they had lost it all to the Assyrians.

The Nubian capital was moved from Napata to Meroe in c. 300 BCE and the powerful Meroitic Kingdom emerged. Meroe became an important center of iron making. In 324 CE, the Meroitic Kingdom collapsed after being defeated by the Ethiopian Axumite Kingdom.

After the fall of Meroe, Nubia broke up into three kingdoms: Nobatia; Makuria (or Makurra); and Alodia (or Alwa). Between 575 and 599, Makuria absorbed Nobatia and formed the larger kingdom of Dongola (or Dunqulah). This kingdom disappeared after Arabs invaded the region in the fifteenth century. Alodia collapsed in c. 1500 when it was overrun by the Funj Kingdom from farther south in present-day Sudan.

Archeological remains

Archeologists have discovered over one hundred ancient burial chambers of Nubian people. The earliest tombs date from c. 300–400 and were found at Qostol. The latest date from c. 500–550 and were found at Ballana. These sites are in present-day Egypt, just north of the second cataract of the Nile. They are attributed to Nubian civilizations that arose after the fall of Meroe – most likely the Nobatia Kingdom. The sites have since been flooded by the building of the Aswan High Dam.

The tombs were buried under mounds of earth from 7 to 40 ft (2–12 m) high. Under these mounds were the remains of mud-brick tombs. Many were obviously the graves of royalty; large numbers of people, horses, camels, and dogs had been put to death to accompany their masters and mistresses into the afterworld. The tombs were full of treasures – gold and silver jewelry, silverware and ironware, and many bronze articles including folding tables and chairs. The presence of many imported goods from Greece, Rome, and Egypt shows that the Nubians engaged in commerce with the rest of the world.

The Nubians were converted to Christianity in the sixth century and some of the later tombs contain Christian inscriptions. Archeologists have also found the ruins of a number of castles and early Christian churches. The Nubians mostly built their churches in brick, but a few were made of stone.

Lion Temple
The northern gateway of the Lion Temple at Naqa, showing Queen Amanitore smiting her foes. Built 2,000 years ago, this Meroitic temple is dedicated to the god Apedemak.

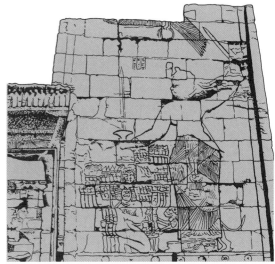

Modern Nubian house
In painting this house, the Nubian artist has used emblems and symbols that date from historical Nubia. Until recently, descendants of the Nubians still lived in the region. After the building of Egypt's Aswan High Dam in the 1960s, however, much of Nubia was flooded and many Nubians were relocated in Sudan or Egypt.

A	B	D	E	Ê	H (KH)	Ḥ (KH)	I	K	L	M	N

Ñ	P	Q	R	S	Š (SH)	T	TE	TÊ	W	Y

Meroitic writing
The people of Meroe developed their own alphabetical script, which used both characters and hieroglyphs (picture symbols).

Refugees

A refugee is basically someone who flees from their home or country to escape danger. The country to which a refugee flees is often called the host country. In general, refugees who do not cross international borders but remain within their own country are referred to as internally displaced people.

Africa has one of the world's largest refugee problems, but African countries are also among the world's most generous in trying to help refugees. Central African countries in particular are both the source and host of many refugees.

Why people become refugees

The reasons behind refugee crises are many and complex. A person may wish to escape from religious or political persecution, civil war, or ethnic conflict.

Some conflicts that have forced people to flee have their roots in colonialism and imperialism. Wars of liberation and the imposition of national boundaries – often with no regard to history, culture, or ethnicity – inevitably caused conflict. More recently, South Africa's occupation of Namibia and funding of rebel groups in Angola and Mozambique – partly responsible for these countries' prolonged civil wars – are the source of a significant proportion of refugees in Central Africa.

Ethnic and religious persecution are also common causes. The recent conflict in Rwanda and Burundi is a major source of refugees. In Zambia, Jehovah's Witnesses have been persecuted for refusing to state their allegiance to the nation (as demanded by their faith). The civil war in Sudan stems, in part, from the attempts of the north to impose Sharia (Islamic holy) law on the largely non-Muslim south.

CONGO (DEM. REP.), formerly Zaire, is host to many people from neighboring countries. In mid-1994, more than two million Rwandan refugees sought asylum in Zaire. In 1995, Zaire began forcibly repatriating the Rwandans but stopped after an international outcry and entrusted the task to the United Nations High Commissioner for Refugees (UNHCR). In 1996, however, thousands more fled to Zaire from Rwanda and Burundi, triggering the outbreak of civil unrest in the Zairean population. There are also many Ugandans in Congo (Dem. Rep.) who have fled political persecution at home as well as Sudanese people and Angolans fleeing the civil wars in their respective countries. Congo (Dem. Rep.) is also the source of many refugees. Burundi, Tanzania, South Africa, Uganda, and Angola all harbor people who have fled persecution there. The conflicts in the Shaba and Kasai provinces in the 1990s have been a major source. Some people suspect these conflicts were fomented by then President Mobutu (q.v.) to distract attention from the tense political situation.

CENTRAL AFRICAN REPUBLIC (CAR) From 1966 to 1979, Jean-Bédel Bokassa (q.v.) ruled CAR. His regime was cruel and despotic. As a result, many thousands fled to neighboring countries. Today, CAR is host to refugees fleeing the civil wars in Sudan and Chad.

ANGOLA For the last twenty years a bloody civil war raged in Angola causing thousands to flee the country while around one million have been internally displaced. Recent peace accords have ended the conflict for now, but it is unlikely Angolan refugees will return until they are sure the peace will last. The presence of an estimated nine million antipersonnel landmines left over from the war is a major deterrent to the return of refugees. Large areas of land are unusable and homelessness and malnutrition have resulted. The majority of Angolan refugees can be found in Congo (Dem. Rep.), Zambia, Congo (Rep.), and Namibia.

ZAMBIA Zambia is a relatively peaceful and stable country so it is an attractive destination for those facing uncertain futures. Zambia provides asylum for refugees from the civil wars of Angola and Mozambique. Although Mozambique is now at peace, many refugees cannot return as their land has been sold to private companies or allocated to civil servants by the new government.

EQUATORIAL GUINEA During Macías Nguema's (q.v.) brutal reign (1968–79), it has been estimated that around one-third of the population left the country. Although Macías was deposed in 1979, few of these refugees have returned to the country as they still fear persecution by the current government, which has a record of human rights abuses.

The effects of large refugee movements

Large refugee movements have an impact on both the source country and the host country. Large numbers of refugees can deprive a country of revenue, labor, markets, and political and economic stability. The refugees who fled Macías' Equatorial Guinea, for example, were often the better skilled and better educated members of the population and their loss has had a great impact on the country's economy. In the host country, the greatest impact that refugees have is often environmental. If they are concentrated in a large camp then often deforestation and perhaps overgrazing of the surrounding area occurs. Refugees can also have political consequences for their host country. The huge numbers of Rwandan and Burundi refugees in Congo (Dem. Rep.), many of them armed, has actually added to the political instability of that country and many antigovernment rebel groups took advantage of this.

International relations can also be adversely affected. The forced repatriation of Zairean refugees from Congo (Rep.) in 1992 soured the relationship between these countries. Neighboring countries such as Angola and Zaire have frequently accused each other of harboring antigovernment rebels as refugees.

Conversely, refugees can also bring benefits to their hosts: by providing a labor force in areas of scarcity, creating new or larger markets and business opportunities, and by farming underutilized land. Occasionally, host countries have benefited from the provision of infrastructure – roads and airstrips, for example – by organizations like the UNHCR.

The map shows refugee movements into, out of, and between the countries of Central Africa and the number* of refugees involved.

1 Rwanda to Zaire: 1,080,000

2 Burundi to Zaire: 120,000

3 Angola to Zaire: 200,000

4 Sudan to Zaire: 111,900

5 Angola to Zambia: 96,000

6 Sudan to Central African Republic: 25,900

7 Zaire to Burundi; 21,900

8 Chad to Central African Republic: 21,500

9 Mozambique to Zambia: 23,000

10 Uganda to Zaire: 18,500

11 Zaire to Tanzania: 15,800

12 Zaire to Zambia: 13,500

13 Angola to Congo: 12,000

14 Zaire to Angola: 10,700

15 Zaire to Uganda: 12,291

16 Chad to Congo: 2,100

17 Zaire to Sudan: 1,800

18 Angola to Namibia: 1,000

19 Zaire to South Africa: 800

20 Somalia to Zambia: 600

21 Angola to South Africa: 600

* Figures are from the period 1994–6. Source: UNHCR

© DIAGRAM

Loading the ship
This old engraving depicts slaves being loaded onto a ship for transportation, probably to the Americas.

Slavery

In the early sixteenth century, European colonists in the Caribbean and Central and South America forced Native Americans and European convicts to work their mines and plantations. Most of these unwilling workers died of disease and cruel treatment, so the settlers turned to Africa to solve their labor needs, believing that Africans could best withstand the harsh working conditions and tropical climate. The Spanish and Portuguese were the first to enter the Atlantic slave trade, but by the late sixteenth and early seventeenth centuries many other European nations had established forts and trading posts along the coast of West Africa from present-day Senegal to Angola. By the time the slave trade was finally halted in the late nineteenth century (over fifty years after it was banned by Britain in 1807 and the United States in 1808), over ten million African men, women, and children had been transported across Atlantic.

Slavery existed before the European arrival in Africa, with prisoners of war, debtors, or criminals being common victims of enslavement. Slavery and slave trading had never been practiced on such a large scale before, however, nor with such a disregard for human suffering. The introduction of material incentives – goods exchanged for slaves – resulted in the established rules governing enslavement breaking down, and "wars" were provoked to legitimize kidnapping. Most slaves originated from relatively short distances from the coast and few peoples were left unaffected by the trade; local economies were distorted and social relationships undermined.

Factors, or resident agents, dealt with local rulers through a web of European and African traders who would skim off a proportion of the goods traded. Slave purchasers developed preferences for particular parts of Africa and crude ethnic stereotypes evolved. For example, the Akan peoples of Ghana were regarded as being rebellious in nature; the Igbo of Nigeria were considered easy to control though prone to moodiness or even suicide; and the Manding peoples from Senegal were seen as excellent house servants. Goods such as iron bars, guns, beads, cloth, and alcohol were traded. In 1756 it was recorded that one man could be traded for 115 gal. (435 l) of rum, and a woman 95 gal. (360 l).

The triangle trade

Most slave ships sailed from European ports carrying goods to trade for African slaves. Slaves were delivered to trading posts and crammed into the ships' holds without delay because ships' crews feared falling prey to fever or dysentery that resulted in a life expectancy of just two years for European residents of West Africa. On board the ships, conditions were appalling with little ventilation, poor food, and no medical care. In general, up to one quarter of the Africans died (and sometimes more) during the three- to six-week journey as a result of disease, suicide, or by being thrown overboard for acts of resistance or because of sickness. On arrival in the Americas, the Africans were sold and the ships were loaded with gold, silver, sugar, tobacco, cotton, and other goods. The ships then returned to Europe, unloaded, and resumed their triangular trading. This trade was also carried out by a smaller number of American slavers who crossed the Atlantic carrying rum, returning to America via the Caribbean.

Africa in the Americas
The tinted areas of the map show where slaves were taken in the Americas. Today, African influences are unmistakable throughout the Americas. Rarely is it possible for individuals to trace their lineage to any particular African people, but contemporary diet, religion, music, language, and folktales often bear witness to a rich African heritage. In Brazil (the most important destination for slaves), African influences are clear, for example, in the rituals of the Candomblé religion, in which the gods are clearly Yoruba-derived.

NORTH AMERICA

SOUTH AMERICA

Below deck
The cramped conditions of a slave ship are shown in this drawing of the floor plan below deck.

Key dates	
1517	Spain officially approves importing of African slaves to the Caribbean, disregarding the Pope's disapproval
1593	The Netherlands starts to establish trading posts along the coast of West Africa
1600s	England, France, Denmark, the Netherlands, Portugal, Spain, and Sweden engage in the Atlantic slave trade
c. 1750s	The Atlantic slave trade reaches its peak with Africans being shipped to the Americas at a rate of around 100,000 per year
1700s	Opposition to slavery and the slave trade develops in Europe and the United States
by 1804	States north of Maryland abolish slavery
1787	Freetown (Sierra Leone) founded by British philanthropists as a settlement for liberated African slaves
1791	Slave revolt in Haiti leading to independence from France in 1804
1807	Britain prohibits slave trade in its colonial possessions
1808	United States prohibits slave trade
1833	Britain abolishes slavery throughout its empire
1847	Liberia founded by the American Colonization Society as a settlement for liberated slaves
1865	The defeat of the Confederacy in the American Civil War; slavery abolished throughout the United States
1888	Slavery abolished in Brazil

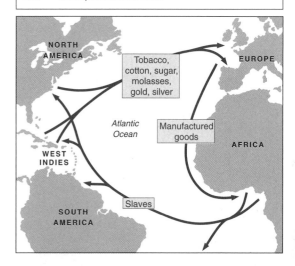

Zimbabwes

In the southeast of Zimbabwe, not far from the town of Masvingo, a small granite hill rises steeply to a height of about 350 ft (100 m) above the surrounding plains. At the top and to the south of the hill, stand the massive granite walls that are the remains of the ancient Shona civilization of Great Zimbabwe.

Great Zimbabwe was the largest of about 200 similar zimbabwes (literally, stone houses) – the palaces of Shona kings and chiefs – scattered throughout Zimbabwe and neighboring parts of Mozambique and South Africa. The Shona first began to construct these impressive dry-wall stone enclosures – built without mortar – in the late 1100s. This building system was perfected in the building of the Great Zimbabwe palace, which reached a peak in the 1300s and 1400s. The quality of the stonework at the site is so impressive that for many years some people believed that no indigenous African people could possibly have been the builders.

Symbol of wealth

For about four hundred years, from the twelfth to the sixteenth centuries, the site of Great Zimbabwe – and the city that grew up around it – was the political, religious, and commercial center of a prosperous Shona civilization.

The great wealth of the Shona people, which enabled them to build Great Zimbabwe, was based on agriculture, mining, and trade. They grew crops; raised cattle; mined and worked iron, copper, and gold; and controlled the trade routes between the interior of Africa and the Arab/Swahili ports on the coast of what is now Mozambique. Through these coastal ports they exported gold, copper, and ivory and imported silks and porcelain from China; glass beads from Indonesia, India, and Europe; and faience (expensive, highly-colored glazed pottery) from Persia (modern Iran).

Walls and buildings

The massive stone walls of Great Zimbabwe form enclosures that contained mud-walled and thatched-roofed circular buildings, some up to 30 ft (9 m) or more in diameter. The largest buildings were often divided internally into separate rooms and had roofs about 20 ft (6 m) high. The stone walls themselves are up to 30 ft (9 m) high and about 16 ft (5 m) thick at the base; their foundations were built in carefully prepared and leveled trenches.

To get the stones with which they built the walls, the Shona masons used a technique probably first developed by their miners. They built fires around boulders

or outcrops of granite to heat them up, then doused the rocks with cold water. This sudden cooling split them into slabs 3 to 7 in. (7.5–17 cm) thick. These slabs were then dragged on sledges to the construction site, where they were cut into small blocks with stone hammers and iron chisels.

Abandonment and plunder

Great Zimbabwe lost its importance as a political center in the middle of the fifteenth century, when the Shona kings abandoned the site and moved their capital north to the area around the Zambezi River; it continued only as a religious and ceremonial site. The site was completely abandoned in the 1830s, when most of its inhabitants were driven out or taken prisoner by Nguni peoples fleeing from the Zulu Mfecane/Difaqane.

The Nguni ignored, or did not find, most of the treasures of Great Zimbabwe. In the late nineteenth century, the ruins were discovered by Europeans and the buried riches were plundered by treasure hunters. Nearly all of the priceless gold artifacts were melted down and so lost forever.

Stonework
Shown here are two examples of stonework from Zimbabwe. One (top) is from earlier buildings and the other is a later example. Technical improvements can be seen in the quality of the stonework.

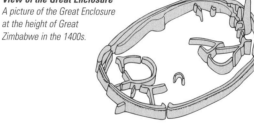

View of the Great Enclosure
A picture of the Great Enclosure at the height of Great Zimbabwe in the 1400s.

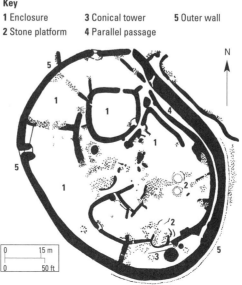

Plan of the Great Enclosure
The Great Enclosure – the finest of the Shona dry-wall zimbabwes (stone houses) – is part of the main Great Zimbabwe site, which also includes the Western and Eastern enclosures. Work on the site was begun in the late 1100s and continued for over three hundred years. All the walls were built without mortar, the earlier parts being undressed stone. Later parts feature dressed stone and beautiful, chevron-patterned friezes.

Key
1 Enclosure 3 Conical tower 5 Outer wall
2 Stone platform 4 Parallel passage

The conical tower (above)
This huge conical tower inside the Great Zimbabwe complex is regarded as the greatest architectural and technical achievement of the early Shona people. Originally thought to be hollow inside, it is now believed to be solid. It is 35 ft (10 m) high and 17 ft (5 m) across at the base.

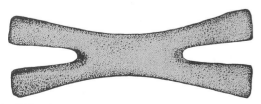

Ingot (above)
The currency of Great Zimbabwe consisted of copper ingots (metal bars). Soapstone molds for making these ingots have been found at Great Zimbabwe and the ingots themselves have turned up as far away as China.

Clay ox
This clay model of an ox dates from the eleventh century and was found in the Western Enclosure of Great Zimbabwe.

© DIAGRAM

Fang sculpture
Fang sculptures and masks are are known to have had a particularly great influence on cubism as well as on the work of artists such as Amedeo Modigliani.

Central African and Western art

The study of the art histories of both Africa and the West reveals a high degree of cross-cultural fertilization that has enriched both African and Western art.

The discovery of African art in the West

African art has been a major influence on twentieth-century modern art in the West. Before the 1900s, few people knew of African art in Europe and America. In 1907, the Spanish painter Pablo Picasso visited the Palais de Trocadero, an ethnographic museum in Paris. The African sculptures that he saw there profoundly affected him. He described them as "...the most powerful and most beautiful things the human imagination has ever produced..." Picasso was transformed by this visit and his next work, Les Demoiselles de Avignon, was heavily influenced by this experience. This painting was a turning point for Western art, cubism developed as a result and flourished as an art form between 1907 and 1914. Cubists represented objects and people using basic geometrical forms and many were strongly influenced by African sculpture. In turn, cubism revolutionized Western art by introducing new ways to portray form and space, allowing the boundaries of art to be redrawn. The style of many major twentieth-century artists, such as the French painters Maurice de Vlaminck, André Derain, and Henri Matisse; the Italian artist Amedeo Modigliani; the French cubist Georges Braque; and the British sculptor Henry Moore, have all been influenced by African art.

The discovery of Western art in Africa

During the colonial era in the early twentieth century, the history of African art was closely linked with the influence and patronage of Europeans. The establishment of formal art schools and the founding of experimental workshops were often undertaken by European expatriates in the first half of the 1900s. At these institutions, artists were introduced to the methods and techniques of Western artists. Although there are painting traditions in Africa – on walls, bodies, and bark, for example – painting permanent pictures on canvas or paper was little known. New materials such as enamel paints, watercolors, and even shoe polish have further broadened the tools available to African artists.

From the 1920s to 1960s, many African artists were being tutored and mentored by Europeans. A typical example is the case of Albert Lubaki. In the 1920s, the wall paintings of this Congo (Dem. Rep.) painter attracted the attentions of a colonial administrator called Georges Thiry. Thiry provided paints, papers, and paid Lubaki for his work, which was shown in Paris, Geneva, Brussels, and Rome. Lubaki's paintings still followed the style of African wallpainting, but were committed on paper.

While many artists readily adapted Western ideas, others refused to. After independence, many countries attempted to discard the overpowering influence of the West. In the 1970s, President Mobutu Sese Seko (q.v.) of Zaire (Congo [Dem. Rep.]) launched his "authenticity" doctrine, which attempted to promote African – and in particular, Zairean – culture above foreign influences. This led to the formation of the avant-gardistes

Figurative pot
This pot was made by the Congo (Dem. Rep.) artist Voania Muba during the colonial era. Muba produced work largely for Europeans and the fact that he signed his work was evidence of European influence. In present-day Africa, demand for African art by non-Africans (for example, tourists and European or American patrons) still exerts a heavy influence on style, because internal artwork markets tend to be underdeveloped or reliant on government support.

Zairean urban art
This painting, Colonie Belge (1973), is by the Congo (Dem. Rep.) artist Nkulu wa Nkulu. Early Zairean urban art of the 1960s and 1970s concentrated on the effects and legacies of colonialism. Popular themes were Belgian colonization and civil war. These have been replaced by a new generation of Congo (Dem. Rep.) artists who did not experience the colonial era but are concerned instead with issues of political instability, urban life, social justice, and crime. In this way, a supposedly foreign art form – painting on paper or canvas – has been creatively reworked into a distinctly Congolese one.

in 1975. This group of ten artists sought to recover the intrinsic personality of African art by using themes and materials that they considered African in origin.

A backlash to this search for innate "Africanness" is expressed by artists who assert their right to use any materials available to them. In reality, African artists' creative and inspirational melding of influences, ideas, traditions, and styles from both Africa and elsewhere has led to a rich variety of contemporary art that reflects modern African society rather than some idealized, so-called "traditional" past.

Central African mask
At one time, this Central African mask was owned by the French painter André Derain. It was Derain who suggested that Picasso visit the Palais de Trocadero. The interest of many European artists in African art at the beginning of the twentieth century freed the study of African art in Europe from the confines of ethnography.

Brides and Grooms

Marriage is a serious business in all societies. Among most North African peoples, marriage is regarded as a tie between two families; it is not just the concern of the individuals involved. The majority of people in North Africa follow the Islamic religion. In general, they obey the Muslim laws on marriage, but with regional variations according to local customs. The non-Muslim people of southern Sudan, however, largely follow their own customs.

Muslim marriages

Islam does not prescribe any particular wedding ceremonies, but Muslim marriages are generally celebrated in style. Customs vary in detail from one ethnic group to another. One that is very common involves the bride having parts of her body painted with designs in henna, a reddish-brown dye made from the henna plant. The henna is applied especially to the hands. Often the bride's attendants decorate her with elaborate patterns on her arms and legs, and even on her face. Before the painting, the bride has a ceremonial bath. Usually, a qadi (a Muslim judge) performs the actual legal part of the ceremony. Elaborate feasting follows. In some groups, men and women hold separate feasts.

Under Islamic law, a man may have as many as four wives, but only if he is sufficiently well off to support them all equally. Each wife normally has her own home. Although most Tuareg are Muslims, polygamy (the practice of having more than one wife) is not widely practiced as it goes against the Tuareg's own monogamous (the practice or state of having only one marriage partner) traditions and few Tuareg women are tolerant of co-wives.

Divorce is simple for men: a man may end a marriage at will, and need not ask a court of law for a divorce. A woman can also divorce her husband, but generally has to pay a fee or go to court to do so. A couple can also divorce by mutual consent.

Bridewealth

A widespread custom is that of bridewealth, which is given by the bridegroom to the bride's family. The bride is not regarded as property; the payment is usually considered to be compensation to the bride's family for the loss of a working member. Part of it may be used by the couple to set up home together.

Among the Berbers and other groups whose living depends on herding animals, the fee is generally in the form of cattle or sheep. For the Nuer, for instance, the standard amount is generally between twenty and forty head of cattle; for the Dinka, the standard amount is between thirty and forty. Local circumstances affect these ideal figures, though. Nuer, Dinka, and Shilluk marriages are not considered legal until the bridewealth has been exchanged.

The bride's father distributes the cattle among her relatives, including uncles and aunts. There are strict rules for this distribution. Among some southern Sudanese ethnic groups, the bridegroom has to perform work for his prospective father-in-law. In farming communities such as the Nuba, this service takes the form of several days' work tilling the ground, or doing other necessary farm tasks.

If a husband divorces his wife, her family may have to pay back at least part of the bridewealth. This can make divorce difficult.

Choosing partners

In all strands of North African society, arranged marriages are traditionally more common than those in which men and women are free to choose partners for themselves. Individuals are increasingly more likely to make their own arrangements now than in the past, however.

In many ethnic groups, certain partnerships are chosen above all others. Marriage between cousins is often favored, especially cousins on the father's side. In some groups, such as the Beja, a man may marry his brother's widow, or the sister of his deceased wife. Among the Dinka, if the widow of a childless marriage remarries, her subsequent children are deemed to be those of her late husband.

One Berber group, the Ait Haddidou of Morocco, holds an annual bride fair. Men seeking wives and women seeking husbands flock to this three-day event. Many of the women are divorced; women are free to divorce as often as they like and can choose whom they wish to remarry. Relatives help men and women to choose their spouses at the fair.

Bride-to-be
The face of a Berber bride in the Atlas Mountains of Morocco is typically hidden by a highly decorated headdress.

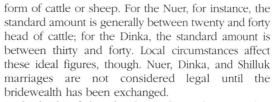

Wedding procession
This Egyptian bride is riding on a camel to the home of the groom accompanied by her friends, family, and some musicians. She sits beneath a decorative canopy, topped by waving palm fronds. Elaborate processions such as this one are customary only in rural, Islamic areas.

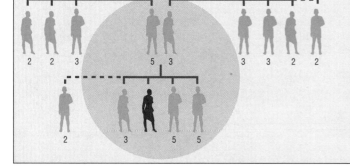

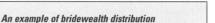

An example of bridewealth distribution
Among the Nuer in Sudan, up to forty head of cattle may be given to the bride's father by the groom's family. The father then distributes the cattle to his family. The immediate family – parents and siblings – is shown in the circle in the diagram, as is the bride (indicated by a dark tint) Members of the extended family – shown outside the circle – also receive cattle. They include aunts, uncles, and even – in this case – a half-brother and a half-uncle (attached by dotted lines). The numbers under each figure indicate the number of cattle received by that person.

Cash crops

Agriculture dominates East African economies. The region has been integrated into the world market for centuries. European colonial penetration of the region in the late nineteenth century, however, established the large-scale production of export-oriented crops, especially sisal (a fiber crop), cotton, tobacco, tea, and coffee. Much of the best land was taken by colonialists to develop plantations, forcing dispossessed Africans to work less desirable land or take up employment as laborers, often on a seasonal basis. Others found it necessary to produce cash crops as a means of paying taxes and school fees.

Coffee

Coffee originates in Ethiopia, with commercial production dating back a thousand years. The crop spread across the Red Sea to Yemen and eventually to other parts of the world. Arabica coffee is a major Ethiopian export, but production is on a relatively small scale. Cultivated and wild bushes are stripped of both ripe and unripe beans and a lot of the coffee produced is low quality and unsuitable for export. Small quantities of good-quality coffee are produced that are highly rated by European consumers.

Coffee is also a major cash crop in Kenya, Rwanda, Burundi, and Uganda, which has its own native coffee variety (Robusta). There have never been coffee plantations in Uganda and production is mainly by peasant farmers who, since about 1950, have produced coffee as their main cash crop instead of cotton. There have been periods when Ugandan farmers have suffered from their dependency on coffee, which is subject to considerable price swings and changes in government purchasing policies.

Tea

In East Africa, small-scale tea production for the local market began in 1924. After World War II, British tea companies feared that their south Asian production base would be nationalized when India and Sri Lanka became independent. So they concentrated on expanding production in Africa. The climate and soils of Tanzania, Malawi, and the Kenyan Highlands are ideal for tea production and there are plenty of available workers for this labor-intensive industry. Today, India is Kenya's main tea producing rival. Kenyan labor is more expensive than Indian and, as a result, Kenyan producers are more capital intensive and more dependent on machinery, fertilizers, and pesticides than labor.

Other cash crops

Tobacco has long been widely produced in East Africa. During the 1980s, it became an important crop for Ugandan smallholders, with some negative environmental consequences. Wood is required to fire the furnaces used for curing tobacco; this has led to widespread deforestation. In turn, deforestation has caused streams and rivers to dry up, forcing women and children to walk farther to collect water. In addition, the loss of forest cover has resulted in the fertile topsoil being washed away.

Ethiopia exports a considerable amount of qat (a mild stimulant) to southwest Asia. Also, until the coun-try lost control of the main area of production along the Sudanese border – because of the war in Sudan – Ethiopia was a significant sesame seed producer. Bananas are the most important export crop of Somalia. When Italy, the main customer, levied a tax on Somalian bananas in the 1980s, the economy was badly affected – this tax has since been abolished. Other important crops grown in East Africa include cotton, cloves, and sugar cane.

New cash crops

In recent years, East African farmers have turned to new types of cash crop production, keen to decrease their dependency on a single earner. Pyrethrum is produced by some East African countries such as Kenya and Rwanda. It is an insecticide ingredient made from chrysanthemums. In Kenya, flowers, fruit, and vegetables (such as green beans and strawberries) produced for the European winter market are now an important source of income for small farmers. The purchasing criteria, however, are extremely rigorous and farmers are subject to the high costs of approved seeds or cuttings, pesticides, and fertilizers, which are either imported or made locally by international chemical giants. The use of pesticides has become an important issue as most spraying is done without protective clothing, and this has serious effects on the farmers' health.

In recent decades, attempts have been made to establish more processing plants such as factories to wash coffee and distilleries to produce clove oil. This is beneficial as more revenue can be earned from the export of processed goods than of raw materials.

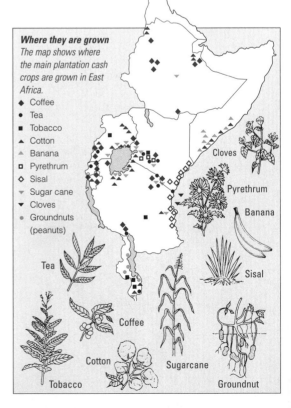

Where they are grown
The map shows where the main plantation cash crops are grown in East Africa.

- ◆ Coffee
- ● Tea
- ■ Tobacco
- ▲ Cotton
- ▲ Banana
- ▫ Pyrethrum
- ◇ Sisal
- ▽ Sugar cane
- ▼ Cloves
- ● Groundnuts (peanuts)

Cloves
Pyrethrum
Banana
Sisal
Groundnut
Sugarcane
Coffee
Cotton
Tobacco
Tea

Fables and proverbs

Some of the most popular and most enduring African storytelling involves animal fables, tales in which familiar animals take on human characteristics – similar to Aesop's "Fables" and Rudyard Kipling's "Just So Stories," which probably borrow from African traditions. These animal fables – explaining how the goat became domesticated, for instance, or describing the cunning of a trickster animal – have been passed down through the ages, and have even made their way to other parts of the world. The West Africans who were taken as slaves to the Americas from the 1500s to the 1800s took with them many aspects of their culture, including dance, music, and storytelling. Many stories originated elsewhere, such as India or Europe, and were brought to Africa by migrants thousands of years ago.

Fables are intended to teach. Some fables explain a natural phenomenon: why the leopard has its spots, for instance. Others illustrate an aspect of human nature or behavior – but manifested by an animal. Trickery and cleverness are among the most common behaviors that appear. Sometimes, a fable contains a moral that is meant as a lesson to humans. Good deeds are rewarded; deceit is always punished; and wit wins over physical strength.

Anansi the spider

Anansi the spider appears in a number of folk tales, in West Africa and the Caribbean, where he is often described as conceited or lazy. Usually Anansi is shown as clever, but in other stories he is outwitted. A tale explaining why spiders hide in the corners of houses describes a feud between rich Anansi and poor Chameleon: Anansi tries to steal Chameleon's field but is fooled by the cleverer animal. Anansi is left with nothing and hides in shame.

Uncle Remus

Many ancient folk tales were transported to the Americas by African slaves. Uncle Remus – a character created by writer Joel Chandler Harris in the late nineteenth century – is a former slave who tells stories to entertain the son of the owner of the plantation where he lives. The stories are versions of fables told by his African ancestors; they feature animal characters such as Brer Rabbit, Brer Fox, and Brer Wolf, tricksters who usually win in the end through cleverness. Rabbits, foxes and wolves aren't found in sub-Saharan Africa; the original fables probably featured spiders, hares, and hyenas.

"Tar Baby" is one such story transferred from West Africa to the American South. The Hausa tell a story called "Rubber Girl," in which Spider steals a neighbor's nuts to cover up for his not having planted any. The neighbor makes a figure of a girl out of sticky rubber resin, and when Spider sees the figure, he tries to touch it. He ends up being stuck fast to the Rubber Girl, and the neighbor beats Spider before letting him go.

Animal proverbs

Many African proverbs featuring animals were sometimes associated with the brass gold-weights made by the Asante people. Antelopes, crocodiles, fish, and scorpions are just a few of the animal forms used in these weights. An antelope with long horns suggests the proverb "Had I known that, but it has passed behind me," meaning have no regrets when something's done, somewhat similar to "Don't cry over spilled milk."

Continuing traditions

Many African writers today incorporate folklore into contemporary themes. Among them are: Duro Lapido, a Nigerian playwright who has composed Yoruba folk operas; Camara Laye, a novelist from a Malinke family in Guinea, who sometimes adopted the style of a griot, or storyteller; Onuora Nzekwu, a Nigerian novelist whose work reflects the influence of Igbo folklore; and Wole Soyinka (q.v.), a Nigerian poet and playwright who uses some of the themes found in Nigerian folklore in his work.

Elephants
This rock painting from Tassili-n-Ajjer in the Sahara Desert depicts an elephant. In folklore an elephant can symbolize a chief, and it appears in the proverb "If you follow an elephant you don't lose your way," which means that you will be protected if you stay close to an important person.

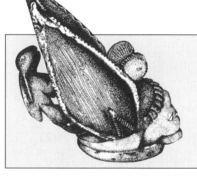

Tortoise and Hare
A hare climbs up the back of this Yoruba mask. Sometimes Hare is a clever character who wins by his wits. But better known is the story of the race between Hare and Tortoise. Hare, obviously faster, challenges the Tortoise to a race. But Tortoise is clever and manages to outwit Hare every time.

Griots
In West Africa, professional storytellers are called griots, and they are highly respected in many cultures. This griot to a royal court (right) was sketched by one of the first visiting Europeans many years ago.

How Leopard got his spots
This ancient leopard from Nigeria is carved in ivory and has copper spots. The leopard features in many folk tales, usually as a fearsome animal widely admired for its strength and speed. In a Sierra Leonean fable explaining how the leopard got its spots, however, the animal is a figure of pity. The story explains that Leopard regularly visited his friend Fire and often asked Fire to visit his home. But when Fire finally visited, Leopard's house was destroyed, and Leopard and his wife were scorched by the flames, resulting in the blackened spots that all leopards have today.

Basket bowl
Baskets are commonly used as containers for food. some baskets are so tightly woven that they can hold liquids, such as palm wine.

Mortar and pestle
A mortar and pestle is used to pound grain. This example is from Benin.

Separating grain
This Fulani woman is using two hollowed gourds to separate grain from its husks.

Food and drink

West African food and drink vary enormously, a reflection of the region's varied geography and cultural diversity. Over a period of centuries, the West African diet has been influenced by contact with other parts of Africa, North and South America, and Europe; while the region has contributed greatly to the creation of cuisines elsewhere, in particular those of the Caribbean, Brazil, and the American South.

In rural areas, most families grow much of their own food. Staples vary according to local climatic and soil conditions, but rice is widely available. It is, however, fairly expensive because much that is consumed is imported. In areas with sufficient rainfall, cassava, yams, and other root vegetables as well as plantains are key cooking ingredients, while in the semidesert Sahel, couscous (made from coarse-ground semolina or other grains) is popular. Vegetables too are varied, and include the leaves of sweet potatoes, pumpkins, cassava, and other plants used to create spinachlike dishes, and beans, peppers, eggplant, and okra. Sauces for vegetable and meat dishes are often based either on groundnut (peanut) paste or on palm oil. Food is typically eaten from a communal dish with the fingers, though in strict Muslim households, men and women often eat out of separate dishes.

Meat and Fish

Both meat and fish form central parts of meals, though many households find their cost prohibitive except for festivals and other special occasions. On the coast, people fish in the Atlantic, but the region's rivers – in particular the Senegal, Niger, and Benue – are important sources of freshwater fish. Today, fish is often frozen, but it is also sun-dried or smoked for ease of storage and transportation, and because these forms are essential ingredients for many recipes. Mutton and goat are the most commonly consumed meats, with beef and chicken reserved for special occasions because they are expensive. Game is a staple in many areas, but overhunting and loss of habitat have resulted in limited availability. Rodents and antelopes are much sought after, but monkeys, snails, cats, and dogs are also sometimes hunted.

Alcoholic drinks

A wide variety of alcoholic drinks is produced in West Africa, though many Muslims in the region do not consume alcohol. A traditional drink that is popular in coastal areas is palm wine: a white, frothy brew made from the naturally alcoholic sap of the species of palm tree that also provides palm nuts and palm oil (used for cooking and frying).

Beer is the most popular alcoholic drink, and cassava flour, millet, sorghum, and corn are used in the fermentation process of homemade brews. Today, however, Western-style beers are also produced in virtually every country, often using a mix of imported hops and locally grown cereals or cassava. Nigeria has the largest range of commercially produced beers, with both light and dark varieties popular.

Cassava balls
Cassava can be pounded, then mixed into a paste and made into balls. The balls are fried and eaten with stew.

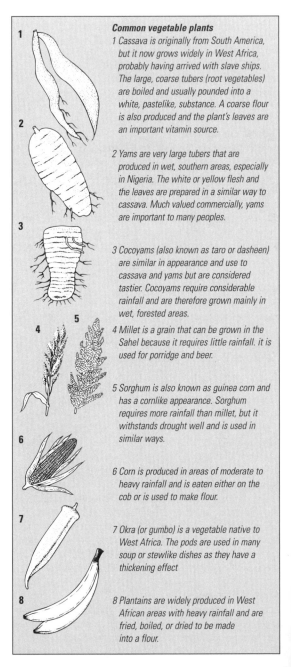

Common vegetable plants
1 Cassava is originally from South America, but it now grows widely in West Africa, probably having arrived with slave ships. The large, coarse tubers (root vegetables) are boiled and usually pounded into a white, pastelike, substance. A coarse flour is also produced and the plant's leaves are an important vitamin source.

2 Yams are very large tubers that are produced in wet, southern areas, especially in Nigeria. The white or yellow flesh and the leaves are prepared in a similar way to cassava. Much valued commercially, yams are important to many peoples.

3 Cocoyams (also known as taro or dasheen) are similar in appearance and use to cassava and yams but are considered tastier. Cocoyams require considerable rainfall and are therefore grown mainly in wet, forested areas.

4 Millet is a grain that can be grown in the Sahel because it requires little rainfall. it is used for porridge and beer.

5 Sorghum is also known as guinea corn and has a cornlike appearance. Sorghum requires more rainfall than millet, but it withstands drought well and is used in similar ways.

6 Corn is produced in areas of moderate to heavy rainfall and is eaten either on the cob or is used to make flour.

7 Okra (or gumbo) is a vegetable native to West Africa. The pods are used in many soup or stewlike dishes as they have a thickening effect

8 Plantains are widely produced in West African areas with heavy rainfall and are fried, boiled, or dried to be made into a flour.

Foods and food taboos

Foods and diets vary greatly in North Africa. In the cities, particularly those of the Mediterranean coast, reasonably well-off people eat a mixed diet comparable in quality, though not necessarily in type, with diets of the West; poorer people tend to eat less well. In the desert and underdeveloped rural areas, people are largely dependent on what they can grow for themselves. In addition, there are many dietary restrictions imposed by religion or custom. The Muslim month of Ramadan is marked by great feasts held at the beginning and end of the month-long fast. During this fast, food and drinks can only be consumed out of daylight hours.

City foods

Generally, food along the North African coast is strongly influenced by Arab, European, and Turkish cultures – the last is a legacy of the Turkish Ottoman Empire, which once ruled much of North Africa. In the Maghreb (Algeria, Morocco, and Tunisia) the two most popular food and drink items in the cities are couscous and mint tea. Couscous is a steamed, coarse-ground grain such as semolina. It is normally eaten with a meat or vegetable stew. Many people eat couscous almost every day and there are a great many variations on the basic recipe. It is a communal dish, so is usually served in large bowls from which everyone can help themselves. Mint tea, made with tea leaves and sprigs of fresh mint, is served hot and sweet in very small cups. People often drink this tea many times a day.

Tunisian cooks favor fish as a main stew ingredient – a wide variety of seafood is available along the northern coast. Vegetables eaten in North African cities include eggplant, broad beans, celery, cucumbers, leeks, lettuce, onions, spinach, sweet peppers, tomatoes, and zucchini. Fruit is varied and plentiful. The shops in the souks (marketplaces) in the old quarters of the cities abound with fruit, vegetables, and great mounds of ground spices. In Algeria and Tunisia, cayenne and chili are popular spices used in cooking.

Rice is a basic dish outside the Maghreb and bread is eaten everywhere. People usually make round, flat loaves of bread using a minimum of raising agent, or leaven. Most bread is made from wheatflour, but Tunisians like a bread made from semolina.

Desert foods

The availability of food in the Sahara Desert depends on the activities of people. In the oases (fertile pockets of the desert), fresh vegetables and fruit are available. Oasis farmers grow barley, corn, millet, and wheat and make unleavened bread and pancakes from flour. Dates, from date palms, are used for food and as trade goods.

Nomadic peoples who travel with their herds in search of pasture and water have a spartan diet relying mainly on milk and milk products such as cheese and yogurt. On treks across the desert, nomads often eat one meal a day, but may have two when in camp. They make a gruel from grain blended with butter or sour milk. Meat tends to be reserved for special feasts, because the animals are more valuable as sources of milk or cash. Old and infirm camels are used as meat

from time to time, and wild animals such as gazelles (small antelopes) and lizards are eaten. Camel meat and fish – when available – are frequently salted and sun-dried to be carried along as iron rations. Nomadic peoples drink tea or coffee when they can obtain them.

Foods of the plains and hills

People who live mainly by agriculture and herding – such as the Dinka and Baggara of Sudan – grow millet, barley, sorghum, and some vegetables for their own use. Pumpkins and melons are also grown. Corn, an American crop, is now grown by many people; sometimes it is ground and made into a porridge. Tamarinds (a type of evergreen tree) produce seed pods that can be pressed into cakes or made into a refreshing drink. These foods are supplemented by the meat of chickens, goats, and sometimes pigs. Fishing is also a major source of food for many coastal and riverine people.

Food taboos

There is a great variety of food taboos (prohibitions) in North Africa. Many Muslims do not eat pork or drink alcohol, as these are forbidden under the Islamic code. In southern Sudan, however, non-Muslims raise pigs for food, and some Algerians make wine for export. Adult Tuareg of a group who live in the Ahaggar Mountains of southern Algeria will not eat chicken or chicken eggs under any circumstances. The reasons behind this taboo are not known.

Couscous utensils
1 A large woven basket called a *tbeck,* used to contain couscous grains that have been sorted according to size.
2 A lidded pot called a *keskes* in which couscous is steamed.
3 An early twentieth-century, terra-cotta couscous dish from Algeria, which is large enough for many people to eat from.

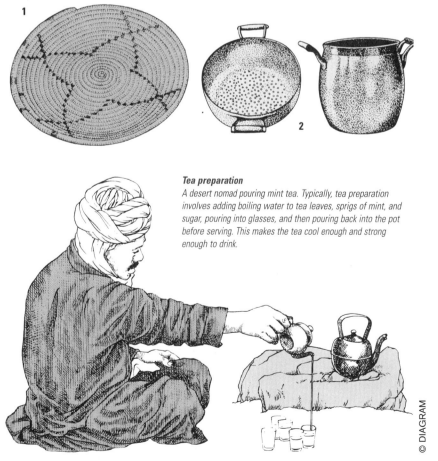

Tea preparation
A desert nomad pouring mint tea. Typically, tea preparation involves adding boiling water to tea leaves, sprigs of mint, and sugar, pouring into glasses, and then pouring back into the pot before serving. This makes the tea cool enough and strong enough to drink.

© DIAGRAM

Colorful hair

In preparation for a dance, this Moorish woman from Morocco has had her hair done in several long, thin braids, which have been interwoven with colorful beads and glass balls.

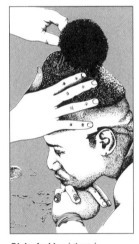

Dinka fashion *(above)*

This young Dinka man from southern Sudan is having an ostrich feather attached to his hair by a friend. His hair has been colored red with ocher and then shaved close to the head in the shape of a bowl.

Hairstyles

For many North Africans, hairstyles have traditionally been symbolic as well as decorative, for both men and women. Hairstyling is a professional, demanding skill, mostly practiced by women though sometimes by men as well. It is also an art, one that is handed down through generations, and it can be a form of self-expression, even of sculpture. But self-expression is only one of the reasons why hairdressing is so important among many African peoples. Hair, and the ability to control it, has great symbolic significance. The Nuba of southern Sudan, for instance, believe that shaving and grooming one's hair is what distinguishes humans from animals – it is a kind of control that animals cannot practice.

Traditional beliefs about hairstyling

The Nuba have many other traditional beliefs about hair. Among the Nuba, only men decorate their hair, although traditionally both men and women oil their hair and dress it with ocher (a reddish brown or yellow clay). Also, women won't groom their hair while they are pregnant and many women shave their hair after they have reached an age when they can no longer have babies. Hair grooming is an essential aspect of being part of society; when outside the normal society – for example, when some members of a village go to farms away from their village to wait for the grain to ripen – the Nuba don't groom their hair. The hair itself is also significant; hair cuttings must be buried to prevent them being stepped on by another, otherwise misfortune could result.

Historically in many African cultures, the way the hair was presented or styled signified a certain role in society or the passing of an important milestone. For example, among peoples living in the Maghreb (Algeria, Morocco, and Tunisia), puberty for both girls and boys was marked with new hairstyles. For many Africans of the southern Sudan area, hairstyle can still indicate the wearer's status in society. The use of hairstyles to distinguish people according to status is, however, less common than it was, as personal preference and fashion increasingly dictate which hairstyle a person chooses. Practices such as shaving one's head

(to signify that a woman has passed childbearing age), or covering the hair with a headdress (to signify that a woman is married), still maintain their traditional meanings in some places. Hair grooming is also a practical concern, especially for warriors; long hair can be dangerous and easy for the enemy to grab hold of. As in most parts of the world, special occasions still demand that extra attention is paid to the hair.

Techniques and materials

Techniques used in hairstyling include braiding and weaving, threading fibers or beads onto the hair, and molding the hair into shapes using clay as a fixing gel. Some elaborate styles can take several hours to create. Different regions and different ethnic groups reflect a wide variety of styles and techniques, and a variety of dressing agents are used. In some parts, ocher is rubbed on the hair to give it an interesting texture and color; among other people, fat or oil is used; and still others use beeswax to coat the hair. Most styling aids are made using locally available ingredients.

False hair

A traditional custom among the Jewish women of Morocco's past involved combining false hair – made from cows' tails or wool – with real hair. This example uses wool wound into hornlike shapes and attached on both sides of the head to hang behind the shoulders.

Giving messages with hair

This Toposa woman from southern Sudan is wearing her hair in lots of tiny pigtails to show that she is married.

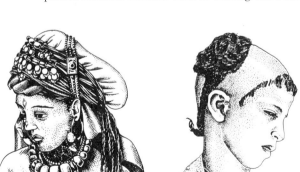

Berber styles

There are many variations of Berber hairstyles. Among the Berber people who live in the Middle Atlas Mountains of north Morocco, a common hairstyle (left, above) involves braiding the hair down the back. Then an elaborate scarf is wrapped around the hair like a turban and held in place with cords. Elsewhere, young Berber girls may have their hair cut into a skullcap shape close to the head (right, above). A "knot" of hair, which is decorated with ribbons and other ornaments, is left to hang down on one side.

Braids

This Tuareg girl has divided her hair into several braids. This style is both practical, as it keeps long hair under control, and attractive.

In East Africa the men generally wear more elaborate hairstyles than the women do, many of whom shave their heads. Young Maasai men, for instance, might spend hours doing one another's hair. Many of the elaborate styles worn by Oromo men are said to resemble the highly stylized coiffures seen in Ancient Egyptian art.

Aside from shaving, one of the most common women's styles is the shiruba, which is composed of many tiny braids that are worn close to the scalp and loose at the ends, fluffing out at the back and over the shoulders. The style, which can take several hours to create, would normally be worn for up to week before being redone. "Western"-style hairdos are also being increasingly adopted, especially by urban women.

Although hairstyling all over the world is a means of personal adornment, it could be said that practicality dictates many of the styles worn in East Africa today, even some of the elaborate ones. Shaving all or most of the hair, cropping bangs over the forehead, and wearing tiny braids secured to the head are all ways of controlling hair that may take time to achieve but which give a conveniently long-lasting style. In contrast, hairstyles described by some nineteenth-century European travelers in East Africa were fantastic productions involving, for example, huge spikes or hoops – so fantastic, in fact, that they might well have been products of European imagination or exaggeration.

Pins and haircombs are among the accessories commonly used by East African women in their hair. They may be made of ivory, wood, and even silver (among Amhara women living in the Ethiopian Highlands especially). Other materials used in hairstyling include feathers, beads, rings, and grass; in southwestern Ethiopia, some women wear tiaras made of woven grass. Beads or pieces of bamboo might be used to close the ends of braids.

Samburu man
This Samburu man from Kenya wears a hairstyle that protects his eyes from the glare of the Sun. It has been created using sisal, cloth, ocher, and animal fat.

Historical hairdos
Among the images brought back to Europe by nineteenth-century travelers to Africa were remarkable hair creations. Clearly they are not worn today, but whether they were actually worn at some point is not known for sure. Among these styles are:

1 Karamojong "hoop"
2 Nyamwezi "spikes"
3 Large spike with a frame for the face from the Horn of Africa region.

Boran woman (left)
This woman from Borana in the south of Ethiopia has elaborately braided hair. Near the roots, the braids are close to the scalp but are then left to hang free.

Fur attachments
Fur from the colobus monkey is incorporated into some hairstyles worn by the men of the Galeb. Feathers and fur are more often found in men's hairstyles than in women's. Maasai men, for instance, sometimes wear projecting cockades of feathers.

Styling gel
Lavishly applied red clay has been used as an easily available gel to style this Ethiopian girl's hair.

Maasai warriors
Traditionally, the Maasai people spend a lot of time on personal adornment and beauty, and this is particularly true of the younger adult men, or moran. They shave their heads when they first become moran, and later grow their hair long. A moran might have a friend spend a day or longer creating an elaborate style. A typical style for a moran incorporates hundreds of twisted strands of hair that have been smeared with clay and ocher, a reddish clay. Strands at the front would be brought together over the forehead. Maasai women, on the other hand, often adopt a more practical and infinitely simpler style, first shaving and then smearing their heads with fat and ocher.

Shiruba style (right)
This Tigre girl from Ethiopia is sporting a typical shiruba hairstyle – braided at the top and loose at the ends.

Fulani fashions
A Fulani woman from Mali (above) wearing an elaborate style that incorporates ring-shaped beads. Many Fulani women wear amber beads or coins worked into the hair. This sometimes signifies that their families are nomads, who travel with their herds of animals in search of water and pasture. Fulani men also decorate their hair and even wrap it in gold. This Bororo Fulani man (below) has had brass wound around sections of braided hair. The brass must be polished daily to keep it shiny.

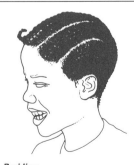

Hairstyling in West Africa is a great art form, and a wide variety of recognizable styles has developed over the years. Many of these styles are still worn today, both in Africa and elsewhere. From the Yoruba, for example, come many styles – using a variety of techniques, alone or combined – that are now fashionable around the world.

Variations
Hair styles vary from region to region and from group to group. Even within one ethnic group many different styles may have emerged. The Fulani, for instance, are scattered over a large part of West Africa, and their hairstyles can vary considerably from one region to aother.

New from old
In the recent past, a certain style signified a time of life or the passing of an important milestone, such as reaching puberty. Some members of a society, such as religious leaders, might wear a particular style to signal their important roles. Today, however, hairstyles are chosen more often for their attractiveness rather than for their symbolism. Traditional hairdressing is still common, but new interpretations of old styles are being created, and hairpieces are often added for more dramatic designs. Hair attachments or extensions are often woven into the hair to give a greater choice of style.

Hairdressing stalls
At Igbo markets there is often a hairdressing booth where women can have their hair styled as part of the social event of going to market. For Igbo girls, hair is important in the transition to adulthood. After she begins puberty, an Igbo girl has her hairstyle redone frequently, and each style is often increasingly elaborate.

Beads
Beads are another common accessory in West African hairstyles. Here, beads of different sizes, shapes, and colors have been threaded on to the hair.

Kanuri style
This Kanuri woman from northeast Nigeria wears a design using braids and, at the top, a cloth wrapping.

Braiding
Braiding (or cornrowing) is a popular and versatile technique. Another is threading, in which the hair is parted in sections and wrapped with thread, making the strands easier to work into designs that stand away from the scalp.

Onigi
In this design, the hair is wrapped to resemble sticks; the word "onigi" means "sticks" in the Yoruba language. It is a relatively simple style to create, and it forms the basis for many of the more elaborate, threaded styles.

Eko Bridge
One of the most widespread of the onigi-based designs is called Eko Bridge. Threaded strands are joined at their ends to form circles, creating a crownlike shape. The design is named for a bridge in Lagos, formerly the capital of Nigeria.

Braids
The braids of this Sara woman from Chad are tightly woven near the scalp and looser at the bottom to soften the effect.

Islam

Within four centuries of the Arab conquest of North Africa, which was completed by 711, the great majority of the region's inhabitants had converted to Islam – the religion practiced by Muslims. Islam is also practiced widely throughout the rest of Africa.

Islam is a monotheistic religion (believing in one God) in which the universe, and all within it, are the creation of Allah who is considered all-powerful, just, and merciful. Islam is very much a communal and practical religion; more than just a moral code, it includes laws that affect all aspects of life. Most North Africans are Sunni Muslims, and Sunnis make up about 85–90 percent of all Muslims worldwide. Sunnis place less emphasis on the importance of a religious hierarchy led by imams (spiritual leaders) than do other Muslims.

Conflicts have existed for some time in North Africa between fundamental Muslims and believers in secular (nonreligious) ideals of government. In recent years, these conflicts have combined with economic and social crises – most notably in Algeria and Egypt – to lead to violent outbursts by radical Islamic fundamentalists, seeking the creation of states governed by Sharia (Islamic holy) law, a detailed code of conduct enforced in law. In Sudan, Sharia law was imposed in 1983. Opposition to Sharia law was a major force in the civil war that has split Sudan into rival north and south factions.

The Prophet Muhammad and the Koran

Muslims believe Muhammad to have been the last messenger of God, completing the sacred teachings of Abraham and Moses, the Jewish prophets of the Old Testament, and Jesus. It was through the Prophet Muhammad that the teachings of Islam were revealed. Muslims often say or write "Peace be upon Him" whenever they refer to Muhammad.

Muhammad was born in Mecca, in present-day Saudi Arabia, in 570. Islamic teaching explains that while Muhammad was meditating one day, the angel Gabriel appeared, instructing him to serve as a prophet. Muhammad started preaching and went on to become the leader of a religious community, his religious message becoming law. Islam's most sacred book, the Koran (or Quran), is believed to be the actual words of Allah as revealed by Gabriel over a period of many years. Muhammad's teachings and sayings – the Hadith – were also collected and written down. They are con-

sidered a vital source for understanding Islam. The third most important Islamic text is the Sunna, a code of behavior based on Muhammad's example recorded in the Hadith.

Mosques

Mosques (Islamic houses of worship) follow a general pattern, based on the first prayer house built by Muhammad at Medina, in present-day Saudi Arabia. The basic plan of North African mosques is a large open space, generally protected by a roof. It contains two essential features. One is the mihrab, a semicircular niche in one wall that indicates the direction of Mecca, the holy city of Islam; Muslims must face toward Mecca when praying. Next to it stands the other feature, the minbar. This is a flight of steps leading up to a seat from which the preacher can address the congregation. Attached to most mosques is a minaret – a tall, slender tower with a platform at the top. From this platform a muezzin, or crier, calls the faithful to prayer. Many mosques are elaborately decorated, with carvings, inlay, and mosaic work.

Religious practices and duties

Devout Muslims must fulfil five duties: to profess the faith ("there is no god but Allah and Muhammad is His Prophet"); to pray five times a day; to try to make at least one pilgrimage (Hajj) to Mecca; to fast during Ramadan, the month that Allah called Muhammad to be His Prophet; and to regularly donate a proportion of their income or possessions to charity – the religious tax, or zakah.

The strictness of adherence to Islamic practices varies according to the traditions of particular societies and between individuals. For example, Islam calls on both male and female followers to dress modestly, but this is interpreted in widely differing ways, with only the strictest wearing all-enveloping veils.

Oldest mosque
The mosque of Ibn Tulun was built in 876–9 and is the oldest surviving mosque in Egypt.

Pottery design
Text from the Koran (Islamic holy book) is sometimes inscribed on North African pottery, such as this Tunisian pot. It is also common for potters to paint an image that only resembles Koranic script. This is to prevent Koranic writings from being used for unholy purposes – to decorate a pot that is used to hold alcohol, for example.

Calligraphic art
Arabic calligraphy is an art form in itself. Here, the phrase "In the name of Allah, the Merciful, the Compassionate" is written in four different styles.

Sufi shrine
Shown here is a Sufi shrine in Melilla, Morocco. Sufis are a small but influential Muslim sect in North Africa. Sufis are mystics who are opposed to materialism. They practice spiritual exercises involving dancing, chanting, and rhythmic movement.

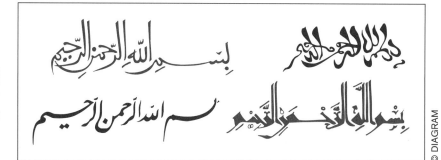

© DIAGRAM

Bagpipes

These North African bagpipes each have a single mouth pipe and double chanters that produce the notes.

Bagpiper

A Tunisian musician plays the mezonad, a mouth-blown bagpipe.

Music and dance

Music and dance are an essential feature of celebrations in North Africa. In the cities, there are professional orchestras complete with singers and dancers, who hire themselves out for celebrations. A female singer is known in Morocco as a chikha. In Tunisia, the equivalent word is mashta. Most players are part-timers, because they find it difficult to make a living from music alone. The instruments they play include violins, lutes, mandolins, flutes, oboes, and drums. The violins are an import from across the Mediterranean Sea, but other instruments tend to be traditional North African ones. For example, the oboe equivalent in a North African orchestra is likely to be a shawm, which is an ancestor of the modern oboe. Many musicians play regional bowed instruments, such as the rabab, a folk fiddle descended from the medieval rebec. The rabab is more likely to be played by a street musician than in an orchestra though. Tunisian instruments include the mezonad, a form of bagpipe, much used by snake charmers.

One form of popular music in Morocco is called chaabi. Chaabi groups can be heard at festivals, in cafes and souks (markets), and in village squares. The music is a mix of Arab, Berber, and contemporary Western styles, and the lyrics tend to highlight political and social issues.

Berber music

Some groups of professional Berber musicians are called rwais. A rwai performance will include poetry and dance as well as music. A rwai group will have several singers; instruments include the rabab, lutes, and cymbals. Another type of Berber group is the imdyazn, usually made up of four musicians, including a poet as leader. Instruments include drums, rabab, and ghaita (a type of reed instrument). Imdyazn usually play during the summer, traveling from village to village and often playing at the weekly markets.

In the High Atlas Mountains of Morocco, professional Berber musician-dancers are known as chleuh. The leader of the group plays on a form of rabab with a single horsehair string. The accompaniment is provided by the gumbri, a small three-stringed lute, with the naqqara, a simple kettledrum, and the bandair, a large tambourine with snares, beating out the rhythm. The Tuareg and other nomadic people play instruments that are easily portable, such as pipes and drums. Berber singers tend to use Arabic, especially for ritual music, but some groups mainly use Berber languages.

Tuareg musician

This Tuareg woman is playing a drum. Among the Tuareg, it is mostly the women who are musicians.

Arab music

The Arab conquerors of North Africa brought with them not only their religion and their language, but also much of their culture. Arab music covers a range of styles, from urban pop to Sudanese swing to the "belly-dance" rhythms. The instruments used are those found all over North Africa, especially those of the Maghreb (Morocco, Algeria, Tunisia). What is different about Arab music is its structure. It uses up to twenty different modes – which compare with the modes or scales of medieval Europe – that are built up from twenty-four quarter-tone intervals; Western scales are based on eight-note sequences. One of the most popular forms is the nuba, a suite of several movements. In Egypt and Libya, the nuba has eight movements, played on lute, zither, violin, flute, and drum. In the Maghreb there is a different style of nuba, which developed in Spain during the "Moorish" (Arab and Berber) occupation of that country. Most musicians only remember a few of these nuba though.

Music of Egypt

Music and dance have been a feature of Egyptian life for over 3,000 years. Tomb wall paintings show people playing flutes, clarinet- and oboe-like instruments, trumpets, harps, lyres, tambourines, castanets, and drums. The remains of harps, lyres, trumpets, flutes, and bells have been found in tombs.

Something of the old traditions survives in folk music. Various kinds of flutes, clarinets, oboes, and drums are common. The traditional instrument of the

Bandair and shawm players

These Algerian musicians are shown playing a bandair, a tambourinelike instrument (right), and a type of reed instrument called a shawm.

Oud player

A Sudanese musician plays the oud, a type of lute that has been at the center of Arabic music for hundreds of years. "Oud" comes from the Arabic word for "lute" which is "al ud," meaning "the wood."

Mulid band
These band members are performing at a mulid, a huge Sufi festival. The Sufis, Islamic mystics, differ from other Muslims in their use of music as a spiritual influence.

rural Egyptians is the arghul, a type of double clarinet. Among the twentieth-century greats of Egyptian music are Muhammad Abd al Wahaab, a singer and composer who is credited with modernizing Arabic music, and Umm Kalthum (q.v.), widely considered one of the greatest singers of the Arab world. Kalthum's legendary status has continued even after her death in 1975.

Music of Sudan
Each of the various ethnic groups of Sudan has its own musical traditions. Most music is associated with religious festivals or social ceremonies and includes singing and dancing. Drums are a major feature, especially in southern Sudan, where a lot of music is based around five notes and is different from the Arabic rhythms of the north. The Baggara, on the other hand, do use Arabic scales, and their music reflects the rhythms of cattle herding.

A common melody instrument is the lyre, which goes under a number of different names, such as tambour among the Nubians and brimbiri among the Nuba; it is also sometimes called a kissar. Most Sudanese lyres have metal strings. Harps and one-stringed fiddles of the rabab type are also used. Sudanese people play a variety of wind instruments, including flutes, trumpets, and horns.

Lyrics
In some North African music, the voice is used for chanting and other wordless sounds rather than to sing lyrics. But many North Africans use lyrics as a powerful medium for conveying a political stance or other

message. In Sudan, for instance, lyrics have been used both by the Dinka – to praise the leader of the Sudanese People's Liberation Army (SPLA), Colonel John Garang (q.v.) – and by followers of the former military dictator Colonel Gaafar Muhammad Nimeri (q.v.) to ignite nationalistic feelings, in an attempt to unite his war-torn country. 1960s Nubian lyrics mourn the loss of their homeland, which was flooded by the building of the Aswan High Dam. In Algeria, the lyrics of the young, antiestablishment rai singers usually express their frustration with both the government and the growing radical Islamic fundamentalist movement.

Rai: a modern twist to an old art
Hugely popular today in Algeria and Morocco, the music known as rai has produced many international stars. Rai has roots in the music of Algerian rural musicians from several centuries ago, called cheikhs, but in the early twentieth century their mostly poetic and nonpolitical songs were dropped by a new generation of rebellious women cheikhas. By the 1970s, rai had developed into a form of protest music for disaffected Algerian youth. The musicians, many of whom prefix their name with Cheb or Chaba, combine traditional instruments such as the darabouka (a clay drum) with synthesizers, bass guitars, and drum machines to create danceable rhythms, which are played in clubs and discos.

Dancing
Music is often accompanied by dancing. In some groups men and women dance together, in others separately. Traditional dance styles include the vertical springing of the Dinka, the loping stomp of some Saharan nomads, and the whirling of some Muslims. At Islamic family celebrations and other gatherings, the women and men are separated. This gives the women more freedom to express themselves through dance, which can be quite erotic. The Koran does not forbid either music or dancing, but strict Muslims make distinctions between what they regard as moral and immoral performances.

Among some of the Tekna peoples of southern Morocco, the women dance on their knees. This is because they live (and dance) in low tents, where there is not enough headroom to stand upright. Rhythm for the dance is provided by a large cooking pot, the guedra, which has an animal skin stretched over it to turn it into a drum. Nomadic peoples like the Tekna cannot afford to carry large numbers of items, so the pot does double duty.

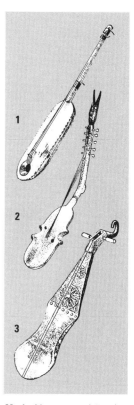

Musical instruments *(above)*
Some typical North African musical instruments.

1 An Egyptian lute, which is played while standing up. Leather thongs are used to hold its strings in place.
2 This Sudanese bow harp has five strings and a fiddlelike body
3 The rabab is a member of the fiddle family that is played widely in North Africa. It is often used to accompany singers. The rabab has two strings and a relatively short neck.

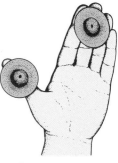

Cymbals
These cymbals are held in the hand and used to accompany dancing.

"King of Rai"
Cheb Khaled is one of the most popular rai singers and is now a star in Europe and India as well as his native Algeria.

Whirling dervishes *(right)*
Dervishes are Sufi Muslims, who follow a special form of Islamic mysticism. Dervishes are dedicated to a life of poverty and chastity. Sufis and dervishes are found throughout North Africa. Their devotional rituals tend to send the dervishes into a trance. In this state, they break into wild dances in which they spin around and around.

© DIAGRAM

Superstars of the West African music scene

Contemporary West African popular music generally involves a fusion of traditional African musical styles with American forms such as jazz, blues, and reggae – themselves styles that derive from West Africa through 500 years of contact. In recent years, West African musicians have attracted a worldwide following. Afro-Beat, juju, Ghanaian highlife and other high-energy dance music styles with their larger-than-life stars have excited tremendous interest, but so too have the sensual music and songs of the jali – the traditional caste of Malian and Guinean musical storyteller or griot.

Abidjan (Ivory Coast) Dakar (Senegal) and Lagos (Nigeria) are the main regional centers of the West African music industry. Because of sophisticated recording facilities and commercial networks, however, European cities such as Paris – and to a lesser extent London – have become major poles of attraction for West African musicians. To reach a wider international audience, many musicians use French or English lyrics.

Instruments

Traditional instruments are fundamentally important for West African musicians, but "Western" instruments have also been widely adopted.

DRUMS A huge variety of drums provides most of the rhythmic qualities so typical of West African music. "Talking drums," so called because they are used to mimic the tonal qualities of African languages, are just one of the many types of traditional drums used widely throughout West Africa.

KORA The kora usually has twenty-one to twenty-five strings and resembles a cross between a harp and a lute. The instrument probably originated in what is now Guinea-Bissau, but today the most famous kora players are from Mali, and they often play electrified

Drum talk
A kalungu, a type of talking drum from Nigeria, imitates the tone of the speech. It is hourglass-shaped, and the pitch can be adjusted by tightening the "waist."

versions of the instrument.

XYLOPHONE The xylophone is widely played, especially in Mali and Guinea. It has eighteen to twenty-one keys suspended on a bamboo frame over gourd resonators, and is often played by two people. The balaphone is one type of xylophone widely used throughout West Africa.

GUITAR The traditional instrument of Cape Verde, the guitar became popular elsewhere in West Africa with the return of African soldiers and sailors from overseas after World War II. Standard and electric guitars are widely played, and distinct African styles have developed, such as the juju style.

BRASS Cuban music has been popular in West Africa since before Word War II, its saxophones and other brass wind instruments have become important features of West African dance music.

Kora players *(left)*
Master kora players performing Casamance-style music, a percussive style from the region of the same name in southern Senegal and Gambia.

Oding player *(right)*
A woman from Cameroon plays the oding, a traditional flute played only by women. The flute is filled with water before being played.

Musical "greats"

Cesaria Evora *(below)*
Cape Verde's music is remarkable for its diversity of styles – many little altered through the centuries. Portugal left a major impact on Cape Verde's music, but mainland African, Brazilian, and Caribbean influences are also clear. Despite its beauty, Cape Verde's music is little known beyond its shores except among the emigrant communities in Portugal and Massachusetts, US . One recent exception is Paris-based Cesaria Evora whose slow-paced, nostalgic ballads sung in a Creole language are typical of Cape Verde.

Angelique Kidjo
Few women from West Africa have made it to superstar status. One who has is vocalist Angelique Kidjo, from Benin. She sings in Fon, and her music reflects the style of zilin, a Fon-region singing style similar to the blues.

King Sunny Ade *(below, q.v.)*
Juju has been a popular music style since the 1920s, when it originated – then called palm-wine music – among the Yoruba in Lagos, but it took on a more modern form when Nigerian musician IK Dairo introduced electric guitars, the accordion, and the talking drum into juju songs. This led to the spread of juju around the globe and made Dairo an international star. In the late 1970s, King Sunny Ade, a Yoruba musician, took over the role of "juju king."

Salif Keita *(below, q.v.)*
To a great extent, it is thanks to Salif Keita's fusion album Soro that Malian music came to international attention in the early 1980s. Keita's high-tech Paris and Los Angeles arrangements are impressive, and he has brought attention to the more traditional Malian musicians, such as the remarkable kora player Toumani Diabaté.

Youssou N'Dour *(right, q.v.)*
Fusing Cuban music and traditional styles from his native Senegal, Youssou N'Dour – born into a griot (storyteller) family – became a superstar at home before conquering the world in the 1980s. N'Dour sings mainly in Wolof, and his lyrics relate to the experiences of his original fans, the inhabitants of the poor neighborhoods of the capital city Dakar. He has recently set up a recording studio in Dakar.

Fela Kuti *(q.v.)*
Born into an elite Yoruba family, Fela Kuti studied trumpet and musicology in London, England before returning to Nigeria in 1963. Kuti's blend of highlife, jazz, and Yoruba music became known as Afro-Beat, and he quickly rose to national stardom. His music is less easily accessible (and less dance oriented) than that of many of his compatriots. As an outspoken critic – in his lyrics and off stage – of Nigerian military regimes and the British and US governments, Kuti has been subject to harassment, house-arrest, and imprisonment in Nigeria.

Rhythms of Central Africa

The music of Central Africa has evolved into a large number of distinct styles, many of which put the emphasis on rhythm rather than melody. The modern music of the region is highly rhythmical and combines distinctively African elements with American and Latin American styles.

Old instruments and new rhythms

Because of the emphasis on rhythm, drums are perhaps the most important of the region's instruments and some have long been used for communication as well as for making music. These talking drums can be heard over long distances and convey their messages by using a range of tones and pitches that mimic those of spoken words.

As well as drums, Central African musicians play a wide range of stringed and wind instruments including lutes, flutes, trumpets, and whistles. These are often made by the musicians themselves from readily-available local materials including wood, gourds, animal horns, shells, metal, bamboo, and the hollow stems of reeds and other plants.

Another important instrument is the mbira, also known as the sansa or thumb piano. It has about ten metal straps attached at one end to a wooden resonator. When plucked with the fingers, as if playing a piano, the strips vibrate to produce notes of definite pitch. The mbira is often found in the instrumental lineup of modern African bands, alongside electric guitars, horns, and synthesizers.

Modern music

The most popular styles of modern Central African music are congo, which developed in Congo (Rep.) and Congo (Dem. Rep.), and makossa, which originated in Cameroon but is hugely popular in Central Africa.

Congo, or soukous, is an exciting, rhythmically complex African version of Cuban rumba music (itself a blend of African and Latin American styles). Soukous was hugely popular in the 1930s and 1940s. During the 1950s, in what was then the Belgian Congo, the rumba was given a distinctively African rhythmic flavor by the pioneers of modern music such as composer and bandleader Joseph Kabasele ("Le Grand Kalle"), guitarist Franco Luambo Makiadi, and singer Tabu Ley (q.v., also known as Rochereau).

This Africanization of the rumba was boosted in the

Marimba
The marimba or balaphone is a type of xylophone. Its tuned wooden bars are played with sticks and the gourds below the bars act as resonators and amplify the sound.

late 1960s, when Zaire's President Mobutu (q.v.) launched his "authenticity" movement to encourage the development of African cultural styles. Today, the stars of soukous include Papa Wemba, Pepe Kalle (q.v.), Kanda Bongo Man (q.v.), and the new wave of female singers such as Deyess Mukangi. It is a major form of modern music not only in Congo (Dem. Rep.) but also in Congo (Rep.), Gabon, and the Central African Republic. Its influence has also spread to other parts of Africa, and can be heard in, for example, the mbira-based rumbira music of Zimbabwe and in Zambian kalindula.

In Central Africa, makossa closely rivals soukous in popularity and, like its rival, it is a powerful dance music with an infectious beat, using drums, horns, and guitars. Makossa developed in Cameroon and combines highlife, the fast-paced dance music that originated in Ghana, with elements of African-American soul, funk, jazz, and rock.

The first star of makossa was Manu Dibango (q.v.), whose 1972 album Soul Makossa is credited with establishing the style as a major music form in the early 1970s. Dibango, a Cameroonian who had formerly played saxophone and keyboards in Joseph Kabasele's soukous band, African Jazz, is still one of makossa's big names. Others include Moni Bilé, Ekambi Brilliant, Toto Guillaume, Sammy Njondji, Sam Fan Thomas, and Tamwo.

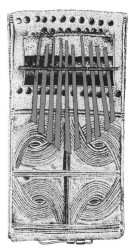

Mbira
The mbira, or sansa, is one of the most popular musical instruments in Central Africa. It is used in a great variety of musical styles, ranging from modern pop songs to those performed at religious ceremonies. This mbira is from Angola. The mbira is widely used by many African peoples, from the Azande of Central Africa to the Shona of Zimbabwe.

Deyess Mukangi *(above)*
One of Congo (Dem. Rep.)'s most popular female soukous singers is Deyess Mukangi, who embarked on a solo career after singing with the band Anti-Choc (Shockproof).

Kettledrums
The drums of Central Africa come in an enormous range of sizes and styles. These Congolese kettledrums are supported by a wooden frame.

Manu Dibango *(left, q.v.)*
Although a Cameroonian, saxophonist and keyboardist Manu Dibango is hugely popular in Central Africa and helped launch the craze for makossa music in the region.

Joseph Kabasele *(right)*
The man considered to be the founder of Zairean soukous music is Joseph Kabasele. In 1953 he formed a band called African Jazz, which developed the soukous style and made over 400 recordings before it disbanded in the mid-1960s. At its peak, it was the most popular dance band in Africa.

© DIAGRAM

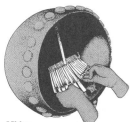

Mbira
In Zimbabwe, the mbira (or thumb piano) is an instrument that forms the basis of the music, chanting, and dancing of the ceremonies at which the Shona make contact with the spirit world.

Thomas Mapfumo *(q.v.)*
Mapfumo is well known for his electric mbira style, which translates the sounds of the mbira into guitar riffs. He is outspoken about political matters and his 1990s single Corruption *sparked controversy in Zimbabwe.*

Valiha horn *(below)*
Consisting of a long bamboo tube with twenty strings stretched lengthwise around its circumference, the valiha is considered the national instrument of Madagascar. Still popular with modern musicians, valihas are now being made in different materials, metal strings are used, and a thirty-eight-stringed chromatic model has even been designed

Tarika *(right)*
Tarika are one of the bands at the forefront of the roots-revival movement in Madagascar.

Rhythms of Southern Africa

The music of Southern Africa is vibrant and varied, blending traditional harmonies, rhythms, and instruments with modern music styles, such as blues and jazz, to create new and exciting musical forms.

Mbaqanga and iscathamiya

As might be expected given its size and dominance, South Africa is the leading musical influence in the region and has produced many unique forms such as the mbaqanga songs of the townships, and the powerful Zulu a capella (unaccompanied) singing style, iscathamiya. The ancestry of the mbaqanga vocal style can be traced back to the four-part harmonies of 1950s African-American bands. South African musicians at first copied these harmonies, but then Africanized them by adding an extra voice, creating a five-part-harmony style that echoed traditional African singing. The Zulu iscathamiya style originated in the all-male workers' hostels of the industrial areas of 1920s Natal. Typified these days by bands such as Ladysmith Black Mambazo, it features unaccompanied close-harmony vocals and sophisticated dance routines.

South African jazz

The post-World War II era saw the growing popularity of jazz music in South African urban areas – Johannesburg in particular boasted many bands with large followings. Township jazz bands combined American swing with marabi (or jive music – an early form of township jazz based around three chords) to create the dynamic African jazz style. In the 1960s, a more self-consciously-artistic style called progressive jazz emerged, often with an overtly antiapartheid stance. Musicians such as trumpeter Hugh Masekela (q.v.) and pianist Dollar Brand (q.v., who became Abdullah Ibrahim) were at the forefront of this movement. Oppressive government policies sadly forced many of this era's best musicians into exile, ending the golden age of South African jazz. In the last few years, however, the end of apartheid and the return of many exiled musicians has revitalized the jazz scene and new styles and faces are emerging.

Mbira, chimurenga, and rumbira

Zimbabwe has also made important contributions to Southern African music, often with styles influenced by the mbira (thumb piano). Although the mbira is traditionally played by men, some of its most prominent players today are women, such as Beulah Diago and Stella Chiweshe. In 1970s, the powerful, hypnotic style

Ladysmith Black Mambazo
The South African group Ladysmith Black Mambazo, led by Joseph Shabalala (q.v.), released their first album in 1973 and it became the first African LP to sell over 25,000 copies. It was their work with Paul Simon in the mid-1980s, however, that helped to make iscathamiya the most widely-recognized South African music style.

of the mbira inspired a unique contemporary music style called chimurenga. Created by Thomas Mapfumo (q.v.), chimurenga – which means "liberation war" – played an important role in the struggle for majority rule in Zimbabwe. During that time, its Shona and Ndebele lyrics contained messages of resistance that few whites could understand but which helped to raise the morale of the liberation movement.

Other distinctive mbira-influenced Zimbabwean music forms are Jit Jive (a term coined by the internationally successful Bhundu Boys), an energetic dance music featuring mbira-style guitars, and rumbira, an exciting blend of electric mbira and Zairean rumba rhythms.

Roots revival

Electric-roots music – combining modern instruments such as electric guitars and synthesizers with traditional instruments and vocals – is a popular modern genre in Southern Africa. Previously marginalized by Western-style pop, Madagascar's music has been undergoing a roots revival in the last few years. Jean Emilien, for example, blends traditional vako-drazana songs with dance music and plays an amplified version of the guitarlike kabosy, while Ricky Randimbiarison plays vako-jazzana, combining vako-drazana and jazz.

Miriam Makeba *(q.v., right)*
Miriam Makeba is probably the best-known singer to emerge from the golden age of South African jazz. Exiled in 1963 for her antiapartheid views, she has now returned to South Africa. Her singing style incorporates the "click" sounds used in many Southern African languages.

Hugh Masekela *(q.v., right)*
After spending over three decades in exile in the US and elsewhere, Masekela's music has expanded to include influences from African-American funk and soul as well as from marabi and mbaqanga music.

Rock art

The Sahara was not always a desert; 10,000 years ago it was a place of rivers and grassy plains. The people who lived there left records of their life in the Sahara from about 6000 to 100 BCE. These records are a series of paintings on the red sandstone rocks of Tassili-n-Ajjer, southeastern Algeria. Tassili-n-Ajjer is a bleak plateau scored with deep canyons and gorges. Its highest point is 7,400 ft (2,250 m) above sea level. The plateau is baking hot by day and bitterly cold at night. Tassili-n-Ajjer means "plateau of the rivers," and from the paintings it is obvious that there was once plenty of water around. The remains of a fossil forest show that its slopes were once wooded, but today it is hard to imagine elephants, giraffes, and other animals roaming the area. Several of the paintings are of hippopotamuses and archeologists have found bones of hippos in a dry riverbed south of Tassili-n-Ajjer. Other rock paintings in North Africa show crocodiles and men hunting from boats in areas that are now waterless.

The earliest pictures show human figures wearing flared leggings and performing some kind of dance. These paintings probably date from 8,000 years ago. A thousand years later, artists were painting cattle, wild sheep, giraffes, and other animals. Giant buffaloes, which are now extinct, are often featured. Later paintings show horse-drawn chariots; camels begin to appear from around 100 BCE. Many of the paintings are on top of earlier ones. In places, there are as many as a dozen layers. This overpainting suggests that the artists regarded certain sites as sacred and that to make a new painting on one was a way of placating the gods.

The ancient artists of Tassili-n-Ajjer used a few bright colors – mostly yellow, red, and brown. They obtained these colors from ocher (a reddish-brown or yellow clay).

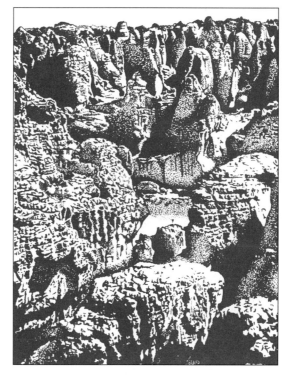

Tassili-n-Ajjer (left and above)
Tassili-n-Ajjer is a block of sandstone that has been carved by the erosive powers of water and wind into a maze of weird, pillarlike columns of rock separated by deep, dry gullies. The rock paintings are mostly found at the feet of these columns. The site lies at the heart of the Sahara Desert in the south of Algeria close to its border with Libya. Some of the ancient trans-Saharan trade routes once passed through this area.

Dance figures (below)
Some of the oldest paintings, probably from around 6000 BCE, show strange, stylized, featureless figures possibly performing a ritual dance.

Hippo hunt {right}
Hunting was a way of life for the people of the Sahara. It is thought that this painting shows a hippopotamus hunt, with the hunter in a canoe. This is further evidence that lakes and rivers once covered the Sahara.

Pastoralists (right)
From about 5000 to 1200 BCE the inhabitants of Tassili-n-Ajjer were pastoral people who herded cattle and other animals. The rock paintings from this time show herds of cattle and flocks of sheep and goats.

Chariots (left)
This chariot painting is probably from around 1200 BCE, when invasions from the north brought chariots and warriors and led to the end of the long pastoral period in Tassili-n-Ajjer. The pastoralists were probably driven southward.

© DIAGRAM

Tourism

Since the early 1970s, East Africa has been a major destination for tourists attracted to the region's varied landscapes, wildlife, and cultures. Tourism, however, is not new to East Africa; the region has been visited by European tourists since the late nineteenth century. Hunters – both tourists and white settlers – were responsible for what amounted to carnage, eliminating entire species such as the blaubok (a large, bluish-gray antelope) and quagga (a type of zebra). Hunters would take pride in slaughtering hundreds of animals on a single expedition: a safari led by former president of the United States Theodore Roosevelt slaughtered five thousand animals, including some of the few remaining white rhinos.

Tourism has become the single most important source of foreign currency and is central for development plans of most countries in the region. Some argue that tourism brings much-needed jobs to regions of high unemployment, but that ignores the fact that service jobs – in restaurants and hotels – are no replacement for the largely self-sufficient ways of life that many people have been able to maintain.

People, parks, and conservation

During the 1940s, in the name of conservation, huge tracts of land in East Africa were designated as parks, with admission reserved for rangers and paying tourists. These areas were not "wilderness," however, but were among the world's longest-inhabited areas: game being concentrated in regions that, with the best grazing land and most reliable water sources, were areas also most suitable for cattle and, of course, people.

Conflicts between the interests of indigenous peoples and wildlife conservation are well illustrated by the case of the Maasai. From the 1940s to the 1980s, Kenya's Maasai were deprived of most of their dry-season pasture because it was said that a human population could not coexist with wildlife within a park. Some conservationists have argued that local people have always endangered wildlife through hunting and overgrazing. Historically, peoples hunted only to survive, however, and most ecologists now agree that overgrazing was rare. Only after the Europeans arrived was wildlife threatened.

There is general agreement that environmental damage would result from unrestricted settlement in

Hot-air ballooning
A hot-air balloon drifting over Masai Mara provides tourists with an aerial view of this national park, which straddles the border between Kenya and Tanzania. Hot-air ballooning is a popular tourist activity.

Trophy-hunters
Buffalo were among the many big-game animals of East Africa that were killed by European and American hunters seeking trophies. Unlike local people, who used every part of any animal caught and rarely killed more game than they needed, the trophy-hunters had no use for anything but the head or horns. In recent decades, while antihunting laws have protected the wildlife, conservation measures often adversely affect locals by keeping them out of the parks.

National parks and game reserves
The map above shows the major national parks and game reserves of Uganda, Kenya, and Tanzania. The establishment of these protected areas curtailed many people's rights of access to vital resources. Some were even evicted from their land. Today, governments are beginning to realize the value of indigenous lifestyles that help maintain the environment and are allowing greater access to national parks and game reserves.

(Names in brackets indicate peoples affected by the establishment of that park or reserve)

1 Ruwenzori
2 Lake Mburo (*Bahima*)
3 Kabelega Falls
4 Kidepo (*Dodoth, Ik, Napore, Nyangia*)
5 Siboli
6 Marsabit (*Boran*)
7 South Turkana (*Turkana*)
8 Mount Elgon (*Maasai*)
9 Laikipia (*Maasai, Laikipiak*)
10 Losai
11 Samburu (*Samburu*)
12 Buffalo Springs (*Samburu*)
13 Shaba
14 Aberdares (*Kikuyu*)
15 Mount Kenya
16 Meru
17 Masai Mara (*Maasai*)
18 Amboseli (*Maasai*)
19 Chyulu
20 Tsavo (West)
21 Tsavo (East) (*Taita*)
22 Shimba Hills
23 Serengeti (*Maasai*)
24 Ngorongoro Crater (*Maasai*)
25 Arusha (*Arusha*)
26 Tarangire
27 Mkomazi (*Maasai*)
28 Ruaha
29 Mikumi
30 Selous

the parks. But many people argue that the Maasai at least be given grazing access. Instead, they are excluded from the best of the lands they regard as theirs, which leads to overgrazing elsewhere, with a result that many of the parks are islands of biodiversity set amid environmental degradation.

Not surprisingly, many of the Maasai expelled from parks feel bitter toward conservation and tourism. Some have taken to poaching, while others are actively hostile toward tourists.

Sea and sand

Coastal tourism in East Africa – particularly the main resorts of Mombasa and Malindi in Kenya – has been expanding without restrictions. Most Kenyan beach hotels have been built in tourist enclaves and have resulted in local people losing their land. Fishermen have lost access to beaches and fishing grounds because of hotel development and the creation of marine parks, while local women can no longer collect crabs, once an important source of food. Scuba diving, reef trips, and sewage from hotels have damaged coral reefs, resulting in local resentment toward tourists.

Elsewhere in East Africa, coastal tourism is either in its infancy or tourist numbers are deliberately limited, so lessening both environmental damage and conflict with local people. This situation is likely to change with Tanzania – in particular on the island of Zanzibar – promoting its beaches.

Kenya

Tourism accounts for forty percent of Kenya's foreign currency earnings, with tourists drawn by the beaches and wildlife safaris. Because of the revenue from tourists, wildlife preservation has been important for the government. With a rising population, however, many Kenyans question the priority given to wildlife tourism, which excludes local people and limits the availability of much of the country's best land for agriculture. Furthermore, the costs of conservation are high and the upkeep of parks and reserves is dependent on foreign aid.

Kilaguni
Tourists get the chance to see wildlife close-up at Kilaguni Lodge in Tsavo, Kenya's largest national park. Recently expanded to include a conference center, Kilaguni attracts a lot of tourist traffic.

Uganda

Two decades of dictatorship and political unrest have meant that only since 1990 has Uganda been in a position to actively promote tourism. Uganda's rare mountain gorillas are its primary attraction, but water-based ecosystems are also promoted, including cruises to view crocodiles and hippos. In recent years, the creation of national parks has led to the displacement of entire peoples; in 1982, for example, the cattle-herding Bahima were expelled from their grazing land in what became Lake Mburo National Park.

Tanzania

Tourism contributes twenty-five percent of Tanzania's foreign currency earnings. As in Kenya, tourism is highly controversial due to the cost of conservation programs, population displacement, and a government legacy of avoiding tourist development as being demeaning and culturally threatening. Foreign tour operators reap most of the financial benefits. This situation is gradually changing as the Tanzanian government encourages tourism away from the congested northern parks near the Kenyan border toward game reserves elsewhere and to Zanzibar's beaches. Nevertheless, the Maasai have been banned from the Ngorongoro Crater and Serengeti National Park – both of which, the country is proud to boast, have been declared World Heritage sites by the United Nations – forcing them into a more sedentary existence that does not suit their cattle-herding lifestyle.

Seychelles

Until the opening of the airport in 1971, only a handful of tourists visited the Indian Ocean islands of the Seychelles each year. Tourism is now the main foreign currency earner, but the Seychelles' Marxist government is keen to limit the social and environmental damage that has blighted the East African mainland. The Seychelles is promoted as an upmarket destination, so bringing maximum revenue from as few tourists as possible. Half the land is designated as a park, but there is little conflict between tourists and islanders as most of the park area is unsuited to agriculture or human habitation.

Photo opportunity
Here a tourist photographs a Maasai woman. People in traditional costume are popular with tourists and can earn welcome extra income by posing for photographs. Others, however, feel that this reinforces negative views of an unchanging, "primitve" Africa.

Local crafts
On a roadside in Kenya, this Kikuyu woman is selling bags and baskets, which are made from sisal and are called ciondo.

Treetops
In the Aberdares National Park, Kenya – once a Mau Mau stronghold – is Treetops Lodge, a world-famous hotel. It was first built in 1934 and has been visited by many European royals.

Camel safaris
Camels have been used in Somalia for centuries and, well suited to the environment, they have recently been introduced elsewhere in East Africa. This Samburu man leads a camel on a tourist trek in Kenya.

© DIAGRAM

SECTION

Algeria

PEOPLE

Ethnic groups: Arab (p 32)**, including Bedouin** (p 50)**, Berber** (p 53)**, other including French**
Population: 29,318,000 (about a tenth of the US population of 267,636,000)
Religions: Islam (99.9%), Christianity (0.1%)
Religions: Islam (99.9%), Christianity (0.1%)

SOCIAL FACTS

- The average life expectancy at birth is 70 years, as compared with 76 years in the US
- Only 56% of the people live in urban areas, as compared with about 76% in the US
- 90% of Algerians live in the northern coastal region
- A million French settlers left Algeria after independence

in 1962
- Muslim fundamentalists oppose westernization, and the government has attempted to curb French influences
- Most people in the cities wear Western dress and they are generally more westernized than rural people

KEY POINTS IN RECENT HISTORY

1954 War for independence from France begins, led by the Front de Libération Nationale (FLN)
1962 Independence day (July 3)
1963 Muhammad Ben Bella (an FLN leader) becomes president
1965 Military coup overthrows government
1991 Fundamentalist Front d'Islamic Salvation (FIS) wins

first round of elections, the government cancels second round; a state of emergency is then declared
1992 A military regime is established and Islamic fundamentalists begin a long terrorist campaign
1995 Liamine Zeroual is appointed president
1999 Zeroual steps down and Abdulaziz Bouteflika is elected president after opposition candidates withdraw

THE NATION

Location: North Africa, facing the Mediterranean Sea
Neighbors: Tunisia, Libya, Niger, Mali, Mauritania, Western Sahara, Morocco
Official name: People's Democratic Republic of Algeria
Divisions: Forty-eight provinces
Capital: Algiers
Largest cities: Algiers, Oran, Constantine, Annaba, Blida, Sétif, Sidi-bel-Abbès (in order of size)
Flag: The Algerian flag is green and white with a red star and crescent. Green is a traditional Islamic color and the red star and crescent, symbols of Islam, also appear on the country's green-and-white coat of arms
National anthem: "We swear by the lightning that destroys"

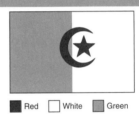

■ Red □ White ■ Green

1963 stamp marking promulgation of the Algerian constitution

Major languages: Arabic (official), Berber, French
Currency: Dinar = 100 centimes

GEOGRAPHY

With an area of 919,355 square miles (2,381,120 sq. km), Algeria is Africa's second largest country. It is nearly three times bigger than Texas in the United States (US).

Northern Algeria consists of the Tell, a region of coastal plains and hill country. Behind this region lie the Atlas Mountains, which extend across the country from Morocco to Tunisia. Plateaus in the Atlas range contain salt lakes, which periodically dry up. Algeria's chief rivers, including the Chelif, rise in the Atlas and flow north into the Mediterranean. Southern Algeria, which makes up about 80% of the country, consists of the Sahara Desert. Much of the Sahara is flat, but the Ahaggar Mountains in the south contain Algeria's highest peak, Mount Tahat, at 9,573 ft (2,918 m) high.

The Tell has hot, dry summers and mild, moist winters, but the rainfall decreases to the south. The Atlas range has

forests of juniper, Aleppo pine, and cork oak. Temperatures in the Sahara often soar to 120 °F (49 °C) by day, but nights can be chilly. The Sahara contains little plant or animal life except at oases, which are fertile pockets.

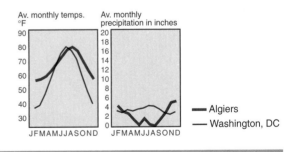

ECONOMY

Chief farm products: barley, citrus fruits, cork, dairy products, dates, grapes, meat, olives, potatoes, wheat
Chief mineral resources: Oil and natural gas, iron ore
Chief industrial products: Cement, liquid natural gas, refined petroleum products, iron and steel, vehicles, textiles, processed food
Exports: Oil and natural gas (97%)
Per capita income: $1,500 (as compared with $29,080 in the US)

Employment:

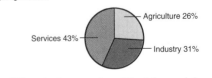

Agriculture 26%
Services 43%
Industry 31%

In the US, agriculture employs 3% of the work force, industry 26%, and services 71%

Angola

PEOPLE

Ethnic groups: Kongo (p 119), **Mbundu** (p 145), **Ovimbundu** (p 177)
Population: 11,659,000 (as compared with the US population of 267,636,000)
Religions: Christianity (90%), African religions (9.5%)

SOCIAL FACTS

- The average life expectancy at birth is 46 years, as compared with 76 years in the US
- Only 31% of the people live in urban areas, as compared with about 76% in the US
- Most Europeans left the country after Angola became independent

- Angola takes its name from Ngola, the title of the early rulers of the country
- Angola, a former Portuguese territory, was a major source of slaves for Brazil
- Ethnic and political differences have caused civil war and marred progress since independence

KEY POINTS IN RECENT HISTORY

1961 Rebellions in Luanda and other parts of the country occur when supporters of the Movimento Popular de Libertaçâo de Angola (MPLA) demand independence from Portugal
1966 Southern rebels set up the Uniâo Nacional para a Independência Total de Angola (UNITA) independence movement
1975 Civil war breaks out between rival groups in Angola, chiefly MPLA and UNITA; civil war continues after

independence on November 11
1992 Parliamentary and presidential elections are won by the MPLA
1994 A peace agreement is signed
1995 United Nations forces arrive to supervise the peace process
1996 Angola joins the Community of Portuguese-speaking Countries
1998 The civil war resumes near the end of the year

THE NATION

Location: Central Africa, facing the Atlantic Ocean
Neighbors: Dem. Rep. of Congo, Zambia, Namibia
Official name: Republic of Angola
Divisions: Eighteen provinces
Capital: Luanda
Largest cities: Luanda, Huambo, Benguela, Lobito, Lubango (in order of size)
Flag: The red and black flag contains an emblem, which includes a star to symbolize socialism; half of a gearwheel, to symbolize industry; and a machete, a large knife that is widely used in agriculture
National anthem: "Oh Fatherland, never shall we forget"

■ Red ■ Black □ Yellow

1975 stamp marking Angola's independence

Major languages: Portuguese (official), Umbundu, Kimbundu
Currency: Kwanza = 100 lei

GEOGRAPHY

With an area of 481,354 square miles (1,246,702 sq. km), Angola is Africa's seventh largest country. It is about 1.8 times as large as Texas in the United States (US).

Most of the land forms part of the huge plateau that makes up Southern Africa. The interior is mainly between 2,000 and 4,000 ft (600–1,200 m) above sea level, but the highest point, Mount Moco, reaches 8,596 ft (2,620 m) in the west. Northeastern Angola forms part of the Congo (Zaire) River Basin. In the south, some rivers, including the Cubango and Cunene, flow into inland drainage basins rather than the sea.

Angola includes a small external enclave, Cabinda, that is cut off from the rest of the country by a strip of land 20 miles (32 km) wide belonging to the Democratic Republic of Congo (formerly Zaire). Cabinda is important because it contains most of Angola's oil reserves.

Angola has a tropical climate, but the altitude lowers

temperatures in the interior. The coast is arid, but the rainfall increases to the east. Tropical savanna covers much of Angola, with open grassland in drier areas. Semidesert occurs on the coast, merging into the bleak Namib Desert in the south.

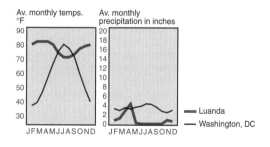

Av. monthly temps. °F

Av. monthly precipitation in inches

━ Luanda
━ Washington, DC

JFMAMJJASOND   JFMAMJJASOND

ECONOMY

Chief farm products: Bananas, cassava, coffee, corn, livestock, millet, palm oil, sugar cane
Chief mineral resources: Diamonds, oil, iron ore
Chief industrial products: Beverages, cement, chemicals, footwear, processed food, textiles
Exports: Oil (90%), diamonds
Per capita income: $260 (as compared with $29,080 in the US)

Employment:

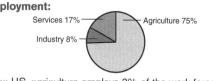

Services 17%   Agriculture 75%
Industry 8%

In the US, agriculture employs 3% of the work force, industry 26%, and services 71%

© DIAGRAM

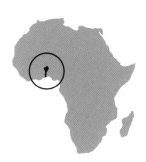

Benin

Ethnic groups: Bariba (p 48), **Fon** (p 83), **Yoruba** (p 218)
Population: 5,796,000 (as compared with the US population of 267,636,000)
Religions: African religions (62%), Christianity (23%), Islam (12%)

SOCIAL FACTS

- The average life expectancy at birth is 53 years, as compared with 76 years in the US
- Only 38% of the people live in urban areas, as compared with about 76% in the US
- Benin was called Dahomey until 1975
- The historic Kingdom of Dahomey, with its capital at Abomey, existed long before the Europeans arrived
- African slaves took the worship of Dahomeyan gods – vodun (singular, vodu) – to the Americas. These gods are still venerated by some Brazilians. "Voodoo" is a corruption of "vodu"

KEY POINTS IN RECENT HISTORY

1960 Dahomey becomes independent from France (August 1)
1960s and 1970s The government changes frequently because of repeated military coups
1975 Dahomey is renamed Benin; it becomes a one-party, Marxist-Leninist "people's republic" (socialist state)
1989 Marxism-Leninism is abandoned after years of economic decline
1990 A national conference discusses a new, multiparty constitution
1991 Benin holds its first multiparty presidential elections; Nicéphore Soglo, a former World Bank executive, becomes president
1994 CFA franc is devalued by 50%
1996 Mathieu Kérékou, Benin's dictator from 1972 until 1990, defeats Soglo in elections and becomes president
1997 Labor unions protest against economic liberalization policies

THE NATION

Location: West Africa, facing the Gulf of Guinea
Neighbors: Togo, Burkina Faso, Niger, Nigeria
Official name: Republic of Benin
Divisions: Six provinces divided into eighty-four districts
Capital: Porto-Novo
Largest cities: Cotonou, Porto-Novo, Djougou, Abomey, Parakou (in order of size)
Flag: The three colors (a vertical strip of green in the hoist and yellow and red horizontal stripes) represent African unity. They are the colors used on the flag of Ethiopia, Africa's oldest independent nation
National anthem: "L'aube nouvelle" ("New dawn")

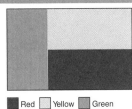

Red ▮ Yellow ▮ Green

1978 stamp depicting Samori Toure, hero of anticolonial resistance

Major languages: French (official), Fon, Yoruba
Currency: CFA franc = 100 centimes

GEOGRAPHY

With an area of 43,484 square miles (112,623 sq. km), Benin is one of Africa's smaller countries. It is a little larger in area than Tennessee in the United States (US).

Benin is a narrow country, and extends about 400 miles (640 km) from north to south. The coast, 77 miles (124 km) long, is lined by lagoons and has no natural harbors. Behind the coast is a broad plain with occasional hills. This region, which includes the marshy Lama Depression, is called the barre, or "clay country." In central Benin, the land rises to a series of low plateaus. The highest part of Benin reaches about 2,100 ft (640 m) in the Atakora Mountains in the northwest. In northeastern Benin, the land slopes down toward the valley of the Niger River.

The longest river is the Ouémé. This river flows south for 280 miles (450 km) to the Gulf of Guinea.

Benin has an equatorial climate. The rainfall is greatest in the central regions of the country. Rainforests once covered much of the south, but have been largely cleared. The rainfall decreases to the north, which has a marked dry season between November and March. Tropical savanna is the typical vegetation in the north.

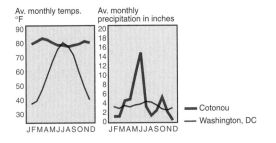

Av. monthly temps. °F

Av. monthly precipitation in inches

— Cotonou
— Washington, DC

ECONOMY

Chief farm products: Beans, cassava, cocoa, corn, coffee, cotton, millet, peanuts, rice, sorghum, sugar cane, yams
Chief mineral resources: Limestone, some offshore oil
Chief industrial products: Beverages, cement, palm oil, sugar, textiles
Exports: Cotton, energy, palm kernels and palm oil, manufactured goods
Per capita income: $380 (as compared with $29,080 in the US)

Employment:

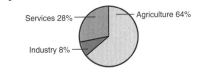

Services 28%
Agriculture 64%
Industry 8%

In the US, agriculture employs 3% of the work force, industry 26%, and services 71%

Botswana

PEOPLE

Ethnic groups: Khoisan, including Kung (p 124), **Shona** (p 186), **Tswana, including Kolong and Hurutshe** (p 205)
Population: 1,533,000 (as compared with the US population of 267,636,000)
Religions: Christianity (50%), African religions (49%)

SOCIAL FACTS

- The average life expectancy at birth is 47 years, as compared with 76 years in the US
- 60% of the people live in urban areas, as compared with about 76% in the US
- Botswana was once known as Bechuanaland

- Botswana is one of the most stable democracies in Africa
- 17% of the country is protected in national parks and reserves, the highest proportion in Africa
- Since 1971, mining has transformed Botswana's economy, which was formerly based on livestock raising

KEY POINTS IN RECENT HISTORY

1961 Seretse Khama forms the Bechuanaland (later Botswana) Democratic Party (BDP)
1966 Bechuanaland becomes independent from Britain as the Republic of Botswana (September 30); Seretse Khama becomes the first president
1980 Seretse Khama dies and Dr Ketumile (Quett) Masire

succeeds him as the head of the BDP
1980s Tension is caused by South African raids on the homes of African National Congress (ANC) refugees
1984 The BDP wins the first elections after Khama's death
1998 Masire retires and Festus Mogae becomes president

THE NATION

Location: Landlocked country in Southern Africa
Neighbors: Zimbabwe, South Africa, Namibia
Official name: Republic of Botswana
Divisions: Eleven districts, one city, and eight towns
Capital: Gaborone
Largest cities: Gaborone, Francistown, Selebi-Pikwe, Molepolole, Kanye (in order of size)
Flag: The flag consists of two blue stripes (top and bottom), with a black stripe, edged with white, in the center. The black-and-white feature is a symbol of racial harmony, while the blue represents much-needed rain
National anthem: "Fatshe leno la rona" ("Blessed noble land")

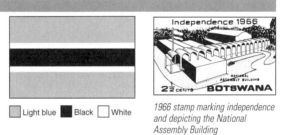

Light blue   Black   White

1966 stamp marking independence and depicting the National Assembly Building

Major languages: English (official), Setswana (national)
Currency: Pula = 100 thebe

GEOGRAPHY

With an area of 224,468 square miles (581,370 sq. km), Botswana is Africa's twenty-first largest country. It is about 1.4 times larger in area than California in the United States (US).

Botswana occupies part of the huge plateau that makes up most of Southern Africa. The average height of the flat or gently rolling land is around 3,300 ft (1,000 m) above sea level.

Large depressions in the north form inland drainage basins. The Okavango Swamps are supplied by the Okavango River, which rises (as the Cubango River) in Angola. Another depression, the Makgadikgadi Salt Pans, is supplied with water by the Botletle River, which flows from the Okavango Swamps when that area is flooded. These northern drainage basins are rich in wildlife. The Kalahari Desert in the southeast has practically no surface drainage.

Botswana has a dry, subtropical climate. The Kalahari

has about 12 in. (30 cm) of rain a year and is really a semidesert, with grass and thorn scrub covering most of the land, though sand dunes occur in the southwest. The east has more rainfall and tropical savanna covers large areas. Some forests occur in the north, which also contains swamp vegetation in the inland drainage basins. Droughts are common throughout the country.

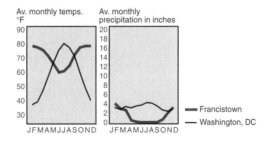

Av. monthly temps. °F

Av. monthly precipitation in inches

Francistown
Washington, DC

ECONOMY

Chief farm products: Beef, corn, cotton, millet, roots and tubers, sorghum, vegetables
Chief mineral resources: Diamonds, copper, nickel, cobalt, coal
Chief industrial products: Chemicals, processed food, textiles, wood products and paper
Exports: Diamonds, copper-nickel, beef products
Per capita income: $3,310 (as compared with $29,080 in the US)

Employment:

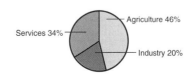

Agriculture 46%
Services 34%
Industry 20%

In the US, agriculture employs 3% of the work force, industry 26%, and services 71%

Burkina Faso

PEOPLE

Ethnic groups: Bariba (p 48), **Bobo** (p 56), **Dyula** (p 72), **Fulani** (p 85), **Lobi** (p 126), **Mossi** (p 155), **Senufo** (p 184), **Soninke** (p 191)

Population: 10,474,000 (as compared with the US population of 267,636,000)

Religions: African religions (45%), Islam (43%), Christianity (12%)

SOCIAL FACTS

- The average life expectancy at birth is 44 years, as compared with 76 years in the US
- Only 16% of the people live in urban areas, as compared with about 76% in the US
- Burkina Faso is a Mossi name, which means "land of the incorruptible men"

- Until 1984, Burkina Faso was known as Upper Volta, because it contained the headwaters of the Volta rivers
- Burkina Faso is heavily dependent on foreign aid and about two million of its citizens work abroad
- The north is part of the Sahel, a dry semidesert region south of the Sahara

KEY POINTS IN RECENT HISTORY

1919 France creates the colony of Upper Volta
1960 Upper Volta becomes independent (August 5) with Maurice Yameogo as president
1966 General Sangoulé Lamizana seizes power in a military coup
1978 Lamizana is elected president
1980 Colonel Saye Zerbo takes power after a military coup
1982 Another military coup brings Surgeon-Major Jean-

Baptiste Ouedraogo to power
1983 Captain Thomas Sankara ousts Ouedraogo and becomes president
1987 Military leaders overthrow Sankara, who is replaced by Captain Blaise Compaoré
1991 Compaoré, the sole candidate, is elected president
1994 After pressure from France, the CFA franc, which is linked to the French franc, is devalued by 50%

THE NATION

Location: Landlocked country in West Africa
Neighbors: Mali, Niger, Benin, Togo, Ghana, Ivory Coast
Official name: Democratic People's Republic of Burkina Faso
Divisions: Thirty provinces
Capital: Ouagadougou
Largest cities: Ouagadougou, Bobo-Dioulasso, Koudougou, Ouahigouya (in order of size)
Flag: The red and green flag, with a yellow star in the center, was adopted in 1984, when Upper Volta was renamed Burkina Faso. The three colors, taken from the flag of Ethiopia, symbolize African unity
National anthem: "Against the shameful fetters"

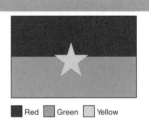

■ Red ■ Green □ Yellow

1993 stamp depicting the red-fronted gazelle

Major languages: French (official), Moré
Currency: CFA franc = 100 centimes

GEOGRAPHY

With an area of 105,869 square miles (274,200 sq. km), Burkina Faso is Africa's twenty-eighth largest country. It is about the same size as Colorado in the United States (US).

The country consists of a large plateau, mostly between about 650 and 2,300 ft (200–700 m) above sea level. The highest point is the Aguille de Sindou, which reaches 2,352 ft (717 m) on the southwestern border with Mali. The soil in Burkina Faso is generally thin and infertile. Soil erosion has given many areas a barren, rocky appearance.

The chief rivers are the Black Volta, the Red Volta, and the White Volta, which flow southward into Lake Volta, in Ghana. However, in the northeast, small rivers flow into the Niger River. During droughts, some rivers stop flowing and parts of their courses become swamps.

Burkina Faso has a tropical climate. It is cool and dry

between November and February, hot and dry from March to June, and hot and rainy for the rest of the year. The rainfall is greatest in the south. Tropical savanna occurs in the north, with stunted trees and thorn shrubs in the dry north.

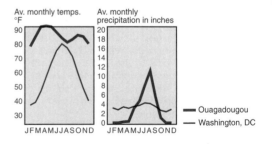

Av. monthly temps. °F

Av. monthly precipitation in inches

— Ouagadougou
— Washington, DC

ECONOMY

Chief farm products: Corn, cotton, livestock, millet, peanuts, rice, shea nuts, sorghum, sugar cane
Chief mineral resources: Gold, silver, other unexploited minerals
Chief industrial products: Beverages, footwear, motorcycles and bicycles, processed food, textiles
Exports: Raw cotton, live animals, manufactured goods, hides and skins
Per capita income: $250 (as compared with $29,080 in the US)

Employment:

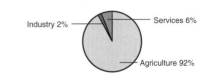

Industry 2%
Services 6%
Agriculture 92%

In the US, agriculture employs 3% of the work force, industry 26%, and services 71%

Burundi

PEOPLE

Ethnic groups: Hutu (p 99), **Tutsi** (p 99), **Twa** (p 145)
Population: 6,435,000 (as compared with the US population of 267,636,000)
Religions: Christianity (79%), African religions (19%) Islam (2%)

SOCIAL FACTS

• The average life expectancy at birth is 42 years, as compared with 76 years in the US
• Only 8% of the people live in urban areas, as compared with about 76% in the US

• The minority Tutsi have controlled the region for hundreds of years
• Burundi is mainland Africa's second most densely populated country after neighboring Rwanda

KEY POINTS IN RECENT HISTORY

1916 Belgium occupies the former German territory of Ruanda-Urundi
1961 Urundi votes to break away from Ruanda-Urundi and become the independent Kingdom of Burundi
1962 Independence day (July 1)
1966 Burundi becomes a republic, with a Tutsi, Michel Micombero, as president
1972 An unsuccessful Hutu revolt results in about 100,000 deaths

1976 Captain Jean-Baptiste Bagaza seizes power
1987 Major Pierre Buyoya takes power
1993 The newly elected Hutu president is killed; Tutsi-Hutu massacres follow
1994 Ethnic conflict follows the probable assassination of Burundi's and Rwanda's presidents in an airplane crash
1996 Burundi expels thousands of Rwandan Hutu refugees. Military coup led by Buyoya ousts president. Ethnic conlict erupts between Hutu and Tutsi

THE NATION

Location: Landlocked country in East Africa
Neighbors: Rwanda, Tanzania, Dem. Rep. of Congo
Official name: Republic of Burundi
Divisions: Fifteen regions
Capital: Bujumbura
Largest cities: Bujumbura, Gitega, Bururi, Ngozi (in order of size)
Flag: The white circle in the center contains three red stars bordered in green. White bands extend from the circle to the corners separating red areas (above and below) and green (left and right)
National anthem: "Uburundi bwacu" ("Dear Burundi")

White ▪ Red ▪ Green

1962 stamp marking independence, and depicting King Mwambutsa IV

Major languages: Rundi and French (both official), Swahili
Currency: Burundi franc = 100 centimes

GEOGRAPHY

With an area of 10,747 square miles (27,834 sq. km), Burundi is one of Africa's smaller countries. It is about the same size in area as Maryland in the United States (US.)

Western Burundi occupies part of the Great Rift Valley. The border with Zaire runs along the floor of the Rift Valley through Lake Tanganyika and along the Ruzizi River, which flows into it from the north. Overlooking the Rift Valley are high mountains, reaching 8,858 ft (2,700 m) in the north. which form part of the divide between the Congo (Zaire) and Nile river systems.

East of the mountains lie plateaus between about 5,000 and 6,500 ft (1,500–2,000 m) high. These plateaus descend toward the east along steep, steplike escarpments. Flowing northeast across the plateau is the Ruvuvu River, the most southerly tributary of the Nile.

Burundi has a tropical climate, though temperatures are moderated by the altitude. The rainfall is plentiful, especially on the mountains. May to August is the dry season. Forests grown on the mountains but they give way to wooded tropical savanna and more open grassland to the east.

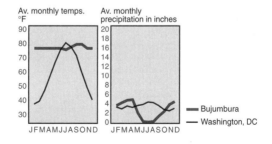

ECONOMY

Chief farm products: Bananas, beans, cassava, coffee, corn, cotton, livestock, peanuts, sorghum, sugar cane, sweet potatoes, tea, yams
Chief mineral resource: Gold
Chief industrial products: Beverages, footwear, leather goods, processed food, sugar, textiles
Exports: Coffee, hides and skins, cotton fabric
Per capita income: $140 (as compared with $29,080 in the US)

Employment:

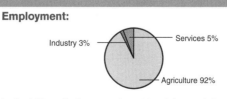

In the US, agriculture employs 3% of the work force, industry 26%, and services 71%

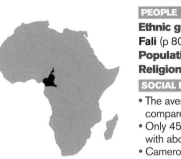

Cameroon

Ethnic groups: Anglophones of Cameroon (p 31), **Bamileke** (p 46), **Bamum** (p 46), **Dyula** (p 72), **Fali** (p 80), **Fang** (p 80)
Population: 13,936,000 (as compared with the US population of 267,636,000)
Religions: Christianity (77%), African religions (21%)

SOCIAL FACTS

- The average life expectancy at birth is 57 years, as compared with 76 years in the US
- Only 45% of the people live in urban areas, as compared with about 76% in the US
- Cameroon is known for its wooden masks and statues

- Cameroon is an ethnic crossroads, containing forest peoples, Bantu-speaking groups, and Sudanic peoples
- Some English-speaking Cameroonians favor secession
- Cameroon was named for the camarões (shrimps) found by the Portuguese in the Wouri River

KEY POINTS IN RECENT HISTORY

1960 French Cameroun becomes the independent Republic of Cameroon; Ahmadou Ahidjo becomes president
1961 British Cameroons votes to join Nigeria; the south votes to join the Republic of Cameroon
1961 The southern part of British Cameroons and the Republic of Cameroon combine to form the Federal Republic of Cameroon
1966 A one-party state is proclaimed

1972 Cameroon becomes a unitary (nonfederal) state
1982 Ahidjo resigns and Paul Biya becomes president
1990 The government legalizes opposition parties
1992 Multiparty elections take place; Biya is reelected president
1994 The CFA franc is devalued by 50% causing economic hardship
1995 Cameroon joins the Commonwealth of Nations
1997 Biya is reelected president

THE NATION

Location: West Africa
Neighbors: Nigeria, Chad, Central African Republic, Congo, Gabon, Equatorial Guinea
Official name: Republic of Cameroon
Divisions: Ten provinces
Capital: Yaoundé
Largest cities: Douala, Yaoundé, Garoua, Maroua, Bafoussam (in order of size)
Flag: The green, red, and yellow stripes symbolize African unity, because these colors come from the flag of Africa's oldest independent country, Ethiopia. The gold star was added in 1975
National anthem: "O Cameroon, thou cradle of our fathers"

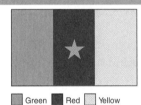

Green Red Yellow Gold

Stamp marking the Union of African and Malagasy States in 1962

Major languages: French and English (both official), Fang
Currency: CFA franc = 100 centimes

GEOGRAPHY

With an area of 183,569 square miles (475,442 sq. km), Cameroon is Africa's twenty-third largest country. It is a little larger in area than California in the United States (US).

Cameroon consists mainly of plateaus that slope down to the north to the Lake Chad basin. Lake Chad, which Cameroon shares with Nigeria, Niger, and Chad, is the largest lake. The southwest is mountainous. Near the coast is an active volcano, Mount Cameroon, which is the country's highest peak, at 13,353 ft (4,070 m).

The narrow coastal plain is crossed by two of the country's largest rivers, the Wouri and Sanaga. Another important river, the Benue, rises in the Adamawa plateau in central Cameroon. It flows north and then west to become a tributary of the Niger River in central Nigeria.

The south is hot and rainy, but inland temperatures are moderated by the altitude. The rainfall decreases to the north, which is hot and dry. Rainforests grow in the south, though farmers have cleared large areas. Tropical savanna is the main vegetation in central Cameroon, but the north is semidesert.

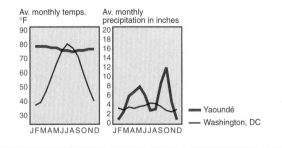

Av. monthly temps. °F

Av. monthly precipitation in inches

Yaoundé
Washington, DC

JFMAMJJASOND JFMAMJJASOND

ECONOMY

Chief farm products: Bananas, cassava, cocoa, coffee, cotton, lumber, millet, palm products, plantains, rice, sugar cane, yams
Chief mineral resources: Oil, tin
Chief industrial products: Aluminum, cement, petroleum products, processed food, wood products
Exports: Oil, cocoa, sawn wood and logs, cotton, coffee
Per capita income: $620 (as compared with $29,080 in the US)

Employment:

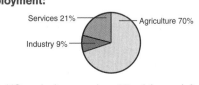

Services 21%
Agriculture 70%
Industry 9%

In the US, agriculture employs 3% of the work force, industry 26%, and services 71%

Cape Verde

PEOPLE

Ethnic groups: Mixed origin: African and European
Population: 401,000 (as compared with the US population of 267,636,000)
Religions: Christianity, including Roman Catholics (93%)

SOCIAL FACTS

- The average life expectancy at birth is 68 years, as compared with 76 years in the US
- Only 54% of the people live in urban areas, as compared with about 76% in the US
- Cape Verde has close historic links with Guinea-Bissau

- Severe droughts periodically cause famine and hardship
- Many Cape Verdeans emigrate to find work; the money they send home is important in the country's economy
- The local Creole dialect contains words from Portuguese and various African languages

KEY POINTS IN RECENT HISTORY

1951 Portugal makes its colony of Cape Verde an overseas province
1956 Nationalists set up the Partido Africano de la Independência do Guiné e Cabo Verde (PAIGC) party; it calls for independence
1974 A military group overthrows the government in Portugal
1975 Cape Verde becomes an independent country
1981 The PAIGC is renamed the Partido Africano da Independência do Cabo Verde (PAICV); the removal of

Guiné (Guinea) from the title reflects a rift with Guinea-Bissau's leaders
1990 Cape Verde's parliament abolishes the PAICV's sole right to rule
1991 Multiparty elections are won by the Movimento para a Democracia (MPD); António Mascarenhas Monteiro is elected president
1996 Cape Verde joins the Community of Portuguese-speaking Countries

THE NATION

Location: Island nation in West Africa
Nearest mainland: Senegal
Official name: Republic of Cape Verde
Divisions: Ten islands and five islets
Capital: Praia
Largest cities: Praia, Mindelo (in order of size)
Flag: Adopted in 1992, the flag consists of a blue field, on the lower half of which are three stripes of white, red, and white. Superimposed are ten yellow stars arranged in a circle
National anthem: As in Guinea-Bissau – "Sun, sweat, the green, and the sea"

Blue ☐ White ■ Red
☐ Yellow

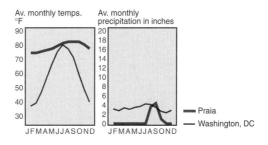

1976 stamp marking the first anniversary of Cape Verde's independence

Major languages: Portuguese (official), Creole
Currency: Escudo = 100 centavos

GEOGRAPHY

With an area of 1,557 square miles (4,033 sq. km), Cape Verde is Africa's smallest country. It is a little larger than Rhode Island in the United States (US).

Cape Verde is a group of volcanic islands in the Atlantic Ocean. The Barlavento, or Windward, group consists of Santo Antão, São Vicente, Santa Luzia, São Nicolau, Sal, and Boa Vista. The Sotavento (Leeward) group of islands, in the south, are Brava, Fogo, São Tiago, and Maio. Santa Luzia and the five islets are uninhabited. The largest island is São Tiago, on which the capital, Praia, is located. This island contains more than three-quarters of the country's population. The highest point on these mountainous islands, called Pico, is on Fogo island. It reaches 9,281 ft (2,829 m) above sea level.

Cape Verde has a warm, dry climate. Dry northeast trade

winds blow for most of the year, but moister southwest winds bring some rain from August to October. Sandstorms from the Sahara sometimes hit the islands. Much of the land is desert, with thorny shrubs in some areas.

Av. monthly temps. °F / Av. monthly precipitation in inches
■ Praia
— Washington, DC

ECONOMY

Chief farm products: Bananas, cassava, coconuts, coffee, corn, fruits, livestock, plantains, sugar cane, sweet potatoes, vegetables
Chief mineral resources: Salt, pozzolana (volcanic rock used tomake cement)
Chief industrial products: Beverages, processed food, rum and molasses
Exports: Oil and oil products, fish
Per capita income: $1,090 (as compared with $29,080 in the US)

Employment:

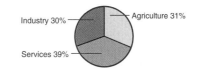

Industry 30% / Agriculture 31% / Services 39%

In the US, agriculture employs 3% of the work force, industry 26%, and services 71%

Central African Republic

PEOPLE

Ethnic groups: Banda (p 47), **Baya** (p 49), **Mandija** (p 142), **Mbun** (p 145), **Sara** (p 183)
Population: 3,418,000 (as compared with the US population of 267,636,000)
Religions: Christianity (68%), African religions (24%), Islam (8%)

SOCIAL FACTS

- The average life expectancy at birth is 45 years, as compared with 76 years in the US
- Only 39% of the people live in urban areas, as compared with about 76% in the US
- National parks and reserves make up 6% of the country
- Slavery greatly depleted the population of the region from the 1500s to the 1800s
- Farming is the main activity, but only 3% of the land is cultivated
- Sango, which is based on the Baya language, includes many French words

KEY POINTS IN RECENT HISTORY

1910 CAR (then called Oubangui-Chari) becomes part of the French Equatorial Africa colony
1960 CAR becomes independent (August 13) and David Dacko becomes the first president
1966 The army leader, Jean-Bédel Bokassa, seizes power
1976 Bokassa makes himself emperor of the renamed Central African Empire; he rules as a dictator
1979 Bokassa is overthrown with French assistance and Dacko becomes president again
1981 Army officers remove Dacko and General André Kolingba takes power
1992 The government introduces a multiparty constitution
1993 Multiparty elections take place and Ange-Félix Patassé beats eight candidates to become president
1994 CFA is devalued by 50%
1996 Bokassa dies

THE NATION

Location: Landlocked country in Central Africa
Neighbors: Chad, Sudan, Dem. Rep. of Congo, Congo, Cameroon
Official name: Central African Republic
Divisions: Sixteen prefectures and the autonomous commune of Bangui
Capital: Bangui
Largest cities: Bangui, Berbérati, Bouar, Bambari, Bossangoa, Carnot (in order of size)
Flag: The top two horizontal stripes of blue and white, together with the vertical red stripe, recall France's flag. The red and the horizontal green and yellow stripes symbolize African unity
National anthem: "La renaissance" ("Rebirth")

| ■ Blue | □ White | ■ Red |
| ■ Green | □ Yellow | |

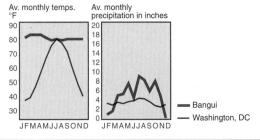

1960 stamp marking CAR joining the UN

Major languages: French (official), Sango (national)
Currency: CFA franc = 100 cents

GEOGRAPHY

With an area of 240,324 square miles (622,437 sq. km), Central African Republic (CAR) is Africa's nineteenth largest country. It is a bit smaller in area than Texas in the United States (US).

The country consists of a rolling plateau mostly between about 2,000 and 2,500 ft (600–760 m) above sea level. The highest point is Mount Toussoro, at 4,462 ft (1,360 m), in the northeast. The plateau is a major divide between the Congo (Zaire), Nile, and Lake Chad river basins. In the south, rivers drain into the Oubangui River, a tributary of the (Congo) Zaire River. The Oubangui and its tributary, the Mbomou River, form much of the country's border with Congo. They form a major waterway for trade. In the north, rivers feed the Chari River that flows north to Lake Chad. In the northeast, a number of rivers flow into the Nile River system.

The altitude moderates temperatures in this tropical country. The main rainy season is from June until October. The rainfall exceeds 60 in. (152 cm) in the south, but it is only 30 in. (76 cm) in the north. Rainforests grow in south, but wooded tropical savanna covers most of the land.

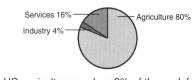

Av. monthly temps. °F / Av. monthly precipitation in inches

■ Bangui
— Washington, DC

ECONOMY

Chief farm products: Bananas, cassava, coffee, corn, cotton, livestock, peanuts, sorghum, yams
Chief mineral resources: Copper, diamonds, gold, iron, uranium
Chief industrial products: Beverages, chemicals, clothing, metal products, textiles, tobacco, wood products
Exports: Diamonds, wood, cotton, tobacco, coffee, gold
Per capital income: $320 (as compared with $29,080 in the US)

Employment:

Services 16%
Industry 4%
Agriculture 80%

In the US, agriculture employs 3% of the work force, industry 26%, and services 71%

Chad

Ethnic groups: Bagirmi (p 43), **Beri** (p 55), **Buduma** (p 57), **Sara** (p 183), **Sudanic Arab** (p 32), **Teda** (p 199)
Population: 7,153,000 (as compared with the US population of 267,636,000)
Religions: Islam (40%), Christianity (33%), African religions (27%)

SOCIAL FACTS

- The average life expectancy at birth is 49 years, as compared with 76 years in the US
- Only 22% of the people live in urban areas, as compared with about 76% in the US
- From the 700s until the 1800s, Chad was part of the Kanem-Borno Empire
- Conflict has occurred between the Muslim Arabs and Berbers in the north and the Black Africans, most of whom follow either Christianity or African religions
- In 1994 the International Court of Justice ruled against Libya's claim to the Aozou Strip in northern Chad

KEY POINTS IN RECENT HISTORY

1960 Chad becomes independent from France (August 11) with François Tombalbaye as the first president
1962 A group of northerners forms the Front de Libération National du Tchad (FROLINAT)
Mid-1960s Civil war breaks out
1971 Libya aids FROLINAT troops in their struggle
1973 Libya occupies the Aozou Strip
1975 A military group kills Tombalbaye and sets up a military regime; the civil war continues
1987 Government forces conquer the north, except for the Aozou Strip
1990 A rebel group overthrows the government; Idriss Déby becomes president; he seeks to unite the country and restore democratic institutions
1994 CFA is devalued by 50%
1996 Déby is reelected president

THE NATION

Location: Landlocked country in West Africa
Neighbors: Libya, Sudan, Central African Republic, Cameroon, Nigeria, Niger
Official name: Republic of Chad
Divisions: Fourteen prefectures
Capital: N'Djamena
Largest cities: N'Djamena, Sarh, Moundou, Abéché, Koumra (in order of size)
Flag: The blue vertical stripe, left, represents the sky and hope; the yellow stripe, center, the Sun; and the red stripe, right, fire and unity. The flag was adopted in 1959 as Chad prepared for independence
National anthem: "People of Chad arise and to the task"

☐ Blue ☐ Yellow ■ Red

1976 stamp depicting decorated gourds and a ladle

Major languages: French and Arabic (both official), Sara
Currency: CFA franc = 100 centimes

GEOGRAPHY

With an area of 495,755 square miles (1,284,000 sq. km), Chad is Africa's fifth largest country. It is 1.2 times larger in area than California in the United States (US).

Northern Chad contains arid plateaus interspersed with rocky mountains. The highest peak, Emi Koussi, at 11,204 ft (3,415 m), is in the Tibesti Mountains in the northwest. The north contains sand dunes, gravel-strewn plains, and large areas of bare rock. The wadis (dry watercourses) are turned into fast-flowing rivers after heavy rainstorms.

The south contains a number of rivers, the most important being the Chari and Logone, which unite before flowing into Lake Chad. This lake, whose area varies greatly from season to season, is the country's largest and occupies an inland drainage basin. Chad shares it with Cameroon, Nigeria, and Niger. Northern Chad is part of the Sahara and the climate is hot and almost rainless. Central Chad contains part of a semidesert region called the Sahel. In the south, where rain occurs from May until September, tropical savanna covers large areas. Some forests occur in the far south.

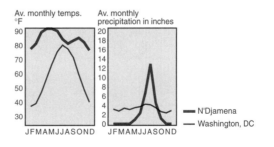

Av. monthly temps. °F

Av. monthly precipitation in inches

■ N'Djamena
— Washington, DC

JFMAMJJASOND   JFMAMJJASOND

ECONOMY

Chief farm products: Beans, cassava, corn, cotton, livestock, millet, peanuts, rice, sugar cane, yams
Chief mineral resources: Salt, bauxite (aluminum ore), gold, and uranium
Chief industrial products: Beverages, cigarettes, cotton fabrics, hides and skins, processed food
Exports: Raw cotton, cattle and meat, hides and skins
Per capita income: $230 (as compared with $29,080 in the US)

Employment:

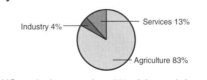

Industry 4%
Services 13%
Agriculture 83%

In the US, agriculture employs 3% of the work force, industry 26%, and services 71%

Comoros

Ethnic group: Comorians (of mixed African and Arab descent)
Population: 518,000 (as compared with the US population of 267,636,000)
Religions: Islam (99.4%), Christianity (0.6%)

SOCIAL FACTS

- The average life expectancy at birth is 60 years, as compared with 76 years in the US
- Only 30% of the people live in urban areas, as compared with about 76% in the US
- Arab sultans ruled the islands from the 1400s until the 1800s

- The Comorians are descendants of Africans, Madagascans, Arabs, and Southeast Asians
- Comorian is a Bantu language, similar to Swahili – the lingua franca in East Africa
- From 1975 until 1995, the Comoros suffered seventeen coup attempts

KEY POINTS IN RECENT HISTORY

1947 France makes the Comoros an overseas territory
1961 The Comoros gain self-rule
1974 The people of three islands vote for independence, but Mayotte opts to remain under French rule
1975 The Comoros become independent (July 6) under President Ahmad Abdullah; a coup led by Ali Soilih overthrows Abdullah

1978 Abdullah regains power after a coup
1989 Abdullah is assassinated; his successor is Said Muhammad Djohar, head of the Supreme Court
1995 Djohar flees after failed coup attempt
1996 Djohar returns; elections bring in new government
1998 Anjouan and Mohéli declare their independence from the Comoros; their action is not recognized internationally

THE NATION

Location: Island nation in the Indian Ocean, off the coast of Southern Africa
Nearest countries: Mozambique, Madagascar
Official name: Federal Islamic Republic of the Comoros
Divisions: Three main islands
Capital: Moroni
Largest cities: Moroni, Fomboni, Mutsamudu (in order of size)
Flag: The white crescent on a green background represent the country's dominant religion, Islam. The four stars represent four islands – the three that make up the Comoros, and nearby Mayotte, which is a French dependency
National anthem: "Udzima wa ya masiwa" ("The union of the islands")

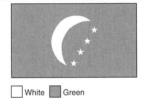

☐ White ■ Green

1977 stamp depicting a big-game fish

Major languages: Comorian and French (both official), Swahili, Arabic
Currency: Comorian franc = 100 centimes

GEOGRAPHY

With an area of 719 square miles (1,862 sq. km), the Comoros is Africa's fourth smallest country. It is smaller in area than Rhode Island in the United States (US).

Geographically, the Comoros is a group of four islands in the Indian Ocean, between mainland Africa and northern Madagascar. The Comoros republic, however, includes only three of these islands – Njazidja (or Grande Comore), Mwali (or Mohéli), and Nzwani (or Anjouan). The people of the fourth island, Mayotte, in the southeast, voted to remain a French dependency.

The highest peak on these volcanic islands is an active volcano, Mont Kartala, which reaches 7,646 ft (2,331 m) above sea level on Njazida. Although largely mountainous, the Comoros also has some fertile lowland.

The climate is tropical, with dry, cool conditions from May

to October and a hot rainy season between November and April. The highest rainfall is usually in January. Mangrove swamps occur on the coast, but much of the inland forest has been cut down. Grasses and heather grow on the mountain slopes.

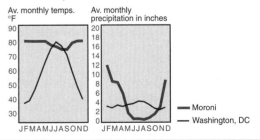

Av. monthly temps. °F / Av. monthly precipitation in inches

■ Moroni
— Washington, DC

ECONOMY

Chief farm products: Bananas, cassava, cloves. coconuts, coffee, copra, corn, rice, perfume oils, sisal, sweet potatoes, vanilla
Chief mineral resources: Sand, gravel
Chief industrial products: Beverages, plastics, textiles, wood products
Exports: Vanilla, perfume oils, cloves
Per capita income: $400 (as compared with $29,080 in the US)

Employment:

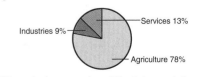

Industries 9%
Services 13%
Agriculture 78%

In the US, agriculture employs 3% of the work force, industry 26%, and services 71%

Congo, Democratic Republic of

PEOPLE

Ethnic groups: Alur (p27), **Azande** (p 39), **Kongo** (p 119), **Luba** (p 129), **Lugbara** (p 131), **Mangbetu** (p 143), **Mongo** (p 152), **Ndembu** (p 161), **Pende** (p 171), **Songye** (p 191), **Suku** (p 194)
Population: 46,709,000 (as compared with the US population of 267,636,000)
Religions: Christianity (94.5%), African religions (3%), Islam (1%)

SOCIAL FACTS

- The average life expectancy at birth is 51 years, as compared with 76 years in the US
- Only 29% of the people live in urban areas, as compared with about 76% in the US
- The province of Kasai uses a different currency from the rest of the country; it has refused to adopt the new zaire notes and still uses the old ones

- In 1971, many names were Africanized; Léopoldville became Kinshasa and President Joseph-Désiré Mobutu became Mobutu Sese Seko
- Secessionist groups, especially in the mineral-rich Katanga (formerly Shaba) region, have caused political instability

KEY POINTS IN RECENT HISTORY

1908 Congo becomes a Belgian colony
1960 Congo becomes independent (June 30); it is known as Congo (Kinshasa) to distinguish it from Congo (Brazzaville)
1960–3 Civil (First Shaba) War
1965 General Joseph-Désiré Mobutu becomes president and puts down rebellions
1970 Mobutu declares the country to be a one-party state
1971 Congo (Kinshasa) is renamed Republic of Zaire

1996 Rwanda/Burundi conflict spreads to Tutsi of eastern Congo and civil disorder follows
1997 Laurent Kabila leading Tutsi forces marches on Kinshasa and becomes president; he renames the country the Democratic Republic of Congo
1998 Civil war begins when forces aided by Burundi, Rwanda and Uganda, rebel; Kabila gets support from Angola, Chad, Namibia and Zimbabwe

THE NATION

Location: Central Africa, facing the Atlantic Ocean
Neighbors: Congo, Central African Republic, Sudan, Uganda, Rwanda, Burundi, Zambia, Angola
Official name: Democratic Republic of Congo
Divisions: Ten regions and Kinshasa
Capital: Kinshasa
Largest cities: Kinshasa, Lubumbashi, Mbuji-Mayi, Kisangani, Kananga (in order of size)
Flag: The flag of the Democratic Republic of Congo contains a dark blue background, with one large yellow star, center right, and six small stars in the row on the left.
National anthem: "La Congolaise"

Blue Yellow

1973 stamp marking Zaire's Third International Fair, Kinshasa

Major languages: French (official), Luba, Kongo, Lingala
Currency: Congolese franc = 100 centimes

GEOGRAPHY

With an area of 905,568 square miles (2,345,412 sq. km), Congo is Africa's third largest country. It is 3.4 times larger in area than Texas in the United States (US).

Congo lies mainly within the Congo River Basin. This river is Africa's second longest, with a length of about 2,900 miles (4,660 km). It carries more water than any other river in the world apart from the Amazon.

The land rises to the east, where mountains border the Great Rift Valley. Congo's highest point is Margherita Peak, 16,762 ft (5,109 m), in the Ruwenzori Range on the Uganda border. There are other highlands are in the south. The Great Rift Valley contains lakes Tanganyika, Kivu, Edward, and Albert. The country's eastern border runs through these lakes.

Northern Congo has an equatorial climate. with high temperatures and heavy rainfall. Rainforests cover large areas, but the south has a marked dry season. There, the forests give way to tropical savanna. The highlands have a cooler climate and bands of vegetation based on altitude.

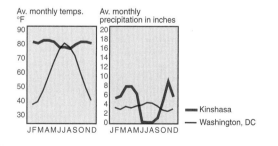

Av. monthly temps. °F
Av. monthly precipitation in inches

JFMAMJJASOND JFMAMJJASOND

— Kinshasa
— Washington, DC

ECONOMY

Chief farm products: Bananas, cassava, coffee, corn, cotton, palm oil, peanuts, rice, rubber, timber
Chief mineral resources: Copper, diamonds, oil, gold, silver
Chief industrial products: Beverages, cement, chemicals, footwear, processed food, textiles, tires
Exports: Copper, industrial diamonds, oil, coffee
Per capita income: $110 (as compared with $29,080 in the US)

Employment:

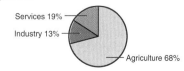

Services 19%
Industry 13%
Agriculture 68%

In the US, agriculture employs 3% of the work force, industry 26%, and services 71%

Congo, Republic of

Ethnic groups: Bakota (p 43), **Bapounou** (p 47), **Kongo** (p 119), **Mbochi** (p 145), **Sango** (p 183), **Teke** (p 199)
Population: 2,708,000 (as compared with the US population of 267,636,000)
Religions: Christianity (93%), African religions (5%)

SOCIAL FACTS

- The average life expectancy at birth is 48 years, as compared with 76 years in the US
- Only 58% of the people live in urban areas, as compared with about 76% in the US
- In 1970, Congo became the first declared communist country in Africa
- Brazzaville was named after the nineteenth-century French explorer Pierre Savorgnan de Brazza
- Congo was once called Congo (Brazzaville) to distinguish it from another Congo – Congo (Kinshasa), now called Zaire
- Dugout canoes are the main form of transportation in northern Congo

KEY POINTS IN RECENT HISTORY

1960 Congo becomes independent from France (August 15); Abbé Fulbert Youlou becomes the first president
1964 Congo adopts a one-party system of government
1968 A military group led by Captain Marien Ngouabi seizes power
1970 Congo declares itself a communist country
1977 Ngouabi is assassinated

1979 Colonel Denis Sassou-Nguesso becomes president
1990 Congo renounces communism
1991 Congo legalizes opposition political parties
1992 Sassou-Nguesso is defeated in national elections by Pascal Lissouba
1997 Civil war breaks out and Sassou-Nguesso, with support from Angolan troops, seizes power

THE NATION

Location: Central Africa
Neighbors: Gabon, Cameroon, Central African Republic, Dem. Rep. of Congo, Cabinda (Angola)
Official name: Republic of Congo
Divisions: Nine prefectures
Capital: Brazzaville
Largest cities: Brazzaville, Pointe-Noire, Loubomo, Mossendjo (in order of size)
Flag: The flag has a diagonal pattern of green, yellow, and red. These are the colors of the flag of Ethiopia, and symbolize African unity. This flag was adopted in 1990, replacing the previous red (socialist) flag
National anthem: "La congolaise"

Green | Yellow | Red

1971 stamp commemorating the eighth anniversary of the 1963 revolution

Major languages: French (official), Kileta, Lingala, and Kongo
Currency: Lilangeni = 100 cents

GEOGRAPHY

With an area of 132,047 square miles (342,000 sq. km), Congo is Africa's twenty-sixth largest country. It is about twice as big as Texas in the United States (US).

Behind the coast, which is 100 miles (160 km) long, lies a narrow plain that extends inland to the steep Mayombe Escarpment. Beyond that lie a series of plateaus, between about 1,600 and 2,600 ft (500–800 m) above sea level. The highest point in the country is Mount Lékéti, at 3,412 ft (1,040 m).

The main river on the coastal plain is the Kouilou. Its main tributary, the Niari River, flows through a fertile region. Northern Congo consists of high plains crossed by many rivers that flow into the Congo (Zaire) River and one of its tributaries, the Oubangui. Many of the river valleys in the north flood annually and contain large areas of swamp.

Most of Congo has high temperatures and abundant rainfall. The cold, offshore Benguela Current lowers temperatures on the coast, which is the driest part of the country. The coastal plain is treeless, but tropical savanna covers the plateaus, with forests in the valleys. The north is largely forested.

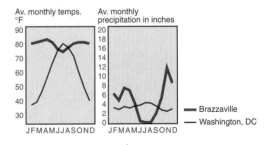

Av. monthly temps. °F

Av. monthly precipitation in inches

Brazzaville
Washington, DC

ECONOMY

Chief farm products: Bananas, cassava, cocoa, coffee, corn, palm products, peanuts, sugar cane, yams
Chief mineral resources: Oil and natural gas, lead, zinc
Chief industrial products: Beverages, cement, fuel oils, processed food, textiles, wood products
Exports: Oil and oil products (90%), manufactured goods, raw materials
Per capita income: $670 (as compared with $29,080 in the US)

Employment:

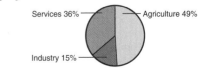

Services 36% — Agriculture 49%
Industry 15%

In the US, agriculture employs 3% of the work force, industry 26%, and services 71%

Djibouti

PEOPLE

Ethnic groups: Afar (p 21), **Somali, including Issa** (p 189)
Population: 636,000 (as compared with the US population of 267,636,000)
Religions: Islam (96%), Christianity (4%)

SOCIAL FACTS

- The average life expectancy at birth is 50 years, as compared with 76 years in the US
- 82% of the people live in urban areas, as compared with about 76% in the US
- Djibouti is strategically placed at the southern end of the Red Sea

- Djibouti was formerly called French Somaliland and, later, the Territory of the Afars and the Issas
- Only about 1% of the land can be used for farming
- Rivalries between the Afar and the Somalis have caused problems in Djibouti

KEY POINTS IN RECENT HISTORY

1917 A railroad to Addis Ababa, Ethiopia, is completed, making Djibouti an important trading center
1947 Nationalists in what was then French Somaliland call for independence for the territory
1967 The country is renamed the Territory of the Afars and the Issas
1977 The country becomes independent (June 26) as the Republic of Djibouti; Hassan Gouled Aptidon is the

first president
1981 Hassan Gouled Aptidon is reelected president
1991 A coup attempt is defeated
1992 A constitution permitting four political parties is adopted; each party must have an ethnic balance
1993 Hassan Gouled Aptidon is again elected president, defeating three opponents

THE NATION

Location: North Africa, facing the Mediterranean Sea
Neighbors: Tunisia, Libya, Niger, Location: East Africa, on the Gulf of Aden
Neighbors: Somalia, Ethiopia, Eritrea
Official name: Republic of Djibouti
Divisions: Five administrative districts
Capital: Djibouti
Largest cities: Djibouti, Ali Sabieh, Tadjoura (in order of size)
Flag: The horizontal stripes of blue (top) and green symbolize the two main peoples, the Afar and the Somalis. The white triangle contains a red star, which represents unity and independence
National anthem: "Hinjinne u sara kaca" ("Arise with strength")

Blue ▢ Green ▢ White
Red

1978 stamp depicting a seashell

Major languages: Arabic and French (both official), Afar, Somali
Currency: Djibouti franc = 100 centimes

GEOGRAPHY

With an area of 8,958 square miles (23,201 sq. km), Djibouti is Africa's eighth smallest country. It is slightly smaller than New Hampshire in the United States (US).

Djibouti is located around the Gulf of Tadjoura, an inlet of the Gulf of Aden. Behind the narrow coastal plain, the land rises to highlands in the north, where Moussa Ali reaches 6,768 ft (2,063 m). The country includes Lake Assal, whose shoreline is Africa's lowest point on land, reaching 509 ft (155 m) below sea level. The country's largest lake is Lake Abba on the Ethiopian border in the west. This lake is fed by the Awash River. The Awash flows through the Great Rift Valley. which cuts across Djibouti.

Djibouti has a hot, dry climate. The annual rainfall is everywhere less than 20 in. (51 cm) and deserts cover

nearly 90% of the land. Only hardy grasses and thorn shrubs can survive there. The mountains contain some wooded areas and date palms and other plants grow at oases.

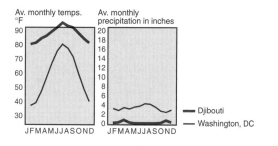

Av. monthly temps. °F

Av. monthly precipitation in inches

JFMAMJJASOND   JFMAMJJASOND

— Djibouti
— Washington, DC

ECONOMY

Chief farm products: Hides and skins, livestock (cattle, camels, goats, sheep), melons, meat, tomatoes, vegetables
Chief mineral resources: Salt, building materials
Chief industrial products: Beverages, furniture, electromechanical products
Exports: Mainly reexports, live animals
Per capita income: $835 (as compared with $29,080 in the US)

Employment:

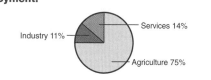

Services 14%
Industry 11%
Agriculture 75%

In the US, agriculture employs 3% of the work force, industry 26%, and services 71%

Egypt

Ethnic groups: Arab (p 32), **including Bedouin** (p 50), **Nubians** (p 165)
Population: 60,348,000 (about a quarter of the US population of 267,636,000)
Religions: Islam (about 90%), Christianity – mainly Coptic Christians (about 10%)

SOCIAL FACTS

- The average life expectancy at birth is 66 years, as compared with 76 years in the US
- 45% of the people live in urban areas, as compared with about 76% in the US)
- Egypt is Africa's second most populous country after Nigeria
- Nearly all Egyptians live in the Nile Valley or along the Suez Canal
- Egypt is Africa's second most industrialized country
- Women have more rights in Egypt than in any other Arab country.
- Egyptian fundamentalists want to return to traditional Muslim culture

KEY POINTS IN RECENT HISTORY

1914 Egypt becomes a British protectorate
1922 Egypt becomes a nominally independent monarchy (February 28)
1948 Egypt is involved in the Arab-Israeli War (1948–9)
1954 Egypt becomes a republic
1956 Egypt nationalizes the Suez Canal; Britain, Israel, and France attack Egypt, but the United Nations ends the fighting and foreign troops withdraw

1967 Israel wins a short war against its Arab neighbors, including Egypt
1973 Renewed fighting between Israel and Arab nations, including Egypt
1979 Egypt and Israel sign a peace agreement
1991 Egyptian troops form part of the Allied military forces against Iraq in the Gulf War
1993 Hosni Mubarak is sworn in for a third term as president

THE NATION

Location: North Africa, with coastlines on the Mediterranean and the Red Sea
Neighbors: Israel, Sudan, Libya
Official name: Arab Republic of Egypt
Divisions: Twenty-six governates
Capital: Cairo
Largest cities: Cairo, Alexandria, Giza, Shubra al Khayma, Port Said, Suez (in order of size)
Flag: The flag has three stripes of red, white, and black. The white stripe contains the national emblem, an eagle, which was the symbol of Saladin (Salah ad-Din), the great Muslim leader and warrior (1137–93)
National anthem: "Biladi, biladi" ("My homeland, my homeland")

Red | White | Black

1951 stamp marking the royal wedding of King Farouk I and Queen Narriman

Major languages: Arabic (official), Berber, English, French
Currency: Pound = 100 piastres

GEOGRAPHY

With an area of 386,095 square miles (1,000,000 sq. km), Egypt is Africa's twelfth largest country. It is nearly 1.5 times as big as Texas in the United States (US).

West of the Nile, the world's longest river, is the Libyan or Western Desert (part of the Sahara). In the northwest is the Qattara Depression, where Egypt's lowest point, 436 ft (133 m) below sea level, is located. Eastern Egypt contains the Eastern Desert (also part of the Sahara) and the Sinai peninsula. The Sinai contains Egypt's highest peak, Jabal Katherina, at 8,851 ft (2,696 m) above sea level. Lake Nasser, a reservoir behind the Aswan High Dam, is the largest lake.

Egypt has a hot, dry climate, though temperatures often fall quickly after dark. Winters are mild. The average annual rainfall is about 8 in. (20 cm) on the coast. Plant life, including date palms, is confined to the Nile Valley and desert oases.

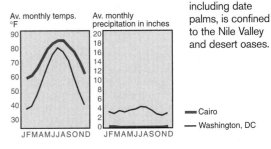

ECONOMY

Chief farm products: barley, citrus fruits, cotton, dates, potatoes, rice, sorghum, sugar cane, wheat
Chief mineral resources: Oil and natural gas, phosphates, iron ore
Chief industrial products: Cars, cement, chemicals, cotton yarn, fertilizers, refrigerators, sugar, TV sets
Exports: Oil and oil products, cotton goods, engineering and metal products
Per capita income: $1,200 (as compared with $29,080 in the US)

Employment:

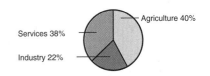

Agriculture 40%
Services 38%
Industry 22%

In the US, agriculture employs 3% of the work force, industry 26%, and services 71%

Eritrea

PEOPLE

Ethnic groups: Afar (p 21), **Issa** (p 107), **Tigre** (p 202)
Population: 3,773,000 (as compared with the US population of 267,636,000)
Religions: Christianity (about 50%), Islam (about 50%)

SOCIAL FACTS

- The average life expectancy at birth is 51 years, as compared with 76 years in the US
- Only 17% of the people live in urban areas, as compared with about 76% in the US
- Officially independent in 1993, Eritrea is Africa's youngest country
- Because of the disruption caused by civil war, adult illiteracy is high at about 80% of the population
- Women played an important part in the civil war, some as commanders, fighting alongside men
- Eritrea's economy depends heavily on overseas aid

KEY POINTS IN RECENT HISTORY

1941 British troops drive out Italian occupation forces and take over the government of Eritrea
1952 Eritrea becomes a self-governing part of Ethiopia
1961 Civil war breaks out
1962 Ethiopia declares Eritrea to be one of its provinces, making Ethiopia a unitary (nonfederal) state
1970 The Eritrean People's Liberation Front (EPLF) is

formed to seek independence for Eritrea
1991 Ethiopia's government is overthrown by rebel forces; a government is set up to rule all of Ethiopia except for Eritrea: Eritrea is considered unofficially liberated
1993 Eritreans vote overwhelmingly for independence, which is officially achieved on May 24
1998-9 Border clashes occur along the Ethiopian frontier

THE NATION

Location: East Africa, facing the Red Sea
Neighbors: Djibouti, Ethiopia, Sudan
Official name: State of Eritrea
Divisions: Ten provinces, each with a governor
Capital: Asmera
Largest cities: Asmera, Aseb, Keren, Mitsiwa, Mendefera (in order of size)
Flag: The flag of Eritrea has three triangular segments. The top segment is green and the bottom one blue. The central segment, the largest of the three, is red and contains a yellow wreath and olive branch.
National anthem: "Eritrea, Eritrea, Eritrea"

■Red □Yellow ▨Green ■Blue

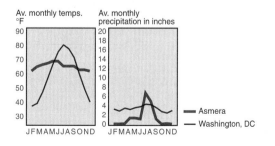

1995 One of the first stamps from newly-independent Eritrea

Major languages: Tigrinya, Arabic (both official), Afar, Beja
Currency: Birr

GEOGRAPHY

With an area of 45,405 square miles (117,598 sq. km), Eritrea is one of Africa's smaller countries. It is about the same size as Pennsylvania in the United States (US).

The Red Sea coast extends northeast for about 620 miles (1,000 km) from the border with Djibouti to the border with Sudan. Behind the coastal plain, which is 10 to 40 miles (16–64 km) wide, the land rises to the central highlands and Eritrea's highest point, Mount Soira, which reaches a height of 9,885 ft (3,013 m) above sea level.

In the west, the land slopes down toward the Sudanese and Ethiopian borders. The country's lowest point, about 361 ft (110 m) below sea level, is located in the Danakil Depression in the southeast. Eritrea's main rivers, including the Baraka and Gash (or Marab), rise in the central highlands.

The coastal plain has a hot climate, with average annual temperatures of around 81°F (27°C). The highlands are

cooler, with average temperatures around 61°F (16°F). The coastal plain has an average annual rainfall of only about 5 in. (13 cm) and most of the land is desert. By contrast, the average annual rainfall in the highlands reaches around 24 in. (61 cm). The rainiest months are usually June and July. Extensive grasslands and forests occur in the uncultivated parts of the highlands.

Av. monthly temps.
°F

Av. monthly precipitation in inches

JFMAMJJASOND   JFMAMJJASOND

■■ Asmera
— Washington, DC

ECONOMY

Chief farm products: Barley, dairy products, millet, sorghum, teff (a kind of grain), vegetables, wheat
Chief mineral resources: Salt, sand, some oil deposits
Chief industrial products: Beverages, glassware, leather goods, oil products, processed food, textiles
Exports: Beverages, leather goods, oil products, textiles
Per capita income: $230 (as compared with $29,080 in the US)

Employment:

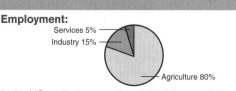

Services 5%
Industry 15%
Agriculture 80%

In the US, agriculture employs 3% of the population, industry 26%, and services 71%

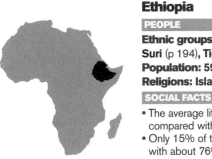

Ethiopia

PEOPLE

Ethnic groups: Amhara (p 28), **Anuak** (p 32), **Issa** (p 107), **Konso** (p 121), **Oromo** (p 173), **Sadama** (p 181), **Suri** (p 194), **Tigre** (p 202)
Population: 59,750,000 (as compared with the US population of 267,636,000)
Religions: Islam (45%), Christianity (40%), African religions (12%)

SOCIAL FACTS

• The average life expectancy at birth is 43 years, as compared with 76 years in the US
• Only 15% of the people live in urban areas, as compared with about 76% in the US
• Ethiopia has more than 70 languages and 200 dialects
• Ethiopia, formerly known as Abyssinia, is Africa's oldest independent country. Its empire lasted from Biblical times until 1974, when the emperor, Haile Selassie I, was overthrown
• The Ethiopian Orthodox (or Coptic) Church has inspired much art
• Many of Ethiopia's "Black Jews" – the Falasha – have emigrated to Israel

KEY POINTS IN RECENT HISTORY

1930 Ras Tafari becomes emperor as Haile Selassie I
1935 Italy invades Ethiopia
1941 The Italians are defeated by Ethiopian and British forces and Haile Selassie returns to the throne
1952 Eritrea becomes part of Ethiopia
1960s Fighting occurs as secessionist groups, including Somalis in the south, demand independence
1974 Haile Selassie is replaced by a socialist military government
1980s A major drought causes great hardship
1991 Mengistu Haile Mariam, head of the government, is overthrown
1993 Eritrea becomes independent
1995 National elections are held under a new federal constitution
1998-9 Border clashes occur along the Eritrean frontier

THE NATION

Location: A landlocked nation in East Africa
Neighbors: Djibouti, Somalia, Kenya, Sudan, Eritrea
Official name: Ityo (Ethiopia)
Divisions: The 1995 constitution created nine provinces
Capital: Addis Ababa
Largest cities: Addis Ababa, Dire Dawa, Gonder, Nazret, Bahir Dahr, Debre Zeyit (in order of size)
Flag: Ethiopia's flag consists of three stripes of green (top), yellow (center), and red. In Africa, these colors now represent African unity, because Ethiopia is the continent's oldest independent nation
National anthem: "In our Ethiopia, our civic pride is strong"

☐ Green ☐ Yellow ■ Red

Stamp marking the first session of the Economic Conference for Africa, in 1958

Languages: Amharic (official), Oromo, Tigrinya
Currency: Birr = 100 cents

GEOGRAPHY

With an area of 435,523 square miles (1,128,000 sq. km), Ethiopia is Africa's tenth largest country. It is a little larger in area than California in the United States (US).

Ethiopia consists mainly of a high plateau, with lowlands in the east and south. Ethiopia's highest peak, Ras Dashen, reaches 15,157 ft (4,620 m) in the north. The plateau is split into two parts by the Great Rift Valley.

Lake Tana, the largest lake and source of the Blue Nile (called the Abay Wenz in Ethiopia), is also in the north. The Blue Nile, flows into Sudan, where it joins the White Nile at Khartoum. Other lakes are in the Great Rift Valley, the northern part of which is drained by the Awash River. The Awash provides hydroelectricity for Addis Ababa and water for irrigation.

The lowlands are hot and dry and desert covers large areas. Forests grow in the hot and wet southwest, but the altitude moderates the climate in plateau regions. Grassland covers large areas in the cool highlands, where the rainfall is generally around 40 in. (102 cm) a year.

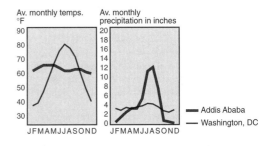

Av. monthly temps. °F / Av. monthly precipitation in inches

— Addis Ababa
— Washington, DC

ECONOMY

Chief farm products: Barley, coffee, corn, hides and skins, oilseeds, sorghum, sugar cane, teff (a kind of grain), wheat
Chief mineral resources: Salt, limestone, gold
Chief industrial products: Beverages, cement, footwear, processed food, textiles
Exports: Coffee, hides, gold, petroleum products
Per capita income: $110 (as compared with $29,080 in the US)

Employment:

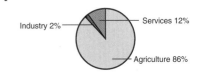

Industry 2% / Services 12% / Agriculture 86%

In the US, agriculture employs 3% of the work force, industry 26%, and services 71%

Equatorial Guinea

PEOPLE

Ethnic groups: Bubi (p 57), **Fang** (p 80)
Population: 420,000 (as compared with the US population of 267,636,000)
Religions: Christianity (89%), African religions (5%)

SOCIAL FACTS

- The average life expectancy at birth is 50 years, as compared with 76 years in the US
- Only 42% of the people live in urban areas, as compared with about 76% in the US
- Bioko was formerly called Fernando Póo and, briefly, Macías Nguema

- The Victorian writer and explorer Mary Kingsley praised the beauty of Bioko in her writings
- A small group of people, the Fernandinos, are Creoles descended from slaves freed by Britain in the nineteenth century
- Many Nigerian migrants work on Bioko

KEY POINTS IN RECENT HISTORY

1900 The mainland territories of what was then Spanish Guinea are fixed by the Treaty of Paris
1968 The country wins independence as Equatorial Guinea (October 12); Macías Nguema becomes president
1970 Equatorial Guinea becomes a one-party dictatorship
1979 Lt.-Col. Teodoro Obiang Nguema Mbasogo seizes power; Macías Nguema, accused of many crimes,

including torture, murder, and persecution of foreigners, is executed
1992 A multiparty constitution is introduced
1993 The Democratic Party wins 68 of the 80 seats in parliment
1996 Obiang Nguema is reelected president amid allegations of vote-rigging

THE NATION

Location: Central Africa
Neighbors: The mainland is bordered by Cameroon and Gabon
Official name: Republic of Equatorial Guinea
Divisions: Mainland Río Muni (or Mbini), plus Bioko and four other islands
Capital: Malabo
Largest cities: Malabo, Bata (in order of size)
Flag: The top horizontal stripe of green represents the country's natural resources, the white stripe stands for peace, and red stripe for the struggle for independence. The blue triangle represents the sea
National anthem: "Let us journey, treading the pathways"

☐ Green ☐ White ■ Red
■ Blue

1971 stamp marking the second anniversary of Equatorial Guinea's independence

Major languages: Spanish (official), Fang, Creole
Currency: CFA franc = 100 centimes

GEOGRAPHY

With an area of 10,831 square miles (28,052 sq. km), Equatorial Guinea is Africa's eleventh smallest country. It is a little larger in area than Maryland in the United States (US).

The mainland part of Equatorial Guinea, called Río Muni or Mbini, makes up 93% of the country. It contains a narrow coastal plain, rising inland to a series of plateaus. The main river, also called Mbini, flows from east to west across the mainland.

The largest island is Bioko, which lies northwest of Río Muni. Bioko is a volcanic island and contains the country's highest point, Pico de Basilé (or Santa Isabel Mountain), which reaches a height of 9,869 ft (3,008 m) above sea level. Equatorial Guinea's capital, Malabo, on Bioko's north coast, stands on a natural harbor formed by a submerged volcanic crater.

The climate is hot, wet, and humid. Because of its rugged terrain, Bioko is especially rainy, but the country has a dry season from December until February. Río Muni has rainforests, with tropical savanna inland and mangrove swamps along the coast. Bioko's vegetation is varied, with vegetation zones determined by the altitude.

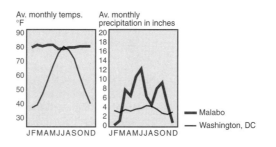

ECONOMY

Chief farm products: Bananas, cassava, cocoa, coconuts, coffee, lumber, palm kernels and palm oil, sweet potatoes
Chief mineral resources: Gold, oil (production began offshore in 1992), some unexploited metal reserves
Chief industrial products: Processed food, wood products
Exports: Timber, cocoa, coffee
Per capita income: $1,060 (as compared with $29,080 in the US)

Employment:

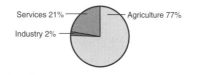

Services 21% — Agriculture 77%
Industry 2%

In the US, agriculture employs 3% of the work force, industry 26%, and services 71%

Gabon

PEOPLE

Ethnic groups: **Bakota** (p 43), **Bapounou** (p 47), **Fang** (p 80), **Mpongwe** (p 158),
Population: 1,153,000 (as compared with the US population of 267,636,000)
Religions: Christianity (96%), African religions (3%), Islam (1%)

SOCIAL FACTS

• The average life expectancy at birth is 52 years, as compared with 76 years in the US
• 50% of the people live in urban areas, as compared with about 76% in the US
• Gabon is one of Africa's most thinly populated countries
• Libreville (meaning "free town") was founded in 1849

by freed slaves
• Albert Schweitzer, who set up a sleeping sickness and leprosy hospital at Lambaréné, won the 1952 Nobel Peace Prize for his humanitarian work
• Some bands of tropical forest-foragers live in the southern forests

KEY POINTS IN RECENT HISTORY

1910 Gabon becomes a French colony within French Equatorial Africa
1960 Gabon becomes independent (August 17) and Léon M'Ba becomes the country's first president
1964 French troops restore M'Ba to power after a military coup
1967 M'Ba dies and is succeeded by Albert-Bernard (later, Omar) Bongo
1968 Gabon becomes a one-party state

1974 Work starts on the Trans-Gabon Railroad, which will open up the mineral-rich interior
1990 Opposition parties are legalized; elections are won by the Parti Démocratique Gabonais (PDG), the former sole political party
1993 Presidential elections are held and Bongo is reelected for fourth time
1994 The CFA, which is linked to the French franc, is devalued by 50% causing hardship and civil unrest

THE NATION

Location: Central Africa, facing the Atlantic Ocean
Neighbors: Equatorial Guinea, Cameroon, Congo
Official name: Gabonese Republic
Divisions: Nine provinces
Capital: Libreville
Largest cities: Libreville, Port-Gentil, Makoku, Lambaréné, Moanda (in order of size)
Flag: Of the three horizontal stripes, the green, top, represents the country's forests; the yellow, center, symbolizes the Equator (which runs through Gabon); and the blue, bottom, symbolizes the sea
National anthem: "Uni dans la concorde" ("United in concord")

■ Green □ Yellow ■ Blue

1965 stamp marking the fifth anniversary of independence and depicting President M'Ba

Major languages: French (official), Fang
Currency: CFA franc = 100 centimes

GEOGRAPHY

With an area of 103,347 square miles (267,668 sq. km), Gabon is Africa's twenty-ninth largest country. It is roughly the same size in area as Colorado in the United States (US).

Gabon's coast is 500 miles (800 km) long and lined with sandy beaches, lagoons, and swamps, Behind it is a narrow coastal plain and inland lie hills, plateaus, and low mountains. The highest point is Mount Iboundji, 3,904 ft (1,190 m) above sea level in the Massif du Chaillu in south-central Gabon.

Most of Gabon lies in the drainage basin of its chief river, the Ogooué. This river, 746 miles (1,201 km) long, rises in Congo and reaches the sea near Port-Gentil, the chief port. It is navigable throughout the year below the port of Lambarene. The climate is hot, rainy and humid. The rainy

season is from October until May. In the dry season (June to August), winds blow from the land to the sea and little rain falls. Rainforest covers about 75% of Gabon. In the east and southeast, the forests merge into tropical savanna.

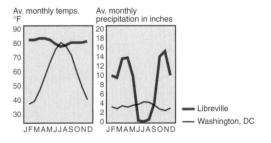

Av. monthly temps. °F

Av. monthly precipitation in inches

■■ Libreville
— Washington, DC

ECONOMY

Chief farm products: Cassava, cocoa, coffee, corn, lumber, palm products, peanuts, sugar cane, yams
Chief mineral resources: Oil and natural gas, manganese, uranium
Chief industrial products: Beverages, cement, cigarettes, processed food, textiles, wood products
Exports: Oil (80%), timber, manganese, uranium
Per capita income: $4,120 (as compared with $29,080 in the US)

Employment:

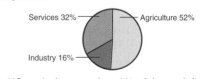

Services 32% — Agriculture 52%

Industry 16%

In the US, agriculture employs 3% of the work force, industry 26%, and services 71%

Gambia, The

PEOPLE

Ethnic groups: Dyula (p 72), **Fulani** (p 85), **Manding, including Malinke** (p 44), **Soninke** (p 191), **Wolof** (p 215)
Population: 1,181,000 (as compared with the US population of 267,636,000)
Religions: Islam (95.4%), Christianity (3.7%), African religions (0.9%)

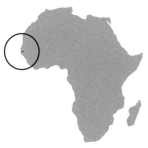

SOCIAL FACTS

• The average life expectancy at birth is 53 years, as compared with 76 years in the US
• Only 29% of the people live in urban areas, as compared with about 76% in the US
• Tourism is a fast-developing industry in Gambia
• The African-American writer Alex Haley traced his ancestors back to The Gambia in his novel Roots
• In the east, people from Senegal, called "strange farmers" help to plant the land and harvest the crops
• "The" was officially adopted as part of the country's name to further distinguish it from Zambia

KEY POINTS IN RECENT HISTORY

1965 Gambia becomes independent from Britain (February 18)
1970 Gambia becomes a republic; Sir Dawda Jawara becomes president
1981 Senegalese troops help Gambia to put down a rebellion
1982 Gambia and Senegal set up a confederation called Senegambia; it unites the countries' defense forces
1989 Senegambia is dissolved

1994 A military coup overthrows the government and Sir Dawda Jawara flees into exile; Lieutenant Yahya Jammeh becomes president and chairman of an Armed Forces Provisional Council
1995 An attempted countercoup led by Vice-President Sana Sabally is foiled
1996 Jammeh wins presidential elections after retiring from military

THE NATION

Location: West Africa, facing the Atlantic Ocean
Neighbors: Gambia is almost completely enclosed by Senegal
Official name: Republic of The Gambia
Divisions: Thirty-five districts
Capital: Banjul
Largest cities: Greater Banjul, Serrekunda, Brikama, Bakau (in order of size)
Flag: The flag of Gambia consists of three horizontal colored bands. The red band, top, stands for the Sun; the blue (edged with white) in the center represents the Gambia River; the green, bottom, is for the land
National anthem: "For The Gambia, our homeland"

■ Red ■ Blue □ White
■ Green

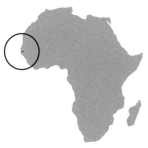

1975 Stamp marking the tenth anniversary of Gambia's independence

Major languages: English (official), Manding, Fulfulde, Wolof
Currency: Dalasi = 100 butut

GEOGRAPHY

With an area of 4,361 square miles (11,295 sq. km), Gambia is the smallest country on the African mainland. It is slightly smaller in area than Connecticut in the United States (US).

Gambia is a long and narrow strip of land, running roughly 180 miles (290 km) from east to west along the banks of the Gambia River, but it measures only between 15 and 30 miles (24-38 km) from north to south. In the east, the river flows through a deep valley cut through a sandstone plateau. In central Gambia, flat, fertile terraces, called banto faros, border the river, but near the coast, saltwater has spread inland, spoiling the soils in the valley.

Gambia has a tropical climate. The summer months (especially June to October) are rainy, but winters, when a dusty wind called the harmattan blows from the Sahara. Mangrove swamps grow along the coast. Inland, much of the tropical savanna has been cleared to make farmland.

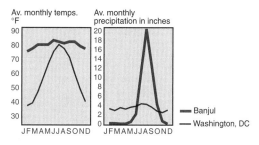

■ Banjul
— Washington, DC

ECONOMY

Chief farm products: Bananas, cassava, cotton, livestock (cattle, goats and sheep), millet, palm kernels, peanuts, rice, sorghum
Chief mineral resources: sand, gravel
Chief industrial products: Beverages, chemicals, leather, palm-kernel oil, processed food, textiles
Exports: Peanuts and peanut products, cotton, fish, hides and skins
Per capita income: $340 (as compared with $29,080 in the US)

Employment:

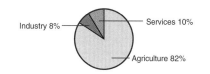

Industry 8%
Services 10%
Agriculture 82%

In the US, agriculture employs 3% of the work force, industry 26%, and services 71%

© DIAGRAM

Ghana

PEOPLE

Ethnic groups: Akan (p 26), **Asante** (p 36), **Ewe** (p 76), **Fante** (p 82), **Lobi** (p 126), **Mamprusi** (p 142), **Mossi** (p 155)
Population: 17,985,000 (as compared with the US population of 267,636,000)
Religions: Christianity (63%), African religions (21%), Islam (16%)

SOCIAL FACTS

- The average life expectancy at birth is 60 years, as compared with 76 years in the US
- Only 36% of the people live in urban areas, as compared with 76% in the US
- Before 1957, Ghana was known as Gold Coast
- Ghana was the first Black African nation to win its independence
- Ghana is the name of a medieval African kingdom that lay to the northwest of present-day Ghana
- About 75 languages are spoken in Ghana, and many Ghanaians also speak English, the official language

KEY POINTS IN RECENT HISTORY

1947 Kwame Nkrumah forms the Convention People's Party, which calls for the independence of Gold Coast
1957 Gold Coast gains independence from Britain (March 6), with Nkrumah as prime minister; it is renamed Ghana
1960 Ghana becomes a republic and Nkrumah becomes president
1966 President Nkrumah is overthrown by military leaders

1969 Civilian rule is restored
1972 A military group again seizes power
1979 Flight Lieutenant Jerry Rawlings becomes head of state, but then steps down in favor of a civilian government
1981 Rawlings returns to power
1993 Civilian rule is restored under a new multiparty constitution, with Rawlings as the elected president
1996 awlings is reelected president

THE NATION

Location: West Africa, facing the Gulf of Guinea
Neighbors: Ivory Coast, Burkina Faso, Togo
Official name: Republic of Ghana
Divisions: Ten regions, each under a Regional Secretary
Capital: Accra
Largest cities: Accra, Kumasi, Tamale, Tema, Sekondi-Takoradi (in order of size)
Flag: The flag of Ghana has three horizontal stripes of red, yellow, and green. These colors are those of the Ethiopian flag and have come to symbolize African unity. In the center is a black star
National anthem: "God bless our homeland, Ghana"

Red Yellow Green

Black

1959 stamp marking Africa Freedom Day

Major languages: English (official), Akan, Moré, Ewe
Currency: Cedi = 100 pesewas

GEOGRAPHY

With an area of 91,985 square miles (238,240 sq. km), Ghana is one of Africa's smaller countries. It is a little smaller in area than Oregon in the United States (US).

The land is generally low-lying. The highest peak is Mount Afadjato, which reaches 2,904 ft (885 m) in the southeast, near the border with Togo. The north lies in the Volta River Basin, which is separated from the rivers that flow south into the Gulf of Guinea in the southwest by the Kwahu Plateau. This plateau forms a divide between the two river systems.

The Black and White Volta rivers, Ghana's main waterways, flow into Lake Volta, which lies behind the Akosombo Dam in the southeast. Lake Volta, 3,275 square miles (8,482 sq. km) in area, covers about 3.5% of Ghana and is one of the world's largest artificial lakes.

Ghana has a hot tropical climate. The southwest has rain throughout the year and rainforests grow there, but the southeast, around Accra, is much drier. The rainfall decreases to the north, which has a marked dry season. Tropical savanna with scattered trees in central Ghana merges into open grasslands in the far north.

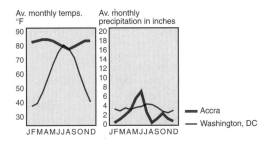

ECONOMY

Chief farm products: Cocoa, coconuts, corn, livestock, lumber, palm oil, peanuts, rice, sorghum, yams
Chief mineral resources: Bauxite (aluminum ore), manganese, gold, diamonds
Chief industrial products: Aluminum, cement, cocoa products, fuels, processed food, textiles
Exports: Cocoa, lumber, gold, manganese, industrial diamonds
Per capital income: $390 (as compared with $29,080 in the US)

Employment:

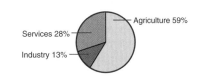

In the US, agriculture employs 3% of the work force, industry 26%, and services 71%

Guinea

PEOPLE

Ethnic groups: Fulani (p 85), **Kissi** (p 118), **Kpelle** (p 121), **Manding, including Malinke** (p 46), **Susu** (p 194), **Tukolor** (p 210)
Population: 6,920,000 (as compared with the US population of 267,636,000)
Religions: Islam (85%), African religions (5%), Christianity (1.5%)

SOCIAL FACTS

- The average life expectancy at birth is 48 years, as compared with 76 years in the US
- Only 29% of the people live in urban areas, as compared with about 76% in the US
- Guinea was once part of the medieval Mali and Songhay empires

- Griots, or storytellers, keep history alive by memorizing and reciting it
- Guinea is the world's second-largest producer of bauxite
- The name "Guinea" once applied to the entire West African coast; it now applies to three African countries: Guinea-Bissau, Equatorial Guinea, and Guinea

KEY POINTS IN RECENT HISTORY

1947 The nationalist political party, the Parti Démocratique de Guinée (PDG), is founded
1952 Sekou Touré becomes leader of the PDG
1958 Guineans vote for independence from France; France withdraws all its investment and stops aid; in a national crisis, Sekou Touré becomes president and introduces socialist policies

1980 An assassination attempt on Sekou Touré fails
1984 Sekou Touré dies and an army coup brings Col. Lansana Conté to power, heading a Military Committee; Conté introduces free-enterprise policies to revive the economy
1993 Conté is reelected president, defeating seven opponents

THE NATION

Location: West Africa, facing the Atlantic Ocean
Neighbors: Guinea-Bissau, Senegal, Mali, Liberia, Sierra Leone
Official name: Republic of Guinea
Divisions: Thirty-three provinces and Conakry
Capital: Conakry
Largest cities: Conakry, Kankan, Labé, Kindia (in order of size)
Flag: The colors of the three vertical stripes – red, yellow, and green – are the same as those on the flag of Ethiopia, Africa's oldest independent nation. They symbolize African unity
National anthem: "People of Africa, the historic past"

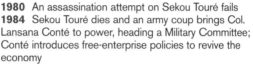

Red | Yellow | Green

1959 stamp marking Guinea's independence and depicting President Sekou Touré

Major languages: French (official), Fulfulde, Manding, Susu, Kissi
Currency: Guinean franc = 100 centimes

GEOGRAPHY

With an area of 94,926 square miles (245,849 sq. km), Guinea is Africa's thirtieth largest country. It is roughly the same size in area as Oregon in the United States (US).

Behind the coastline, which is 190 miles (300 km) long, is a swampy plain. Inland, the Futa Djallon plateau covers central Guinea. This region rises to heights of more than 3,000 ft (900 m) and contains much fine scenery. To the northeast, the land slopes gently down to the high plains of Upper Guinea. The Guinea Highlands in the southeast contain Mount Nimba, the highest peak. Located where Guinea's border meets those of Ivory Coast and Liberia, it reaches a height of 5,748 ft (1,752 m) above sea level.

Three major rivers rise in the Futa Djallon plateau. These are the Gambia, Niger, and Senegal rivers.

The climate is tropical. The rainy season is from May until October, and in the dry season, hot winds blow from the Sahara. Mangrove swamps grow on the coast, and there are rainforests inland, especially in the southeast. Tropical savanna is the main vegetation on the Futa Djallon plateau, with more-open grassland in the drier northeast.

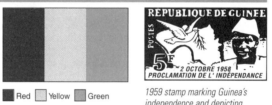

Av. monthly temps. °F / Av. monthly precipitation in inches

—— Conakry
—— Washington, DC

ECONOMY

Chief farm products: Bananas, cassava, coffee, corn, livestock, palm products, peanuts, sugar cane
Chief mineral resources: Bauxite (aluminum ore), diamonds, gold
Chief industrial products: Alumina, beverages, iron, plastics, processed food, textiles, tobacco
Exports: Bauxite, alumina, diamonds, gold, coffee, fish
Per capita income: $550 (as compared with $29,080 in the US)

Employment:

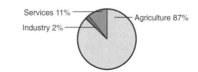

Services 11% | Agriculture 87%
Industry 2%

In the US, agriculture employs 3% of the work force, industry 26%, and services 71%

Guinea-Bissau

PEOPLE

Ethnic groups: Balanta (p 44), **Fulani** (p 85), **Manding, including Malinke** (p 142), **Manjaco** (p 143)
Population: 1,137,000 (as compared with the US population of 267,636,000)
Religions: African religions (54%), Islam (38%), Christianity (8%)

SOCIAL FACTS

- The average life expectancy at birth is 44 years, as compared with 76 years in the US
- Only 22% of the people live in urban areas, as compared with about 76% in the US
- Slaves were taken from Guinea-Bissau to Cape Verde and Brazil

- Guinea-Bissau was formerly called Portuguese Guinea
- Guinean and Cape Verdean people collaborated in opposing Portuguese rule, but a movement to unite the two countries failed in 1977
- The lingua franca Crioulo contains African and Portuguese words

KEY POINTS IN RECENT HISTORY

1951 Portuguese Guinea becomes an overseas province of Portugal
1956 Nationalists form the Partido Africano da Independência do Guiné e Cabo Verde (PAIGC); it demands freedom for Cape Verde and Guinea-Bissau
1963 The war for independence begins
1973 By now, nationalists control 75% of the country
1974 Guinea-Bissau wins independence (September 10) with Luiz Cabral as president

1980 Major João Bernardo Vieira seizes power from Cabral
1984 A new constitution creates a new National People's Assembly and a Council of State
1991 The law making the PAIGC the sole political party is abolished
1994 Vieira wins presidential elections
1996 Guinea joins the Community of Portuguese-speaking Countries

THE NATION

Location: West Africa, facing the Atlantic Ocean
Neighbors: Senegal, Guinea
Official name: Republic of Guinea-Bissau
Divisions: Eight regions
Capital: Bissau
Largest cities: Bissau, Bafata (in order of size)
Flag: The flag uses the three colors from the flag of Ethiopia, Africa's oldest independent country, with a red vertical stripe and two horizontal stripes of yellow (top) and green (bottom)
National anthem: As in Cape Verde – "Sun, sweat, the green, and the sea"

Red Yellow Green
Black

ESTADO DA GUINE-BISSAU

1976 stamp commemorating Amílcar Cabral, a former PAIGC leader

Major languages: Portuguese (official), Crioulo
Currency: CFA franc = 100 centimes

GEOGRAPHY

With an area of 13,945 square miles (36,117 sq. km), Guinea-Bissau is one of Africa's smaller countries. It is about 1.33 times as large as Maryland in the United States (US).

Guinea-Bissau is a low-lying country. The broad coastal plains are swampy and many of the flat islands in the Bijagós Archipelago and elsewhere are also waterlogged. Geologists believe that the coast was submerged in recent geological times, cutting off the islands from the mainland and creating drowned river valleys (called rias) along the coast. The highest land, reaching a height of about 800 ft (240 m). The ridges and hills found here are an extension of an extension of the Futa Djallon plateau in Guinea.

The coast is hot and rainy, but inland it is drier. The dry season is from November until April. Mangrove swamps line parts of the coast and the islands, with rainforests flourishing on the coastal plain. Inland, the forests merge into tropical savanna, with more open grassland on higher ground.

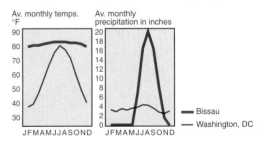

ECONOMY

Chief farm products: Cashews, cassava, corn, lumber, millet, palm products, plantains, rice, sorghum, sugar cane, sweet potatoes
Chief mineral resources: Undeveloped reserves of bauxite (aluminum ore) and phosphate
Chief industrial products: Beverages, clothing, processed food
Exports: Cashews, peanuts, frozen fish
Per capita income: $230 (as compared with $29,080 in the US)

Employment:

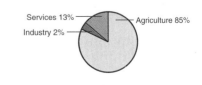

Services 13% Agriculture 85%
Industry 2%

In the US, agriculture employs 3% of the work force, industry 26%, and services 71%

Ivory Coast

PEOPLE

Ethnic groups: Akan (p 26), **Baulé** (p 48), **Dyula** (p 72), **Lobi** (p 126), **Malinke** (p 44), **Kru** (p 122), **Mole-Dagbane** (p 151), **Senufo** (p 184), **Soninke** (p 191), **Mande** (p 142)

Population: 14,211,000 (as compared with the US population of 267,636,000)

Religions: Islam (39%), Christianity (27%), African religions (17%)

SOCIAL FACTS

- The average life expectancy at birth is 47 years, as compared with 76 years in the US
- Only 43% of the people live in urban areas, as compared with about 76% in the US
- More than 60 languages and dialects are spoken in Ivory Coast

- Ivory was a major export from the 1400s until the 1800s
- Abidjan is one of the world's most expensive cities
- The new capital, Yamoussoukro, contains the world's largest church: the Basilica of Our Lady of Peace
- Ivory Coast is also known as Côte d'Ivoire

KEY POINTS IN RECENT HISTORY

1960 Ivory Coast becomes independent from France (August 7) Félix Houphouët-Boigny becomes the first president

1980 An attempted coup fails

1983 Parliament agrees to build a new capital at Yamoussoukro, Houphouët-Boigny's birthplace

1990 Pope John Paul II dedicates Yamoussoukro's huge new basilica

1990 The government introduces a multiparty constitution

1990 The first multiparty elections are held; Houphouët-Boigny is reelected for the seventh time

1993 Houphouët-Boigny dies; his successor is Henri Konan-Bédié

1994 CFA franc is devalued by 50%

1995 Konan-Bédié's party wins a majority in the National Assembly

THE NATION

Location: West Africa, facing the Gulf of Guinea
Neighbors: Liberia, Guinea, Mali, Burkina Faso, Ghana
Official name: République de la Côte d'Ivoire
Divisions: Forty-nine departments
Capital: Yamoussoukro
Largest cities: Abidjan, Man, Bouaké, Yamoussoukro, Daloa (in order of size)
Flag: The vertical orange stripe, left, represents the savanna country in northern Ivory Coast; the white stripe, center, represents peace and unity; and the green stripe, right, represents the forests in the south
National anthem: "L'Abidjanaise ("Hail, o land of hope")

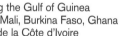

☐ Orange ☐ White ☐ Green

Stamp marking the 1963 Conference of African Heads of State

Major languages: French (official), Akan, Dyula
Currency: CFA franc = 100 cents

GEOGRAPHY

With an area of 124,504 square miles (322,464 sq. km), Ivory Coast is Africa's twenty-seventh largest country. It is a little larger than New Mexico in the United States (US).

The country's coastline, 315 miles (507 km) long, changes in character from east to west. In the east, sand bars hold back lagoons, while the west has a rocky, cliff-lined coast. Abidjan, the chief port, stands on a lagoon in the east. A canal links the lagoon to the sea.

The narrow coastal plain, up to 40 miles (64 km) wide, gives way to plateaus inland. The plateaus rise in the west to the country's highest point, Mount Nimba, which reaches 5,748 ft (1,752 m). The principal rivers are the Bandama, which is 300 miles (480 km) long; the Cavally, which forms part of the border with Liberia; the Komoé; and the Sassandra.

The south is hot throughout the year, with two main rainy seasons – from May until July and in October and

November. The north is much drier, with one rainy season and a marked dry season. A rainforest once covered much of the south, but farmers have cut down large areas of it. Tropical savanna covers most of the north.

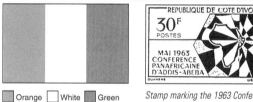

Av. monthly temps. °F

Av. monthly precipitation in inches

— Abidjan
— Washington, DC

ECONOMY

Chief farm products: Cassava, coffee, corn, cotton, livestock, lumber, palm products, rice, sugar cane, yams
Chief mineral resources: Diamonds, oil, gold
Chief industrial products: Beverages, cement, oil products, processed food, textiles, wood products
Exports: Cocoa, oil products, wood and wood products, coffee, cotton
Per capita income: $710 (as compared with $29,080 in the US)

Employment:

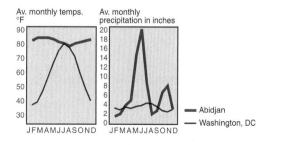

Services 30% — Agriculture 60%

Industry 10%

In the US, agriculture employs 3% of the work force, industry 26%, and services 71%

Kenya

PEOPLE

Ethnic groups: Acholi (p 20), **Gusii** (p 93), **Iteso** (p 107), **Kalenjin, including Kipsigis, Nandi, Pokot, Okiek** (p 109), **Kambe** (p 109), **Kikuyu** (p 115), **Luo** (p 133), **Luyia** (p 133), **Mbeere** (p 144), **Mijikenda** (p 151), **Turkana** (p 210)
Population: 28,612,000 (about a tenth of the US population of 267,636,000)
Religions: Christianity (73%), African religions (19%), Islam (6%)

SOCIAL FACTS

- The average life expectancy at birth is 52 years, as compared with 76 years in the US
- Only 29% of the people live in urban areas, as compared with about 76% in the US
- 75% of Kenyans live in the southwestern highland region

- 51% of Kenyans are under 15 years of age; in the US, only about 22% are under 15 years of age
- Fossils of some of the earliest of human ancestors have been found near Lake Turkana
- Many tourists visit Kenya to see its magnificent wildlife

KEY POINTS IN RECENT HISTORY

1920 Kenya becomes a British colony
1952 Mau Mau rebellion (1952–6) begins and the Kikuyu leader Jomo Kenyatta is convicted of being its leader
1963 Kenya becomes independent (December 12)
1964 Kenya becomes a republic and Kenyatta becomes president
1978 Kenyatta dies and is succeeded by Daniel arap Moi

1982 Kenya becomes a one-party state, ruled by the Kenya African National Union (KANU)
1991 Under pressure from aid donors, the government legalizes opposition parties
1992 Elections are held; Moi reelected; KANU remains the majority party, but accusations of autocratic rule continue

THE NATION

Location: East Africa, facing the Indian Ocean
Neighbors: Ethiopia, Somalia, Tanzania, Uganda, Sudan
Official name: Republic of Kenya
Divisions: Seven provinces and Nairobi district
Capital: Nairobi
Largest cities: Nairobi, Mombasa, Kisumu, Nakuru, Machakos, Meru, Eldoret (in order of size)
Flag: The flag has three stripes of black, red (edged with white), and green. In the center is a Maasai warrior's shield and crossed spears. The shield and spears represent the defense of freedom
National anthem: "Ee Mungu nguvu yetu" ("Oh God of all Creation")

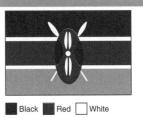

Black ■ Red □ White
Green

Stamp marking Kenyatta Day, 1978

Major languages: Swahili (official), English, Kikuyu, Maa
Currency: Shilling = 100 cents

GEOGRAPHY

With an area of 224,961 square miles (582,647 sq. km), Kenya is Africa's twenty-second largest country. It is about twice as big as Arizona in the United States (US).

Behind the narrow coastal plain, the land rises in a series of plateaus to a highland region in the southwest. The highlands slope down to Lake Victoria, Kenya's largest lake, which Kenya shares with Tanzania and Uganda. Rising above the plateau is Kenya's highest peak, the extinct volcano Mount Kenya, at 17,057 ft (5,199 m) above sea level.

An arm of the steep-sided Great Rift Valley cuts across Kenya from north to south. This huge trough contains several lakes, including Naivasha and Nakuru in the south and Turkana in the north. The Athi and Tana, Kenya's two main rivers, drain into the Indian Ocean.

Kenya lies on the equator and the coast is hot and humid. The generally dry plateaus, covered mainly by tropical savanna, are cooler. The weather is especially pleasant in the rainier southwest highlands, Kenya's most densely populated and chief farming region. Only 15% of Kenya gets a reliable rainfall of 30 in. (76 cm). Some forests grow in the southwestern highlands, but the north is mainly desert.

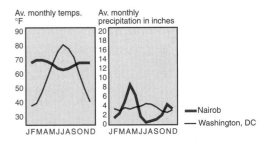

ECONOMY

Chief farm products: Bananas, beef, coffee, corn, pineapples, sisal, sugar cane, tea, wheat
Chief mineral resources: Soda ash, fluorspar
Chief industrial products: Cement, chemicals, petroleum products, processed food, textiles, vehicles
Exports: Tea, coffee, fruits and vegetables, petroleum products
Per capita income: $340 (as compared with $29,080 in the US)

Employment:

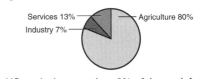

Services 13%
Industry 7%
Agriculture 80%

In the US, agriculture employs 3% of the work force, industry 26%, and services 71%

Lesotho

PEOPLE

Ethnic groups: Sotho (p 191), **Zulu** (p 220)
Population: 2,014,000 (as compared with the US population of 267,636,000)
Religions: Christianity (about 93%), African religions (about 7%)

SOCIAL FACTS

- The average life expectancy at birth is 56 years, as compared with 76 years in the US
- Only 24% of the people live in urban areas, as compared with about 76% in the US
- About 60% of working-age men are employed in South Africa's mines

- Most Sotho people live in villages; the center of the village is the kgotla (meeting place or court)
- Because Lesotho is so mountainous, less than 12% of the land is suitable for farming
- Many houses are painted in bright colors and striking designs

KEY POINTS IN RECENT HISTORY

1966 Basutoland becomes independent from Britain (October 4) as the Kingdom of Lesotho
1979 Opposition parties are banned, their leaders are arrested, and the constitution is suspended
1986 Military leaders overthrow the civilian government
1990 King Moshoeshoe II is removed from office and his

son, Letsie III, is installed as monarch
1993 Civilian rule restored after elections
1995 Moshoeshoe II is restored as King of Lesotho, but is killed in a car crash (1996); Letsie III becomes King
1998 Protests against election results cause conflict and South African troops try to restore order

THE NATION

Location: Landlocked country in Southern Africa
Neighbors: Lesotho is completely surrounded by South Africa
Official name: Kingdom of Lesotho
Divisions: Eleven districts
Capital: Maseru
Largest cities: Maseru, Maputsoe, Teyateyaneng, Mafeteng, Butha-buthe (in order of size)
Flag: The white, blue, and green flag of Lesotho was adopted in 1987. The white area occupying the upper diagonal half of the flag contains a brown emblem that represents a Basotho shield, a spear, and a club.
National anthem: "Lesotho, land of our fathers"

White ▨ Blue ▨ Green
▨ Brown

INDEPENDENCE 1966
MOSHOESHOE I
MOSHOESHOE II
LESOTHO 2½ cents

1966 stamp marking the independence of the Kingdom of Lesotho

Major languages: Sesotho, English (both official), Zulu, Xhosa
Currency: Loti = 100 lisente

GEOGRAPHY

With an area of 11,720 square miles (30,355 sq. km), Lesotho is Africa's twelfth smallest country. It is a little larger in area than Maryland in the United States (US).

Lesotho is a mountainous country, where all the land is above 3,300 ft (1,000 m). The highest point, Thabana Ntlenyana, reaches 11,424 ft (3,482 m) in the northeast. It is the highest point in Southern Africa. The mountains form part of the Drakensberg range, which is made up of the eroded southeast corner of the high plateau that makes up most of Southern Africa.

The Orange River rises in the northeast and flows across southern Lesotho, through South Africa, and into the Atlantic Ocean. The main centers of population are in the lower Orange River Valley and on the western lowlands, where the capital, Maseru, is located.

The climate is greatly influenced by the altitude. The mountains are snow-capped in winter and temperatures

sometimes fall below freezing on the western lowlands. Summers are warm, and the average rainfall is around 28 in. (71 cm) a year. Most of the rain occurs in the summer months, between October and April. Mountain grassland covers most of Lesotho, with trees, such as willow, growing in sheltered areas.

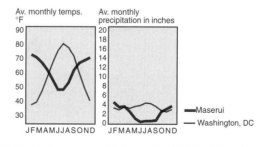

Av. monthly temps. °F

Av. monthly precipitation in inches

JFMAMJJASOND   JFMAMJJASOND

■ Maserui
— Washington, DC

ECONOMY

Chief farm products: Beans, cattle, corn, hides and skins, mohair, sorghum, wool, wheat
Chief mineral resources: Diamonds, sand and gravel
Chief industrial products: Beverages, chemicals, clothing, leather goods, processed food, textiles,
Exports: Manufactured goods, food and live animals, raw materials
Per capita income: $680 (as compared with $29,080 in the US)

Employment:

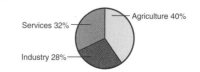

Agriculture 40%
Services 32%
Industry 28%

In the US, agriculture employs 3% of the work force, industry 26%, and services 71%

Liberia

Ethnic groups: Americo-Liberians (p 28), **Bassa** (p 48), **Dan** (p 65), **Grebo** (p 92), **Kpelle** (p 121), **Kru** (p 122), **Ma** (p 134)
Population: 2,886,000 (as compared with the US population of 267,636,000)
Religions: Christianity (68%), Islam (14%), African religions (18%)

- The average life expectancy at birth is 47 years, as compared with 76 years in the US
- Only 44% of the people live in urban areas, as compared with about 76% in the US
- Liberia's name comes from the Latin word "liber," meaning "free"

- Monrovia was founded in 1822 by the American Colonization Society
- Descendants of the original freed slaves who settled in Monrovia are called Americo-Liberians
- Americo-Liberians dominated the government until 1980, when people from local ethnic groups seized power

1926 The American Firestone Company sets up huge rubber plantations in Liberia
1944 William Tubman, an Americo-Liberian, becomes president
1971 William Tolbert becomes president when Tubman dies
1979 People demonstrate against price rises
1980 President Tolbert is assassinated; an army sergeant, Samuel Doe, becomes president
1989 Civil war breaks out between various ethnic groups
1990 Doe is assassinated; rival leaders declare themselves president
1995 A cease-fire holds after the heads of warring factions join in a transitional government
1996 Fighting recurs in Monrovia

Location: West Africa, facing the Atlantic Ocean
Neighbors: Sierra Leone, Guinea, Ivory Coast
Official name: Republic of Liberia
Divisions: Thirteen counties
Capital: Monrovia
Largest cities: Monrovia, Buchanan, Yekepa, Tubmanburg (in order of size)
Flag: The flag was inspired by the US Stars and Stripes. The eleven red and white stripes represent the eleven men who signed Liberia's Declaration of Independence in 1847. The white star is set on a blue field
National anthem: "All hail, Liberia, hail"

■ Red □ White ■ Blue

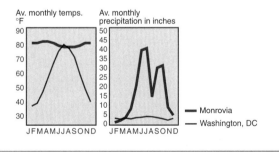

1952 stamp honoring the United Nations (UN)

Major languages: English (official), Mende, Kwa
Currency: Liberian dollar = 100 cents

With an area of 42,990 square miles (111,344 sq. km), Liberia is one of Africa's smaller countries. It is a little larger in area than Ohio in the United States (US).

Behind the coastline, which is 350 miles (560 km) long, lies a coastal plain between 15 and 25 miles (24–40 km) wide. Inland, the ground rises to low hills and plateaus. The highest point is Mount Nimba, which reaches a height of 5,748 ft (1,752 m) on Liberia's border with Ivory Coast and Guinea.

The chief rivers are the Cavally, which forms part of the border with Ivory Coast, and the Mano and Morro rivers that form the border with Sierra Leone. The St. Paul River reaches the sea near Monrovia. A hydroelectric power station at rapids on the St. Paul River is a major source of electricity for Liberia.

Liberia has a tropical climate, with high temperatures and the heavy rainfall. The coast has a relatively dry season from December until March. The rainfall diminishes inland, where the dry season is longer. Rainforests cover about 40% of the land and there is tropical savanna in the drier interior. The average annual rainfall on the coast is around 200 in. (510 cm), but inland it is lower at 85 in. (220 cm).

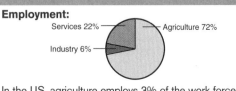

Av. monthly temps. °F — Av. monthly precipitation in inches

JFMAMJJASOND   JFMAMJJASOND

—— Monrovia
—— Washington, DC

Chief farm products: Bananas, cassava, cocoa, coffee, fruits, livestock, palm products, rice, rubber, sugar cane, sweet potatoes
Chief mineral resources: Iron ore, diamonds, gold
Chief industrial products: Beverages, cement, palm oil
Exports: Iron ore, rubber, wood, diamonds, gold, coffee
Per capita income: $390 (as compared with $29,080 in the US)

Employment:

Services 22% — Agriculture 72%
Industry 6%

In the US, agriculture employs 3% of the work force, industry 26%, and services 71%

Libya

PEOPLE

Ethnic groups: Arab (p 32)**, including Bedouin** (p 50)**, Berber** (p 53)
Population: 5,201,000 (as compared with the US population of 267,636,000)
Religions: Islam (97% of Libyans are Sunni Muslims)

SOCIAL FACTS

- The average life expectancy at birth is 70 years, as compared with 76 years in the US
- About 85% of the people live in urban areas, as compared with about 76% in the US
- The first people to settle in Libya were the Berbers
- The Arabic language was introduced into Libya in the 600s
- Tripoli was once a base for Barbary pirates, or corsairs; the US fought a war against the corsairs in the early 1800s
- Libya is known for its active support of radical movements around the world

KEY POINTS IN RECENT HISTORY

1911 Italy conquers northern Libya
1942 Britain and France take over Libya during World War II
1951 Libya becomes an independent kingdom (December 24), formed from three provinces – Cyrenaica, Fezzan, and Tripolitania
1969 Army officers declare Libya to be a republic; Col. Muammar al Qaddafi becomes head of the government

1977 Libya becomes a one-party socialist jamahiriya, or "state of the masses" – every adult is supposed to have a share in policy-making
1986 The United States bombs Libya as a reprisal for alleged Libyan involvement in terrorist activities
1994 The International Court of Justice rejects Libya's claims to the Aozou Strip in Chad; Libya becomes increasingly isolated internationally

THE NATION

Location: North Africa, facing the Mediterranean Sea
Neighbors: Egypt, Chad, Niger, Algeria, Tunisia
Official name: Great Socialist People's Libyan Arab Jamahiriya
Divisions: About 1,500 communes
Capital: Tripoli
Largest cities: Tripoli, Benghazi, Misratah, Zawiyah (in order of size)
Flag: Libya's plain green flag, the world's simplest, symbolizes Islam and the country's commitment to creating a green revolution (based on irrigation) in agriculture. The flag was officially adopted in 1977
National anthem: "Allahu Akbar" ("God is great")

Green

1978 Stamp marking International Antiapartheid Year

Major languages: Arabic (official), Berber
Currency: Dinar = 100 dirhams

GEOGRAPHY

With an area of 679,180 square miles (1,759,069 sq. km), Libya is Africa's fourth largest country. It is two and a half times as large in area as Texas in the United States (US).

Desert landscapes dominate all of Libya apart from the narrow coastal regions in the northeast and northwest. The Sahara covers most of Libya and it contains huge areas of sand dunes and bare rocky mountains, which rise to Bette Peak in the south, near the Chad border. Bette Peak is Libya's highest point at 7,500 ft (2,286 m) above sea level.

Under the barren desert are huge aquifers – layers of rock saturated with water. Water from the aquifers appears at the surface at oases, and engineers have tapped many aquifers and piped water to the north. This scheme is called the "Great Man-made River Project."

The northeast and northwest coast, where nearly all Libyans live, have hot, dry summers and mild, moist winters – the typical climate of Mediterranean lands. But most of

Libya is hot desert, with an average yearly rainfall of 4 in. (10 cm) or less. Temperatures are high and Al-Aziziyah southeast of Tripoli holds the world record for the highest shade temperature, 58°C (136°F). Scrub and woodland grow in the coastal regions, while date palms flourish around oases in the desert.

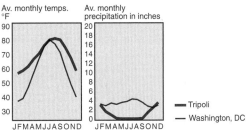

ECONOMY

Chief farm products: Barley, citrus fruits, dates, livestock (sheep, goats, camels, cattle), olives, onions, potatoes, tomatoes, watermelons, wheat
Chief mineral resources: Oil and natural gas
Chief industrial products: Cement, oil products, steel
Exports: Oil and oil products
Per capita income: $6,510 (as compared with $29,080 in the US)

Employment:

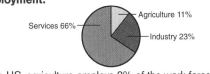

In the US, agriculture employs 3% of the work force, industry 26%, and services 71%

Madagascar

Ethnic groups: Madagascan Peoples (p 138)**, including Merina and Betsimisaraka**
Population: 14,148,000 (as compared with the US population of 267,636,000)
Religions: Christianity (51%), African religions (47%), Islam (2%)

SOCIAL FACTS

- The average life expectancy at birth is 57 years, as compared with 76 years in the US.
- Only 26% of the people live in urban areas, as compared with about 76% in the US
- Madagascar is the world's fourth largest island
- Madagascans are of mixed African and Southeast

Asian descent
- The official language, Malagasy, resembles Malay and Indonesian, with Arabic, Bantu, and European words
- Deforestation has caused widespread soil erosion
- Cyclones (tropical storms) frequently hit Madagascar

KEY POINTS IN RECENT HISTORY

1960 Madagascar becomes independent from France (June 26) as the Malagasy Republic; Philibert Tsiranana becomes president
1972 Army officers seize power; Gabriel Ramanantsoa becomes president
1975 The country's name is changed from Malagasy Republic to the Republic of Madagascar; Didier Ratsiraka

becomes leader of the country's ruling Supreme Revolutionary Council
1991 After much unrest, an interim government is formed to introduce a new multiparty constitution
1993 Professor Albert Zafy defeats Ratsiraka in presidential elections
1997 Ratsiraka becomes president after elections in 1996

THE NATION

Location: Island country off the southeast coast of Southern Africa
Nearest mainland: Mozambique
Official name: Democratic Republic of Madagascar
Divisions: Six provinces
Capital: Antananarivo
Largest cities: Antananarivo, Toamasina, Antsirabe, Mahajanga, Fianarantsoa (in order of size)
Flag: The white of the vertical stripe, and the red and green of the horizontal stripes, are colors used on historic flags of Southeast Asia, reflecting the country's ancient ties with that region
National anthem: "Ry tanindrazanay malalaô" ("O our beloved fatherland")

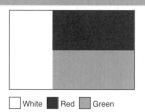

White ■ Red ■ Green

1962 stamp marking the UNESCO Conference on Higher Education in Africa

Major languages: Malagasy (official), French
Currency: Malagasy franc = 100 centimes

GEOGRAPHY

With an area of 226,658 square miles (587,042 sq. km), Madagascar is Africa's twentieth largest country. It is about 1.4 times larger than California in the United States (US).
  Madagascar consists of one large island and many tiny ones dotted around it. The length of the coastline of the main island is about 2,600 miles (4,180 km). The east coast is narrow and the land rises steeply to the central highlands. The highest point, Maromokotro, reaches 9,436 ft (2,876 m) above sea level in the north. Western Madagascar consists of low plateaus and broad plains. Many rivers flow across this region into the Mozambique Channel which separates Madagascar from mainland Africa. The lowlands are hot and wet, except in the arid southwest. The altitude moderates temperatures in the highlands. Grassland and scrub occurs

in the south. Rainforest once covered much of central Madagascar, but deforestation has meant that tropical savanna and open grassland now cover large areas.

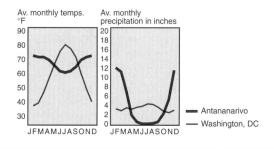

Av. monthly temps. °F

Av. monthly precipitation in inches

— Antananarivo
— Washington, DC

ECONOMY

Chief farm products: Bananas, cassava, cloves, coffee, corn, cotton, fruits, livestock, rice, sweet potatoes, taro (an edible tuber), vanilla
Chief mineral resources: Chromite (chromium ore), salt, mica
Chief industrial products: Beverages, cement, palm oil, processed food
Exports: Vanilla, shrimp, coffee, cloves and clove oil, cotton fabrics
Per capita income: $250 (as compared with $29,080 in the US)

Employment:

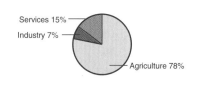

Services 15%
Industry 7%
Agriculture 78%

In the US, agriculture employs 3% of the work force, industry 26%, and services 71%

Malawi

PEOPLE

Ethnic groups: Maravi (p 143), **Ngonde** (p 162), **Tonga** (p 203), **Yao** (p 217)
Population: 10,276,000 (as compared with the US population of 267,636,000)
Religions: Christianity (64%), African religions (19%), Islam (16%)

SOCIAL FACTS

- The average life expectancy at birth is 43 years, as compared with 76 years in the US
- Only 13% of the people live in urban areas, as compared with about 76% in the US
- Malawi has one of Africa's highest rates of HIV infection
- Malawi is heavily dependent on foreign aid; most aid was suspended in the early 1990s because of the country's poor human rights record
- Malawi was a center of the slave trade in the early 1800s
- Tourism is an expanding industry in Malawi

KEY POINTS IN RECENT HISTORY

1953 Britain makes Nyasaland part of the Central African Federation (CAF) despite African protests against white-minority domination
1963 CAF is dissolved and Nyasaland prepares for independence
1964 Nyasaland becomes independent as Malawi (July 6)
1966 Malawi becomes a republic; the prime minister, Dr

Hastings Kamuzu Banda, becomes the first president
1971 Banda becomes president-for-life and Malawi adopts a one-party system
1993 A multiparty system is restored
1994 Bakili Muluzi defeats Banda in presidential elections
1997 Despite criticisms of his conduct, Banda is given a state funeral following his death in November

THE NATION

Location: Landlocked country in East Africa
Neighbors: Tanzania, Mozambique, Zambia
Official name: Republic of Malawi
Divisions: Three regions and twenty-four districts
Capital: Lilongwe
Largest cities: Blantyre, Lilongwe, Mzuzu, Zomba (in order of size)
Flag: A rising Sun on the top black stripe, added in 1964 when Malawi became independent, represents the beginning of a new era for the country. The other stripes are red, center, and green, bottom
National anthem: "O God bless our land of Malawi"

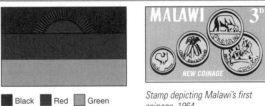

■ Black ■ Red □ Green

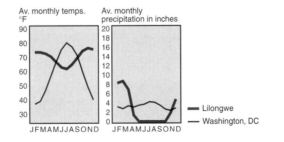

Stamp depicting Malawi's first coinage, 1964

Major languages: Chichewa and English (both official)
Currency: Kwacha = 100 tambala

GEOGRAPHY

With an area of 45,747 square miles (118,484 sq. km), Malawi is one of Africa's smaller countries. It is a little larger in area than Tennessee in the United States (US).

Malawi includes part of Lake Malawi, which is called Nyasa in neighboring Tanzania and Niassa in Mozambique. This lake, one of the world's deepest at more than 2,300 ft (700 m), occupies part of the floor of the Great Rift Valley and covers a total area of about 11,000 square miles (28,500 sq. km). Malawi's chief river, the Shire, flows south from the southern end of Lake Malawi to the Zambezi River.

West of the deep Great Rift Valley, the land rises to plateaus at about 2,500 to 4,000 ft (760–1,200 m) above sea level. The land rises to more than 8,000 ft (2,400 m) in the north, but the country's highest peak, Mulanje, which reaches 9,843 ft (3,000 m), is in the southeast, on a plateau not far from the Mozambique border.

The Great Rift Valley is hot and humid, but the highlands

have a pleasant, much cooler climate. The average annual rainfall ranges from around 70 in. (178 cm) in the highlands to 30 in. (76 cm) in the lowlands. Open grassland and tropical savanna cover most of Malawi, with woodland in river valleys and other wet areas.

ECONOMY

Chief farm products: Bananas, cassava, corn, cotton, livestock, peanuts, potatoes, sorghum, sugar cane, tea, tobacco
Chief mineral resources: Limestone and marble
Chief industrial products: Beverages, cement, chemicals, processed food, textiles, tobacco
Exports: Tobacco, tea, sugar, cotton
Per capita income: $210 (as compared with $29,080 in the US)

Employment:

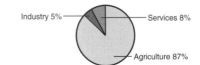

In the US, agriculture employs 3% of the work force, industry 26%, and services 71%

© DIAGRAM

Mali

Ethnic groups: Bambara (p 44), **Dogon** (p 69), **Dyula** (p 72), **Fulani** (p 85), **Manding, including Malinke** (p 144), **Senufo** (p 184), **Songhay** (p 191), **Soninke** (p 191)
Population: 10,290,000 (as compared with the US population of 267,636,000)
Religions: Islam (90%), African religions (9%), Christianity (1%)

SOCIAL FACTS

• The average life expectancy at birth is 50 years, as compared with 76 years in the US
• Only 27% of the people live in urban areas, as compared with about 76% in the US
• Only about 2% of the land in Mali is cultivated
• Mali was part of three major medieval African civilizations:
the Empire of Ghana, Empire of Mali, and Songhay
• Timbuktu (modern Tombouctou) was a great Islamic center of learning in the 1300s
• Prolonged and severe droughts in the Sahel in the 1970s and 1980s caused great suffering

KEY POINTS IN RECENT HISTORY

1959 The French colony of Soudan unites with Senegal to form the Federation of Mali
1960 The Federation breaks up and Soudan becomes the independent Republic of Mali (June 20)
1968 A military coup sweeps Modibo Keita, Mali's first president, from power; he is succeeded by Lt. Moussa Traoré
1974 Mali becomes a one-party state

1991 A coup brings Lt.-Col. Amadou Toumani Touré to power
1992 Multiparty elections are held and Alpha Oumar Konaré becomes president
1993 A coup to restore Traoré to power is unsuccessful
1994 CFA franc, which is linked to the French franc, is devalued by 50%.
1996 Konaré is reelected president

THE NATION

Location: Landlocked country in West Africa
Neighbors: Algeria, Niger, Burkina Faso, Ivory Coast, Guinea, Senegal, Mauritania
Official name: Republic of Mali
Divisions: Eight regions
Capital: Bamako
Largest cities: Bamako, Ségou, Mopti, Sikasso, Gao (in order of size)
Flag: The colors of the three vertical stripes – green, yellow, and red – are those of the flag of Ethiopia, Africa's oldest independent nation. As on several other African flags, the colors symbolize African unity
National anthem: "A ton appel, Mali" ("At your call, Mali")

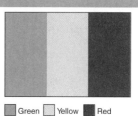

Green   Yellow   Red

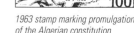

1963 stamp marking promulgation of the Algerian constitution

Major languages: French (official), Manding, Fulfulde, Songhay
Currency: CFA franc = 100 cents

GEOGRAPHY

With an area of 478,821 square miles (1,240,142 sq. km), Mali is Africa's eighth largest country. It is 1.8 times larger in area than Texas in the United States (US).

Mali is a largely flat country. The main highland region is the Adrar des Ifôghas in the northeast, but the highest point is Hombori Tondo, which reaches 3,798 ft (1,158 m) and is in the south, near the Burkina Faso border.

The chief river, the Niger, makes a large loop called the Niger Bend, through south-central Mali. In the Niger Bend, the river divides into several channels. The south, with its rivers, contrasts with the desert landscapes in the north.

Mali has a tropical climate. The south has an average annual rainfall of 40 in. (102 cm) or more, with the rainy season from May until October, but the north has 4 in.

(10 cm) or less. The north lacks plants except around oases. Central Mali belongs to a semidesert zone called the Sahel, and tropical savanna occurs in the south.

Av. monthly temps. °F

Av. monthly precipitation in inches

━━ Bamako
── Washington, DC

JFMAMJJASOND   JFMAMJJASOND

ECONOMY

Chief farm products: Cassava, corn, cotton, livestock, millet, peanuts, rice, sorghum, sugar cane, sweet potatoes, yams
Chief mineral resources: Limestone, phosphates, gold, diamonds
Chief industrial products: Beverages, cement, processed food, textiles
Exports: Cotton and cotton products, live animals, gold, diamonds
Per capita income: $260 (as compared with $29,080 in the US)

Employment:

Industry 2%   Services 12%

Agriculture 86%

In the US, agriculture employs 3% of the work force, industry 26%, and services 71%

Mauritania

PEOPLE

Ethnic groups: Black African, Moors (p 154)
Population: 2,461,000 (as compared with the US population of 267,636,000)
Religions: Islam (99.4%), Christianity (0.4%)

SOCIAL FACTS

- The average life expectancy at birth is 53 years, as compared with 76 years in the US
- Only 51% of the people live in urban areas, as compared with about 76% in the US
- Mauritania is a very sparsely populated country
- Mauritanian Moors include White Moors or Bidanis (who

are of Arab-Berber origin) and Black Moors or Sudanis (of Black African origin)
- Historically, White Moors were divided into two castes: warriors and marabouts (scholars or priests)
- Droughts in the 1970s and 1980s caused great hardship

KEY POINTS IN RECENT HISTORY

1903 France makes Mauritania a protectorate (colony)
1960 Mauritania becomes independent (November 28) with Moktar Ould Daddah as president
1965 Mauritania is a one-party state
1976 Mauritania occupies the southern third of Western (formerly Spanish) Sahara and Morocco takes the north; Western Saharan guerrillas launch a war for independence

1978 Military leaders overthrow President Ould Daddah
1979 Mauritania gives up its claims to Western Sahara; Morocco takes the entire territory
1991 Mauritania adopts a multiparty constitution
1992 The people elect Maaouiya Ould Sidi Ahmed Taya as elected president
1997 Taya is reelected president

THE NATION

Location: West Africa, facing the Atlantic Ocean
Neighbors: Western Sahara, Algeria, Mali, Senegal
Official name: Islamic Republic of Mauritania
Divisions: Twelve regions and thecapital district
Capital: Nouakchott
Largest cities: Nouakchott, Nouadhibou, Kaédi, Kiffa (in order of size)
Flag: The green color of the flag and the yellow star and crescent are symbols of Islam, the country's official religion. The flag was officially adopted in 1959, one year before the country became independent
National anthem: "Mauritania"

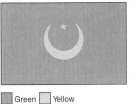

Green | Yellow

1976 stamp celebrating the reunification of Mauritania with southern Western Sahara

Major languages: Arabic (official), Soninke, Wolof
Currency: Ouguiya = 5 khoums

GEOGRAPHY

With an area of 395,955 square miles (1,025,519 sq. km), Mauritania is Africa's eleventh largest country. It is about 1.5 times larger in area than Texas in the United States (US).

Mauritania is a mainly low-lying country, with flat coastal plains and rocky plateaus at about 600 to 900 ft (200–300 m) above sea level. A few isolated peaks rise above the plateaus. These include Mauritania's highest point, Kediet Ijill, which is a huge mass of hematite (an iron ore) and reaches 3,002 ft (915 m).

Northern Mauritania is part of the Sahara and is thinly populated. Its features include drifting sand dunes, bare rocky areas, and wadis (dry watercourses). The chief river is the Senegal, which forms the southeast border with Senegal. Most Mauritanians live in the south of the country.

Mauritania has a hot, dry climate, though temperatures often fall from about 100 °F (38 °C) in the afternoon to

45 °F (7 °C) at night. The north is almost rainless, but the south has 12 to 15 in. (30–38 cm) of rain a year. The desert in the north merges into the semidesert Sahel, where droughts are common. Tropical savanna occurs in the far south of the country.

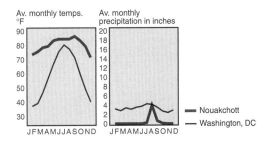

ECONOMY

Chief farm products: Beans, corn, dates, gum arabic, livestock (cattle, sheep, goats), millet, peanuts, pulses, rice, sorghum, sweet potatoes
Chief mineral resources: Iron ore, gypsum (calcium sulfate)
Chief industrial products: Dairy products, meat, hides and skins
Exports: Iron ore, fish (both ocean and freshwater)
Per capita income: $440 (as compared with $29,080 in the US)

Employment:

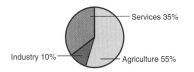

In the US, agriculture employs 3% of the work force, industry 26%, and services 71%

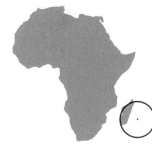

Mauritius

Ethnic groups: Chinese, Creoles (p 64), Ilois of Diego Garcia (p 104), Indo-Pakistanis
Population: 1,148,000 (as compared with the US population of 267,636,000)
Religions: Hinduism (50%), Christianity (32%), Islam (16%)

SOCIAL FACTS

- The average life expectancy at birth is 71 years, as compared with 76 years in the US
- Only 41% of the people live in urban areas, as compared with about 76% in the US
- Mauritius was colonized first by France and then by Britain
- Mauritius claims the island of Diego Garcia in the British Indian Ocean Territory
- The population increased quickly after the eradication of malaria
- Mauritius is a tax haven: from 1992 through 1995, the number of offshore (mainly Indian) registered companies rose from ten to more than 2,500

KEY POINTS IN RECENT HISTORY

1968 Mauritius becomes independent from Britain as a constitutional monarchy (March 12), with Queen Elizabeth II as head of state; Sir Seewoosagur Ramgoolam heads the government as prime minister
1982 Elections are won by the Mouvement Militant Mauricien (MMM) and Aneerood Jugnauth becomes the prime minister

1983 Jugnauth founds a new party, the Mouvement Socialiste Mauricien (MSM), which wins the elections
1992 Mauritius becomes a republic on March 12; Cassam Uteem becomes the first president, while Jugnauth continues as prime minister
1995 Dr Navinchandra Ramgoolam replaces Jugnauth as prime minister

THE NATION

Location: Island country in the Indian Ocean, to the east of Southern Africa
Nearest country: Madagascar
Official name: Republic of Mauritius
Divisions: The islands of Mauritius, Rodrigues, and some smaller islands
Capital: Port Louis
Largest cities: Port Louis, Beau Bassin-Rose Hill (in order of size)
Flag: The four horizontal bands, from top to bottom, are red, for the struggle for independence; blue, for the ocean; yellow, for sunlight and the bright future; and green, for agriculture and the country's lush vegetation
National anthem: "Glory to thee, motherland"

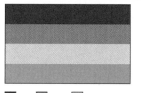

Red | Blue | Yellow
Green

1971 stamp commemorating the twenty-fifth anniversary of Plaisance Airport

Major languages: English (official), Creole, French
Currency: Mauritian rupee = 100 cents

GEOGRAPHY

With an area of 788 square miles (2,041 sq. km), Mauritius is Africa's third smallest country. It is about two-thirds the size of Rhode Island in the United States (US).

Mauritius consists of one large island, Mauritius, which covers 720 square miles (1,865 sq. km). Rodrigues, with an area of 40 square miles (104 sq. km), lies about 340 miles (550 km) to the east. The two small islands of Agalega lie 580 miles (930 km) to the north, and the Cargados Carajos Shoals are about 250 miles (400 km) to the north. Mauritius, a volcanic island, rises to a central plateau ringed by some higher areas. The highest point, the Piton de la Petite Rivière-Noire, reaches 2,711 ft (826 m). Major rivers include the Grand River South East and the Grand River North West. The climate is tropical, though the altitude moderates temperatures. December to April is

the hottest period. The rainfall ranges from about 200 in. (508 cm) a year in the north to about 35 in. (89 cm) in the southwest. Mauritius is densely populated and most of its forest has been cleared to make way for farms.

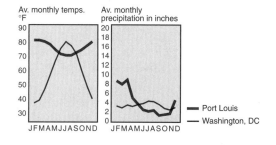

Av. monthly temps. °F
Av. monthly precipitation in inches

Port Louis
Washington, DC

ECONOMY

Chief farm products: Bananas, corn, livestock, peanuts, pineapples potatoes, sugar cane, tea, tobacco, vegetables
Chief mineral resources: Sand, salt
Chief industrial products: Beverages, sugar and molasses, tea
Exports: Clothing and textiles, sugar, yarns, diamonds and synthetic gemstones
Per capita income: $3,870 (as compared with $29,080 in the US)

Employment:

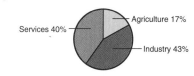

Services 40%
Agriculture 17%
Industry 43%

In the US, agriculture employs 3% of the work force, industry 26%, and services 71%

Morocco

PEOPLE

Ethnic groups: Arab (p 32)**, including Bedouin** (p 50)**, Berber** (p 53)
Population: 27,310,000 (about a tenth of the US population of 267,636,000)
Religions: Islam (98.7%), Christianity (1.1%)

SOCIAL FACTS

- The average life expectancy at birth is 67 years, as compared with 76 years in the US
- Only 52% of the people live in urban areas, as compared with about 76% in the US
- The Berbers live mainly in the mountain areas
- Morocco claims authority over Western (formerly Spanish) Sahara, a region to its south some 102,703 square miles (266,000 sq. km) in area, but its claim is disputed
- Morocco produces excellent leather goods, metalware, pottery, and rugs
- The University of Kairaouin, Fez, was founded in 859 and is the world's oldest

KEY POINTS IN RECENT HISTORY

1956 Morocco, divided into French and Spanish territories in 1912, gains its independence
1957 The Sultan takes the title of King Muhammad V
1961 Hassan II succeeds Muhammad V
1976 Spain withdraws from Western Sahara, which is partitioned between Morocco and Mauritania
1979 Mauritania withdraws from Western Sahara; Morocco annexes the entire territory
1982 The Sahrawi Arab Democratic Republic, proclaimed by Western Saharan opponents of Moroccan rule, joins the Organization of African Unity
1999 A UN referendum on the future of Western Sahara is scheduled for July 2000. Sidi Mohamed succeeds Hassan II

THE NATION

Location: North Africa, facing the Mediterranean Sea and Atlantic Ocean
Neighbors: Algeria, Western Sahara
Official name: Kingdom of Morocco
Divisions: Thirty-six provinces and eight prefectures
Capital: Rabat
Largest cities: Casablanca, Rabat, Fez, Marrakech, Meknès, Kenitra (in order of size)
Flag: The flag of Morocco is a plain red color and features a green, five-pointed star at its center. This star is also a part of the country's coat of arms, which depicts the Atlas Mountains, the Sun, a crown, and two lions
National anthem: "Fountain of freedom, source of light"

■ Green ■ Red

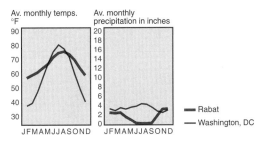

1960 stamp marking the inauguration of the Arab League Center

Major languages: Arabic (official), Berber, French, Spanish
Currency: Dirham = 100 centimes

GEOGRAPHY

With an area of 175,115 square miles (453,546 sq. km), Morocco is Africa's twenty-fourth largest country. It is about the same size as Washington state in the United States (US).

Most Moroccans live on the fertile coastal plains in the north and west. Mountain ranges occupy much of the interior, and the High Atlas Mountains, which run across the country from southwest to northeast, contain Morocco's highest peak, Djebel Toubkal, at 13,665 ft (4,165 m). Other ranges include the Anti Atlas range in the south, the Middle Atlas in the center, and the Rif Atlas in the north.

Most of Morocco's rivers flow from the mountains to the Atlantic Ocean or vanish in the Sahara, a region of sand, bare rock, and stony plains in the south. The Moulouya is the main river flowing into the Mediterranean.

The coastal lowlands have hot, dry summers and mild, moist winters. Uncultivated areas have typical Mediterranean scrub vegetation. The cooler, wetter mountain regions contain forests of cedar, fir, and juniper, with grasslands at higher levels. In the hot, dry Sahara, date palms grow around the scattered oases.

Av. monthly temps.
°F

Av. monthly precipitation in inches

— Rabat
— Washington, DC

J F M A M J J A S O N D   J F M A M J J A S O N D

ECONOMY

Chief farm products: Barley, citrus fruits, corn, dairy products, meat, vegetables, wheat
Chief mineral resources: Phosphates, copper, lead, zinc
Chief industrial products: Cement, chemicals, metal products, olive oil, sugar, textiles, vehicles, wine
Exports: Phosphate rock and phosphates, food products, textiles
Per capita income: $1,260 (as compared with $29,080 in the US)

Employment:

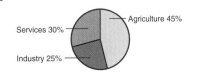

Agriculture 45%
Services 30%
Industry 25%

In the US, agriculture employs 3% of the work force, industry 26%, and services 71%

© DIAGRAM

Mozambique

PEOPLE

Ethnic groups: Makua-Lomwe (p 141), **Ngoni** (p 162), **Shona** (p 186), **Tsonga** (p 205), **Yao** (p 217)
Population: 16,630,000 (as compared with the US population of 267,636,000)
Religions: African religions (48%), Christianity (39%), Islam (13%

SOCIAL FACTS

- The average life expectancy at birth is 45 years, as compared with 76 years in the US
- Only 34% of the people live in urban areas, as compared with about 76% in the US
- Mozambique was once a major slave-trading area
- Mozambique is the world's poorest country in terms of per capita GNP
- Most Portuguese left Mozambique after independence in 1975
- Mozambique's railroads link neighboring landlocked countries, such as Zimbabwe, with its seaports and are a major source of revenue

KEY POINTS IN RECENT HISTORY

1961 The Frente de Libertação de Moçambique (Frelimo) is formed
1964 Frelimo launches a guerrilla war against Portuguese colonial rule
1974 A coup occurs in Portugal; the new leaders negotiate with Frelimo
1975 Mozambique becomes an independent one-party state (June 25)
1980s A guerrilla force, the Resistência Nacional Moçambicana Movement (Renamo), fights government forces
1990 Opposition parties are allowed
1992 A cease-fire is signed
1994 Multiparty elections are won by Frelimo; Renamo states that it will cooperate with the government
1995 Mozambique joins the Commonwealth of Nations
1996 Mozambique joins the Community of Portuguese-speaking Countries

THE NATION

Location: Southern Africa, facing the Indian Ocean
Neighbors: South Africa, Swaziland, Zimbabwe, Zambia, Malawi, Tanzania
Official name: Republic of Mozambique
Divisions: Ten provinces and Maputo
Capital: Maputo
Largest cities: Maputo, Beira, Nampula, Nacala (in order of size)
Flag: The flag's green stripe symbolizes fertile land, the black stripe (edged with white) represents Africa, the yellow stripe stands for minerals. The red triangle contains a star with a rifle, a hoe, and a book
National anthem: "Viva, viva a Frelimo" ("Long live Frelimo")

| ■ Green | ■ Black | □ White |
| ■ Yellow | ■ Red | |

1980 stamp marking the independence of neighboring Zimbabwe

Major languages: Portuguese (official), Makua, Shona, Tsonga
Currency: Metical = 100 centavos

GEOGRAPHY

With an area of 309,496 square miles (801,592 sq. km), Mozambique is Africa's sixteenth largest country. It is nearly twice as big in area as California in the United States (US).

The coastline is bordered by coral reefs, with swamps and sand dunes along the shore. Plains cover nearly half of Mozambique, with hill country and plateaus inland. The highest peak, Mount Binga, reaches 7,992 ft (2,436 m) near the Zimbabwe border. The chief river is the Zambezi. The Cahora Bassa Dam on the Zambezi has a hydroelectric power station that exports electricity to South Africa.

The climate is tropical. Summers (November-March) are wet and hot, while winters are milder and drier. The average annual rainfall varies from 20 to 50 in. (51-127 cm). Tropical savanna covers large areas.

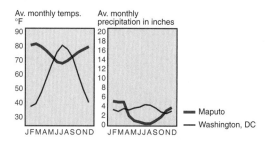

ECONOMY

Chief farm products: Bananas, cashew nuts, cassava, corn, cotton, livestock, palm products, peanuts, rice, sorghum, sugar cane
Chief mineral resources: Bauxite (aluminum ore), coal, salt
Chief industrial products: Beverages, cement, processed food, textiles
Exports: Shrimp, cashew nuts, cotton, sugar, lobster
Per capita income: $140 (as compared with $29,080 in the US)

Employment:

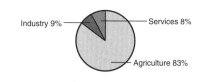

Industry 9% — Services 8% — Agriculture 83%

In the US, agriculture employs 3% of the work force, industry 26%, and services 71%

Namibia

PEOPLE

Ethnic groups: Herero (p 96), **Kung** (p 124), **Nama** (p 158), **Ovambo** (p 175), **whites**
Population: 1,623,000 (as compared with the US population of 267,636,000)
Religions: Christianity (90%), including Lutheran (51.2%)

SOCIAL FACTS

- The average life expectancy at birth is 56 years, as compared with 76 years in the US
- Only 36% of the people live in urban areas, as compared with about 76% in the US
- The whites in Namibia are of Dutch, English, and German descent

- The earliest inhabitants of Namibia were the Khoisan
- Namibia is sparsely populated, because it is one of the world's driest countries
- Northern Namibia's Skeleton Coast was the scene of many shipwrecks

KEY POINTS IN RECENT HISTORY

1915 South Africa takes South West Africa (Namibia) from Germany
1920 The League of (later, United) Nations gives South Africa a mandate to govern South West Africa
1945 South Africa refuses a United Nations (UN) request that South West Africa be placed under UN trusteeship
1948–89 Form of apartheid in practice

1966 Guerrilla warfare begins
1969 The UN declares South African rule in South West Africa to be illegal
1990 Namibia independent (March 21); Sam Nujoma becomes president
1994 Walvis Bay, a South African enclave (external territory) on the Namibian coast, is returned to Namibia

THE NATION

Location: Southern Africa, facing the Atlantic Ocean
Neighbors: Angola, Zambia, Botswana, South Africa
Official name: Republic of Namibia
Divisions: Thirteen regions and ninety-three local government areas
Capital: Windhoek
Largest cities: Windhoek, Swakopmund, Rundu, Rehoboth, Keetmanshoop (in order of size)
Flag: The flag of Namibia features a red diagonal stripe, with white borders, running from bottom left to top right. This stripe separates a blue triangle with a yellow Sun, top left, from a green triangle, bottom right
National anthem: "Namibia, land of the brave"

Red | White | Blue
Yellow | Green

1990 stamp marking Namibia's independence and depicting President Sam Nujoma

Major languages: English (official), Ovambo, Kavango, Afrikaans, Herero
Currency: Dollar = 100 cents

GEOGRAPHY

With an area of 318,261 square miles (824,293 sq. km), Namibia is Africa's fifteenth largest country. It is about 1.2 times as large as Texas in the United States (US).

Behind the narrow coastal plain, Namibia forms part of the Southern Plateau, which makes up most of Southern Africa. Central Namibia lies mainly between about 3,000 and 6,500 ft (900–2,000 m) above sea level, though Brandberg, Namibia's highest point, reaches 8,465 ft (2,580 m) on the west of the plateau. In eastern Namibia, the land descends to the Kalahari basin.

The Orange River borders South Africa in the south, while the Kunene and Okavango rivers form parts of the northern border with Angola. In the far northeast, the Zambezi River flows along the border with the Caprivi Strip, a narrow corridor of land linking Namibia with Zambia.

Namibia has a warm, dry climate. North-central Namibia

has about 20 in. (51 cm) of rain a year, and the tropical savanna provides a habitat for many animals. The rainfall on the plateau decreases to the south. The coastal Namib Desert is one of the world's bleakest areas. The Kalahari Desert, in the east, is actually a semidesert.

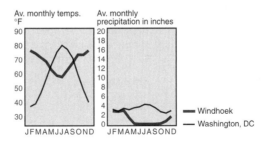

Av. monthly temps. °F / Av. monthly precipitation in inches

— Windhoek
— Washington, DC

ECONOMY

Chief farm products: Corn, dairy products, livestock, millet, sorghum, vegetables, wheat, wool
Chief mineral resources: Diamonds, uranium, copper, gold, lead, zinc
Chief industrial products: Cut diamonds, karakul sheep pelts, refined metals, processed food, textiles
Exports: Diamonds and other minerals; farm products, including cattle
Per capita income: $2,110 (as compared with $29,080 in the US)

Employment:

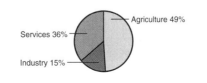

Agriculture 49%
Services 36%
Industry 15%

In the US, agriculture employs 3% of the work force, industry 26%, and services 71%

© DIAGRAM

Niger

PEOPLE

Ethnic groups: Hausa (p 94), **Fulani** (p 85), **Songhay** (p 191), **Tuareg** (p 207), **Wodaabe** (p 214), **Zerma** (p 220)
Population: 9,799,000 (as compared with the US population of 267,636,000)
Religions: Islam (98.6%), African religions (1.4%)

SOCIAL FACTS

- The average life expectancy at birth is 47 years, as compared with 76 years in the US
- Only 18% of the people live in urban areas, as compared with about 76% in the US
- Droughts have caused great hardship since the 1960s
- Mobile "tent schools" provide education for the children of nomads
- 85% of the people live by farming, but only 3% of the land is farmed
- Tuareg in northern Niger have conducted guerrilla warfare in an attempt to achieve self-rule

KEY POINTS IN RECENT HISTORY

1906 France fixes Niger's boundaries
1946 The Parti Progressiste Nigérien (PPN) is formed under Hamani Diori
1960 Niger becomes independent, with Diori as president
1974 A military coup overthrows Diori; Lt.-Col. Seyni Kountché becomes head of a military government
1987 Kountché dies; Col. Ali Saïbou succeeds him

1992 A multiparty constitution is approved
1993 Mahamane Ousmane is elected as president
1996 A coup brings Ibrahim Bare Mainassara to power (January); he is elected president in June
1999 Mainassara is assassinated and Daouda Malem Wanke becomes head of state

THE NATION

Location: Landlocked country in West Africa
Neighbors: Algeria, Libya, Chad, Nigeria, Benin, Burkina Faso, Mali
Official name: Republic of Niger
Divisions: Eight departments
Capital: Niamey
Largest cities: Niamey, Zinder, Maradi, Tahoua, Agadez (in order of size)
Flag: The orange stripe, top, represents the Sahara and the white stripe stands for the Niger River, with the circle symbolizing the Sun. The green stripe at the bottom represents the grasslands in the south of the country
National anthem: "By the banks of the mighty great Niger"

☐ Orange ☐ White ☐ Green

1961 stamp marking the first anniversary of Niger's admission into the United Nations

Major languages: French (official), Hausa, Songhay, Arabic
Currency: CFA franc = 100 centimes

GEOGRAPHY

With an area of 489,191 square miles (1,267,000 sq. km), Niger is Africa's sixth largest country. It is 1.8 times larger in area than Texas in the United States (US).

Southern Niger consists of plains that slope down to the Lake Chad basin in the southeast. The northern two-thirds of the country consists of plateaus, which are broken by the volcanic Aïr Mountains. These mountains contain Niger's highest point, Mount Gréboun, which reaches 6,552 ft (1,997 m) above sea level. Northern Niger forms part of the Sahara, though the Aïr Mountains have a little more annual rainfall than the surrounding plateaus.

The chief river is the Niger, which flows from Mali through Niger and into Nigeria in the southwest. The Niger Valley, which contains the capital, Niamey, is the country's most fertile and most heavily populated region.

Niger is one of the world's hottest countries. The north is extremely arid and the rainfall is unreliable in the south. From March until May, a hot, dusty wind, the harmattan, blows from the Sahara over the south. The north is desert, but the Sahel in the south is semidesert. Tropical savanna occurs in the far south of the country.

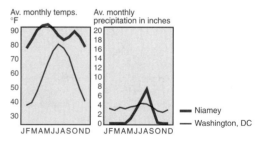

Av. monthly temps. °F

Av. monthly precipitation in inches

JFMAMJJASOND   JFMAMJJASOND

— Niamey
— Washington, DC

ECONOMY

Chief farm products: Cassava, corn, cotton, livestock, millet, peanuts, rice, sorghum, sugar cane, sweet potatoes, tobacco, vegetables, wheat
Chief mineral resources: Uranium, natron (sodium carbonate), phosphates, salt, gold
Chief industrial products: Beverages, cement, processed food, textiles
Exports: Uranium, live animals, beverages, tobacco
Per capita income: $200 (as compared with $29,080 in the US)

Employment:

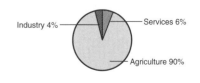

Industry 4%   Services 6%

Agriculture 90%

In the US, agriculture employs 3% of the work force, industry 26%, and services 71%

Nigeria

PEOPLE

Ethnic groups: **Bariba** (p 48), **Edo** (p 75), **Fulani, including Wodaabe** (p 85), **Hausa** (p 94), **Ibibio** (p 101),
Igbo (p 103), **Kanuri** (p 109), **Rukuba** (p 181), **Tiv** (p 202), **Yakurr** (p 217), **Yoruba** (p 218)
Population: 117,897,000 (as compared with the US population of 267,636,000)
Religions: Islam 48%; Christianity 34%; African religions 18%

SOCIAL FACTS

- The average life expectancy at birth is 54 years, as compared with 76 years in the US
- Only 40% of the people live in urban areas, as compared with about 76% in the US
- Nigeria has the highest population in Africa
- Nigeria's external debts are the highest in Africa

- Conflict exists between northerners, who are mainly Muslim, and southerners, who are Christians or followers of African religions
- Nigeria's great artistic and historical centers include Nok, Ife, Oyo, and Benin

KEY POINTS IN RECENT HISTORY

1914 Britain forms the colony of Nigeria
1960 Nigeria becomes an independent federation (October 1)
1966 Military leaders overthrow the civilian government
1967 Civil war breaks out and the eastern state of Biafra proclaims its independence
1970 Civil war ends with Biafra's defeat
1979 Civilian rule is restored

1983 A military regime is established
1993 Presidential elections are annulled and military rule under General Sani Abacha continues
1995 The Commonwealth suspends Nigeria's membership
1998 Abacha dies and his successor continues the process of restoring civilian government
1999 Obansanjo Olesegun is elected president as Nigeria returns to civilian rule

THE NATION

Location: West Africa, on the Gulf of Guinea
Neighbors: Benin, Niger, Chad, Cameroon
Official name: Federal Republic of Nigeria
Divisions: Thirty states and the Federal Capital Territory
Capital: Abuja
Largest cities: Lagos, Ibadan, Kano, Ogbomosho (in order of size)
Flag: The Nigerian flag has three broad vertical stripes of equal width. The two outer stripes are of green, which represents agriculture. The stripe in the center is white, which stands for unity and peace
National anthem: "Arise O compatriots, Nigeria's call obey"

Green ☐ White

1961 Stamp marking Nigeria's admission into the Universal Postal Union

Major languages: English (official), Hausa, Yoruba, Igbo, Fulfulde
Currency: Naira = 100 kobo

GEOGRAPHY

With an area of 356,669 square miles (923,769 sq. km), Nigeria is Africa's fourteenth largest country. It is about 1.33 times bigger than Texas in the United States (US).

Northern Nigeria consists of high plains and plateaus, which are drained by the Niger and Benue rivers. But in the northeast, rivers drain into Lake Chad, which occupies an inland drainage basin. Lake Chad, which Nigeria shares with Niger, Chad, and Cameroon, is the country's largest lake.

Southern Nigeria contains hilly regions and broad plains. The land rises to the southeast, with highlands along the border with Cameroon. Nigeria's highest point, Vogel Peak, reaches 6,669 ft (2,033 m) in these highlands. Nigeria's coastline, which contains many lagoons and the huge Niger delta, is 478 miles (769 km) long.

Nigeria has a tropical climate. The south, which is hot and rainy throughout the year, was once covered by dense rainforests, but large areas have been cleared for farming. The north is hotter and drier, with a dry season from November until March. Tropical savanna merges into thorn scrub in the far north.

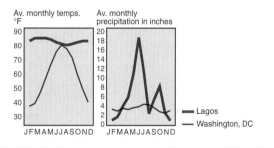

Av. monthly temps. °F

Av. monthly precipitation in inches

■ Lagos
— Washington, DC

ECONOMY

Chief farm products: Beans, beef and hides, cocoa, cassava, corn, cotton, millet, palm products, peanuts, rice, rubber, yams
Chief mineral resources: Oil and natural gas
Chief industrial products: Cement, chemicals, fertilizers, food products, textiles, vehicles
Chief export: Oil (98%)
Per capita income: $280 (as compared with $29,080 in the US)

Employment:

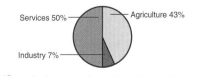

Services 50%
Agriculture 43%
Industry 7%

In the US, agriculture employs 3% of the work force, industry 26%, and services 71%.

Rwanda

PEOPLE

Ethnic groups: Hutu (p 99), **Tutsi** (p 99), **Twa** (p 145)

Population: 7,895,000 (as compared with the US population of 267,636,000)
Religions: Christianity (74%), African religions (17%), Islam (9%)

SOCIAL FACTS

- The average life expectancy at birth is 40 years, as compared with 76 years in the US
- Only 6% of the people live in urban areas, as compared with 76% in the US
- The Tutsi people have ruled the area for hundreds of years, often treating the Hutu like serfs in the past
- Rwanda is mainland Africa's most densely populated country
- Soil erosion, a serious problem in Rwanda, has helped to make the country one of the world's poorest

KEY POINTS IN RECENT HISTORY

1916 Belgium occupies the former German territory of Ruanda-Urundi
1961 Following a Hutu rebellion against the Tutsi monarchy, the people of Ruanda vote in a referendum to make their country a republic
1962 Independence is achieved for the new Republic of Rwanda (July 1); Grégoire Kayibanda becomes president
1973 General Juvénal Habyarimana overthrows Kayibanda
1983 Habyarimana elected president
1990 10,000 guerrillas of Tutsi-based Front Patriotique Rwandais (FPR) invade northeast Rwanda from Uganda starting a civil war
1991 Tension between Hutu and Tutsi is increased by conflict. A multiparty system of government is introduced
1993 One million refugees flee conflict in Rwanda, many Tutsi civilians and moderate Hutu are massacred by other Rwandans. Ceasefire is declared
1994 Habyarimana dies in plane crash; assassination is suspected; war erupts. Pasteur Bizimungu becomes president

THE NATION

Location: Landlocked country in East Africa
Neighbors: Uganda, Tanzania, Burundi, Dem. Rep. of Congo
Official name: Republic of Rwanda
Divisions: Ten prefectures
Capital: Kigali
Largest cities: Kigali, Ruhengeri, Butare, Gisenyi (in order of size)
Flag: The red, yellow, and green stripes symbolize African unity; they are the colors of the flag of Ethiopia, Africa's oldest independent nation. The "R" in the center distinguishes Rwanda's flag from that of Guinea
National anthem: "My Rwanda, Rwanda who gave me birth"

■ Red ☐ Yellow ■ Green

1962 stamp marking independence and depicting President Kayibanda

Major languages: Rwanda and French (both official), Swahili
Currency: Rwanda franc = 100 centimes

GEOGRAPHY

With an area of 10,169 square miles (26,338 sq. km), Rwanda is Africa's ninth smallest country. It is a little larger in area than Vermont in the United States (US).

The Great Rift Valley, which cuts through western Rwanda, contains part of the country's largest lake, Kivu. Overlooking the Rift Valley are mountains, including Mount Karisimbi, Rwanda's highest peak at 14,787 (4,507 m). The mountains bordering the Rift Valley form part of the divide between the Congo and Nile river systems. Eastern Rwanda consists of plateaus that slope down to the Kagera River Valley in the east. The Kagera flows into Lake Victoria and is one of the most remote sources of the Nile.

Rwanda has an equatorial climate, though the altitude moderates temperatures. The hottest region is the Rift Valley floor, while the wettest places are the western mountains. The rainforests in the west once also covered the east, but they have been largely cleared for farming.

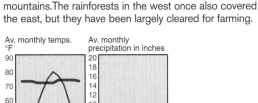

Av. monthly temps. °F

Av. monthly precipitation in inches

— Kigali
— Washington, DC

ECONOMY

Chief farm products: Bananas, beans, cassava, coffee, corn, livestock, peanuts, potatoes, pyrethrum (a plant used in insecticides), tea, tobacco
Chief mineral resources: Tin ore, tungsten ore, gold, natural gas
Chief industrial products: Blankets, cement, processed food, soap
Exports: Coffee, tea, pyrethrum
Per capita income: $210 (as compared with $29,080 in the US)

Employment:

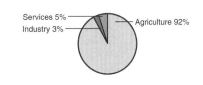

Services 5%
Industry 3%
Agriculture 92%

In the US, agriculture employs 3% of the work force, industry 26%, and services 71%

São Tomé and Príncipe

PEOPLE

Ethnic groups: Mixed Black African and European ancestry
Population: 138,000 (as compared with the US population of 267,636,000)
Religions: Christianity (100%)

SOCIAL FACTS

• The average life expectancy at birth
is 64 years, as compared with 76 years in the US
• Only 43% of the people live in urban areas, as compared
with about 76% in the US
• About 95 percent of the population lives on São Tomé
island
• São Tomé was a Portuguese slave-trading center in the

1500s
• Most farms produce crops for export; food has to be
imported
• Most of the people are descendants of slaves, contract
laborers and European settlers; they are called "filhos da
terra" ("sons of the land")

KEY POINTS IN RECENT HISTORY

1953 Portuguese troops kill hundreds of workers during a
protest
1972 The country's nationalist party is named the
Movimento de Libertação de São Tomé e Príncipe (MLSTP)
1975 The country becomes independent from Portugal
(July 12) and the MLSTP leader, Manuel Pinto da Costa,
an economist, becomes president
1983–4 An acute drought occurs

1990 A new constitution makes the formation of
opposition parties legal
1991 The MLSTP is defeated in elections and da Costa
retires; Miguel Trovoada becomes the new president
1994 The MLSTP regains power when it wins 27 out of
the 55 seats in the National Assembly
1996 São Tomé and Príncipe joins the Community of
Portuguese-speaking Countries

THE NATION

Location: Island country off the coast of Central Africa
Nearest mainland country: Gabon
Official name: Democratic Republic of São Tomé and
Príncipe
Divisions: Two main islands and several islets
Capital: São Tomé
Largest cities: São Tomé, Trinidade, São Antonio (in
order of size)
Flag: The two stripes of green, the yellow stripe, center,
and the red triangle use the three colors of the flag of
Ethiopia, Africa's oldest independent nation. The black
stars represent the two main islands
National anthem: "Total independence, glorious song of
the people"

Green Yellow Red

Black

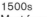

REPÚBLICA DEMOCRÁTICA
12 de Julio de 1976 · L'Aniversario

independencia Nacional 12$ 50
DE SÃO TOMÉ E PRÍNCIPE

*1963 stamp marking promulgation
of the Algerian constitution*

Major languages: Portuguese (official), Creole, Fang
Currency: Dobra = 100 céntimos

GEOGRAPHY

With an area of 372 square miles (963 sq. km), São Tomé
and Príncipe is Africa's second smallest independent
country after Seychelles. It is less than a third of the size of
Rhode Island in the United States (US).

São Tomé, the country's main island, makes up about 86%
of the total area. It is largely mountainous and consists of the
remains of extinct volcanoes, with fertile plains formed from
volcanic ash in the south. The highest point, Pico de São
Tomé, reaches 6,640 ft (2,024 m) in the west. Príncipe is
another volcanic island. Its highest point is 3,107 ft (947 m)
above sea level. The country's other islands are tiny.

The climate is tropical, but temperatures are moderated by
altitude and by the cold Benguela Current, which flows
north along the western coast of Africa. The rainfall is

abundant, though a marked dry season occurs from June
until September. Rainforest covers the higher land, but
farmers have cleared most of the forest on the lower slopes.

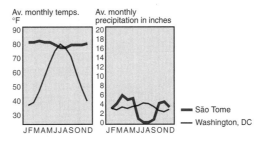

Av. monthly temps.
°F

Av. monthly
precipitation in inches

━━ São Tome
━━ Washington, DC

ECONOMY

Chief farm products: Bananas, cassava, cocoa, coconuts,
coffee, copra, livestock, palm oil, sweet potatoes, yams
Chief mineral resources: Some quarrying for
construction materials
Chief industrial products: Bricks, processed food, soap,
textiles, wood products
Exports: Cocoa (60%), copra, coffee, bananas, palm oil
Per capita income: $290 (as compared with $29,080 in
the US)

Employment:

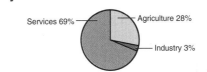

Services 69%
Agriculture 28%
Industry 3%

In the US, agriculture employs 3% of the work force,
industry 26%, and services 71%

Senegal

Ethnic groups: Dyula (p 72), **Fulani, including Tukolor** (p 210), **Manding** (p 142), **Serer** (p 184), **Wolof** (p 215)
Population: 8,790,000 (as compared with the US population of 267,636,000)
Religions: Islam (94%) **Christianity** (5%), **African religions** (1%)

SOCIAL FACTS

- The average life expectancy at birth is 52 years, as compared with 76 years in the US
- Only 44% of the people live in urban areas, as compared with about 76% in the US
- Dakar is a major African seaport
- In colonial times, Dakar was the capital, main port, and industrial center of French West Africa, which included eight countries
- Many Senegalese belong to brotherhoods (Islamic groups), headed by marabouts (religious leaders), who have much political influence

KEY POINTS IN RECENT HISTORY

1959 Senegal unites with French Soudan to form the Federation of Mali
1960 Senegal leaves the federation and becomes independent (June 20)
1966–74 Senegal is governed by a one-party system
1980 Senegal's first president, Léopold Sédar Senghor, resigns; Abdou Diouf becomes president
1981 Senegalese troops help to put down a rebellion in Gambia

1982 Senegal and Gambia form a confederation called Senegambia
1989 Senegambia is dissolved
1993 Diouf is reelected president for the third time; his Parti Socialiste wins the majority of the seats in the National Assembly
1994 CFA franc, which is linked to the French franc, is devalued by 50% causing widespread economic hardship and civil unrest

THE NATION

Location: West Africa, facing the Atlantic Ocean
Neighbors: Mauritania, Mali, Guinea, Guinea-Bissau, Gambia
Official name: Republic of Senegal
Divisions: Ten regions
Capital: Dakar
Largest cities: Dakar, Thiès, Kaolack, Ziguinchor, Saint-Louis (in order of size)
Flag: The green, yellow, and red vertical stripes symbolize African unity; these are the colors of the flag of Ethiopia, Africa's oldest independent nation. The green star symbolizes Islam
National anthem: "All pluck the koras, strike the balafons"

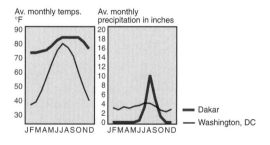

Green Yellow Red

1970 stamp marking the twenty-fifth anniversary of the United Nations (UN)

Major languages: French (official), Wolof, Fulfulde, Manding
Currency: CFA franc = 100 centimes

GEOGRAPHY

With an area of 75,955 square miles (196,723 sq. km), Senegal is Africa's thirty-third largest country. It is about the same size as South Dakota in the United States (US).

Senegal's coastline, which is 310 miles (499 km) long, is lined with sandy beaches, with high sand dunes in the north and mangrove swamps in parts of the south. The capital, Dakar, stands on a volcanic promontory, Cape Verde. Inland are rolling plains, and the land rises in the southeast to a height of 1,634 ft (498 m), the country's highest elevation. This area is an extension of the Futa Djallon plateau in Guinea.

Major rivers include the Senegal, which forms the northern border, and the Casamance in the south. The Gambia River flows from northern Guinea through Senegal into Gambia, a narrow country surrounded by Senegal.

The climate is tropical, with a rainy season from July until October. The northeast is arid, but the northwest and center are part of the semidesert Sahel. Tropical savanna occurs in the far south. Forests grow only in river valleys.

Av. monthly temps. °F

Av. monthly precipitation in inches

— Dakar
— Washington, DC

ECONOMY

Chief farm products: Cassava, corn, cotton, livestock, millet, peanuts, rice, sorghum
Chief mineral resources: Phosphates
Chief industrial products: Beverages, cement, fish products, processed food and edible oils, fertilizers
Exports: Canned fish, phosphates, fresh fish, peanut oil, shellfish, cotton
Per capita income: $540 (as compared with $29,080 in the US)

Employment:

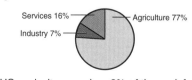

Services 16%
Industry 7%
Agriculture 77%

In the US, agriculture employs 3% of the work force, industry 26%, and services 71%

Seychelles

PEOPLE

Ethnic groups: Chinese, Creole (p 64), **English, Indian, Madagascan Peoples** (p 138)
Population: 78,000 (as compared with the US population of 267,636,000)
Religions: Christianity (97%), Hinduism

SOCIAL FACTS

- The average life expectancy at birth is 71 years, as compared with 76 years in the US
- About 55% of the people live in urban areas, as compared with about 76% in the US
- More than 80% of the people live on Mahé island
- Most people are Creoles, of mixed African and European descent; the Creole language used in the Seychelles is considered to be a French dialect
- The islands were uninhabited when they were first discovered in the early 1500s
- Tourism is a major and expanding industry in Seychelles

KEY POINTS IN RECENT HISTORY

1976 Seychelles becomes independent from Britain (June 29); James Mancham, leader of the Democratic Party, becomes the first president
1979 A military coup ousts Mancham and the opposition leader, France-Albert René, becomes president
1977 René's Seychelles People's Progressive Front (SPPF) becomes the sole party; the government pursues Marxist policies

1981 A coup attempt fails
1984 René is reelected president
1989 René is reelected president
1991 The government legalizes opposition parties and relaxes its socialist policies
1993 René is reelected president and the SPPF wins 28 of the 33 seats in the People's Assembly
1998 René and his SPPF are again reelected

THE NATION

Location: Island country in the Indian Ocean, off the coast of East Africa
Nearest mainland: Mainland Africa lies about 1,000 miles (1,600 km) to the west
Official name: Republic of Seychelles
Divisions: 115 islands in two main groups, the Granitic and Coralline
Capital: Victoria
Largest city: Victoria
Flag: The red stripe, top, represents revolution and progress; the wavy white stripe symbolizes the Indian Ocean; and the green stripe, bottom, stands for agriculture. The flag was first introduced in 1977
National anthem: "With courage and discipline, we have broken down all barriers"

■ Red □ White ■ Green

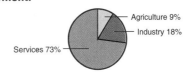

1976 stamp marking both the independence of Seychelles and the US Bicentenary

Major languages: French, English (both official), Creole
Currency: Seychelles rupee = 100 cents

GEOGRAPHY

With an area of 176 square miles (456 sq. km), Seychelles is Africa's smallest nation. It is about one-seventh of the size in area of Rhode Island in the United States (US).

The 32 islands in the Granitic group cover a total area of 92 square miles (238 sq km). This mountainous island group includes the largest island, Mahé, which contains the country's highest point, at 2,893 ft (882 m) above sea level. The 83 Coralline, or Outer Islands, are low-lying coral islands or reefs. Many of them are uninhabited.

The climate is tropical, though the highlands are cooler than the humid coasts. The rainfall is moderate to heavy, being greatest on the south-facing slopes of the Granitic Islands, which lie in the path of the prevailing southeast trade winds. The vegetation is lush, but most of the original rainforest has been cut down.

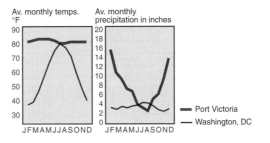

Av. monthly temps. °F

Av. monthly precipitation in inches

■ Port Victoria
— Washington, DC

JFMAMJJASOND JFMAMJJASOND

ECONOMY

Chief farm products: Bananas, cassava, cinnamon, coconuts, copra, livestock, sugar cane, sweet potatoes, tea, vegetables, yams
Chief mineral resources: Guano
Chief industrial products: Beverages, canned fish, petroleum products
Exports: Petroleum products, canned tuna and other fish, cinnamon, food, beverages, tobacco, chemicals
Per capital income: $6,910 (as compared with $29,080 in the US)

Employment:

Agriculture 9%
Industry 18%
Services 73%

In the US, agriculture employs 3% of the work force, industry 26%, and services 71%

© DIAGRAM

Sierra Leone

PEOPLE

Ethnic groups: Creoles (p 64), **Fulani** (p 85), **Kono** (p 121), **Limba** (p 126), **Mende** (p 148), **Temne** (p 201)
Population: 4,748,000 (as compared with the US population of 267,636,000)
Religions: Islam (60%), African religions (30%), Christianity (10%)

SOCIAL FACTS

- The average life expectancy at birth is 37 years, as compared with 76 years in the US
- Only 33% of the people live in urban areas, as compared with about 76% in the US
- Freetown was set up in 1787 as a settlement for freed slaves
- The country was once named the "white man's grave" because of its climate and its tropical diseases
- Sierra Leone means "lion's mountain," possibly because the shape of the coastal peninsula resembles that of a lion
- Civil war has caused much destruction since 1991

KEY POINTS IN RECENT HISTORY

1952 Dr Milton Margai of the Sierra Leone People's Party is elected prime minister
1961 Sierra Leone becomes independent from Britain (April 27)
1964 Milton Margai dies and his brother Albert becomes prime minister
1967 A military coup overthrows the civilian government
1968 Civilian rule is restored with Siaka Stevens as prime minister

1971 The country becomes a republic
1978 Sierra Leone becomes a one-party state
1991-6 Civil war; the military take power in 1992
1996 Ahmad Tejan Kabbah is elected president in multiparty elections
1997 Kabbah flees after a military coup
1998 Kabbah is restored to power after intervention by a Nigerian-led force
1999 Rebel forces attack Freetown

THE NATION

Location: West Africa, facing the Atlantic Ocean
Neighbors: Guinea, Liberia
Official name: Republic of Sierra Leone
Divisions: Four provinces
Capital: Freetown
Largest cities: Freetown, Koidu-New Sembehun, Bo, Kenema, Makeni (in order of size)
Flag: The green stripe, top, symbolizes agriculture; the white stripe, center, stands for peace; and the blue stripe, bottom, represents the waters of the Atlantic Ocean
National anthem: "High we exalt thee, realm of the free"

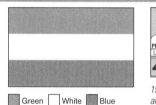

Green ☐ White Blue

1975 stamp marking the first anniversary of the Mano River Union

Major languages: English (official), Mende, Temne, Krio
Currency: Leone = 100 cents

GEOGRAPHY

With an area of 27,699 square miles (71,740 sq. km), Sierra Leone is one of Africa's smaller countries. It is a little smaller in area than South Carolina in the United States (US).

Deep estuaries and swamps occur along the northern coast, but lagoons border the southern shore. Freetown, which stands on the rocky Sierra Leone peninsula, has one of West Africa's finest natural harbors.

Behind the coast is a broad plain, extending up to 100 miles (160 km) inland in the north, but plateaus and mountains make up about half of the country. The mountains rise to Mount Mansa, which reaches 6,391 ft (1,948 m) above sea level near the northeastern border. Many rivers flow across Sierra Leone, running generally from northeast to southwest. They include the Great and Little Scarcies, Rokel, Jong, Sewa, Moa, and Mano.

The climate is tropical, with rains from April to November.

The south is dry in January and February. The dry season in the north runs from December to March. The coast is swampy, while inland, the rainforest has been largely cut down. Farther inland are grasslands, with tropical savanna in the north.

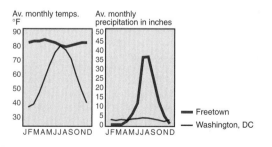

Av. monthly temps. °F

Av. monthly precipitation in inches

JFMAMJJASOND   JFMAMJJASOND

Freetown
Washington, DC

ECONOMY

Chief farm products: Cassava, cocoa, coffee, corn, livestock, millet, palm oil and kernels, peanuts, plantains, rice, sorghum, sweet potatoes
Chief mineral resources: Bauxite (aluminum ore), rutile (titanium ore), diamonds, gold
Chief industrial products: Beverages, furniture, processed food, salt
Exports: Rutile, bauxite, diamonds, cocoa, coffee
Per capita income: $160 (as compared with $29,080 in the US)

Employment:

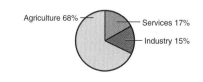

Agriculture 68%
Services 17%
Industry 15%

In the US, agriculture employs 3% of the work force, industry 26%, and services 71%

Somalia

PEOPLE

Ethnic groups: Issa (p 107), **Somalis** (p 189), **divided into several clans; some Arabs** (p 32) **and Bantu** (p 47)
Population: 8,775,000 (as compared with the US population of 267,636,000)
Religions: Islam (99.8%)

SOCIAL FACTS

- The average life expectancy at birth is 47 years, as compared with 76 years in the US
- Only 37% of the people live in urban areas, as compared with about 76% in the US
- The Somalis have a rich oral literature
- The Somali language did not have a written form until the early 1970s
- Somali-speaking people live in Djibouti, Ethiopia, and Kenya; some Somalis would like to create a Greater Somalia to include these people
- Somalis are divided into clans; clan rivalries have led to civil war

KEY POINTS IN RECENT HISTORY

1905 Italy takes over southern Somalia (northern Somalia is a British protectorate)
1941 During World War II, Britain occupies Italian Somaliland
1960 The two Somalilands unite to form independent Somalia (July 1)
1969 A military regime is set up
1970s Somalia supports Somali-speaking guerrillas in Ethiopia
1988 Somalia and Ethiopia sign a peace treaty
1991 Civil war occurs; the north "secedes," but it is not recognized internationally as a sovereign state
1993–4 US Marines sent by the United Nations oversee food distribution
1995 Somalia has no effective central government, and political power is in the hands of clan leaders
1997–8 Attempts are made to end clan warfare

THE NATION

Location: East Africa, facing the Gulf of Aden and the Indian Ocean
Neighbors: Kenya, Ethiopia, Djibouti
Official name: Somali Democratic Republic
Divisions: Eighteen regions
Capital: Mogadishu
Largest cities: Mogadishu, Hargeisa, Kismatu, Berbera, Merca (in order of size)
Flag: The blue flag is based on that of the United Nations (UN). The five points of the white star represent regions where Somalis live, namely the former British and Italian Somalilands, Kenya, Ethiopia, and Djibouti
National anthem: "Somalia"

Blue ☐ White

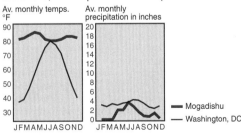

1967 stamp marking the visit of King Faisal of Saudi Arabia

Major languages: Somali and Arabic (both official); English, Italian
Currency: Somali shilling = 100 cents

GEOGRAPHY

With an area of 246,201 square miles (637,658 sq. km), Somalia is Africa's eighteenth largest country. It occupies the Horn of Africa and in area is a little smaller than Texas in the United States (US).

In the north, a narrow coastal plain facing the Gulf of Aden extends to the tip of the Horn of Africa. Behind this hot and arid plain, which is called the Guban (meaning "burned"), lie mountains that rise to a height of 7,900 ft (2,408 m) at Surud Ad mountain, Somalia's highest peak.

Central and southern Somalia, facing the Indian Ocean, consist of low plateaus and plains. The only permanent rivers, the Juba and Shebelle, are in the south. These rivers rise in Ethiopia and they provide valuable water resources.

Somalia has a tropical climate, but the altitude moderates temperatures in the north. The average annual rainfall seldom exceeds 20 in. (51 cm), even in the wetter south, and is unreliable. Semidesert and dry grassland cover much of the land, with tropical savanna in parts of the south.

Av. monthly temps. °F
Av. monthly precipitation in inches

JFMAMJJASOND   JFMAMJJASOND

■ Mogadishu
— Washington, DC

ECONOMY

Chief farm products: Bananas, citrus fruits, corn, cotton, dates, livestock, rice, sorghum, sugar cane
Chief mineral resources: Deposits of many minerals have been found
Chief industrial products: Beverages, hides and skins, processed food, petroleum products, textiles
Exports: Live animals, fish products, bananas, hides and skins
Per capita income: $150 (as compared with $29,080 in the US)

Employment:

In the US, agriculture employs 3% of the work force, industry 26%, and services 71%

South Africa

PEOPLE

Ethnic groups: Afrikaner (p 23), Asian (p 38), Cape Colored (p 58), Cape Malay (p 58), European, Griqua (p 93), Khoisan (p 205), Ndebele (p 159), Sotho, including Pedi (p 191), Swazi (p 197), Tswana, including Kolong and Hurutshe (p 205), Venda (p 211), Xhosa, including Mpondo and Thembu (p 215), Zulu (p 220)
Population: 40,604,000 (as compared with the US population of 267,636,000)
Religions: Christianity (78%), African religions (10.5%)

SOCIAL FACTS

- The average life expectancy at birth is 65 years, as compared with 76 years in the US
- Only 49% of the people live in urban areas, as compared with about 76% in the US
- The most widely spoken of the official languages are Zulu and Xhosa

- South Africa is the continent's most developed and richest country, but most of the wealth is in the hands of the white minority.
- Afrikaans is a language that developed from Dutch; it was spoken by people once called Boers but now called Afrikaners

KEY POINTS IN RECENT HISTORY

1910 Union of South Africa is formed
1912 South African Native National Congress – renamed African National Congress (ANC) in 1923 – is formed
1934 South Africa approves independence from Britain
1948 National Party is elected to power by the whites-only electorate and apartheid is officially introduced
1961 South Africa becomes a republic
1986 State of emergency declared
1989 F. W. de Klerk becomes president and starts to

ease apartheid laws
1990 ANC leader Nelson Mandela is released after twenty-six years in prison
1991 Apartheid laws abolished
1994 ANC wins multiracial elections and Mandela becomes president
1996 New constitution adopted
1999 Mandela retires; the ANC wins elections and Thabo Mbeki becomes president

THE NATION

Location: Southern Africa, facing both the Indian and Atlantic oceans
Neighbors: Namibia, Botswana, Zimbabwe, Mozambique, Swaziland, Lesotho
Official name: Republic of South Africa
Divisions: Nine provinces
Capitals: Pretoria (administrative), Cape Town (legislative), Bloemfontein (judicial)
Largest cities: Cape Town, Johannesburg, Durban, (in order of size)
Flag: The South African flag combines the red, white, and blue colors of the flags of the former colonial power Britain and of the Boer republics with the green, black, and gold of African nationalist organizations
National anthem: "Nkosi sikelel'i, Afrika" ("God bless Africa")

☐ Red ☐ White ☐ Blue ☐ Green
☐ Black ☐ Gold

1986 stamp marking the twenty-fifth anniversary of the Republic of South Africa

Major languages: Afrikaans, English, Ndebele, Sesotho, Tsonga, Setswana, Tshivenda, Xhosa, Zulu (all official)
Currency: Rand = 100 cents

GEOGRAPHY

With an area of 473,290 square miles (1,225,816 sq. km), South Africa is Africa's ninth largest country. It is nearly twice as big in area as Texas in the United States (US).

South Africa consists largely of a plateau. The highest peak, Champagne Castle, rises to 11.073 ft (3,375 m) in the southwest. The longest river is the Orange. The climate is mostly mild and sunny. Only 25% of South Africa has more than 25 in. (64 cm) of rain per year and the country contains parts of the Kalahari and Namib deserts. Forests cover only 3% of the land, but grasslands cover large areas.

Av. monthly temps. °F

Av. monthly precipitation in inches

— Pretoria
— Washington, DC

JFMAMJJASOND JFMAMJJASOND

ECONOMY

Chief farm products: Apples, beef, citrus fruits, corn, potatoes, tobacco, sugar cane, wheat, wool
Chief mineral resources: Coal, copper, diamonds, gold, uranium
Chief industrial products: Chemicals, iron, steel, machinery, metal products, processed food, textiles, vehicles
Exports: Gold, metals and metal products, diamonds, food products
Per capita income: $3,210 (as compared with $29,080 in the US)

Employment:

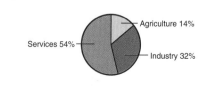

Services 54%
Agriculture 14%
Industry 32%

In the US, agriculture employs 3% of the work force, industry 26%, and services 71%

Sudan

PEOPLE

Ethnic groups: Acholi (p 20), **Anuak** (p 32), **Arab** (p 32), **Azande** (p 39), **Beja** (p 50), **Beri** (p 55), **Dinka** (p 66), **Funj** (p 89), **Fur** (p 89), **Nuba** (p 163), **Nubians** (p 165), **Nuer** (p 165), **Suri** (p 194)

Population: 27,737,000 (as compared with the US population of 267,636,000)

Religions: Islam (75%), African religions (17%), Christianity (8%)

SOCIAL FACTS

- The average life expectancy at birth is 55 years, as compared with 76 years in the US
- Only 31% of the people live in urban areas, as compared with about 76% in the US
- Khartoum is a center of Islamic fundamentalism
- Conflict between Muslim northerners and mainly Christian southerners has gone on for hundreds of years
- Sudan's Muslim leaders have been accused of trying to destabilize Egypt, Eritrea, Libya, and Uganda
- Nearly all of Sudan's Christians are Black Africans who live in in the south of the country

KEY POINTS IN RECENT HISTORY

1956 Sudan becomes independent (January 1) from Anglo-Egyptian rule

1958 An army group seizes power

1964 Civil war breaks out between the north and the mainly Christian south

1969 Col. Gaafar Muhammad al Nimeri seizes power

1972 The government grants southern Sudan regional autonomy, ending the civil war

1983 Nimeri introduces Sharia (Islamic holy) law throughout Sudan and the civil war starts again

1985 A military group overthrows Nimeri

1989 Another coup brings Brig. Omar Hassan Ahmad al Bashir to power; he abolishes all political parties

1990s The civil war continues

1998 The government announces that it is prepared to hold a referendum on the secession of southern Sudan

THE NATION

Location: North Africa, facing the Red Sea

Neighbors: Ethiopia, Kenya, Dem. Rep. of Congo, Central African Republic, Chad, Libya, Egypt

Official name: Republic of Sudan

Divisions: Twenty-six states

Capital: Khartoum

Largest cities: Khartoum (including Omdurman and Khartoum North), Port Sudan (in order of size)Flag: The red, white, and black horizontal stripes are colors associated with the Pan-Arab movement. The green triangle is a symbol of Islam. Sudan adopted this flag in 1969

National anthem: "Nahnu djundullah" ("We are god's army")

☐ Red ☐ White ☐ Black
☐ Green

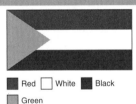

1969 Stamp marking the fifth anniversary of the African Development Bank

Major languages: Arabic (official), Nuer, Beja, Dinka, Koalib, Tegali, Katla, Tumtum, Shilluk

Currency: Dinar = 10 Sudanese pounds

GEOGRAPHY

With an area of 967,245 square miles (2,505,155 sq. km), Sudan is Africa's largest country. It is 3.6 times larger in area than Texas in the United States (US).

Most of Sudan is flat, but a hilly region runs parallel to the Red Sea coastline.West-central Sudan is a badland region of ancient lavas and compacted volcanic ash. Mount Kinyeti in the far southeast is the highest peak, at 10,456 ft (3,187 m).

The chief rivers are the Nile, the world's longest, and its tributaries, the Bahr al Arab, the Blue Nile, and the Atbara. In the south, where the Nile winds through a vast swamp called the Sudd, the river is called the Bahr al Jabal. It is called the White Nile between the Sudd and Khartoum, where it is joined by the Blue Nile and becomes simply the Nile.

The land north of Khartoum has a hot desert climate, but heavy rains occur in the far south. The north is desert, except along the Nile Valley and at oases. Central Sudan is a dry grassland where farming depends on irrigation. Tropical savanna, rainforest and swamp occur in the south.

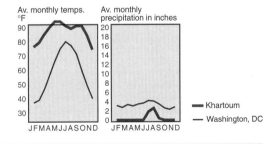

ECONOMY

Chief farm products: Cotton, gum arabic, livestock, millet, peanuts, sesame seeds, sugar cane, wheat

Chief mineral resources: Chromite (chromium ore), gold, gypsum, salt

Chief industrial products: Cement, fertilizers, hides and skins, processed food, textiles

Exports: Cotton, sesame seeds, sheep and lambs, gum arabic, hides and skins

Per capita income: $290 (as compared with $29,080 in the US)

Employment:

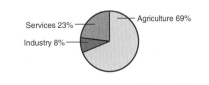

In the US, agriculture employs 3% of the work force, industry 26%, and services 71%

© DIAGRAM

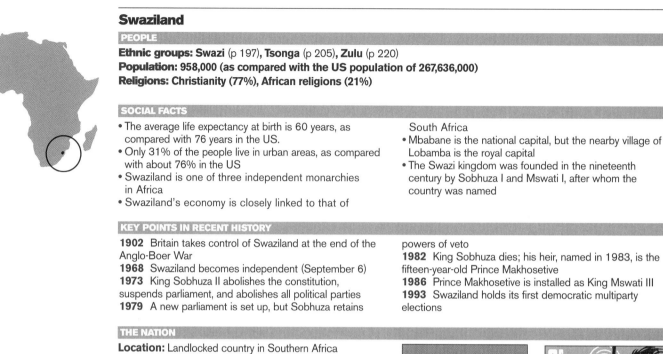

Swaziland

PEOPLE

Ethnic groups: Swazi (p 197), **Tsonga** (p 205), **Zulu** (p 220)
Population: 958,000 (as compared with the US population of 267,636,000)
Religions: Christianity (77%), African religions (21%)

SOCIAL FACTS

• The average life expectancy at birth is 60 years, as compared with 76 years in the US.
• Only 31% of the people live in urban areas, as compared with about 76% in the US
• Swaziland is one of three independent monarchies in Africa
• Swaziland's economy is closely linked to that of South Africa
• Mbabane is the national capital, but the nearby village of Lobamba is the royal capital
• The Swazi kingdom was founded in the nineteenth century by Sobhuza I and Mswati I, after whom the country was named

KEY POINTS IN RECENT HISTORY

1902 Britain takes control of Swaziland at the end of the Anglo-Boer War
1968 Swaziland becomes independent (September 6)
1973 King Sobhuza II abolishes the constitution, suspends parliament, and abolishes all political parties
1979 A new parliament is set up, but Sobhuza retains powers of veto
1982 King Sobhuza dies; his heir, named in 1983, is the fifteen-year-old Prince Makhosetive
1986 Prince Makhosetive is installed as King Mswati III
1993 Swaziland holds its first democratic multiparty elections

THE NATION

Location: Landlocked country in Southern Africa
Neighbors: Mozambique, South Africa
Official name: Kingdom of Swaziland
Divisions: Four regions
Capital: Mbabane
Largest cities: Mbabane, Manzini, Nhlangano, Piggs Peak, Siteki (in order of size)
Flag: The flag of Swaziland has horizontal blue stripes at the top and bottom. Thin yellow stripes separate these from the central red stripe, which contains a warrior's shield, two assegais (spears), and a fighting stick
National anthem: "O Lord our God, bestower of blessings upon the Swazi"

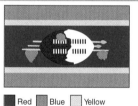

Red ■ Blue ■ Yellow □
Black ■ White □

1968 stamp depicting a Swazi warrior

Major languages: Swazi, English (both official), Zulu
Currency: Lilangeni = 100 cents

GEOGRAPHY

With an area of 6,704 square miles (17,363 sq. km), Swaziland is Africa's seventh smallest country. It is a little larger in area than Hawaii in the United States (US).

Swaziland's land regions run north-south. The Highveld in the west covers 30% of Swaziland and includes Mount Emlembe, the country's highest point at 6,109 ft (1,862 m). To the east lies the Middleveld, which is from 1,150 to 3,300 ft (350–1,000 m) above sea level. The Middleveld makes up 28% of the land, and the third region, the Lowveld, makes up another 33%. Here the average height is around 900 ft (270 m). The fourth region is the Lebombo Mountains along the Mozambique border in the east. These mountains reach a height of about 2,600 ft (790 m). The chief rivers are the Komati, the Umbeluzi, the Great Usutu, and the Ingwavuma.

Swaziland has a subtropical climate, though the altitude moderates the climate. While the Lowveld is hot and fairly dry, the Highveld has warm summers, cool winters, and abundant rainfall. Grasslands cover about two-thirds of the country, and pine forests planted by Europeans cover large areas in the Highveld.

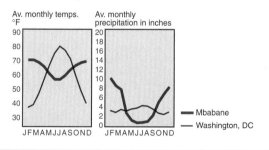

Av. monthly temps. °F
Av. monthly precipitation in inches

— Mbabane
— Washington, DC

JFMAMJJASOND   JFMAMJJASOND

ECONOMY

Chief farm products: Citrus fruits, corn, cotton, livestock, pineapples, sorghum, sugar cane, vegetables
Chief mineral resources: Asbestos, diamonds, quarry stone
Chief industrial products: Cement, beverages, fertilizers, processed food, sugar, textiles, wood pulp
Exports: Sugar, wood and wood products, canned fruit, diamonds
Per capita income: $1,520 (as compared with $29,080 in the US)

Employment:

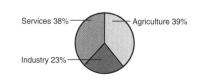

Services 38%   Agriculture 39%
Industry 23%

In the US, agriculture employs 3% of the work force, industry 26%, and services 71%

Tanzania

PEOPLE

Ethnic groups: **Bondei** (p 56), **Chagga** (p 59), **Fipa** (p 83), **Haya** (p 96), **Hadza** (p 94), **Iraqw** (p 106), **Luo** (p 133), **Nyamwezi** (p 167), **Nyakyusa** (p 167), **Pare** (p 179), **Sandawe** (p 183), **Shambaa** (p 184), **Sukuma** (p 194), **Swahili** (p 194), **Yao** (p 217), **Zaramo** (p 219)
Population: 31,316,000 (about a ninth of the US population of 267,636,000)
Religions: African religions (35%), Islam (35%), Christianity (30%)

SOCIAL FACTS

- The average life expectancy at birth is 48 years, as compared with 76 years in the US
- Only 24% of the people live in urban areas, as compared with about 76% in the US
- Tanzania has one of Africa's highest literacy rates
- About 13% of Tanzania is protected in reserves
- Though Tanzania has many ethnic groups (about 120), it has not suffered from ethnic conflicts
- The beautiful carvings and masks made by the Makonde people of Tanzania are among Africa's finest artworks

KEY POINTS IN RECENT HISTORY

1918 Britain takes over Tanganyika (formerly German East Africa)
1961 Tanganyika becomes independent (December 9)
1962 Tanganyika becomes a republic; Dr Julius Nyerere is elected president
1964 Tanganyika and Zanzibar, independent from Britain in 1963 (December 10), unite to form Tanzania
1965 Tanzania becomes a one-party state and pursues

Ujamaa policies (a form of rural socialism)
1985 New president, Ali Hassan Mwinyi, aims to reduce state control
1992 A democratic multiparty constitution is introduced
1993 Regional parliaments are set up for mainland Tanganyika and Zanzibar
1995 Multiparty elections take place

THE NATION

Location: East Africa, facing the Indian Ocean
Neighbors: Mozambique, Malawi, Zambia, Burundi, Rwanda, Uganda, Kenya
Official name: United Republic of Tanzania
Divisions: Twenty-five regions
Capital: Dodoma
Largest cities: Dar es Salaam, Mwanza, Dodoma, Tanga (in order of size)
Flag: The flag of Tanzania has five diagonal stripes. These stripes are green, representing agriculture; gold, which represents minerals; black, which symbolizes the people; gold again; and blue, for the ocean
National anthem: "Mungu ibariki Afrika" ("God bless Africa")

Green | Gold | Black
Blue

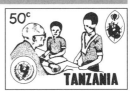

Stamp marking the International Year of the Child, 1979

Major languages: Swahili, English (official), 120 African languages
Currency: Shilling = 100 cents

GEOGRAPHY

With an area of 364,900 square miles (945,087 sq. km), Tanzania is nearly 1.34 times as big in area as Texas in the United States (US).

Behind the narrow coastal plain on the Indian Ocean, the land rises in a series of plateaus. Rising above the plateaus in the northeast is Africa's highest peak, a dormant volcano called Kilimanjaro, at 19,341 ft (5,895 m) above sea level.

In the west, the Great African Rift Valley contains Lake Tanganyika. Another arm of the Rift Valley runs through central Tanzania. The largest lake, Victoria, is shared with Kenya and Uganda and the chief river is the Rufiji. The islands of Zanzibar and Pemba are made of coral. The coast is hot and humid, but it is cooler and drier inland.

Mangrove swamps occur on the coast. Inland, miombo (wooded tropical savanna) or grassland cover large areas.

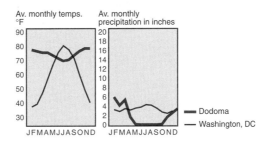

Dodoma
Washington, DC

ECONOMY

Chief farm products: Bananas, beef, cloves, coconuts, coffee, corn, millet, rice, sisal, sorghum, sugar cane, tobacco, wheat
Mineral resources: Diamonds, gold
Chief industrial products: Petroleum and chemical products, processed food, textiles
Exports: Coffee, manufactured goods, cotton, minerals, tea, tobacco
Per capita income: $210 (as compared with $29,080 in the US)

Employment:

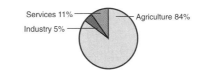

Services 11% — Agriculture 84%
Industry 5%

In the US, agriculture employs 3% of the work force, industry 26%, and services 71%

© DIAGRAM

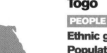

Togo

Ethnic groups: Bariba (p 48), **Ewe** (p 76), **Temba** (p 201), **Yoruba** (p 218)
Population: 4,345,000 (as compared with the US population of 267,636,000)
Religions: African religions (59%), Christianity (28%), Islam (12%)

• The average life expectancy at birth is 55 years, as compared with 76 years in the US
• Only 31% of the people live in urban areas, as compared with about 76% in the US
• The port of Lomé also handles trade for Niger and Burkina Faso

• From the 1400s until the 1800s, Togo was called "the coast of slaves"
• Togo is an Ewe word meaning "behind the sea"; the Ewe form the largest single ethnic group
• Germany, France, and Britain all once colonized Togo

1919 After World War I, the League of Nations partitions the former German Togoland between Britain and France
1957 British Togoland joins Ghana, which becomes independent
1960 French Togoland becomes the independent Republic of Togo (April 27); Sylvanus Olympio becomes the first president
1963 Olympio is assassinated; his successor is

Nicolas Grunitzky
1967 Army officers led by Gnassingbe Eyadéma seize power
1992 Togo adopts a new constitution
1994 The Rassemblement du Peuple Togolais (RPT), formerly the sole party, sets up a coalition government with one of the opposition parties. CFA franc, which is linked to the French franc, is devalued by 50%

Location: West Africa, facing the Gulf of Guinea
Neighbors: Ghana, Burkina Faso, Benin
Official name: Republic of Togo
Divisions: Five regions
Capital: Lomé
Largest cities: Lomé, Sokodé, Kpalimé, Atakpamé, Tsévié, Bassari (in order of size)
Flag: The three horizontal stripes of green stand for agriculture, the yellow for minerals, and the red square for blood shed during the struggle for independence. The white star stands for purity
National anthem: "Let us sweep aside all ill feelings that foil the national unity"

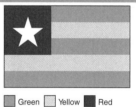

■ Green □ Yellow ■ Red
□ White

1963 stamp marking promulgation of the Algerian constitution

Major languages: French (official), Ewe, Akan
Currency: CFA franc = 100 centimes

With an area of 21,925 square miles (56,786 sq. km), Togo is one of Africa's smaller countries. It is just over twice the size of Maryland in the United States (US).

Togo is a narrow country, measuring about 360 miles (580 km) from north to south. The coastline on the Gulf of Guinea is only 40 miles (64 km) long, while the greatest east-west distance is only 90 miles (145 km).

The country is divided into two main regions by the Togo-Atakora Mountains, which extend diagonally across the country from the southwest to the northeast. South of the mountains is a plateau that descends to a narrow but densely populated coastal plain. To the north is another low plateau region. The highest point is Mount Agou in the southwest. It is 3,235 ft (986 m) above sea level.

The climate is tropical and it is hot throughout the year. The

main rainy season runs from March to May, with a lesser rainy season in October and November. The north is drier with one rainy season. Tropical savanna covers most of Togo, with some patches of rainforest in the center of the country.

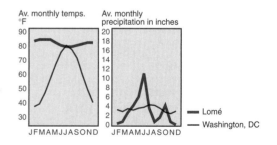

Av. monthly temps. °F
Av. monthly precipitation in inches

JFMAMJJASOND   JFMAMJJASOND

■ Lomé
— Washington, DC

Chief farm products: Bananas, cassava, cocoa, coffee, corn, cotton, kola nuts, livestock, millet, palm oil and kernels, peanuts, rice, sorghum, yams
Chief mineral resources: Phosphates, iron ore, limestone
Chief industrial products: Beverages, cement, processed food, textiles
Exports: Phosphates, cotton, lime and cement
Per capita income: $340 (as compared with $29,080 in the US)

Employment:

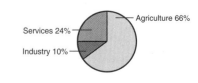

Agriculture 66%
Services 24%
Industry 10%

In the US, agriculture employs 3% of the work force, industry 26%, and services 71%

Tunisia

PEOPLE

Ethnic groups: Arab (p 32), **including Bedouin** (p 50), **Berber** (p 53), **French** (p 85), **Italian** (p 107)
Population: 9,215,000 (as compared with the US population of 267,636,000)
Religions: Islam (99.4%), Christianity, Judaism

SOCIAL FACTS

• The average life expectancy at birth is 70 years, as compared with 76 years in the US
• Only 62% of the people live in urban areas, as compared with about 76% in the US
• More than three million tourists visit Tunisia every year
• Kairouan in Tunisia is the fourth holiest city of Islam, after Mecca, Medina, and Jerusalem; Kairouan was founded in 671
• The site of ancient Carthage is just north of the city of Tunis
• Tunisia's educational system is one of the best in Africa

KEY POINTS IN RECENT HISTORY

1934 Habib Bourguiba sets up the nationalist Néo-Destour (New Constitution) Party, later called the Parti Socialiste Destourien (PSD)
1956 Tunisia becomes independent from France as a monarchy (March 20); Bourguiba is prime minister
1957 Tunisia becomes a republic; Bourguiba becomes president
1987 The prime minister, Zine al Abidine Ben Ali, removes Bourguiba from office and becomes president
1988 Opposition parties are allowed
1989 Ben Ali, leader of the Rassemblement Constitutionnel Démocratique (formerly the PSD), is elected president
1992 A fundamentalist Islamic group, Nahda, is banned
1994 Ben Ali is reelected unopposed

THE NATION

Location: North Africa, facing the Mediterranean Sea
Neighbors: Libya, Algeria
Official name: Republic of Tunisia
Divisions: 23 governorates
Capital: Tunis
Largest cities: Tunis, Sfax, L'Ariana, Bizerte, Djerba, Gabès, Sousse, Kairouan (in order of size)
Flag: The white circle in the center of the flag contains two symbols of Islam – the crescent and the star. The flag dates from 1835 and is based on that of Turkey, but it did not become Tunisia's national flag until 1956
National anthem: "Humata al hima" ("Defenders of the homeland")

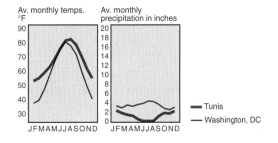

■ Red ☐ White

1978 stamp marking International Antiapartheid Year

Major languages: Arabic (official), French, Berber
Currency: Dinar = 1,000 millimes

GEOGRAPHY

With an area of 63,360 square miles (164,102 sq. km), Tunisia is Africa's thirty-fourth largest country. It is a little larger in area than Georgia in the United States (US).

The eastern ranges of the Atlas Mountains, extend into northern Tunisia. The country's highest point, Mount Chambi, is in the southern branch of the Atlas Mountains, which is called the Tebessa Mountains. Mount Chambi reaches a height of 5,066 ft (1,544 m) above sea level.

Fertile plains lie to the north and east of the Atlas ranges, but to the south, the land descends in a series of plateaus into the barren Sahara. Central Tunisia contains several depressions, which are salt pans. Tunisia has only one permanent river, the Medjerda in the north.

Northern Tunisia has hot, dry summers and mild, rainy winters, the climate of Mediterranean lands. The rainfall decreases to the south. Forests of cork oak and other trees grow in the mountains, but the northern plains support only scrub vegetation. Dry grassland in central Tunisia merges into desert in the south.

Av. monthly temps. °F / Av. monthly precipitation in inches

JFMAMJJASOND   JFMAMJJASOND

— Tunis
— Washington, DC

ECONOMY

Chief farm products: Almonds, barley, citrus fruits, dates, grapes, livestock, olive oil, sugar beets, vegetables, wheat
Chief mineral resources: Oil and natural gas, phosphates, iron ore
Chief industrial products: Cement, phosphoric acid, processed food
Exports: Clothing and accessories, oil and oil products, olive oil
Per capita income: $2,110 (as compared with $29,080 in the US)

Employment:

Agriculture 28%
Services 39%
Industry 33%

In the US, agriculture employs 3% of the work force, industry 26%, and services 71%

Uganda

PEOPLE

Ethnic groups: Acholi (p 20), **Alur** (p 27), **Ganda** (p 89), **Iteso** (p 107), **Langi** (p 125), **Lugbara** (p 131), **Luyia** (p 133), **Soga** (p 189), **Toro** (p 205)
Population: 20,317,000 (as compared with the US population of 267,636,000)
Religions: Christianity (78%), African religions, Islam

SOCIAL FACTS

- The average life expectancy at birth is 42 years, as compared with 76 years in the US
- Only 13% of the people live in urban areas, as compared with about 76% in the US
- Uganda has one of the world's highest rates of HIV infection
- Rivalries between people of the diverse ethnic groups

has led to much bloodshed and instability
- Most Ugandan Asians were forced to leave the country in the early 1970s
- Before Europeans arrived, much of Uganda was divided into centralized kingdoms, such as Buganda, Bunyoro, Ankole, and Toro

KEY POINTS IN RECENT HISTORY

1962 Uganda becomes independent from Britain (October 9); Dr Milton Obote becomes prime minister
1963 The Kabaka (king) of Buganda is elected head of state
1966 Obote dismisses the kabaka; he becomes president, and abolishes the four kingdoms of Toro, Ankole, Buganda, and Bunyoro
1971 Idi Amin Dada seizes power
1972 Ugandan Asians expelled by Amin

1979 Amin is deposed with the help of Tanzanian troops and Obote is restored to power in 1980
1985 Obote is overthrown and, in 1986, guerrilla leader, Yoweri Museveni, takes power and restores order
1993 The four kingdoms are restored, but only as cultural institutions
1996 Museveni is reelected president
1998 Uganda supports rebel forces in the civil war in the Democratic Republic of Congo

THE NATION

Location: Landlocked nation in East Africa
Neighbors: Tanzania, Rwanda, Dem. Rep. of Congo, Sudan, Kenya
Official name: Republic of Uganda
Divisions: Thirty-eight districts
Capital: Kampala
Largest cities: Kampala, Jinja, Mbale, Masaka, Gulu, Entebbe, Soroti, Mbarara (in order of size)
Flag: The six horizontal stripes on the flag of Uganda are, from top to bottom, black, yellow, red, black, yellow, and red. The bird depicted within the white central disk is a crested crane, Uganda's national emblem
National anthem: "Oh, Uganda, may God uphold thee"

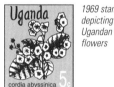

Black Yellow Red White

1969 stamp depicting Ugandan flowers

Major languages: Swahili, English (both official), Ganda, Luo, Nyoro
Currency: Shilling = 100 cents

GEOGRAPHY

lWith an area of 93,074 square miles (241,061 sq. km), Uganda is one of Africa's smaller countries. It is about the same size as Oregon in the United States (US).

Uganda lies mainly on the high East African plateau, east of an arm of the Great Rift Valley that contains lakes Edward and Albert. However, Uganda's largest lake, Victoria, is not in the Rift Valley but occupies a shallow depression in the plateau. The highest mountains are in the southwestern Ruwenzori Range, where Margherita Peak reaches a height of 16,762 ft (5,109 m) above sea level.

The chief river of Uganda is the Nile, which is the only outlet of Lake Victoria. Called the Victoria Nile when it leaves the lake, it flows through lakes Kyoga and Albert before flowing north, as the Albert Nile, into Sudan.

Uganda has an equatorial climate. The wettest region lies

north of Lake Victoria. Some rainforest grows in the south, but much of the original forest is now farmland. Wooded tropical savanna covers much of the center and north. Giant herbs grow to tree size along the Ruwenzori Range.

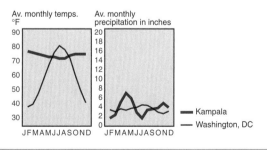

Av. monthly temps. °F

Av. monthly precipitation in inches

JFMAMJJASOND

Kampala
Washington, DC

ECONOMY

Chief farm products: Bananas, beans, cassava, coffee, corn, cotton, meat, sugar cane, tea, tobacco
Chief mineral resources: Gold, copper, tungsten
Chief industrial products: Beverages, cement, footwear, processed food, textiles
Exports: Coffee, cotton, gold, tea, tobacco, copper
Per capita income: $330 (as compared with $29,080 in the US)

Employment:

Services 10%
Industry 5%
Agriculture 85%

In the US, agriculture employs 3% of the work force, industry 26%, and services 71%

Zambia

PEOPLE

Ethnic groups: Alur (p 27), **Bemba** (p 51), **Lugbara** (p 131), **Mangbetu** (p 143), **Maravi** (p 143), **Ndembu** (p 161), **Pende** (p 179), **Songye** (p 191), **Suku** (p 194), **Tonga** (p 203)
Population: 9,443,000 (as compared with the US population of 267,636,000)
Religions: Christianity (72%), African religions (27%)

SOCIAL FACTS

- The average life expectancy at birth is 43 years, as compared with 76 years in the US
- Only 43% of the people live in urban areas, as compared with about 76% in the US
- Zambia is one of the world's top ten copper producers
- From 1911 until 1964, Zambia was called Northern Rhodesia, after the British imperialist Cecil Rhodes
- Zambia was named after the Zambezi, Africa's fourth longest river after the Nile, Congo (Zaire), and Niger rivers
- Woodcarving, basketry, and pottery are important art forms

KEY POINTS IN RECENT HISTORY

1924 Northern Rhodesia becomes a British territory
1953 The territory becomes part of the Central African Federation (CAF) with Southern Rhodesia and Nyasaland; many Africans oppose this step
1963 The CAF is dissolved
1964 The country becomes independent as Zambia (October 24); Kenneth Kaunda, leader of the United National Independent Party (UNIP), becomes president
1972 UNIP becomes sole legal party
1990 Opposition parties are legalized
1991 The Movement for Multiparty Democracy (MMD) defeats UNIP in parliamentary elections, and Frederick Chiluba defeats Kaunda in presidential elections
1996 Chiluba is reelected president

THE NATION

Location: Landlocked country in Central Africa
Neighbors: Tanzania, Malawi, Mozambique, Zimbabwe, Namibia, Angola, Dem. Rep. of Congo
Official name: Republic of Zambia
Divisions: Nine provinces
Capital: Lusaka
Largest cities: Lusaka, Ndola, Kitwe, Mufulira, Chingola (in order of size)
Flag: The background field of green stands for the country's natural resources. An orange eagle, top right, flies over three vertical stripes of red, for freedom; black, for the people; and orange, for Zambia's great mineral wealth
National anthem: "Stand and sing of Zambia, proud and free"

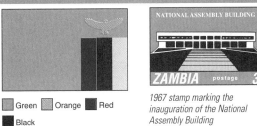

Green — Orange — Red — Black

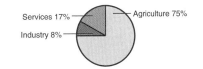

1967 stamp marking the inauguration of the National Assembly Building

Major languages: English (official), eight major African languages
Currency: Kwacha = 100 ngwee

GEOGRAPHY

With an area of 290,587 square miles (752,617 sq. km), Zambia is Africa's seventeenth largest country. It is nearly 1.1 times as large as Texas in the United States (US).

Zambia consists mainly of gently rolling plateaus from 3,000 to 5,000 ft (900–1,500 m) above sea level. The Muchinga Mountains, in the northeast along the Malawi border, have peaks topping 7,000 ft (2,100 m).

Southern Zambia is part of the Zambezi River basin. The Zambezi River has been dammed to create the artificial Lake Kariba along the border with Zimbabwe. There are several natural lakes in the north. Lake Bangweulu is fed by the Chambeshi River. Its outlet, the Luapula River, feeds Lake Mweru, which in turn is drained by the Luvua, a headwater of the Congo River.

Zambia lies within the tropics, but its altitude moderates temperatures. The rainy season runs from November to March, and the rainfall is highest in the north. Wooded tropical savanna covers much of Zambia, with swamps in some areas. The southwest has some evergreen forest.

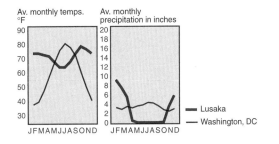

ECONOMY

Chief farm products: Cassava, corn, cotton, fruits, livestock, millet, peanuts, sorghum, soybeans, sugar cane, tobacco, vegetables, wheat
Chief mineral resources: Copper, zinc, cobalt, lead, silver, gold
Chief industrial products: Cement, processed food, refined metals, sulfuric acid
Exports: Copper, cobalt, zinc, tobacco, lead
Per capita income: $370 (as compared with $29,080 in the US)

Employment:

Services 17%
Industry 8%
Agriculture 75%

In the US, agriculture employs 3% of the work force, industry 26%, and services 71%

Zimbabwe

PEOPLE

Ethnic groups: **Matabele** (p 159), **Shona** (p 186), **Sotho** (p 191), **Tonga** (p 203), **Venda** (p 211)
Population: 11,468,000 (as compared with the US population of 267,636,000)
Religions: Christianity (45%), African religions (40%)

SOCIAL FACTS

- The average life expectancy at birth is 52 years, as compared with 76 years in the US
- Only 32% of the people live in urban areas, as compared with about 76% in the US
- Zimbabwe literally means "house of stone." Dry-wall (without mortar) structures, such as those at Great

Zimbabwe, are unique in Southern Africa. They were built by a historic Shona civilization
- Zimbabwe has one of the world's highest rates of HIV infection
- Zimbabwe was once called Southern Rhodesia and then Rhodesia, after the British imperialist Cecil Rhodes

KEY POINTS IN RECENT HISTORY

1923 The country becomes a British colony called Southern Rhodesia
1953 The country becomes part of the Central African Federation (CAF) with Southern Rhodesia and Nyasaland
1963 CAF is dissolved; Ian Smith becomes prime minister of Rhodesia (as the country is named when Northern Rhodesia becomes Zambia and Nyasaland becomes Malawi)
1965 The white government declares Rhodesia

independent (November 11), an action which is widely condemned as illegal
1970 Rhodesia becomes a republic
1970s Black African guerrillas fight for majority rule and independence
1980 The country becomes legally independent as Zimbabwe (April 18)
1996 Robert Mugabe wins a fourth successive term as president

THE NATION

Location: Landlocked nation in Southern Africa
Neighbors: Botswana, Zambia, Mozambique, South Africa
Official name: Republic of Zimbabwe
Divisions: Eight provinces and two cities with provincial status
Capital: Harare
Largest cities: Harare, Bulawayo, Chitungwiza, Mutare, Gweru (in order of size)
Flag: The flag of Zimbabwe has horizontal stripes of green, yellow, red, black, red, yellow, and green. The triangle on the left contains a star and a depiction of the Great Zimbabwe soapstone bird
National anthem: "Ishe komborarei Africa" ("God bless Africa")

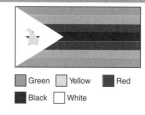

Green		Yellow		Red
Black		White		

1989 Stamp depicting the black rhinoceros, an endangered species

Major languages: English (official), Shona, Ndebele
Currency: Zimbabwe dollar = 100 cents

GEOGRAPHY

With an area of 150,873 square miles (390,760 sq. km), Zimbabwe is Africa's twenty-fifth largest country. It is about the same size as Montana in the United States (US).

The land consists mainly of plateaus. On either side of the central High Veld is a lower region, the Middle Veld. The smaller Low Veld consists of plains in the Limpopo, Sabi and Zambezi river basins. The Eastern Highlands contain the highest peak, Mount Inyangani, at 8,514 ft (2,595 m). Lake Kariba, which Zimbabwe shares with Zambia, was created when the Kariba Dam was built across the Zambezi.

The climate is tropical, but temperatures are moderated by the altitude. Summers (October to March) are generally hot and wet. Winters are cool and dry. Forests grow in wet

areas. such as the Eastern Highlands, with grasslands at higher levels. Woodland savanna covers most of the country.

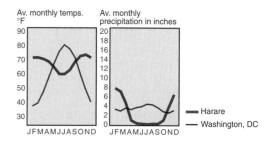

ECONOMY

Chief farm products: barley, beef, coffee, cotton, maize, millet, peanuts, sorghum, soybeans, sugar, sunflower seeds, tea, tobacco, wheat
Chief mineral resources: Gold, asbestos, nickel, chromium
Chief industrial products: metal and wood products, processed food, textiles
Chief exports: Metals and metal products, tobacco
Per capita income: $720 (as compared with $29,080 in the US)

Employment:

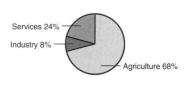

Services 24%
Industry 8%
Agriculture 68%

In the US, agriculture employs 3% of the work force, industry 26%, and services 71%

SECTION 4

BIOGRAPHIES

Sanni Abacha

Abd al Kadir

Abacha, General Sanni (1943–1998)

Sanni Abacha became head of Nigeria's military government in November 1993. His postponement of the return to civilian rule, together with alleged abuses of human rights, provoked international criticism. In 1995, Nigeria's membership of the Commonwealth was suspended after the execution of nine political dissidents, including KEN SARO-WIWA. His successor, General Abdulsalami Abubakar, pushed ahead with the restoration of civilian rule.

Abbas, Ferhat (1899–1985)

One of the leaders of Algeria's fight for independence, Ferhat Abbas was the first president of the Algerian provisional government in exile (1958–61). He also served as president of Algeria's National Assembly (1962–4), until differences with AHMED BEN BELLA led to his resignation and house arrest (1964–5). Abbas was rehabilitated shortly before he died.

Abd al Kadir (1807–1883)

Abd al Kadir, Emir (ruler) of Oran, led the resistance to the French conquest of Algeria. He fought the French from 1832, scoring several victories, but was eventually defeated and surrendered in 1847. Imprisoned in France, he was freed by Emperor Napoleon III in 1852 and died in Damascus, Syria.

Abd al Krim (1882–1963)

A Berber chief and a great Moroccan resistance fighter, Abd al Krim – "the Wolf of the Rif Mountains" – was founder and president of the Republic of the Rif (1921–6). He was defeated by a combined French and Spanish army of 250,000 troops in May 1926, and exiled to the island of Réunion in the Indian Ocean. He was freed in 1947 and went to Egypt.

Abd al Mumin (c. 1094–1163)

Abd al Mumin was a Berber chief who founded the Almohad dynasty in North Africa. He succeeded IBN TUMART, founder of the Almohad sect, and proclaimed himself caliph (ruler) of the dynasty. He overthrew the Almoravid dynasty, conquered Morocco, Tunis, and Tripoli, and paved the way for the Almohad conquest of Islamic Spain.

Abdullah, Ahmad (1919–1989)

Ahmad Abdullah became the first head of state of the Comoros in 1975, but later that year he was deposed in a coup. He was elected president after another coup in 1978, made the Comoros into an Islamic one-party state, and was reelected in 1984. In 1989, he was assassinated by his presidential guard and succeeded by SAID MUHAMMAD DJOHAR.

Abeni, Queen Salawo (born 1965)

Queen Salawo Abeni is a Nigerian singing prodigy who recorded her first album, *The Late Murtala Mohammed*, at the age of twelve. She specializes in Waka, a singing style featuring a female vocalist and drums. She sings mostly in the Yoruba language.

Abiodan, Dele (born 1955)

A Nigerian singer and composer, Dele Abiodan created the style called Adawa, a mixture of Afro-Beat and juju, a Yoruba music style based on guitars. It includes talking drums and the Hawaiian steel guitar.

Abiola, Chief Moshood (1938–1998)

Chief Abiola, a Yoruba Muslim, led the Social Democratic Party to victory in elections in Nigeria in 1993, but the military government suspended the results and, in 1994, he was arrested and charged with treason. He was replaced by the dictator General SANNI ABACHA. Abiola's wife Kudirat – a campaigner for the restoration of democracy in Nigeria – was murdered in 1996.

Abrahams, Peter (born 1919)

Peter Abrahams is a major South African novelist who wrote about the political struggles of black people, notably in *A Wreath for Udomo* (1956), *The View from Coyaba* (1985), and *Tell Freedom* (1954), his autobiography. He left South Africa at the age of twenty and wrote most of his works in exile.

Achebe, Chinua (born 1930)

A Nigerian poet and novelist, Chinua Achebe won the Commonwealth Prize for his book *Beware, Soul Brother* (1971). He is probably the most widely-read African writer, and his *Things Fall Apart* (1958) has been translated into over forty languages.

Ade, King Sunny Adeniyi (born 1947)

Now a world-famous musician, King Sunny Ade came from a Yoruba royal family and was one of the leaders of the Nigerian juju music craze of the 1980s. He was greatly influenced by IK DAIRO, one of the founders of juju (which came from an amalgamation of a kind of African blues with traditional Yoruba music).

King Sunny Ade

Afewerki, Issaias (born 1945)

Afewerki was a former guerrilla leader in the struggle against the Ethiopian government of HAILE MENGISTU MARIAM. He secretary-general of the Eritrean People's Liberation Front and was elected president of Eritrea in May, 1993, when the country became independent. He was reelected in 1997.

Africanus, Leo see **Leo Africanus**

Ahidjo, Ahmadou (1924–1989)

As prime minister of Cameroon (1958–60), Ahmadou Ahidjo led his country to independence and was its first president (1960–82). He achieved the complex task of uniting the French- and English-speaking parts of the country. In November 1982, he resigned the presidency and handed over his responsibilities to the prime minister, PAUL BIYA. In 1983, he went into exile in France.

Aideed, Muhammad Farrah (1934–1996)

A soldier and former diplomat, Muhammad Farrah Aideed was the best-known of the clan leaders who struggled for power in Somalia in the 1990s. He became internationally famous when his militia killed members of the United Nations peacekeeping mission, forcing it to withdraw. Aideed declared himself president of Somalia in 1995 but died as a result of fighting in 1996.

Aidoo, Ama Ata (born 1942)

Ama Ata Aidoo is a Ghanaian writer noted for her novels, plays, and poems about women in modern Africa. A chief's daughter, for twelve years she was a university professor of English. She lived in Zimbabwe for some time, but moved to the United States in the 1990s.

Akendengue, Pierre (born 1944)

Pierre Akendengue, a Gabonese musician, was forced into exile in 1972 after criticizing his country's government. He studied literature and psychology at French universities, but then lost his sight. *Nandipo*, the first major recording by his band, blended music, poetry, and politics, with both traditional and modern instruments providing the backing. He received a presidential pardon in 1977.

Al Hajj Umar (1794–1864)

Al Hajj Umar, born Umar Said Tall in Futa Toro, northern Senegal, was the Fulani Muslim leader who founded the Tukolor Empire. In the 1840s, he established a fortress in the the town of Dinguiray (in present-day Guinea), where he trained and armed a powerful army. From there, in 1852, he began a jihad (Islamic holy war) during which he conquered the West African states of Kaarta, Segu, and Macina, but was driven out of Futa Toro by the French. In 1864, he was killed during a battle with Fulani, Bambara, and Tuareg forces who had rebelled against his rule and besieged the Macina town of Hamdullahi.

Alkali, Zaynab (born 1950)

Zaynab Alkali was the first woman novelist from northern Nigeria. She was born in Borno State to an Islamic family, but was brought up in a Christian community in eastern Nigeria. Her first novel, *The Stillborn* (1984), dealt with the ambitions of women in a male-dominated world.

Amin Dada, Idi (born 1925)

Commander of Uganda's army from 1968, Idi Amin seized power in January 1971. On becoming president of the country, he declared himself champion for life. His regime was harsh and brutal, and he murdered thousands of his opponents and expelled Uganda's Asian population. Amin was deposed by rebels led by YOWERI MUSEVENI and backed by the Tanzanian army in 1979 and fled into exile, finally settling in Saudi Arabia. Amin was once the heavyweight boxing champion of Uganda, a title he held from 1951 to 1969.

Idi Amin

Ampadu, Kwame (born c. 1946)

A leader of Ghanaian popular music (1965–75), Kwame Ampadu dominated the guitar-based highlife style. This style relies on traditional African sources and jazz influences. "Nana" ("King") Ampadu, as he became known, formed the African Brother International band, which became the premier band in Ghana.

Annan, Kofi Atta (born 1938)

On January 1, 1997, Annan became Secretary-General of the United Nations, the first to have come from Africa south of the Sahara. Born in Kumasi, Ghana (then the Gold Coast), he worked for the UN from 1962, except for two years when he was head of the Ghana Tourist Development Company. From March 1, 1993, he was under-secretary-general of peace-keeping operations and worked in Somalia and Bosnia-Herzegovina.

Anthony of Egypt (or Thebes or Memphis), Saint (c. 250–356)

Saint Anthony was an Egyptian Copt who founded the first Christian monastery. From the age of twenty, he lived as a hermit near the Red Sea, and in 305, he organized his fellow hermits into a monastery. At the age of one hundred he preached against false beliefs in Alexandria.

Aouita, Said (born 1959)

Said Aouita, a Moroccan runner, won gold in the 5,000 meters finals in the 1984 Los Angeles Olympics. Over the next four years, he broke the world records for 2,000 meters, 1,500 meters, and 5,000 meters.

Arabi, Ahmad (Arabi Pasha) (1839–1911)

Ahmad Arabi, an Egyptian soldier and revolutionary popularly known as Arabi Pasha, led a rebellion to overthrow the Egyptian rulers Ismail Pasha in 1879 and Tewfik Pasha in 1881. Britain invaded Egypt in 1882 to maintain control of the Suez Canal, and defeated him at the Battle of Tell al Kebir. The British captured him and tried him for sedition, exiling him to Ceylon (now Sri Lanka) until 1901.

Armatto, Raphael Ernest Grail Glikpo (1913–1953)

Raphael Armatto was born in Togoland, now part of Ghana, and was one of Ghana's leading poets. His work describes the African experience in colonial times. He studied medicine in Scotland and Germany, anthropology and French literature in France, and worked as a doctor in Northern Ireland.

Asabia (born 1957)

Asabia (Eugenia Asabia Cropper) is a Ghanaian singer and saxophonist. She turned professional after a successful tour of Togo as an amateur singer and has performed with several bands, preferring to work in her homeland.

Askia Muhammad (c. 1450–1528)

In 1493, Muhammad Toure seized the throne of the Songhay Empire (in present-day Mali) and took the title of Askia ("Usurper"). A devout Muslim, he overthrew the non-Muslim Sunni Baru, the son of SUNNI ALI, who rebuilt Songhay after its domination by the Empire of Mali. Muhammad greatly extended the empire and made it prosperous, but was deposed and exiled by his eldest son in 1528.

Awolowo, Obafemi (1909–87)

A major Yoruba leader, Nigerian statesman, and influential writer, Obafemi Awolowo was premier of Nigeria's Western Region (1954–9) and leader of the opposition in the federal parliament (1960–2) after independence. In 1962, Awolowo and other opposition leaders were arrested on charges of treasonable felony. Awolowo was eventually jailed.

Awoonor, Kofi Niydevu (born 1935)

Kofi Awoonor is a leading West African writer in Ewe and English. His poems and novels reflect African cultural traditions, especially those of the Ewe people. He was a university professor both in the United States (1967–75) and in Ghana, and has won prizes for his poetry and written histories of Ghana and studies of African literature.

Azikiwe, Nnamdi (1904–96)

Nnamdi Azikiwe was Nigeria's first president, from 1963 until 1966. In 1937, he took a leading part in the Nigerian nationalist movement, becoming president of the National Council of Nigeria and the Cameroons. He became prime minister of the eastern region (1954–9) and Governor-General of Nigeria (1960–3). During the Biafran (Nigerian Civil) War (1967–70), he first acted as spokesman for his fellow Igbo people, but he later supported the federal government.

Mariama Ba

Ba, Mariama (1929–81)

A Senegalese teacher and champion of women's rights, Mariama Ba sprang to fame with her prizewinning first novel *Une Si Longue Lettre* (1979). She died just as her second novel, *Le Chante Ecarlate*, was about to be published. Separated from her politician husband, Obeye Diop, she raised her nine children singlehanded.

Babangida, Ibrahim Badanosi (born 1941)

In 1985, as commander-in-chief of the army, Ibrahim Babangida led a coup against President Buhari and assumed the presidency himself. He held office until 1993, when, after declaring void the results of a general election won by Chief MOSHOOD ABIOLA, he stood down in favor of a nonelected interim government.

Balewa, Sir Abubakar Tafawa (1912–1966)

Abubakar Tafawa Balewa was elected first federal prime minister of Nigeria in 1959. A Muslim northerner, he was spokesman for the Northern People's Congress (NPC). The NPC was determined that a federal Nigeria would not be dominated by Western-educated southerners, and argued for official recognition of Islam and for at least half of federal representatives to be northerners. He was knighted when Nigeria became independent in 1960, and assassinated in January 1966 during a military coup.

Sir Abubakar Balewa

Ballinger, Margaret Hodgson (1894–1980)

Ballinger was a Scottish-born South African lecturer and a campaigner against apartheid. She also did pioneering historical research at the University of Witwatersrand. She and ALAN PATON formed the Liberal Party in 1953, and for many years she was one of four whites elected to represent black South Africans in parliament. She retired from politics by 1960 and devoted herself to campaigning for African women's rights.

Banda, Dr Hastings Kamuzu (c. 1902–1997)

Hastings Banda was appointed prime minister of Malawi in 1963 and president in 1966. His policies contrasted strongly with the socialist aims of some of his neighbors, and he encouraged officials to follow his example in buying farms and investing in businesses. He was voted "president-for-life" in July 1971, but that title was withdrawn when multiparty government was restored in 1993. He lost the 1994 elections and Bakili Muluzi became president. In 1995, he was cleared of murdering four of his former ministers.

Barnard, Dr Christiaan Neethling (born 1922)

Christiaan Barnard, a South African surgeon, performed the world's first human heart transplant, in 1967. The patient, Louis Washkansky, died of pneumonia eighteen days later, but other patients lived much longer. Barnard studied in South Africa and at the University of Minnesota. His books include an autobiography and works on medicine.

Bashir, Omar Hassan Ahmad al- (born 1944)

Brigadier-General (later Lieutenant-General) Omar al-Bashir overthrew Sudan's civilian government led by Sadiq al-Mahdi in June 1989. He served as president of the Revolutionary Command Council for National Salvation and, in 1993, he was appointed president of Sudan. He was reelected in 1996.

Bédié, Henri Konan (born 1934)

Bédié succeeded FÉLIX HOUPHOUËT-BOIGNY as president of Côte d'Ivoire in December 1993. The formerly speaker of the country's National Assembly, he was re-elected president of Cote d'Ivoire in 1996. Before entering politics, Bedie served in the diplomatic service and was Ambassador in the United States and Canada in the 1960s.

Bekederemo, John Pepper Clark (born 1936)

John Bekederemo is one of Nigeria's leading writers and was professor of English at the University of Lagos until 1980. The son of an Ijaw chief, he wrote under the name "John Pepper Clark" for some years, reverting to his full name in 1985. His most important work is *The Ozidi Saga* (1976), a series of plays based on Ijaw epic drama.

Ben Ali, Zine al Abidine (born 1936)

In a peaceful takeover in November 1987, Zine al Abidine Ben Ali, prime minister of Tunisia since early October, replaced former President HABIB BOURGUIBA as head of state. He was reelected in 1989 and 1994. His government has been criticized for abuses of human rights, but praised for its economic reforms.

Ben Bella, Muhammad Ahmad (born 1916)

The first prime minister of Algeria (1962–3), Ahmad Ben Bella became the first elected president, in 1963. His dictatorial style of government aroused opposition, and he was deposed and arrested in a bloodless military coup in 1965, led by HOUARI BOUMEDIENNE. He was detained until 1979. One of the leaders of the struggle for Algerian independence, Ben Bella was twice imprisoned by the French (1950–2 and 1956–62).

Beti, Mongo (born 1932)

Mongo Beti (real name Alexandre Biyidi) is one of Cameroon's leading writers, and his novels reflect the adverse effects of colonialism on African ways of life. He uses the French language, having studied at the Sorbonne in Paris, where he obtained a doctorate in literature. His best-known novel is *Poor Christ of Bomba* (1965), about a missionary's failure to understand African culture.

Bikila, Abebe (1932–73)

Abebe Bikila, the great Ethiopian marathon runner, then virtually unknown and running barefoot, won the gold medal in the marathon at the 1960 Rome Olympics. He was the first Black African to do so and also set a new world record time of 2 hrs 15 mins 16.2 secs. He went on to take gold at the 1964 Tokyo Olympics, where he again set a new world record, of 2 hrs 12 mins 11.2 secs. He was paralyzed in an automobile accident in 1969, but became a paraplegic athlete (archery and javelin) and founded the Ethiopian Paraplegic Sports Association.

Biko, Steve (Stephan Bantu) (1946–1977)

A founder of South Africa's Black Consciousness movement, Steve Biko was the first president of the all-black South African Students' Organization. He was also an organizer of the Black Community Program, which encouraged black pride and opposition to apartheid, and the government banned him from political activity in 1973. He died of head injuries while in police custody.

Biya, Paul (born 1933)

Paul Biya, prime minister of Cameroon (1975–82), became the country's second president when AHMADOU AHIDJO resigned in 1982. He survived a coup attempt in 1984, which caused considerable loss of life, and after widespread protest, he legalized opposition parties in 1991. Biya was reelected president in an uncontested election in 1988 and in multiparty elections in 1992.

Hastings Banda

Steve Biko

Jean-Bédel Bokassa

P. W. Botha

Hassiba Boulmerka

Houari Boumedienne

Boutros Boutros-Ghali

Blondy, Alpha (born 1953)

An Ivory Coast singer and composer, Alpha Blondy was greatly influenced by the reggae music of the West Indies. He studied trade and English at Columbia University in the United States, but was sent to a psychiatric hospital for two years by his parents when he returned home a Rastafarian. He sings in English, French, and the Dyula language of his mother.

Blyden, Edward Wilmot (1832–1912)

Edward Blyden was born in the Virgin Islands, but became a professor and major political leader in Liberia, where he settled in 1853. He served as secretary of state there (1864–6), but had to flee to Sierra Leone when his enemies tried to lynch him. He campaigned for African unity and opposed the idea of white superiority.

Bokassa, Jean-Bédel (1921–96)

As the Central African Republic's supreme military commander, Bokassa seized power from DAVID DACKO in 1966 and served as president until 1976, when he made himself "Emperor" of the "Central African Empire." His rule was harsh and dictatorial and he was responsible for many deaths, including those of children. The republic was restored by a coup in 1979, led by Dacko, and Bokassa went into exile. He returned in 1986 and served six years in prison for murder and fraud before dying from a heart attack in 1996.

Bongo, Omar (born 1935)

Omar (formerly Albert-Bernard) Bongo has been president of Gabon since 1967. He also served as prime minister from 1968 until 1976. He made Gabon a one-party state in 1968, and despite some discontent, the country retained its political stability until the late 1980s, when increasing unrest forced a switch to multiparty politics in 1990.

Botha, P. W. (Pieter Willem) (born 1916)

Botha was prime minister (1978–84) and then president (1984–9) of South Africa. His attempts to modify apartheid while maintaining white supremacy alienated the right wing of his National Party, while failing to satisfy black or international opposition to apartheid. He resigned, unwillingly, in 1989 and was replaced by F. W. DE KLERK.

Boulmerka, Hassiba (born 1968)

After becoming the first Algerian to win a world running championship in 1991, Hassiba Boulmerka was denounced by Muslim clerics for "running with naked legs in front of men." Despite this criticism, she went on to take gold in the 1,500 meters at the 1992 Barcelona Olympics.

Boumedienne, Houari (1925–1978)

Boumedienne replaced BEN BELLA as president of Algeria after a coup in 1965. He established an Islamic socialist government and served as president until 1978. Before independence, he had led guerrilla operations against the French.

Bourguiba, Habib ibn Ali (born 1903)

A radical nationalist, Habib Bourguiba was Tunisia's first prime minister (1956–7) and its first president (1957–87). He attempted to curb Islamic fundamentalists during his years as president and maintained moderate, pro-Western foreign policies. He was declared president-for-life in 1975, but was deposed by his prime minister, BEN ALI, in 1987 on the grounds that he was unfit to continue due to senility and ill-health.

Boutros-Ghali, Boutros (born 1922)

In 1992, Boutros-Ghali, an Egyptian, became the first African Secretary-General of the United Nations. Egypt regarded his appointment as recognition of its moderating influence in the region. He had earlier served in the Egyptian government as deputy prime minister and, as foreign minister, he helped to win Arab support for the 1991 Gulf War. He was succeeded as Secretary-General by KOFI ATTA ANNAN on January 1, 1997.

Brink, André (born 1935)

André Brink is a dissident South African writer who caused a sensation in the 1960s with his politically inspired novels in Afrikaans, which won widespread acclaim in English translation. *Kennis van die aand* (1973), which he translated as *Looking on Darkness*, was banned by the South African government. He won the Martin Luther King Memorial Prize in 1980.

Brutus, Dennis (born 1924)

Dennis Brutus, a South African poet of mixed parentage, had his works banned by the government in the 1960s because of his antiapartheid views. He was arrested, shot in the back while trying to escape, and then jailed. He went into exile in 1966, settling first in England and then the United States. His *Letters to Martha* are poems written while in prison.

Buthelezi, Chief Mangosuthu Gatsha (born 1928)

A member of Zulu nobility, Chief Buthelezi became chief executive in the KwaZulu "homeland" in South Africa in the early 1970s. At first a supporter of the African National Congress (ANC), he later formed the Zulu Inkatha movement, which developed into the Inkatha Freedom Party (IFP). This party, which favors maximum autonomy for KwaZulu/Natal (formerly KwaZulu) province, won the provincial elections in 1994, but it finished third in the national elections. Buthelezi then became Minister for Home Affairs in the new South African government.

Chief Buthelezi

Buyoya, Pierre (born 1949)

A Tutsi army officer, Pierre Buyoya became president in Burundi in 1987, displacing Jean-Baptiste Bagaza. In 1993, Buyoya was defeated in multiparty elections, but his successor, a Hutu named Melchior Ndadaye, was assassinated later that year, sparking off widespread ethnic conflict. Buyoya again became president in 1996 displacing the Hutu president Sylvestre Ntibantunganyu.

Cabral, Amílcar (1931–1973)

Leader of the independence struggle against Portuguese rule in Guinea-Bissau, Amílcar Cabral was assassinated in 1973. He was the founder of the independence movement Partido Africano da Independência do Guiné e Cabo Verde (PAIGC) in 1956.

Cabral, Luiz (born 1929)

Brother of AMÍLCAR CABRAL and a prominent leader in the independence struggle, Luiz Cabral became the first president of Guinea-Bissau in 1974. Cabral promoted the interests of Cape Verdeans in Guinea-Bissau while allowing the economy to decline. He was overthrown in a coup led by the prime minister, joão vieira, in 1980.

Cetshwayo (c. 1826–1884)

Cetshwayo, a nephew of the great Zulu leader SHAKA, ruled the Zulu kingdom from 1872 and resisted British and Boer colonialism. In 1879, he defeated the British at Isandhlwana but was later defeated and captured at Ulundi. Part of his kingdom was restored to him in 1883, but soon after he was driven out by an antiroyalist faction.

Cetshwayo

Cheops *see* Khufu

Chilembwe, John (c. 1860–1915)

John Chilembwe, a Baptist minister, studied theology in the United States and founded the Providence Industrial Mission at Mbombwe, Nyasaland in 1900, which set up seven schools. In 1915, he led an attack against British rule in Nyasaland (now Malawi). This attack was provoked by the cruelty of white plantation owners. It failed, and Chilembwe was captured and shot.

Chiluba, Frederick (born 1943)

Frederick Chiluba, a former labor leader, became the second president of Zambia by defeating KENNETH KAUNDA in multiparty presidential elections in 1991. His Movement for Multiparty Democracy (MMD) party also won the majority of seats in the National Assembly elections.

Chipenda, Daniel (1931–1996)

From l962, Daniel Chipenda was a prominent guerrilla leader of the Movimento Popular de Libertação de Angola (MPLA) in the independence struggle against the Portuguese. In 1975, the MPLA split and Chipenda became allied with the rival Frente Nacional de Libertação de Angola (FNLA). Following the defeat of the FNLA by the MPLA, Chipenda went into exile in Portugal. He returned to Angola in 1992 and tried to negotiate peace in the ongoing civil war. He managed to make peace with rebel leader JONAS SAVIMBI, and attempted to mediate between him and Angolan president JOSÉ EDUARDO DOS SANTOS.

Chissano, Joaquim Alberto (born 1939)

Joaquim Chissano became prime minister of Mozambique in 1974 and president in 1986. He took over as president after the death of SAMORA MACHEL, with whom he had worked closely in the Frente de Libertação de Moçambique (Frelimo) during its fight against Portuguese colonial rule. In 1992, he signed a peace treaty with AFONSO DHLAKAMA, leader of the rebel Resistência Nacional Moçambicana (Renamo). Chissano was reelected president in multiparty elections in 1994.

Cleopatra VII (69–30 BCE)

Cleopatra VII was the last of the Ptolemy dynasty (who were of Macedonian (Greek) origin) to rule Egypt. She took a great interest in her subjects' welfare and won their affection. Cleopatra became queen in 51 BCE but was deposed by supporters of her husband (and younger brother), Ptolemy XIII. She was restored to the throne in 47 BCE by Julius Caesar, a Roman general. Later, she became the lover of another Roman general, Mark Antony. They set up an empire based on Egypt, but were defeated by the Romans at the naval Battle of Actium (31 BCE). In 30 BCE, Antony committed suicide after hearing a false report that Cleopatra had died. Later that year, Cleopatra – unable to save her dynasty – also committed suicide, supposedly by causing a poisonous snake to bite her breast.

Cleopatra VII

Lansana Conté

Samuel Ajayi Crowther

F. W. de Klerk

Coetzee, J. M. (John Michael) (born 1940)

Coetzee, an Afrikaner, is a South African academic and novelist who has won many literary prizes for his vivid novels, which deal with social and political themes. Among them, *Life and Times of Michael K* (1983), which won the Booker Prize in Britain, is outstanding. Coetzee also won the Jerusalem Prize in 1987 for his opposition to apartheid.

Compaoré, Captain Blaise (born 1951)

Blaise Compaoré became president of Burkina Faso after a coup in 1987 and was reelected in 1991. In 1983, he had helped to organize the coup that brought his predecessor, THOMAS SANKARA, to power. Sankara was killed in the 1987 coup, a fact that made Compaoré widely unpopular.

Conté, Lansana (born 1945)

Lansana Conté took power in Guinea in 1984, when he led a bloodless coup a few days after the death of the first president, SEKOU TOURÉ. At first, he introduced liberal policies, but after a failed coup in 1985, he adopted a more repressive approach. After the introduction of a multiparty system in 1991, he was elected president in 1993. In 1996, he survived a crisis when the army mutinied over pay.

Crowther, Bishop Samuel Ajayi (c. 1809–1891)

Samuel Crowther was a pioneer of Yoruba language studies and the first West African to become a bishop. A Creole born in Yorubaland, in what is now Nigeria, he was captured by slave traders in 1819 but rescued and freed by the British in 1822. He was ordained as a priest in London in 1825 and returned to Yorubaland as a missionary. Crowther became Bishop of Niger in 1864 and translated the Bible into Yoruba. He also wrote *Grammar and Vocabulary of the Yoruba Language*.

Dacko, David (born 1930)

In 1960, David Dacko became the first president of the Central African Republic. He was deposed in a coup led by his nephew JEAN-BÉDEL BOKASSA in 1966 and placed under house arrest, but he returned to office when he overthrew Bokassa, with French assistance, in a popular bloodless coup in 1979. Although committed to political liberalization, Dacko attempted to curb opposition parties. After reports of ill-health, he was persuaded to hand over power to a military government, led by ANDRÉ KOLINGBA, in 1981.

Dadié, Bernard Binlin (born 1916)

Bernard Dadié is a militant Ivory Coast nationalist who combined a career as a politician with a huge volume of writing. His output included essays, novels, plays (often satirical), poetry, and short stories, greatly influenced by folk tales. He served as Ivory Coast's Minister of Cultural Affairs from 1977 to 1986.

Dairo, IK (Isaiah Kehinde) (1931–1996)

IK Dairo was one of the founders of modern Nigerian juju music. In 1956, he formed the Morning Star Band (later the Blue Spots Band), in which he played guitar, talking drum, and accordion. He often toured overseas, and was made a Member of the Order of the British Empire by Queen Elizabeth II. A devout Christian, he founded the Eternal Sacred Order Church in Lagos. For a year, he was visiting professor of African music at Washington State University, Seattle.

Darko, George (born 1951)

George Darko is a Ghanaian guitarist who scored a hit when he blended two styles: highlife (a mixture of African dance music with Western music) and funk (a form of modern jazz). He won international fame when he toured the United States and Europe with his band, Bus Stop.

de Klerk, F. W. (Frederik Willem) (born 1936)

F. W. de Klerk succeeded P. W. BOTHA as president of South Africa in 1989. Under his leadership, the racial policies of apartheid were swiftly dismantled. The release of NELSON MANDELA in 1990 led to multiracial negotiations and elections in 1994, when a multiparty government was set up. Mandela became president and THABO MBEKI and de Klerk became deputy presidents. De Klerk shared the 1993 Nobel Peace Prize with Nelson Mandela.

Dempster, Roland Tombekai (1910–1965)

Roland Dempster was Liberia's first poet laureate. His poetry, published in several books, echoes the forms and manners of the English classics. Dempster was successively a civil servant, a journalist, and finally a professor at the University of Liberia.

Dhlakama, Afonso (born 1953)

In 1982, Afonso Dhlakama became president of the Resistência Nacional Moçambicana (Renamo), a guerrilla force founded in 1976, with Rhodesian and later South African support, to destabilize Mozambique. A former member of the Frente de Libertação de Moçambique (Frelimo), which had fought for Mozambique's independence from Portuguese colonial rule, he joined Renamo shortly after it was formed.

Dhlomo, Herbert Isaac Ernest (1903–1956)

Herbert Dhlomo was a Zulu novelist, playwright, and poet who wrote in both Zulu and English. His poetry reflects his anger at the plight of the Zulu people under white rule. Dhlomo was successively a school teacher and a journalist, and was a great influence on other Zulu writers in English. He was the younger brother of ROLFUS DHLOMO.

Dhlomo, Rolfus Reginald Raymond (1901–1971)

Rolfus Dhlomo wrote what is believed to be the first novel in English by a Zulu writer, *An African Tragedy* (1928). Most of his other novels were historical stories written in the Zulu language. Dhlomo, the elder brother of HERBERT DHLOMO, spent most of his life as a journalist.

Dibango, Manu (born 1933)

Manu Dibango, a Cameroonian saxophonist, pianist, and composer, dominated African music for more than fifty years. He studied classical music in Paris, then switched to jazz, playing in Belgium, Zaire, and New York City, NY.

Dingane (died c. 1840)

In 1828, after he and his brother Mhlangane assassinated their half-brother SHAKA, Dingane killed Mhlangane and proclaimed himself king of the Zulu. In 1838 he made a pact with PIET RETIEF, one of the Boer leaders of the Great Trek, then treacherously killed the Boers. A few months later, the Boers routed the Zulus at the Battle of Blood River and Dingane fled to Swaziland, where his half-brother Mpande killed him.

Manu Dibango

Dingiswayo (c. 1770–1818)

Dingiswayo was ruler of Mthethwa, a kingdom that dominated present-day KwaZulu/Natal in the late 1700s and early 1800s. He became overlord of thirty chiefdoms, including the Zulu chiefdom ruled by SHAKA, one of his generals and military advisors. He was killed when his army was defeated by that of a neighboring kingdom, Ndwandwe, in 1818. This defeat led to the breakup of the Mthethwa kingdom and the rapid expansion of Zulu power.

Diop, Alioune (1910–1980)

Alioune Diop was a Senegalese writer who founded the journal *Présence Africaine*. Many African political leaders wrote for it, and it was published in Paris, where Diop was senator for Senegal and worked as a professor of classical literature.

Diop, Bigaro Ismail (1906–1989)

Bigaro Diop was a Senegalese poet who popularized the traditional folk tales of the Wolof people. He qualified as a veterinarian in France, then set up in practice in what was then French West Africa. He worked in Paris, France from 1942 until 1944.

Diori, Hamani (1916–1989)

Hamani Diori became the first president of Niger when the country gained independence from France in 1960. After an assassination attempt in 1965, Diori harshly repressed criticism of his regime, but when Niger was badly hit by drought in 1973, some of his ministers were found with stocks of food and accused of hoarding food aid and selling it at inflated prices. In 1974, amid accusations of high-level corruption, Diori was overthrown by Seyni Kountché in a military coup and imprisoned (his wife died during the fighting). He was released from prison in 1980, but stayed under house arrest until 1984.

Diouf, Abdou (born 1935)

Abdou Diouf became Senegal's first prime minister from 1970 until 1981, when he succeeded LÉOPOLD SÉDAR SENGHOR as president. Diouf set about reorganizing Senegal's political system and allowed opposition parties to proliferate. In 1981, he used Senegalese troops to reinstate the Gambian president, Alhaji Sir DAWDA JAWARA, who had been ousted by a military coup. In 1982, Diouf and Jawara united their countries to form the confederation of Senegambia, with Diouf as president. He was elected president of Senegal in his own right in 1983 and reelected in 1988 and 1993. The Senegambia confederation dissolved in 1989.

Djohar, Said Muhammad (born 1918)

Said Djohar, head of the Comoros Supreme Court, became interim president of the country in 1989, following the assassination of AHMAD ABDULLAH. Elected in 1990, Djohar sought to balance the ethnic and political factions in his country. In 1995, he fled after a failed coup and returned in 1996 to be given a symbolic position, but only after he agreed not to contest the elections.

Doe, Samuel Kenyon (1951–1990)

A former army sergeant, Samuel Doe became president of Liberia in 1980, following a military coup in which President WILLIAM TOLBERT was killed. Doe was elected president in 1985, despite allegations of vote rigging, and he was accused of human rights abuses. A civil war broke out in 1989. In 1990, Doe, a member of the Krahn people, was captured, tortured, and killed by a rival group. His death led to the escalation of Liberia's civil war.

Samuel Doe

Dollar Brand *see* Ibrahim, Abdullah

dos Santos, José Eduardo (born 1942)

Dos Santos became president of Angola on the death of ANTONIO AGOSTINHO NETO in 1979. He was reelected in 1985 and 1992, and in 1994–5 negotiated the end of the war with South African-backed rebels.

Ekwensi, Cyprian Odiatu Duaka (born 1921)

Cyprian Ekwensi is a Nigerian novelist who took as his main theme immoral lives of some African city-dwellers. This was the theme of his first major novel, *People of the City* (1954). He also wrote children's books. He studied pharmacy in England and taught it in Nigeria. After supporting the Biafran rebellion of 1967–70, he returned to pharmacy as a career, while continuing to write.

El Anatsu (born 1944)

El Anatsu is a Ghanaian-born sculptor who has won wide acclaim for his innovative approach to woods and styles. He studied at the University of Science and Technology at Kumasi, Ghana, served as artist-in-residence at the Community of Arts in Cummington, Massachusetts, in 1987, and then became sculpture professor at the University of Nigeria.

Emecheta, Buchi Florence Onye (born 1944)

Buchi Emecheta is an Igbo Nigerian novelist who uses the position of women in Africa today as her central theme. She married at sixteen and moved to London, England in 1962, but her marriage broke up and she raised her five children on her own. Among her best books is *The Bride Price* (1976), whose theme is Nigerian marriage taboos. In *The Family* (1990), she deals with the problems black people and single mothers face in Western society.

Buchi Emecheta

Emin Pasha, Mehmed (1840–1892)

Emin Pasha was born in Germany and originally named Eduard Schnitzer. He adopted the name Mehmed Emin in Albania in 1865, when he became a Muslim, and later became Pasha (administrator) of Equatorial Province in Sudan. An explorer and physician, Emin Pasha was also a skilled linguist and his studies added enormously to the knowledge of African languages. He also wrote valuable geographical papers and collected many specimens of African flora and fauna. He fought against slavery and was murdered by Arab slave traders at Stanley Falls (now Boyoma Falls, Zaire).

Eyadéma, Gnassingbe (formerly Etienne) (born 1937)

Following a bloodless coup in 1967, Gnassingbe Eyadéma – who had served in the French army – became president of Togo, ousting NICOLAS GRUNITZKY. In 1969, he set up the Rassemblement du Peuple Togolais (RPT), which later became the sole political party. He was reelected president under a new constitution in l993. An unpopular leader, he has begun to make Togo's political system more democratic but there have been many attempts to overthrow him.

Farah, Nuruddin (born 1945)

Nuruddin Farah is Somalia's leading modern writer. After studying in Somalia and India, he worked in Somalia, but emigrated to Europe when his writings were censored. He is best known for his novels in English, such as *A Naked Needle* (1976), and for his plays for the British Broadcasting Corporation (BBC). Unable to return to Somalia, he has settled in Nigeria.

Farouk I (1920–1965)

Farouk I, a descendent of MEHEMET ALI, was the last king of Egypt. He reigned from 1937 until 1952, when he was deposed by army officers led by General MUHAMMAD NEGUIB. He was known for his extravagance, which, together with the defeat of Egyptian forces by Israel in 1948–9 and his failure to end the British military occupation of Egypt, made him unpopular. In 1959, he became a citizen of Monaco.

First, Ruth (1925–1982)

Born in Johannesburg, South Africa, Ruth First was a leading campaigner against South Africa's apartheid policies. She joined the Communist Party as a student and married Joe Slovo, a South African lawyer, in 1949. She was charged with treason in 1956 and, in 1964, she left South Africa. She was assassinated in Maputo, Mozambique by a parcel bomb sent to her office there.

Fodio, Usman dan *see* Usman dan Fodio

Franco (1939–1989)

Franco (original name L'Okanga La Ndju Pene Luambo Makaidi) was a virtuoso Zairean guitarist and a leader of African popular music for more than thirty years. He headed TPKO Jazz, Africa's most famous band. The initials stand for Tout Puissant Orchestre Kinois, "All-Powerful Kinshasa Band." His use of the Swahili and Lingala languages has led to Lingala becoming a cult language among young people in East Africa. Franco had several wives and eighteen children.

Fugard, Athol (born 1932)

Athol Fugard is a South African playwright and actor of mixed Afrikaner and English parentage. He attacked apartheid in his plays and frequently tangled with the authorities, notably over his greatest play – "*Master* *Harold*"... *and the Boys* (1982) – which was banned in South Africa because it dealt with the friendship between a white boy and a black waiter.

Garang de Mabior, John (born 1945)

In 1983, John Garang, a Dinka from southern Sudan, became leader of the rebel Sudanese People's Liberation Movement (SPLM) and its military wing, the Sudanese People's Liberation Army (SPLA). His movement opposes such government policies as the use of Arabic in schools and the imposition of Sharia (Islamic holy) law.

Gebrselassie, Haile (born 1973)

Ethiopian Gebrselassie is one of the world's top runners in 5,000 meters and 10,000 meters events. Having set the 5,000 meters world record in June 1994, he went on to slice 8.5 seconds off the 10,000 meters record a year later. In 1995, he also set a new world record in the 5,000 meters, removing nearly 11 seconds from the record he had lost to Kenyan MOSES KIPTANUI earlier in the summer. He is a current Olympic champion after taking gold in the 10,000 meters at the 1996 Atlanta Olympics.

Glover, Emmanuel Ablade (born 1934)

Emmanuel Glover is a Ghanaian painter, sculptor, and textile designer, who combines African art styles with modern European styles. He studied art in Ghana, England, Kent State University (Ohio), and Ohio State University. He became professor of art education at the University of Science and Technology at Kumasi, Ghana, and was elected a fellow of the Royal Society of Arts in London, England.

Gordimer, Nadine (born 1923)

Nadine Gordimer is an outspoken white critic of apartheid who won South Africa's first Nobel Prize for Literature, in 1991. Before apartheid was abolished, the government had banned four of her novels, including *The Late Bourgeois World* (1966) and *Burger's Daughter* (1979), dealing with the Soweto riots of 1976, because of their political views.

Nadine Gordimer

Gouled Aptidon, Hassan (born 1916)

Hassan Gouled, who was born into a nomadic Somali family, became the first president of Djibouti when it gained independence in 1977. He was reelected in 1981, 1987, and 1993.

Gowon, Yakubu (born 1934)

Yakubu Gowon became Nigeria's head of state and commander-in-chief of its armed forces in 1966, and led the country during the Biafran (Nigerian Civil) War (1967–70). He was deposed in 1975 and went into exile first in Britain and then in Togo.

Grunitzky, Nicolas (1937–1994)

Nicolas Grunitzky served as prime minister of Togo (1956–8) and became president of Togo in 1963 after the overthrow of SYLVANUS OLYMPIO. Dependence on France increased under him and, in 1967, he was ousted in a bloodless coup by GNASSINGBE EYADÉMA and exiled.

Habyarimana, Juvénal (1937–1994)

Juvénal Habyarimana, an army officer, took power in Rwanda in a bloodless coup that ousted President GRÉGOIRE KAYIBANDA in 1973. He ruled the country until he was killed, together with President Cyprien Ntaryamira of Burundi, when their plane was shot down in April 1994. Both presidents were Hutu and their deaths provoked terrible conflict between the Hutu and Tutsi in Rwanda, Burundi, and Congo (Dem.Rep.).

Haile Selassie I (1892–1975)

Originally Ras (Prince) Tafari, Haile Selassie was Emperor of Ethiopia from 1930 until the army deposed him in 1974. He was exiled to Britain during the Italian occupation of Ethiopia (1936–41), and after his return he sought to introduce reforms, but his critics considered that the rate of change was too slow. He was a prominent figure in African affairs, especially in the Organization of African Unity (OAU). He also came to be revered as a divine being by the Rastafarian religious group, which is named after him.

Emperor Haile Selassie I

Hamilcar (c. 270–228 BCE)

Hamilcar, father of HANNIBAL, was a Carthaginian general who resisted Roman attempts to capture the city-state of Carthage, in modern Tunisia. His full name, Hamilcar Barca, means "Hamilcar Lightning."

Hannibal (247–182 BCE)

Hannibal was Carthage's greatest general, and is best known today for taking an army, equipped with elephants, through Spain and France and across the Alps to attack the Romans. The son of HAMILCAR, he fought the Romans in Spain and Italy from 221 to 203 BCE, when he was recalled to defend Carthage. He was defeated by the invading Romans at the Battle of Zama. For a time, he ruled Carthage, but was driven into exile and later committed suicide.

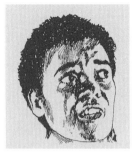

Bessie Head

Félix Houphouët-Boigny

King Idris I

Hassan II (1929 – 1999)

King of Morocco since 1961, Hassan II became commander of the armed forces in 1956 and prime minister in 1960. He became chairman of the Organization of African Unity (OAU) in 1972, but Morocco suspended its participation in the OAU in 1985 when representatives of the rebel Polisario group – the Sahrawi Arab Democratic Republic – were admitted. He died in July 1999 and was succeeded by his son, Sidi Mohamed.

Hatshepsut (c. 1540 – c. 1481 BCE)

Hatshepsut was one of the few women to rule Ancient Egypt in her own right. She became queen in about 1505 BCE, probably jointly with Tuthmosis III, who was her nephew and stepson. She was devoted to religion, and built a magnificent temple at Deir al Bahri and two obelisks at the Karnak temple complex. She also sent an expedition to the Land of Punt (probably in modern Somalia), an exploit depicted in the Punt Hall at Deir al Bahri.

Head, Bessie (1937–1986)

Bessie Head, daughter of a white woman and a black stablehand, was a South African novelist who wrote powerful novels drawing on her own experiences in a racist society. In *A Question of Power* (1974) she coupled that with the problems of mental breakdown. From the mid 1960s, she lived as a refugee in Botswana with her son.

Houphouët-Boigny, Félix (1905–1993)

Félix Houphouët-Boigny became the first president of Ivory Coast, in 1960, and he continued in this office, exercising a paternal style of government, until his death in 1993. He was born in Yamoussoukro, which in 1983 became the new political and administrative capital of Ivory Coast; Abidjan, the former capital, remains the economic and financial capital. During a visit in 1990, Pope John Paul II consecrated a basilica in Yamoussoukro; it is the largest Christian church in the world, and cost over US$800 million to build.

Ibn Battuta (1304–1368)

Ibn Battuta, born in Morocco, was probably the greatest Arab explorer and geographer. From 1325 to 1349, he traveled through East Africa and the basin of the Niger, as well as large parts of Asia including India and China. In the 1350s, he crossed the Sahara Desert and visited the medieval Songhay and Mali empires, of which he left graphic descriptions.

Ibn Khaldun (1332–1406)

Ibn Khaldun was a leading Arab philosopher and historian and has been called the "father" of sociology. Born in Tunis, he held posts in Morocco and Spain before settling in Egypt, where he was chief judge five times. His writings include histories of the Arabs and the Berbers.

Ibn Tumart, abu Abdullah Muhammad (c. 1078–1130)

Ibn Tumart was a Berber religious leader who founded the Almohad religious sect in Morocco. He proclaimed himself Mahdi (one who is guided) and gathered a following of Berbers from the Atlas Mountains, paving the way for the Almohad dynasty that ruled North Africa and Spain from 1150 to 1269. He was succeeded by ABD AL MUMIN.

Ibrahim, Abdullah (born 1934)

Abdullah Ibrahim is a jazz pianist, cellist, saxophonist, and flautist who recorded South Africa's first black jazz album with his band, Jazz Epistles, in 1960. He combines jazz techniques with the melodies and rhythms of African music. He went to the United States in 1962 to play with Duke Ellington, and has since toured in the US and in Europe. His name was originally Adolph Johannes Brand, and he changed it to Abdullah Ibrahim after becoming a Muslim in 1968. Many of his earlier performances and recordings were under the name of Dollar Brand.

Idris Aloma (c. 1575–1617)

Idris Aloma was the greatest ruler of the Muslim empire of Kanem-Borno in what is now northern Nigeria, southeast Niger, and western Chad. He equipped his soldiers with firearms and conquered Borno's neighbors, and the empire he built lasted fifty years.

Idris I (1890–1983)

Idris I was king of Libya from 1951, when the country became independent, until 1969, when he was deposed in a coup led by MUAMMAR AL QADDAFI and the monarchy was abolished. He had earlier led Libyan resistance to Italian rule.

Imhotep (2900s BCE)

Imhotep was an Ancient Egyptian sage and architect. He was adviser to Pharaoh Zoser, for whom he designed the Step Pyramid at Saqqara – the first true (smooth-sided) pyramid ever built. He was also the only physician to have been venerated as a god after he died. In around 500 BCE, he was worshipped as the son of Ptah, the god of Memphis (once the capital of Egypt), and the Greeks identified him with Asclepius, their god of medicine.

Ishola, Haruna (1918–1983)

Nigerian composer and singer Haruna Ishola popularized the Apala style, originally a music of Yoruba Muslims, in which talking drums and other drums accompanied singers.

Jabavu, John Tengo (1859–1921)

John Tengo Jabavu was a South African journalist and lay preacher who founded *Imvo Zabantsundu* ("Native Opinion"), the first newspaper edited by a black South African. Jabavu, a Xhosa, fought for higher education for black people, and established the "Native College" at Fort Hare, South Africa, which is now Fort Hare University.

Jammeh, Captain Yahya (born 1965)

Jammeh seized power during a military coup in Gambia in 1994, when he became Chairman of the Armed Forces Provisional Ruling Council. He was elected president in 1997. He joined the army in 1984 and was commissioned in 1989, becoming a captain in 1994.

Jawara, Alhaji Sir Dawda Kairaba (born 1924)

Sir Dawda Jawara was the longest-serving Gambian head of state. He was prime minister from 1963 to 1970, and president from 1970 until 1994. He survived several attempted coups, but was finally deposed by a military junta in 1994.

Jonathan, Chief (Joseph) Leabua (1914–1987)

Chief Leabua Jonathan was the first prime minister of Lesotho when it became independent in 1966, and he ruled the country for the next twenty years. A great-grandson of Lesotho's founder, MOSHOESHOE I, Jonathan was a leading nationalist politician before independence. After independence, he forced King MOSHOESHOE II to become mainly a figurehead and, in l970, suspended the constitution and ruled by decree. He was overthrown by a military coup in 1986.

Jordan, Archibald Campbell (1906–1968)

Archibald Jordan was a Xhosa novelist, poet, and teacher who made a study of Xhosa language and literature. The only one of his three novels to be published, *Iggoumbo yeminyanya* ("The Wrath of the Ancestral Spirits"), contrasted Xhosa and Western customs. He lectured at the University of Cape Town, then traveled to the United States, where he became a professor of African languages and literature at the University of Wisconsin.

Joseph, Helen Beatrice May (1905–1992)

British-born Helen Joseph was one of the first whites in South Africa to take a prominent part in the struggle against apartheid. In 1955, she was a founding member of the Congress of Democrats, the white wing of the African National Congress (ANC).

Juba I (c. 85–44 BCE)

Juba I, a Berber king of Numidia (Algeria), considered himself ruler of all North Africa. He was defeated by the Romans, committed suicide, and was succeeded by his son, JUBA II.

Juba II (c. 50 BCE – c. 24 CE)

Juba II was made ruler of Numidia by the Romans after they defeated his father, JUBA I. He married a daughter of CLEOPATRA and Mark Antony.

Jugnauth, Sir Aneerood (born 1930)

Aneerood Jugnauth became prime minister of Mauritius in 1982 and introduced economic policies that increased the country's prosperity. However, in elections in December 1995, he was swept from power by an opposition alliance that favored a fairer distribution of the fruits of economic success.

Kabbah, Alhaji Ahmad Tejan (born 1932)

A former civil servant and diplomat, Kabbah was elected president of Sierra Leone in 1996. He was overthrown in 1997 by a military junta but, in 1998, a Nigerian-led force overthrew the military regime and Kabbah returned to Sierra Leone as president on March 10.

Kabila, Laurent Desire (born 1939)

In October 1996, Kabila became head of the Alliance of Democratic Forces for the Liberation of Congo-Zaire, a rebel force, consisting mainly of Tutsis from eastern Zaire. Following the flight of President Mobutu, Kabila proclaimed himself head of state in May 1997 and renamed the country the Democratic Republic of Congo. Kabila is a member of the Luba ethnic group. In the 1960s, when the country was in turmoil, Kabila was a Marxist politician and a known opponent of Mobutu.

Kagame, Alexis (1912–1981)

A Rwandan Roman Catholic priest, Alexis Kagame was the historian and chief philosopher of the Tutsi people. He wrote most of his many historical and philosophical works in French, and his poetry and some other works in the Rwandan language. He advocated the Africanization of Christianity in Africa, rather than maintaining traditional European missionary ideas.

Kalle, le Grand (1930–1982)

Le Grand Kalle (Joseph Kabaselle Tshamala) led the transition from traditional to modern in the music of his native Zaire. He influenced such musicians as FRANCO and TABU LEY, who issued an album of songs in his memory after his death. His band, African Jazz, played rumbas and sambas with an African flavor.

Kallé, Pepé (born 1951)

Pepé Kallé is a Zairean bandleader who became a star in the 1970s with his band Empire Bakuba. The band's music is characterized by a fast beat and fascinating cross rhythms. Among its most typical recordings is *Kwassa Kwassa* (1989). Kallé is called the "Elephant of Zaire" because of his height and fame.

Kalthum, Umm (1910–1975)

Umm Kalthum was an Egyptian singer of classical Islamic music. When she was young, her father, embarrassed at seeing a girl publicly singing religious songs, dressed her as a boy. She never sang "pop" music, but her music was – and still is – extremely popular, and for over fifty years she dominated the classical music scene in Egypt and other parts of the Arab world.

Kanda Bongo Man (born 1955)

Kanda Bongo Man, a Zairean singer and composer, emigrated to France in 1979 because he saw no prospect of a successful recording career in his home country. He is now based in Paris and internationally famous.

Kante, Mory (born c. 1951)

Mory Kante, a member of a musical family in Guinea, performs regularly in Europe and Africa. He uses the kora, a West African double harp, with brass and electric piano to create a sound combining funk, rock, and soul. He maintains that all modern dance rhythms originated in Africa.

Kasavubu, Joseph Ileo (1913–69)

In 1960, Joseph Kasavubu, who favored a federal system of government for the Congo Republic (now Congo [Dem.Rep.]), became the country's first president. Faced with an army mutiny and the secession of Katanga (now Shaba) province, Kasavubu dismissed his prime minister PATRICE LUMUMBA, who favored the creation of a strong central government. Kasavubu was deposed in 1965 by General MOBUTU SESE SEKO.

Kaunda, Kenneth David (born 1924)

The first president of Zambia, Kenneth Kaunda was born in Nyasaland (now Malawi). He became a major figure in the late 1950s for his opposition to the white-minority ruled Central African Federation. Kaunda served as president from 1964 until 1991, when he was defeated in multiparty elections. He gave help and support to many black nationalist groups in the white-minority ruled countries of Southern Africa.

Kenneth Kaunda

Kayibanda, Grégoire (born 1924)

Grégoire Kayibanda, a Hutu, became the first president of Rwanda when the country became independent in 1962. He was reelected in 1965 and 1969, but he was overthrown by a military group in 1973 and replaced by JUVÉNAL HABYARIMANA.

Keino, Kipchoge Hezekiah (born 1940)

Kipchoge Keino, a Kenyan athlete, was one of the world's greatest long-distance runners. He set world records in 1965 for the 3,000 meters and 5,000 meters, and won gold medals at the Olympic Games in Tokyo (1968) and Munich (1972). After retiring in 1980, he and his wife have devoted themselves to caring for homeless and abandoned children.

Keita, Modibo (1915–77)

In 1959, Modibo Keita became president of the Mali Federation, consisting of Senegal and French Soudan. This federation broke up in August 1960, and French Soudan became independent as Mali, with Keita as its first president. He was deposed by a military group led by MOUSSA TRAORÉ in 1968.

Keita, Salif (born 1949)

A Malian composer and singer, Salif Keita is descended from the kings of medieval Mali. His music with the band Les Ambassadeurs, later reformed as Super Ambassadeurs, combines Islamic vocals with solos on saxophones and guitars.

Salif Keita

Kenyatta, Jomo (c. 1889–1978)

Jomo Kenyatta was prime minister of Kenya (1963–4) and president from 1964 until 1978. He studied anthropology at London University, England, in the 1930s, and wrote a major study of Kikuyu life, *Facing Mount Kenya* (1938). In 1952, he was arrested and imprisoned for his alleged role in managing the Mau Mau rebellion against British rule. Released from prison in 1959, he spent a further two years under house arrest. When he was eventually freed, in 1961, he assumed leadership of the Kenya African National Union (KANU), which won the preindependence elections in 1963. During his time as president, he used the slogan *Harambee* ("pull together") to encourage ethnic and racial harmony in Kenya.

Kenyatta, Margaret Wambui (born 1928)

The daughter of the Kenyan leader JOMO KENYATTA and his first wife, Margaret Kenyatta became an active campaigner on behalf of third-world women. During her father's jail term she helped him to keep in touch with his supporters. In 1960, she entered local politics and became mayor (1970–6) of Nairobi, the capital.

Kerekou, Mathieu Ahmed (born 1933)

Mathieu Kerekou became president and head of the government of Dahomey (now Benin) in 1972, following a coup. He proclaimed the country a Marxist-Leninist (socialist) state, but the government abandoned Marxism-Leninism in 1989. Kerekou was defeated by Nicéphore Soglo in multiparty elections in 1991, but regained power in 1996.

Khama, Sir Seretse (1921–1980)

Seretse Khama became the first prime minister of Botswana (formerly Bechuanaland) in 1965, and the country's first president from its independence in 1966 to his death in 1980. He was exiled from Bechuanaland from 1950 to 1956 because of his marriage to a white British woman in 1948. As president, he helped to make his country one of Africa's most stable democracies.

Khufu (Cheops) (2500s BCE)

Khufu – also known as Cheops, the Greek name for him – was ruler of the kingdom of Memphis in Ancient Egypt. He ordered the building of the Great Pyramid at Giza, which is the largest of the Egyptian pyramids, plus smaller pyramids for three of his wives. One of his successors was his son Khafre (Chephren), who built the second-largest of the Giza pyramids.

Kimathi, Dedan (1931–1957)

Dedan Kimathi was the leader of the Mau Mau rebellion that opposed British rule in Kenya in the 1950s. He was captured in 1956 and executed.

Kiptanui, Moses (born 1971)

One of the world's top runners, Kenyan Kiptanui has broken an unprecedented seven world records, including the 3,000 meters (indoor and outdoor), the 3,000 meters steeplechase, and the 5,000 meters. In 1995, he became the first man to run the 3,000 meters steeplechase in under eight minutes; an event for which he won a silver medal at the 1996 Atlanta Olympics.

Kolingba, André Dieudonné (born 1936)

André Kolingba became head of state of Central African Republic in 1981, when he seized power from david dacko in a peaceful coup, but he was defeated by ANGE-FÉLIX PATASSÉ in multiparty elections in 1993. Kolingba had earlier served in the army, reaching the rank of general in 1973. During the years of JEAN-BÉDEL BOKASSA'S dictatorship, Kolingba was abroad, in the diplomatic service.

Konaré, Alpha Oumar (born 1946)

A former teacher and writer, Konaré was elected president of Mali in 1992, following a period of military rule. He was re-elected in 1997, taking 84 per cent of the vote, the opposition groups having boycotted the election.

Kutako, Chief Hosea (1870–1970)

Paramount chief of the Herero people of South West Africa (now Namibia), Chief Kutako opposed German colonization and the subsequent rule of the territory by South Africa. He was wounded in the Herero revolt in 1904–5, when around three-quarters of his people were either killed or driven from the country. From the 1950s, he regularly petitioned the United Nations for independence.

Kuti, Fela Anikulapo- (1938–1997)

Fela Kuti was a Yoruba musician who became a major musical influence in Nigeria. His musical style, known as Afro-Beat, combined African rhythms and styles with American jazz and blues. His outspoken political views have earned him several terms of imprisonment and house arrest. He married twenty-seven women in 1978, as a protest against Western ways, and openly opposed feminism.

Lamizana, Sangoulé (born 1916)

Sangoulé Lamizana, who became army chief of staff of Upper Volta (now Burkina Faso) in 1961, led a military coup to overthrow MAURICE YAMEOGO and became head of state in 1966. He served as president until 1980, when he was ousted by a military coup led by Colonel Zerbo.

Leakey, Louis Seymour Bazett (1903–72)

Louis Leakey was one of Africa's greatest archeologists and anthropologists, and he proved that the first human beings appeared in that continent. Leakey was a Kenyan, the son of British missionaries. With his wife MARY LEAKEY, and later with their son RICHARD LEAKEY, he found important fossil remains in East Africa, especially in Olduvai Gorge, Tanzania. These fossils included the 2-million-year-old remains of an early hominid (humanlike) species, *Homo habilis* ("Handy Man"). Leakey also discovered evidence that human beings were living in California over 50,000 years ago. His work, and that of his family, suggests that Africa is one of the first homes of humankind.

Leakey, Mary Douglas (1913–1996)

Mary Leakey was an English-born archeologist who moved to Kenya after marrying LOUIS LEAKEY in 1936. In 1948, she discovered the fossil remains of a primitive ape thought to have lived twenty-five to forty million years ago. Together with her husband she made many other important discoveries and she wrote several books including *Africa's Vanishing Art: The Rock Paintings of Tanzania* (1983).

Leakey, Richard Erskine Frere (born 1944)

Richard Leakey is a Kenyan who has a double career as an anthropologist and a politician. He is the son of LOUIS LEAKEY and MARY LEAKEY, and with them found many important fossils of early apes and humans. From 1968 to 1989, he was a director of the National Museum of Kenya, later becoming head of the Kenya Wildlife Service. His political views led the Kenyan government to remove him from his wildlife post, but in 1995 he founded a new political party, Safina ("Noah's Ark").

Leo Africanus (c. 1494–c. 1552)

Leo Africanus (real name Al Hassan ibn Muhammad al Wazzan) was a Spanish-born Arab traveler and geographer. He traveled extensively in Africa and Asia Minor, and documented his African experiences in his book *Africa Descriptio* (1526). He was captured by Venetian pirates and taken to Rome, where he lived for twenty years and became a Christian. He then returned to Africa and died in Tunis.

Letsie III (born 1964)

The son of King MOSHOESHOE II of Lesotho, Crown Prince David Mohato Bereng Seeisa was made king, with the title Letsie III, by the country's military government in 1990. In 1995, he voluntarily abdicated to let his father, who had been deposed by the military, return. When his father was killed in a car crash in 1996, however, Letsie III once again became king.

Ley, Tabu (born 1940)

Tabu Ley led the development of "Congo" music and is ranked second only to FRANCO as a performer of African popular music. He was born in Zaire, and is also known as Rochereau. He has written more than 2,000 songs and produced over 150 albums. He moved to exile in Paris when the political situation in Zaire deteriorated in the late 1980s, and in 1993 he produced an album, *Exil-Ley*, commenting on his exile.

Louw, Nicholaas Petrus van Wyck (1906–1970)

Nicholaas Louw was one of South Africa's leading Afrikaans academics and writers. His three volumes of poetry all won literary prizes, and he also wrote essays and radio plays. In 1950 he became professor of Afrikaans language and literature at the University of Amsterdam, in the Netherlands. He returned to South Africa, to teach at the University of the Witwatersrand, in 1958.

Lumumba, Patrice Emergy (1925–1961)

Patrice Lumumba was the first prime minister of the Congo Republic (now Congo [Dem.Rep.]) from June to September 1960, when he was dismissed by President JOSEPH KASAVUBU. Lumumba was shot dead in 1961, allegedly by rebels from Katanga (now Shaba) province. His death caused a strong reaction throughout Africa, where he was widely regarded as a hero.

Luthuli, Chief Albert John (1898–1967)

Chief Luthuli, a leading Zulu figure in the struggle against apartheid in South Africa, was awarded the 1960 Nobel Peace Prize. President-general of the African National Congress (ANC) from 1952 until it was banned in 1960, he was arrested in 1956 and charged with treason, but released in 1957. His autobiography, *Let My People Go*, appeared in 1962.

Chief Albert Luthuli

Maathi, Wangari Muta (born 1940)

Wangari Maathi, a Kenyan scholar and feminist, founded the Greenbelt Movement in 1977. This is a reforestation program whose fifty thousand women members plant trees to replace those felled for lumber. When she started the movement, she was a professor in biology at the University of Nairobi; she resigned to stand for parliament, was disqualified, and was not allowed back into the university. Her husband, a member of parliament, was pressured into divorcing her.

Machel, Samora Moises (1933–1986)

Samora Machel became the first president of Mozambique when the country gained its independence in 1975, and remained in office until he was killed in a plane crash in 1986. Machel had been active in the independence war against the Portuguese (1964–74) and was president of the ruling Frente de Libertação de Moçambique (Frelimo) party, which followed Marxist-Leninist (socialist) policies.

Macías Nguema, Francisco (1922–1979)

The first president of Equatorial Guinea (1968–79), Francisco Macías Nguema was a brutal dictator whose reign of terror led to the flight of up to two-thirds of the population. He was deposed in a military coup in 1979, led by his nephew OBIANG NGUEMA MBASOGO, and was executed.

Mahdi *see* **Muhammad Ahmad al Mahdi**

Mahfouz, Naguib (born 1911)

Naguib Mahfouz, an Egyptian novelist, won the 1988 Nobel Prize for Literature, the first writer in Arabic to do so. Among his forty novels are the three books of *The Cairo Trilogy* (1956–7), in which he portrays the city where he was born and has lived all his life. He also wrote movie scripts for Egyptian director SALAH SEIF. Some of his work has aroused fierce criticism in the Arab world, and in 1995 two men were sentenced to death for trying to murder him.

Mainassara, Ibrahim Bare (1949-1999)

General Mainassara seized power during a bloodless coup in January 1996. In June 1966, he was elected president. However, he was assassinated in April 1999 by members of his presidential guard, one of whom, Daouda Malam Wanke, took over as head of state.

Makeba, Miriam Zensi (born 1932)

Miriam Makeba is a leading South African singer who was forced to leave the country in 1963 because of her opposition to apartheid. She settled in the United States, where she won fame as "the empress of African song" and became an international star. Forced to leave the United States because of her marriage to Black Panther leader Stokely Carmichael, she settled in Guinea for some years and represented that country at the United Nations. (She was married twice, her first husband being the trumpeter HUGH MASEKELA.) She returned to South Africa in 1990.

Miriam Makeba

Malan, Daniel François (1874–1959)

Daniel Malan became prime minister of South Africa after defeating JAN SMUTS in the 1948 elections. He is best known for the official introduction of apartheid. He retired from office in 1954.

Mambety, Djibril Diop (born 1945)

Djibril Mambety, a Wolof from Senegal, is an actor turned film producer who emphasizes the clashes between African and Western culture in his films. In *Badou Boy* (1972), he did this through the story of a street urchin in Dakar, the capital.

Daniel François Malan

Mancham, James Richard (born 1929)

James Mancham became the first president of the Seychelles when the country became independent in 1976, but he was deposed by his prime minister FRANCE- ALBERT RENÉ in 1977. He had earlier served as chief minister, from 1970 until 1974.

Mandela, Nelson Rolihlahla (born 1918)

Nelson Mandela, leader of the African National Congress (ANC), was elected president of South Africa in the country's first multiracial elections in 1994. Mandela qualified as a lawyer and worked with OLIVER TAMBO. He became a leader of the ANC before it was banned in 1960 and founded Umkonto we Sizwe (the military wing of the ANC) in 1961. He was one of the defendants in the so-called Treason Trial (1956–61) of 156 antiapartheid activists, every one of whom was acquitted. Mandela continued his antiapartheid activities and in 1962, along with WALTER SISULU and seven others, he was arrested and charged with sabotage and terrorism. All except one were sentenced to life imprisonment. Mandela was released in 1990, having become an international symbol of the struggle against apartheid. During his imprisonment, his wife WINNIE MANDELA did much to ensure that his plight was not forgotten by the outside world. After his release, he successfully led negotiations for a new, nonracial constitution for South Africa. He shared the 1993 Nobel Peace Prize with F. W. DE KLERK, and retired in June 1999.

Nelson Mandela

Mandela, Winnie (born 1934)

Winnie (Nomzano Zaniewe Winnifred) Mandela emerged as a major opponent of apartheid and a controversial figure in her own right during her husband NELSON MANDELA'S twenty-eight-year imprisonment. After qualifying as a social worker, she married him in 1958. Her first arrest took place three months later, and in 1962 she was banned from political activity for the first time. For the next twenty years she was banned, restricted, detained, and jailed a number of times. In 1990, after her husband's release from prison, she took a prominent role in the African National Congress (ANC) until her 1991 conviction for assault and kidnapping. She was divorced from Nelson Mandela in 1996.

Manga, Bebe (born 1948)

Bebe Manga (full name Elizabeth Prudence Manga Bessem), is a Cameroonian singer-songwriter and pianist. She won fame in 1982 with *Amie*, a song recorded in Paris, France, which sold more than a million copies.

Sir Milton Margai

Mansa Musa (c. 1264–1337)

Musa became mansa (king) of the medieval Empire of Mali in 1307, and set about reorganizing trade (especially the exporting of copper and gold) and spreading Islam. In 1324, he set off on pilgrimage to Mecca with a large retinue and about twenty tons of gold. On the way, he stopped off in Cairo, where his lavish spending caused severe inflation.

Mapfumo, Thomas (born 1945)

Thomas Mapfumo is a pioneer of popular African music in Zimbabwe. He devised the chimurenga music style, which combines the rhythms of the thumb piano (mbira) with more modern instruments. His first recording in Shona, *Hoyoka* ("Watch Out"), made with the Acid Band in 1977, was banned by the then white-minority government.

Margai, Sir Milton Augustus Stiery (1895–1964)

Milton Margai was chief minister of Sierra Leone from 1954 to 1958, and the country's first prime minister from 1958 until his death in 1964. He was succeeded as prime minister by his half-brother Albert Margai.

Thomas Mapfumo

Hugh Masekela

Masekela, Hugh Ramopolo (born 1939)

Hugh Masekela, a trumpeter, became South Africa's leading jazz artist but spent thirty-four years in self-imposed exile because of apartheid. For some years he was married to the singer and fellow South African exile MIRIAM MAKEBA. In 1960, he went to the United States to study at the Manhattan School of Music, New York, and his record *Grazin' in the Grass* topped the charts in the United States in 1968. He left the United States and settled in West Africa, then returned to South Africa in 1994.

Masire, Sir (Quett) Ketumile Joni (born 1925)

A founder of the ruling Botswana Democratic Party (BDP), Ketumile Masire became Botswana's vice-president in 1966. He became president in 1980, following the death of SERETSE KHAMA, and he was reelected in 1984, 1989, and 1994. He returned in 1998 and was succeeded by Vice-President Festus Mogae

M'Ba, Léon (1902–1967)

Léon M'Ba became president of Gabon in 1960 when the country became independent. He had earlier served as head of the government from 1957 until 1960. In 1964, with the help of French troops, he survived an attempted coup. He was reelected in 1967, but died later that year and was succeeded by OMAR BONGO.

Mbarga, Prince Nico (born 1950)

West African singer Prince Nico Mbarga (real name Nicholas Mbarga) had a major hit with his song *Sweet Mother* in 1976. Sung in pidgin English, it was a bestseller for two years. Mbarga's father was a Cameroonian and his mother was Nigerian. He worked in Nigeria with his band, Rockafil Jazz, but the government expelled four of the band's members who were Cameroonians, and he had to recruit Nigerians to replace them.

Mbeki, Thabo (born 1942)

Thabo Mbeki became First Deputy President of South Africa in 1994 and succeeded NELSON MANDELA as leader of the African National Congress (ANC) and president of South Africa following the elections of 1999. Born in Transkei, Mbeki studied economics in Britain and became active in the ANC. In 1975, he became the youngest member of the ANC executive, and in 1993, he became ANC chairperson.

Mehemet Ali

Mboya, Thomas Joseph (1930–1969)

Tom Mboya, a Luo, was general secretary of the Kenya Federation of Labour from 1953 until 1962. He was prominent in opposing British colonial rule in the late 1950s when JOMO KENYATTA and other older leaders were in prison. He helped to found the Kenya African National Union (KANU) in 1960 and became its general secretary, and was later a member of the Kenyan government. He was assassinated in 1969.

Mehemet Ali (1769–1849)

Mehemet Ali, also known as Muhammad Ali, was an Albanian-born Ottoman (Turkish) soldier who became viceroy (ruler) of Egypt in 1805, ruling on behalf of the Ottoman Empire. He massacred his main enemies, the Mamluks, who were the remnants of a Turkish dynasty that had been defeated by the Ottomans in 1517. He also reformed the Egyptian administration, army, and navy, and conquered large parts of Sudan, and when he fell out with his Turkish masters, his army defeated them. As a result, the Ottomans made him hereditary ruler of Egypt, and his descendants ruled until a republic was declared in 1953. The last of them to rule was FAROUK I, deposed in 1952.

Menelik II (1844–1913)

Menelik II was the king of Shoa, the central province of Ethiopia, and he became Emperor of Ethiopia in 1889. He modernized Ethiopia and kept it from Italian invasion, defeating an Italian army at the Battle of Adowa (modern Adwa) in 1896 and thus preserving Ethiopian independence.

Mengistu, Haile Mariam (born 1937)

Haile Mariam Mengistu seized power in Ethiopia in 1974 after a revolution that removed the emperor, HAILE SELASSIE I. In 1977, he became Ethiopia's first president. Mengistu pursued socialist policies and received aid from the former Soviet Union, but his period in office was marked by famine and civil war. He was overthrown by rebel forces in 1991 and took refuge in Zimbabwe.

Mensah, E. T. (1919–1991)

E. T. Mensah, a Ghanaian composer, saxophonist, trumpeter, and bandleader, became the leader of the highlife style of playing in West Africa in the 1950s. When the West African big-band era ended in 1969, Mensah retired, becoming a government pharmacist. He made a comeback in the 1970s and was known as "The King of Highlife."

Mensah, Kwaa (1920–1991)

Kwaa Mensah was a Ghanaian guitarist who became known as the "Grandfather" of the palm-wine style of popular music, which evolved into the highlife style. He rose to fame in the 1950s with his guitar band, but then his popularity waned. His work was revived for a time in the 1970s.

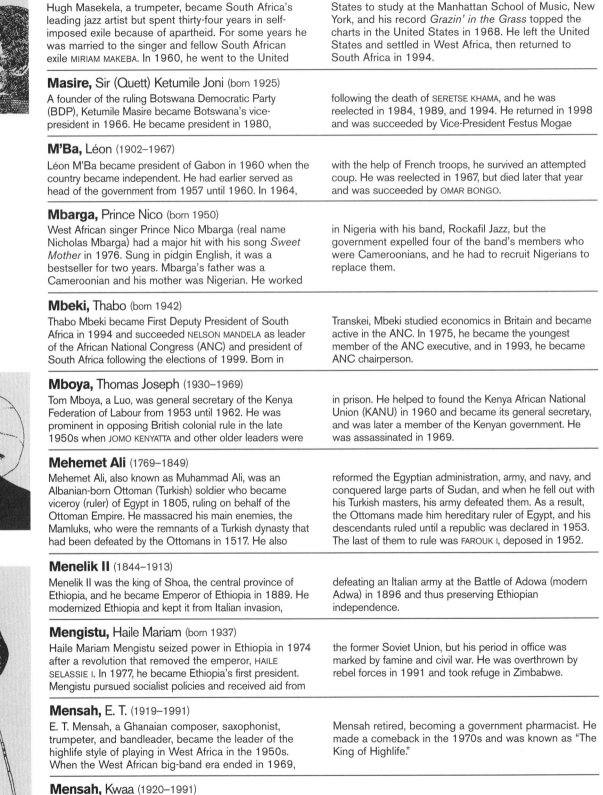

Emperor Menelik II

Micombero, Michel (1940–1983)

In 1966, while the mwama (king) of Burundi was abroad, Micombero, the prime minister, declared the country a republic and made himself president. Micombero, a Tutsi, consolidated Tutsi supremacy in Burundi and purged the army and government of Hutus. After an abortive coup attempt in 1972, between one hundred thousand and two hundred thousand Hutu were brutally massacred. He was deposed in 1976 by Colonel Jean-Baptiste Bagaza and arrested.

Mkapa, Benjamin William (born 1938)

Mkapa, a former civil servant and journalist, was elected president of Tanzania in 1995, winning 61.8 per cent of the total votes cast. He is chairman of the Chama Cha Mapinduzi (Revolutionary Party).

Mobutu Sese Seko (1930–1977)

Mobutu Sese Seko, originally named Joseph-Désiré Mobutu, was Zaire's head of state from 1965. He became an army commander in 1960, and briefly led a provisional government in Congo (Léopoldville), which is now Congo (Dem.Rep.). In 1965, he again took power and became president, restoring the power of the central government and making Zaire a one-party state. He promised a multiparty system in 1990, but he set no election dates. Accused of corruption, he went into exile in 1997 and a new regime was set up under LAURENT KABILA.

Mobutu Sese Seko

Mogae, Festus (born 1939)

A former planning officer, financial administrator and Vice-President of Botswana, Mogae was sworn in as President of Botswana in April 1998. He succeeded Sir KETUMILE MASIRE who had announced his impending retirement in 1997.

Moi, Daniel arap (born 1924)

Daniel arap Moi was Kenya's vice-president from 1967 until 1978, when he succeeded JOMO KENYATTA as president. His party, the Kenya African National Union (KANU) was the sole legal party from 1982 until 1991 – when opposition parties were legalized. In elections in 1992, Moi, who has been criticized for human rights abuses, was reelected president.

Mokhehle, Ntsu (1919–1999)

A nationalist leader, Ntsu Mokhehle won Lesotho's 1970 elections but the results were declared void and Mokhehle was imprisoned until 1972. After a failed coup attempt in 1974 – allegedly by Mokhehle's supporters – he was forced to flee the country. Following the introduction of a democratic constitution, Mokhehle's Basotho Congress Party (BCP) won elections in 1993 and he became prime minister. He survived two attempted coups in 1994.

Momoh, Joseph Saidu (born 1937)

Joseph Momoh became commander of the Sierra Leone army in 1983, and in 1985, he was the sole presidential candidate of Sierra Leone's only political party, the All-People's Congress (APC). Initially popular, Momoh used tough measures to crack down on the corruption that had flourished under his predecessor, Siaka Stevens. He refused to consider adopting multiparty politics, however, and was removed from office in l992 by a military coup led by Valentine Strasser.

Mondlane, Eduardo (1920–1969)

A prominent Mozambican nationalist, Eduardo Mondlane became president of the liberation movement Frente Nacional de Libertação de Angola (Frelimo) in 1962. He led a guerrilla war against the Portuguese rulers of Mozambique from 1964, and was assassinated in Tanzania in 1969.

Morceli, Noureddine (born 1970)

Morceli, an Algerian, is one of the greatest runners ever. He has broken world records in the 1,000, 1,500, 2,000, and 3,000 meters and the mile. At the 1996 Atlanta Olympics, he took gold in the 1,500 meters.

Moshoeshoe I (1786–1870)

Moshoeshoe I, sometimes known as Moshesh, was a Sotho chief who created the kingdom of Basuto (now Lesotho). He united the various clans of the Sotho people, fought off numerous attacks by neighboring peoples, and fought the British and the Boers. In 1868, at his request, the British annexed his land (as the Basutoland protectorate) to prevent it being taken over by the Boers.

Moshoeshoe II (1938–1996)

Born Constantine Bereng Seeiso, Moshoeshoe II was the grandson of MOSHOESHOE I. He became king of Lesotho in 1960, but went into exile for eight months in 1970 after a clash with the country's first prime minister, Chief LEABUA JONATHAN. He continued as king, with reduced powers, until 1990, when he was deposed and exiled after refusing to sanction changes proposed by the then military government. He was restored to the throne in January 1995, but was killed in a car accident the following year and succeeded by his son, LETSIE III.

Moshoeshoe I

Moutawakel, Nawal al (born 1962)

Nawal al Moutawakel, a Moroccan runner, won the first-ever Olympic 400 meters hurdles for women when the event was introduced in the 1984 Los Angeles Olympics. She was the first woman from an Islamic nation and the first African woman, other than a white South African, to win a solo Olympic medal. She was also the first Moroccan to win an Olympic gold medal.

Nawal al Moutawakel

Mphalele, Es'kia (born 1919)

South African writer Es'kia (formerly Ezekiel) Mphalele was exiled for twenty years from his homeland because he protested against apartheid. His novels and short stories reflect the struggles of black people in a racist society. He spent part of his exile in teaching in Nigeria and Kenya, then went to the United States where he obtained a doctorate in literature at the University of Denver. He subsequently became a professor at the University of the Witwatersrand, South Africa. His books include the autobiography *Down Second Avenue* (1959).

Mpiosso, Matima Kinuani (1951–1996)

Matima Mpiosso, a Zairean guitarist, was leader of the group Zaïko Langa Langa, which he founded while still at school. He combined Zairean folk tunes and rhythms with rock to produce an individual sound that was popular in Europe and Japan. Arthritis forced him to stop playing guitar some time before his early death.

Mqhayi, Samuel Edward Krune Loliwe (1875–1945)

Samuel Mqhayi was a leading Xhosa-language poet and novelist, and also a teacher and scholar who helped to standardize Xhosa spelling and grammar. His first novel was *Ityala lama-wele*, the story of twins quarreling over which of them was the heir to their father's inheritance. He published several volumes of verse and three biographies.

Mswati I (c 1820–1865)

Mswati I founded the Swazi nation, which was named after him. He was the king of the Ngwane kingdom that had been united by his father, Sobhuza I. Mswati, who ruled from 1845 until 1865, was a great general and made his kingdom one of the most powerful in the region.

Mswati III (born 1968)

Mswati III, son of SOBHUZA II, is the king of Swaziland. Educated in Britain, he was formerly named Prince Makhosetive. He was chosen as heir to the throne following the death of his father in 1982, and was officially installed as king when he reached the age of eighteen in 1986. He reorganized the government, but there has been growing public dissatisfaction with the political system, with many opposition groups demanding change.

Mswati I

Muana, Tshala (born 1950s)

Tshala Muana is a Zairean singer who made her name first as a dancer, especially as a modern interpreter of traditional dances. In the 1970s, she moved to Ivory Coast as a singer, and she was voted Best African Female Singer in 1984 for her album *Tshala Muana*, which was recorded in Paris.

Mubarak, Muhammad Hosni (born 1928)

A former air force officer, Hosni Mubarak became president of Egypt in 1981 following the assassination of ANWAR SADAT, having served as vice-president from 1975. Mubarak has pledged to deal firmly with Muslim extremists in Egypt and to continue the peace process with Israel. In 1990, he sent Egyptian troops to help defend Saudi Arabia after Iraq's invasion of Kuwait, and in 1995, he survived an assassination attempt during a visit to Ethiopia.

Hosni Mubarak

Mugabe, Robert Gabriel (born 1924)

Robert Mugabe, president of Zimbabwe, was a largely self-educated teacher who founded the anticolonialist Zimbabwe African National Union (ZANU) with NDABANINGI SITHOLE in 1963. He was detained by the then ruling British authorities in Southern Rhodesia (now Zimbabwe) in 1964, and imprisoned until 1974 for his nationalist, anticolonial activities. From 1976 until 1979, Mugabe was joint leader – with JOSHUA NKOMO – of the Patriotic Front guerrilla movement, which fought IAN SMITH's illegal white-minority regime in Rhodesia. As leader of ZANU, Mugabe was elected prime minister of Zimbabwe (defeating Bishop ABEL MUZOREWA) when it became fully independent in 1980. In 1988, ZANU merged with the main opposition party – Joshua Nkomo's Zimbabwe African People's Union (ZAPU) – and Zimbabwe became a one-party state. Mugabe became executive president in 1987 and was reelected in 1990 and 1996.

Muhammad Ahmad al Mahdi (1848–1885)

Muhammad Ahmad, who assumed the title of Mahdi (Muslim Messiah) in 1881, was a former civil servant turned slave trader who went on to lead the Sudanese rebellion against Anglo-Egyptian rule in 1882. He captured eastern Sudan in 1883, made Al Obeid his capital, and annihilated an Egyptian army that had been sent to retake it. In 1885, he captured Khartoum after a five-month siege and moved his capital to Omdurman, where he died later that year. The Islamic state he had established lasted until 1898, when the Mahdist forces were defeated by General Kitchener's Anglo-Egyptian army at the Battle of Omdurman. His great-grandson, Sadiq al Mahdi, has been prime minister of Sudan two times.

Muhammad Ali *see* Mehemet Ali

Al Mahdi

Muhammad Toure *see* **Askia Muhammad**

Muluzi, Bakili (born 1943)

Following the adoption of a multi-party constitution in Malawi in 1994, Bakili Muluzi, leader of the United Democratic Front since 1992, was elected president of Malawi, defeating former President Banda and two other candidates.

Musa *see* **Mansa Musa**

Museveni, Yoweri Kaguta (born 1945)

Yoweri Museveni took part in the overthrow of Uganda's dictator IDI AMIN DADA in 1979. Museveni became president of Uganda in 1986 after his National Resistance Army had defeated government forces, ending a five-year conflict. He has been criticized for his ban on political parties which, he claims, encourage tribal divisions.

Yoweri Museveni

Muzorewa, Bishop Abel Tendekayi (born 1925)

Abel Muzorewa became the first black bishop of the United Methodist Church, in 1968. He was a prominent opponent of IAN SMITH'S illegal white-minority government in Zimbabwe in the 1970s. In elections in 1979, Muzorewa became the country's first black prime minister, but he was heavily defeated by ROBERT MUGABE in 1980. Muzorewa returned to politics in 1994, but he withdrew his candidacy in the 1995 presidential elections, criticizing the way in which they had been conducted.

Mveng, Engelbert (born 1930)

Engelbert Mveng, a Jesuit scholar from Cameroon, is a historian, artist, and theologian. For some years he was head of cultural affairs for the Cameroon Ministry of Education and Culture, and in 1980 became secretary- general of the Ecumenical Association of Third-World Theologians. He painted a huge mural for the Afro-American Catholic Church of Holy Angels in Chicago.

Mwinyi, Ali Hassan (born 1925)

Ali Hassan Mwinyi became president of Tanzania in 1985, after President JULIUS NYERERE retired. He was reelected in 1990 and served until 1995, when, having completed the maximum of two terms in office, he was replaced by Benjamin Mkapa. Mwinyi pursued liberal economic policies and introduced a multiparty constitution in 1993.

Mzilikazi (c. 1790–1868)

Mzilikazi established the Ndebele/Matabele kingdom around Bulawayo, in what is now Zimbabwe. His territory became known as Matabeleland. Mzilikazi led a number of Ndebele north from Natal to Transvaal to escape from the Zulu under DINGANE, and then farther north still to escape from the Boer settlers.

Gamal Abd an-Nasser

Naidoo, Jay (Jayaseelan) (born 1954)

A leading trade unionist and opponent of apartheid, Jay Naidoo was elected general secretary of the Congress of South African Trade Unions (COSATU) in 1985. He played a major role in organizing the mass protests against apartheid policies during the 1980s. After the democratic elections in 1994, he was appointed as Minister for Reconstruction and Development.

Nasser, Gamal Abd an- (1918–1970)

Nasser was prime minister of Egypt (1954–6) and president from 1956 until 1970. He was one of the leaders of a military coup that overthrew King FAROUK I in 1952, and took power after ousting General MUHAMMAD NEGUIB in 1954. Nasser pursued socialist policies aimed at raising living standards and was widely respected by the Arab world. To finance the building of the Aswan High Dam, he nationalized the Suez Canal, provoking an invasion by British, French, and Israeli troops – a conflict that was ended by the United Nations. Nasser offered to resign after military failures in the 1967 Six-Day War with Israel, but the Egyptian people refused to accept his offer.

Youssou N'Dour

Ncube, Sister Bernard Nekie Zellie (born 1935)

A member of the Companions of Angela religious order in South Africa, Sister Bernard is a leading women's activist. She is also a member of the African National Congress (ANC) national executive committee, and a member of the South African parliament. She was an active opponent of apartheid and has been imprisoned six times.

N'Dour, Youssou (born 1959)

Youssou N'Dour is a Wolof musician and singer from Senegal. He created the mbalax style of African music by adding African elements to the Cuban and American soul music then common in Senegal, and later experimented by adding rock and jazz. Internationally famous, he has made two tours of the United States and took part in the 1988 Amnesty International Human Rights Tour.

Nefertiti (c. 1385–c. 1350 BCE)

Nefertiti helped her husband, the Egyptian pharaoh (king) Amenhotep IV (Akhnaton), in his attempt to change the religion of Ancient Egypt from worship of its numerous traditional gods to worship of just one – Aton, the Sun. Nefertiti, who was famed for her beauty, had six daughters. One, Ankhesenpaaten, married Tutankhamen, who became pharaoh of Egypt at the age of twelve, restored the worship of the old gods, and died at eighteen.

Nefertiti

Neguib, Muhammad (1901–1984)

An Egyptian general, Muhammad Neguib became prime minister and president of Egypt after the overthrow of King FAROUK I in l952. Popular for his condemnation of British policies in Egypt, Neguib was a conservative Muslim. He was removed from office in 1954 and replaced by the more radical GAMAL ABD AN-NASSER.

Neogy, Rajat (1938–1995)

Rajat Neogy, a Ugandan journalist, was the founder/editor of *Transition*, an influential literary magazine. He criticized the government for many years and was jailed for sedition. After his release, he edited the magazine in Ghana, then emigrated to the United States, where he died.

Neto, Dr Antoniu Agostinho (1922–1979)

A poet and Marxist politician, Agostinho Neto became the first president of Angola (1974–9). He had led the Movimento Popular de Libertação de Angola (MPLA) forces in the guerrilla war against the Portuguese colonial regime from 1961 until 1974. Neto presided over the beginning, in 1975, of Angola's civil war between the government and rebel forces (principally those of JONAS SAVIMBI), which continued for sixteen years after his death.

Ngouabi, Marien (1938–1977)

Marien Ngouabi seized power in Congo in 1968 in a coup that deposed Alphonse Massamba-Débat. He adopted Marxist-Leninist policies and became president in 1970. Power struggles and ethnic tensions during Ngouabi's presidency led to political instability in the country and he was assassinated in 1977.

Ngugi, John (born c. 1963)

A Kikuyu athlete from Kenya, John Ngugi won the 5,000 meters gold medal at the 1988 Seoul Olympics. He has won the World Cross Country Championships a record five times, winning in four consecutive years from 1986 onward.

Ngugi wa Thiong'o (born 1938)

Ngugi wa Thiong'o (formerly known as James Ngugi) is a Kenyan novelist and playwright who wrote the first novel in English by an East African, *Weep Not, Child* (1964). He later switched to writing in Kikuyu, and in 1977 he co- wrote a play with Ngugi wa Marii that offended the government. This led to his detention without trial for a year, and he later went into exile.

Nico, Dr (1939–1985)

Dr Nico (real name Kasanda wa Mikalay Nicholas), a Zairean guitarist and composer, was a leading exponent of "Congo" music, which combines jazz and African styles. He was a dominant figure on the music scene for ten years and made many records, but very little money.

Gaafar Nimeri

Nimeri, Gaafar Muhammad (born 1930)

Gaafar Nimeri was president of Sudan from 1969 until 1985. A professional soldier, he seized power in a coup in 1969. He was elected president in 1971 and worked to raise food production throughout the country, but his attempts to introduce Sharia (Islamic holy) law alienated many people in the non-Muslim, largely Christian south. He was deposed by a coup in 1985.

Nkomo, Joshua Mqabuko Nyongolo (1917–1999)

Joshua Nkomo was the leader of the nationalist Zimbabwe African People's Union (ZAPU) from the 1960s. Nkomo and ROBERT MUGABE were joint leaders of the Patriotic Front guerrilla movement which campaigned against IAN SMITH'S illegal white-minority government of Rhodesia from 1976 until 1979. In the 1980 elections, however, Nkomo's ZAPU was defeated by Mugabe's Zimbabwe African National Union (ZANU). Nkomo was given a cabinet position in Mugabe's government but was dismissed in 1982 after conflicts between ZAPU and ZANU. In the 1980s, Nkomo's native Matabeleland harbored dissidents from Mugabe's rule and this led to further tensions between ZAPU and ZANU. In 1988, however, the two parties merged and Nkomo became one of Zimbabwe's two vice-presidents. He died in office in 1999.

Kwame Nkrumah

Nkrumah, Dr Kwame (1909–1972)

Kwame Nkrumah became prime minister of Gold Coast (later Ghana) in 1951, and then the first president of Ghana, in 1960. He was overthrown in a military coup in 1966. A campaigner against white domination, Nkrumah was widely respected throughout Africa. He became increasingly autocratic, however, and economic crises dogged his final years in office.

Nujoma, Sam Daniel (born 1929)

Sam Nujoma founded the South West African People's Organization (SWAPO) in 1958, and from 1966 led it in a guerrilla war against the illegal occupation of South West Africa (present-day Namibia) by South Africa. Nujoma became president of Namibia on its independence in 1990 and was reelected in 1994.

Sam Nujoma

Nyame, E. K. (1927–77)

E. K. Nyame was Ghana's most popular guitar band leader. With his Akan Trio he played at state functions when President Kwame Nkrumah visited Liberia. His early songs were written in English, but later songs were all in the Twi language. His popularity was such that he was given a state funeral when he died, in 1977.

Nyerere, Julius Kambarage (1922–1999)

Julius Nyerere, leader of the Tanganyika African National Union (TANU) – later named Chama Cha Mapinduzi (CCM) – became Tanganyika's first prime minister in 1961 and its first president in 1962. In 1964, he became president of the united Tanzania (Tanganyika and Zanzibar). He retired in 1985, but remained chairman of the CCM until 1990. A pioneer of ujamaa (self-help) policies and African socialism, Nyerere was successful in introducing social reforms, but his economic policies were less successful. In the mid 1990s, he acted as mediator in Burundi peace talks.

Julius Nyerere

Nzinga Nbandi, (Anna) (1582–1663)

Nzinga was a queen of Ndongo and later queen of Matamba (both in what is now Angola). As queen of Ndongo, she tried to keep her country free from Portuguese control and fought the slave trade. In 1623, she went to the Portuguese colony of Angola to negotiate with the governor, and while there, she was baptized a Christian as Dona Aña de Souza. The negotiations failed, however, and the Portuguese drove her out of Ndongo in 1624. She then conquered the kingdom of Matamba, which allied itself with the Dutch and became prosperous by collaborating with the Portuguese slave trade.

Obasanjo, Olesegun (born 1937)

Lieutenant-General Obasanjo became Nigeria's military head of state in 1976, following the assassination of Brigadier Murtala Mohammed, but he returned the country to civilian rule in 1979. In 1999, as part of another process to return Nigeria to civilian rule, Obasanjo led his People's Democratic Party to victory and was himself elected president. A member of the Yoruba ethnic group, Obasanjo joined the army in 1958 and distinguished himself in the Biafran War. After 1979, when he retired from the army, he became a mediator in African affairs. In 1995 he was imprisoned for allegedly plotting a coup against General SANI ABACHA, but he was released in 1998.

Obey, Ebenezer (born 1942)

Ebenezer Obey, a Nigerian bandleader, pioneered modern juju, a guitar-based musical style that originated in Yoruba-speaking western Nigeria. Obey called his version of juju the Miliki System. Many of his songs reflect his strong Christian beliefs. He has made several tours of the United States.

Obiang Nguema Mbasogo, Teodoro (born 1942)

Obiang Nguema became president of Equatorial Guinea in 1979 after leading a coup against his uncle, President MACÍAS NGUEMA. Under Obiang, power remained highly centralized and, despite the introduction of a multiparty system, Obiang was elected in 1996 with more than ninety-nine percent of the vote. His opponents had withdrawn, objecting to voting irregularities.

Obote, Apollo Milton (born 1924)

Milton Obote led Uganda to independence in l962, serving as its first prime minister. In 1966, he deposed the head of state, King Mutesa II of Buganda, and made himself executive president. In 1971, he was himself deposed, by IDI AMIN DADA. Obote returned from exile in Tanzania to regain the presidency in 1980 but was again deposed in 1985.

Ogot, Grace Emily Akinyi (born 1930)

Grace Ogot is a Kenyan who won fame as a novelist and short story writer and worked to preserve the folk tales of the Luo people. She combined her writing with politics, serving as a member of parliament and as a delegate to the United Nations. Her earlier career was as a midwife in Uganda and England.

Ojukwu, Chukwuemeka Odumegwu (born 1933)

Chukwuemeka Ojukwu was president of the breakaway state of Biafra during the Biafran (Nigerian Civil) War (1967–70). He went into exile after the rebellion collapsed.

Okigbo, Christopher (1932–1967)

Christopher Okigbo was one of Nigeria's finest poets, and has been an inspiration to other Nigerian writers. Most of his poetry, all written in English, survives in the collection *Collected Poems* (1986). Many of his poems have a mystical element. He worked as a teacher and librarian, but in 1967, he joined the army of Biafra, which tried to break away from Nigeria, and was made a major. He was killed in action within a month.

Chukwuemeka Ojukwu

Okosun, Sonny (born 1947)

Sonny Okosun, a Nigerian guitarist and composer, is a former actor who created a mixture of reggae and rock styles that he named ozzidi. This name was derived from the Igbo words "ozi di," meaning "there is a message," and his songs contain much social and political comment.

Okri, Ben (born 1959)

Ben Okri is a Nigerian broadcaster, poet, fiction writer, and journalist. He moved to Britain at the age of nineteen to study at the University of Essex, and later settled in London. His novel *The Famished Road* won the 1991 Booker Prize in Britain.

Olajuwon, Hakeem (Born 1963)

Hakeem Olajuwon is a Nigerian basketball player who made his name in the United States with the Houston Rockets, whom he joined in 1984. He became an American citizen in 1993, and in 1994 was voted Most Valuable Player in the National Basketball Association. A devout Muslim, he converted a disused building in Houston, Texas, into a mosque.

Olympio, Sylvanus (1902–1963)

Sylvanus Olympio was prime minister of Togo (1958–60) and became the country's first president when it gained independence in 1960. Olympio was a prominent campaigner for reunification of the Ewe people, who are divided between Togo and Ghana. He was killed in a military coup in 1963 and replaced by NICOLAS GRUNITZKY.

Ongala, Remmy (born 1947)

Remmy Ongala, born in Zaire, is Tanzania's most popular musician. In 1980, he formed the band Super Matimila, of which he is lead singer and guitarist, and later recorded with it in England. His lyrics attack the evils of racism and poverty.

Opoku Ware II (1919–1999)

A Ghanaian lawyer, Opoku Ware succeeded his uncle Sir Osei Agyeman-Prempe II as asantehene (king) of the Asante people in 1970. He was succeeded by Nana Kwako Dua.

Opoku Ware, Lady Victoria (1929–1996)

The senior wife of OPOKU WARE II, Lady Victoria was an influential figure at court and accompanied the king on foreign trips. In 1981, she helped to arrange the Asante exhibitions that were staged in London and New York. A powerful personality, she used her influence to defend the Asante kingdom's interests while maintaining an allegiance to the Ghanaian state.

Lady Victoria Opoku Ware

Osei Bonsu (1779–1824)

Osei Bonsu expanded the Asante Empire to its greatest size, covering modern-day Ghana and parts of Togo, Burkina Faso, and Ivory Coast. The seventh Asante king, his name means "Osei the Whale." He encouraged Asante arts and crafts and made the nation rich from their goldmines.

Osei Tutu (died 1717)

Osei Tutu united the separate Asante chiefdoms in the 1670s to create the Asante Empire, now part of Ghana as the Asante Kingdom. To join the empire, the chiefdoms had to acknowledge the authority of the Golden Stool. This was a wooden stool, covered in gold and said to have been conjured from the sky, that symbolized the spirit of the Asante. Osei Tutu embarked on a series of wars of expansion in 1701, and was killed in battle in 1717.

Ouédraogo, Idrissa (born 1954)

Ouédraogo is a distinguished movie director from Burkina Faso, whose work, which is concerned with the sufferings and aspirations of African people, has attracted international attention. His motion pictures include *Karim and Sala* (1983), and *Heart's Cry* (Le Crie de Coeur) (1994).

Ould Daddah, Moktar (born 1924)

The first president of Mauritania (1960–78), Moktar Ould Daddah worked to unify his ethnically divided people. Dissatisfaction with Mauritania's unsuccessful and costly attempt to take over the southern part of Spanish (now Western) Sahara, however, led to his overthrow.

Ousmane Sembene (born 1923)

Sembene Ousmane was the first major African moviemaker. Born in Senegal, he wrote several novels before directing *La Noire de... (Black Girl)*. His other movies include *Mandabi* (1968) and *Ceddo* (1977), considered to be his masterpiece.

Oyono, Ferdinand Leopold (born 1929)

Leopold Oyono is a Cameroonian writer and diplomat who wrote several novels in the 1950s and 1960s critical of colonial rule. Brought up as a Roman Catholic, Oyono completed his education in Paris, France, where he obtained a law degree. Following Cameroon's independence, he served as an ambassador to the United States and other countries, and in the 1990s was minister of external relations.

Patassé, Ange-Félix (born 1937)

Former prime minister (1976-8), Patassé became president of the Central African Republic in 1993, when he defeated the military dictator Andre Kolingba. In 1996, the government and opposition parties agreed to set up a government of national unity.

Ange-Félix Patassé

Paton, Alan Stewart (1903–1988)

Alan Paton was a white South African writer whose best-selling novel *Cry, the Beloved Country* (1948) helped to alert the world to the problems of apartheid. He had seen many of those problems in his years as principal of a reformatory. His second novel, *Too Late the Phalarope* (1953) dealt with the relationship between a white man and a black woman, and was banned by the government. He founded the South Africa Liberal Party with MARGARET BALLINGER in 1953, and was its president until 1960.

P'Bitek, Okot (1931–1982)

Okot P'Bitek, a Ugandan poet and anthropologist, did much to promote African culture and values. He wrote in both English and in Luo, and his first novel, *Lar tar miyo kinyero wi lobo*, was in Luo. He studied law and anthropology at British universities, and had an academic career in Uganda and later in exile in Kenya. For a time he was writer-in-residence at the University of Iowa.

Piankhy (died c. 712 BCE)

From 751 to 712 BCE, Piankhy was the Nubian king of Kush (part of modern Sudan). He was a brilliant general, and he conquered Egypt and became its pharaoh (king). When he invaded Egypt, his forces were moving down the Nile while a Libyan chief, Tefnakht, was advancing upriver. Piankhy defeated Tefnakht and some Egyptian forces, seized the throne, then sailed back up the Nile to Kush with a great haul of loot.

Plaatje, Solomon Tshekiso (1876–1932)

In 1912, Sol Plaatje was a cofounder of the South African Native National Congress, which became the African National Congress (ANC) in 1923. His book *Native Life in South Africa* (1916) was an indictment of the misery caused by the Natives Land Act of 1913, while his novel *Mhundi* celebrates the importance of African culture and African history. Largely self educated, Plaatje also translated several of Shakespeare's plays into the Setswana language.

Player, Gary (born 1936)

Gary Player was one of the world's leading golfers of the 1960s and 1970s. In 1959, he won the British Open championship, at twenty-four the youngest player to do so. He has won all the major international golf championships, including the US Open, the US Masters, and the US PGA title. He spends part of his time in Florida and part on a farm near Johannesburg, South Africa, where he breeds horses and supports a school for 430 poor black children.

Pukwana, Dudu Mtutuzel (born 1938)

Dudu Pukwana is a South African musician who had to move to Europe in 1964 because the band he was in, the Blue Notes, contained both white and black musicians, which was illegal under apartheid laws. He settled in London, playing and recording with numerous bands.

Qaddafi, Muammar al (born 1942)

Muammar al Qaddafi became leader of Libya and commander-in-chief of the armed forces in 1969 after the overthrow of King IDRIS I. At home, Qaddafi sought to reorganize Libyan society along socialist, nationalist lines. Abroad, his support for radical movements, such as the Black Panthers in the United States and the Irish Republican Army (IRA) in Northern Ireland, made him a controversial figure. In 1986, US planes bombed several sites in Libya, missing Qaddafi but killing thirty-seven people, many of them civilians.

Muammar al Qaddafi

Rabéarivelo, Jean-Joseph (1901–1937)

Jean-Joseph Rabéarivelo was Madagascar's leading poet. Most of his poems were written in French, on themes including death and catastrophe, but he also wrote in his mother tongue, Hova. Unable to find what he considered a worthwhile job, he became depressed, took to drugs, and committed suicide.

Rabeh Zobeir see Rabih bin Fadl Allah

Rabemananjara, Jean-Jacques (born 1913)

A Madagascan politician and poet, Jean-Jacques Rabemananjara played an important role in the liberation struggle against French colonial rule. As a deputy of the Mouvement Démocratique pour la Rénovation Malagache (MDRM), he was imprisoned and exiled to France from 1947 until 1950 after extremist MDRM members organized a violent revolt in which about eighty thousand people were killed. From 1960, he served in the government of PHILIBERT TSIRANANA as foreign minister.

Rabih b. (bin) Fadl Allah (c. 1840–1900)

Rabih b. Fadl Allah was a Sudanese adventurer who carved out a huge empire in west-central Africa, south of Lake Chad. A former slave, he became an Egyptian soldier, then took to slave trading himself. He raised a large army, based himself in what is now Chad, and began twenty years of conquest. He was eventually killed by a French army at the Battle of Lakhta.

Ramanantsoa, Gabriel (1906–1979)

Gabriel Ramanantsoa, Madagascar's armed forces commander, became president in 1972, when PHILIBERT TSIRANANA relinquished power to him in the face of widespread strikes and riots. He was initially popular for his maintenance of order and prosecution of corrupt officials, but in 1975, after several coup attempts, he handed over power to a military government and was succeeded by DIDIER RATSIRAKA.

Ramgoolam, Sir Seewoosagur (1900–1985)

Seewoosagur Ramgoolam served as chief minister of Mauritius from 1961 and became the country's first prime minister in 1964. He was prime minister when Mauritius became independent in 1968, but was defeated in the 1982 elections by ANEEROOD JUGNAUTH.

Ramses II (reigned 1304–1237 BCE)

It has been suggested, but never proved, that Ramses II was the Egyptian pharaoh (king) who oppressed and enslaved the Israelites, as described in the Bible. Known as Ramses the Great, he was one of the most successful pharaohs and left many fine buildings, including the huge temple at Abu Simbel. His mummified body was discovered at Queen HATSHEPSUT'S temple at Deir al Bahri in 1881.

Ransome-Kuti, Funmilayo (1900–1978)

Funmilayo Ransome-Kuti was a Nigerian feminist leader who helped to save market women from exploitation. She formed working women into the Nigerian Women's Union, which founded clinics for mothers and children and helped to teach people to read and write. She died from injuries received when troops, who were raiding her son's house to punish him for criticizing the authorities, threw her from a second floor window.

Ratsiraka, Didier (born 1936)

Didier Ratsiraka, a former naval officer, became head of state in Madagascar in 1975, after the downfall of GABRIEL RAMANANTSOA. He was popular with both students and the bourgeoisie for his nationalist sentiments, and pledged to carry out administrative and rural reforms. He was elected president in 1976 and, despite several coup attempts, remained in office until he was defeated by Albert Zafy in the 1993 presidential elections.

Rawlings, Jerry John (J. J.) (born 1947)

Son of a Scottish father and a Ghanaian mother, Jerry John Rawlings seized power in Ghana in a peaceful coup in 1979, but ruled for only 112 days before restoring civilian government. Rawlings, an air force officer, was immensely popular for his anticorruption policies. He again seized power in 1981, but his reluctance to return power to a civilian government after this second coup lost him some support. In 1992, however, he was elected president in democratic multiparty elections.

Jerry Rawlings

René, France-Albert (born 1935)

France-Albert René, prime minister of Seychelles, seized power in 1977 to become the country's second president, replacing JAMES MANCHAM. René created a one-party state and followed policies of nonalignment. He was reelected in multiparty elections in 1993.

Retief, Piet (1780–1838)

Piet Retief was a leader of the Voortrekkers, the South African Boer farmers who migrated north on the Great Trek to escape British rule in the Cape. In 1837, he published a declaration listing the grievances of the Boers against the British, and led a party into Natal, stronghold of the Zulu. The Zulu king, DINGANE, refused to grant him land and in 1838 killed Retief and his followers.

Piet Retief

Ribas, Oscar Bento (born 1909)

Oscar Ribas, an Angolan of mixed African and European parentage, was the leading novelist and ethnologist of Portuguese colonial Africa. He became totally blind at the age of twenty-one, but continues to research and write. He made an influential study of the Kimbundu people, but his most important work is a study of Angolan literature.

Roba, Fatuma (born 1973)

Fatuma Roba, an Ethiopian runner, was the women's marathon gold medalist in the 1996 Atlanta Olympics. Roba, a policewoman who had won marathons in Marrakech and Rome in 1996, is the first African woman to take a gold medal in the Olympic marathon.

Robert, Shaaban (1909–1962)

Shaaban Robert was a Tanzanian poet and novelist who wrote a number of verse novels with anticolonial themes and turned Swahili from a classical tongue into a modern language. He also began the practice of writing it in Roman script instead of Arabic.

Fatuma Roba

Rochereau *see* Ley, Tabu

Saadawi, Nawal al (born 1931)

An Egyptian doctor and novelist, Saadawi became Egypt's Director of Public Health but her books, which focus on the lives of women in the Arab world, antagonized the authorities and she was dismissed. She went on to work as an advisor on women's programs for the United Nations. Her long campaign for women's rights in Egypt led to her imprisonment under ANWAR SADAT. She has since devoted her time to writing, journalism, and speaking on women's issues. Saadawi's books, which have won many literary awards, include *The Hidden Face of Eve: Women in the Arab World* (1980), *Woman at Point Zero* (1983), and *God Dies by the Nile* (1985).

Anwar al Sadat

Sadat, Muhammad Anwar al (1918–1981)

Anwar Sadat, vice-president of Egypt, became president on the death of GAMAL ABD AN-NASSER in 1970. He is remembered for his dramatic peace initiative that led to the Camp David peace treaty, signed in 1979, ending the conflict between Egypt and Israel. He shared the 1978 Nobel Peace Prize with Israel's Menachem Begin. Sadat was assassinated in 1981 by Muslim extremists.

Samori Toure (c. 1830–1904)

Samori Toure led West African resistance to French colonialism. At first a trader, he served in the army of the Sise people for several years, then formed his own army and built up the Second Mandinka Empire, which by 1881 stretched from Guinea to Ivory Coast. He fought of French advances for seven years, but, after years of fighting he was captured and imprisoned in 1898, then exiled.

Oumou Sangare

Sangare, Oumou (born 1968)

Oumou Sangare, a Malian singer, is the most popular female vocalist in West Africa and has been called the "Madonna of Mali." She has been singing in public since she was six, and her music is based on the hunting and harvest dances of her native land. The songs on her 1996 album *Worotan* deal with love, jealousy, and the position of women in society.

Sankara, Thomas (1949–1987)

Sankara became prime minister of Burkina Faso in 1982, after a military coup led by Colonel Ouédraogo, who became president. Frustrated by Ouédraogo's failure to tackle the country's dire economic problems, Sankara staged another coup in 1983 and took over as president. A popular leader, he embarked on a series of ambitious development programs intended to restructure the economy and make the rural areas self-reliant. To do so, Sankara had to cut government spending in other areas. This brought him into conflict with the country's powerful trade unions, and the subsequent discontent led one of his closest advisors, BLAISE COMPAORÉ, to mount a coup in 1987 in which he was killed.

Samori Toure

Saro-Wiwa, Kenule Beeson (1941–1995)

Ken Saro-Wiwa, a Nigerian writer, campaigned for his fellow Ogoni people, whose region had been polluted by the oil industry. In 1994, he was charged with the murder of four moderate Ogoni leaders. Despite international pleas for leniency, he was executed in 1995.

Sassou-Nguesso, Denis (born 1943)

Sassou-Nguesso became president of Congo in 1979, promising to continue the government's Marxist policies, though his policies were, in practice, more liberal than those of his predecessors. In 1990, bowing to public pressure, the government renounced Marxist ideology, and in 1991, it legalized opposition parties and stripped Sassou-Nguesso of all his powers. In the 1992 multiparty elections, Sassou-Nguesso was defeated by Pascal Lissouba.

Ken Saro-Wiwa

Savimbi, Jonas (born 1934)

Jonas Savimbi led the forces of the União Nacional para a Independência Total de Angola (UNITA), formed in 1966 to fight in the Angolan war of independence from Portuguese rule (1961–74). After independence (in 1975), UNITA fought a twenty-year war against AGOSTINHO NETO'S government forces, which finally ended in 1994–5.

Schreiner, Olive (Emilie Albertina) (1855–1920)

Olive Schreiner was a South African writer who sprang to fame with her novel *The Story of an African Farm* (1883), originally published under the pen-name "Ralph Iron." She was a pioneer of feminist writing and a campaigner for women's rights.

Seif, Salah Abou (1915–96)

Salah Seif, formerly a civil servant and then a journalist, was one of Egypt's most important film directors. He made eight films with the Nobel prizewinner NAGUIB NAHFOUZ as scriptwriter, and his 1977 production *The Death of the Waterbearer* was chosen as the Egyptian Film Association's film of the year.

Senghor, Léopold Sédar (born 1906)

A distinguished poet, Léopold Senghor became the first president of Senegal in 1960. He favored moderate "African socialism" and restricted political activity – by 1966, Senegal was a one-party state. He worked to modernize agriculture, prevent corruption, and establish close ties with neighboring countries. He also developed a philosophy called "negritude" that celebrated African culture and values. A declining economic situation and pressure for political reforms led to Senghor's resignation in late 1980. He was succeeded by ABDOU DIOUF.

Shaka

Ian Smith

Shabalala, Joseph (born c. 1940)

Joseph Shabalala is a Zulu singer who created the South African vocal group Ladysmith Black Mambazo. The ten-man group, singing mainly gospel songs, perfected a distinctive Zulu harmonic style. In 1981, Shabalala became a priest in the Church of God of the Prophets.

Shaka (1787–1828)

A brilliant military strategist, Shaka became a general in the army of DINGISWAYO, king of Mthethwa, and founded the Zulu kingdom in 1818. He won many victories in what is now KwaZulu/Natal, practicing the strategy of total warfare – complete annihilation of the enemy. In 1828, he was murdered by his half-brothers Mhlangane and DINGANE.

Siad Barre, Muhammad (born 1919)

Muhammad Siad Barre became president of Somalia in 1969, following a military coup. His rule was marked by civil war and war with Ethiopia, and he was overthrown by rebel forces in January 1991.

Sisulu, Nontsikelelo Albertlna (born 1918)

Albertina Sisulu and her husband WALTER SISULU were leading figures in the struggle against apartheid in South Africa and were imprisoned or placed under house arrest for long periods. She was a leader of the African National Congress (ANC) Women's League, became president of the Federation of African Women in 1984, and was elected a member of parliament in 1994.

Sisulu, Walter Max Ulyate (born 1912)

Walter Sisulu, like his wife ALBERTINA SISULU, was a prominent South African antiapartheid campaigner. Together with NELSON MANDELA, he was one of the 156 black activists tried and acquitted in the so-called Treason Trial (1956–61). In 1962, Sisulu and Mandela were arrested again, along with seven others, and charged with sabotage and terrorism. All except one were sentenced to life imprisonment in 1964. Sisulu was released in 1989, and in 1991 he became deputy president of the African National Congress (ANC).

Sithole, Rev. Ndabaningi (born 1920)

Ndabaningi Sithole, a clergyman, politician, and influential writer, was a major figure in the nationalist struggle in Rhodesia (now Zimbabwe) in the 1960s and 1970s. He founded the anticolonialist Zimbabwe African National Union (ZANU) with ROBERT MUGABE in 1963. He was imprisoned from 1965 until 1974, but in 1978 he helped to achieve an agreement with IAN SMITH'S white-minority government for constitutional change. This agreement was considered inadequate by the other leading nationalists, Robert Mugabe and JOSHUA NKOMO, and Sithole's political influence declined when a new agreement was negotiated in 1979. In November 1996, he was taken to court charged with planning to assassinate Mugabe and overthrow the government.

Skunder Boghassian (born 1937)

Skunder Boghassian is an Ethiopian painter who has achieved worldwide fame as an abstract and surrealist artist. His style reflects elements of Coptic, European, and West African art. He taught at the Fine Arts School at Addis Ababa, Ethiopia's capital, but after the 1974 revolution he took up a teaching post at Howard University in Washington, DC.

Slovo, (Yossel) Joe Mashel (1926–1995)

Born in Lithuania, Joe Slovo became a leading South African opponent of apartheid. A member of the Communist Party of South Africa (CPSA), he was barred from political activity in 1954. He later helped to found the military wing of the African National Congress (ANC), but he spent many years in exile before returning to South Africa in 1990. He was appointed minister for housing in South Africa's first multiracial government in 1994.

Smith, Ian Douglas (born 1919)

Ian Smith became prime minister of the white-dominated Rhodesia (now Zimbabwe) in 1964 and in 1965 he made an illegal Unilateral Declaration of Independence (UDI) from Britain in order to maintain white domination of the government. This eventually led to civil war between Smith's government forces and those of ROBERT MUGABE and JOSHUA NKOMO. Smith continued to serve as prime minister until 1979, when an interim multiracial government led by Bishop ABEL MUZOREWA was established.

Smuts, Jan Christiaan (1870–1950)

A South African politician and prime minister, Jan Smuts fought against the British in the Anglo-Boer War (1899–1902), becoming a general. Later, he worked to reconcile the Boer and British populations. He served as South Africa's prime minister from 1919 until 1924, and again from 1939 until 1948.

Sobhuza II (1899–1982)

Sobhuza II was king of Swaziland from 1921 and made his country strong and prosperous. As head of state from 1968, when Swaziland became independent from Britain, he regained large areas of land that had been taken by European settlers. He abolished the country's democratic constitution in 1973 and ruled the country with a council of ministers, but introduced a new constitution in 1979, allowing for a partly elected parliament and a "traditional" Swazi National Council. After his death, he was succeeded by his son MSWATI III.

Sobukwe, Robert Mangaliso (1924–1978)

A founder of the antiapartheid Pan-Africanist Congress (PAC) in South Africa, and its president from 1959, Robert Sobukwe helped to organize demonstrations against the Pass Laws in 1960. During one of these, at Sharpeville, the police opened fire on demonstrators and 69 people were killed and 180 wounded. This event, which became known as the Sharpeville massacre, focused world attention on the antiapartheid struggle. Sobukwe was banned from political activity and imprisoned – under a law used only against him and nicknamed the "Sobukwe clause" – from 1960 until 1969.

Zulu Sofala

Sofola, Zulu (born 1935)

Zulu Sofola, Nigeria's first woman playwright, writes on a variety of themes. She was educated in the United States, and became professor of performing arts at the University of Ilorin, Nigeria.

Sonni Ali *see* Sunni Ali

Soyinka, Wole (born 1934)

The first Black African to win a Nobel Prize in literature (1986), Wole Soyinka is an outstanding and prolific Nigerian playwright, novelist, critic, editor, and poet. His first play (*Invention*, 1955) was staged in London, England, as were *Brother Jero*, *Kongi's Harvest* (both 1965), and *The Swamp Dwellers* (1958), which he has adapted for a 1967 film. His first novel, *The Interpreters* (1965), has been called the first truly modern African novel. In 1984, he directed his first feature film, *Blues for a Prodigal*. Much of Soyinka's work dwells on the interplay of African and Western cultures in African society. He has been harshly critical of both the colonial and independent regimes in Africa, which has earned him periods of house arrest, exile, and imprisonment. Since 1988, Soyinka has been the professor of African studies and theater at Cornell University, NY.

Sundiata Keita (died 1255)

Sundiata, who founded the medieval Empire of Mali, was a member of the royal family of Kangaba, a kingdom close to historic Ghana. Because he was disabled from birth, when the Susu people murdered his brothers in 1224 they spared him as they thought he would be no threat. But despite his lameness, he became a great soldier and defeated the Susu in 1235. By 1240, he had conquered all of the Empire of Ghana. Sundiata was known as the "Lion of Mali."

Sunni Ali (died 1492)

Sunni Ali built the Songhay Empire of West Africa in the fifteenth century, after his people's domination by the Empire of Mali. He was at first ruler of the kingdom of Gao, which was controlled by Mali, and in about 1464, he began to free Gao from Mali and unite the Songhay people. He conquered large areas of Mali, and captured the important cities of Timbuktu and Djenné. His son and successor, Sunni Baru, was overthrown by ASKIA MUHAMMAD.

Efua Sutherland

Sutherland, Efua Theodora (1924–1996)

Efua Sutherland was a major Ghanaian poet and dramatist. She founded the Ghana Drama Studio in Accra, and in 1963 began a research program into African literature at the University of Ghana. She wrote several books for children, and her plays *Foriwa* and *Edufa* (both 1967) focused on women's roles.

Suzman, Dame Helen (born 1917)

Between 1953 and her retirement in 1989, Helen Suzman was the chief voice of liberalism in South Africa's parliament. Daughter of a Lithuanian Jewish immigrant, she was first elected to parliament in 1953 as a member of the United Party. After the United Party split in 1959, she became a member of the antiapartheid Progressive Party, and from 1961 until 1974, she was its sole representative in parliament. She was awarded the United Nations Human Rights Award in 1978.

Tala, André-Marie (born 1950)

André-Marie Tala is a Cameroonian guitarist who lost his sight as a teenager. He gave his first major concert in 1971, in Yaoundé, the capital of Cameroon. In 1972, he went to Paris to record his first singles, and he settled there in 1979. He has written film scores, and in 1994 produced his first CD, *Bend Skin*, based on Cameroonian folklore.

Oliver Tambo

Tambo, Oliver Reginald (1917–1993)

Oliver Tambo directed the activities of the African National Congress (ANC) while in exile from South Africa from 1960 until his return in 1990. He had joined the ANC in 1944 and, like his friend and former law partner NELSON MANDELA, was one of the defendants in the so-called Treason Trial (1956–61). He became acting president of the ANC in 1967 and was president from 1977 until 1991, when Mandela succeeded him. In July 1991, he was named ANC vice-president.

Taya, Maaouiya Ould Sidi Ahmed (born 1943)

Colonel Taya became Mauritania's head of state when he seized power in 1984. Under a new constitution introduced in 1991, he was elected president of Mauritania in 1992 and reelected in 1997. Taya served in the war in Western Sahara between 1976 and 1978 and later served as prime minister and minister of defence.

Taylor, Charles Ghankay (born 1948)

Charles Taylor, leader of the rebel National Patriotic Front of Liberia, launched the country's seven-year-long civil war in 1989 when he invaded Liberia from Côte d'Ivoire. However, in 1997, he was elected Liberia's president.

Tekle, Afewerk (born 1923)

Afewerk Tekle, Ethiopia's leading artist, was effectively court painter to Emperor HAILE SELASSIE. He had planned to be a mining engineer, but trained in art in London, England. He combined both African and European styles in his work, and is famous for his stained glass windows.

Tewodros (or Theodore) II (c. 1816–1868)

Tewodros II, born Theodore Kassai, reunified Ethiopia, then called Abyssinia, by conquering rival chiefs who had split the country between them. He was crowned king in 1855 as Tewodros II. After failing to form alliances with Britain and France against Ethiopia's Muslim neighbors, he developed a hatred of Europeans and imprisoned a number of them at the fort of Magdala. A British army sent to free them defeated him, and he then shot himself.

Tlali, Miriam (born 1933)

Miriam Tlali, a South African novelist and journalist, had her first two novels banned under the apartheid regime because they criticized its policies. Much of her work is concerned with the troubled black township of Soweto. She studied at universities in South Africa and Lesotho, but had to give up through lack of funds.

Todd, Sir Reginald Stephen Garfield (born 1908)

Garfield Todd was prime minister of the Federation of Rhodesia and Nyasaland from its formation in 1953 until 1958, when his party's policies were rejected as too liberal by the white-dominated electorate. Born in New Zealand, Todd went to Southern Rhodesia (now Zimbabwe) as a missionary in 1934. An opponent of the illegal regime of IAN SMITH, he was detained from 1965 until 1966 and again from 1972 until 1976.

Tolbert, William Richard Jr. (1913–1980)

William Tolbert was vice-president of Liberia from 1951 to 1971, and succeeded WILLIAM TUBMAN as president in 1971. During his time in office, Liberia's economy suffered because of falls in the prices of iron ore and rubber, and a rise in rice prices in 1979 led to rioting. He was assassinated during an army coup, led by SAMUEL DOE, in 1980.

Tombalbaye, Ngarta (1918–1975)

Ngarta Tombalbaye (formerly François Tombalbaye) was the first president of Chad, serving from 1962 until he was assassinated during an army coup, led by Félix Malloum, in 1975. He had earlier served as prime minister (1959–62).

Touré, Ahmad Sekou (1922–1984)

A major figure in the struggle for independence from colonial rule, Sekou Touré became president of Guinea in 1958. From 1971, following an unsuccessful invasion by opposition forces based in Guinea-Bissau, Touré imposed restrictions on the opposition, but improved his human rights record before his death in 1984. He was succeeded as president by LANSANA CONTÉ.

Toure, Ali Farka (born 1939)

Ali Farka Toure is a Malian musician who took up the guitar when he was eighteen. He soon became well known in Mali, and international success came in the late 1980s, when recordings and concerts made him popular in Britain.

Traoré, Moussa (born 1936)

Moussa Traoré, an army officer, became head of state of Mali in 1968 after leading a military coup that deposed MODIBO KEITA. He was himself deposed by another coup in 1991, led by Amadou Toure. During his period in office, droughts in the semidesert Sahel region caused widespread famine in Mali.

Tshombe, Moïse Kapenda (1919–1969)

Moïse Tshombe led the mineral-rich "Republic of Katanga" (now the province of Shaba) that declared itself independent from the Congo Republic (now Congo [Dem.Rep.]) in 1960. Following the occupation of Katanga by United Nations troops in 1963, Tshombe went into exile. In 1964 he returned to become head of the central government of the Congo Republic, but he was dismissed in 1965. He again went into exile, in Spain, after MOBUTU SESE SEKO took power, and a Congolese court sentenced him to death in his absence. In 1967, he was kidnapped and taken to Algeria, where he remained under house arrest until his death.

Moïse Tshombe

Tsiranana, Philibert (born 1912)

Philibert Tsiranana became the first president of Madagascar in 1959. He was reelected in 1972, but his poor health, accompanied by demonstrations against his regime, led him to appoint GABRIEL RAMANANTSOA in his place and he resigned as president.

Tubman, William V. S. (Vacanarat Shadrach) (1895–1971)

William Tubman was president of Liberia from 1944 until his death in 1971, when he was succeeded by WILLIAM TOLBERT. Through his "open-door" policies, he attracted foreign investment and reduced the country's dependence on the United States.

Tutu, Desmond Mpilo (born 1931)

Desmond Tutu was a powerful and eloquent antiapartheid campaigner. His emphasis on nonviolent resistance to the apartheid regime earned him the 1984 Nobel Peace Prize. His appointment as Archbishop of Cape Town, in 1986, made him head of the Anglican Church in South Africa, Lesotho, Mozambique, Namibia, and Swaziland; he retired in 1996. After the downfall of the apartheid regime, he set up the Truth and Reconciliation Commission to give the enforcers of apartheid the opportunity to confess their crimes and seek forgiveness. This has been opposed by many of apartheid's victims and their families, who feel that the guilty should be tried for their crimes. His demand that the African National Congress (ANC) also seek amnesty for its past human rights abuses has sparked controversy.

Adaora Ulasi

Ulasi, Adaora Lily (born c. 1932)

Adaora Ulasi is a Nigerian journalist and author who used pidgin English in her first novel, *Many Thing You No Understand* (1970), to highlight the relationship between colonial administrators and local people before independence. The daughter of an Igbo chief, she studied in the United States and later divided her time between Nigeria and England.

Usman dan Fodio (1754–1817)

In 1804, Usman dan Fodio, a Fulani ruler and Islamic scholar, proclaimed a jihad (Islamic holy war) that led to the creation of a Fulani-Hausa empire – the Sokoto Caliphate – in present-day Benin, Cameroon, Niger, and northern Nigeria. He later handed over power to his son Muhammad Bello, and retired to teach and write.

Uwaifor, "Sir" Victor (born 1941)

"Sir" Victor Uwaifor is a Nigerian musician who began his career as an amateur wrestler. As a bandleader and playing many instruments himself, he created fresh rhythms and dances. His recording *Joromi* was a major hit in West Africa, and financial success enabled him to open a hotel and set up his own television studio.

van Riebeeck, Jan (1618–1677)

Jan van Riebeeck, an official in the service of the Dutch East India Company, headed the first Dutch settlement at the Cape of Good Hope, in 1652. In 1657, he allowed some of the soldiers under his command to set up farms on Khoikhoi grazing lands. These soldiers became the first of South Africa's Boers – "boer" is the Dutch word for "farmer" and the historical name of the Afrikaners.

Hendrik Verwoerd

Verwoerd, Dr Hendrik Frensch (1901–1966)

Hendrik Verwoerd was prime minister of South Africa from 1958 until his assassination in 1966; he was succeeded by JOHN VORSTER. He favored the breaking of his country's ties with the Commonwealth, which it left in 1961. He had earlier served as minister of "native affairs," when he developed strict apartheid policies with the support of the premier, Johannes Strijdom, whom he succeeded. His administration was marked by further development and ruthless application of the highly controversial apartheid policy. In fact, he has been called the architect of apartheid for his efforts to enforce it.

Vieira, João Bernardo (born 1939)

In 1980, João Vieira, prime minister of Guinea-Bissau, led a military coup against LUIZ CABRAL and became head of state. He was made executive president in 1984, then reelected in 1989 and again in 1994 in the country's first multiparty elections.

Vorster, John (1915–1983)

John (formerly Balthazar Johannes) Vorster was the prime minister of South Africa following the assassination of HENDRIK VERWOERD in 1966 until 1978. He was elected president in 1978, but resigned in 1979 following a political scandal. He enforced apartheid policies, but sought to make contacts with other African governments.

Weah, George (born 1966)

George Weah, a Liberian soccer player, became in one year (1996) African Player of the Year, European Player of the Year, and World Footballer of the Year. He has played in more than fifty international games and also for the French league teams AC Monaco and Paris St. Germain, and scored seventy-five goals in six seasons. In 1996, the Italian team AC Milan paid US$10 million for him. He supports his national team financially, paying for their uniforms and fares to overseas games.

Welensky, Sir Roland (Roy) (1907–1991)

Roy Welensky was prime minister of the Central African Federation (CAF) from 1956 until 1963, when it was broken up to form Malawi, Zambia, and Rhodesia (now Zimbabwe). A former trade unionist and heavyweight boxing champion, Welensky entered politics in 1938 and worked for the creation of the white-minority ruled CAF. When it collapsed, he retired from politics.

Yameogo, Maurice (1921–1993)

Maurice Yameogo was the first president of Upper Volta (now Burkina Faso) from 1958 until 1966, when he was deposed by a military coup led by SANGOULÉ LAMIZANA. He was imprisoned from 1966 until 1970, when he went into exile.

Youlou, Abbé Fulbert (1917–1972)

A Roman Catholic priest, Abbé Youlou became the first president of Congo in 1959. In 1963, he was forced to resign and went into exile after widespread unrest and a general strike. He was succeeded as president by Alphonse Massamba-Débat.

Zenawi, Meles (born 1955)

Meles Zenawi, an opponent of the military regime of HAILE MARIAM MENGISTU, became head of state of Ethiopia in 1991, at the end of the civil war. He was elected by the Council of Representatives set up by the ruling coalition, the Ethiopian People's Revolutionary Democratic Front. He was reelected in 1994.

Zéroual, Liamine (born 1941)

Zéroual was appointed president of Algeria in 1994 and elected in 1995. In 1999, when he stepped down and was replaced as president by Abdelaziz Bouteflika. As president, Zéroual tried to resolve Algeria's domestic crisis and unsuccessfully attempted to negotiate peace with the Islamic Salvation Front. Zéroual fought against France in Algeria's war of independence and he rose to become land forces chief in 1989. He then resigned from the army and became defence minister in 1993.

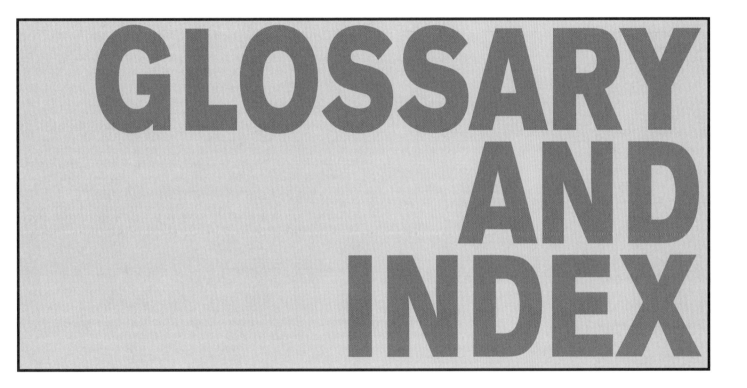

Glossary

Bold words are cross-references to other glossary entries.

a cappella Music without instrumental accompaniment.

Abarusura The historic army of the Bunyoro Kingdom.

Abuk An important **yath** in the Dinka religion. Abuk was the first woman and is associated with rivers.

adoimara The "whites" (or lower class) in Afar society.

African Franc Zone A group of African countries whose currencies are linked with the French franc at a fixed exchange rate. The currency that these countries use is called the **CFA** or CFA franc. The African Franc Zone, or Franc Zone, countries of Central Africa are Congo, Gabon, Equatorial Guinea, and the Central African Republic. The remainder of the African Franc Zone countries are in West Africa.

Afro-Beat A form of popular West African music.

age-grades The various social levels in certain societies. Each person belongs to a particular age-set that moves up through the various age-grades.

age-regiments A largely historical feature common to many Southern African peoples. Basically, men or women were organized by age into these groups, which were usually used as mobile sources of labor or occasionally provided the army. Different societies structured or organized their age-regiments in various ways. The Zulu age-regiments under Shaka, for instance, were largely concerned with battle and remained together for much longer than in other societies. Age-regiments were an important way of providing social unity.

age-set see **age-grades**

akhnif A long, embroidered cape once worn by Jewish men in North Africa.

akiwor Initiation of Karamojong girls into adulthood.

akple A mixture of corn and cassava flour used to make a food that is usually eaten with meat or vegetable stew.

Akuj The supreme god of the Karamojong religion.

Ala In the Igbo religion, Ala is generally considered to be the Earth goddess. Shrines are dedicated to Ala, and the Igbo's most important festival, the Yam Festival, is celebrated in her honor.

Allah The Muslim name for God.

aloalo A carved wooden pole on a Mahafaly tomb.

amaNdlozi The revered ancestors of a Ndebele family, who are believed to be spirit guardians.

amenokal In the past, the Tuareg were divided into seven main **confederations**. Each was led by an amenokal, or king.

Amma The Dogon supreme god.

Amon In Ancient Eygpt, Amon was a local Theban god depicted with a ram's head and symbolizing life and fertility. Over time, Amon became identified with **Re** and eventually became known as Amon-Re.

Amon-Re see **Amon**

Anansi A spider character, known as a trickster, who features in many West African folktales. Anansi also appears in Caribbean storytelling as African folklore was taken to the Americas by slaves taken from Africa.

ankh A T-shaped cross with a loop at the top. It is based on the Ancient Egyptian **hieroglyph** for eternal life.

apartheid An Afrikaans word meaning "apartness" or "separateness." It is generally used to refer to the South African government's policy of racial and ethnic segregation and white domination. Officially, apartheid was in effect from 1948 to 1991, though racist policies had been in place before this date and the legacy of apartheid can still be seen today. The government definition of apartheid was "separate development of the races" – a euphemism for oppression.

Apedemak An ancient Nubian god.

aperit An overnight Karamojong festival for elders.

appliqué A decoration or trimming of one material sewn or fixed onto another.

arghul An ancient instrument from rural Egypt, a type of double clarinet.

ari An Afar house of flexible sticks covered with mats.

asaimara The politically dominant class in Afar society.

asantehene The Asante king.

asapan Initiation of Karamojong boys into adulthood.

askari Africans who fought in the colonial armies of German East Africa during World War I.

Astarte The Phoenician Moon goddess, renamed "Tanit-Pene-Baal" (meaning "Tanit the Face of Baal") by the Carthaginians.

avant-gardistes A Congo (Dem. Rep.) art movement of the 1970s that attempted to create a uniquely "African" art style unaffected by foreign influences.

awoamefia The **dukowo** head of the Anlo Ewe.

ayana A saint of the Oromo religion.

Baal-Haman see **Baal-Moloch**

Baal-Moloch The Phoenician Sun god, renamed Baal-Haman by the Carthaginians.

badima Pedestal-based drums used at Tonga funerals.

badimo Offerings that Sotho people make to their ancestors to ask for assistance or in gratitude.

bakama A Bachwezi king.

balaphone see **marimba**

balopwe A group of official ministers (rather like a government cabinet) that helped the Luba king with certain duties.

banda In Herero society, a **lineage** of ancestors that is traced through a person's female relatives.

bandair A large Berber tambourine with an extra set of strings (snares) across its surface for added vibrations.

Bantustan An alternative name for a **homeland**.

bany In the political structure of the Dinka, each group has a priestly or religious **clan**, called a bany, whose historical role was to control and safeguard the land.

bao kiswahili An East African version of **mankala**.

basango Spirits in the Tonga belief system. They are associated with particular regions or neighborhoods.

Baswezi A Nyamwezi society devoted to **Swezi**.

bataka The Ganda term for the head of a **clan**.

bavide In the Luba religion it is believed that these spirits exert a bad influence on people.

bebtara A Falasha religious official.

Bena Yanda A Bemba **clan**. The name literally means Crocodile Clan.

beng The head of the **bany** in Dinka society. The name means "Master of the Fishing Spear."

bieri A form of ancestral reverence practiced by the Fang as part of the Fang religion.

Black Consciousness A movement that emerged in the 1970s and had medical student Steve Biko as one of its leading thinkers. Biko formed the South African Students Organization (SASO), which was based on the principles of Black Consciousness. The movement stressed pride in being black, emphasized black values and culture, and rejected white culture and white liberalism.

Boeremusiek Light, danceable Afrikaner country music.

bokulaka A Mongo village chief.

bolombatos Manding gourd harps.

braaivleis An Afrikaner barbecue.

bridewealth A practice common among African people in which a marriage between a couple is sealed with a gift – often cattle, but it may be cash or other animals – from the groom to the bride's family. The bride is not regarded as property. It is usually considered to be compensation to the bride's family for loss of a working member or a token of respect. Part of it may be used by the couple to set up home together.

brimbiri A Nuba stringed musical instrument.

bugalli A Nyamwezi porridgelike dish.

bulogi Witchcraft as believed in by many Nyamwezi.

burra An Afar camp, usually comprising one or two **ari**.

butala granary A mud and grass **granary** with a thatched roof.

bwiti A politico-religious movement practiced by the Fang, which has replaced **bieri** as the main religious force. Bwiti combines aspects of both Christianity and bieri.

cahen A Falasha religious official. The plural is cahenet.

cahenet *see* **cahen**

calabash A type of gourd whose hollowed-out shell has a wide variety of uses from container to musical instrument. Calabashes often figure in African legends and mythology where the two halves are used, for example, to symbolize the union of Heaven and Earth, Man and Woman, or Land and Sky.

caliph The Arabic for "successor": an Islamic ruler.

canopy A layer in a forest formed by the crowns (branches and leaves) of trees. **Rainforests** have more than one canopy. The upper canopy occurs at a height of 90 to 150 ft (30–45 m), but this layer is pierced by occasional tall trees called **emergents**. One or two lower canopies occur at roughly 60 ft (20 m) and 30 ft (10 m). The canopies are inhabited by tree-dwelling species such as birds, bats, and monkeys. The sunlight is strong and the vegetation is thick and virtually impenetrable. Below the canopies, relatively little sunlight penetrates down to ground level where the vegetation is sparser.

caravan A company of travelers journeying together, often with a train of animals loaded with goods.

Casamance-style music A percussive style from a region of the same name in Senegal and Gambia.

caste A rigid class distinction generally based on birth, wealth, and occupation. The Hindu (Indian) caste system consists of four main castes, called varnas, into which a person is born. The top varna is occupied by Brahmans (religious leaders and scholars); the next consists of Kshatriyas (rulers, nobles, and warriors); then come the Vaisyas (bankers and other kinds of business people); and the lowest varna comprises the Sudras (artisans and laborers). Besides the four varnas there is a fifth category of "outcastes," called panchamas (fifths), untouchables, or the "children of god". Many attempts have been made to eliminate the system, and laws and modern urban life have lessened its rigidity somewhat.

cataract An unnavigable or hazardous stretch of river, perhaps created by rapids, waterfalls, or a narrowing of the riverbanks. There are six major (numbered) cataracts on the Nile River between Aswan and Khartoum, some of which once formed political frontiers.

CFA An abbreviation for "Communauté Financière Africaine," CFA is the currency used by the Central and West African countries that form the **African Franc Zone**. The CFA franc is on a fixed exchange rate with the French franc. The initials originally stood for "Colonies Français d'Afrique," but were changed after Central Africa became independent from colonial rule.

CFA franc *see* **CFA**

chaabi A form of popular music in Morocco; a mix of Arab, Berber, and contemporary Western styles, the lyrics tending to highlight political and social issues.

cheikhas Women musicians from rural Algeria from several centuries ago. The male equvalent is cheikhs.

chikha A female singer in Morocco. (Note that it can also have negative connotations; chikha can also mean "prostitute.")

chimurenga A contemporary African music based on the rhythms of the **mbira**. Created by Thomas Mapfumo, chimurenga – which means "liberation war" – played an important role in the struggle for majority rule in Zimbabwe (then Rhodesia).

Chitimukulu The name and title of the Bemba kings. It literally means "Chiti the Great" and refers to Chiti, the leader of the **Bena Yanda**, who founded the Bemba kingdom. All the following kings were named after him.

chleuh Professional Berber musician-dancers of the High Atlas Mountains of Morocco.

Chukwu A supreme being acknowledged by some Igbo groups. Chukwu is the creator of the visible universe.

cicatrix *see* **scarification**

cikunza A Chokwe mask used as part of the initiation of boys into adulthood.

ciondo A Kenyan bag made from **sisal**.

circumcise To carry out **circumcision**.

circumcision A relatively simple, if painful, procedure (removal of all or part of the foreskin) for boys but a much more serious operation (ranging from minor to severe genital mutilation) with long-lasting consequences for girls. This practice is highly controversial, however, and is opposed by many African women.

clan A group of people, usually several **lineages**, who claim descent from a common ancestor or ancestors.

compound An enclosure containing living quarters. Compound is often used to refer to a group of buildings lived in by members of the same family or extended family. One compound may include several buildings.

confederation An alliance of political groupings.

congo A popular style of Central African music that developed in the Congo (Rep.) and Congo (Dem. Rep.). Also referred to as **soukous**.

copra The dried "meat" of the coconut. Copra is the source of coconut oil.

Coptic The word "Coptic" is derived from "aiguptios," the Greek word for Egyptian, which comes from an Ancient Egyptian name for Memphis. Today, the word "Coptic" has acquired many different meanings. As a noun, it is the name of an Afroasiatic language written in the Greek alphabet that is now largely extinct. Used as an adjective, Coptic can refer to the Copts (the Christian minority in Egypt); the Coptic (Christian) churches of Egypt and Ethiopia; to a historical period inEgypt's history; and to certain artifacts.

Not all Copts are members of the Egyptian Coptic Church, some are Roman Catholics or belong to various evangelical sects. Those that are members of the Coptic Church are sometimes called Orthodox Copts. The historical Coptic Period is basically Egypt's Christian era, which can be dated from either the 200s to 642 or from 451 to 642. "Coptic" is also used to refer to artifacts that were produced in Egypt during its Coptic Period, but not necessarily by Coptic artists. Finally, "Coptic" can be used to describe the Ethiopian Christian Church, which traces its history back to the Egyptian Coptic Church.

couscous A spicy dish originating in North Africa that consists of a steamed, coarse-ground grain such as semolina. Couscous is popular in the semidesert Sahel region of West Africa.

crux ansata A cross used from the fifth century onward in Egypt (during the **Coptic** Period), the shape of which is based on the Ancient Egyptian **hieroglyph** for "life" (the **ankh**). These crosses often decorated gravestones.

cubism An early twentieth-century Western art movement. Cubism was characterized by the separation and abstract arrangement of subjects into cubes and other geometrical forms. This was a move away from the portrayal of subjects in a more realistic and natural way.

Dak The legendary son of **Nyikang**.

darabouka A Moroccan clay drum.

dardar The head of an Afar sultanate.

deforestation The clearing of trees in a forest. In the African **rainforests**, huge tracts of land are being cleared of trees every year. The reasons are primarily economic. In poorer countries, where most rainforests are, their clearance is a way of raising much-needed cash to pay off debts to foreign banks and governments. Also, the growth of urban areas has led to the intensification and extensification of agriculture: more land is needed to farm and this land is farmed more intensively, leaving it little time to recover. In forest areas, this can result in a permanent loss of forest if the land is not allowed time to recover from cultivation. Deforestation causes soil deterioration, which can lead to soil erosion. It can also indirectly lead to a decrease in rainfall as trees are an essential part of the climatic processes that produce rain.

delta An apron of land made from sediment deposited at the mouth of a river where the main stream splits up into several distributaries.

demotic A simplified system of Ancient Egyptian **hieroglyphic** writing.

Deng An important **yath** in the Dinka religion, Deng is associated with rain, thunder, and lightning.

derra A colored blouse once worn by Jewish women in North Africa.

dervishes Members of a branch of Islam called **Sufism**. Dervishes are dedicated to a life of poverty and chastity.

desertification A process of land degradation in which previously fertile land can be turned into barren land or desert. It is usually caused by **drought** or the overuse of fragile lands. Desertification only occurs in drylands, which have low, infrequent, and irregular rainfall and high temperatures. This includes the Sahel semidesert region in West Africa, where desertification has become an increasingly urgent problem in recent decades, and, in Southern Africa the fringes of the Nambi Desert and the semidesert Kalahari.

dhow A cargo ship with a raised deck at the stern (rear end) and sails, which is used along Indian Ocean coasts.

diel The founding family of a Shilluk village.

Difaqane A Sotho-Tswana word meaning "scattering." It is used to refer to the period (1819–39) of mass migrations and wars in the southeastern half of Southern Africa. The Difaqane was triggered by the rise of the Zulu kingdom. This period is known as the **Mfecane** by the Nguni peoples east of the Drakensberg Mountains.

disenfranchisement Depriving a person of the right to vote or other rights of citizenship.

divination A common feature of many African religions, divination is practiced by diviners who use various tools (such as wooden figures, plants, bones, or seeds) to divine the spiritual cause of a specific problem such as illness, accident, or misfortune.

diviner A Practioner of **divination**.

Dja-gay The first human according to the Nuer religion. Dja-gay is said to have emerged from a hole in the ground at a holy place called Duar.

domba In Venda society, girls who have completed the **vhusha** initiation process attend a school known as the domba to learn the duties expected of wives and mothers. Domba can also refer to the process of initiation itself.

drought Water shortage caused by a prolonged period of inadequate rainfall. Drought can have a devastating affect on the land and people who make their living from the land, in particular reducing the number of **nomads**, for example in the Sahel region of Western Africa in recent decades.

dufia The head of a village in Ewe society.

dukowo A council of Ewe **dufias** who would advise the overall leader of a whole region. In the past, the Ewe were divided into ten such dukowo.

durra An alternative name for the cereal sorghum.

dyamu Malinke word for a group of people who share the same name, male ancestors, and **taboos**.

dyeli A name for professional singers (bards) among the Bambara and Malinke. Dyeli are often involved in maintaining oral history as their songs retell and preserve Manding history.

Ehi The people of the historic Kingdom of Benin believed that every human had a spirit of destiny, called a Ehi, which the soul created before birth in conversation with **Osanobua**.

ekitela Subsections of Karamojong society whose members gather for festivities relating to the seasons and the harvest. Ekitela is literally the name of a reddish soil.

electric mbira A contemporary African style of music that translates the sounds of the **mbira** into guitar riffs accompanied by complicated drum patterns and vocals based on traditional singing styles.

emahiya A brightly-colored body wrap worn by Swazi men and women.

embalming The treatment of a dead body, usually after removing the internal organs, with various chemicals to prevent it from decaying. The Ancient Egyptians embalmed bodies so that the dead could use their own bodies in the afterlife. Early embalmers probably used tarlike substances as embalming solutions, but more successful techniques using dry natron (a naturally-occurring salt) were developed over time.

emergents Occasional tall trees that rise above the upper **canopy** of a tropical **rainforest**. The upper canopy occurs at a height of 90 to 150 ft (30–45 m), but emergents can reach a height of over 190 ft (60 m).

emir The ruler, prince, or commander of an Islamic state.

enkang Maasai rainy-season homes.

Epiphany A yearly festival held on January 6 in many Christian churches commemorating both the revealing of Jesus as Christ and the baptism of Jesus.

epiphytes A plant that grows on another plant but is not a parasite – an epiphyte does not obtain its nourishment from its host or cause the host any harm, found particularly in rainforests.

erg An area of shifting sand dunes in a desert.

erosion Can be used to refer to the loss of soil cover, which has been eroded by the action of wind or rain.

Esu A god of the historic Kingdom of Benin and of the Yoruba people. Often described as the " trickster god," Esu (or Eshu) tells **Olodumare** of the activities of other **orisa** and of people.

Ethiopian faunal realm A biogeographical zone that includes most of sub-Saharan Africa. Animals of this realm include lions, elephants, and giraffes.

fama A Bambara local leader.

feluccas Small, narrow boats propelled by oar or wind that have been used on the Nile River for centuries.

fez A brimless felt hat shaped like a truncated cone.

forest-foragers Forest-dwelling peoples who are mainly **hunter-gatherers**.

fou-fou Cassava root turned into flour and made into a kind of dough.

gadaa The historic Oromo democratic system.

gandu The basic unit of the cooperative system in which most Hausa agricultural work is carried out.

Garang An important **yath** in the Dinka religion. Garang was the first man and is associated with the Sun. Garang is also a common Dinka family name.

garigue Heath and poor **scrub** with patches of bare rock and soil.

Gaua An evil god of some Khoisan religions, also called Gawama, who tries to disrupt the work of **Nadi**.

Gawama *see* **Gaua**

geerewol A dance performed at a Fulani **worso**. These dances prove the ability of men to attract women.

Gelede Festivals incorporating masked dancers held by the Yoruba at regular intervals. Now largely to entertain, they were once intended to appease local witches.

Genna Christmas in Ethiopia.

gerber An Oromo water container made from a whole goatskin with the leg, tail, and neck openings tied.

ghaita A Berber reed instrument.

ghana The title – meaning war-chief – of the kings of the ancient empire of Wagadu. It later came to be used as the name for the medieval Empire of Ghana.

Gikuyu According to the Kikuyu religion, the Kikuyu are descended from Gikuyu, the son of **Ngai**.

ginna The "great house," generally lived in by the male head of a Dogon village or **lineage**.

global warming An increase in the average global temperature believed to be caused by the **greenhouse effect**.

gorfa A Bedouin **granary**.

granary A building or room in which grain is stored.

Great Vidye The creator-god of the Luba religion.

greenhouse effect The greenhouse effect is a natural – and extremely important – phenomenon. It keeps the Earth's surface some 30 °C (86 °F) warmer than it would be otherwise, so enabling life on the planet to exist. Carbon dioxide (CO_2) and other gases act like glass in a greenhouse; they let the Sun's rays in but trap some of the heat that would otherwise be radiated into space. Human activity is beginning to alter the greenhouse effect, however. The burning of fossil fuels and **deforestation** are increasing the level of CO_2 in the atmosphere. As levels go up, more heat is retained and the average global temperature could rise. If the Earth's surface warms enough, ice caps would melt; sea levels would rise; low-lying areas would disappear underwater; and farming would be adversely affected, resulting in widespread famine and social disruption.

griot A general West African name for storytellers, singers, and musicians.

groundnut A group of plants including the peanut, which is a major cash crop and food item in many African countries.

groundnut A group of plants including the peanut, which is a major cash crop and food item in many West African countries.

guedra A Moroccan drum made from a cooking pot with a skin stretched over its opening.

gum arabic A gum exuded by certain acacia trees. It has many uses and is used in the manufacture of ink, food thickeners, and pills.

gumbri A small, three-stringed Berber lute.

Hadith A Muslim holy book providing guidance on all aspects of life, attributed to the Prophet Muhammad.

haikal A screen that seperates the sanctuary from the choir in a **Coptic** church.

Hajj One of the five holy duties of Muslims, the Hajj is a pilgrimage to Mecca, in Saudi Arabia – the Islamic holy city. After making the pilgrimage, a person can use a prefix such as Haji before their name.

hakpa A session at a Ewe festival that is a general singing practice for everybody.

hale Societies to which many Mende belong. Among the most important hale are **Poro** and **Sande**. Others include **Humui**, **Njayei**, **Yassi**, and **Kpa**. Until recently the working of these socieites was kept from noninitiates, so they are often refered to as "secret" societies.

halo A feature of some Ewe festivals, it is an exchange of insulting songs between neighboring villages.

hammada An area of rock platforms and boulders in a desert, covered with a thin layer of sand and pebbles.

haratin Lower-class Berber **oasis** cultivators.

harayto A traditional top worn by rural Afar men.

harmattan A cool, dry, dusty wind from the Sahara Desert that blows toward the West African coast, especially from November through March.

havalu A session at a Ewe festival in which the composer teaches a new song to his fellow drummers.

hazomanga A village ritual post used by the Sakalava.

henna A reddish-orange dye made from plants and used as a paint with which to decorate skin or dye hair.

hieratic A rapid, handwritten form of Ancient Egyptian **hieroglyphics** largely used by priests.

hieroglyph Picture symbol used in **hieroglyphics**.

hieroglyphics A form of writing, especially used in Ancient Egypt and Nubia, that uses pictures and symbols to represent concepts, objects, or sounds.

highlife A dance music that is often considered the national music of Ghana. Early forms of it originated in Ghana's southern Cape Coast area in the 1880s. The name "highlife" was coined during the 1920s in the context of high-class Ghanaian ballroom dance orchestras. Highlife incorporates African guitar techniques brought from Liberia by Creole mariners in the beginning of the twentieth century, and has also been influenced by colonial military bands. It became very popular during and after World War II but declined in the 1980s. More recently, Ghanaian musicians have been using computer aids to produce disco-orientated forms.

hogon The spiritual leader of the Dogon, responsible for, among other things, preserving myths.

homeland Usually meaning the land or country in which one lives or was born, it also refers to the South African Bantustans. Created by the South African government during the **apartheid** era, these were artificial homelands in which Black African peoples were forced to live. They often bore no relation to the areas in which groups had historically been associated with. The ten homelands were created from 260 "native reserves" that had been in existence since 1913. Homeland facilities and infrastructure were poor and their inhabitants suffered from overcrowding and poverty.

Horus An Ancient Egyptian Sun god, usually depicted with a falcon's head; the lord of heaven.

Humui A Mende **hale** that helps to regulate sexual behaviour. The rules of Humui prohibit certain kinds of sexual relationships, such as those with girls under the age of puberty or with nursing mothers.

hunter-gatherers People who live off food that can be hunted or collected from the wild and do not cultivate crops or raise livestock.

Ifijoku A god worshipped by the Igbo as the giver and protector of yams – a form of sweet potato that plays a central part in the village economy.

igikubge A Tutsi headdress worn by royals.

iklan The third and lowest class within the Tuareg social structure.

ikula A wooden Kuba knife. Introduced by the peace-loving Kuba king Shamba Bolongongo, the ikula replaced the **shongo**.

ilterekeyani The name of the most recent Maasai **age-set** to make the **age-grade** of elder.

imajeghen The Tuareg nobility, one of whom is elected as the **amenokal** of each **confederation**.

Imam A Muslim religious leader. An imam often leads the prayers at a **mosque**. The **Ismaili** Muslim subsect have an Imam as their leader.

Imana The benevolent god of the Hutu and Tutsi.

imdyazn A type of Berber band usually made up of four musicians, including a poet as leader.

imghad A Tuareg social classification refering to the ordinary citizen.

imraguen A Moorish social class of largely itinerant fisherman who live along the coast of Mauritania.

imwu A rounded bunlike hairstyle worn – more commonly in the past – by Teke men of noble rank.

imzi A Zulu homestead.

inabanza The inabanza, one of the Luba **balopwe**, had charge of ritual matters concerning the **Mulopwe**'s sacred role.

inakulu The principal wife of an Ovimbundu chief. They are believed to have supernatural powers in the Ovimbundu religion.

Incwala A three-week-long period, also called the First Fruits Festival, when the king and nation of Swaziland reaffirm their relationship.

indigo A deep blue dye usually made from certain plants.

indlu The basic social unit in Swazi society is the indlu (a husband and wife and their children). Several indlu make up an **umuti**. The members of an **umuti** share agricultural tasks.

ineslemen *see* **marabout**

ingondo Small Twa pots that were intended to contain love charms. Twa women would wear them tied around the waist to ensure their husband's affections.

injera A pancakelike bread made from **teff**.

inkosi Historically, the Xhosa's allegiance was to their **clan**, led by an inkosi whose status was gained through his mother. Inkosi (which actually means "thank-you") were obliged to be hospitable and generous and their powers were limited by public opinion and counselors.

inselbergs Isolated rocky hills rising abruptly from a flat plain or plateau.

invertebrates Any animal without a backbone.

iscathamiya An **a cappella** Zulu singing style originally from the all-male workers' hostels of 1920s Natal.

Isis An Ancient Egyptian fertility goddess, usually depicted as a woman with cow's horns; wife and sister of **Osiris** and mother of **Horus**.

Ismailis A Muslim subsect that has as its spiritual leader the Aga Khan. The Ismailis believe that the office of **Imam** should have gone to a descendant of Ismail (died 760) when Jafar the sixth Imam died in 765.

itoom A type of sculpture used in **divination** by the Kuba. A moistened disk would be rubbed on the back of the sculpture while the diviner recited certain phrases. The phrase at which the disk stuck would reveal the answers to the client's question.

iwisa A knobkerrie – a stick with a round knob at the end – used as a club or missile by Zulu warriors.

izar Long, striped garment, usually red or white, once worn by Jewish women in North Africa.

jalabiya A long, loose robe often worn by Arab men.

jali Manding term for **griot**; the traditional caste of musician storytellers.

jihad An Islamic holy war against nonbelievers undertaken by Muslims. (In the 1670s, the Fulani began a series of jihads against their non-Muslim neighbors, which lasted for almost the next two centuries. During this period Futa Toro, Futa Djallon, Wuli, and Bundu were established as jihadist states.)

jile An Afar dagger.

Jit Jive A term coined by the internationally-successful Zimbabwean group, the Bhundu Boys. It is an energetic dance music featuring **mbira**-style guitars.

juju Yoruba urban music of Nigeria.

Juok The god of the Shilluk people. Juok is an abstract divine being who is thought to have created the world.

kabaka A Bugandan king.

kabosy A Madagascan instrument similar to a guitar.

kafu A group of Malinke villages making up a distinct social unit, headed by a **mansa**.

Kaikara The Nyoro harvest goddess.

kalindula A Zambian bass instrument and the very fast-paced form of music of the same name.

Kalunga The supreme god of the Chokwe. Also known as Nzambi.

kalunga A type of **talking drum** from Nigeria.

Kanaga The "Hand of God," the name of a Dogon mask worn by newly initiated young men.

kente Colorful cloth generally made by Asante weavers and considered the national dress of Ghana. Kente cloth is famous for its complex patterns.

Keskes A lidded pot in which **couscous** is steamed.

kess A Falasha community priest, similar to a **rabbi**.

keta Strip-woven cloth generally made by Ewe weavers that uses contrasting **warp** and **weft** colors with inlaid designs. It is similar to Asante **kente** cloth.

kettledrum A drum made from a hollow metallic hemisphere with a flexible top that can be tightened or loosened to change the pitch.

kgotla A Sotho-Tswana term that can be used to mean both meeting place and court.

Khalifa A variation of **caliph**, the Arabic word for "successor." (In particular, it is used to refer to Abdullah ibn Muhammad who succeeded the **Mahdi** in 1885.)

khamsa Arabic for "five." A symbol of the hand that is used in jewelry worn by Berber women is also called khamsa. It represents the five holy duties of Muslims.

khamsin A strong local wind of Egypt.

khanga A rectangular cloth printed with a border and a design that includes a Swahili proverb.

kia A trancelike state that Kung healers usually achieve by performing a dance. This activates **num** (an energy from the gods), which is then used as a healing force.

Kibuka The Ganda god of war, brother of **Mukasa**.

kidumu A mask worn by Tsaayi (eastern Teke) dancers at funerals and celebrations.

Kintu The first man and the ancestor of the Ganda.

kissar A Sudanese stringed instrument similar to a lyre.

kitumpa kya muchi One of the names a Luba **diviner** could call a **mboko**.

kize-uzi Fonio grain, the smallest cultivated seed. The Dogon call it "the little thing."

Kongolo The Songye ruler of the Luba kingdom.

kontingo A three-stringed, Manding musical instrument.

kora A popular stringed musical instrument played widely throughout West Africa but thought to originate from Manding culture.

Koran The sacred book of the Islamic religion, believed by Muslims to be the word of **Allah**.

Kowth The creator-god of the Nuer religion. The Nuer pray to Kowth for health and good fortune.

Kozo The name of a particular **nkisi nkondi** used in matters concerning women's affairs.

Kpa A Mende **hale**. Kpa members, who are largely men, are trained to use herbs to treat minor ailments such as toothache or earache.

kpegisu One of the oldest traditional Ewe drums, kpegisu was probably originally a war drum.

kpezi A clay and raffia drum used at Fon funerals.

Kuomboka Festival An annual Lozi festival centered on the rise and fall of the Zambezi waters and the transfer of the king's capital from Lealui to Limulunga.

kuuarmuon A magistrate figure among the Nuer peoples; also known as the "leopard-skin chief" as, in the past, he would wear a leopard skin to indicate his status.

kwosso A fast ball game played by the Afar.

laibon A Maasai prophet or healer.

lamba A wraparound dress that is a very traditional style of Madagascan clothing rarely worn today.

leaven Any substance, such as yeast, that helps dough to rise. Many people in North Africa make round, flat bread using a minimum of leaven.

Leza The creator god of the Tonga religion, now generally thought to be identical with the Christian God.

lifela Sotho songs describing the life of migrant laborers.

Likube The supreme god of the Nyamwezi religion, variously referred to as Limatunda (the Creator), Limi (the Sun), or Liwelelo (the Universe).

Limatunda *see* **Likube**

Limi *see* **Likube**

lineage An extended family that shares a common ancestor. If descent is traced through the male line, the lineage is patrilineal. If descent is traced through the female line, the lineage is matrilineal. Several related lineages make up a **clan**.

Lisa The Sun god of the Fon religion who represents strength and endurance and who causes day and heat. He is the son of **Mawa**.

lithoko Sotho poetry praising a noble person.

litunga A Lozi king.

Liwelo *see* **Likube**

lobola The name used by many Bantu-speaking people of Southern Africa for **bridewealth**.

lolwapa A low-walled courtyard that lies at the heart of a Tswana **compound**.

lost-beetle *see* **lost-wax**

lost-wax A metal-casting method used by Asante goldsmiths and other metalworkers for centuries. A wax model of the object is made and encased in a clay mold. When the clay mold is heated, the wax melts and molten metal is poured into its place through a hole in the mold. The lost-beetle method, which may be even older, is similar but uses a real object such as a beetle or seed rather than a wax model.

Lukiko The **kabaka's** council of ministers.

Macardit A **yath** in the Dinka religion. Macardit is the source of death and sterility.

Maghreb The Arabic name for the region comprising Morocco, Algeria, and Tunisia.

mahamba Chokwe ancestral and nature spirits that act as intermediaries with **Kalunga**.

Mahdi In Islam, a Mahdi is a holy messiah (an expected savior or liberator). (In particular, it refers to Muhammad Ahmad who founded the nineteenth-century Mahdist State in present-day Sudan.)

maina A male Kikuyu social division that shares political power with the **mwangi**.

makossa A fast and popular style of Central African dance music that originated in Cameroon. It combines **highlife** with elements of African-American soul, jazz, funk, and rock.

mangrove forests A forest of mangrove trees – tropical evergreen trees with intertwining roots that form a dense thicket. Mangrove forests generally occur along coasts and rivers, where their networks of roots help to anchor the silty soil. This can create areas of swampy land, hence their alternative name of mangrove swamps. Many West African mangrove forests have been cleared for rice cultivation. This **deforestation** is a threat to the great variety of animal and marine life that inhabits these areas.

mangrove swamps *see* **mangrove forests**

mani The title of the Kongo king. Also, it is the name of an Azande initiation society that flourished in the early twentieth century.

mankala An ancient game, played in many parts of the world, in which seeds are moved around a board.

mankuntu Cylindrical Tonga drums of varying pitch.

mansa A Malinke chief or king.

manyatta A camp in which, for their initiation into adulthood, young Maasai men of about sixteen years of age live away from the village.

mapoto A beaded apron worn by a married Ndebele woman.

maquis Shrubby mostly evergreen vegetation.

marabi An early form of **township** jazz based around three chords.

marabout A Muslim holy man or hermit, especially among the Moors of Mauritania and the Berbers of North and West Africa.

marimba A type of xylophone, also called a **balaphone**. Its tuned wooden bars are played with sticks, and gourds below the bars act as resonators to amplify the sound.

masabe Spirits of the Tonga belief system. Masabe are considered to be invasive and are thought to attack and possess people. Also, the name of a Tonga drum.

mashta A female singer in Tunisia.

masquerade A festival at which masks and costumes are worn. Many African cultures have rich heritages that include masquerades, which when taken to the Americas by slaves became the ancestors of many modern carnivals.

matano Made from clay or wood, matano figures are used to illustrate the stories and **milayo** that are part of the teaching process of Venda girls undergoing initiation.

matrilineal *see* **lineage**

Mawa The creator god of the Fon religion. Mawa is the Moon god and has both male and female characteristics. Mawa is also associated with **Mawu**, the supreme god of the Ewe religion, which is related to the Fon religion.

mawe The basic Mende social and economic unit.

Mawu The supreme god of the Ewe religion. Mawu is usually only approached through the **trowo**. Mawu is associated with **Mawa**, the creator god of the Fon religion, which is closely related to the Ewe religion.

mbanje Long **calabash** pipes still occasionally smoked by some Tonga women. The mbanje used by men tended to be smaller and made from clay.

mbaqanga A vocal style that can be traced back to the four-part harmonies of 1950s African-American bands. South African musicians at first copied these harmonies, but then added an extra voice, creating a five-part harmony style reminiscent of African singing.

mbar The first man according to Lunda legend.

mbari A political division in Kikuyu society, literally meaning "ridge" – of which Kikuyuland has many.

mbira An instrument used widely by many African peoples. It consists of tuned metal strips, attached to a resonating metal box which are plucked with the thumbs. One of the most popular musical instruments in Central Africa, it is used in both traditional and modern music. Also called a sansa or thumb piano.

mboko A carved wooden figure used in Luba **divination**.

mboli The all-powerful god of the Azande religion.

mbweci A Chokwe staff used by men on long journeys as a walking stick.

mebere The one god of the Fang religion.

medina Literally meaning "town" in Arabic, a medina is usually the ancient quarter of a North African city.

mesgid A Falasha **synagogue**.

mezonad A Tunisian musical instrument similar to a bagpipe.

Mfecane The Nguni word meaning "crushing." It is used to refer to the period (1819–39) of mass migrations and wars in the southeastern half of Southern Africa. The Mfecane was triggered by the rise of the Zulu kingdom. It is known as the **Difaqane** by the Sotho-Tswana people west of the Drakensberg Mountains.

mfumu Nyamwezi **diviners**.

mhondoro In the Shona religion, the ancestral spirits of influential people. Mhondoro spirits provide the link between mortals and god.

mihrab A semicircular niche in one wall of a **mosque**; it indicates the direction of Islam's holy city, Mecca.

mikisi mihasi Commemorative sculptures made by the Luba people that are named after certain ancestors.

milayo A Venda saying that expresses a wise or clever observation or a general truth or belief.

minaret A slender tower, topped by a platform and attached to a **mosque**.

minbar A flight of steps in a **mosque**, leading up to a seat from which the speaker can address the congregation.

minsereh Carved wooden female figures used by the Mende **Yassi** society for healing and **divination**.

mint tea A North African drink made with tea leaves and sprigs of fresh mint that is served hot and sweet.

mishiki In the Luba religion, it is believed that these spirits control the supply of game and fish.

mizimo Spirits of dead ancestors revered by the Tonga. They are particular to certain families only.

Mkhulumnqande The creator-god of the Swazi religion.

mogho naba The supreme ruler, or king, of the Mossi.

Molimo The creator-god of the Tswana religion.

monoculture The continuous growing of one particular type of crop.

monogamous The practice or state of having only one marriage partner.

monogamy The practice of having only wife or husband.

Monophysite doctrine The **Coptic** Christian doctrine that asserts the unity of both the human and the divine in the nature of Christ.

monotheistic The practice or state of believing in only one god.

monsoon A seasonal wind of the Indian Ocean, or the (rainy) period during which it blows from the southwest.

montane forests "Montane" literally means from or inhabiting mountainous regions. A montane forest is made up of trees and vegetation that prefer the cool and moist conditions of highland areas. These forests are also sometimes known as mist or cloud forests.

Moombi In the Kikuyu religion, the wife of **Gikuyu**. According to legend she bore him nine daughters, the origin of the nine main **clans** of the Kikuyu.

moran After they have undergone **circumcision**, young Maasai men join the **age-grade** of moran, often translated as "warriors." Moran did act in the past as the Maasai army, but they mainly provide a flexible pool of labor for specific tasks such as herding.

mosque A Muslim place of worship.

mpsikidy A Madagascan **diviner**.

mud cloths Bambara mud cloths are woven by men but bear geometric designs applied by women. A pattern is painted onto a just-dyed cloth using mud, then soap, then more mud. When the cloth is dry, the mud is scraped off, which removes the dye from the area beneath and leaves the pattern exposed. Usually, mud cloths are made with a pale pattern on a dark background.

mudzimo The ancestral spirit of an ordinary person according to the Shona religion.

muezzin A crier who calls the Muslim faithful to prayer. The muezzin stands on the platform of a **minaret**.

Mugizi The Bachwezi god of Lake Albert.

Muhingo The Bachwezi god of war.

Mukasa The great god of the Ganda religion.

mulena mukwae The princess chief of the Lozi kingdom, who was based in Nalolo.

mulid A huge **Sufi** festival.

Mulopwe The Kunda ruler of the Luba kingdom. The Mulopwe was the head of the government and also the religious leader, believed to have supernatural powers.

mummy A dead body artificially preserved, as by the Ancient Eygptians. "Mummy" is a shortening of the term "mummification," which refers to the whole process of preserving and **embalming** a dead body.

murundu A **circumcision** ceremony for boys entering adulthood in Venda society.

Murungu see **Mwari**

musang The first woman according to Lunda legend.

mushal *see* **shash**

musimbo A type of Tonga drum.

mvet A stringed Fang instrument that is a cross between a zither (a musical instrument that has strings stretched over a resonating box) and a harp.

Mwaash a Mbooy Masks made from wood, beads, cowrie shells, and fibers that were used as a tool of royal justice by the Kuba. They were supposed to be able to assess everyone's behavior. When they appeared before their subjects, the king or chief wore the whole costume.

mwadi Made by the Tetela people, a Mongo subgroup, a mwadi is a mask that is part of a costume worn by dancers who performed at funerals and weddings.

mwaku The son of **Musang** and **Mbar**.

mwami A Tutsi king.

mwana pwo The name for the mask and raffia (palm fiber) costume used by the Chokwe to represent the ideal wife and beautiful woman.

mwangi A male Kikuyu social division that shares political power with the **maina**.

Mwari The supreme god of the Shona religion, referred to as **Murungu** in historical documents.

Mwata Yamvo The title of the king of the Lunda Empire. It comes from an early Lunda ruler of the same name.

mwenge A beer brewed in Uganda from certain bananas.

n'anga Religious and medical practitioners of the Shona religion, who both heal illnesses with herbs and diagnose evil forces at work through **divination**.

naba Chiefs in Mossi society.

Nadi The supreme god of some Khoisan religions.

nakomsé Literally meaning "the right and power to rule," the nakomsé is the Mossi ruling class, and was made up of chiefs, kings, and emperors in the past.

nalikwanda The royal barge of the **litunga**.

Nambi A goddess of the Ganda religion; the daughter of the King of Heaven, and wife of **Kintu**, the first man.

naqqara A kettledrum played by Berber musicians.

nazir Leader of a Baggara group. The nazir acts as the official link with the Sudanese government.

ndilo A bowl used in the past for **divination** at the courts of Venda chief's, in particular to identify witches.

Ndlovukazi The title of mother of the Swazi king; it literally means "Lady Elephant," a reference to her considerable influence and power.

ndop A series of wooden sculptures that represent Kuba kings. The statues were used to both commemorate a dead king and initiate a new one. Ndop were considered to be the receptacle of the king's spirit and would be placed by the king's bed. After his death, the statue would be placed next to the new king in order that the spirit could be passed on. Although over one hundred Kuba kings were known, only nineteen ndop survive.

Nduala The Bachwezi god of pestilence.

Ngai The all-powerful god of the Kikuyu religion. Also, the name of the supreme god of the Maasai religion.

Ngewo The supreme god of the Mende religion.

ngikenoi Subsections of Karamojong society whose members gather for certain ceremonies. Ngikenoi literally means, "fireplaces with three stones."

ngil A pre-twentieth century Fang society whose members had both political and judicial powers.

ngitela Social groupings of the Karamojong people of Uganda that celebrate religious and social events together. They are determined by geography.

ngoma A Venda drum played at a chief's court.

ngombo wa tshisuka A **divination** tool used by Chokwe diviners. It comprises a basket that contains over sixty carved wooden objects – each with a fixed symbolic meaning.

ngoni A four-stringed lute, in the past played by Bambara musicians to inspire men to fight.

ngozi In the Shona religion, harmful ancestral spirits that are thought to cause evil; they can be the spirits of people who were murdered.

Ngwenyama The title of the Swazi king; it literally means "Lion."

Nhialac A Dinka divinity or **yath**, Nhialac can be several things: the sky; what is in the sky; an entity sometimes called "father" or "creator"; and also a power that can be possessed by any yath or even a particular man.

Njayei A Mende **hale**. Njayei initiates use herbs and other substances to cure mental illness, which is attributed to breaching this society's rules.

nkisi nkondi The Kongo people make different figures out of wood, iron, and other materials that they call nkisi nkondi or "power figures." Nails, spikes, or blades would be embedded into the figure to mark an occasion or to deal with a particular problem, grievance, or other matter or to rouse the figure's magical or medicinal properties.

nomad Used to describe a particular lifestyle followed by many desert-living peoples. Nomads are "wanderers" (the word derives from "nomas," Latin for "wandering shepherd"), but they usually travel well-used paths, and their movements are dictated by the demands of trade or the needs of their herds for pasture and water.

nomadic Characteristic of, or like, **nomads** and their ways of life.

nomadism Used to describe the lifestyle of a **nomad**.

nomori A type of figurine made by Mende artisans.

nsikala The nsikala acted as a temporary ruler when the reigning **Mulopwe** died or was unwell.

ntemi Self-governing Nyamwezi chiefdoms.

ntomos Societies among the Bambara and Malinke whose responsibility it is to prepare young boys for **circumcision** and initiation into adulthood.

nuba A form of traditional Arab music comprising a suite of several movements.

nubsa The Fang term for **bridewealth**, which in this case became due on the birth of a couple's first child.

num *see* **kia**

nyamakala Professional groups representing different craftworkers among the Bambara and Malinke.

Nyambe The supreme god of the Lozi religion.

Nyame The supreme god of the Asante religion.

nyangas Male herbalists in the Ndebele religion.

Nyikang The hero-god of the Shilluk religion. He is thought to have founded the Shilluk and to be reincarnated in the figure of the **reth**.

nyonyosé A Mossi social class comprising the ordinary civilians. Nyonyosé literally means "ancient ones" or "children of the earth."

Nzambi The creator god of the Lunda religion.

Nziam The creator god of the Teke religion.

oasis A fertile pocket in the desert where the underground water reaches the surface.

oba A position held by a descendant of a town's founder in Yoruba society, passing in turn to princes from several ruling houses. Also, the title of the king of the historic Kingdom of Benin.

Obatala The most important of the Yoruba **orisa**, Obatala is the chief representative of **Olodumare** on Earth. Obatala was taught to create the human form into which Olodumare then put life.

ocher A yellow or reddish-brown clay. Many people use ocher to color and style their hair or paint their bodies.

oding A traditional flute from Cameroon usually played only by women. The oding is filled with water.

Ogun A god of the historic Kingdom of Benin, Ogun was the god of farmers, hunters, and metalworkers. In the Yoruba religion, Ogun is the god associated with iron and is often shown respect by taxi

drivers who have singled him out for protection while they drive their vehicles.

ohemmaa Commonly refered to as the "**queen mother**" in some literature, the ohemmaa is actually the most senior Asante woman and not neccessarily the mother of the **asantehene**.

Ohiguwu A god of the historic Kingdom of Benin, Ohiguwu is the bringer of death.

olaiguenani A chairman of Maasai **age-grade** meetings.

Olodumare The supreme god (the owner of Heaven) in the Yoruba religion.

Olukon A god of the historic Kingdom of Benin, son of **Osanbua**, who brought prosperity and long life.

omakipa Ivory clasp-buttons that were given by an Ovambo bridegroom to his bride in the past.

omda An official of a Baggara group responsible for collecting taxes and settling disputes.

omukama A king of the Bunyoro Kingdom.

onigi Meaning "sticks" in Yoruba, onigi refers to hairstyles in which the hair is wrapped to resemble sticks.

orinka A Maasai ceremonial club.

orirembo A Bachwezi royal enclosure.

orisa Yoruba spirits or deities, each with its own cult, priests, temples, and shrines. There are more than four hundred orisa (or orisha) in the Yoruba religion.

Orit The Falasha name for the **Torah**.

oruzo In Herero society, a **lineage** that is traced through a person's male relatives.

Osanobua The creator-god of the historic Kingdom of Benin, Osanobua brought prosperity and long life.

Osiris An Ancient Egyptian god, ruler of the underworld and judge of the dead.

oud A stringed instrument of southwest Asia and North Africa that resembles a lute.

ozonganda A Herero **compound**.

Palearctic faunal realm A biogeographical zone that includes Africa north of the Sahara, Europe, and most of Asia north of the Himalayas.

papyrus A tall, reedlike water plant, or the writing material made from it by the Ancient Egyptians. The Ancient Egyptians also used papyrus to make boats.

Parsee A follower of the **Zoroastrian** religion descended from Persian refugees who fled to India during the Muslim persecutions of the 600s to 700s.

Passover An eight-day Jewish festival commemorating the deliverance of the ancient Hebrews from slavery in Ancient Egypt.

pastoral Characteristic of, or like, **pastoralists** and their ways of life.

pastoralism Used to describe the lifestyle of a **pastoralist**.

pastoralist A person who raises livestock.

patrilineal see **lineage**

pharaoh The title of the kings of Ancient Egypt.

pitsos Sotho term for public meetings.

polygamy The practice of having more than one wife or husband.

pongo A decorated and patterned bark cloth typical of the forager art of Congo (Dem. Rep.).

Poro A Mende **hale** for men. Initiates are taken to a camp in the forest where they live in seclusion for weeks. Poro teaches Mende ideals of manhood, settles local disputes, and regulates market trading.

protectorate A state or territory that is controlled by a usually stronger nation. In particular it is used to refer to the colonies established by Europeans in Africa. African rulers were often misled, forced, or tricked into signing protectorate treaties on the understanding that they were only a promise by the Europeans to protect their country from agression, and were not told that the agreement gave away sovereignty over their land.

Ptah An Ancient Egyptian god, worshipped as the creator of both gods and mortals.

pylon A monumental gateway, such as one at the entrance to an Ancient Egyptian temple. Ancient Egyptian pylons often resembled shortened pyramids.

pyrethrum A plant of the chrysanthemum family, or the insecticide made from the dried heads of certain varieties.

qabiil The Somali **clans**.

qadi A Muslim judge.

qalittis Female religious leaders in the Oromo religion.

qat A plant of the staff-tree family. The fresh leaf is chewed for its stimulating effects or used in tea.

quallus Hereditary Oromo religious leaders.

queen mother A position of prestige conferred on the most senior woman in Fon and Asante society. Also, used in the past in the historic Kingdom of Benin.

qumqum An Arabic perfume sprinkler.

rabab A bowed instrument, similar to a fiddle, largely used in the **Maghreb**.

rabbi A Scholar and teacher of Jewish law who is qualified to decide questions of law and ritual and to perform ceremonies such as marriages.

rai A hugely popular form of music in Algeria and Morocco, rai has its roots in the Algerian rural musicians of several centuries ago, but has been adopted by a new generation of young, disaffected Algerians as a form of protest music. It is becoming very popular in France, where many people from North Africa live.

rainforest Dense forest found in tropical areas with heavy rainfall. The trees are nearly all broadleaved evergreens, such as ironwood and mahogany. The crowns of these trees merge to form several canopies of leaves and branches. The upper **canopy** is pierced by even taller trees called **emergents**. The temperature is about 80 °F (27 °C) throughout the year with eighty-percent humidity. Up to fifty percent of the rain that falls on a rainforest consists of water released into the atmosphere by the forest itself, so without the forest, the rainfall in the region would be greatly reduced. Also, rainforests are ecologically very rich and house a greater variety of flora and fauna than most other environments. **Deforestation** is the biggest threat to the rainforests and great stretches are cut down every year for fuelwood, to clear land for farming, or to provide timber to export. Central Africa has the largest area of rainforest inAfrica.

Ramadan The ninth month of the Muslim year, during ·which Muslims fast between sunrise and sunset. Ramadan is the month that **Allah** called Muhammad to be His Prophet.

Re The Ancient Egyptian Sun god, depicted as a man with a falcon's head. Also known as Ra.

rebec A medieval fiddle and ancestor of the **rabab**.

reg An area of gravel and pebbles in a desert.

reliquary figure Carved wooden statues designed to protect Fang ancestral relics.

reth A king who is the ruler of the Shilluk people of southern Sudan, believed by his subjects to be the incarnation of the legendary hero-god **Nyikang**.

rias Long narrow inlets of the seacoast that were formerly valleys which have been submerged by a rise in the sea level.

riika The Kikuyu name for an **age-set**.

rumba A rhythmic Cuban dance and the music played to accompany it.

rumbira A contemporary style of Zimbabwean music that blends **electric mbira** with Congo (Dem. Rep.) **rumba** rhythms.

rwais A group of professional Berber musicians who mix poetry, dance, and music in their performances.

Sabbath The Jewish holy day of rest, usually Saturday.

salinization The buildup of salts in the soil that often occurs in poorly-drained, irrigated drylands. As the water level rises, evaporation also increases, leaving behind the salts from the water. The concentration of salts in the soil impairs plant growth and causes crop yields to drop.

sanafil A traditional garment worn by the Afar; it is wrapped around the waist and tied on the right hip.

Sande A Mende **hale** for women. Initiates are taken to a camp in the forest where they live in seclusion for weeks. Sande mostly teaches Mende ideals of womanhood though it also provides healthcare and advice for women.

Sango The Yoruba **orisa** associated with thunderstorms and the anger of **Olodumare**. Sango (or Shango) artefacts are usually recognizable for the inclusion of a double ax-head motif.

sangoma A Nguni word for a **diviner** or prophet. "Sangoma" literally means "people of the drum."

sansa see **mbira**

sanza An Azande musical instrument made of wood or hollowed gourds and similar to a **balaphone**.

sari The main outer garment worn by Indian women, consisting of a long piece of cloth worn wrapped around the body with one end forming an ankle-length skirt and the other end draped over one shoulder.

savanna Open grasslands, often with scattered bushes or trees, characteristic of tropical Africa.

saza Historic provinces of the Bunyoro Kingdom.

scarification The practice of making scratches or shallow cuts to adorn the body or face. The scar formed when such a cut heals is called a cicatrix.

scribe A professional writer who copied manuscripts before the advent of printing.

scrub Dense vegetation consisting of stunted trees, bushes, and other plants. Also referred to as bush.

secondary forest When a **rainforest** is cut down by **slash-and-burn** cultivators, the new vegetation that eventually grows back (if left to nature) is generally called secondary (or disturbed) forest. They are not the same as the original forest and have different species of tree. After a few decades, they are hard to distinguish from primary rainforest. Therefore, **deforestation** – if practiced carefully – does not have to lead to a permanent loss of forest. For centuries, the farmers of Central Africa have been cutting down parts of the forest and allowing it to regrow in this fashion.

seminomadic pastoralism A form of **pastoralism** involving the seasonal movement of livestock.

seminomadic Used to describe lifestyles that involve a seasonal or regular movement from place to place.

Sharia The body of doctrines and laws that regulate the lives of those who profess Islam – Islamic holy law.

shash A black, cloth headdress traditionally worn by a married Afar woman. Also known as a mushal.

shawm A musical instrument used in the **Maghreb**; an ancestor of the modern oboe.

shifting cultivation A land use system in which a patch of land is cleared and cultivated until its fertility diminishes, and then abandoned until restored naturally. This type of farming has long been practiced in Africa.

Shiite A member of one of the two main branches of Islam, Shiites regard Muhammad's son-in-law Ali and his descendants as the true Imams (leaders).

shikuki Ovambo reed baskets used for catching fish.

shiruba A women's hairstyle common in East Africa, composed of tiny braids worn close to the scalp at the roots and loose at the ends.

shongo A multibladed throwing knife. A deadly weapon, the shongo spins through the air when thrown allowing it to inflict the maximum damage. Shongo were used by many people in East and Central Africa, the Azande and Kuba in particular.

sibhaca A Swazi dance performed by men.

Sigd A unique Falasha festival that celebrates the return of the exiles from Babylonia, led by Ezra and Nehemia.

sikidy A form **divination** practiced in Madagascar.

simoom A hot, violent, sandladen wind of the desert.

sirata Designs on Maasai shields that indicate the **age-group** and family of the shield's owner.

sirocco A hot, steady, oppressive wind that blows from the Libyan Desert (which is part of the Sahara Desert) across the Mediterranean into southern Europe, often accompanied by rain and dust.

sisal A strong durable fiber made from leaves of the sisal plant; it is used to make rope, baskets, and other goods.

sistrum A rattlelike musical instrument with bells.

siwa A Swahili brass horn used to announce ceremonies and religious events.

slash-and-burn A form of **shifting cultivation** practiced in forest regions. It is a short term method of cultivation in which forest is cleared by cutting down and burning trees and other vegetation for temporary agricultural use. Although labor intensive, this method is ideally suited to the tropics. It allows the soil to recuperate, and the burning of vegetation fixes nutrients in the soil.

souk The Arabic word for marketplace. Souks are usually in the old part of a town or village and are often in the open air.

soukous An African version of Cuban **rumba** music. Also a generic term for all Congo-Zairean dance music. It can also refer to a particular style of folk dancing.

Sowo The spirit of **Sande**.

Sowo-wui Wooden heads that are part of **Sowo** costumes of the **Sande** society of the Mende people.

steppe An extensive grassy plain, usually without trees.

subsistence agriculture A type of agriculture in which all or most of the crop is consumed by the farmer and his family, leaving little or nothing for other uses.

Sufi A Muslim ascetic (one who leads a life of strict self-discipline) who adheres to **Sufism**.

Sufism A branch of Islam that is a special form of Islamic mysticism.

sungu The **sungu**, one of the Luba **balopwe**, was a sort of prime minister who mediated between the people and the **Mulopwe**.

Sunna A code of behavior based on the Prophet Muhammad's words and deeds.

Sunni One of the two main branches of Islam, it consists of those who accept the authority of the Sunna. Sunnis make up about ninety percent of all Muslims.

Swezi A spirit in the Nyamwezi religion that is believed to influence people. Individuals who have been attacked or possessed by Swezi must join the **Baswezi** society in order to obtain relief from its influence.

synagogue A Jewish house of worship.

taboo A social prohibition or restriction laid down by culture, tradition, or convention that forbids, for example, certain actions and helps to define acceptable behavior.

tagelmust A long strip of cloth worn over the head and face by Tuareg men.

Tahi A Chokwe **diviner**.

talking drum A drum that can be used to mimic the tonal qualities of African languages. The pitch of talking drums can be adjusted by tightening the "waist" of these drums, which are often hour-glass shaped. Talking drums probably originate from Wolof culture (a West African ethnic group).

Talmud From the Hebrew for "learning," the Talmud is a collection of writings and instructions on the Jewish way of life (especially civil and religious law), based on oral teachings from the time of Moses.

tambour A Nubian stringed musical instrument.

Tanit-Pene-Baal *see* **Astarte**

Tata A senior male elder in Mongo society, it literally means "Father."

tbeck A large basket in which couscous grains, sorted according to size, are stored.

teff A small, cultivated grain rich in iron and protein.

Timkat The Ethiopian name for **Epiphany**.

tinkhundla Local authorities in Swaziland based on small groups of chieftaincies. In 1978, the Swazi king revived parliament (which he had previously dissolved in 1973) with a system of indirect, nonparty elections based on tinkhundla. This system allows the king to preserve his hold on power.

Tisiefa In the Ewe religion, Tisiefa means the "Other World," which is where people go after death.

togu na An open-sided building in the main square of a Dogon village. It is used for council meetings.

Torah From the Hebrew "to instruct," Torah refers to the first five books of the Old Testament regarded collectively. It can also refer to the scroll on which this is written, as used in **synagogue** services, or the whole body of traditional Jewish teaching, including Oral Law.

Towahedo The Orthodox Christian Church in Ethiopia, which has close links with the Egyptian **Coptic** Church.

townships Government-built towns in South Africa that were created during the **apartheid** era to house people evicted from "white" towns. Townships often had poor facilities and high population levels. As their inhabitants' labor was still needed in the "white" towns, however, the government developed "subsidized busing" to take people from the townships to their place of work.

The journey could take up eight hours and could cost a person a quarter of their wages.

trekboer A migrant Afrikaner farmer. Trekboers led the colonization of areas inland from the Cape in the 1700s.

tro A spirit or deity in the Ewe religion. The plural is trowo. Trowo are similar to the Fon **vodun**.

trowo *see* **tro**

tsetse fly A Bantu word, "tsetse" literally means "the fly that kills." Tsetse flies carry organisms that can cause severe illnesses in both animals and humans. They flourish near rivers and in swamps and their presence can make a region uninhabitable. The tsetse fly is particularly widespread in Central Africa.

tukl A Nuba building with a thatched, cone-shaped roof.

tumba A Kongo tomb sculpture.

tumellano Sotho songs in which groups of people sing together in harmony.

twite The twite, one of the Luba **balopwe**, was the army and police commander of the Luba kingdom.

Tyi-wara A mythical half-man, half-antelope attributed with the introduction of cultivation to the Bambara.

ubuhake A system whereby a Hutu could enter into a client relationship with a Tutsi, who would provide cattle to herd and general protection, in return for menial tasks.

ujamma A rural village in Tanzania established as part of the **villagization** policies as set out in the Arusha Declaration in 1967, after which attempts were made to reorganize Tanzanian society along socialist lines.

Umhlanga Every September in Swaziland, unmarried girls perform the Umhlanga, or Reed Dance, to pay homage to the queen mother.

umnumzana Each Swazi **umuti** has as its head an umnumzana, who is usually male but can be a woman. The umnumzana settles disputes, allocates land, and organizes workers.

umuti *see* **indlu**

underemployment A situation in which although few people are totally unemployed many do not have enough work to provide for their needs. For example, this can mean that people may have a few part-time, low-paid jobs that do not fully exploit their potential. In Africa, few people can afford to be unemployed as there are rarely social security systems on which they can rely. A lack of job opportunities, however, means that people are forced to take or create whatever work is available.

urbanization The process of making a predominantely rural area more industrialized and urban. This can involve the migration of rural people into towns.

vako-drazana Traditional Madagascan songs.

vakojazzana A contemporary Madagascan music style that combines jazz with **vako-drazana**.

valiha A Madagascan horn consisting of a long tube (in the past, it was usually of bamboo) with twenty or more strings stretched lengthwise around its circumference.

vhusha In Venda society, girls who have reached puberty undergo this six-day initiation process.

villagization The process of restructuring rural communities into planned, often cooperatively-run and state-controlled, villages.

vodoun *see* vodu

vodu A spirit or deity of the Fon religion. The plural of vodu is vodun (or vodoun, which is also an alternative name for the Fon

religion). Vodun are very similar to the **trowo** of the Ewe religion. "Vodu" is probably the origin of the word "voodoo," a term that embodies Western misunderstandings about the Fon religion – "voodoo" is often incorrectly described as involving "black magic," witchcraft, and the worship of fetishes (idols).

vodun *see* **vodu**

Voortrekker An Afrikaner who took part in the Great Trek (1836–45).

wadi A normally dry **watercourse** in the desert that is subject to flash flooding after heavy rain.

Waqaayo The supreme god of the Oromo religion.

warp Lengthwise threads in a woven cloth.

watercourse A dry or seasonally dry river.

wattle-and-daub A building technique using a woven latticework of sticks thickly plastered with clay.

waya A togalike garment worn by Oromo men.

weft Threads that go across the **warp** in a woven cloth.

worso A Wodaabe (Fulani) annual festival that celebrates marriages and births of the previous year.

yaake A dance performed at a **worso** in which men are judged for charm, magnetism, and personality by elders.

yad A hand indicator for use while reciting the **Torah**.

Yanda A carved wooden figure used in the Azande religion to represent the Yanda spirit.

Yassi A Mende **hale** that is devoted to the art of spiritual healing. Female Yassi **diviners** use **minsereh** figures.

yath A divinity or power of the Dinka religion. The plural is **yeeth**.

yeeth *see* **yath**

Yemoja A female **orisa**, associated with water, rivers, lakes, and streams.

zakah A form of religious tax in Islam. Paying zakah is one of the five holy duties of Muslims and is derived from the Arabic word meaning "to purify."

zilin A Fon singing technique similar to the blues.

zimbabwe A dry-wall (without mortar) stone house or enclosure built by the Shona. The Shona probably began building zimbabwes in the late 1100s.

Zoroastrian Characteristic of, or relating to, Zoroaster or Zoroastrianism; or a follower of Zoroastrianism – the religion of the Persians before their conversion to Islam. It was founded by Zoroaster (who probably lived in about the 1200s BCE), and it includes belief in an afterlife and in the continuous struggle between good and evil. Zoroastrians pray in the presence of fire, which is considered to be a symbol of order and justice.

Index